Social P
The Second Edition

1. u

25

11. 0

- i r

16.

Social Psychology
The Second Edition

Roger Brown

THE FREE PRESS
A Division of Macmillan, Inc.
NEW YORK

Collier Macmillan Publishers
LONDON

The Free Press
A Division of Macmillan, Inc.
866 Third Avenue, New York, N.Y. 10022

Collier Macmillan Canada, Inc.

Printed in the United States of America

printing number

4 5 6 7 8 9 10

Library of Congress Cataloging-in-Publication Data

Brown, Roger William
    Social psychology, the second edition.

    Includes bibliographies and index.
    1. Social psychology. I. Title.
HM251.B73 1986   302   85-13114
ISBN 0-02-908300-1
ISBN 0-02-946040-9 (I.S.E.)

To Albert Gilman

Contents

Preface

When friends ask me whether the manuscript for this book was typed on a word processor, I can truly say it was but the answer is misleading since it was not I who mastered the word processor but my secretary Mrs. Sarah Goldston. Mrs. Goldston mastered the word processor—and also proofreading and reference checking—even as she has, for many years, mastered every new task that came along. She was *born* knowing correct spelling, grammar, and punctuation. She is pure gold and looks after my affairs in just two and a half days a week. Her family may require another day and I speculate that she runs General Motors in what remains. Thanks, Sarah, my good friend and accomplished collaborator.

The Free Press has lavished a series of fine editors on this book. Ms. Kitty Moore kept my spirits up early on. Ms. Laura Wolff has been the main editor. She read all the manuscript very closely and told me what things were wrong and firmly stood up to both bullying and blandishment. Where mistakes have been made, you may count on it that I had my way.

The copy-edited manuscript arrived just as I had checked into Harvard's Stillman Infirmary for a week of bed rest to treat an ailing back. My copy editor was Mr. Norman Sloan, and since I spent all day every day responding to his queries on the manuscript I had a period of total immersion in his company and it was a great pleasure. Mr. Sloan not only corrected all my inconsistencies and omissions, he also entertained me. Since I had written, in Chapter 6, about the television play *Twelve Angry Men* Mr. Sloan wrote: "I've seen this so often on the tube that I will keep you alert by writing in the names of all twelve actors in the play." Try it, all twelve. Mr. Sloan is not just a great copy editor; he must be the Cape Cod champion of Trivial Pursuits.

Mr. Robert Harrington was in charge of production. I was somewhat behindhand in getting permissions to represent tables and figures—so behindhand that if I had known in June all that had still to be done I would have gone into a panic. But Mr. Harrington gently led me through what had to be done, and it was done with no great strain.

Elizabeth Weiss, the author of the *Instructor's Manual*, taught the Harvard undergraduate social psychology course with me for several years. When I learned that someone would have to be asked to write a *Manual*, I knew at once whom to ask. Elizabeth's understanding of concepts in social psychology had always been exact, and I knew that she wrote beautifully. My jacket blurb for her would read: "Best *Instructor's Manual* I have ever seen."

Some chapters of the book were read and improved upon by Professor Elizabeth Loftus of the University of Washington, Professor Reid Hastie of Northwestern University, Professor Sandra Bem of Cornell University, and others who are anonymous to me. Thank you all.

Introduction

THIS SECOND EDITION is not a revision in any ordinary sense but a new book with a new organization and many new topics. Hardly any sentences from the 1965 edition reappear here. With an interval of twenty years, new topics are inevitable in a discipline as alive as social psychology. Would it have been necessary to write a new book had I revised after a sensible interval of five years or so? For me it would, because I think the best way to introduce social psychology is in terms of the pros and cons of currently interesting arguments. What arguments are interesting changes with the state of the evidence and of the world, and the change is rapid, even though there is a set of deep questions, central to the discipline, that changes hardly at all. Selection of a new argument entails new figure–ground decisions about experiments and a general reordering of information. Multiple new arguments mean a totally new organization, a new book, a lot of work.

Several research stories told in the first edition have been omitted from the second because the stories were largely complete in 1965 and the contributions —substantial ones—were already made. This is what happened, for instance, to the Authoritarian Personality. A few topics, e.g. crowd behavior, have been dropped because, while they were interesting though little developed scientifically in 1965, 1985 finds them still interesting but not much more developed. Some chapter titles in the first edition, which are standard "classical" titles, do not appear in this book, notably "Attitude Change" and "Group Dynamics." It is only the titles that are missing, not the subject matter.

The subject matter is to be found in new patterns in many places throughout the book.

Two chapters in *The Second Edition* are clear continuations of chapters in the first. Chapter 6, "Group Polarization," tells what has become of the "risky shift" problem central to "Group Dynamics" in the 1965 book. Chapter 11, "Impressions of Personality," tells what has become of the phenomena of "primacy" and "centrality," which were already important in the 1965 chapter that bore the "Impressions" title. Those two chapters seem to me to describe impressive advances in knowledge. The same problems have been studied for twenty years, and after twenty years and some hundreds of experiments, we have something better than a collection of "findings"; we have some answers that are not likely to be turned back.

There are in *The Second Edition* many matters not treated at all in the first. Those include two very general theories: Attribution and Equity. These are expounded in depth and repeatedly invoked throughout the book. There are a number of applied topics, full of promise and controversy: the "Psycholegal Issues" of "Eyewitness Testimony" and "Jury Size and Decision Rule," the "Issues of Sexual Liberation" concerning "The Androgynous Personality" and "Sources of Sexual Orientation," and an introduction to the vast domain of "Health and Social Behavior."

The Second Edition includes, as did the first, a substantial treatment of language, but there is no overlap of contents. In the first edition the focus was on linguistic structure and the acquisition of the native language. Those are great subjects, but they are also linguistically technical subjects. I have often wondered how many of the instructors who used the 1965 book assigned the chapters on language, because, although the content belongs conceptually in social psychology, it is pretty unreasonable to expect social psychologists to "work it up" in their spare time. In *The Second Edition*, "Language (and Communication)" treats just those matters that are most central to social psychology, and while they are fairly technical, they are not technical in an alien sense; they are technical psychologically rather than linguistically.

Finally, *The Second Edition* devotes three chapters to "Ethnic Hostilities," perhaps the most difficult subject to write about, though the most interesting for me to read about. The section is unusual, perhaps unique among American textbooks, in its heavy reliance on European social psychology, especially on the theory of social identity and the phenomenon of minority influence. It is not an optimistic section that cheerily looks forward to the imminent resolution of ethnic conflict. How could it be, in view of world realities? I think European social psychology has managed better than American social psychology to keep in focus how intractable the problems are and has found sources of ethnic conflict that are as deeply rooted as the true sources must be.

Every chapter in this book is intended to be fully understandable in isolation from the rest. There are, however, some cross-references and interconnections. For the chapters grouped under the same part title they are, as you would expect, especially rich. There is definitely something to be gained from reading all the chapters in any one part, yet it is not necessary to do so. There is no great advantage in reading the chapters in the order in which they appear in the book except for the two general theories, Attribution and Equity, which are more useful early than late.

No one, I am sure, can teach the entire book in one semester. At any rate, I cannot. I always include Attribution and Equity and then some selection from the remaining chapters. Some texts cover a range as great or greater and yet can be read or taught in one semester. This one cannot because I am committed to the idea that participation in the process of making social psychology is more important than knowing the "findings" of social psychology, and if a reader is to participate in the process, some things must be treated in detail and at length. In order to reconcile the goal of full participation and the goal of reasonably full coverage of the domain of social psychology, it has been necessary to write long chapters and a long book, expecting everyone to choose what is wanted and to omit the rest.

The 1965 edition was a more personal book than textbooks usually are, and 1985 is personal again. It is not the overuse of the first-person pronoun that makes the books personal, but the inclusion of anecdotes and judgments that cannot be said to be fully objective. Perhaps the real reason why I have allowed the books to be fairly personal is that I, like most people, would rather write an autobiographical novel but lack the art to bring it off. There are, however, less self-indulgent reasons. It seems to me that books in psychology ought not to omit things the author believes to be important simply because there are not fifty supporting experiments. I also think that the best technique for producing comprehension of abstract concepts and principles in psychology is to activate in the reader a flow of relevant memories and introspection, and for that, some person-to-person contact is perhaps essential. We are not writing physics, you know.

Having implicitly admitted that social psychology is a less objective discipline than physics, I want also to say why I think it is an important discipline. The unchanging agenda of basic questions such as "What arouses hostilities between races and nations?" is obviously important but not peculiar to social psychology. Philosophy, history, political science, anthropology, some of biology, and all humanistic studies share our agenda. However, social psychology brings something distinctive to the basic questions of human life; it brings empirical and, especially, experimental evidence. Our experiments do not settle any of the great questions, but they certainly refresh arguments that otherwise tend to be too wordy in the manner of philosophy or too particularistic in the manner of history.

Consider the sources of ethnic hostility. In any particular case we are likely to learn most from political science, history, and investigative journalism. However, Henri Tajfel's "minimal group" experiment, showing that hostility arises immediately whenever humans are divided into groups, even on a random basis, moves the topic to a level of breathtaking generality. Consider discussions of the nature of authority, legitimacy, obedience, and rebellion. When they are purely philosophical or sociological, they tend to become moralistic and abstract. Stanley Milgram's obedience experiments, showing that most ordinarily decent people will, in certain situations, obey a malevolent authority that commands them to punish an innocent person with life-threatening electric shocks, add concrete information that curbs any tendency to preach. Consider the "opinions" of the Supreme Court on the size of jury and rule of decision necessary to ensure full and fair debate. The experiments of Michael Saks and of Reid Hastie show that opinions can be informed by something better than everyday observation.

When social psychologists are so naive and arrogant as to suggest that our experiments "generate" the answers to great questions, other disciplines understandably bridle, but when we suggest that an experiment makes a distinctive contribution to the argument, that contribution is welcome.

1

Social Forces in Obedience and Rebellion

THE PUBLICATION IN 1983 of *Eichmann Interrogated* (Von Lang and Sibyll, 1983), a partial transcript of the interrogation in 1961 of Adolf Eichmann preliminary to his trial and eventual execution by hanging in Jerusalem for "causing the killing of millions of Jews," renewed worldwide puzzlement over the discrepancy between the ordinariness of the man and the monstrosity of his deeds. The late Hannah Arendt, a distinguished social philosopher, covered the Eichmann trial for *The New Yorker*, and her subsequent book *Eichmann in Jerusalem* (1963) was subtitled *A Report on the Banality of Evil*. Because Eichmann was on trial for his life, he naturally enough denied responsibility for the death of the six million Jews whose transport he supervised as a Nazi bureaucrat with the modest rank of lieutenant colonel. Arendt believed Eichmann's contention that he was no "innere Schweinehund," which is to say not in his heart a "dirty bastard," not even a fanatic anti-Semite, but rather an ambitious functionary who at first felt that it was his personally distasteful *duty* to obey the Führer's orders and transport Jews to their death, a duty he carried out with meticulous care. Many students of the Holocaust have sharply disagreed with Arendt, and Jacob Robinson in his book *And the Crooked Shall Be Made Straight* (1965) castigated her for defending Eichmann. And yet the editors of the 1983 book, after close study of the 275 hours of interrogation of Eichmann, describe him as "an average man of middle class origins and normal middle class upbringing, a man without identifiable criminal tendencies."

The words that must haunt a social psychologist were spoken by Eichmann himself and were among his last: "I am not the monster I am made out to be. I am the victim of a fallacy." It is not Eichmann's fate that matters to us as social psychologists; that is something to interest history, perhaps, and Holocaust studies. The question for social psychology is: What sort of fallacy, if any, was invoked in thinking that the doer of monstrous deeds must necessarily be a monster? If there is a fallacy here, how general is it? Who subscribes to it? Is social psychology free of it?

To say that monstrous actions entail a monster as actor is to say more generally that we expect to find continuity in the things a person does over time and over relationships. Some of those expectations of continuity are disappointed in Eichmann's case. Half a dozen psychiatrists examined him and found him sane. His sentiments for and actions toward his parents, wife, and children were all normal, even more than ordinarily ideal. After escaping the Nuremberg trials and taking up residence under a false identification in Buenos Aires, Eichmann took serious personal risks in order to inform his family that he was still alive and later in contriving to have his wife and children join him—though he knew the Israeli Secret Police were searching the world for him. Before getting his orders to participate in what the Nazis called the "Final Solution of the Jewish Problem," Eichmann was himself an active Zionist who believed the right "solution" was to find a separate territory for the Jews to emigrate to—Madagascar, he thought, or a not very attractive part of Poland. He actively expounded Zionist ideas to his fellow officers in Hitler's security service, the infamous SS. Eichmann always insisted that he had no anti-Semitic sentiments and, indeed, had good personal reasons for not having them; for a time in Vienna he had a Jewish mistress (a very dangerous crime for an SS officer), and he had a Jewish half-cousin whom he personally arranged to protect from the general destruction. He himself never committed an overt act of killing. In short, over the span of his entire life and all his relationships, it is difficult to find the monster.

To say that monstrous deeds presuppose a monster as actor is also to say that the deeds would not be performed by most or many people because monsters are fairly rare. However, Eichmann's defense attorney insisted again and again that the fate of the Jewish people would have been no different at all if Eichmann had not lived; if he had not done his job, someone else would have. And it is difficult to argue otherwise just because Eichmann seemed so ordinary, so like bureaucrats everywhere. The things he cared most about, the events he remembered best, all concerned his own career, not the fate of the Jewish people. The things he felt ashamed of, the things that gave him anguish, were trifling breaches of German etiquette: For example, he once invited senior officers to join him for a glass of wine when that was not his prerogative. What he felt proud of was his strict adherence to duty in transporting Jews and his efficiency in the job. What he regarded as a temptation successfully resisted was the occasional sentiment of pity for individual victims. Perhaps Hannah Arendt and all those who have agreed with her about Eichmann were too

Figure 1–1. Adolf Eichmann

Captain Avner W. Less, who interrogated Eichmann for 275 hours, wrote: "My first reaction when the prisoner finally stood facing us in the khaki shirt and trousers and open sandals was one of disappointment. I no longer know what I had expected—probably the sort of Nazi you see in the movies: tall, blond, with piercing blue eyes and brutal features expressive of domineering arrogance. Whereas this rather thin, balding man not much taller than myself looked utterly ordinary" (Von Lang and Sibyll [eds.], 1983; photo by Stern/Black Star).

credulous; the man was, after all, on trial for his life. Yet she made the startling claim that "in certain circumstances the most ordinary decent person can become a criminal." That should not be so if monstrous deeds presuppose a monstrous character. However, the most famous series of experiments in social psychology, Stanley Milgram's (1974) experiments on obedience to malevolent authority, confirm Arendt's prophetic claim.

Milgram created a simple situation that turned out to be very powerful: Someone taking orders from a scientist-experimenter in a laboratory is brought to throw a switch delivering 450 volts, a very dangerous shock, to an innocent likable victim who, furthermore, has a heart problem. The work was begun in the 1960s, and its exact significance is still debated today. That is partly because the results were news to everyone. It is an experiment that cannot be said only to demonstrate common knowledge. We can be sure about that because Milgram, in fact, asked various kinds of people to predict in advance what subjects would do. The experimental protocol was described in great detail to groups of laymen, college students, behavior scientists, and psychiatrists, and they were told that subjects like themselves would be ordered to deliver shocks, starting with a very mild 15 volts and proceeding in increments of 15 volts to the very high level of 450 volts, to a victim who would plead to be released. The question was at what point, what level of shock, would subjects disobey the scientist and refuse to go on.

The predictions of the various groups, in spite of the presumed variation in their expertise, were much the same. Everybody guessed that all subjects would defy the experimenter long before being asked to deliver 450 volts; on the average they thought that rebellion would come as soon as the victim asked to be released, which would be at about 140 volts. The facts of the experiment were otherwise: 63 percent of actual subjects obeyed the scientist to the limit and delivered 450 volts. Milgram himself was surprised by the outcome. He had started with a procedure in which the victim made no complaint, because Milgram thought that the levels of shock, clearly marked as "severe," "dangerous," and so on, would be enough to cause defiance of the experimenter but found that in the absence of expressed protest, virtually all subjects blithely obeyed to the end. It was necessary to introduce expressed protest as a counterforce in order to get any disobedience at all.

The unexpectedness of the Milgram result is partly due, I think, to an assumption we make about the relations between moral judgment and morally relevant behavior. We are inclined to believe that a rational man, if he knows what is morally right in a situation, will be able to act rightly. Indeed, moral philosophers usually make just this simplifying assumption in explicit form. Milgram (1977a) asked twenty undergraduates to say, with respect to the shock scenario, how *should* one act in this situation? All thought one should disobey the experimenter, and they placed the shock level at which one should disobey, on the average, at 150 volts, which is almost identical with the level at which other subjects, on the average, said one *would* disobey. The average level at which subjects did, in fact, disobey was 360 volts, and 63 percent never disobeyed at all. In short, neither expectations of how people would behave nor judgments of how they should behave predicts at all well how they do behave. Something intervenes between the description of the scenario and action, something not easy to imagine realistically, the force of the actual situation.

Milgram's obedience research is not a single study but a set of twenty-one variations, and the figure of 63 percent obedience applies to what he calls the "baseline condition." That baseline condition has been reproduced in about half a dozen countries, and there is one great unchanging result. About two-thirds of every sample tested proved willing under orders to shock to the limit: 450 volts. The percentage obedient proved slightly higher in a study done in West Germany (Mantell, 1971), and in Amman, Jordan, it was 80 percent (Shanab and Yahya, 1977). In Australia (Kilham and Mann, 1974) the obedience percentage was slightly lower. But two-thirds obedient, everywhere the experiment has been tried, is a fair summary. It is also true that people everywhere who have not been in the experiment think that only the rare pathological personality would obey the orders. Yet when Elms and Milgram (1966) compared a sample of maximally obedient subjects with a sample of maximally rebellious subjects with respect to scores on some standard personality tests, no significant differences at all appeared. We seem then to have in obedience to authority something we do not understand at all: a situation having a power, impossible to imagine from a verbal report, to cause a majority of people regardless of personal character to do something they think they would not do and should not do. "Eichmann's fallacy" is perhaps the belief that behavior springs from character and is consonant with personal morality.

I am not going to claim that Milgram's experiments on obedience to malevolent authority teach us that about 65 percent of middle-class Americans stand ready to play a role like Eichmann's. Eichmann's actions were carried out over many years, and he had plenty of time to reflect on what he was doing, discuss it with others, and suffer recurrent nightmares. Milgram's situation lasted just one hour; a subject confronted authority all alone and had no opportunity to reflect. Yet Milgram's contrived situation was in some ways weaker than the one the Third Reich contrived for Eichmann. The Jews had been systematically denigrated by the state to the point where they no longer seemed fully human, whereas the victim in Milgram's experiment was a likable new acquaintance. Eichmann worked at a great distance from his victims, both geographically and in terms of the chain of command, whereas Milgram's subjects themselves administered the shock to a victim whose protests they could hear and, in some conditions, see.

There is a third case of obedience to authority that helps define the relevance of Milgram to Eichmann. During the war in Vietnam a platoon of American soldiers "wasted" (shot dead) all the inhabitants they could round up of a village called My Lai, and those inhabitants were mostly women, old men, and children (Hersh, 1970). The man commanding the platoon, Lieutenant William Calley, made the same plea that Eichmann made: Orders had been received from a superior, and it was his duty as a soldier to obey. There was some doubt about whether such orders had been explicitly given, and Calley was adjudged guilty but given a light sentence. Calley's situation would seem to fall somewhere between Milgram's scenario and Eichmann's term of duty: The occasion to rebel was brief, the atmosphere emotional, the contact with victims direct, all as in Milgram's scenario; the victims were a denigrated enemy population, as in Eichmann's case. In all three cases idealistic reasons had been given for the larger cause: in Milgram's scenario the advancement of science; for the war in Vietnam, halting the advance of Communism; and for the Final Solution Hitler did not, of course, give hatred as a reason, but rather the purification of the Aryan race, making Europe *Judenrein*.

The Calley case seems to argue that Milgram's experiments are not entirely irrelevant to the case of Adolf Eichmann, because it is in some ways like the one and in some ways like the other. However, William Calley was one particular individual, and we have no data comparable to Milgram's to show that 65 percent of a population would have done what he did. Still, Calley—like Eichmann—had shown no criminal tendencies before My Lai and lives today in quiet civilian respectability. As it happens, a national survey was made of the reaction of the American public to Lieutenant Calley's trial (Kelman and Lawrence, 1972), and 51 percent of the sample said that they would follow orders if commanded to shoot all inhabitants of a Vietnamese village. The authors conclude: "Yet our data suggests that many Americans feel they have no right to resist authoritative demands. They regard Calley's actions at My Lai as normal, even desirable, because (they think) he performed them in obedience to legitimate authority." I think, therefore, that while differences between the Milgram experiment and the deeds of Adolf Eichmann are great, we cannot comfortably dismiss the laboratory results as irrelevant to the historical case.

Obedience to Authority and Rebellion Against It

Until 1981 the Milgram procedure was the only laboratory method used in studying obedience, and even that method was used only a very few times. The failure to stimulate a large number of replications and variations is truly extraordinary in view of the high social importance of the topic and the great surprise value of the initial findings; a much less dramatic topic like attribution theory has, in about the same period, inspired more than a thousand experiments. What can account for the fact that obedience research is not a major research tradition? The original reception was certainly warm enough. It may, in fact, have been too hot. Baumrind (1964) and others criticized the experiment for exposing human subjects to excessive stress. There is no doubt that most subjects ordered to give dangerous shocks to an innocent person pleading to be spared do experience some division of mind. However, Milgram (1977a) sent all subjects follow-up questionnaires, and he reported that over 99 percent felt either good or neutral about having participated and less than 1 percent had any regrets. One might have expected more regrets, considering that a majority of subjects behaved in a way (obedience to malevolent authority) they themselves disapproved of, once out of the situation. However, they seem to have been able to receive the news as we do—as an interesting revelation about human nature. Milgram had an impartial psychiatric examiner interview, one year after the event, forty subjects judged most likely to have suffered some ill consequence of the experiment. The psychiatrist's report said that "none was found by this interviewer to show signs of having been harmed by the experiment."

As far as the ethics of research on human subjects is concerned, I think Milgram is absolutely in the clear and deserves to be praised for doing research of the highest human consequence while showing great concern for the welfare of his subjects. The slight personal risk involved is justified by the importance of the topic. However, universities nowadays have committees that review plans for research on human subjects because national granting agencies require such review. I have been a member of the Harvard committee since its creation, and while I think our committee (which is probably fairly representative) is wise to be extremely cautious about somatic risk from shock, drugs, and the like, I think it tends to be excessively cautious about behavioral and mental risk for normally functioning adults (as opposed to children or special populations). Higher levels of psychological stress than any an experimenter creates are frequent in ordinary life, and people seem to be able to handle them. I know of no case in which it has been demonstrated that a psychological or behavioral manipulation in an experiment caused serious injury to anyone. Nevertheless, the Milgram procedure is widely regarded by committees on the use of human subjects in research as a marginal case; in fact, it effectively defines the boundary on which votes for and against approval would be about equal. Very probably, therefore, the imaginations of young social psychologists have veered away when they approached this boundary, and we have a lot of routinely approvable research and not enough for which approval could not be taken for granted but which, if it could be made safe and approved, would certainly be consequential.

In 1981 Gamson and his colleagues (Gamson, Fireman, and Rytina, 1982) devised a new procedure (called the MHRC Encounter) for the experimental study of encounters with unjust authority. Their new procedure, like Milgram's, was powerful. One participant said, "I'm glad to have done it, but I'm really shook and my blood pressure will be high for hours." Another said, "It's okay to look back now. But the pressure was too much. I've got the *shakes!*" One called the experiment "the most stressful experience I've had in the past year" (p. 39). In the end the investigators, sensitive to the ethics of research, felt they had to stop without completing their research design. They had intended to run eighty groups but stopped with thirty-three. I myself am rather sorry they stopped but glad that they elected to publish a full report on the thirty-three completed groups. I am glad because those groups present a marked contrast in outcome with Milgram's results. In all but four of the thirty-three groups, more or less successful rebellions against authority occurred.

Milgram's shock experiment and the MHRC Encounter of Gamson and his co-workers (to be described) differed in that the former produced obedience in the majority of individuals and the latter produced rebellion in the majority (of groups). Why the difference? That is the question to be answered in this chapter. We shall pursue the answer by looking closely at Gamson's thirty-three groups and Milgram's twenty-one variations and by introducing Latané's (1981) Law of Social impact and Asch's work on conformity (1956) and in the process will learn a good deal about the social forces determining obedience and rebellion.

Milgram's Basic Experiments

Suppose that you are a subject in what Milgram has called his "baseline condition." Your career as a subject begins when you read an advertisement in a New Haven newspaper offering to pay $4.00 plus carfare for one hour of your time if you will participate in a study on human memory being done at Yale University. Five hundred New Haven men are sought; no students but, rather, factory workers, city employees, barbers, businessmen, salespeople, construction workers—any adult male not in high school or college. You decide to do it and in due course arrive at Yale's quite elegant Interaction Laboratory where you are met by a thirty-one-year-old male scientist in a technician's gray coat. Arriving with you is another volunteer who looks to be about forty-five, a cheerful Irish-American type, rather likable. (He is a trained, paid confederate of the experimenter and a very good actor, but you know nothing of this.)

It seems, as you two volunteers are told, that while psychologists have learned quite a bit about human learning, there are some unanswered basic questions concerning the role of punishment on learning, and the present experiments are designed to answer those questions. Participants are being scheduled as pairs, and one of you two is going to be asked to serve as *teacher* and one as *learner*—on a chance basis. You each draw slips of paper and yours reads "teacher," so that will be your role. Just as well, you think; it will probably be the easier part to play. (The assignment has been rigged; both slips read "teacher.")

You and the learner go into the next room to see how the punishment will be administered. In that room there is a kind of "electric chair" apparatus, and the learner is strapped into it; the straps, it seems, are to prevent excessive movement. An electrode is attached to the learner's wrist and some electrode paste applied to prevent burns or blisters. The electrode is connected to a shock generator in the next room, which you will operate. You leave the learner strapped in his chair and return to the first room to inspect the generator, a splendid new piece of equipment with thirty switches, each one labeled with the voltage it delivers to the learner. The range is from 15 to 450 volts, and there are verbal designations from left to right; "Slight Shock," "Moderate Shock," and so on up to, over toward the right, "Very Strong Shock," "Intense Shock," "Extreme Intensity Shock," "Danger: Severe Shock," and, opposite the thirtieth and last switch, simply "XXX." So that you may have some idea of what the learner's experiences will be, you are given a sample shock of 45 volts, which makes you jump but does not really hurt. To allay a certain gathering concern, the experimenter says: "Although the shocks can be extremely painful, they cause no permanent tissue damage." (In fact, the whole apparatus is a fake, and the only real shock that will ever be delivered is the sample you got.)

The experiment itself goes like this. Teacher reads to the learner a set of words as paired associates: *blue–sky, nice–day, wild–duck*. After that comes the testing sequence, when the teacher reads the first word (e.g. *blue*) plus a set of alternative second words: *sky, ink, box, lamp.* The learner makes his choice, pressing one of four switches, which lights one of four bulbs in front of the teacher (remember the learner is in the next room). The teacher (you, the naive subject) is to administer a shock for each wrong answer and to move one level higher on the generator each time the learner makes a wrong answer, calling out the voltage as he does so—lest anyone not notice.

You find it not uninteresting watching the lights to see how the dumbo learner does and flipping switches to help him get on the ball. The experimenter seems to think you are doing a good job, and you think you rather enjoy research work. At 75 volts the learner can be heard to grunt on being shocked. He does so again as you move from switch to switch. A necessary part of the experiment, you suppose, if psychological science is going to learn how punishment affects learning. But at 120 volts the learner shouts that the shocks are becoming painful and at 150 volts he yells: "Experimenter, get me out of here. I won't be in the experiment any more! I refuse to go on!" What now do you do, o sorcerer's apprentice?

If you hesitate and ask whether you should go on, the experimenter gives you a gelid "Please continue." It is almost certain that you are the sort of person who would continue, though you probably think not, because in the baseline condition 100 percent of Milgram's subjects did continue beyond 120 volts. The learner also continues, with rising insistence, to say that he wants out. At 180 volts it is: "I can't stand the pain," and at 270, an agonized scream. Perhaps you would like to stop. The experimenter firmly says: "The experiment requires that you continue." More than 75 percent did. At 300 volts the learner desperately shouts that he will no longer answer. Now what? The experimenter says to treat no response as a wrong answer. Oh no! At 315 volts a violent scream. You may feel that you have had enough of this research, but the implacable experimenter says: "It is absolutely essential that you continue." From 315 to 330 no answers, just shrieks, and beyond 330 an ominous total silence. The experimenter says, "You have no other choice, you *must* go on." It seems incredible, but 63 percent did—in New Haven, other American cities, and other countries on several continents.

To say that the behavior in the baseline condition is *obedience to authority* sounds reasonable, but what about conceptualizing the behavior in some other way? Perhaps what it should be called is "aggression." Perhaps what the baseline condition shows is that aggression is a powerful human drive that will be expressed when one person is given complete power over another. If aggression is the right concept, if the subject really wants to deliver those shocks, then the experimenter's orders to keep elevating the level should not be necessary. All that should be required, one might argue, is simple permission to use any shock level the teacher likes, including the high and painful levels. Milgram did a variation in which forty subjects were told to set whatever shock level they wished, over a series of thirty errors by the learner. The average level set was about 50 volts, at which point the learner would have expressed no discomfort. Evidently flipping the switches is not aggression but, rather, obedience.

For most, the behavior is best construed as *obedience*, but must it be obedience to *authority*? Suppose an ordinary man, not an authority figure, were to give the orders. "Why not find out?" was Milgram's characteristic response, and a new variation was created. The experimenter made all preparations for the learning task in the usual way, but then a prearranged phone call made it necessary for him to leave. Anxious not to lose time on his research, the experimenter turned over his task to an extra volunteer (actually a confederate) but gave his replacement no directive on shock levels to be used. The substitute experimenter pretended himself to hit on the scheme of raising the shock level each time the learner made a mistake and he likewise prodded the teacher to continue just as the experimenter would have done. The percentage of subjects obeying all the way dropped to 20 percent, enough of a difference to show that *authority* was necessary for high obedience and not simply somebody giving orders.

There is one alternative to Milgram's conceptualization that remains. To say that a learner was shocked in obedience to authority is to imply a relation among roles rather than among personalities; the formulation suggests that the critical events would generalize across individuals. In the baseline condition the learner had been a soft avuncular sort of person and the experimenter, a contrasting body type and temperament, was lean and hard, in manner severe. It seemed possible that subjects found the experimenter the more striking personality and followed him because of his personal traits rather than the authority of his position. To check that possibility, a second team was created, reversing the personality types in the two roles. The change made a difference, but only a small one: 50 percent still shocked to the limit, and the mean highest shock was 305 volts. Extreme contrasts of personality, in short, made so little difference that we must judge the roles of experimenter and learner to be the effective factors.

Since Milgram's first call for subjects was for men only, probably many of you have wondered whether the obedience results would generalize to women. Consulting gender stereotypes, we can find reason to predict either way: If women are compassionate, they should obey less; if compliant, more. In fact, the baseline condition run with forty women subjects produced results in no way different from male subjects. Obedience to authority in the situation created seems really to be just that, *obedience* to *authority*, and it seems to be a result that generalizes across gender as well as occupation and nationality.

The MHRC Encounter

MHRC stands for Manufacturer's Human Relations Consultants, and with your knowledge of the duplicity of social psychologists you will have guessed that the organization is an imaginary one and that the common man's jarring encounter with MHRC is going to involve a lot of play-acting. There are good plays and bad; this is a good one. The plot is more complex than Milgram's; quite a lot goes on, and it takes a while to realize that what is going on is outrageous.

The work was done in a small city in southeastern Michigan; my guess is Ypsilanti, a city that is near Ann Arbor but definitely not a university town. Recruitment is by advertisement for participation in market research to be paid at the rate of $10 for two hours. The first step is a phone call, and the caller is asked to say whether he is willing to participate in any or all of the following kinds of research:

Research on brand recognition of commercial products
Research on product safety
Research in which you will be misled about the purpose until afterward
Research involving group standards

Most callers would say "okay" to all four kinds and would then be told that only the last kind of research (community standards) was currently in progress but, if interested, the caller would be given an appointment at a nearby Holiday Inn.

The very ethical research team of Gamson et al. did not propose to practice deception upon subjects without getting their prior consent, and they found a devilishly clever way of getting people to agree to be deceived that did not, in the process, undeceive them. The four kinds of research that callers agreed to participate in are not all of the same logical type; the first, second, and fourth possibilities are topical (brand recognition, product safety, community standards) and, as such, mutually exclusive. The third "kind of research" is a procedure—deception—and therefore could occur in conjunction with any of the three topics. However, when the four are listed together and worded in a parallel way, one tends not to notice the disparity of logical type, but to assimilate the third variety to the rest and think of it as another topic. The result is that when the caller is told that the only type of research now going on involves group standards, he unwittingly (and incorrectly) infers that it cannot also involve deception even as it cannot involve brand recognition or product safety. By this ingenious means, he is set up to be deceived most royally and at the same time has given permission to be deceived. Nothing untrue has been said—in words at least. To be sure, a false inference has been made almost inevitable: The caller has said that he is willing to be misled, but he infers that he will certainly not be misled on the occasion of his immediate appointment.

The Holiday Inn lists on its schedule of the day's events: "MHRC: Room __", just in case a subject checks. At the designated room he is greeted by a young man in a business suit who introduces himself, hands out a name tag and a letter on MHRC stationery explaining that legal cases sometimes hinge on supposed community standards and when that is so, MHRC sometimes collects evidence on existent standards by bringing together concerned citizens for a group discussion. That is what is scheduled for today. In the room is a U-shaped table with nine places. Three video cameras are directed at the table, and at each place there is a microphone. In a short time nine citizens are present, both males and females, and all genuine subjects.

The man in charge (he calls himself "the coordinator") and an assistant distribute questionnaires asking for opinions on a wide variety of issues, including attitudes toward large oil companies, employees' rights, and sentiments on extramarital affairs. In addition, age, sex, race, organizational membership, and the like are asked for. Subjects are also asked to sign a "participation agreement," which acknowledges receipt of payment and states that the subject is willing to be videotaped and that he understands the videotapes made will be the sole property of MHRC. The cameras are turned on, the coordinator gives the name of the project and date of meeting, and each member introduces himself on camera. The taping is stopped, and the coordinator reads a summary of the current legal case requiring evidence of community standards:

> This case is now before the courts. To protect the identity of the parties involved, names are not used.
>
> From June of 1967 until February of 1976 Mr. C. managed a service station, holding a franchise from a major oil company. On February 10, 1976, his franchise was revoked. Mr. C. filed a legal suit against the oil company two weeks later.
>
> The oil company maintains that they terminated Mr. C., only after they were convinced that his immoral behavior made him unfit to serve as their local representative in his community. This information came from a private investigator hired by the company to look into disturbing reports about Mr. C.'s lifestyle. Through conversations with Mr. C.'s neighbors and landlady, the investigator learned that Mr. C., who is 39, was living with a 24-year-old woman to whom he is not married. Although the two of them shared the same apartment for a year and a half, no one had heard them mention any intention of ever getting married.
>
> The company contends that a station manager who represents the company must be beyond moral reproach. Their local business depends, in part, upon the image that the community has of the local station manager. But Mr. C. is not living up to the community's moral standards, according to the company, and he would no longer be able to maintain good relations with customers. It is written in Mr. C.'s contract that his franchise may be revoked at any time if he ". . . is no longer fit to represent the company due to arrest, drug addiction, insanity, or similar condition." Moral turpitude is one such "similar condition," according to company lawyers. They claim Mr. C. is morally unfit, and the oil company has every right to revoke his franchise.
>
> Mr. C. is suing the company for breach of contract and invasion of privacy. He asserts that his relationship with Miss R. does not affect his competence on the job and is no business of the company. He claims that he was having no problem with customers. According to Mr. C. the oil company was "out to get him" because he criticized the company's gas pricing policies in an interview that appeared on local TV. (An official of the company was later given an opportunity to defend company

policies on the same TV station.) It was not until shortly after the TV interview, according to Mr. C., that the company began investigating him.

The oil company, on the other hand, claims that it decided to investigate Mr. C. only after other information had raised doubts about his conduct. Disturbed by this information but unwilling to act on the basis of rumors, the company commissioned a complete investigation. The company contends that it was trying to protect Mr. C. by refusing to act on reports of his immoral lifestyle until they were thoroughly verified. Mr. C.'s TV interview, the company claims, was irrelevant to the investigation of Mr. C. and irrelevant to the subsequent revoking of his franchise. [Gamson, Fireman, and Rytina, 1982, pp. 45–46]

The coordinator asks the group: "Would you be concerned if you learned that the manager of your local gas station had a life-style like Mr. C.'s? Please discuss why you feel the way you do." The cameras are turned on, and the coordinator goes into the next room to watch a console. After about five minutes he reenters, turns off the cameras, and designates specific people— three of them—to argue as if they were offended by Mr. C.'s conduct, turns the cameras back on and leaves. After another five minutes he returns once again, turns off the cameras, gives the group a short break, and designates three additional members to argue as if offended by Mr. C.; cameras on once more, and he leaves. Two-thirds of the participants are now arguing as if offended by Mr. C., having been assigned to do so. There are several additional short breaks, giving the group members opportunity to talk privately among themselves, and then the coordinator says that each individual in turn is to have a few minutes alone on camera and in that time is to speak from the viewpoint of one offended by Mr. C.'s affair, saying why he will not do business with the station and why he thinks the manager should lose his franchise. Finally, there is an affidavit to be signed and notarized which gives MHRC the right to introduce the tapes as evidence in court, editing them in any way they see fit.

All of the foregoing describes what would have happened in the MHRC encounter for any group that was totally obedient or compliant. In fact, only one group of the thirty-three even came close. At varying points, the real nature of MHRC's effort dawned on group members, and they began to bridle and boil, producing remarks like these:

"Would you mind leaving the tape on while you give us these instructions, so that it doesn't appear . . ." [p. 65]

"Can you assure us that the court is going to know these aren't our real opinions? [p. 62]

"Do these professional people know what you're doing in fact is suborning perjury?" [p. 62]

"This, ladies and gentlemen, is what Watergate is all about." [p. 62]

"I can't sign this [the affidavit]. I'm sorry." [p. 63]

"No way." [p. 63]

One participant, when instructed to argue as if offended by racy Mr. C., nicely defeated the purpose by using a Gabby Hayes voice and saying something like the following: "Next to ma waaf, ma car is my favritt thing, an ah ain't sending neither of 'em tuh that gas stoishen" (p. 61). One group carried its rebellion into action:

> JACK: [*gathering material from the table and folding them up*] I'm going to take these things over to the *News* right afterward. I'm going to talk to an editor.
>
> LEIF: Have them publish something about this, so they don't sucker more people into it.
>
> CHUCK: Go to the *News!* Go to the *News!* [p. 64]

If there had been paving stones handy, one feels this group would have taken them up.

The original experimental design of Gamson and his colleagues called for a total of eighty groups: Twenty would be baseline groups following the protocol described above; the remaining sixty were to include twenty groups for each of three experimental modifications. The modifications were all to involve one confederate in a group who would take a more or less active role in mobilizing rebellion. The least active role was that of exemplar, someone who would be prepared to provide an example, late in the proceedings, of one who saw through the MHRC purpose and objected to it. The most active role was that of organizer, someone who late in the proceedings would propose collective action the group might take against the MHRC. The twenty groups in the baseline condition, made up entirely of naive subjects, would face authority on their own. Unfortunately, the eighty-group design was aborted after just thirty-three groups had been run, because two successive groups became so excitedly and angrily rebellious that the investigators decided the level of emotional involvement created by their procedure entailed excessive risks for subjects and, therefore, they could not, in good conscience, continue.

The thirty-three groups run were a bit of a hodge-podge: Nine groups intended to serve as pretests, eighteen baseline groups, and six groups with confederates in mobilizing roles. As it turned out, the confederates who were prepared to take active roles mobilizing resistance at a late point in the procedure were never called upon to play their roles for the reason that resistance in their group always developed independently and early. The pretest groups were not significantly different from the baseline groups, and so the simplest, approximately accurate, way to think of the outcome is as thirty-three baseline groups.

In the MHRC Encounter we have an experiment with no independent variable—all groups were treated in essentially the same way. Why should we be interested in an experiment that failed? We are interested primarily because it provides a striking contrast in outcome with the Milgram experiments; the MHRC Encounter produced mainly rebellion, whereas Milgram's shock scenario produced mainly obedience. Of course, the MHRC–Milgram contrast is not an experimental one, because the differences between the two are manifold, and so it is not obvious how the contrast can teach us anything about the determinants of the two opposite outcomes. However, we have more to go on than a contrast between two baseline conditions; Milgram ran twenty-one variations, and some of those resemble the MHRC Encounter more closely than others. In addition, the outcomes of the MHRC Encounter were not entirely uniform: Sixteen groups rebelled to the point of unanimous refusal to sign the final affidavit; nine groups rebelled to the point where a majority of the members, but not all, refused to sign; the remaining eight groups expressed more or less rebellious sentiments, but in the end majorities obeyed and signed the affidavit. There was, in other words, some variation in the degree of rebellion. There is also some information to use to postdict group outcomes, to relate, after the fact, to variation on the dependent variable of rebellion: the information obtained on the initial questionnaires asking for sex, age, education, and so on, as well as attitudes of various kinds. Between the Milgram variations and the *post hoc* analyses of factors relating to degree of rebellion in the MHRC Encounter we can build a shaky sort of bridge and make informed guesses about what factors favor obedience and what factors, rebellion.

Similarities and Differences

Milgram's "experiment on the role of punishment in learning" and the MHRC's "inquiry into community standards" bring together previously unacquainted people for a rather brief time to perform specific tasks. In both cases there are agents of authority, the experimenter and the coordinator, and the initial intention of subjects is certainly to comply with the authorities. In short, neither encounter was anything like a protest gathering, and they seem to have nothing in common with full-scale revolutions and social upheavals. Subjects do not share any ideology of protest; they are not organized together; they seek no radical redistribution of social goods. All those factors, so important in such social movements as the unionization of labor, blacks' civil rights, equal rights for women, and the French, American, and Russian revolutions were not important in our two kinds of experimental authority encounter, and so the latter may seem totally unrelated to social change on a large scale. But they are not unrelated.

The important point is that most authority encounters in life—those with parents, teachers, government officials, and so on—result in uncomplicated compliance. Authority is not automatically resisted or even questioned and certainly *ought* not to be, because authority–agent relations are, as Milgram (1974) emphasizes, the simple machinery of social routine. What is special about our two encounters, and they are the same in this respect, is that authority oversteps its proper bounds and, in terms of a larger moral perspective, can be seen to be acting *unjustly*. The larger moral perspective that matters is not that of the investigators, of course, but rather that of the subjects themselves. For both encounters, when subjects were free of immediate pressures and emotion, and when they thought about what went on, it was clear that the authorities had acted unjustly and ought to have been resisted.

Our two authority encounters are related to social movements in that they are potential "incidents." When authority acts unjustly, there is the possibility of a small-scale rebellion, a micro-rebellion, and as Gamson and his co-workers (1982) point out, such micro-rebellions play a part in mobilizing for mass social action. Milgram's experiment can be seen as a stripped-down version of an encounter between a German citizen and a Nazi official. If enough actual little encounters of this sort had had rebellious outcomes, world history might have been different. The MHRC Encounter can be seen as an abstraction of an encounter between individuals and powerful business interests, and it is known that the organization of labor in Detroit factories, for instance, was preceded by many such little incidents leading to rebellion.

Our two authority encounters are like one another but unlike many of the little rebellions of history in that authority and agent are not fully institutionalized, well-practiced roles. Eichmann was an SS officer responding to superior SS officers and ultimately to the Führer in ways prescribed by law and symbolized by uniforms and enforceable with guns. A worker in an auto factory in the 1920s responding to his foreman was doing what plant regulations specified, and there was blue collar–white collar symbolization and firing as a possible punishment. We can be sure that if our two encounters had involved such institutionalized relations, obedience would have been even stronger than it was in the Milgram case.

The many similarities between the Milgram and MHRC cases, in conjunction with the sharp divergence of outcomes, make it interesting to search for differences in the situations that might account for the outcomes. One possibility is a historical change in the respect felt for authority in this country. Milgram's baseline experiment was done in 1963, whereas the MHRC baseline groups were run in 1981. Both occurred in the United States. Between 1963 and 1981 much happened to affect our view of authority. The civil rights movement, the Vietnam War and the opposition to it, and, of course, Watergate had all weakened the belief that legal authority ought always to be obeyed. More Americans in 1981 than in 1963 had come to believe that there were moral imperatives that transcended legal authority, and more had had actual experience in disobeying authority because of moral principle. It seems possible that the change of national climate made people in 1981 readier to resist authority than they were in 1963. We have, unfortunately, no way of knowing. The MHRC Encounter had never been staged before 1981; Milgram's baseline condition was reproduced a few times in the 1970s, but always in countries other than the United States. In the MHRC groups one person actually cited the Milgram experiment as a reason to resist, and others cited Watergate and the Vietnam War, so it is likely that the national climate was a factor, but we cannot be sure.

There is a striking difference also in the degree of respect, or legitimate authority, people might be expected to have accorded Yale University and the MHRC outfit, and so perhaps Yale's great reputation is what made so many subjects deliver 450 volts. On that point we do have information. In one variation Milgram moved his setup from New Haven to the city of Bridgeport and changed auspices from Yale University to Research Associates of Bridgeport (an invention). The parallel with MHRC is almost ideal since Research Associates was simply described as a private firm doing research for industry. They were quartered in a three-room office suite in a slightly run-down building; the laboratory was respectable looking but less than elegant. One subject said afterward:

> "What dopes we were not to check up on this deal. How do we know that these guys are legit? No furniture, bare walls, no telephone. We could of called the police up or the Better Business Bureau. . ." [1974, p. 69]

The less "legit" setting did make a difference: 48 percent of subjects, rather than 63 percent, were fully obedient. Probably then the difference of respect accorded the two institutions (Yale and the MHRC) was a factor in the differential outcomes. It cannot, however, have been the only factor, because the MHRC groups were not simply a little less obedient than Milgram's subjects; they were often actively and angrily rebellious.

The social historian Michael Walzer has made this trenchant generalization: "Disobedience when it is not criminally but morally, religiously or politically motivated is always a *collective* act and it is justified by the values of the collectivity and the mutual engagements of its members" (1970, p. 4; italics added). The disobedience in the MHRC groups was morally and not criminally motivated. In Walzer's generalization we have found the single most important determinative difference in the two authority encounters. In the MHRC Encounter the possibility of collective action always existed; eight or nine members were naive subjects. Milgram's procedure, strangely enough, has never been tried with more than one naive subject in the teacher role, and so the possibility of collective action of the MHRC type has never been studied.

The experiment that would determine whether the possibility of collection action, which existed for the MHRC Encounter but not for the obedience experiment, is the factor favoring rebellion in the former case and obedience in the latter is easily imagined. It would be a simple crossover design. Let one subject alone face the MHRC coordinator and let three or more naive subjects simultaneously play the teacher role. I even feel confident predicting the results: I think a majority of single subjects alone in the MHRC Encounter would obey, and I think a majority of groups in the Milgram experiment would rebel.

An experiment is an empirical test, and doing the experiment would settle the simple empirical question: Does the number of subjects to whom orders are given in the two situations that concern us affect the probability of obedient and rebellious outcomes? Knowing the answer would give us a limited power of prediction. It would not, however, give us much understanding, because understanding entails more than prediction. Every person on earth has, from infancy, been able to predict that almost all objects will fall if dropped. This great power of prediction was not accompanied by understanding until the laws of the force of gravity were discovered by Newton and his successors. Understanding means being able to *deduce* particular phenomena from general laws, including some phenomena never yet experienced, such as which objects will not fall if dropped, whether objects will fall on the moon, and whether a heavier-than-air object can every fly. Are there any general principles in social psychology from which the effect of groups as opposed to individuals in an obedience–rebellion dilemma might be deduced? There is one such, a very general law of social forces. The difference between collective and individual action can, in fact, be derived from that law, but in order to understand the derivation it is first necessary to understand the law as a whole and to become familiar with its application to several kinds of concrete case.

The Law of Social Impact

In 1981 Latané proposed that we think of the individual exposed to social influences as operating in a social force field, which determines what he does in lawful ways that can be partially specified even at this early date in the history of social psychology. Theorizing in terms of social forces—by analogy with physical forces such as light, sound, gravity, and magnetism—is an old and honorable tradition in social psychology, associated most closely with the work of Kurt Lewin (1935). Latané has been more audacious than any predecessor and has proposed an explicit quantitative law that captures, however roughly, several relationships that are well founded in experimental research. In addition, his formulation of those relationships as a completely general Law of Social Impact identifies abstract similarities in research areas that have long been isolated from one another. It is already clear that the law is in some ways imprecise and in some ways wrong (Tanford and Penrod, 1984), but it also seems to be correct in several important ways and highly suggestive of systematic research.

The Law of Social Impact conceives of persons as directing social forces on a target person very much in the way that light bulbs cast light on a surface. The total amount of light falling on such a surface would depend on the strength (or wattage) of the bulbs, the number of bulbs beaming light at the surface, and the closeness of the bulbs to the surface. By analogy, the total social impact of a set of individuals on a single target person will increase, Latané suggests, with the strength (in a sense to be defined) of the individuals, the number of the individuals, and their immediacy (in a sense to be defined) to the target.

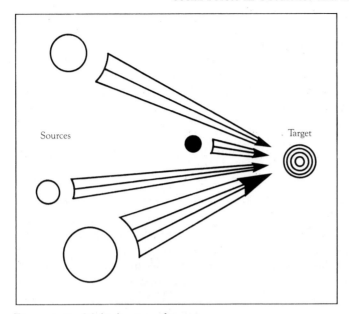

Figure 1-2. Multiplication of impact

(After B. Latané, The psychology of social impact, *American Psychologist, 36* [1981], p. 344, Fig. 1. Copyright 1981 by the American Psychological Association. Reprinted by permission of the publisher and author)

Strength or power, Latané says, would depend on such things as the source person's status, age, and prior relationship with the target. Immediacy is proximity in space and time as well as the absence of intervening barriers or filters.

The effect on the target person of increasing numbers of source persons should, Latané suggests, be something like the effect of increasing numbers of dollars on the value we set on each additional dollar. As any economist will tell you, a gain of one dollar is psychologically greater if you have only two dollars than if you have one hundred dollars. In general, the psychological value of money *increases at a decreasing rate*, which is to say that while $n + 1$ dollars is always more valuable than n dollars, the size of the psychological increase gets smaller as n gets larger. In economics one says that money exhibits a decreasing marginal utility. Latané's idea is that the social impact of numbers of person-sources will similarly decrease at an increasing rate. One person added to two persons will exert a much greater increase in impact on a target than one person added to a hundred.

Latané calls his formulation of the effect of increasing numbers a "Psychosocial Law," a term meant to bring forward an analogy with what is known as the "Psychophysical Law." The Psychophysical Law, formulated by S. S. Stevens in 1957, is a simple equation that describes how the physical intensities of stimuli are related to our psychological impressions of them. The nature of the relationship is such that for each sense modality (e.g. loudness, brightness, pressure, warmth, and so on), the magnitude of the sensation (or psychological experience) is some power exponent of the stimulus intensity. The Psychophysical Law, as formulated by Stevens (1957), is one of the very greatest achievements of psychological science. Latané's social law is more a suggestive idea than an achievement.

The Simple Effects of Strength, Immediacy, and Number

In Milgram's twenty-one variations on obedience there are good examples of the operation of two of the three variables: strength and immediacy, but not number. The target is very clearly the naive subject, the teacher. In most variations the source of the obedience force on the target was the experimenter, and in most variations there was only one such source. We have already described a variation in which the experimenter, being called out of the room, asked an ordinary man to play his role and give the orders. That is a reduction of status, and so of what Latané calls "strength." The number of teacher-targets shocking to the limit fell from the baseline value of 63 percent to 20 percent, and so it seems that the intensity of impact fell as Latané's law predicts. The variation moving the experiment from Yale to Research Associates of Bridgeport is also interpretable as a reduction in the status of the experimenter-source and, as the law predicts, the effect of the target declined. We have called the kind of social force exerted in the Milgram experiments "obedience," but Latané's law does not as now formulated make any qualitative distinctions among forces; his intention is to begin by calling all alike "social impact," though in the end distinctions of quality may be necessary.

Immediacy is the variable most fully explored in the obedience experiment, though it takes a little explanation to see that this is so. If Milgram had been interested, as he was not, in a direct test of the effect of immediacy, in Latané's sense, on the intensity of impact of the force to obey, he would have proceeded as follows. The naive subject is, of course, the target of the obedience force, and the experimenter is the source. To vary immediacy of the source to the target, since immediacy means proximity in space or time and presence or absence of barriers, one would just move the experimenter in one or another variation closer to or farther from (perhaps in the next room) the target or introduce intervals between orders and actions or supernumeraries between source and target to relay orders. In part, that is what Milgram did.

The meaning of immediacy in Milgram's experiment is complicated by the fact that there are two persons exerting forces on the target; the suffering victim must be supposed to have some impact. However, the impact of the victim (call it compassion or guilt) is a force directly contrary to that issuing from the experimenter, for its effect is to impel the target to disobey. It therefore makes sense in this experiment to speak of a "net force of obedience" and to mean by that the impact of the experimenter *minus* the impact of the victim. By the same logic, it makes sense to speak of a "net immediacy," which is the immediacy of the experimenter minus the immediacy of the victim. Making those assumptions and allowing ourselves a little latitude in what to count as immediacy, we can identify a total of seven variations in immediacy (with forty subjects run in each variation).

In applying the ideas of social force and immediacy to some of Milgram's experimental variations, we are only taking a little further an idea he himself introduced. Under the titles "closeness of the victim" and "closeness of authority" Milgram changed proximity relations and explicitly suggested that the teacher seemed to find himself in a force field between two poles so that the strength of the force to obey depended on the teacher's position in that field. We identify more different degrees of immediacy (seven) than Milgram did by interpreting immediacy a little more liberally.

The seven variations on immediacy appear in Table 1-1. They are ordered from high to low (top to bottom) in terms of the net immediacy and so presumed net force to obey, which always means the force generated by the teacher minus the force generated by the victim. In Table 1-1 each immediacy level (7 to 1) is briefly charcterized and stands opposite the group obedience results (forty subjects always), which are summarized in terms of percentage of subjects who shocked to the limit ("STL") and the mean highest or maximum

TABLE 1-1.   Results with Decreasing Immediacy in the Obedience-Inducing Force

Immediacy Level	Characterization	Results
7	No feedback at all from victim	$\overline{M}$ = 450V; 100% STL
6	Victim pounds on wall at 300 volts	$\overline{M}$ = 405V; 65% STL
5	Baseline: Audible protests from next room	$\overline{M}$ = 370V; 63% STL
4	Like baseline plus victim visible in same room	$\overline{M}$ = 310V; 40% STL
3	Teacher forces victim's hand down onto shock plate	$\overline{M}$ = 265V; 30% STL
2	Experimenter gives directions by telephone	$\overline{M}$ = 270V; 20.5% STL
1	No orders from experimenter; teacher has free choice in choosing shock levels	$\overline{M}$ = 45V; 2.5% STL

NOTE: $\overline{M}$ is mean maximum shock level for subjects in this group. STL means "shock to limit," and the limit is 450 volts.

shock level ("$\overline{\text{M}}$"). Some of the variations are already familiar, and some are described here for the first time.

For levels 7 through 3, the experimenter holds the same position—close to the teacher—while the victim is brought nearer and nearer to the teacher, thereby *reducing* the net immediacy and presumed net force to obey, one step at a time. For levels 2 and 1, the victim stays in place—close to the teacher—and the experimenter is moved father away, reducing the net immediacy two more steps.

Maximal net immediacy (level 7) is represented by the preliminary experiments in which Milgram had no learner-reaction feedback at all because he thought the designations on the generator (e.g. "Danger: Severe Shock") would be enough to deter some teacher-subjects. In fact, none was deterred, and so that seems to be a case in which the force to disobey had a value of zero. The lowest level at which a force to disobey existed was level 6, at which the learner in the next room made no spoken protest but did, at 300 volts, pound protestingly on the wall; thereafter, the learner was silent. With that somewhat ambiguous feedback, 35 percent of the teachers eventually disobeyed, though at a quite high mean shock level. Level 6 does not bring the victim as source closer to the target in either space or time over level 7 and so does not strictly represent an increase in victim "immediacy" as Latané has defined immediacy. However, Latané seems to offer his definitions of "immediacy" and "strength" in a tentative, suggestive spirit rather than as definite formal commitments. Already it seems reasonable to extend immediacy so as to give it a psychological sense such as salience in consciousness for the target, and that kind of extension will become increasingly attractive with more results. Level 5 is the baseline condition already described in detail in which the victim produces programmed complaints, groans, and screams from the next room. If we count this as an increase of victim immediacy and so a decline in net immediacy, in the psychological sense, then the drop in obedience is what the Law of Social Impact predicts.

Level 4 was called the "Proximity Condition" by Milgram: The learner is in the same room with the teacher, and his sufferings are visible. That is an increase in victim immediacy and, therefore, a decrease in net immediacy of the obedience-inducing source, and obedient behavior declines accordingly. At level 3 the learner is up next to the teacher and shock is administered by way of a hand plate. Beyond a certain point, the teacher must actually force the protesting victim's hand down onto the plate (see Figure 1–3), and it is a pretty startling finding that 30 percent were willing to do so even unto 450 volts.

The general lesson of levels 7–3 is that willingness to shock a victim, though always the same in its supposed ultimate effect, declines from 100 percent to 30 percent as the person administering the shock becomes more immediately and intimately acquainted with the suffering he believes he is producing. This is an important series of experiments because it captures the essence of

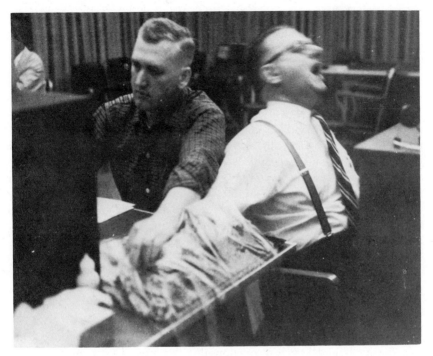

Figure 1–3. Level 5

Teacher presses learner's hand down on a shock plate. (Figure 7 from *Obedience to Authority: An Experimental View* by Stanley Milgram. Copyright © 1974 by Stanley Milgram. Reprinted by permission of Harper & Row, Publishers, Inc., and Tavistock Publications, London)

the difference between dropping bombs from 10,000 feet and attacking someone close up. It is an experimental series that accounts for the horror we feel at the close-up atrocities of My Lai and Auschwitz and the probably lesser horror we feel at the remote leadership that was primarily responsible. Adolf Eichmann took care to see as little as he possibly could of the sufferings his office helped to bring about.

Level 2 is the variation in which the experimenter gives his orders by telephone. The obedience-inducing source declines in immediacy and the obedience behavior decreases as the Law of Social Impact says it should. At level 1 the experimenter tells the teacher he is free to set whatever level of shock he chooses, and almost all choose a very low level. Immediacy affects intensity of impact in the obedience experiments exactly as the Law of Social Impact says it should.

The third variable in the Law of Social Impact is number of sources, and Milgram did not, we know, include any variations to provide a measure of the effect of number of naive subjects. However, there are examples of the effect of number in many other experimental situations. Just to fill out our examples of the effects of each variable taken one at a time with some work done by Milgram, we shall use his experiment on social contagion (Milgram, Bickman, and Berkowitz, 1969).

Milgram's laboratory at the Graduate Center of the City of New York was on 42d Street.[1] In the late 1960s his interest in crowd behavior led him to devise this simple experiment. Varying numbers of passersby on 42d Street (confederates all) stopped and looked up at a sixth-floor window. Behind that window was Stanely Milgram, filming the crowd craning and gawking on the street below. The independent variable was the number of persons who stopped to stare, and the dependent variable was the percentage of pedestrians (not confederates) passing that spot in an interval of one second who stopped to stare where others were staring. The size of the stimulus crowd ranged from one to fifteen. With one confederate craning and gawking, only about 45 percent of those who came along in one second did the same, but with additional persons the percentage rose steadily until, with an initial fifteen confederates, 85 percent of the passersby joined the crowd. The targets in this situation are the naive passersby, and the sources are the staring confederates. As the number of sources increased, all else equal, the intensity of the social impact seems also to have increased since the percentages imitating the sources went steadily up. We would call the social force here contagion or imitation, certainly not obedience to authority, but qualitative distinctions do not matter in social impact theory.

Strength, Immediacy, and Number in Combination

Latané's formal statement of the Law of Social Impact is:

$$I = f(SIN)$$

I   means Intensity of social impact or force
S   means Strength of each impact source
I   means Immediacy of impact sources
N   means Number of impact sources

The formula says more than that the intensity of impact increases with the strength of each source, the immediacy of the sources, and the number of them. It says that total intensity is to be found by multiplying the three values together. In the absence of well-defined units of measurement, the formulation is just a guess that the three forces are likely to combine in a multiplicative rather than additive way. One implication of multiplicative combination that is different from additive combination is that if any of the three values should be zero (zero strength or zero immediacy or zero number), then the total impact

---

[1] Stanley Milgram, perhaps the most gifted experimentalist in the social psychology of our time, died on December 20, 1984, at the age of 51.

would be zero. It seems more reasonable to make that assumption than the additive assumption that one (or two) values could be zero without eliminating all impact. Surely there must be some individuals exerting some force at some immediacy, if there is to be any impact at all. There are many interesting examples of the effects on intensity of changing more than one variable.

NEWS VALUE

On any newspaper the editor who decides how much space to give each story on a given day makes an interesting kind of magnitude estimate. Essentially he is estimating for the paper's readership the relative interest of each story and allotting space on the surely correct assumption that the amount of detail a reader will want to have on a story will vary directly with his interest. This estimated "interest value" would seem to be the same thing as potential impact on readers, and if you think about what makes a story interesting, the top three considerations seem to be the strength of the story, how close to home it is (immediacy), and the number of people involved. In a rough way, one can see those ideas confirmed by the front page of almost any newspaper.

Figure 1-4 shows the top half of the front page of the *Boston Sunday Globe* for February 6, 1983, an issue that appeared just at the time I was thinking about this subject. As an estimate of the editor's judgment of news value and so of presumed social impact on the reader—who is the target—the number of column inches assigned a story will serve very well. The February 6 issue of the *Globe* gives nearly equal space to "3 Boys Found Alive in Swamp" and "20 Killed, 136 Hurt in Beirut Explosion" (actually a little more space to the first story). How should we think of strength, immediacy, and number in connection with those stories? Number is straightforward: 136 + 20 or 156, opposed to three suggests that the Beirut story would have much the greater impact. Immediacy is also straightforward: The three boys were found in a swamp in Hamilton, Massachusetts, a town very near Boston, whereas Beirut is about six thousand miles away. So geographic immediacy greatly favors the Hamilton story. For Hamilton, number is low and immediacy high; for Beirut, number is high and immediacy low, and it seems as though they are pretty well balanced for total estimated impact (column inches on the front page) on the target-reader.

How do we estimate strength values in the two *Globe* stories? An experiment by Bassett and Latané (1976) suggests that it is not simply the social status of the persons involved, but something like the extremity or severity of the event in conjunction with its unexpectedness. The investigators had Ohio State University students play the role of campus newspaper editors and recommend the amount of coverage (in column inches) for various stories. The stories were twenty headlines involving either a fire or a bombing; professors or secretaries (status) at Ohio State University or Arizona State (immediacy); and 2, 5, 9, 14, 27, or 54 individuals. Two sample headlines: "14 Professors

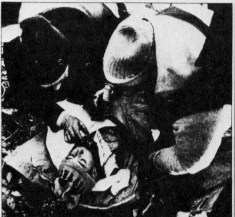

Figure 1–4. The social impact of two stories varying in strength, immediacy, and number

(Courtesy *The Boston Sunday Globe*, Feb. 6, 1983)

Hospitalized After a Fire in Arizona State Lounge"; "Bomb Disrupts Columbus Meeting of Secretaries, Two Killed." The results showed that coverage went up sharply for immediacy (Ohio over Arizona) and regularly for number of individuals (54 hospitalized much more newsworthy than 14), but not at all for status. The campus "news editors" considered secretaries to be just as newsworthy as professors when bombed or hospitalized. However, the severity of the event did strongly affect impact; a bomb was a bigger story than a fire. For the *Boston Globe* also, a car-bomb would usually be a stronger story than someone getting lost in a swamp, but, of course, bombings had become almost commonplace in Beirut in 1983.

While the variable "strength" must be better defined in order to apply the Law of Social Impact to the news value of stories, the general aptness of the characterization is great. In the spring term of 1983 Mr. Stuart Levey, a student in our "Introduction to Social Psychology" course, carried out a naturalistic study that demonstrates the high promise of impact theory for the study of news coverage and also the need to define immediacy in a psychological rather than geographic sense. He took a single historical event and compared magnitude of news coverage for twenty-four newspapers in cities at various distances from the scene of the event. The event was *Kristallnacht*, two days in November 1938 of rioting against Jews in Germany and Austria, rioting of unprecedented savagery which was clearly organized by Nazi officials. Nearly a hundred Jews were killed, seven thousand businesses destroyed (the name *Kristallnacht* derives from the splintered glass of shattered windows), 191 synagogues burned down, and thirty thousand Jews arrested and sent to concentration camps. The event was the historical turning point that marked the start of what was to become the Holocaust. The coverage of it in newspapers did not regularly decrease in magnitude as geographic distance from the scene increased. To be sure, the Berlin *Volkischer Beobachter* gave its entire front page to the story, but *Le Temps* in Paris gave less coverage than either the *Jerusalem Post* or the *New York Times*. Mr. Levey hit on the bright idea of rank-ordering the twenty-four cities where newspapers he studied were published in terms of the percentage of the population that was Jewish in 1938 and correlating that rank order with the magnitude of news coverage given *Kristallnacht* in the cities' newspapers. There was a significant ($p < .05$) relation between the two. His index of Jewish representation in a city is an ingenious way of assessing psychological immediacy.

Social impact theory applied to newsworthiness promises to make interesting distinctions among kinds of newspapers. Informal study suggests that the archival role of the *New York Times* is manifest in a less-than-average attention to geographic (and probably also psychological) immediacy. The *Times*, as a paper with a large national readership and an obligation to history, looks at the news from a position somewhere between Manhattan and a space satellite. By contrast, we have the tabloid *Boston Herald*, which seldom puts anything on its front page that takes place more than 10 miles from city hall. The *National Enquirer* is, I think, a kind of family newsletter relaying the more prurient events in the lives of The Family of Us All: Auntie Elizabeth Taylor, Uncle Sinatra, Sister Farrah Fawcett, and all the rest. Psychological immediacy dominates everything else.

Division of Impact

We have been considering social force fields involving a single target and multiple sources, but the case also exists in which the targets are multiple (see Figure 1–5). In such circumstances Latané suggests that the impact is diffused or divided over the target, and it is the principle of divided impact from which the

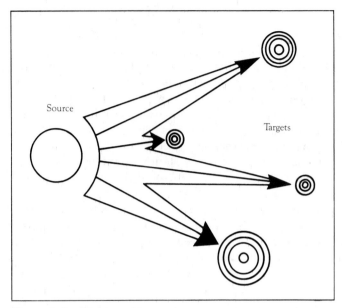

Figure 1–5. Division of impact

(After B. Latané, The psychology of social impact, *American Psychologist, 36* [1981], p. 349, Fig. 5. Copyright 1981 by the American Psychological Association. Reprinted by permission of the publisher and author)

difference between groups and individuals in an obedience–rebellion situation can be deduced.

Jackson and Latané (1981) have provided a good naturalistic example of the division of impact by numbers in the case of the social force commonly called "stage fright" or "performance anxiety." The first week in May at Ohio State University is "Greek Week," and in that week the sixty-three fraternities and sororities at the university compete in a talent show. The show is held in a large campus auditorium that seats about 2,500. The 2,500 are the sources of whatever stage fright performers feel, but that number, being constant, is not the number of interest. Acts at the talent show of 1979 ranged in size from one to ten performers, and those are the numbers of interest. The performers are all targets, but they work together, and so the expectation is that the terrible force of 2,500 spectators will be diffused over them or, more exactly, the force on any one target will be divided by the number of co-acting targets. One person singing or being comic all alone should feel a maximum impact, but ten persons singing or being comic should individually feel much less force.

In fact, Latané proposes that just as the power of a number of sources increases at a decreasing rate, so should the reduction of power in a number of co-acting targets decrease at a decreasing rate. The addition of one member to an act of two should reduce the felt impact much more than the addition of one member to an act of nine. The same negatively accelerated kind of curve ought to apply to increasing numbers of co-acting targets as to increasing numbers of sources.

For the talent show of 1979 the acts involving few persons and the acts involving larger numbers were about equally often musical or comic in nature. One hour before show time individual participants were asked to assess the magnitude of the performance anxiety they felt at that point. They were also asked to estimate the level of anxiety they would experience on stage. The point of getting two estimates for different times was to assess the effect of immediacy, not, as heretofore, geographic immediacy, but immediacy in time. The prediction for temporal immediacy is the same as for geographic (or psychological): Greater immediacy should mean greater impact, the impact being stage fright or performance anxiety in this case.

The effect of number of fellow targets was as predicted. One performer alone felt, on the average, about six times as anxious as one performer in an act of ten. The effect of number was, incidentally, also negatively accelerated. Adding one person to an act of one reduced the anxiety by about 75 percent, whereas adding one person to an act of nine produced a barely perceptible decrease in anxiety. Immediacy also had the expected effect. Anxiety an hour beforehand was estimated to be significantly less than anxiety on stage.

Division of impact by number of co-acting targets can be demonstrated for several sources other than stage fright. The most massive evidence comes from studies of bystanders in an emergency, a topic that Latané and Darley introduced into social psychology in 1970. Chapter 3 describes that work in considerable detail.

Emergencies that have been simulated in experiments include these: A woman in the next room falls and sprains her ankle; smoke begins to pour under a door suggesting fire; someone down the hall is apparently having an epileptic seizure; a briefly unattended cash register is robbed. The single person in an emergency situation is the source of a force to give aid, to respond with help. The independent variable in bystander experiments has been number of bystanders. The bystanders are targets of the force to help. Does it matter whether a bystander confronts an emergency alone or in the company of one, two, three, or more other bystanders? In some thirty-one experiments carried out since 1970 (Latané and Nida, 1981), the number of bystanders has always made a difference. The probability that any individual will help is maximal if he stands alone, and it decreases with the number of fellow bystanders. In short, the impact of an emergency, the force to help, is divided by the number of persons on whom it impinges, exactly as social impact theory predicts.

Division of Impact in Obedience–Rebellion Situations

The generalization that intensity of impact is divided by the number of persons at whom a social force is directed is the principle from which rebellion in the

MHRC Encounter (nine target persons) and obedience in the Milgram experiment (one target person) can be deduced—if we add one existent fact to the picture. The difficulty with simply deducing more rebellion in the MHRC case than in the Milgram case on the principle of division of impact is that the cases are not otherwise equal. How can we exclude the possibility that the Milgram situation may be simply so much more powerful than the MHRC Encounter that it would always elicit obedience from any number of subjects? Happily we *can* exclude that possibility, because Milgram (1977b) did one last valuable variation that involves multiple persons (three) in the administration of shock. Even though only one of them was a naive subject, the variation demonstrates that collective action can reduce obedience in the shock experiment.

The role of teacher, the role ordinarily assigned to the single naive subject, was fractionated into three roles: Teacher 1 read the nonsense syllables to the learner (who was, as always, a confederate acting his agonies); teacher 2 pronounced the answer correct or incorrect; and teacher 3 threw the switch that delivered the shock. The shock, as in the baseline condition, was to be increased 15 volts each time the learner was incorrect. With three persons involved in carrying out the experimenter's commands, the possibility of collective disobedience was created. We would very much like to know what would have happened if all three teachers had been naive subjects, for then the conditions would have approximated those of the MHRC Encounter. However, only one teacher was a genuine subject—the third person, the one who threw the switch. The first two teachers, in the sequenced action, were confederates who had been programmed to facilitate disobedience in the genuine naive subject by acting as exemplars of rebellion, a role that the Gamson group planned also to introduce in one set of variations but it was never really needed.

At the punishment level of 150 volts, by which point the learner had complained and told the experimenter that he wanted to withdraw, the first teacher (T1), the confederate who read the words, informed the experimenter that he was not going to continue. The experimenter insisted, but T1 was not swayed; he left his place behind the generator with the other two teachers and took a seat in another part of the room. The experimenter, somewhat exasperated, assigned T1's task, the reading of word pairs, to T3, the naive subject who also administered the shocks. At the punishment level of 210 volts, by which point the learner had said he could not stand the pain, T2 announced that he would go no further, and while the experimenter made a strong effort to change his mind, T2 was obdurate and moved to a seat in another corner of the room. The experimenter assigned T2's task, announcement of the outcome of a trial as correct or incorrect, to T3, who now handled the full teacher assignment, which was exactly the same as the starting assignment of the single teachers in the usual experiment.

The one real subject in this Milgram variation was, as in all variations, a target of the authoritative experimenter's orders, but from the subject's point of view the orders have been directed not at him alone but also at two peers. He, of course, did not know that the peers were confederates of the experimenter and so thought he had witnessed two instances of successful rebellion against the orders. In effect, it was for the real subject a situation in which collective action could and indeed had occurred. The behavior of the subject in this group situation was strikingly unlike that of subjects who confront authority alone. Of forty subjects, twenty-five immediately joined the rebels. In the baseline condition (individuals alone) only eight of forty had refused to continue at the same shock level. And the fifteen who did not at once follow the example of their rebellious peers were, nevertheless, affected by that example. In the end, only four subjects (10 percent) shocked to the limit, whereas 63 percent did so in the baseline condition.

The results of single subjects in the company of two rebels show that number of subjects definitely can reduce the amount of obedience in the Milgram situation. With such evidence that the Milgram situation is far from totally resistant to collective action, it seems safe to invoke the principle of division of force intensity by number of subjects at whom the force is directed and conclude that the usual difference of outcome for the MHRC Encounter and the Milgram situation is explained by the fact that the former situation always involved groups and the latter usually involved single individuals. Number of subjects is the crucial difference. The prediction ought actually to be tested, but it would probably be confirmed and now we know why: It is because of the principle that intensity is divided by number. Curious, though, how unsatisfying that explanation is. Strange that we still seem not fully to understand. There seems to be something missing.

The Law of Social Impact is a very remote, "action of the moon on the tides" sort of law. It says nothing at all about the mental processes that would mediate the effects of number, neither the effect of multiplication nor the effect of division, in those cases where the law seems to convey some real understanding. I think it is because we are able to supply the missing mental states. For instance, consider the fact that the larger the number of people who were already staring up at Milgram's sixth-floor window, the larger the percentage of passersby who joined the crowd. It stands to reason that something up there that interests fifteen people is more likely also to interest me than something that interests two people. For another instance, if fifteen professors at your university are injured in a bombing rather than just two, the chances are greater that your own life will be somewhat affected by the event. For another instance, and it is the best instance, why is the probability that an individual will help in an emergency greater if the individual is alone than if he is with others? In this case we need not rely on common sense to supply the mediating mental considerations, because Latané and Darley (1970) worked them out in a long research program.

The full story of the effect of numbers on bystanders in an emergency is told in Chapter 3. In summary, the mediating mental processes are of two kinds:

1. Social definition. If an individual sees others *not responding*, that fact helps to define the situation as not really an emergency, not really a situation to which anyone need respond.

2. Diffusion of responsibility. When one person alone is attendant at an emergency, then it is clear that the responsibility to help is his; there is no one else. When others are present, it is possible for each to think that someone else must bear the greater responsibility by virtue of ability to help, proximity to the victim, prior relationship to the victim, or some other consideration. Responsibility is diffused; it is ambiguous rather than well defined.

The mediating mental processes supplied by the work of Latané and Darley (1970) are what make the division of intensity really convincing as an explanation. The remote law by itself is not fully satisfying, and that is in part because it would not actually always be true but is so only in certain cases, the cases Latané considered, for which plausible mental mediation is easily found. The social force that most concerns us, obedience, would not in all cases be reduced by increasing the number of targets. Suppose that the Milgram experiment were truly represented by its cover story, a study of verbal learning, and not even a study of the effects of punishment on learning, but something more routine like a study of massed practice versus spaced practice—in short, innocuous. Subjects then, like subjects in experimental psychology everywhere, would be disposed to follow directions (a form of obeying orders), and ten subjects together or one hundred together would probably follow directions about as well as one subject at a time. Suppose that the MHRC Encounter were rendered innocuous by turning it into a study of brand name recognition. Probably again subjects would obey the authoritative experimenter as well in groups as they would individually.

The fact is that the MHRC Encounter and the Milgram situation are not simply cases in which a force of obedience is directed at one or more targets. That description underspecifies them. Situations satisfying such a description would not uniformly satisfy the division-of-intensity-by-numbers principle. It is necessary to define the situations more closely. It is necessary to add that in both situations a large majority, or even all, subjects came into the situation with beliefs and values that implicitly defined the obedience demanded as immoral or illegitimate. Milgram (1977a), we know, simply asked persons comparable to his subjects to judge from a detailed verbal account what a teacher *should* do, and almost everyone said he should refuse to obey. Gamson and his co-workers in a preliminary questionnaire inquired whether subjects thought large oil companies acted in the public interest, whether an employer's right to investigate the private life of employees should be limited, and whether they would mind associating with someone having an extramarital affair. Between 80 percent and 90 percent of their subjects were critical of oil companies, were tolerant of affairs, and thought an employee's private life was none of an employer's business. In short, the two critical situations are like one another, and unlike the majority of authority encounters, in that those required to obey came into the situation with beliefs and values that should have required them to rebel. It is in just this latter situation that numbers make a difference, that the possibility of collective action is a near-prerequisite to rebellion. And it is in just that situation of latent, well-rooted opposition to the force of obedience that we can easily imagine mediating processes.

In the case of Milgram's experiment, we have somewhat explored the larger historical climate that made the authority of the experimenter latently immoral. Eichmann, Nazism, My Lai, Soviet Communism, the whole recent history of authoritarianism—all were represented in the minds of subjects and created the potential for identifying the present events at Yale University or at Research Associates of Bridgeport as wrong. In the case of the MHRC Encounter, nothing really has been said about the larger historical climate represented as beliefs and values in the minds of subjects. It included recent acute shortages of gasoline for cars and oil for heating that the public suspected the large oil companies might have helped to create. It included the General Motors Corporation's efforts to silence Ralph Nader's criticism of their safety standards by putting a private investigator on his trail. It included all the spying, taping, deceit, and treachery exposed in the Watergate hearings. So subjects in both cases came into a situation well prepared to identify an authority extended beyond its proper limits and to rebel against it.

In the situation described, an external force to obey is in potential conflict with privately held attitudes and beliefs. Why should numbers or the possibility of collective action make the difference between rebellion and obedience? There seem to be three kinds of mediating event: exchange of information, triggering, and conformity.

Exchange of Information

What can the opportunity to exchange information, which exists for a group but not for an individual, do to transform a latent conflict into an open rebellion? The first problem, probably the most difficult, is simply to recognize the present situation as an instance of illegitimate authority. Situations do not come labeled as morally relevant or irrelevant. Many things operate to prevent both the learning experiment and the MHRC research from being recognized as moral tests.

From things said in MHRC groups, we can see the possibilities of information exchange for defining the kind of moral test in progress.

"Did you see the movie, *Kurlack's View?* In it, an ad was placed in the paper for help wanted, and what it turned out to be was trained killers. A very innocuous beginning and they wound up as trained killers." [Gamson, Fireman, and Rytina, 1982, p. 101]

"This isn't public opinion, because we're giving false opinion." [p. 129]

"How are people going to know that these aren't our opinions?" [p. 102]

"And we don't want to be faced with the situation where you read in the *New York Times* one day that thanks to a new method of litigation [*group laughter*] that this poor schnook [*group laughter*] lost his license." [p. 101]

As each individual contributes his mite to the general fund for information, the situation becomes clearly defined for all.

Milgram's (1974) subjects (whom he quotes extensively) also thought of many reasons to rebel, but each had the advantage of only those that came into his own head, and for the majority of individuals those were not enough to define the moral relevance of the situation. Surely things would have gone differently if subjects had had an opportunity to exchange ideas.

"I have no choice but to go on? In Russia maybe, but not in America." [p. 48]

"What about the fear that man had? It's impossible for you to determine the effect that had on him." [p. 48]

"What if he's dead in there?" [p. 76]

"Worried he had a heart attack. He said he had a bad heart." [p. 79]

Of course, if subjects can talk together, they can exchange all kinds of information, not only information helping to define the experiment as illegitimate, but also information helping to define it as legitimate and arguing in favor of rebellion. Why should one think that the larger number of statements and the more persuasive statements that would come out in group discussion would help to identify the situation as improper instead of perfectly appropriate? The reason for expecting the exchange of information to flow predominantly in one direction is simply that we know that that is the direction of the inner conviction of a majority of subjects.

Gamson and his colleagues made a comparison between the twenty-three groups in which a majority of subjects held values and beliefs favoring rebellion (anti large oil companies, tolerant of sexual affairs, opposed to employer meddling, and so on) and the ten groups that had the least rebellious views in advance (at least a third did not hold the rebellious views). It turned out that 65 percent of the former groups brought off completely successful rebellions (all refused to sign the affidavit) whereas only 10 percent of the latter did so. In eight of the latter groups, the majority eventually obeyed and signed the affidavit. That is evidence that the exchange of information in defining the situation will chiefly flow in the direction of prior beliefs. The well-established role of exchange of information in polarizing a group—making the group more extreme in the direction of its original inclination—is described in Chapter 6.

Triggering

Exchange of information when the latent stock of beliefs and values favors rebellion will prepare a majority for action—prepare them, but not inevitably propel them into action. There is a kind of surface tension to be penetrated if unaccustomed action is to be taken. It just is not easy definitely to refuse even when you and most others know that refusal is called for. Some of Milgram's subjects who actually shocked to the limit, when queried about their behavior afterward, insisted that they had not wanted to deliver the shocks and had refused to do so. "Refused? But you did it?" "Yes, but I objected; I told you it was wrong." In the setting it was not always clear that one could just say "no" and stick by it. Objections sometimes felt like refusals. And that also was true for some who signed the MHRC affidavit.

It is important in a group to have one or more individuals with low thresholds for action. An exemplar of rebellion can show others that nothing terrible follows. That is for some reason a difficult lesson to learn. My guess is that it cannot be well learned by instruction and that "disobedience drills," comparable to fire drills, may be necessary to break the habit of obedience, the cake of custom.

From the questionnaires given in advance of the MHRC Encounter, Gamson and his co-workers were able to determine which subjects had a prior history of political and organizational activism, which ones had participated in the past in protests and strikes. The experimenters had themselves supplied (as confederates) such "exemplars" and "organizers" in a few groups and had originally planned to do so in many more, precisely because they thought such persons might be essential "resources" in group rebellion. As it turned out, most groups (twenty-two) had people with activist experience and needed no confederates. However, a minority of groups (eleven) had a deficit of activists. The interesting question was whether deficit groups differed from the rest in the frequency of fully successful rebellions. Was it important to have triggers to action, people who had had the experience of rebelling? It clearly was. Of the eleven groups deficient in such triggers, only one (and that one just barely) rebelled, whereas two-thirds of the groups with a threshold number of activists successfully rebelled.

Conformity

Once the authority encounter has become defined as a case of a large oil company prying into the private life of an employee, a private life that involves nothing more startling than an extramarital affair, and some "triggers" have shown that action is possible, those factors will serve to cause the majority in an MHRC group to rebel. We cannot know, but may speculate, that in Milgram's experiment, if it were run with groups, the same sorts of preliminaries (information exchange and triggering) would activate a majority to rebel. For the MHRC case there is evidence that while exchange of information and triggers are enough to start a rebellion, they are not enough alone to produce the completely successful rebellion defined by unanimous refusal to sign the affidavit. To obtain that result, an additional factor was important: the force of conformity.

To say that conformity is, like obedience, a social force is simply to say that it refers to effects exerted on the behavior of some people by other people. In the case of obedience those who affect behavior do so by direction, not example, and they are invested with the special status called authority. In the case of conformity behavior is affected by example rather than direction, and those setting the example are not authorities but equals or peers. Conformity, therefore, is much like imitation or social contagion, but when the term is carefully used, there is a difference. Conformity is properly distinguished from imitation by limiting its use to cases in which the affected individual on his own definitely would not perform the action modeled for him by his peers, cases in which the individual has his own reasons for thinking the modeled action is a mistake and yet, because of the force of example, performs it.

Conformity played a significant role in the rebellions against the MHRC:

> [T]he challengers succeeded in defining resistance to the affidavit as a group norm to which the uncertain and wavering felt pressure to conform. Some, who had already signed, crossed their names out or tore up the form. Overt attempts to influence are frequently made on waverers in such groups, and signers must be prepared to accept some public scorn from other participants [Gamson, Fireman, and Rytina, 1982, p. 64].

Some participants told the coordinator,

> "I didn't personally say anything I didn't believe, but I'm not going to sign this either, if the rest of the group isn't signing." Many were uncertain at this point, waiting to see what others would do, delaying decision as long as possible. Ultimately, they were faced with an unavoidable choice—to sign or not to sign—and loyalty to the group became one major factor in their decision. [p. 99]

The classic experiments on conformity were done by Solomon Asch in the 1950s (1951, 1952, 1956), and their fame is probably second only to Milgram's obedience experiments. Milgram has acknowledged that the simple but powerful situation invented by Asch was his own ideal model of research.

If you were to serve as a subject in the Asch experiment, you would have been recruited for a study of visual perception. You would find yourself in Asch's laboratory with a number of other subjects (often seven to nine others), the experimenter would ask you to take seats in two rows facing the front of the room, and you would find yourself in the second row with just one person behind you. You would not realize that you had been jockeyed into that position by a well-practiced team of seven to nine confederates.

The experiment itself seems to you extremely casual. The problem is one of judging the lengths of vertical lines. On pieces of cardboard propped against the blackboard the experimenter displays one standard line and three comparison lines (as in Figure 1–6) and asks that each subject announce the comparison line that is equal in vertical length to the standard. The correct answer

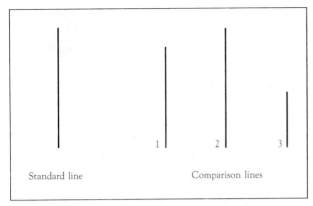

Figure 1–6. Lines to be judged in vertical length

(From Brown and Herrnstein, 1975, p. 292)

(2) is obvious since its best competitor is more than one inch shorter than the standard. Answers are to be called out from front to back, down one row and then the other, which makes you next to last. As you were sure he would, the first subject says "2" and so do all, including yourself. The experimenter then puts up a new set of lines, one standard and three comparisons, and while the whole set is shorter than the first set, the correct answer is again very obvious (1), and each subject in turn gives that obvious answer. Now comes a third set of lines; what a prehistoric method of running an experiment this is, you think, the experimenter fumbling around with cardboards, time not standardized, data collected from one subject at a time. Not only that, but the correct answer is once again obvious, suggesting that the experimenter has no sense of the range of visual lengths that will serve really to test discrimination. Ho hum, it's an easy three bucks.

The first subject in line must really have dozed off; he gives a wrong answer (1), and the line is nearly an inch shorter than the standard. The second subject unaccountably gives the same answer and so, in turn, do six others. By the time your turn comes, you have really become *interested* and have tried looking at the lines with your head cocked one way and another and through your fingers and upside down, but it is still perfectly clear to you that "2", not "1", is the right answer (see Figure 1–6). Is "2" what you would say?

For the basic procedure described in Asch's 1956 monograph there was a one-in-three chance that you would go along with the group rather than with your own clear visual impression. We know that the visual impression was clear, because Asch carried out a control series in which subjects reported their judgments privately (on paper), and those judgments were almost totally error-free (less than 1 percent mistakes). However, in the full experimental series of twelve problems in which a unanimous majority disagreed with a minority of one (interspersed were six trials like the first two on which the majority

Figure 1–7. A minority of one faces a unanimous majority

(Courtesy William Vandivert and *Scientific American*, November 1955)

reported truly), about one-third of the minority responses conformed to the majority. There was some tendency for individual subjects to respond in a consistent way—either as independents or as conformists—though only 24 percent of subjects never followed the group on a single trial. The specific percentages are not important since conformity can be increased by making the judgments more difficult or ambiguous, and just about everyone can be made independent if the wrong answer reported by the majority is made hugely, grotesquely wrong. The stable powerful effect Asch demonstrated is that over a range of judgments that are actually perfectly clear, a substantial percentage of persons can be induced to report falsely by a falsely reporting set of confederates.

The method Asch used in the 1950s was, of course, a slow way to accumulate data, for there was only one subject to a group. Crutchfield invented a more economical procedure (see Krech, Crutchfield, and Ballachey, 1962, for a comprehensive report). All subjects become real subjects; groups work simultaneously but not face to face. Each subject is in a booth, which screens him from the others. The lines to be judged are projected on a wall (or console) visible to all subjects. Each one has in his booth a set of switches for signaling judgments, and each one sees lights that are purpoted to reveal the judgments of other subjects. Decisions are made one at a time and in a fixed order. In fact, the lights are not responsive to subjects' actual judgments but are controlled by the experimenter in such a way as to confront each subject with a unanimous majority. Crutchfield's method really speeded things up, and thousands of subjects have by now been subjected to conformity pressures in connection with a very wide variety of problems: perceptual judgments of shape and color, statements of opinion and of presumed fact, and so forth. The basic finding remains the same. Substantial numbers will go along with the majority against their own private judgment, and the numbers who will do so increase with the difficulty or ambiguity of the judgment.

Asch intended to create a situation in which the relevant visual reality would be clear. One cannot easily believe that each subject really comes to "see" what the group tacitly agrees to "see." To be sure, there was one subject (Asch, 1952), who, after going with the majority on every critical trial, insisted in the interview following the experiment that he had only reported what he had seen, and he would not retreat from this position when pressed fairly hard. In general, however, it was rare for anyone who went with the majority to say that he had seen what he reported. There were half-hearted attempts to reconcile a sincerely reported group response with a contradictory but sincerely reported individual response by means of fanciful theories of optics and vision. Perhaps the line of regard from the subject's unique position made a difference, or perhaps eye level or angle of head—something. Some even proposed that the first subject to report, and just that subject, had defective vision, and then all the rest like sheep followed his lead. None of those is the most common reaction, however.

For every subject the situation changed dramatically the first time he made a minority response, on whatever trial he made it. At that point and from then on, he felt himself to be the focus of the group's attention, and no subject could be indifferent to that fact, although some were able to report independently in spite of it. For every person who became a minority of one, the situation was powerfully emotional; the evidence is both physiological (Bogdonoff et al., 1961) and behavioral (Asch, 1951, 1952, 1956). How people felt as a minority of one is very clear from Asch's interviews: Like a "silly fool," a "misfit," "queer," "conspicuous," "objectionable," "crazy," "wet blanket," "sore thumb," and so on (1956, p. 31). Our language is rich in terms for the feeling of nonconformity.

It is very important to know exactly what people did when they felt out of step with Asch's unanimous majority. In the first place, a substantial number (24 percent) became firmly independent. In Asch's experiment, it is the amount of conformity that is contrary to common sense and surprising and memorable, but one must not forget that in the major series of experiments (1956), on two-thirds of the trials, the subjects gave independent responses; only on one-third were responses conforming. But, when a subject did conform to a majority, to push our question a little harder, we ask again: "What exactly was he doing?"

The conforming subject was not reporting what he privately thought he saw. His perception, his mind, had not, for the most part, been changed by the force of conformity. What most conforming subjects really did was bring their overt behavior into *compliance* with the majority without any alteration of *internal* belief (Kelman, 1958). "I was beginning to think that 140 million Frenchmen can't be wrong, which is hypocritical, of course." "After all the majority rules. . . " "They had the power of numbers . . ." (Asch, 1956, p. 28). Outside the interaction, once again, each subject knew perfectly well the correct answers.

In the obedience experiment and in the MHRC Encounter, change of values and attitudes was not necessary as a preliminary to rebellion. The majority in each situation arrived with values opposed to illegitimate authority, needing only to identify the present case as an instance of such authority. Probably each person thought of one or two things that made him think delivering high voltage shocks or giving false testimony on videotape was illegitimate, but for the individual alone those clues to the immorality of it all were usually not sufficient to motivate rebellion, but for individuals in groups (the MHRC Encounter) clues could be shared, and in sum they were usually sufficient to produce rebellion in some—the triggering exemplars.

A fully successful rebellion was defined as one in which all group members refused to sign the affidavit, and since a minority in some groups did not hold anti-authoritarian values and was not persuaded to rebel by group exchange of information, an additional force was needed to make them refuse to sign the affidavit: the force of conformity. There was considerable evidence that majorities successfully exerted this force by making affidavit rejection a group norm.

There were, finally, ten groups in which the majority did not hold anti-authoritarian values, and in eight of them the majority ended up obeying the coordinator and signing the affidavit. To get those groups to rebel, it would have been necessary to change privately held beliefs and values, and group membership and the processes of information exchange and conformity that group membership makes possible seem not to be sufficient conditions to produce that result.

Summary

Milgram's shock experiment and the MHRC Encounter differed in that the former produced obedience in the majority of individuals and the latter produced rebellion in the majority (of groups). Why the difference? The answer at the first level is simply that the latter encounter involved groups, and therefore the possibility of collective action existed, as it did not in the obedience encounter. A simple crossover experiment (groups for Milgram and individuals for MHRC) would determine whether or not that is the critical variable, and probably it is. To know that groups behave differently from individuals in obedience encounters is not to understand why. The Law of Social Impact offers some understanding, as that law holds that the intensity of a social force is divided by the number of target persons across whom it is dispersed. Still, that understanding at the second level is not very satisfying, because the law proposes no mediating mechanisms and does not appear even to be true for all cases.

Groups are more likely than individuals to rebel only when the tacit beliefs and values of a majority already favor rebellion. In order to transform this tacit or covert readiness into active unanimous rebellion, three things seem to be necessary. Exchange of information, possible only in groups, puts each individual in possession of the sum total of beliefs and values favoring rebellion and so increases readiness. Triggering exemplars, identifiable by a history of activism, are necessary to show others in the majority that rebellion is possible. For unanimous rebellion, it is finally necessary to invoke the force of conformity, which will carry along the minority not individually disposed to rebel.

References

Arendt, H. 1963. Eichmann in Jerusalem: A Report on Banality of Evil. New York: Viking Press.

Asch, S. E. 1951. Effects of group pressure upon the modification and distortion of judgments. In H. Guetzkow (ed.), Groups, Leadership, and Men. Pittsburgh: Carnegie Press.

———. 1952. Social Psychology. Englewood Cliffs, N.J.: Prentice-Hall.

———. 1956. Studies of independence and conformity: I. A minority of one against a unanimous majority. Psychological Monographs, vol. 70, no. 9 (whole issue, No. 416).

Bassett, R. L., and B. Latané. 1976. Social influences and news stories. Paper presented at the meeting of the American Psychological Association, Washington, D.C., September.

Baumrind, D. 1964. Some thoughts on ethics of research: After reading Milgram's "behavioral study of obedience." American Psychologist, 19 421–23.

Bogdonoff, M. D.; R. F. Klein; E. H. Estes, Jr.; D. M. Shaw; and K. W. Back. 1961. The modifying effect of conforming behavior upon LIPID responses accompanying CNS arousal. Clinical Research, 9: 135.

Elms, A. C., and S. Milgram. 1966. Personality characteristics associated with obedience and defiance toward authoritative command. Journal of Experimental Research in Personality, 1: 282–89.

GAMSON, W. A.; B. FIREMAN; and S. RYTINA. 1982. *Encounters with Unjust Authority.* Homewood, Ill.: Dorsey Press.

HERSH, S. 1970. *My Lai 4: A Report on the Massacre and Its Aftermath.* New York: Random House.

JACKSON, J. M., and B. LATANÉ. 1981. All alone in front of all those people: Stage fright as a function of number and type of co-performers and audience. *Journal of Personality and Social Psychology, 40:* 73–85.

KELMAN, H. C. 1958. Compliance, identification, and internalization: Three processes of attitude change. *Journal of Conflict Resolution, 2:* 51–60.

KELMAN, H., and L. LAWRENCE. 1972. Assignment of responsibility in the case of Lt. Calley: Preliminary report on a national survey. *Journal of Social Issues, 28* No. 1: 177–212.

KILHAM, W., and L. MANN. 1974. Level of destructive obedience as a function of transmitter and executant roles in the Milgram obedience paradigm. *Journal of Personality and Social Psychology, 29:* 696–702.

KRECH, D.; R. S. CRUTCHFIELD; and E. L. Ballachey. 1962. *Individual in Society.* New York: McGraw-Hill.

LATANÉ, B. 1981. The psychology of social impact. *American Psychologist, 36:* 343–56.

LATANÉ, B., and J. M. DARLEY. 1970. *The Unresponsive Bystander: Why Doesn't He Help?* New York: Appleton-Century-Crofts.

LATANÉ, B., and S. NIDA. 1981. Ten years of reseach on group size and helping. *Psychological Bulletin, 89:* 308–24.

LEWIN, K. 1935. *Dynamic Theory of Personality.* New York: McGraw-Hill.

MANTELL, D. M. 1971. The potential for violence in Germany. *Journal of Social Issues, 27* No. 4: 101–12.

MILGRAM, S. 1974. *Obedience to Authority.* New York: Harper & Row.

———. 1977a. Ethical issues in the study of obedience. In Milgram, S., *The Individual in a Social World.* Reading, Mass.: Addison-Wesley, pp. 139–46.

———. 1977b. Liberating effects of group pressure. In Milgram, S., *The Individual in a Social World.* Reading, Mass.: Addison-Wesley, pp. 188–99.

MILGRAM, S.; L. BICKMAN; and L. BERKOWITZ. 1969. Notes on the drawing power of crowds of different size. *Journal of Personality and Social Psychology, 13:* 79–82.

ROBINSON, J. 1965. *And the Crooked Shall Be Made Straight: The Eichmann Trial, the Jewish Catastrophe, and Hannah Arendt's Narrative.* New York: Macmillan.

SHANAB, M. E., and K. A. YAHYA. 1977. A behavioral study of obedience in children. *Journal of Personality and Social Psychology, 35:* 530–36.

STEVENS, S. S. 1957. On the psychophysical law. *Psychological Review, 64:* 153–81.

TANFORD, S., and S. PENROD. 1984. Social influence model: A formal integration of research on majority and minority influence processes. *Psychological Bulletin. 95,* 189–225.

VON LANG, J., and C. SIBYLL (eds.). 1983. *Eichmann Interrogated.* Translated from the German by Ralph Manheim. New York: Farrar, Straus & Giroux.

WALZER, M. 1970. *Obligations.* Cambridge, Mass.: Harvard University Press.

I

Exchange, Equity, and Altruism

IF YOU WERE SITTING on a bridge watching a sunset, and the person next to you fell into the water and screamed, "Help! I can't swim!" you would be under no legal obligation to throw him a life preserver even if one lay close to hand. In not giving aid, you would commit no tort and would not be liable for damages to the drowned person's family. As far as the law is concerned, one is free to enjoy drownings with sunsets so long as one takes no active part in the total production (Zeisel, 1966).

The absence of law in a domain of social welfare suggests the absence of a need for a law, and so perhaps Good Samaritanism is guaranteed by human nature, though the Christian parable from which the term derives suggests otherwise. So, I am afraid, does research, the daily news, and casual observation. The Good Samaritan in the New Testament went out of his way to give aid to a man who had been stripped and beaten by robbers, whereas pious priests and Levites passed him by. I am almost sorry to report that two irreverent American psychologists (Darley and Batson, 1973) had the wicked thought of finding out how pious types (theology students) would fare today in a comparable situation, and I am definitely sorry to report that they fared badly. Even though they had recently been reminded of the parable of the Good Samaritan, when they were caused to be in a hurry to get somewhere, they unconcernedly passed by an unfortunate man coughing and groaning in a doorway. One seminarian delicately stepped over the body.

The Good Samaritan experiment belongs to a large literature on unresponsive bystanders (Latané and Darley, 1970). That literature took its start from a famous news story. At 3 A.M. on a night in 1964, Catherine (Kitty) Genovese was set upon and murdered in the respectable Kew Gardens neighborhood of New York City. The murderer, a blood-chilling, psychopathic figure, took half an hour to accomplish the act, leaving the scene three times and then returning to finish off his victim, who, crawling toward her apartment door, repeatedly screamed that she was being murdered and pleaded for help (Rosenthal, 1964). Two weeks after the event, *The New York Times*, following up a police tip, carried the horrifying news that thirty-eight neighbors of Kitty Genovese had witnessed the event from their windows, and none had responded even to the point of calling the police. No Good Samaritans in that building—in fact, editorialists and writers of letters to the editor said, no one of ordinary human decency. With the Genovese case, American newspapers were sensitized to the phenomenon of the unresponsive bystander and found it to be very common. Two young social psychologists, Latané and Darley, were stimulated to initiate a series of experiments, which in the end succeeded in explaining the bystander phenomenon. The explanation proved to be quite different from either advance common sense or expert opinion—a genuine contribution to knowledge. More of that later.

The Genovese murder was an emergency, and emergencies do not happen every day, but there is an unresponsiveness fully as horrifying that does: The unconcern of the very rich for the very poor even when the contrast in their conditions is made salient. You see it in big cities everywhere: Manhattanites pushing aside bag ladies to get into Van Cleef & Arpels on Fifth Avenue; high-fashion Egyptians disdainfully striking away starving children in Cairo; owners of large estates quite "overlooking" nearby tin shacks in Caracas—or Miami.

One concrete episode has stayed vivid in my memory for many years. At a glorious buffet supper in the Hilton Hotel in Mexico City, American tourists struggled with themselves (on account of their diets) not to go back for desserts as often as they really wanted and then bulged forth into the night chattering their way past half-starved nursing mothers who sat begging on the pavement. Not just tourists of course; they at least occasionally looked startled (and then peevish to think management could so threaten their pleasure); the local rich, used to that sort of thing, registered nothing at all.

It is easy to think of times when we are less altruistic than we think we ought to be, but it is almost as easy to think of good cases of altruism. Or at least it seems to be. Wealthy benefactors are not uncommon. One of them in the early 1980s gave millions to save from bankruptcy the Metropolitan Center in Boston. Of course, he exacted an almost prohibitive price—renaming it the Wang Center. But I do not really know that Mr. Wang exacted the price; the honor probably was forced on him by a grateful Board of Directors. Does the fact that his benefaction was rewarded make him less the altruist? It does at least cloud the issue. There must be clearer cases.

Many universities have programs of continuing education for senior citizens. They typically involve lectures, symposia, and group discussions on all manner of subjects. The elderly students are usually very enthusiastic and interested, and it obviously does them a world of good. One hears that some such programs are funded in part by life insurance companies, and that is surely an act of altruism on the organizational level. Of course, actuarial data do show that old people who keep active . . . Forget this example.

The Red Cross collects blood from each according to ability and willingness to give and dispenses it according to individual need. Donations are anonymous—no public credit. Dispensations are anonymous—no one to whom gratitude can be expressed. Donors enjoy no advantage over nondonors should they or their families be in need of blood. Donation involves some "costs" to the donor: time, slight pain, and residual weakness. And yet there are many who habitually donate, who return again and again. Surely they are true altruists. Some might grant the altruism but think it rather unimpressive since the costs to the individual are not great. And some might deny that habitual blood donation is a case of true altruism since interviews with approximately two thousand habitual donors at the University of Wisconsin revealed that all "felt good" afterward—improved in mood and self-esteem (Piliavin, Callero, and Evans, 1982). It seems, after all, that the donor does not do something for nothing; he has his reward. Does that matter? Does that make him any the less an altruist?

The costs of blood donation are not great enough to make heroes or saints of donors, but heroes and saints also exist. Near the Museum of the Holocaust in Jerusalem there are avenues of memorial tablets to non-Jews who sacrificed their lives to help rescue Jews. London (1970) has carried out psychiatric interviews with a sample of twenty-seven similar rescuers who survived. A minority of those rescuers seem not to have been altruistically motivated but were, rather, people whose entire lives had been characterized by an extraordinary adventurousness—adventurers, therefore, more than altruists. Others, however, seem to have risked their safety primarily in order to realize an altruistic, sometimes religious ideal. They would seem to be altruists, unless a feeling of religious obligation and a rich sense of having done the right thing counts as a disqualification.

Finally, there is my favorite case, favorite because it is relevant to so many theories of altruism both biological and psychological: the living, genetically unrelated kidney donor (Sadler et al., 1971). He is a rare person, but we do not know whether the rareness derives from personal characteristics that are very uncommon or from the fact that most kidney transplant centers do not use that kind of donor. The cost of altruism of this kind is high—a long-lasting, inconvenient preliminary procedure of interviews, blood-typing, and psychiatric evaluation; a major operation and hospital stay; an enhanced lifetime risk that they themselves will need either a kidney transplant or dialysis. Unrelated kidney donors have no ties of kinship or friendship to motivate them. They are subject to no social pressures of the sort that genetically related potential donors may be; in fact, their families and friends tend to think they are crazy. Some donors have no contact with the recipient and will not allow themselves to be thanked. Some donors have reported that they were admired for what they did but that the admiration was short-lived and, in any case, not very important to them. In such circumstances, it is of the highest interest that all donors studied have reported, for years afterward, that the act of donation was the best thing they had done in their lives, *for themselves.* Their altruistic act seemed to them a high privilege, vastly gratifying, deepening the value of their lives. They, too, had not done something for nothing. Does that make them as selfish as the rest of us? Are we all in the end equally nonaltruistic in the sense that each acts so as to maximize his actual or anticipated rewards, whatever those rewards may be?

In social psychology two influential theories of human interaction are often thought to deny the existence of altruism: the theories of exchange and of equity. The two theories are really one, with exchange being a particular case of equity. Both theories explain human interaction in terms of rewards and costs, and both say that relationships among individuals survive only as long as they are "profitable" to all members. Exchange and equity, with their vaguely economic terminology, are sometimes thought of as cynical theories founded on the premise that nobody does something for nothing. I think this is not the case and that exchange and equity not only allow for the existence of altruism, but provide the conceptual ground for clarifying the several senses of altruism and delimiting their areas of operation. In order to appreciate what exchange and equity bring to the subject of altruism, we must first study the theories as such.

2

Exchange and Equity

EVEN THOSE SOCIAL PSYCHOLOGISTS who find unacceptable the notion that all human interaction is based on rewards and costs admit that the idea does apply well to some human interaction. In this chapter we review the domains in which exchange and equity clearly do apply, and we shall find those domains surprisingly extensive. In this chapter also we attempt to make the basic concepts and propositions of the theories maximally clear and to set aside several distracting misconceptions. Although exchange and equity are really one theory, with exchange being the less general case, exposition is easier if the two are described separately, exchange coming first.

Both exchange theory and equity theory take it as established that in all societies at all times it is and has been considered right (normative) that people should benefit those who benefit them. Indeed, the rule seems universally to take the stronger form: For a benefit received, an *equivalent* benefit ought eventually to be returned. Gouldner in 1960 marshaled all the evidence for that rule, which he called the "universal norm of reciprocity." He also cited authorities from ancient times to the present, and the norm of reciprocity is so important in exchange and equity that it is worth hearing some of those voices. Cicero said: "There is no duty more indispensable than that of returning a kindness." Hobhouse (1951) held that reciprocity is a primordial imperative which "pervades every relation of primitive life" (p. 12). Simmel wrote that "all contacts among men rest on the schema of giving and returning the equivalence" (1950, p. 387). Marx, Durkheim, Malinowski, Lévi-Strauss, Homans, and probably every other master of social theory identified reciprocity of benefits as a universal and central principle of social life. Gouldner's own statement summarizing all the evidence and argument he put together in 1960 is: "A norm of reciprocity is, I suspect, no less universal and important an element of culture than the incest taboo." (p. 171).

Exchange Theory

The exchange theory of social behavior has been called a kind of economic theory, and it is clear that it is conceived by analogy with economics since the basic concepts in the theory are benefits or rewards, costs, profits, and marginal utility. However, all those concepts are used in much more extended senses than in economics. For instance, a reward is simply anything desirable and a cost anything undesirable. In our use of the theory of social exchange, it will be important precisely to distinguish social from economic exchange.

Consultation Among Colleagues

We begin with an example of social exchange not involving money. It is a historically important example that appeared in Peter Blau's 1955 study of government bureaucracy and launched Blau's 1964 version of exchange theory. It has made it possible for a generation of social scientists to "see" interaction as exchange.

The scene is a federal agency concerned with investigating businesses for violations of federal law. There are sixteen agents, one clerk, and one supervisor. A given case is assigned to an individual agent, and the agent works with a manual of regulations more than a thousand pages thick. The decisions to be made are sometimes very delicate, requiring long investigation and a high degree of personal discretion. The findings and actions in a given case are eventually checked by the supervisor and a review board, and each agent is periodically rated by the supervisor on the quality of his performance. If an agent has difficulties with a case that he cannot resolve, the rule is that he must consult the supervisor, not another agent. And the supervisor told Peter Blau that that is what agents did. Blau was there on the scene for several months, observing and taking notes, and it did occur to him, very early on, that an agent must feel somewhat reluctant to consult his supervisor, because frequent consultations would indicate a lack of competency and adversely affect his rating.

"They are not permitted to consult other agents. If they have a problem, they take it up with me." So said the supervisor, but Blau found that an agent averaged five contacts per hour with his colleagues, and most of them were consultations on a case. One agent (p) would take some knotty problem to another (o) and ask him what he thought. The other would stop his own work and take time to think about a problem not assigned to him. In fact, *o helped p*. That looks like altruism. Examining the interaction more closely, however, Blau decided that there was a certain reciprocity involved; *o* gained something from the contact. What *o* gained is made explicit in this remark: "I like giving advice. It's flattering, I suppose, if you feel that others come to you for advice" (Blau, 1955, p. 130). Call *o*'s gain "esteem," and we have a pure social exchange: help for esteem. It was quite clear that the esteem was part of the bargain, for anyone who defaulted on that end by implying that the second opinion had not really been needed or that it was not very valuable soon had trouble getting second opinions. Whether or not the dependence of help on a social reward should disqualify the help as altruism is a question for the next chapter.

Everyone has had the experience of asking for or simply being offered help from someone whose "job description" does not include the giving of such help. Recalling that experience, we shall see that we already know a good deal about exchange theory. Consider the interaction between tellers in a bank and bank clients. The essential core of such interaction is defined by the teller's job description—which is the teller's institutionalized role—and by procedures for clients who desire one service or another. Procedures for clients are also a kind of institutionalized role, and somewhere or other it is written down how to proceed, for instance, in order to cash a check, but we learned those procedures a long time ago, and they are second nature to us now. Complementary roles such as teller and client have a well-defined reciprocity of rights and obligations. Many of the most essential exchanges of human benefits are defined as role obligations in such pairs as parent–child, husband–wife, and teacher–student. What each "owes" the other may be long established but never verbalized, or it may actually be written into contracts, ceremonies, handbooks, and the like. There is reciprocity of benefits in complementary roles, but Gouldner's universal norm applies mainly to fill the gaps between roles, to define proper behavior in every kind of informal case, a sort of universal moral cement.

For teller and client the norm of reciprocity may come into play when a check is to be cashed and the teller is not well acquainted with the client and so is obliged by job description to ask for identification. It is a tiresome cost to clients who are always in a hurry to have to fish out a driver's license. A neighboring teller or a teller two or three places down the line may know the client well and can do the client the "favor" of vouching for him, but that is no part of the teller's job description; it is out-of-role behavior. It is when favors are done that the force of the norm of reciprocity is felt. The client must at a minimum say thanks for the favor, and it should not be too perfunctory but ought to be accompanied by a warm smile and perhaps an inquiry about the health of the family of the gracious teller. If many favors are done for one client by one teller, the client may come to feel that a card or a token gift at Christmas is in order.

When help is needed from someone not obliged to give it and the help is not offered as a favor but must be asked for, we all know from experience that the asking can be a difficult thing to do, requiring some calculation. The person to be consulted is not picked at random. Think of a case in which you have had to ask a classmate for help in some subject. Ideally, you will ask someone who "owes you a favor," someone obligated in advance to help by the norm of reciprocity. If no such helper is available, then at least it should be someone to whom you can render up esteem and thanks without too much pain, someone who will make light of his or her superior knowledge, not, please, someone who will "rub it in."

We can now represent the agent consultation case in exchange theory terms. Rewards (or benefits or positive outcomes) are simply anything that is desirable: gifts, help with any undertaking, esteem, affection, conformity, or obedience. Rewards also include the avoidance of anything undesirable: failure, pain, hardship, humiliation. Costs (or negative outcomes) are simply anything undesirable (failure, pain, etc.) as well as any rewards forgone (gifts, help, independence, etc.). Profits (or net benefits or net outcomes) are defined as rewards minus costs: $P = R - C$.

The first proposition in exchange theory is that the tendency to engage in a social action will be stronger in the degree that it promises to be more profitable than alternative actions. Consider now, p and o, two friendly colleagues in Blau's federal agency, of approximately equal competence. We can imagine rewards, costs, and profits as indicated in Table 2-1A; p has both rewards and costs, and so does o, but the values have been invented so as to make the interaction profitable for both. But we must also consider whether it is more profitable for each than available alternatives (Table 2-1B). If p goes to the supervisor, he will get a second opinion more expert than o can provide, but p will incur the prohibitive cost of disclosing a degree of incompetency, and so this alternative is unattractive. If p simply chooses to work on his own, even though he is not sure about the right decision to make on the case, he will avoid going to the supervisor and not have to express any esteem, but will feel uncomfortable about the decision. That alternative is better than going to the supervisor but not so attractive as going to friend o. What option other than helping is available to o? Refusing to help. He would save his time but he would forgo p's esteem and, still worse, be guilty of rudeness. That should be less appealing than giving the help requested. And so, in view of all this calculation, the interaction, more profitable to each than the alternatives, ought to take place, and of course it does.

The consultation between p and o entails reciprocity of net rewards or profits. However, the profits of p and o, as represented in Table 2-1A, are not equivalent, and Gouldner's universal norm calls for reciprocation of profits with *equivalent* profits. That is not to say, however, that profits in every individual interaction need be equivalent. What seems, rather, to be true is that there must be equivalence of exchange in a relation between two individuals over a more or less long term. And there is a second proposition in exchange theory, a proposition that sounds very cold-blooded. A relationship will

TABLE 2-1. A Consultation in Exchange Theory Terms

A. Profits for *p* and *o* in the consultation

For p who asks help of o	Rewards:	Second opinion	+1
		Avoiding asking supervisor	+3
	Costs:	Giving esteem	−1
	Profits		+3
For o who gives help to *p*	Rewards:	Getting esteem	+1
		Avoiding rudeness	+1
	Costs:	Spending his time	−1
	Profits		+1

B. Profits for *p* and *o* in alternative actions

If *p* asks help of supervisor	Rewards:	Expert opinion	+2
	Costs:	Disclosing incompetence	−3
	Profits		−1
If *p* works on his own	Rewards:	Avoiding asking supervisor	+3
		Preserving esteem	+1
	Costs:	Uncertainty about case	−2
	Profits		+2
If *o* refuses to help p	Rewards:	Saving time	+1
	Costs:	Rudeness to *p*	−1
		Forgoing esteem	−1
	Profits		−1

endure only as long as it is profitable to both in approximately equivalent degree. Such a proposition must be qualified by saying that the duration of the term over which nonequivalence can be tolerated, the term of trust as it were, varies from one relationship to another.

Concerning determinants of the term of trust, it is possible to make suggestions. Probably the length of time over which nonequivalence is tolerable to the one profiting less depends on the profitability of available alternative relationships; a rather unprofitable marriage can last a long time if no more attractive partner shows interest. Probably also, the period over which one will tolerate nonequivalence in a relationship increases with experience that nonequivalence in that relationship is always temporary, with balance always being eventually restored; marriages that have lasted a long time can weather sustained periods of unprofitability.

The rule of equivalence in the exchange of benefits is a general rule of fairness, the simplest of such rules. From that starting point, we will eventually develop more complicated general rules of fairness and ultimately a conception of justice.

Blau's study of a federal agency provides some nice evidence for the proposition that it is equivalence over time in a large number of interactions that matters. Blau kept track of who consulted whom in the agency over some months and found that the consultation patterns revealed consistent partnerships. A given p and o, of roughly equal competence, would confine their consultations to one another, more or less taking turns in giving and receiving help. This meant that though receiving help on any given occasion would be more profitable than giving it, in the long run p and o would receive and give about equally often, and so long-term equivalence existed and held a partnership together over time.

In Blau's federal agency there were three agents more expert than the others. The pattern of consultation entered into by the experts was different from the partnerships of the agents of average competence, and exchange theory casts some light on the difference. The experts were often consulted by nonexperts, but they did not in return ask the nonexperts for help, for obvious reasons. An expert was not repeatedly consulted by any single agent of average competence but, rather, occasionally consulted by all. If we imagine rewards and costs as in Table 2-2, it is clear why an average agent would consult an expert; the interchange would be highly profitable for him. Giving the advice requested would also be profitable for the expert, though not very profitable, indeed, only a little more profitable than not giving the advice. That slight margin of profit would decline at a rapid rate if the same average agent were to apply again and again to the same expert. The profit would decline and, indeed, disappear, because the average agent's power to reward the expert with

TABLE 2–2. A Consultation Between an Expert (o) and an Average Agent (p)

For p who asks help of o	Rewards:	Expert advice	+2
		Avoiding asking supervisor	+3
	Costs:	Giving esteem	−1
	Profits		+4
For o who gives help to p	Rewards:	Getting esteem	+1
		Avoiding rudeness	+1
	Costs:	Spending his time	−1
	Profits		+1
For o who refuses help to p	Rewards:	Saving time	+1
	Costs:	Rudeness to p	−1
		Forgoing esteem	−1
	Profits		−1

his esteem must fall off. If superior expertise has been acknowledged once, twice, thrice, there is very little or no additional information or pleasure in having it acknowledged yet again. That situation has been called, by analogy with economics, a declining marginal utility, and it helps to account for the fact that consultations with experts were dispersed across nonexperts (each has a little esteem to offer up) rather than concentrated on any one.

Economic Exchange and Social Exchange

There is, as already noted, a difference between purely economic exchange and social exchange, but money is not the difference. If you walk into a Mercedes-Benz dealer intending to buy model D300, champagne color, and speak with a salesman, you initiate an exchange that is primarily economic in nature. One thing that makes it economic is explicit definition of equivalence: A definite number of thousands of dollars will be exchanged for an automobile with properties specified down to the last detail of interior trim. The explicit exchange can be said to occur at a definite time when the car and certain papers change hands. Economic exchanges are, furthermore, enforceable by law, as the dealer will demonstrate if you fall behind in your payments and as you will demonstrate if the dealer does not make good on his warranty.

Economic exchange is also unlike social exchange in that the terms are discussable. It is okay to bargain, haggle, and quote competitive offers and foolish or terribly trusting not to do so.

Some people find bargaining over prices distasteful and, of course, no inexperienced American can stomach the level that is routine in an Arab *medina*. The reason it can seem distasteful is that we confuse it with social exchange. The terms of social exchange are never explicit, never enforceable at law; above all, the definition of equivalency is not discussable. If you are invited to a wedding or a bar-mitzvah, you can hardly ask: "What price gift will you settle for?" And while a guest at dinner may well be thinking: "Pot roast does not repay rack of lamb," he or she does not say it. The ban on discussion applies only to the parties directly exchanging. One can and does ask third parties: "How much should I spend on a wedding gift to a niece?"

Economic exchange is not always kept clearly distinct from social exchange. In fact, when exchanges are made face to face, economic and social aspects are almost always combined. One party, the salesman, has reliably an interest in adding an overlay of friendship. The car dealer will insist on telling you his name, asking yours, shaking hands, and so on. The only difference between Chevrolet and Mercedes in this respect is that the Chevrolet dealer at once calls you "Robert" and probably "Bob," whereas at Mercedes they start respectfully with the last name and title. The reason for getting friendly, of course, is to make it a little awkward to haggle and a little "unfriendly" to buy elsewhere. The customer may prefer to hold aloof, but it is not so easy, partly because he also has some need to feel that this is more than a business relation and so surely the dealer would not tell outright lies or fail in the future to deliver the promised good service. Professors tend to be especially squeamish about recognizing economic exchange where there is a social overlay. When a publisher "friend" phones me to ask if I would just glance over a proposal for a book, I have trained myself to reply: "What rather large fee did you have in mind?" Sometimes a business, like a cafeteria, will go in for quite a lot of social exchange at quiet times—chitchat with the cashier—and in rush hours will drop the social dimension, like squeezing the fat out of the economy, as Mr. Reagan would say.

Finally, economic exchange in the pure form is understood to be a matter of calculated costs and benefits, and it would be absurd to suggest that sales were motivated by spontaneous bursts of good feeling. In social exchange the situation is complicated. To talk about helping, charity, hospitality, friendship, attraction, and marriage in terms of exchange theory is, by definition, to analyze those relations in terms of rewards and costs, and most people do not, at first, find such analyses either persuasive or appealing. In fact, such analyses frequently seem downright offensive. "Feelings are more spontaneous than that," some will say, and "Who believes in this cynical theory?" some will ask.

Malinowski reports that Trobriand Islanders think it very bad form to exchange gifts as if engaged in economic exchange, and so it is with us and perhaps with people in all societies. In Japan friends sometimes do not like to "split the check" at a restaurant. To do so is to suggest an unwillingness to take turns, an inability to sustain trust and enter upon real friendship. We have similar feelings even when we do split the check. To insist on *exactly* equal shares is either gauche or a joke: "I owe you twenty dollars *and seven cents.* " To return hospitality at once and in almost objectively identical form is again too economic a procedure. Did I have dinner at your house last night with six guests, two wines, and five courses? Very well, you must have six, two, and five with me tonight. It is not done.

Feeling or Obligation and Calculation

Gouldner, in calling reciprocation of equivalent benefits a universal norm, is sensitive to the fact that "norm" has two senses. A norm is a regularity in social behavior and can be thought of as simply descriptive, as what people in a certain situation usually do. The word "norm" also has a prescriptive sense according to which it says what people ought to do. For the most part the two senses apply to the same phenomena since people generally do what they think they ought to do. With the norm of reciprocity of benefits, however, the two senses raise an interesting question: Does man return good for good because that is the kind of creature he is, that is what he feels like doing? If reciprocity is simply human nature, then that is why it is a universal. It is possible, however, that cultures universally prescribe returning good for good because that is a necessity for stable social life, and that men do it not so much because they feel so inclined as because they feel the moral obligation.

I think social exchange involves both feeling and calculation, and the problem to my mind is working out some generalization about the admixture of the two. Let us have a few examples. The library of the medical school at Harvard —Countway is its name—is in Boston across the river from the arts and sciences library in Cambridge and not easy to get to either by car (where to park?) or public transport (very indirect). A psychologist will quite often need an article found only in Countway, and it is exasperating to have to take the time to go there. One day I needed such an article and—with no hope in my heart—asked in our psychology library if there was any regular messenger service. Of course not. However, a young woman working as an aide in the library piped up: "I go to Countway quite often and I would be glad to get it for you." A clear case of social exchange, a proffered favor outside her defined role. "I would appreciate it very much if it is not too much trouble," and the next morning when I got to my office, early and wishing to work, the article was there, having been slid under my door.

What was my reaction? An immediate warm rush of gratitude. There is no doubt in my mind of that. But of course the delivery of the paper in my absence, a graceful feature of the favor, did not relieve me of the responsibility to reciprocate. But how? The definition of equivalence in social exchange is subjective, not objective, and it is here that some calculation must occur. One cannot return a given benefit with just any benefit; it must not be too little or too great. In fact, my first impulse was quite bizarre. A friend had recently sent me five pounds of pecans, and I was prompted to rush down to the library and bury my benefactor in pecans. Too much? It would have seemed so to her, but actually, of course, with five pounds on my desk, the marginal utility of pecans for me was not great. A few seconds later, in a calmer mood, I thought, "No, a simple note of thanks would be the right thing." But what kind of a note? Something typed by my secretary on departmental bond? Definitely not. A handwritten note on personal notepaper. The librarian later told me it had been just right. Is all this book-of-etiquette calculation an unrepresentative academic curiosity? Don't you believe it.

At Christmas time in 1982 I had a chance to talk (in a hospital waiting room) with a gentleman whose occupation was doorman at an expensive Park Avenue apartment house, and his Christmas tips were on his mind. His in-role tasks probably involved opening doors and asking questions, and his out-of-role social fringes would have been expressed warmth and respect, perhaps helping with bundles. His strict policy, he told me, was to treat all tenants with exactly the same courtesy. Their immediate reciprocations would have also been courtesies, but at Christmas, of course, something additional is expected —the Christmas tip. Expected but not explicitly required. Not written into leases, not enforceable by law, and certainly not discussable between tenant and doorman, but perfectly discussable between doorman and me. It turned out that he had a very definite idea about what constituted a fair tip. To each tenant he gave the same benefits and from each tenant he expected an equivalent benefit, not objectively defined, but subjectively. He expected a tip proportionate to tenant income—as roughly assessed by him from apartment occupied, automobile owned, and so forth—with a kind of corollary that five dollars was the smallest amount acceptable. His message to me was that I probably could not imagine how tight some people could be.

Works of fiction, personal experience, and general observation suggest several unproved propositions about the contributions of feeling and calculation to social exchange. In doing good we are perhaps generally more conscious of the role of feeling—goodness of heart or nature—than we are of the role of calculation, and that may be why calling attention to calculation seems cynical. But it appears that there must always be some calculation, however subliminal, because it really is necessary to reciprocate the approximate *equivalence*, and equivalencies across infinitely various benefits are certainly not wired-in functions but must always be worked out. Finally, it seems as if there is a kind of tradeoff or negative correlation between feeling and cooly calculated obligation. If the good deed is to be done at all, it is necessary that something motivate it. So long as feeling is strong—gratitude, love, or attraction—obligation will scarcely be felt, as in love, close friendship, or simply a generous unexpected favor. When feeling is not strong, obligation is felt, reciprocity becomes a prescriptive norm, and awareness of calculation is likely to be high, partly because in the absence of good feeling the calculation of what is due can be exceeding fine.

Mood and Altruism

The feelings that are relevant to helping behavior and benign acts generally are not only those that focus on the object person, such as liking and admiration. There is also the real possibility that generalized mood is a factor, and on that point there are some nice experiments.

For benefits that are reciprocal, it is difficult to determine whether spontaneous good feeling for the benefactor or a sense of obligation plays the greater determining role. The same problem arises for experiments on mood, though it is not so immediately obvious. It is less obvious because mood experiments generally have dealt not with direct reciprocation but rather with benevolence to a third party. An experiment by Isen and Levin (1972) is representative.

Small boys know that returned coins are sometimes left in pay telephone slots, and they go hunting for them. Adults do not hunt, but most of the time they do check the slot of a pay phone either before or after calling. It is agreeable, very mildly so, to find something there. Isen and Levin guaranteed that experience for some callers in a shopping mall by planting dimes in some phones and making sure nothing was in others. Finding or not finding was their nicely natural independent variable. Immediately after the experience of finding, a subject found himself walking behind a young woman who dropped a manila folder full of papers and thereby created an option: to help or not to help. The young woman was, of course, an experimenter's confederate, and the sequence of events had been carefully planned.

Would a person feeling the slight glow that finding a dime can give be especially likely to give unsolicited aid to a stranger? Isen and Levin obtained the following strong effect:

	Coin	Not
Helped	14	2
Not	1	24

The results seem to show that a small bit of luck produces a good mood, which immediately facilitates benevolent behavior. It is possible, however, to think of the transaction in exchange theory terms, not necessarily involving feeling. To do so, however, one must extend the theory, because the person benefited is not the person responsible for the initial benefit, and so the exchange is not a case of reciprocation. Suppose, however, that we posit a kind of central exchange; it will prove interesting to do so. One might suppose, and it does not contradict intuition, that the rule of fairness we follow with respect to a central exchange is: A benefit withdrawn calls for a benefit deposited. With whom the deposit is made could be a matter of indifference; the point is to maintain a balance in the centrally kept accounts. Whether one believes there is Someone actually keeping those accounts seems to be a question of religion, but many act as if there were even though they do not say they believe it.

Zuckerman (1975) has provided an example of the "Good Deed In—Good Deed Out" principle in which mood is definitely not involved, because the deposit precedes the withdrawal and, in fact, represents an effort to coerce the central exchange. Students close to a time when a difficult and consequential exam would be given (and others not in that position) were asked to donate some time to read for a blind student. Those worried about the impending exam were more likely to do so, and they would not have been put in a good mood in advance, so perhaps exchange is the real determinant of this sort of low-cost helping. (Is it altruism?)

Isen and Levin (1972) so arranged matters that the chance to help immediately followed the small benefit, and it is interesting to ask whether a good mood of this sort, if indeed there was a good mood—and that has not yet been directly demonstrated but only inferred—lasts more than a few seconds. Isen, Clark, and Schwartz (1976) have done a very clever, completely natural experiment to check on the time course of good moods induced by minor benefits. Their experimental subjects were visited by a young woman going door to door distributing sample packages of an attractive notepaper—but making no effort to sell the paper. Control subjects did not receive the samples. At programmed intervals, from one minute to twenty after receiving the unexpected gift, house-holders were telephoned by a "wrong number" who asked to speak to Victor. "No Victor here." "Oh, damn! Information must have given me the wrong number and now I have run out of coins for this pay phone. The problem is that my brother Victor is expecting me to pick him up and I'm going to be late. Could you possibly look up the number, if I give you the name, and make the call for me?" Who would and who would not? Doing the favor would be a fairly low-cost bit of altruism but something of a nuisance all the same. Some people just hung up without a word; others agreed to call, and if they said they would, they did (a confederate "Victor" was on the other end of the line). If we can suppose that the free sample created a good mood, we have a test of the time course of mood decay.

Making the call must have seemed quite an imposition, because only 12 percent of thirty control subjects did it (Figure 2-1). The sample notepaper had an effect. Of people called within seven minutes, 83 percent did the favor. It is interesting that people called within one minute obliged the caller less often, and we may guess that their benign mood was reduced by the irritation of two interruptions so close together. Doing the favor fell off with minutes elapsed since the call and, indeed, after twenty minutes was down to 12 percent—no different from the control group. If, indeed, it is the warm glow produced by a gift that makes one willing to do a favor, the glow produced by a sample of notepaper wears off rather quickly.

One cannot help wondering about the time course of the happiness pro-duced by a really substantial undeserved bit of luck, such as winning a lottery. The chances are against any of us ever finding out from personal experience. One wonders also about the effect over time on mood of catastrophes, acci-dents resulting in paraplegia or quadriplegia. Brickman, Coates, and Janoff-Bulman (1978) have found out. Winners of $50,000 to $1 million, after one month or more, could not be distinguished in ratings of happiness from matched controls who had won nothing at all. There's some comfort in that. However, accident victims were otherwise; their problems stayed with them, and they were less happy than controls for many months afterward, though actually not so unhappy as you and I think we would be.

Everything reviewed so far really leaves unresolved the question as to whether it is mood or central exchange calculation that motivates helping behavior. Brickman and colleagues studied happiness only, not helping. The Isen team studied the time course of helping as a consequence of receiving a gift, but they had no direct indication that the gift induced a good mood; that is an inference, and the calls to Victor may simply have been deposits in central exchange, in which case the deposits fell off with the passage of time just because the unexpected gift faded from memory.

Isen et al. (1978) have evidence that trifling free samples do change outlook

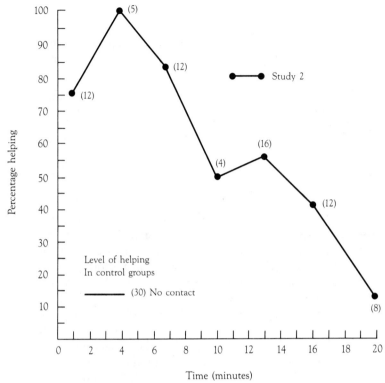

Figure 2–1. Percentage of subjects helping in each condition

N indicated in parentheses. (After A. M. Isen, M. Clark, and M. F. Schwartz, Duration of the effect of good mood on helping: "Footprints on the sands of time," *Journal of Personality and Social Psychology, 34* [1976]. Copyright 1976 by the American Psychological Association. Reprinted by permission of the publisher and author)

or mood quite independently of deposits in the Banque Centrale. Once again in a shopping mall some shoppers were given samples—and others not—and then immediately afterward had an opportunity—not to help—but rather to express what might be called their brightness of outlook, the degree to which they looked on the good side. A consumer survey person asked them, among other things, to rate the quality of performance and service record of the car and refrigerator they had at home. This was quite ingenious. Control and experimental subjects ought to have about equally good possessions, and so if asked to rate from memory, average ratings should primarily reflect current mood. The "gifted shoppers" took a quite significantly more favorable view. In this experiment subjects were not asked to help one another; the index of mood was independent of helping, but the stimulus for the mood was the same as that used to induce helping, so it is a fairly safe conclusion that mood can facilitate low-cost helping. Indeed, there is a great deal of confirmatory research, so much that the relationship may be considered one of the best established in social psychology. Success as well as receipt of an unexpected gift has been used to produce a good mood. It has even been shown (Cunningham, 1979) that restaurant tips are higher on sunny days than cloudy, and sunshine, we know, is a potent creator of good cheer.

In sum, it seems likely that the effect of general moods on helping a third party are the same as the effect of feelings for a second party on helping the second party. The mood is salient, more salient than any calculation of exchange, and yet the exchange calculation seems always also to be there.

Equivalence in Social Exchange

Sometimes the benefits or goods exchanged are objectively equivalent. This was the case in an experiment by Wilke and Lanzetta (1970). They created a business game in which p served as head of one shipping department and o of another. Each was responsible for allocating transport for forty consignments of a certain good, and both had the same number of trucks available for the job. The experimenters programmed a number of different games so that p would sometimes have enough trucks to handle his work and sometimes would need help, which meant borrowing trucks from o. Matters were arranged so that when p needed help he received help 0 percent of the time, 10 percent, 20 percent, 30 percent, or up to 100 percent. The tables were later turned, in a credible sort of way, and it became o's turn to need help. The question of interest was the amount of help p would give to o when he had received help from o one or another percentage of the time. The answer was that p would give back almost the exact equivalent of what he had received. The Wilke and Lanzetta experiment is the prototype for many others demonstrating objective equivalence in exchange (e.g. Kahn and Tice, 1973; Pruitt, 1968). Objective equivalence as a rule of fairness appears to operate when p and o have approximately equal needs and resources, are unacquainted, and feel no particular attraction to one another. When the parameters are changed, objective equivalence fails to be realized, but exchanges do not become lawless; subjective equivalence is the new rule.

Consider tipping once again. The Park Avenue doorman saw himself as rendering the same courtesies and services to all tenants, but the Christmas tips he considered to be fair returns were not objectively equivalent for rich p and less-rich o. His subjective rule was something like "x" percent of presumed income, and that rule rendered equivalent the unequal sums of money he received. The tips given to waiters in restaurants set an interesting test for the principle of subjective equivalence. Clearly tips are not objectively equal. There is, however, a very widespread norm to guide tipping: 15 percent of the check before taxes. Why just that rule? I cannot explain why it should be 15 percent rather than 10 percent or some other value, but "of the check" is explicable.

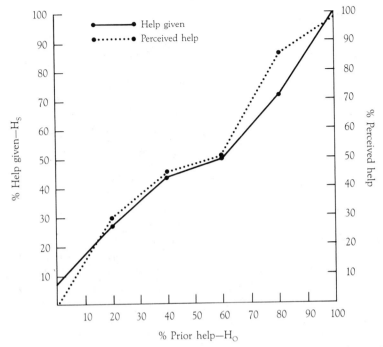

Figure 2–2. Amount of reciprocated help and degree of perceived help as a function of degree of prior help

(H. Wilke and J. T. Lanzetta, The obligation to help: The effects of amount of prior help on subsequent helping behavior, *Journal of Experimental Social Psychology*, 6 [1970]. Used by permission)

The size of the check is a very rough index of ability to pay—of client resources. People who eat at Joe and Nemo's are presumed to have less ability to pay than people who dine at Le Cirque. Of course, that is not necessarily so, but if you dine (once) above your means, you must be prepared to reciprocate service at the proper level, and people who are dining above their means on a given occasion tend to be particularly careful about leaving a large enough tip.

In tipping, the rule of 15 percent of check is a version of "from each according to his means." It is slightly modified, research (Freeman et al., 1975) has shown, by two limiting conditions. The percentage tends to rise as checks get very small; people who pay two dollars for breakfast are likely to leave more than thirty cents (15 percent) as a tip. There is some mad notion in our heads of what constitutes a "decent" or "acceptable" lower limit; it was five dollars for the doorman. It also happens that as checks get very high, the percentage tends to fall slightly, and so there seems to be an absolute upper limit, some notion of how great a sum it is sane to give away. Even those limits-at-the-extreme, however, do not necessarily violate the general principle, because just as there is a lower limit on the amount one can decently give, so is there a lower limit on the amount of service a waiter can deliver in setting up a meal and an upper limit on how good, gracious, or servile service can possibly be.

The principle "from each according to his means" serves to render the objectively nonequivalent subjectively equivalent in quite a wide variety of cases. In gift giving, rich relatives may be expected to, and sometimes do, give more. Governments are not persons, but when representatives of governments discuss foreign aid in an international forum such as a conference sponsored by the United Nations, the reasoning about what is fair is quite familiar. The United States has generally been inclined to stress the fact that its aid to less developed countries has been objectively greater than that of any other country. The less developed countries themselves, however, have been so rude as to argue a "means rule": 1 percent of the gross national income, for instance. By such a rule, it is sometimes pointed out, the United States gives less than most other countries.

I know of only one case in which total exchanges of gifts and hospitality were actually recorded for an entire community to see if the rule of equivalence was realized, and in that case the investigators concluded that it was not. I interpret their findings differently. The Eskimo village of Sugluk has 254 inhabitants, and for a period of six weeks Pryor and Graburn (1980) actually recorded all visits and exchanges, three hundred of the former and more than a thousand of the latter. The authors title their report "The Myth of Reciprocity," because they found that quite a few of their indices were not perfectly balanced at the end of the period of record-keeping. One reason for disagreeing with the conclusion of the authors is that six weeks is an arbitrary period, and the theory of reciprocal exchange does not specify a term over which perfect reciprocity should be realized. Indeed, it is a part of the theory that such terms should vary from one relationship to another.

I think Pryor and Graburn have not made a fair test of reciprocity, but beyond that I think there is evidence in their data that specifically argues for subjective equivalence and gives us a broader definition of it. Comparing disabled Eskimos with able-bodied Eskimos, they found that the former received more than they gave. Comparing unmarried males with married males, they found that the former were net receivers of hospitality and the latter net givers. Probably the same *objective* inequalities hold true in our society, but surely that is just the sort of *objective* inequality to be expected if subjective equality is the rule of fairness. In fact, the inequalities associated with health and marital status follow the same rule as inequalities of wealth—a means rule, with "means" defined abstractly enough to capture the lesser ability to extend hospitality of the disabled and unmarried. Translating the means rule into the concepts of exchange theory yields a fully general rule for transforming objective inequality into subjective equality: The value of a benefit or reward to o varies with its cost to p. The Sugluk villagers themselves believed, Pryor and Graburn admit, that equivalence reciprocity governed their social relations, and it appears to me that the villagers understood their culture in the only relevant way, subjectively, from the inside, and that objective inequality is simply irrelevant.

The principle that benefits are valued more when they cost more (e.g. the "widow's mite") has been demonstrated in many experiments (e.g. Nadler, Fisher, and Streufert, 1974; Tesser, Gatewood, and Driver, 1968). Gergen and his associates (1975) conducted one experiment in three countries, the United States, Sweden, and Japan, and in all three found that donations from lesser resources were valued more highly than the same donation from larger resources. The principle applies not only to tangibles such as gifts and hospitality and physical aid, of course, but also to intangibles like time and sympathy. A brief phone call every month or so from an extremely busy person may be accepted as fair exchange for several letters from a person with a great deal of free time.

When Help Cannot Be Returned

Some of the federal agents whom Blau observed were experts, superior in knowledge and judgment to the majority of agents. The experts by definition were able to give a kind of help that could not be reciprocated, and what happened in Blau's agency forewarns us that help that cannot be reciprocated presents a special puzzle. The less expert agents generally consulted just once with any expert, receiving good advice and in turn offering up their esteem (like the male praying mantis his life), but they did not return for more (the mantis could not).

One can easily see why a continuing partnership would have no attraction for experts; the nonexperts' admiration would have a rapidly dwindling marginal utility. The puzzling thing, however, is not that the experts ceased to offer help, but that the average agent ceased to apply. In Table 2–2 the less-expert agent is represented as enjoying profits of +4 from his single consultation with an expert. Surely this implies that he ought to have gone back again and again. If his marginal utility declined, he might attempt to restore it by increasing the extravagance of his gratitude and admiration. If that effort failed, then it would be for the expert to decline to help, not for the less-expert to stop asking. Perhaps you think the nonexpert would know the expert was enjoying no profits and so would stay away in order to spare himself the humiliation of a rebuff. But it is not at all certain that applications would have been rebuffed or that nonexperts thought they would have been; politeness is a powerful force.

Greenberg and Shapiro (1971) have done an experiment that actually shows it is not fear of rebuff that deters us from asking for help we cannot reciprocate. Some of their subjects were ill qualified (by reason of a physical handicap) for a job that others were well qualified to perform, and when the ill-qualified could not expect ever to be able to reciprocate help, they did not ask for it. In addition, Greenberg and Shapiro asked the ill-qualified whether they thought help would be refused if asked for. They thought it probably would not be refused. Nevertheless, they were not about to ask. Of course, asking is more difficult than accepting. Broll, Gross, and Piliavin (1974) showed that many more students were willing to accept help with a difficult problem in logic when the help was offered than were willing to go to a peer and ask for help. However, needed help very often is not offered but has to be requested, and even offered help is not always accepted (DePaulo and Fisher, 1980).

There is a real puzzle about help that cannot be reciprocated. Why do we not ask for it when we do not expect refusal, and why will we sometimes not accept it when it is offered? It is important to know, because the class of cases in need of help but unable to reciprocate includes the physically handicapped or disabled, welfare clients, underdeveloped nations, and all of us, some of the time. In addition, we must wonder how it happens that help that cannot or will not be reciprocated is available at all. On the face of it, unreciprocated help is altruism, which we have so far found to be a scarce or at least elusive quality. Yet some data would suggest that most people want to be altruists. Muir and Weinstein (1962) reported that in a survey study *all* respondents stated that they "like to do favors for others." Only 8.9 percent said they "like being obligated to others."

The general answer to the puzzles presented by help that cannot be reciprocated is that recipients believe, in accordance with the universal norm of reciprocity, that help *must* be reciprocated, and if it cannot be reciprocated in kind, then some other sort of subjectively equivalent return is expected. Accepting help entails obligation, and obligations are uncomfortable, especially so perhaps when their exact nature is vague. The suspicion arises that the return exacted will be more costly than the help, that it may involve influence, compliance, even a ruinous loss of self-esteem.

Consider the case of help between nations, help not possible to reciprocate in kind. Such foreign aid was quite uncommon before World War II, but since then almost all nations are involved as either donors or recipients, or as both. Gergen and Gergen (1971) interviewed sixty officials involved in international aid, including officials from Tunisia, Algeria, Morocco, Italy, and Greece. Very generally, all believed that foreign aid was really a process of reciprocal exchange. In return for aid (often low-cost surplus commodities), a nation might obtain military bases, economic concessions, protection of business investments, and political influence. One even called foreign aid a psychological substitute for war. The officials interviewed laughed at the idea that the United States or any nation might offer aid and expect nothing in return. They considered such claims to be either dangerously naive or seriously manipulative. On the whole, officials thought what recipient countries needed to hear was not that aid was being freely given, but rather a frank admission that something was expected and explicit specification of just what.

Some aspects of exchange may be explicit in foreign aid. In the degree that they are it resembles an economic transaction, but the full terms are almost never explicit, so there is a residual social exchange dimension. With respect to the dimension of implicit social exchange, misunderstandings sometimes arise. Soviet aid to Egypt some years ago became so extremely generous, so very intimate, that the Egyptian leaders threw the Soviets out of their country. On one occasion in the 1980s the American government presumed that its "generous" aid to Israel gave it the right to reprove Israel for its foreign policy and to ask for a certain amount of compliance. Menachim Begin thereupon exploded and told the U.S. government that Israel owed it nothing, that the aid was given out of American self-interest, and that Israel was a sovereign state that took orders from nobody. The U.S. government made no public reply.

When it comes to U.S. aid to underdeveloped, so-called third world countries, the beliefs of recipient countries are well expressed in the following quotation from an editorial that appeared in the *Pakistan Times* in the late 1960s:

> Primarily, U.S. aid seeks to gain full economic and political control over the aided country; its secondary objectives are to help crush nationalist revolts and to oppose Communism and Communist States. Defense of freedom or democracy as law does not seem to enter into their calculations at any stage. The pacts inspired by the U.S. are only to be presented as the expression of altruism, so that underdeveloped countries can be inveigled to walk into the U.S. parlour and accept a little economic aid. Such aid will be given in a manner that drives the country to a closer alliance. [Andreas, 1969]

So strong is the norm of reciprocity that even federal welfare, as in the program of Aid to Families with Dependent Children, tends to create feelings of obligation. If such feelings were at all realistic, they would be directed at no person or agency but at the generalized state, the collectivity of taxpayers. In fact, however, in the past, before families on welfare learned to think of welfare as a right rather than a charity, most felt that in accepting aid they had implicitly ceded various powers to, especially, the social worker who was the representative of the system. Briar (1966), in a paper called "Welfare from Below," reported some of the obligations felt by women on AFDC. "If the social worker were to call on you at some late and inconvenient hour, could you ever refuse admission?" Ninety-two percent thought not. "If the social worker gave you specific advice like seeking psychiatric help, would you be obliged to follow it?" Most thought they would be.

In 1980–81, a Harvard senior wrote his honors thesis with me. That student, now in Harvard Law School, is congenitally blind, and so I learned from him many things about social psychology, including the social psychology of help that cannot be reciprocated. One day, talking about a questionnaire he might use in his thesis, I made the routine suggestion: "Pretest it on your roommate." Undergraduates at Harvard who are concentrating in psychology do this all the time, very much in the spirit of trying a suspicious food on the dog. My student hesitated a minute and then said: "I don't see how I could ever help him with his thesis." In fact, he felt the force of the norm of reciprocation and articulated for me the special problems it posed for him and must pose for people with any sort of physical handicap.

It was not, the student assured me, that his roommate would be unwilling to do him the favor of filling out the questionnaire. In fact, he would certainly offer if he knew of the need. It was not an expectation of refusal that made the problem. There seemed to be two principal factors making the obligation aversive. One was the possibility of eventual, gradual, tacit resentment and withdrawal. Social isolation is a terrible threat to the blind person.

Another cost associated in the blind student's mind with asking help was a possible implication of inferiority and loss of self-esteem. That is a prominent theme in the interviews that Ladieu and her colleagues (1947) held with persons having various sorts of handicap. It could be heard whenever they tried to distinguish between forms of help they would welcome or at least find inoffensive and forms they would reject. It would often be quite subtle, a matter of the way in which help was offered or something helpful done, but what it seemed to come to was: Any implication that I am less able in a general way, even if more or less true, is disagreeable. Any implication that I need help or that it is troublesome to you to give it is unacceptable. A serious loss of self-esteem is again a cost too great to risk.

The psychological costs of isolation and self-depreciation, though perhaps more generally and keenly felt by persons with serious physical handicaps, are, of course, perfectly familiar to all of us as individuals and even as nationalities. It seems not at all unlikely that those implicit costs of asking help from experts operated in the federal agency Blau studied and prevented such consultations from becoming frequent.

Jane Austen's 1814 novel *Emma* (1972) tells of two ladies, Mrs. Bates and Miss Bates, who are permanently in the position of accepting (never asking for) benefits, chiefly hospitality, which they cannot possibly reciprocate in kind. The ladies qualify for the hospitality they receive because Mrs. Bates is the widow of a former vicar of Highbury and so belongs to the gentry. Jane Austen describes brilliantly the plight of Miss Bates in a society governed by the principle of exchange:

> [She] stood in the very worst predicament in the world for having much of the public favour; and she had no intellectual superiority to make atonement to herself, or frighten those who might hate her into outward respect. She had never boasted either beauty or cleverness. Her youth had passed without distinction, and her middle of life was devoted to the care of a failing mother, and the endeavour to make a small income go as far as possible. [p. 12]

Jane Austen also shows how Miss Bates recompensed the kindness of her richer neighbors:

> She loved every body, was interested in every body's happiness, quick-sighted to every body's merits; thought herself a most fortunate creature, and surrounded with

blessings in such an excellent mother and so many good neighbours and friends, and a home that wanted for nothing. The simplicity and cheerfulness of her nature, her contented and grateful spirit, were a recommendation to every body and a mine of felicity to herself. [p. 12]

From Miss Bates we can learn something about the interplay of feeling and calculation in social exchange. She is someone who must always be in the position of help-recipient and whose circumstances are such that the only benefits she can deliver are psychological. It is clear, however, that the right name for what she does is not "ingratiation." It would be inaccurate to say that, in return for hospitality, she "makes herself agreeable." It would be inaccurate because there is never any conscious calculation; all her expressions of gratitude, admiration, and concern spring from true feeling. The result of this representation of Miss Bates is that she is a sympathetic figure to us, though also one that can be comic. When Emma Woodhouse, the grandest young lady in Highbury, calls on the Bateses (with her friend, Harriet Smith), Miss Bates fairly turns herself inside out trying to recompense such extreme kindness:

> The visitors were most cordially and even gratefully welcomed; the quiet neat old lady, who with her knitting was seated in the warmest corner, wanting even to give up her place to Miss Woodhouse, and her more active, talking daughter, almost ready to overpower them with care and kindness, thanks for their visit, solicitude for their shoes, anxious inquiries after Mr. Woodhouse's health, cheerful communications about her mother's, and sweet-cake from the beaufet. "Mrs. Cole had just been there, just called in for ten minutes, and had been so good as to sit an hour with them and *she* had taken a piece of cake and been so kind as to say she liked it very much; and therefore she hoped Miss Woodhouse and Miss Smith would do them the favour to eat a piece too." [p. 103]

The effect of a figure in a disadvantageous social position who admires and thanks as extravagantly as Miss Bates but who has no corresponding feelings and acts entirely out of calculation is very different. In such a case "ingratiation" is the right word. When the novelist who creates the figure goes one step further and reveals to us feelings directly contrary to the gratitude and admiration expressed and also puts the calculation in the service of self-interest, we have a character not just unsympathetic, but a hypocritical, slimy villain. In fact, Mr. Uriah Heep of *David Copperfield*. It seems clear that while feeling and calculation combine, in life in widely various proportions, we like best the person whose benefits to another are most purely motivated by feeling.

The Unresponsive Bystander

There is not now and never has been a Good Samaritan law in the United States or in England, but since the Kitty Genovese case the desirability of such a law has been much discussed, most exhaustively in 1965 at a "Conference on the Good Samaritan and the Bad: The Law and Morality of Volunteering in

Situations of Peril, or of Failing to Do So" held at the Law School of the University of Chicago (Ratcliffe, 1966). There are many models for a Good Samaritan law, because a majority of European countries have them (including Germany, France, Italy, and the U.S.S.R.). All of the existent laws as well as the arguments for and against them clearly presuppose a reward–cost analysis of the unresponsive bystander situation, which is exactly the analysis Exchange Theory dictates. A witness to an emergency, whether that emergency results from an accident or a crime, finds himself in a situation where he has much to lose (immediate assault, reprisals, reprimands for interference, and so on) and almost nothing to gain (a possible thank you), a profitless situation from which he can only wish to be delivered. A Good Samaritan Law to be effective must change the reward–cost matrix for witnesses to an emergency either by increasing the rewards for helping (e.g. financially) or by increasing the costs of not helping (e.g. a fine or jail sentence).

Also in the late 1960s and also as a result of the Genovese case, Latané and Darley (1970) conducted a series of experiments on simulated but very realistic emergencies to see what the methods of social psychology would reveal about unresponsive bystanders. Their basic theoretical analysis of the problem was again an Exchange Theory analysis in terms of rewards and costs. Let us first see how such an analysis would be applied to one of their own ingenious experiments.

The "Nu-Way Beverage Center" is a discount beer store in Suffern, New York. The store cooperated with Latané and Darley in 1968 by allowing itself to be the scene of ninety-six robberies in one week. The robbers (experimenter confederates) were two husky young men dressed in chinos and T-shirts.

The major variable was the number of customers (subjects, not confederates) who were in the store and could function as onlookers. The robbers bided their time so they could carry off the crime with two onlookers half the time (forty-eight robberies) and just one the other half (forty-eight robberies). Following their scenario, the robbers asked the cashier if he would mind checking how many bottles of Löwenbrau beer he had in stock. While the proprietor was out of sight in the back of the store, the robbers picked up a case of beer near the front of the store, remarked to nobody in particular, "They'll never miss this," and carried it to their car. Then they drove off. There was no possibility that the bystanders could fail to notice the theft.

The cashier then returned to the counter and resumed waiting on his genuine customer or customers. The customer(s) had ample time spontaneously to report the theft, but only 20 percent of all subjects did so. When no report was made, the cashier prodded for one by asking what had become of the two men and whether the customer(s) had seen them leave. Fifty-one percent of the remaining subjects responded to the prompt. Putting all reports together, prompted or spontaneous, 65 percent of the onlookers who had been alone with the robbers told of the theft. The effective individual probability of helping in groups of two was substantially lower; only .34.

With two naive subjects together, the formula for calculating the effective individual probability of helping is: $P_1 = 1 - \sqrt[2]{1 - P_g}$ where P_1 is the individual probability of helping and P_g is the proportion of groups of two in which at least one person helps (Latané, Nida, and Wilson, 1981). For the effective individual probability in groups of two to be as high as the 65 percent of individuals alone who helped, at least one person would have had to report the theft in 87 percent of the groups of two. It is the effective individual probability we want because once one person in a group has helped (reported the theft), the situation is entirely changed. In the thefts at the "Nu-Way Beverage Center," one person helped in just 56 percent of all groups, which yields an individual probability of .34.

In the Beverage Center experiment there are two striking results: (1) The very low level of reporting in any circumstances and (2) a substantially greater probability of reporting in the case of one onlooker than in the case of two. For the moment, we shall stay with the main result, the bystander phenomenon of failing to intervene. With some modifications, the Latané and Darley book suggests the matrix of Table 2-3. For a p who intervenes, there are many possible heavy costs (including, for instance, being assaulted by the robbers and, if the store should be badly damaged by his efforts at intervention, being sued by the store owner) whereas there are few significant rewards (thanks of the owner). The reward–cost consequences of intervening strongly suggest that it is not the thing to do. The reward–cost analysis of not intervening suggests the same thing. The significant rewards are not anything new added for p but simply avoidance of the possible costs of intervention—which, however, will not seem insignificant to any p who thinks of them. There are some possible costs of doing nothing, chiefly self-reproach, but those costs are psychological and, in certain circumstances, as when there is more than one bystander, escapable. They

TABLE 2-3. A Reward–Cost Analysis of Intervening in a Theft

For a p who intervenes	Possible rewards:	Thanks of the store owner
		Newspaper write-up
	Possible costs:	Assault by the robbers
		Ridicule of nonintervening bystanders
		Misunderstanding—the two men are entitled to the beer
		Owner sues for damage done store by attempted intervention
		Questioning by police, lawyers, etc.
For a p who does not intervene	Possible rewards:	Avoiding all five costs of intervention
	Possible costs:	Empathic distress with store owner
		Shame at cowardly inaction
		Reproach of others
		Forgoing rewards of intervention

can, in effect, be "thought away." Everything then favors nonintervention, which is what most people (80 percent) did when they confronted the robbers all alone.

Is it really the case, one might ask, that a witness to an emergency accident or crime runs over in his mind the possible rewards and costs? That is most convincingly answered by interrogating witnesses who have not read Latané and Darley and never heard of Exchange Theory, I myself am convinced by the experiences I have had as a witness—seldom intervening, I confess—and by the many reports of such experiences that students have made to me. It seems not really to make much difference in what you think or do whether or not you have read about the unresponsive bystander.

My most recent failure to be a Good Samaritan occurred around Christmastime in 1983, early in the evening in Cooley's China Shop on Newbury Street in Boston. The shop is a small one with three connecting display rooms. Numerous quite expensive and very fragile glass and china pieces were on open shelves, and I and about fifteen others were poking around hoping to find a gift inspiration. One tiny lady about sixty-five years old was there to wait on us and also, I suppose, to watch us—as best she could—but really there was no possibility of keeping everyone at once under surveillance. Two young men, not at all fragile, came in. They wore very large, shabby overcoats, and in those coats there were capacious pockets. I had the bad luck to see them whip a couple of pieces of china into their pockets. Whether anyone else had seen them, I could not tell. They moved toward the door. What to do?

Well, first I did a lot of quick thinking, and it was all about rewards and costs. Suppose, unimaginably, that I were to call out, "Stop, thief!" (I could not have managed "Stop, thieves"), and if they did stop (conceive it if you can), attempted forcibly to apprehend them. What would have followed?

1. They would have laid me out with one blow, kicked me in the kidneys, and perhaps carved me up a little.
2. Plenty of glass and china would have been broken.
3. They would have escaped.
4. They would have located my champagne-colored Mercedes and worked that over.
5. The lady who owned the store and her customers, even if not injured in the fracas, would have cursed me for being an interfering fool.
6. The police, when at length they arrived, would have said: "Why don't you leave these things to us, Bud?"

Just not much incentive there.

Well, but what about the costs of failing to live up to my moral principles? I knew all about unresponsive bystanders and did not want to act like one of Genovese's neighbors. However—I thought—the thieves looked poor and probably needed money more than Mrs. Cooley. Who was undoubtedly insured against theft. In case all those customers better positioned than I to intervene failed to do their obvious duty. Such situations do indeed quickly register as profitless at best, and one's unworthy thought is likely to be: "Why me?"

If a reward–cost analysis of the unresponsive bystander is the right analysis, and I am sure it is, then it might seem to be easy to draft legislation that would make more bystanders helpfully responsive. In France a citizen can receive a jail sentence for as long as five years and a fine of some thousands of francs for being an unresponsive bystander (Tunc, 1966). Would it be right for me to have been given some such sentence for what I failed to do in Cooley's China Shop? The penalties seem too severe for failure to prevent a mere theft. Actually, they seem so to the French also, and their law applies only to a failure to rescue someone whose life is in danger, which was not the case in Cooley's. But even if it had been, even if the thieves had been about to shoot someone, would it be right for the law to require me to risk my own life to save another's? The French legislators clearly thought not, because their law holds that the obligation to intervene exists only if one can do so without *onerous risk* to oneself. Clearly then, the French law would hold me guiltless in the case of Cooley's. It probably would not, however, do the same for the thirty-eight witnesses in Kew Gardens because they could have stayed indoors and phoned the police. In many other cases it would be a matter of legal argument whether or not onerous risk existed, and a jury might find the judgment difficult to make.

In Cooley's at Christmastime in 1983, while I stood immobile reckoning up possible rewards and costs, the problem was resolved by the woman in charge of the shop, who went up to the two thieves saying, "Can I help you gentlemen?" and she actually was able to edge them out the door with no weapon but a slightly menacing tone. Afterward she told us that she had seen the theft, that it happened every now and then, and that it simply did not pay to attempt a "citizen's arrest." In fact, then, in this case the reward–cost analysis that led to inaction produced the outcome the injured party preferred. Indeed, in American law, if one engages in a rescue attempt that the law does not require and botches the attempt, doing damage in the process, it is possible to be sued and found guilty of actionable negligence. American law punishes malfeasance but does not require *bonfeasance*, and in such circumstances it is, perhaps, not surprising that people so often decide not to *fease* at all.

For a social psychologist the most difficult and interesting problem in drafting a Good Samaritan Law is deciding to whom it applies, who is responsible to act. Rudzinski (1966) writes of the Polish Criminal Code: "It provides that no offense is being committed when there exists a strong possibility of prompt and effective aid by another person or institution whose duty to render aid is obviously greater or when the potential rescuer, having good reasons for it, was convinced that such a strong possibility exists" (p. 103). The problem of deciding whether another person has a greater responsibility to act than oneself leads us directly back to the second finding of Latané and Darley's study of thefts in the Nu-Way Beverage Center: (2) a substantially greater probability of reporting in the case of just one onlooker than in the case of two.

If there is only one onlooker in an emergency, the responsibility to rescue unambiguously falls on him. When there are two or more, primary responsibility becomes problematic. Latané and Darley created many simulated emergencies: a young woman falls and sprains her ankle; a briefly unattended cash register is raided; someone in the next room suffers an epileptic seizure. In all these experiments the principal dependent variable was either the effective individual probability of helping or else the temporal delay in helping, and the main independent variable was the number of other onlookers the subject or subjects believed to be present. The results are consistent across all experiments and, incidentally, directly contrary to commonsense expectations. The larger the number of onlookers, the *smaller* the individual probability of helping, and the longer the delay. By far the greatest effect of increasing numbers occurs between one and three onlookers (Morgan, 1978). Ten years after the original bystander experiments, Latané and Nida (1981) reviewed the fifty-six studies that had been done by then and concluded that the effect of number of onlookers on individual likelihood of helping had been consistently confirmed—with the minor qualification that when all comparisons involve numerous onlookers, increases are not necessarily significant (Piliavin, Rodin, and Piliavin, 1969).

Why should one be less likely to help in an emergency if others are believed to be present? The answer seems mainly to be that responsibility is "diffused" as numbers increase. Whose duty, whose obligation is it to report the crime or come to the aid of a Kitty Genovese? If you are the only witness, the responsibility is yours, and there is no denying it, though you may not fulfill it. Probably the Genovese murder progressed through an entire half-hour without so much as a single call to the police, not *in spite* of there being thirty-eight witnesses, but precisely *because* there were thirty-eight. Although probably no witness knew there were thirty-seven others, all knew there were many. All saw the lights in other apartments and silhouettes at the windows. Granting that there is some potential cost in getting "involved" at all, even to the minimal extent of calling the police, each one may think that some one of the many others watching would have felt a responsibility greater than his, someone who was related to or at least acquainted with the victim, or was nearer the ground floor, or was less in need of a night's sleep, or whatever. Individuals seem to ask themselves, "Why me?" when there are multiple witnesses.

The credibility of Latané and Darley's "diffusion of responsibility" theory is increased by experiments in which the apparent responsibility of an onlooker was varied by causing that onlooker to appear to be more or less qualified to help in a given situation. Schwarz and Clausen (1970), for instance, showed that when an additional onlooker was known to be a premedical student, with experience working in the emergency ward of a hospital, a medical emergency (seizures) was especially likely to be left to him. And, of course, we need no experiments to demonstrate that numbers do not matter when responsibilities are well defined: a pilot for his passengers on a plane, a parent for his child in the subway.

From newspaper stories about unresponsive bystanders, we gather that it is large numbers that make the event newsworthy. In the Genovese case the papers and commentators repeated again and again: "Thirty-eight. There were thirty-eight people who did nothing. Isn't that incredible?" One gathers that a single unresponsive person in Kew Gardens that night would not have made the papers. The "diffusion of responsibility" explanation predicts that it is just when the numbers are large that unresponsiveness is most probable. That would make numerous bystanders the usual thing, the thing to be expected and so the thing that ought not to be newsworthy. Clearly then, newspapers and people generally do not bring the diffusion of responsibility theory to bear on the problem. They hold a quite different theory, a theory that makes large numbers of unresponsive bystanders surprising.

The layman's approach to bystander behavior seems to me to be the same as the layman's approach to all behavior: The unit of lay psychology is personality, and the main determinants of behavior are aspects of personality—traits, values, abilities, and so on. Helping in an emergency then should occur or not, according to the strength of some trait like helpfulness or some value like altruism or social responsibility. Individual differences are to be expected in all aspects of personality, and so individuals ought to vary in their threshold for helping in an emergency. The larger the sample of individuals (number of onlookers), the greater the probability that at least one will help, that there will be at least one for whom the situation is "above the threshold." It is perfectly correct that the probability of finding an individual of a given type in a group must increase with the size of the group; that is simple mathematics. Indeed, the lay analysis as a whole is sound so long as one disregards social forces, but social forces are precisely what cannot be disregarded in the bystander situation. Because two or more onlookers together create the social force called "diffusion of responsibility," the effective individual probability of helping in a group is lower than the probability that an individual alone will help. What the victim wants to know is the probability that anyone will help, and even that is usually lower for a group than for one person alone.

The ambiguities of responsibility help us to see why an effective Good Samaritan law is hard to write, but it does not help us to see why, among Western industrialized societies, it should be the United States and England, in particular, that have not thus far found any such law good enough to adopt. No one knows the answer for sure, but it has been pointed out that indifference is the other side of privacy, and the Anglo-Saxon countries may feel especially attached to the "right to be let alone" (Gregory, 1966).

In any case there is no evidence that a Good Samaritan law results in more Good Samaritan behavior; indeed, there is no sociological, legal, or historical evidence of any kind on the frequency of Good Samaritanism. Zeisel (1966) has done the only relevant experiment. He presented three bystander dilemmas to samples of university students (not including law students) in Germany, Austria, and the United States and asked what percentage of compatriots would fail to be Good Samaritans in the cases described. In general, Germany and Austria are culturally very similar, and Germany has a Good Samaritan law whereas Austria does not, nor, we know, does the United States. The results are almost the same for all three: Germany, 37 percent; Austria, 39 percent; United States, 44 percent. And the German respondents knew they had the law.

The kind of case for which countries have been willing to legislate costs for not helping or rewards for helping has these properties: a clear threat to someone's life that can be relieved without onerous risk to oneself, where it is clear that oneself is the responsible party. In such circumstances it is likely that no law is needed and that the vast majority of citizens in all three countries would help. It is the remaining large class of cases that frequently produces unresponsive bystanders: There is an ambiguous threat to someone's life or else something less serious, involving difficult-to-assess risks to oneself with, above all, diffuse or unclear responsibility. In such cases I would guess that large numbers of citizens in all three countries would not help, but those are the cases for which countries have been unwilling to legislate. In short, the circumstances for which it is most difficult to write a law are the circumstances most in need of remedial legislation.

Equity Theory

Equity is simply a more general form of Exchange Theory. The basic concepts—reward, cost, and profit—are the same in both. However, Equity Theory adds one additional concept: investment. "Investment" is borrowed from economics, as are "reward," "cost," and "profit," and in the psychological theory investment is as extended in sense as are reward, cost, and profit. A person's investments are not just financial; they are *anything at all* that is believed to entitle him to his rewards, costs, and profits. An investment is any factor to be weighed in determining fair profits or losses.

A person who invests more money in a business is, we think, entitled to larger rewards and profits if there are any, because he risks suffering greater costs. Indeed, in business, we commonly think that investors are entitled to profits proportional to investments and would agree that for a p (person) and o who made unequal investments, a fair rule of distribution would be:

$$\frac{[\text{Rewards}_p - \text{Costs}_p] \text{ or Profits}_p}{\text{Investments}_p} = \frac{[\text{Rewards}_o - \text{Costs}_o] \text{ or Profits}_o}{\text{Investments}_o}$$

If a $1,000 investment yields a $100 profit, then if profits are distributed fairly, a $100 investment should yield a $10 profit. A state of equity is said to exist between p and o when their ratios of profit to investment are equal. Equity offers a rule of fairness more complex than the rule of fairness in Exchange

Theory, which simply holds that between a p and o who directly exchange with one another, the profits of p should be equivalent to the profits of o in the more or less long run.

Anything is an investment if people think it is, just as anything is a reward or cost if people think it is. If everyone in the banking business believes that men make better tellers—or managers or presidents—than women do, then male tellers, managers, or presidents can claim that they ought, in equity or fairness, to be paid more than their female counterparts, and the claim will be found credible in the banking business. If both labor and management think that seniority on the job entitles production line workers to higher hourly pay, then seniority on the job is an investment, and unequal pay for identical jobs will be thought fair if seniority is in line with pay. From those two examples, it should be apparent that the determination of what is to count as an investment is not an objective matter but is, rather, subjective; it is the perception or belief of one or more persons. It should also be apparent that the determination of investments varies from one society to another and one historical period to another and that the definition of investments has often in our society been a subject of dispute.

Exchange Theory, when it is carefully used, applies to just two persons, p and o, who exchange directly. Equity Theory always refers to comparisons between p and o with respect to the fairness with which they are rewarded, and the comparisons may be made in the mind of either p or o, as in Exchange Theory, but Equity also embraces the case in which the comparisons between p and o are made by a third party or parties as prototypically by an employer when both p and o are employees. The scope of the theory is further generalized in that p, o, and third parties comparing them can be groups rather than individuals.

In sum, Equity Theory goes beyond exchange in three principal respects: (1) The concept of investments is added to rewards, costs, and profits; (2) the rule of fairness is not that p and o should have equal profits but that they should have equal ratios or proportions of profits to investments; and (3) comparison of the outcomes of p and o may be made by not only p or o, but also by a third party. Exchange and equity are just alike in the way that they extend the meanings of terms borrowed from economics and also just alike in that they always refer to subjective impressions in someone's mind and never to objective facts. Exchange is really a special case of equity; it is the case in which investments are thought of as equal and so can be canceled from the rule of fairness. Everything we have learned about exchange can be reformulated in terms of equity. However, equity captures, as exchange does not, a profoundly important generalization about social life: Humans in society always acquiesce in some forms of inequality, always find it fair that rewards (or benefits or goods) should be unequally distributed among individuals. What manner of distribution of rewards is right? That is the problem of distributive justice, and it is one of the great problems of moral philosophy. Equity theory provides just the right concepts for a social psychological discussion of distributive justice.

Race is a human characteristic that has generally been counted as an investment in the United States, though the arguments and social forces against doing so are so great that such counting is often denied. Baseball is commonly thought to offer the same rewards (or profts) to blacks as to whites, but does it do so? What do the facts (Rae, 1981) suggest when they are cast into equity terms? In 1970 the average salary of black major league ballplayers was actually higher than that of whites. That holds true position by position, with black pitchers earning on the average $21,000 more than white pitchers, black infielders about $12,000 more, and black outfielders about $9,000 more. Such differences also existed among superstars; seven of the ten players making more than $100,000 were black in 1970. It looks then as if blacks in baseball have achieved equality and, in fact, surpassed it. Nevertheless, most black ballplayers in 1970 believed they were "underpaid," which is to say they believed they suffered from inequity. On what could they base their case?

Everything depends on what people count as investments. If two values of race (black or white) and the various team positions (pitcher, catcher, infielder, outfielder) are the only investments recognized, then either blacks are getting overpaid and whites have a right to complain of unfairness or else "Black is Better in Baseball" and so blacks are entitled. Neither of those formulations captures something we recognize as a familiar American idea. What we recognize as historically familiar is the idea that black is less good and what one expects to find, and practically always does find, is that black Americans are paid less than their occupational counterparts. And that is the way it was in baseball in 1970, if you consider batting average, as an index of quality of performance, the most relevant investment. It turns out that white infielders who bat around .280 earn approximately $4,000 more than black infielders with the same average, and black outfielders, holding batting average constant, earned about 25 percent less than whites. Of the ten players earning over $100,000, seven were black. However, Carl Yastrzemski earned $50,000 more than Hank Aaron and Willie Mays, though "Yaz" had been playing fewer years and had not come close to matching Aaron's and Mays's performances.

In 1970 black ballplayers were on the average playing better (or, at any rate, batting better) than white players, and so the fact that the average pay was higher is misleading; when blacks are equated for performance with whites, they turn out to have been paid less well. Therefore, the conclusion that black players had achieved and surpassed equality in 1970 is unwarranted. One is tempted to continue and conclude, as did the black players themselves, that black players were unfairly or inequitably treated in 1970. It is very important to understand that this conclusion does not necessarily follow from Equity Theory; it follows only if batting average is conceived to be the one relevant investment. A manager might argue that popularity with the fans is a significant investment entitling rewards and that Yastrzemski was more popular than either Mays or Aaron. In professional basketball some such argument has been made with managers claiming that a team having too many black players cannot engage the loyalties of white fans.

In this country today there is a strong tendency to believe that honors and exceptional remunerations should be assigned on the basis of meritorious performance and so to believe that the right answers, the final answers to disputes about equity in these areas, are reached when merit is counted as the only investment. However, from the disinterested viewpoint of Equity Theory, merit is only one of many characteristics that may happen to be reckoned as investments, and meritocracy only one of many possible principles for the just distribution of rewards.

Nothing in Equity Theory establishes meritocracy as superior to, for instance, aristocracy. Nothing in Equity Theory says that political offices should be assigned on the basis of qualifications or of election rather than kinship (nepotism). Nothing in Equity Theory says that sexual favors should be allocated on the basis of reciprocal attraction rather than money (prostitution). Nothing in Equity Theory says that need is the only investment relevant to medical care and that money and position ought to be kept out of that domain as well as out of the domain of criminal justice. To argue that one conception of investments is better than another, it is necessary to go beyond equity and argue in terms of moral philosophy.

Social scientists, whether to make light of their discoveries or to claim a respectable antiquity, are fond of finding roots in classical philosophy, usually in Aristotle. The idea of equity is a bit exceptional in that one finds in Aristotle, specifically in the *Nicomachean Ethics*, not just the germ of the idea of equity, but the very ratio itself.

There are several contemporary formulations of Equity Theory, but while the terms differ, the ideas are the same. The terms used by Homans (1974) are the ones we have adopted: "rewards," "costs," "profits," and "investments." Adams's (1965) terms are a little different. For "rewards" he uses "positive outcomes," for "costs" he uses "negative outcomes," for "investments" he uses "inputs." "Profits" are "net outcomes." The formula defining a state of equity between p and o is then very simply stated if net outcomes are symbolized O and inputs I.

$$\frac{O_p}{I_p} = \frac{O_o}{I_o}$$

In Table 2–4 the Homans and Adams formulations are summarized together with the basic propositions on which the two theorists agree.

A third formulation of Equity by Hatfield, Walster, and Berscheid (1978) adds something to the formulations of Homans and Adams. Investments are divided into liabilities (or negative inputs), which entitle one to costs, and assets (or positive inputs), which entitle one to rewards. The equity formula is then written so as to allow for cases in which the costs of an individual exceed his

TABLE 2-4. Two Conceptually Equivalent Formulations of Equity

Homans	Adams
p = person	p = person
o = other (may be p at another time or in another role)	o = other
Rewards = anything agreeable	Positive outcomes = anything agreeable
Costs = anything disagreeable	Negative outcomes = anything disagreeable
Investments = anything entitling to rewards	Inputs = anything entitling to rewards
Profits = rewards − costs	Net outcomes = positive outcomes − negative outcomes
Distributive Justice:	Equity:

Homans:

$$\frac{\text{profits}_p}{\text{investments}_p} = \frac{\text{profits}_o}{\text{investments}_o}$$

Adams:

$$\frac{\text{net outcomes}_p}{\text{inputs}_p} = \frac{\text{net outcomes}_o}{\text{inputs}_o}$$

Symbolized: $\dfrac{O_p}{I_p} = \dfrac{O_o}{I_o}$

Distributive Injustice to p's disadvantage:

$$\frac{\text{profits}_p}{\text{investments}_p} < \frac{\text{profits}_o}{\text{investments}_o}$$

Inequity to p's disadvantage:

$$\frac{O_p}{I_p} < \frac{O_o}{I_o}$$

Distributive Injustice to p's advantage:

$$\frac{\text{profits}_p}{\text{investments}_p} > \frac{\text{profits}_o}{\text{investments}_o}$$

Inequity to o's disadvantage:

$$\frac{O_p}{I_p} > \frac{O_o}{I_o}$$

NOTE: Homans and Adams make just the same sort of predictions. For instance:

a. In case p perceives inequity to his disadvantage, he will feel the form of distress called righteous anger.

b. In case p perceives inequity to his advantage, he will feel the form of distress called guilt.

c. The thresholds for the two forms of distress (from a base of equity are unequal) with the threshold for guilt being higher than that for anger (more inequity in absolute terms is necessary to generate guilt than anger). For instance, in one study British workers underpaid by 10 percent showed an "active sense of grievance" while those overpaid by the same amount showed, at most, a certain sheepishness.

d. Both guilt and anger (the two forms of distress produced by inequity) are motivating. They cause p and/or o to undertake to create or restore equity either by changing actual outcomes and inputs or by changing the way they think of existing outcomes and inputs.

rewards so that there are no net profits but only negative net outcomes. The formula, as written by Homans and Adams, does not allow for that outcome. The Hatfield, Walster, and Berscheid treatment is not itself the last word on formulations of equity. There is a small literature in mathematical psychology (e.g. Harris, 1983; Romer, 1977) on how best to formulate equity. However, there is no reason for us to go beyond the Homans–Adams version, using Homans's terms, because the sophistication of the more advanced formulas far exceeds the sophistication of research results. There is nothing by way of research or ideas that we will need that is not captured by Homans's version.

Even the Homans formulation suggests more power than research on Equity Theory has often attained. The high water mark is, I think, the survey research study of distributive justice and earned income in the city of Baltimore carried out by sociologists Jasso and Rossi (1977). Each respondent was given a set of vignettes such that each vignette described a hypothetical person with respect to such investments as sex, marital status, number of children, education, and occupation plus annual earnings ranging from $2,000 to $40,000. Respondents rated each described case on a scale from -4 (extremely underpaid) through 0 (fairly paid) to $+4$ (extremely overpaid). Using 200 respondents and 600 vignettes, Jasso and Rossi were able to work out the normative conception of fair earnings, for every combination of usual investments in the city of Baltimore in a given year. This study is very unusually complete in measuring the variables that are involved in equity.

Some research on equity (e.g. Adams and Jacobsen, 1964) simply tells subjects that they are getting the pay for which they are qualified or that they are under- or overqualified and then determines whether the overqualified do a less good job ("restriction of output") and the underqualified a better job in order to restore equity—as predicted. Some research (e.g. Kiesler and Baral, 1970) intervenes to raise p's perception of his inputs and determines whether he seeks to bring about a (now deserved) better outcome. In general, research on equity has started with a situation in which many things are assumed to be constant and then made one change of a particular type to see whether it produces another change of the sort predicted.

Equity with the World and Beyond

Most research on equity is concerned with the two-person comparison of p and o, made either by one of the two or by a third party and judged to be equitable or not in accordance with the profits-to-investments ratios. There is considerable evidence (Austin and Hatfield, 1975) that individuals also compare their own profits-to-investments ratios with those of other people in general. How does my net equity compare with that of everyone else I know about? Am I getting what is coming to me in view of my investments and by comparison with the net profits-to-investments ratio of others? That kind of equity calculation has been called "equity with the world."

When people think in terms of equity with the world, how might we expect them to act? The Kerner Commission Report in 1965 on urban riots in Detroit and Newark describes the justifications looters gave for their action. They felt that they had a right to the merchandise they had stolen because of the hardship and deprivation in their lives relative to most people. They felt, in fact, that equity with the world left them unfairly treated and that it was fair to act to even the balance by stealing—even though the victims of the stealing were store owners in no way responsible for the hardship of those who stole from them or even necessarily better off. Thinking in terms of equity with the world is marked by an indifference to whom you choose to harm or to benefit. The net fairness of your outcomes relative to everybody else's can be improved by operating on the outcomes of any others. There is considerable experimental evidence (Austin and Hatfield, 1975) that people do sometimes operate in that way.

The two rules of fairness that we have considered, reciprocity in exchange and ratio equivalence in equity, often seem not to be met in the world generally. People who have been kind and charitable all their lives are sometimes stricken with terrible disease at an early age, while scoundrels of the worst sort live long lives of luxury. Melvin Lerner (1970, 1971; Lerner and Meindl, 1981) has argued in many influential publications that most people have difficulty accepting the manifest injustices of life and have, indeed, a strong need to believe that the world is just. A just world would be a world in which people get what they deserve. It would also be describable as a world in which general equity prevails. We would like to believe that the world is just in part, because that would mean our own outcomes are controllable. If we do good, we can expect good returns or profits. Rubin and Peplau (1975) have shown that belief in the just world hypothesis varies from person to person and tends to be stronger in those who have less formal education and who are strongly attached to institutionalized religion.

Probably the most interesting discovery made in Lerner's just world research is the phenomenon called derogation of the victim (Lerner, 1970). What is invoked essentially is the switch from believing that people get what they deserve to believing that they deserve what they get. In a variety of experiments it has been shown that persons who are seen to suffer (only a simulation, of course) are credited with various defects of character and ability. Stephen Gould (1977) has made the interesting suggestion that research purporting to demonstrate a genetic inferiority in disadvantaged groups like black Americans is a form of derogation of the victim. Are they badly off? Do they suffer? In a just world they must have deserved it.

Some people who believe in a just world even blame themselves if they suffer bad luck or an accident—seemingly preferring to bear blame rather than to live in a world in which such things can happen at random. One naturally wonders how far such self-derogation can go. Would victims of really terrible accidents, clearly random accidents, feel that they had deserved their fates? Bulman and Wortman (1977) interviewed twenty-nine victims of spinal cord injuries, 16–35 years old, left paraplegic or quadriplegic by the injury. When asked "Was it deserved?" all but two quickly said no. There are limits on derogation of the victim. However, ten of the twenty-nine said: "God had a reason."

The reference to God reminds us that many religions include beliefs that have the function (I would not say the purpose) of explaining the inequities, the failures of justice, in the world that one simply cannot rationalize away. Equity may be restored in Heaven; the meek, the poor, the oppressed are promised better fates after life, eternal better fates. That should have gone a long way to make up for the inequities of feudalism and slavery. It also helps to explain why black militants in this world are often critical of the role the church has played in their history. In Hinduism, of course, equity is attained only across incarnations. Are you a flea in this life? Try hard to be a meritorious flea. You may yet be a Brahmin. Those ideas are certainly well designed to reconcile the oppressed to their lot, though it would be too strong to say that anyone had actually designed them with that in mind.

Arguing Investments

In the United States in recent decades controversy over human investments has been unremitting. That is what civil rights, female liberation, gay liberation, Chicano power, deaf pride, and the like are about: investments and the calculation of equity. All of those ideological protest movements have the same logical structure.

One first shows that there are inequalities in the distribution of rewards, inequalities to the disadvantage of blacks, women, gays and lesbians, Chicanos, the elderly, the deaf, whomever. The rewards may be financial, wages and salaries; such inequalities are ubiquitous and fully documented for blacks and whites, men and women. The rewards need not be financial. They can be access to political power, to higher education, to legal justice, to medical care, to insurance premiums, to childrearing, to tax-supported facilities of any kind. Rewards are anything people value. And, of course, it is very easy to document inequalities with respect to one or more domains for blacks, women, gays and lesbians, Chicanos, the elderly, the deaf, and otherwise handicapped persons.

Demonstration of existing unequal distribution of rewards is only one leg of the argument, the easier leg. One must go on to prove, argue, or maybe just assert that the inequalities are *unfair* or *unjust*. So long as differences of race, sex, sexual orientation, ethnic origin, age, and physical condition are accepted as unequal investments, there is no unfairness, no injustice, in unequal rewards. Equity ratios can be equal. If any of the many characteristics of minorities that have been listed counts as an investment of say, just arbitrarily, .5

whereas the contrasting majority characteristic counts as 1.0, then individuals having the majority characteristic are *legitimately entitled* to twice the rewards of the individuals having the minority characteristic. It is as simple as:

$$\frac{\text{Rewards of 2}}{\text{Investments of 1}} = \frac{\text{Rewards of 1}}{\text{Investments of .5}}$$

What makes such inequalities equitable? Thinking so. Nothing more. But nothing less.

It follows that those who seek to change existing rules of distribution in a society must not only demonstrate inequalities but also change the way the majority thinks about the value of human qualities, the way the majority calculates investments. It is not at all obvious how that can be done. Many think it is impossible to prove that one way of thinking about investments is better than another. George Homans puts it well:

> And all the arguments about surplus value from John Ball to Karl Marx are one long attempt to prove that what employers count as investment ought not be so counted, and that, therefore, they get more than their fair share of the returns of economic enterprise and exploit the workers. Of course, none of the arguments prove it; such things are not capable of proof: they are matters of taste. [1961, pp. 246–47]

Maybe so. But if tastes cannot be proved, they definitely can be disputed.

Probably the simplest form of dispute is assertion. The point of slogans like "Black is Beautiful" and "Gay is Good" is to attempt to change minds about investments by simple assertion. Assertion probably does not work very well. The problem is that assertions are as easy to refute as to create. All it takes is a counter-assertion, spoken aloud or in the mind: "The hell it is." And the only way to continue such disputes is in the form of argument favored by small children:

"Girls are as good as boys."

"They are not."

"They are."

"Aren't."

"Are too."

Something a little more sophisticated by way of dispute can be accomplished by appealing to a value the majority holds and pointing out that its present way of thinking contradicts that value. America has a historical commitment to equality of opportunity, and in some domains the course of historical change has steadily been one of expanding equality. That is the case, for instance, with respect to the right to vote (Rae, 1981). The progression has been:

1. One vote for each propertied white man
2. One vote for each white man

3. One vote for each man
4. One vote for each citizen

In succession, over a period of about two hundred years, the qualifications of property, race, and sex have been dropped. If this country feels that it is right to drop such qualifications with respect to the vote, which is also a reward to be distributed, then why not also with respect to all other rewards? There is some persuasive force in that kind of argument for those who value equality strongly and who mean to be progressive in this area, but it has no force for those who judge that voting is not the same kind of reward as political power, high office, access to education, and so on.

Justice

In the end, however, if one is to argue entitlements and distributive justice, it is necessary to turn to moral reasoning. More and more people are doing so. It is not easy to prove things in ethics or moral reasoning, but it is possible to construct arguments that go beyond simple assertion or appeal to historic ideals. There have been many forces for social change in recent years, and the view that those things are a matter of taste or that morality is necessarily relative and arbitrary simply does not meet the need we all feel for somehow adjudicating among rival claims—in our own country most pressingly, but also, of course, internationally. Some Israelis believe that they are entitled to the land they now govern because God promised it to them in the Old Testament and because they lived in it for centuries. Lots of Palestinians think they are entitled to the very same land because they too had been living there for a very long time before the State of Israel was created. How on earth can such rival claims be justly settled?

Many philosophers think the greatest contribution in this century to the general problem of distributive justice is John Rawls's A Theory of Justice (1972). It is a theory that we are well prepared to appreciate at this point. In human societies rewards are distributed in accordance with characteristics that are often disputed, and the problem of justice is to find principles that will adjudicate among conflicting claims. Rawls proposes that in order to find such principles— principles everyone can assent to—it is necessary to take up a special position or frame of mind: We must mentally divest ourselves of all the characteristics of race, sex, nationality, and so forth that constitute possible entitlements.

Rawls's theory is a kind of social contract theory, but he does not intend to say that his contract is an anthropological event, a contract men have actually made in some prehistoric past or are about to make in a science fiction future. It is the contract we would be willing to make if we followed a certain procedure, which everyone will agree is a fair procedure. We are assumed to be rational in that each seeks his own welfare, and we are also assumed to have no prior conception of what is right or just. The problem is to select general principles for the distribution of rewards that all rational men will agree to. Principles must be selected under an assumption of moderate scarcity, so that not everyone can have all the rewards he wants. Otherwise there would be no problem to solve.

Since, in a state of nature, one man will be rich and on that account, perhaps, opposed to taxation for welfare measures, whereas another man will be poor and in favor of such taxation, it is clear that if all are to assent to the same principles, all must reason as if they did not know whether they were rich or poor. For the same sort of reason none can know his sex or age or race or lineage or talents or any possible asset or liability. Nor can one know his generation since each generation must be fair to each other generation in the way it utilizes resources. The relation of each person to each other must be the same and must be affectively indifferent. The claims of kinship and friendship and empathic feeling are, and this is an important and brilliant point, irrelevant to the definition of justice. From this "Original Position," as Rawls calls it, under the "Veil of Ignorance" the principles of justice must be sought. My own silly image is of the unborn, waiting to be born and not knowing what statuses each will be born into, but somehow developed enough to be rational.

What are the principles that all would accept under the Veil of Ignorance? Only the most general ethical principles are to be considered, not particular cases of contested claims. One general ethical principle is Utilitarianism—the greatest good for the greatest number, or the greatest net good. Could humans in the Original Position all accept that principle? No, because one could argue for slavery or serfdom in the name of Utilitarianism; such systems might maximize the net good. In the Original Position one does not know whether he would be master or slave; it is not possible to accept a principle that might leave one enslaved. The rational effort to seek one's own welfare is what prohibits that choice, not concern for one's fellow man—we do not have that concern in the Original Position.

The first principle that should be acceptable to all concerns liberty—a salient good or reward. To each the maximum liberty consistent with an equal liberty for all. Presumably everyone wants as much liberty as possible, and if you don't know how you are going to be placed in life, you must choose to have maximal liberty up to the point where it limits the liberty of another. You might be that other, and so liberty up to the point of interference is as much as you can wish for.

With respect to the distribution of rewards of every sort, equality must be presumed to be the only thing a rational person can accept not knowing what position he will occupy. Would inequalities ever be acceptable? Rawls's argument on this point is complex and subtle, but if we ignore some of the complexities he deals with, the rightness of the conclusion is intuitively compelling. Inequalities are justified only when everyone is better off as a result of the inequality than he would be with equality, especially the least advantaged. If it takes very great natural talent to be a good surgeon and if all feel the need of good surgeons, but training in surgery is long and onerous and the work hard, it may be that exceptional remuneration or honor is necessary to recruit surgeons. Outsize rewards for surgeons will be justified if everyone gets the benefit of better medical treatment as a result, including the poor and indigent. Such an inequality of reward will not be justified if talented surgeons confine their attention to the very rich.

"A conception of right is a set of principles, general in form and universal in application, that is to be publicly recognized as a final court of appeal for ordering the conflicting claims of moral persons" (Rawls, 1972, p. 135). That is what Rawls has undertaken to give us. His principles are *not* intended to describe human behavior; many things can prevent us from seeing what is right in concrete situations, even though we may be clear about general principles, and many things can keep us from doing the right thing even when we are clear about what it is. Much of the content of social psychology concerns the factors that intervene between general principles of morality and moral action. If one thinks of the Milgram obedience experiment from the Original Position—not knowing whether one will be teacher or learner, but subject to the experimenter's deception—one must choose to have no painful shocks administered (you might be the learner). In fact, that is how everyone reading about the experiment judges the morality, but it is not how most people act in the situation. If one reads about bystanders and persons in need of emergency help, one must judge that helping is the right thing to do (you might be the victim), but that is not what most bystanders do.

John Rawls's great book has not, of course, settled the problems of morality for all time. Michael Walzer (1983) is one eminent social theorist who thinks that Rawls's theory of justice is not much help. Walzer grants that ideally rational humans, knowing nothing of their own situation and so barred from particularist claims, might choose one, and only one, distribution system. But he finds the force of that conclusion hard to measure. "It is surely doubtful that these same men and women, if they were transformed into ordinary people, with a firm sense of their own identity, with their own goods in their hands, caught up in everyday troubles, would reiterate their hypothetical choice or even recognize it as their own" (p. 5). Walzer does not attempt to formulate universal principles of justice and thinks it is a very strange idea that the same principles should be applicable to ancient Babylon and the contemporary United States.

Summary

The theory that social interaction is a process of exchange employs such simple economic terms as *reward*, *cost*, and *profit* in greatly extended psychological senses so that help with a problem, giving esteem, favors, tips, gifts, and so on all count as rewards, whereas spending time, sustaining rudeness, losing status, and the like all count as costs, and profits are defined as rewards minus costs. The fundamental principle of Exchange Theory is that parties to a relationship must derive from that relationship *subjectively equivalent profits* if the relationship is to be experienced as fair. A second principle is that profits must be greater in the ongoing relationship than in alternative relationships if the relationship is to endure. A corollary principle, believed to be a universal social norm, is that benefits received must be reciprocated, not necessarily at once, but over the more or less long run.

Economic exchange differs from social exchange in the following ways. In economic exchange, but not in social: (1) the terms of equivalence, the goods to be exchanged, are explicitly defined; (2) the terms are discussable between parties; and (3) the terms are enforceable. Economic exchange clearly involves conscious calculation of rewards, costs, and profits and is not simply motivated by good feeling. Social exchange must involve some calculation since the rewards given in return for rewards received cannot be just any rewards at all, but must be subjectively equivalent. However, social exchange often, though not always, involves benevolent feeling; indeed, the feeling between the exchanging parties may be more salient for them than any calculation or sense of obligation.

In addition to the feelings specific to a relationship, it seems that general mood can affect the readiness of one person to help another. Some experiments that purport to show the effect of mood on helping are subject to the alternative interpretation that anyone who is the recipient of a benefit feels obliged to dispense a benefit to someone or other, not necessarily the one to whom a benefit is owed, in order to keep some sort of central exchange accounts balanced. However, Isen and her associates have found evidence that mood, benevolent feeling, is the mediator and not a central exchange calculation.

Sometimes the rewards or benefits in an exchange relation are objectively equivalent, but usually not; usually the equivalence is subjective. One conception of subjective equivalence that governs much exchange, including tips, gifts, hospitality, time, and expressed sympathy is that each party must give the same percentage of what he has to offer. That means an objectively small gift (in financial cost, for instance) from a poor person is worth more than the same gift from a rich person, and a small gift from a poor person may be subjectively equivalent to a large gift from a rich person.

Help that cannot be reciprocated poses a special problem for the recipient. Because benefits must be reciprocated in some subjectively equivalent way, accepting offered help or, worse, asking for needed help does produce a feeling of obligation in the recipient, and feelings of obligation are unpleasant. When the recipient cannot reciprocate with help, he or she is likely to feel that power or esteem must be returned, and those psychological returns may feel too costly. Handicapped persons, individuals on welfare, and have-not nations all testify to the psychological discomfort of needing help that cannot be reciprocated.

In emergency situations where the victim of assault or robbery or accident is a stranger to persons witnessing the emergency, the witnesses or onlookers have proved surprisingly unresponsive in both life cases (e.g. Kitty Genovese) and experiments. If proving responsive or not depended primarily on individual personality characteristics (e.g. sense of social responsibility), then the probability that someone or other would help in a given emergency would (for sampling reasons alone) increase with the number of bystanders. Because most people think personality *is* what makes a Good Samaritan, emergencies in which large numbers of bystanders prove unresponsive occasion much amazement. Latané and Darley have, however, shown that large numbers of bystanders make unresponsiveness more probable, because unresponsive others suggest a situation not really requiring intervention and because responsibility is diffused by numbers. Unresponsiveness results from a reward–cost analysis that makes it seem unprofitable to intervene, and so Good Samaritan laws have been passed in some countries, basically designed to change the reward–cost matrix (e.g. by punishing nonintervention) so as to make benevolent intervention more likely. However, legislative experience shows that Good Samaritan laws can be written only for cases in which there is a clear threat to someone's life that can be relieved without excessive risk to the helper and in which the person responsible for helping can be clearly defined. That is just the class of cases for which no law is needed.

Equity Theory goes beyond Exchange Theory in three ways: The concept of investments is added; the rule of fairness becomes one of equal ratios of profits to investments; comparisons between p and o may be made by a third person. Equity captures, as exchange does not, the fact that humans in society always acquiesce in some forms of inequality. If one investment (white race or male sex) is valued more highly than another (black race or female sex), then proportionate inequalities of profit will seem equitable or fair. If a person perceives inequity that is to his disadvantage, he is expected to feel anger, whereas perceiving equity that is to one's advantage should produce guilt. In either case the theory predicts efforts to bring about a state of equity.

Equity with the world involves comparing one's own ratio of profits to investments—not with some specific other, but with people in general. In efforts to attain Equity with the world, benefit and harm are dispensed without regard for specific individuals. The Just World Hypothesis is the belief that people get what they deserve, that equity prevails in the world, and derogation of the victim carries this belief to the point of supposing that victims of misfortune must somehow merit their misfortune.

Such contemporary social movements as the drive for racial equality, female liberation, Chicano power, gay pride, and so on may all be interpreted as assertions that certain investments ought to be reassessed and raised in value. When their value is raised, existent inequalities will be seen to be not just inequalities but injustices. The problem of distributive justice is the problem in moral philosophy of adjudicating among contending claims concerning the relative value of social investments. John Rawls's *A Theory of Justice* proposes that such adjudication must take place under the Veil of Ignorance with each person ignorant of his station in life: his sex, race, and lineage. Under those circumstances, there must be universal assent to: (1) the maximum liberty consistent with an equal liberty for all, and (2) equality except for those inequalities that benefit all.

3

Altruism and Affection

STEPHEN JAY GOULD, in one of his readable essays on biology, writes: "Altruistic acts are the cement of stable societies, yet they seem to defy a Darwinian explanation" (1977). The seeming defiance of Darwinism is serious. Gould himself is definitely a Darwinian and, in fact, all modern biologists are Darwinians in the sense that they believe in the theory of natural selection as the force giving direction to evolution. There are differences between evolutionary biologists and molecular biologists on natural selection and also differences between evolutionary biologists like Gould and those evolutionary biologists who sometimes, nowadays, like E. O. Wilson (1975) call themselves "sociobiologists," but all alike agree that altruism in animal societies, including, especially, the human animal, poses a problem for natural selection.

Darwin begins the exposition of his theory of natural selection in *The Origin of Species* (1859) by making an analogy with artificial selection in animal breeding. Everyone is familiar with the fact that animals (plants also) can be selectively bred for any sort of well-defined feature: appearance (size, coloring), temperament (pugnacity in bulldogs and fighting cocks), fertility, resistance to a disease, and so on. The selective force in the artificial case is the breeder who chooses the trait he wants to bring out and enables individuals possessing that trait to breed and produce progeny while denying that privilege to individuals lacking that trait until he has the distinctive strain he wants. In natural selection there is no great divine breeder, but rather an environment to which some of the traits in individuals, produced by random genetic variation, will be better adapted than will the traits of other individuals. The better-adapted individuals will, on the average, have more offspring and since those offspring will tend to carry the genes for the adaptive traits, those genes and those traits will become increasingly prevalent in the population. In this way animal populations differentiate, and when distinct strains become unable to interbreed because their genotypes are too unlike, new species have evolved. When the environment changes—in food supply, predators, climate, and so on—new selection pressures are created and some species become extinct (e.g. the dinosaurs) while new species evolve (e.g. the mammals, the primates, Homo sapiens). Evolution has no direction but adaptation. The idea of progress with man at the top of the ladder is an anthropocentric prejudice; insects, it may be supposed, take a different view.

Why does altruistic behavior raise a paradox for natural selection? To answer that, one must first define altruism in a biological sense, as opposed to a psychological sense, and this is a distinction of great importance for our entire discussion. An act is altruistic in the biological sense if it increases the prospects for survival and, ultimately, the reproductive success (which is the only thing that finally matters in natural selection) of an organism (o), other than the one performing the act (p), at some cost to the survival prospects and reproductive success of p, the organism acting. The acting organism, the one that sustains the costs, is, by definition, the altruistic one. In the definition of biological altruism, motives, intentions, and rewards play no part, though they will be important in our eventual definition of another sort of altruism, psychological altruism. It follows that a plant, lacking all motives and intentions as plants do, can nevertheless show biological altruism. It follows that a parent bird or an insect in feeding its young (and so contributing to its prospects for survival) is performing a biologically altruistic act—even though the meddling naturalist might find that some small change in the noise the young animal makes or a trifling arbitrary alteration of appearance would cause the parent to kill it rather than to feed it. That kind of outcome, jarring to human sensibilities, casts doubt on the intentions and motives of the parent, but since those are irrelevant to biological altruism, the status of the act in this respect is unaffected.

Natural selection should make it impossible for any animal species to evolve so as to have the genetic potential for consistent biological altruism. Why? Because natural selection, as formulated by Darwin, operates single-mindedly and relentlessly in favor of traits that improve the chances of survival and the number of offspring of the individual acting. Natural selection forbids the appearance of traits harmful to the animal acting. Any individual that regularly acted altruistically, that is, in a way that benefited others at some cost to itself, would put itself at a disadvantage and would have few offspring. Such individuals should not last long. Chance mutations would permit any sort of short-term altruism but selection pressures ought always speedily to eliminate altruism of any kind. Natural selection predicts that individuals will act so as to benefit not their group or their species, but themselves alone.

Biological Altruism in Animals Other Than the Human

Biological altruism is a circumstance that can be given an exact definition (individual *p* acts so as to benefit individual *o* at some cost to itself), but it is a circumstance that ought never to be realized as a regular thing in either the animal or the plant world, because natural selection must always forbid it. The outcome of that simple and clear Darwinian reasoning is, however, paradoxical. The paradox lies in the fact that the biological world, the world of plants and animals of which we shall henceforth consider only animals and, for a time, only animals other than the human, abounds in examples of altruism. Or, at least, of *seeming* altruism. And it is in the difference between actual and seeming biological altruism that the resolution of the paradox lies. The neo-Darwinian argument is always essentially the same. Whatever example of animal altruism is brought forward, the Darwinian always shows that it is only *seeming* altruism—in the biological sense.

Natural selection is on home ground with clearly "selfish" behavior. The female praying mantis will, if she gets the chance, chew the head off the male as he copulates with her. Splendid! His performance suffers not at all (it may be improved), the eggs are fertilized, and the female has a good meal. Blackheaded gulls nest in closely packed colonies, and it is common when the eggs are first hatched for a gull to wait until its neighbor's back is turned and then snap up whole the chick next door. Once again, splendid. Individual interest relentlessly pursued is what natural selection calls for (Dawkins, 1976). More awkward for natural selection, though only briefly so, is the seeming altruism of the bird that calls upon sight of a predator and causes its entire flock to freeze into a pattern of camouflage. The calling bird seems to be altruistic, for it benefits others by inviting hazardous attention to itself. The probable explanation, which turns seeming altruism into no altruism at all, lies in the fact that a moving flock is a danger to each individual when a predator such as a hawk is overhead, and it pays, in individual terms, to call and cause all to freeze, thereby concealing all.

Kin Selection

The most general explanation of seeming altruism was provided in 1964 by Hamilton in the theory of kin selection. The general idea is beautifully simple, though the details that make it finally convincing are not. Because animals that are related will share genes, it is theoretically possible for an individual to preserve its genes, though not itself, by behaving altruistically with respect to kin. In the theory of natural selection it is not exactly individual fitness that must be maximized, but "inclusive fitness." Or—in a metaphor—the individual as a set of genes is properly thought of as *distributed* across kin. For example, the individual derives half of its chromosomes (and so genes) from one parent and half from another. There is a fifty-fifty chance that a given gene will be shared by parent and offspring. Their "relatedness" (r) is .5. A parent that loses its life in preserving the lives of more than two offspring will actually maximize its inclusive fitness. The seeming altruism of parental sacrifice is not actual biological altruism if we understand the parent individual to be a set of genes rather than an autonomous organism. The parent—defined as a set of genes—does not act so as to benefit a different set of genes at cost to itself.

Suppose a mother bird puts on what is called a "distraction display" that leads predators away from a nest full of eggs. Such displays make sense in terms of natural selection on the individual level, because they will, on the whole, operate to produce more of the parent bird's genes than would be produced if predators were not distracted and regularly ate the eggs in the nest. The altruism is only "seeming." The parent seems to act in a way that benefits others at a cost to itself. But in the proper *distributed* sense of itself, which includes the genes of the eggs in the nest, it does nothing of the sort. There is no real biological altruism here or, generally, in the care that parent animals give their young. That is a statement not about motives or about selfishness, but simply about gene preservation.

Hamilton's theory applies to kin generally and not only to parents and offspring. The circumstances in which seeming biological altruism should be selected for can be described in a simple formula: r is "relatedness," the probability that two individuals (p and o) share a gene; B is "benefits," which means anything that contributes to survival and reproductive success; C is "costs," which means anything that subtracts from chances of survival and reproductive success. Then we should expect an individual p to behave altruistically with respect to a relative o (various other things being equal) whenever the costs to p are lower than the benefits to o, times the relatedness between p and o. Or, in a formula, whenever $C_p < B_o \times r$. In the parent–offspring case, r is .5, and if the risky distraction display has, for the parent, a cost of 1, whereas the benefit of such a display for the offspring is 8, then $C_p(1) < B_o(8) \times r(.5)$ or $1 < 4$, and the distraction display should be selected for on grounds of purely individual selection.

Because offspring are as closely related to parents as parents to offspring (relatedness is a symmetrical matter), offspring should, on the theory of kin selection, be as disposed to sacrifice themselves for parents as parents should be for offspring. Except for the fact that offspring will, on the average, have more life remaining to them at any given time than will their parents and so have superior reproductive prospects, which ought to select for greater altruism from parents to offspring than the other way around. That fits the facts for social animals generally.

The great success stories of the theory of kin selection, which are what makes it really convincing, lie in the explanation of certain odd features of the social behavior of the *Hymenoptera*—ants, bees, and wasps. The theory explains the evolution of sterile worker castes, the ultimate in altruism. It explains why such castes are always female in ants, bees, and wasps, but both male and female in termites. It explains (Trivers and Hare, 1976) why queen bees act so as to favor a 1:1 ratio of males to females (the queen is equally related to her sons and daughters) whereas workers act so as to favor fertile sisters over brothers (workers' relatedness to sisters is .75 whereas it is only .25 to brothers).

Hamilton's theory of kin selection neatly accounts for the seeming altruism of animal family life (not including human family life) by amending Darwinian natural selection in such a way as to define the individual in terms of his genes as distributed across kin rather than in terms of the bounded organism. The "distributed individual" never acts so as to benefit others at a cost to himself, but only seems to do so when we make the mistake of thinking of the bounded organism rather than a set of genes as the unit of evolution. Kin selection, however, does not eliminate the full paradox of animal altruism. The remaining problem is that seeming altruism also occurs among unrelated animals.

Delayed Reciprocal Altruism

To account for altruism among non-kin, Trivers (1971) has proposed a mechanism of delayed reciprocal altruism. In explaining this mechanism, I borrow from Dawkins (1976), who has us imagine a species of bird that suffers from a certain disease-carrying parasite and so must devote a good deal of time to searching its feathers for the little beggars and removing them with its beak, a process called grooming. The birds and this example are entirely *imaginary*, invented to illustrate a theory. I mention that because when I have used the example in teaching, it has sometimes come back to me on exams as a real bird, often as "Skinner's pigeons," sometimes the black-headed gull, and once the robin. It is none of those, but only an imaginary example. The bird in question must be supposed to be able to groom all parts of its body quite satisfactorily by itself—except for the top of its head, which it cannot reach. For the top of the head the imaginary birds need help from one another. They are not kin, but only members of the same species. Under what circumstances might a genetic basis for altruistic grooming evolve?

Imagine first that these birds operated on a rule of uncontingent altruism. The uncontingent altruist would cheerfully groom the top of the head of any bird that applied for help with that awkward spot. We must suppose that the act of grooming costs something, not much, only a short time taken from self-grooming, food seeking, predator-watches, and mating. The cost, though tiny, would ultimately, over many bird generations, subtract something from the groomer's survival and reproductive prospects. We must also suppose that being groomed counts as a benefit, small but not insignificant, for it frees the groomed one of parasites that could cause disease and death. If all birds in an interacting population were to operate on a rule of uncontingent altruism, things would go well for them; each individual would sometimes bear the costs of grooming and sometimes enjoy the benefits of being groomed. A population of uncontingent altruists would be something like a community of ideal Christians. The problem with uncontingent altruism is vulnerability to wickedness.

Suppose random genetic variation produces the kind of bird we will call a "cheater." Cheater birds do not groom but willingly accept grooming. Since cheaters enjoy benefits but incur no costs, they have a survival edge on uncontingent altruists and in time (as a computer simulation of this imaginary case has shown) cheaters would entirely supplant uncontingent altruists. The avian Christians would altruize themselves into extinction. And once grooming birds had become extinct, so eventually would cheaters; one imagines a pathetic final act in which all birds on stage present to one another heads that none will groom.

Between cheating and uncontingent altruism there is a rule or strategy superior to either: contingent (or reciprocal) altruism. The contingent altruist would start out grooming all who applied for the service, but unlike the uncontingent altruist, he would keep records of which birds whom he had groomed in turn groomed him when requested to do so. When a bird applied for grooming a second time, he would be groomed only if he had proved willing to return the favor, to reciprocate. How should contingent or reciprocal altruism fare as a survival strategy? If contingent altruists were combined with uncontingent altruists, one could not tell them apart, because, though some were keeping records and were prepared to refuse nonreciprocators, they would never have to do so because all would reciprocate. There is really nothing to choose between contingent and uncontingent altruism as comparative strategies.

The special strength of contingent or reciprocal altruism is that it is not vulnerable to cheating. Contingent altruists combined with cheaters would at first not fare well, because they would groom cheaters but not be groomed by them. In time, however, the contingent altruists would come to be most prevalent in a population. It must be so, because a cheater, each time he fails to reciprocate, will add one individual no longer willing to groom him, and in time there will simply not be enough left unaware of his bad name to keep him alive. The contingent altruist, on the other hand, will steadily increase the number of those willing to groom him. Actually a small number of very lucky cheaters could survive in a population largely composed of contingent altruists; the luck would lie in not applying to the same birds twice, too often. There are technical problems with the theory of reciprocal altruism (Wilson, 1978), but it does offer a reasonable explanation for the existence of *seeming* altruism among individuals who are not kin (e.g. rhesus macaques, baboons, and anthropoid apes).

It is important to hold fast to the fact that the theory of delayed reciprocal altruism, although called by Trivers a theory of "altruism," is still, just like Hamilton's theory of kin selection, only a theory of *seeming* altruism, so long as altruism is understood in the clear and strict biological sense. What Trivers has done is show that, for instance, the animal that grooms unrelated members of its species could still be operating in a way that is consistent with Darwinian individual natural selection. The grooming individual appears to sustain costs, in the sense of survival and reproductive prospects, while benefiting other individuals in the same sense, but ultimately that is not true. Ultimately, because of record-keeping and reciprocation by groomed individuals, the groomer contributes to its own survival and reproductive success. There is no *real* biological altruism in the grooming, because when fully understood it is not a case in which individuals sacrifice their own interests in favor of the interests of others. Trivers's accomplishment is to show that still another class of apparent altruism is really consistent with Darwinian principles. A biologist does not expect to find any behavior that is not consistent with Darwinian principles since he believes in those principles. The task the evolutionary biologist sets himself with respect to altruism is always the same: to show that some apparent exception to Darwinism is really not an exception.

Equity in Animal Societies

Good, clear examples of reciprocal altruism in nonhuman animal societies are not numerous; Trivers and Wilson, between them, have come up with just a few, not all of them convincing. There is, however, another sort of seeming altruism between animals that are not kin which is so common that it is almost a universal of animal social life: deference or giving way on the part of one animal (the seeming altruist) to others in approaching food, water, space, and mates. That kind of seeming altruism occurs within the social structures called dominance orders and territories. Those structures are essentially rules governing the distribution of goods and so are functionally analogous to the calculation of equity in human social life.

When the farmer puts feed for his chickens in one pile in the henyard, the following will occur. One hen (biologists say the *alpha* animal) will step forward with every sign of confidence that she has the right to do so and feed while the rest hang back. When *alpha*, the top hen, has had her fill, *beta* will step forward, and so on, with each hen apparently knowing when its turn has come. If the experiment is repeated, the birds feed again in the same order. Access to feed in the henyard then is not an unstructured competitive struggle but, rather, governed by linear order of precedence, an order of rank or dominance, popularly called the "pecking order." If there is not enough feed for all on a given occasion, then the top birds will eat their fill and the bottom birds will do without. Here, then, is an unequal distribution of rewards. Extended studies over time and situation show that in general a hen retains its rank in every sort of competition; the order of precedence for favored roosting places and water is the same as for food. Roosters are generally dominant over all hens, and for roosters, prior rights include choice of mates.

The pecking order is not innate but is learned in a set of pairwise encounters, which occur as the birds mature and which establish a linear structure that generally lasts the lifetime of the birds. It is important to know that these encounters are not all-out combats in which the stronger and fiercer necessarily prevails. Hens and indeed all animals that establish dominance orders hold back in combat; they seldom do serious injury but, rather, engage in ritualized displays of feinting, threat, display, and assertiveness, which eventually cause one animal to make submissive signs, in effect confessing itself defeated or, more exactly, "psyched out."

Pecking, though noticeable in hens, is not important. The essential thing is the dominance order, which is a very stable rule for the unequal allocation of rewards. Dominance orders are found in many animal species. Among birds they include sparrows, finches, wrens, larks, and crows; jackdaws, parrots, cockatoos, and woodpeckers; owls, budgerigars, color-ringed black-capped chickadees, and great tits. The dominance order is not limited to birds but appears (with variations of detail) to occur in all classes of vertebrates, including moles, voles, lions, *anubis* baboons, and chimpanzees (Brown and Herrnstein, 1975).

What are the "investments" that determine the unequal distribution of rewards in animal dominance orders? In hens, size, strength, and vigor seem to be prime investments, and those attributes have a natural rather than arbitrary or conventional relation to rank, or they would have if rank were determined by actual combat. Since, however, rank is largely determined by ritual display and threat, the characteristics counting as investments are somewhat arbitrary. If we look at many animal species, the distribution of unequal rewards seems always to be based on characteristics in some degree arbitrary. Where it is weaponry that matters, as in the claws of the fiddler crab and the antlers and horns of ruminants, it is the brandishing of weapons rather than their deployment that settles contests. In many species the individual characteristics entitling unequal rewards are not weapons at all: the mane of the male lion; the songs of birds and crickets; the musk of alligators and death's-head moths; the tail feathers of pheasants; and the neck ruffs of lizards. It is not, I think, too fanciful to suggest that threats, displays, and makeup in animal species that have dominance orders are analogous to the skin colors, sex membership, age, lineage, seniority, and talents that function as investments in human societies (Brown and Herrnstein, 1975).

Territoriality is really the same kind of thing as a dominance order; it is a rule of distribution for animals that do not find their food piled in one spot but have to forage over an area. Sometimes the same species will be structured territorially if free to roam and linearly if caged (e.g. primates such as baboons), and sometimes a species will be territorial at one phase of its life cycle and ranked at another. Both structures accomplish the same thing: unequal distribution of rewards on the basis of somewhat arbitrary characteristics.

The familiar songbirds of the temperate zone of the United States are mostly territorial. The sparrows of Boston, Cleveland, Detroit, or Chicago wax territorial in the mating season, which is springtime. Each male leaves the winter flock, finds itself a conspicuous spot, and sings at sunrise to advertise his tenancy of a given area. If another male, perhaps a migrant back from the South, approaches to within an acre or so, the first male begins to keep a close eye on him, and if he approaches still nearer—too near—then the first male will try to chase him off. The song (actually a kind of threat) and the chase may be sufficient to keep male sparrows as widely spaced as they need to be in consideration of the density of food resources, but sometimes one will move too near and not retreat under threat, and a fight will ensue, which leaves the victor with a land holding and requires the loser to try his luck elsewhere.

What is a territory good for? Everything, practically. The females arrive only after land holdings are settled and will mate only with a male that has a territory. Males without territories must do without mates and so leave no offspring. The territory is the area in which parent birds can forage for food without interference from others of their species. There is a good deal of evidence that the average size of territories varies inversely across the years with richness of the food supply.

Territoriality, like dominance, is not limited to birds but extremely widespread in the animal kingdom. How much actual fighting goes on over territories? There may be some when territories are first claimed, as in the case of the sparrow, but that fighting, like the fighting associated with the establishment of dominance, generally stops short of serious injury. Neighbors in established territories do not continually fight to expand at one another's expense. The most prevalent behavior is some conventional display that makes it clear where established boundaries lie. Birds sing, howler monkeys howl, male fur seals flop on their bellies and slide toward one another, bumping noses at the border. The male stickleback (a fish) performs a kind of headstand exposing his red belly, which apparently signals his irritable state of mind.

Territoriality, like the dominance order, is a rule for distributing rewards that is analogous with the equity rules of human societies. The investments on which distribution is based include songs, howls, and red bellies and so are at least partially arbitrary. The important similarity among dominance, territory, and equity is that all represent rules for distributing resources to which a community seems to acquiesce.

Animals when they peacefully defer on account of dominance or territoriality seem to act altruistically. The rewards they forgo or postpone are food, water, space, and mates and so are very directly relevant to survival and reproductive success. That seeming altruism is really the most common kind of all, and superficially it looks like the genuine thing: biological altruism with some individuals acting in a way that lowers their own reproductive prospects and improves the prospects of others. Evolutionary biologists are agreed, however, that the seeming altruism arising out of animal social order is not really biological altruism and does not contradict Darwinian natural selection on the individual level. There is disagreement on the details but not on the general line of argument.

Guhl (1953) has shown what can happen when an animal group that ordinarily manifests a rank order is prevented from developing one. He compared two groups of hens that were allowed to stabilize pecking orders with two groups in which individuals were interchanged so frequently that the groups never had a chance to stabilize. The structured groups pecked less but ate more, gained more weight, and laid more eggs. When there was no rank order, no rule of distribution, the hens spent most of their time fighting to settle rank disputes. In effect, the pecking order was, and rank orders generally are, substitutes for fighting. Established territory rights have the same function; time is freed from fighting and threatening for food gathering and other productive activities. It is to the advantage of each individual in the social group to have a stable rule of distribution. The nature of the rule seems almost irrelevant in biological evolution; the important thing is to have a rule so that distribution of food, space, and water can proceed without continual conflict. Because the apparent altruism arising out of social order in animal societies ultimately benefits the individual that appears to act altruistically, the behavior does not contradict the Darwinian theory of natural selection and so is not biological altruism. Biological altruism, in the Darwinian sense, is not acknowledged to exist at all in nonhuman animal societies.

Biological Altruism in Human Life

All of the varieties of seeming altruism found in animal life—kin altruism, delayed reciprocal altruism, and equity altruism—are found in human life and, indeed, are universal in human societies. It seems probable, therefore, that the evolutionary mechanisms accounting for the occurrence of those forms of seeming altruism in animals account for the biological substrate of the same varieties of altruism in man. In the human case, however, kin altruism, reciprocal altruism, and equity altruism do not stay within the bounds defined by Darwinian theory, and in the human case, therefore, biological altruism in the strict sense does occur. Human altruism goes beyond the confines of Darwinism because human evolution is not only biological in nature, but also cultural and, indeed, in recent time primarily cultural.

Kin Altruism

Casual observation suggests that humans are generally less selfish, more altruistic, with kin than with non-kin. Biological parents do commonly feed, clothe, house, and protect their offspring. In societies where people make wills they are more likely to bequeath property to kin than to strangers. Occasionally the bond of kinship seems to operate with a mysterious Darwinian power, as when the elderly rich widow who has been squired for years by a nonprofessional gigolo disappoints his "expectations" and leaves her entire estate to a third cousin in Tennessee whom she has never met.

Beyond the most casual observation, however, altruism among kin does not satisfy the requirements of Hamilton's theory of kin selection. That theory requires that the amount of altruism shown should increase with the level of biological genetic relatedness (r). In Stephen Gould's (1977) amusing example, a man walking down a road with three brothers should, upon the approach of a monster intent on murder, rush ahead, sacrificing his life, in order to give his brothers a chance to hide and survive. The altruistic brother will have propagated 150 percent of his genes. Extending the example to first cousins whose relatedness is .125, a man walking with nine cousins should do the same thing. No data are available on that point. There are, however, data for less fanciful cases.

The most general problem with predicting human altruism from Hamilton's theory of kinship selection stems from the fact that closeness of kinship is construed very differently from one society to another, and the various known cultural kinship systems sometimes depart radically from biological relatedness, which is unlearned and uniform for the species. On the whole, furthermore, the flow of altruistic acts fits learned conceptions of kinship much more closely than it fits biological relatedness. Even cultural conceptions of kinship are clearly irrelevant in many cases. Adopted children who have no biological relatedness at all to their adopting parents are probably cared for at least as well as biological children.

There are numerous speculative attempts to explain one or another awkward fact about human altruism in terms of kin selection, and those I know range from strained to absurd. E. O. Wilson, for instance, has argued (1975) that homosexuality is a largely genetic trait, and for some kinds of exclusive homosexual there is weak evidence to support that view. How could a genetic basis for homosexuality have evolved, given the fact that homosexuals have no genetic offspring? Wilson's notion is that homosexual individuals may, like worker bees, invest their lives in helping to rear the offspring of their brothers and sisters and so promote their survival and, incidentally, the survival of genes for homosexuality, which the nephews and nieces would have a probability of .25 of carrying. There is no evidence for that proposal but also no evidence against it, if it is meant to apply only to the prehistoric past. However, in historical times no one has ever recorded exceptional kin altruism as a characteristic of homosexuals, and if the theory is meant to apply to present-day populations in cities like New York and San Francisco, it is downright risible. A more realistic theory would be that homosexual inclinations survive in the human species because large numbers of adults who have them also have heterosexual inclinations and produce offspring. This theory has the interesting implication that if a society should cease to disapprove of homosexuality and cause the number of homosexuals who enter into heterosexual marriages to decline, the genetic base of the inclination might be lost.

Studies of living kidney donors who are genetically related to the individual (Fellner and Marshall, 1981) are uniquely valuable for determining how well the theory of kin selection fits the facts of human kin altruism. In the first place the donation represents a clear cost in terms of survival prospects and reproductive potential, since we all need one healthy kidney, and the donation will reduce the two we start with to the minimum. The volunteer donor puts his or her life at some increased risk, which doctors explain to prospective donors; they also explain that the donation may do no good because the transplant may fail. When a donor is to be found from among a patient's relatives, it is necessary to carry out a long series of tests on a large population of kin to find the single best match. When that person has been identified, physicians privately offer him or her a medical excuse that will provide a graceful way out, relieving the individual of the worst sort of external pressure to comply. The question the theory of kin selection raises is: How does the percentage of prospective donors who agree to donate vary with the level of genetic relatedness between prospective donor and patient?

For parents donating to offspring agreement is 86 percent; for offspring to parents, 67 percent; for one sibling to another, 50 percent. All alike are first-degree relatives with a relatedness of .5, and that fact alone predicts that all percentages of compliance should be the same, which they clearly are not. However, the asymmetry in the parent–offspring case is in conformity with the kin theory of selection because, as noted previously, the reproductive prospects of offspring will, on the average, as a consequence of age, be greater than the prospects of parents, so parents should be more altruistic to offspring than are offspring to parents. However, the percentage for siblings is not consistent with that reasoning since it is only 50 percent, whereas the offspring-to-parents rate is 67 percent. Brothers and sisters are less altruistic to one another than to their parents, but they ought not to be, because siblings, being more nearly of the same age than offspring and parent, ought to have better prospects of reproductive success than parents. One is inclined to guess, knowing the culture in which the work was done, that children tend to feel closer to their parents on the average than to their siblings.

The evidence cited shows that altruism among kin does not conform to relatedness as it should if the theory of kin selection is to explain it, and so *true* biological altruism among kinfolk does exist in human animals though not in other animals. That is not surprising since human behavior is shaped by culture as well as biology.

Delayed Reciprocal Altruism

There is something about reciprocal altruism—even in the parable of the birds—which strongly suggests human social life. For the rule to operate, certain cognitive capacities are necessary: the ability to recognize individuals as individuals and not simply as members of one's species (how else could records be kept?) and a large long-term memory store (how else can the records of many individuals be retained over time?). Humans have those capacities, as do anthropoids and higher monkeys, but many other animal species lack them.

For reciprocal altruism to operate as a successful Darwinian strategy, groups of individuals, not too large in number, must live together for periods of time protracted enough to allow mutual reciprocation to occur. Primitive man lived in such enduring groups. The mode of life of *Homo sapiens* (our species) for about 40,000 years involved groups not exceeding about one hundred members. The large city-state, too large for individual reciprocity to be the primary principle, is only a few thousand years old.

One even feels, as Trivers pointed out, that certain human sentiments are essentially involved in reciprocal altruism. "Trust" would be a good name for the sentiment necessary to sustain a long-delayed reciprocation, "guilt" a good name for one's own failure to reciprocate, and "righteous anger" a good name for one's reaction to another's failure to reciprocate.

In addition, I think it must be more than a coincidence that uncontingent altruism is the highest moral principle not only of Christianity but of all the great world religions: Hinduism, Islam, Buddhism, Judaism. It is as if the greatest religious teachers had all recognized that there is no genetic foundation in our species for "Do unto others as ye would have them do unto you," no genetic foundation for uncontingent helping and trust, and so no possibility that this will be the natural usual way of behaving.

Finally, delayed reciprocal altruism seems human because examples of it in human life are manifold. Most of the examples of social exchange described in Chapter 2 may equally well be considered examples of reciprocal altruism: consultation among colleagues in which esteem is exchanged for help; the reciprocation of favors, gifts, Christmas cards, and so forth; the exchange of tips for good service—all involve giving benefits, keeping records, and reciprocating. In Chapter 2 also we have seen that Gouldner (1960) considers the rule that individuals should benefit those who benefit them to be a universal human norm, the norm of reciprocity.

Trivers's theory of reciprocal altruism may account for the evolution of the biological basis of exchange in human interaction, but a close look at phenomena of human exchange shows that they go beyond Trivers's theory. To begin with, the exchanges involved in reciprocal altruism are relevant to survival and reproductive prospects and so ought to include not just fringe exchanges like gifts, tips, and Christmas cards, but the more important exchanges of food, shelter, and services that are economic in nature as well. So long as economic exchange is conducted by direct bartering of goods and services, it looks very much like the reciprocal altruism of the birds in the parable. However, there is some finite, and not very large, limit on the size of society that can confine economic exchange to direct bartering. One can learn to recognize and keep accounts on only so many individuals.

With large and complex societies it becomes impossible to conduct economic exchange as barter. The newspaper vendor in Harvard Square can hardly keep mental accounts for even his regular customers, some hundreds in number, waiting for a fresh fish from one, a bunch of radishes from another, repairs on his car from a third. Instead, he receives then and there, as he hands over copies of the *Boston Globe*, 25 cents from each, and when he has enough quarters, he can exchange them with third parties for fish, radishes, and repairs. In short, the invention of money as a general medium of exchange adapted to the necessities of societies with very many members and a very complex division of labor causes economic exchange to look like a domain entirely distinct from the exchange of Christmas cards, phone calls, and favors, which resemble reciprocal altruism. There is no provision in Trivers's theory or in the parable of the birds for money.

One more example, and it should be perfectly clear that human exchange behavior is far more complex than reciprocal altruism. The universal norm of reciprocity requires the reciprocation of *equivalent* benefits; when the equivalence is not objective, it must be subjective. There is definite calculation involved when impoverished p reckons that his modest gift or modest hospitality is subjectively equivalent to rich o's lavish gift or hospitality, because the same percentage of total financial worth may be given in each case. In the parable of the birds, the benefits exchanged are *identical*—grooming of one bird by another—and it is vastly simpler to imagine an evolutionary mechanism for that kind of exchange than it is for the exchange of subjective equivalents.

Equity Altruism

We have seen that the rules of distribution implicit in a dominance order or in territoriality are functionally analogous to the human consideration of investments in calculating equity. We can see how it happens that social theorists who are political conservatives tend to find the study of the social behavior of animals appealing. If the lesson of animal social structure is that a rule, a common understanding of distribution, is advantageous to all, and the actual character of the rule a matter of comparative indifference, then there is much to be said for the *status quo*, for things as they are. Societies always do have rules of distribution, and if the premium is on having a rule of some sort, any sort, then the rule that exists has an advantage over any rule that might conceivably exist, because changing a rule means conflict, which is a general waste of everyone's time.

There is certainly an analogy, a close one, between human conceptions of equity and the operation in animal societies of rank and territory. Each animal species has its own set of relevant and recognized investments for the distribution of rewards like food, water, mates, and space. The investments of one species must seem bizarre to all other species: the mane of the lion, the pincer of the crab, the horns of the antelope, the tail feathers of the pheasant. They seem as varied and bizarre as the considerations of race, sex, genealogy, income, and caste that human societies recognize as investments. Furthermore, animal societies seem quite content, as do human societies, with inequalities of distribution, even vast inequalities, so long as individual rewards are consonant with whatever counts as investments. The principal stimulus to anger and aggression in animals, as in man, is not inequality as such but illegitimate inequality, inequality not in accord with investments as they are reckoned in a given society.

The difference between animal equity and human equity is, however, profoundly important. The reckoning of investments in an animal species changes only by the glacially slow process of biological evolution. In any human society tremendous changes in conceptions of investment can occur in one's own lifetime. In animal societies rewards are distributed in accordance with entitling characteristics that are largely innate; the problem of justice does not arise. In human societies, rewards are distributed in accordance with characteristics that are often disputed, and the problem of justice is to find principles that will adjudicate among conflicting claims, principles like those proposed in John Rawls's *A Theory of Justice* (1972).

Altruism governed by considerations of equity in the human case is, obviously, very much more complicated than the animal altruism governed by dominance and territoriality. The animal altruism can be explained in terms of individual natural selection and so is not true biological altruism at all. Equity-based human altruism cannot be explained by Darwinian selection alone and is real biological altruism. Humans do defer to one another on grounds of race, caste, lineage, seniority, or ability in ways that damage the survival prospects and reproductive potential of the one that defers, enhancing the prospects and potential of others.

Summary

There is much human behavior that reminds us of the kinds of seeming altruism in animals that can be explained by kin selection, delayed reciprocal altruism, or equity-like rules of dominance and territory. In the animal cases the altruism is only *seeming*, but in the full range of human cases the altruism is real in the biological sense. To cap the argument, we need only recall human acts benefiting others where the others were not kin, could not possibly reciprocate, and were not "owed anything" in an equity sense. People really have risked their lives for unknown strangers, for example, the rescuers of Jews from Nazis and the donors of kidneys to unrelated individuals whom they do not meet. Altruism, in a biological sense, certainly exists.

Psychological Altruism

Biological altruism is defined essentially as behavior that violates Darwin's theory of natural selection. In psychology there is a theory of behavior that was conceived by deliberate analogy with natural selection, and that is reinforcement theory, which has historically taken several forms (e.g. Hull, 1943; Skinner, 1938) and has also been known as trial-and-error learning (Thorndike, 1933). The most influential contemporary version of reinforcement theory is B. F. Skinner's (1938) theory of operant conditioning. An operant is a response that an organism *emits* (operants are not *elicited* by specifiable stimuli), and an operant becomes more probable, is strengthened, if it is followed by positive reinforcement (reward). The strengthening of one operant, from a pool of operants, by a history of contingent positive reinforcement is a process of selection occurring in the lifetime of an individual analogous to the selection of a gene across individual lifetimes by its contribution to the survival and reproductive success of the individuals bearing it. Psychological altruism, by direct analogy with biological altruism, would then be an act that positively reinforces (or rewards) an individual other than the one performing the act at some cost (negative reinforcement) to the individual acting. Bypassing all the lower orders of the animal kingdom, the question is: "Do we find psychological altruism in human behavior?"

Social exchange is not altruism since rewards or benefits or positive reinforcements are reciprocated and so neither person rewards the other at a lasting cost to himself. To be sure, reinforcement theory must be considerably loosened to permit that generalization, because we know that rewards may sometimes be reciprocated only after long delays, but then, reinforcement theory must lose most of its precision in *any* application to human behavior. Certain kinds of low-cost altruism seem to be quite common: giving to a stranger, who may not even smile or say thanks, such requested benefits as "any spare change," directions how to get somewhere, and the time of day. Latané and Darley (1970), as a not very serious preliminary to their work on the unresponsive bystander, turned loose in New York City students from introductory psychology courses at Columbia with instructions to ask from passersby just such routine small courtesies. More than 1,500 people were approached, and substantial percentages (from 34 percent to 85 percent, depending on the request) proved to be what the authors call "low-cost altruists." Favors of this kind are called "routine courtesies," not only because they are low-cost but also because they are so ordinary as to raise no questions in the mind of the person approached. However, asking a stranger his or her name, without further explanation, drew refusals from the majority, who probably were set to wondering about possible hidden costs.

In emergencies like robberies, accidents, and assaults, we know from the work of Latané and Darley, most bystanders remain unresponsive, and that is because probable costs in such situations look high and rewards either nonexistent or trivial (see Chapter 2). High-cost altruists were not very numerous. It is important to remember, however, that the probability that someone would help in an emergency increased as the number of candidate helpers or bystanders declined. The governing principle was shown to be the clarity with which the *responsibility* to help fell to a particular person or persons, and that is an important fact to which we shall return.

In exchange theory all human interaction depends upon giving and returning the equivalence, and so there seems to be no provision for psychological altruism. Exchange is a special case of a more comprehensive theory: Social equity. Equity starts with a proposition of pure selfishness: Individuals will try to maximize their profits. That pristine selfishness is modified by the necessity that maximizing individuals have of dealing with maximizing others, which leads to a rule of fairness or equity according to which individuals who compare themselves with one another must have the same ratio of rewards to investments. Again, there is no apparent provision for psychological altruism. Exchange and equity are supposed to apply to all human relationships, but most of the research that has been done and most of the examples of Chapter 2 deal with casual relationships: co-workers in a bureaucratic agency; employer-employee; philanthropist–recipient. Almost everyone acknowledges that considerations of exchange and equity are evident in such time-limited, non-disclosing, circumscribed relations. Not everyone, by any means, is willing to say that exchange and equity govern intimate relationships. Friendship, romance and marriage seem to many to be exempt from vulgar pseudo-economic calculation.

Zick Rubin in his book *Liking and Loving** is especially eloquent:

The notions that people are "commodities" and social relationships are "transactions" will surely make many readers squirm. Exchange theory postulates that human relationships are based first and foremost on self-interest. As such, it often seems to portray friendship as motivated only by what one person can get from another and to redefine love as a devious power game. Such characterizations contrast sharply with what many of us would like to think of friendship and love, that

---

*Copyright © 1973 by Holt, Rinehart and Winston, Inc. Reprinted by permission of Holt, Rinehart and Winston, a division of CBS College Publishing.

they are intimate relationships characterized at least as much by the joy of giving as by the desire to receive. But although we might prefer to believe otherwise, we must face up to the fact that our attitudes toward other people *are* determined to a large extent by our assessments of the rewards they hold for us.

It is difficult to imagine that there has ever been a human society in which some generally agreed upon standards of a person's worth and desirability did not exist. And as long as there are such standards, our interpersonal preferences and relationships will share some of the features of the marketplace. We will typically want to associate with those people who are "valuable" and to shun those who are not. As a result, people's relative value on the marketplace will often structure their relationships, with the more desirable member of a pair also being the one who exerts the greater power. Much of the time these effects will take place more or less automatically, like the operation of the economic laws of supply and demand. In at least some cases, however, conscious tactical considerations play a demonstrable role on the interpersonal marketplace, just as they do in the financial world. . . .

Having said all this about the value of exchange theory, however, it is time to consider its limitations. For the fact is that, even when presented in its most enlightened form, a theory that presumes an overriding human desire to maximize one's own— and only one's own—profits inevitably falls short of providing a complete understanding of human relationships. Contrary to the guiding assumption of the exchange perspective, human beings are sometimes altruistic in the fullest sense of the word. They make sacrifices for the sake of others without any consideration of the rewards they will obtain from them in return. Such selfless concern for the welfare of others may emerge even in interactions among strangers, but it emerges most often and most clearly in close interpersonal relationships. [Rubin, 1973, pp. 82–83]

Many social theorists agree with Rubin that in close relationships psychological altruism, self-sacrifice for the welfare of others, is common (e.g. Douvan, 1972; Wexler, 1980). Many others distinguish between "true" love or friendship, taken to be altruistic, and less admirable forms, which are marked by considerations of exchange. Erich Fromm in *The Art of Loving* (1956) defines true love as giving and contrasts it with the false love of the "marketing character" that depends upon expected reciprocity at some later time. Mills and Clark (1980) distinguish two kinds of intimate relationship: the *communal* couple in which each individual gives out of concern for the other, and the *exchange* couple, which keeps mental records of who is ahead and who is behind. Murstein (e.g. Murstein, 1978; Murstein, MacDonald, and Cerreto, 1977) holds that a scorekeeping mentality in a close relationship guarantees that both parties will be dissatisfied. He has created an Exchange Orientation Scale designed to identify individuals with an extreme conscious concern with short-term equity. There is some research (Murstein, MacDonald, and Cerreto, 1977) suggesting that such exchange types are suspicious, fearful, paranoid, and insecure, whereas those less oriented to exchange are giving and trusting persons.

There is general agreement that psychological altruism is more evident in intimate relations than in casual. We shall therefore look for altruism in intimate relations, seeking to find it where it is supposed to be (Kelley, et al, 1983).

We will not, however, overlook manifestations of exchange and equity just because seeing them has been impugned as a characteristic of marketing characters incapable of true or communal love.

The Matching Hypothesis

Exchange theory and equity theory both clearly predict that individuals who are willing to become a romantic couple should be rather closely matched in ability to reward one another. In exchange terms, what p and o, who may pair up, have to offer one another is themselves, and each self is a combination of more or less rewarding or valuable attributes, including sexual attractiveness, personal wealth, character, a house with a mortgage, and two kids from a prior marriage. The principle of exchange requires that the two prize packages be subjectively equivalent or no deal. Equity says that each person seeks to maximize his or her own profits, and so we might expect all to pursue the rich and beautiful, were it not for the fact that the rich and beautiful, as would-be maximizers, will be pursuing the more-rich and the more-beautiful, and so most of us need not apply and, indeed, had better not lest we incur the cost of a painful rebuff. Perfect selfishness in everyone requires realistic compromise if any couples at all are going to be formed. The best general bargain that can be struck is a value-match, or subjective equivalence. Matching does not necessarily mean similarity, good looks with good looks, rich with rich, and so on; it means subjectively equivalent total value or power to reward, and so the elderly rich widower and his beautiful but poor bride may be a well-matched pair.

In Boston, as in many cities, there is a radio program that plays matchmaker. One "single" calls in and describes himself or herself and then specifies the requirements for a desirable date. Telephone numbers and addresses are not broadcast since that could lead to harassment; the station makes the connections. If you listen to that kind of program even once, you will be convinced that people have a sense of their own market value and of the value of the date they can hope to interest. Irritable, impoverished, elderly widowers do not put themselves up to be bid for by Bo Derek blondes. The lady who might easily pass for forty-three "in the dusk with the light behind her" stresses her sense of humor and love of the movies rather than her allergies and taste for world travel. In such public broadcasts there is a certain reluctance to inventory physical assets and liabilities, and the party on the other end of the line can get impatient and say: "Yes, but what do you look like?" One answer that should give pause is: "Well, you know, two eyes, one nose, and a mouth." Look out! Personals ads in some magazines and newspapers, because of the anonymity that is possible, are much more explicit about physical features and erotic tastes, and the matches proposed may be very highly spiced indeed.

In 1937 Waller published a famous article called "The Rating and Dating Complex" in which he wrote:

> Courtship may be defined as the set of processes among the unmarried from which, in time, permanent marriages usually ensue. . . . For the average college student, and especially for the man, a love affair which led to permanent marriage would be tragic because of the havoc it would create in his scheme of life. Nevertheless, college students feel strongly the attractions of sex, and the sexes associate with one another in a peculiar relationship known as dating. Dating is not true courtship since it is supposed not to eventuate in marriage; it is a sort of dalliance relationship. [Waller, 1937, p. 729]

There is something delicious about Professor Waller describing the peculiar ways of college students as if they were a species of grooming birds.

At the state university on which Waller reported, most students belonged to fraternities or sororities, and the unaffiliated male student, like the unterritoried songbird, either had to go dateless or else had to go "prowling about in small industrial communities nearby" or "take on the role of misogynist—and read Schopenhauer." Students rated one another on a scale from A to D, and dates occurred primarily between men and women of the same "class." What factors entered into the determination of class? A class A male had to belong to one of the better fraternities, be prominent in student activities, have spending money, be well-dressed, have a *smooth* manner, a good *line*, and an automobile. A class A female had to belong to one of the better sororities, have good clothes, smooth looks, dance well, and be much sought after. It was a great mistake for a girl ever to accept a last-minute date, and it were no bad thing if she delayed answering the phone so as to be much paged.

I wonder if the rating and dating complex sounds ridiculously antiquated to college students today. The fully ritualized date with the man calling for the woman, paying the check, and seeing her home is less common than it used to be, but students still do form dating pairs. The factors that count in reckoning social value are transitory, and the language (a *smooth* manner and a good *line*) still more so. The journal copy of Waller's article has been in our library since 1937, and so the overwriting of generations of Harvard and Radcliffe students almost hides the text. Though not always so tamely expressed, the verdict is nearly unanimous: "This is so much rot." The marginal commentaries are, however, mistaken. A 1984 Hollywood masterpiece called *Revenge of the Nerds* might have hired Professor Waller as technical consultant, so exactly does it represent what he wrote about fraternities, sororities, and the unterritoried, undatable nerds. A nerd, of course, is someone not prominent in student activities, someone who lacks spending money, dresses like a nerd, and does not have either a *smooth* manner or a good *line*.

Still, *Revenge of the Nerds* is not realistic cinema, and many students in 1984 say that just about the only thing that matters on first encounters at, say, a "get-acquainted freshman mixer," is personal attractiveness. There are studies that support this claim. A "computer dance" is one for which men and women independently buy tickets and then fill out detailed questionnaires about themselves, which the computer is supposed to use to compute ideal matches. Such a dance was held at the University of Minnesota (Hatfield et al., 1966) for the entire freshman class in the first week of a new term. The four bureaucrats who seemed to be managing the ticket sales and questionnaires were actually rating each client for physical attractiveness on a nine-point scale. The computer in question was not programmed to do the subtle matching tests clients supposed. Men and women were, in fact, paired on a random basis, and many must have been quite puzzled about what that computer knew and what rules it had been given for matching. Outcome data were collected after the dance, both immediately and some days later, and included a listing of all the men who followed up on the first mechanically arranged date by asking for a second voluntary date. Many things were known about the men and women—social skills, intelligence, personality characteristics—but a single factor controlled the probability that a woman would be asked for a second date: her physical attractiveness, without regard to his.

The matching hypothesis makes a clear prediction about attempts to date: Only those men should have asked for a second date who had happened to be matched (by chance) with women whose attractiveness level closely matched their own. The hypothesis follows directly from the principle of exchanging the subjective equivalent. For this experiment the matching hypothesis was wrong. The men acted on a principle of pure selfishness. The more attractive the woman each man had met, the greater the probability that a second approach would be made—completely independent of the man's own attractiveness.

Follow-up studies have shown that the pure selfishness effect in the first computer dance was not representative of dating generally but was an artifact of experimental design. Equity theory holds that pure selfishness is transformed into matching by the fact that persons approached, because they are also selfish, will not ordinarily accept dates from classes below their own, and so offers will not be made for fear of rebuff. That usual curb on sky-high aspirations seems to have been lifted from the men in the first study by their belief that a wise and subtle computer had found in their questionnaire data reason to match them with the women who were their dates. When those men thought about asking for a second date, they felt no need to accommodate what they desired to what they might hope to attain, because the computer had decided that some of even the least attractive men *deserved* (and so had been dated with) the most attractive women.

When a few small changes were made in the computer dances at Minnesota to make them more like ordinary dating situations, the matching hypothesis was confirmed (Berscheid et al., 1971). As before, the men and women who bought tickets were, unknown to themselves, rated for physical attractiveness. They were, however, given an opportunity this time to specify characteristics they hoped to find in their dates, including some level of physical attractiveness on a nine-point scale. They were told that the computer would be able to meet this specification, so large was the pool upon which it could draw. In those circumstances men and women made requests in close agreement with the matching hypothesis; the less attractive asked for the less attractive, the moderately attractive for the moderately attractive, and the highly attractive for the highly attractive. It was not even necessary that the men and women should believe they might be turned down by their choices. So long as they knew their choices would know that they had exercised a choice, they did not *presume* to ask for too much. The result suggests that matching results from a well-learned sense of what is "fitting" more than from fear of actual rebuff in a given case. The purely selfish approach of all to the most attractive in the first experiment came about because the supposed computer-generated matches upset the individual male's sense of his own social value.

Undoubtedly matching for physical attraction is a prime determinant of couple formation, and it is probably maximally influential in college. Students at a college have already been selected, as a population, for their comparative homogeneity in intelligence, social class, knowledge, and values. Many dimensions of individual variation remain and play a role in matchmaking, but physical attraction is probably the most important. Murstein (1972) very neatly demonstrated attraction-matching by having photos of the male and female members of ninety-nine engaged or steady couples rated for physical attractiveness by judges who did not know couple status. It was then only necessary to correlate attractiveness ratings of genuine couples and attractiveness ratings of artificial couples, randomly created. Real couples were much closer in attractiveness than were artificial couples, and Murstein concluded: "Individuals with equal market value for physical attractiveness are more likely to associate in an intimate relationship, such as premarital engagement, than individuals with disparate values" (1972, p. 11). That correlation is so familiar that when it is strikingly violated, it gives rise to such comment as: "I wonder what she sees in him." The *him* in question, by the way, is likely to be quite content with this state of affairs, because his unformulated knowledge of the matching principle tells him that people will assume that "he must have something."

From the matching hypothesis it follows that genuine couples will be more like one another than random couples on any dimension that enters into the calculation of social value. Hatfield, Walster, and Berscheid (1978) summarize a large literature showing that couples tend to be similar in IQ, education, and other characteristics. Similarity on any single value dimension follows from matching, but it is also attributable simply to a tendency for like to select like, assortative mating or *homogamy*—the union of similars (Buss, 1985). Good evidence of matching must show not just similarity but value tradeoffs: beauty for brains, a distinguished lineage for money, and so forth. There is evidence for this that goes beyond the few famous instances we know about from the media.

In the 1930s the Oakland Growth Study (Elder, 1969) rated fifth- and sixth-grade girls for physical attractiveness, and years later the social status of the men the girls had married was independently rated. In general, the more attractive the girl had been in her pre-teen years, the "better" she had done in a status sense in her marriage. Berscheid, Hatfield, and Bohrnstett (1973) had a large sample of persons currently in a stable couple relationship rate their own sexual desirability and that of their partners and obtained substantial numbers of "more desirables" and "less desirables" on that one dimension. The question then was whether the less desirables in some way were compensating for their perceived lower value in one respect by delivering higher value in some other respect—as the matching hypothesis predicts. It was clear that they were. The less attractive partners had, on the average, higher socioeconomic status than the more attractive partners. The lesser partners also put more effort into their marriages and expressed more affection. It seems then that those steady relations were characterized by matching that went beyond similarity and could be described as an equivalence of general, cross-domain, reward value.

Strong support for the matching hypothesis comes from Kiesler and Baral (1970), who managed to vary the value individual men set on themselves and to show that their levels of romantic aspiration varied accordingly. Some were led to believe that they had just done badly on an intelligence test and some that they had done unexpectedly well. Immediately after receiving the self-enhancing or self-diminishing information, each man had a natural-seeming opportunity to become acquainted with, and eventually try to date, either a very attractive young woman or a quite unattractive young woman. The experiment showed that the men who had recently had their values elevated "came on" to the attractive girl, while the men who had recently been depreciated more often approached the unattractive girl.

The Kiesler and Baral experiment gives the man the opportunity to win the reward of an attractive partner by means of other assets, and we do think of that asymmetrical tradeoff as the common one. A man is free to marry for love, but a woman must be more practical. It is interesting to know that there has been some change in recent years in the rewards women will settle for in marriage. The question was asked of both men and women: "If a woman (man) had all the qualities you wish for in a mate but you were not in love with him (her), would you marry?" Twenty years ago, 65 percent of men said no and only 24 percent of women, but in 1976, 86 percent of men said no and 80 percent of women said the same—an indirect indication, I think, of increasingly equal freedom, the freedom to marry for love (Kephart, 1967; Berscheid and Campbell, 1981).

Karl Marx (1963) had a sharp eye for exchange processes in supposedly noneconomic human relations, and one example is unforgettable: "I am ugly, but I can buy the most beautiful women for myself. Consequently I am not ugly, for the effect of ugliness is annulled by money" (p. 191). Michael Walzer in *Spheres of Justice* (1983) argues that this kind of exchange is immoral for the reason that every kind of good has its own proper criterion of distribution, and money ought properly only to be exchangeable for commodities and services, love for love. Observance of Walzer's idea would produce a complex equality in which each person would do well in some areas, less well in others. Walzer would have Marx stay ugly. I think it is obtuse of both not to realize that Marx, if he had money, could buy only "services," not love.

Jane Austen in all her novels implicitly accepts the matching hypothesis and then shows with incomparable subtlety how it operates among three or four "good" families in some country village in nineteenth-century England. The "problem" posed in her novel *Emma* is the discovery of suitable matches for just six persons: Emma Woodhouse, Harriet Smith, Jane Fairfax, Frank Churchill, Mr. Knightly, and Mr. Elton. Emma herself has many assets: "Emma Woodhouse, handsome, clever, and rich, with a comfortable home and happy disposition, seemed to unite some of the best blessings of existence; and had lived nearly twenty-one years in the world with very little to distress or vex her.... The real evils indeed of Emma's situation were the power of having rather too much her own way, and a disposition to think a little too well of herself" (1972, p. 1).

The brilliant comedy of Volume I stems from Emma's efforts to make a match between her chosen companion, Harriet Smith, who is beautiful and engaging but not sensible and not of very good family, and a certain Mr. Elton, who is handsome and clever and "could marry anyone." Emma does not scruple to interfere between Harriet and the intelligent gentleman-farmer Robert Martin, who is in love with Harriet. For nearly a hundred pages Emma is persuaded that Mr. Elton wishes to marry Harriet and persuades Harriet that that is so, but in a climax of high comedy it turns out that Mr. Elton has all this time been courting Emma herself and has had the effrontery to think himself worthy. Emma has mistaken Harriet's market value because Emma has "a disposition to think a little too well of herself." Harriet, Emma has calculated, must be the equal of Mr. Elton for the reason that Harriet is the chosen best friend of Emma Woodhouse. In representing assets and equivalence as subjective calculations, and even in treating a valuable companion as an asset, Jane Austen only shows herself to have had a good unformulated sense of equity; it is in her development of exquisite intertwined ironies out of all this that we see the great novelist.

In Jane Austen's world there is no good match without love, and love is more than a matter of equivalent social value, but then love does not ever develop between seriously unsuitable pairs; eligibility is defined by social strata as it is in nonfictional social life. In other worlds, however, social suitability is overridden by intense immediate attraction. It is for Shakespeare's Romeo and Juliet, Dante's Paolo and Francesca, Wagner's Tristan and Isolde, and all those have their real-life counterparts. In Zandonai's opera *Francesca da Rimini*, Francesca and Paolo, the brother of the man she is supposed to marry, see one another for the first time near the end of Act I, and then, for about fifteen minutes, stare deeply into one another's eyes—speechless and songless—while the orchestra expresses the rapture they feel. Francesca and Paolo are not doing equity calculations; nor are Tristan and Isolde when they sing Wagner's love music. It is not true either, as some say, that such attraction occurs only in opera—or poetry or the movies. Most people fall in love, and more than once in a lifetime. It may be the best experience life offers, in part, perhaps, because self and other and all exchange calculations are suspended (Pope, 1980; Sternberg and Grajek, 1984; Tennov, 1979). Of course, Romeo and Juliet, Paolo and Francesca, Tristan and Isolde all died soon after they met. None of those couples went on to arrange a wedding, buy a house, and raise a family. If they had, issues of equity might have arisen. If you experience rapture and are unwilling ever to come down, there probably is nowhere to go but death.

Compatibility

Once a man and woman have met and judged themselves well enough matched to meet again, what happens next—outside of opera? As self-disclosure becomes more complete and more candid, they will discover themselves to be compatible or not. Compatible couples are, most notably, couples that stay together, that become stable. In addition, compatible couples, other things being equal, are happier, more content, than incompatible couples. There is evidence that matching (or equity) is an important factor in compatibility.

From four Boston-area colleges and universities 231 steadily dating couples volunteered to have their "affairs" studied over a two-year period (Hill, Rubin, and Peplau, 1976). At the end of two years 103 couples had broken up, 45 percent of the initial pairs, and the chief question the researchers asked was whether the eventual outcome, breaking up or staying together, could have been predicted from data collected in the initial questionnaire. Each individual boyfriend and girlfriend had answered the questionnaire, in private and under an absolute guarantee of confidentiality, so that no participant would ever know the answers of his or her partner. To a considerable degree eventual outcomes were predictable. About 80 percent of the couples who described themselves as "in love" at the start were still together after two years, whereas only about 56 percent of those who did not so describe themselves stayed together. Two aspects of initial intimacy proved totally unrelated to outcome: having sexual intercourse and living together. Those actions probably reflect a couple's social values as much as the depth of attachment.

Each person described herself or himself in terms of age, height, SAT scores, religion, and many social attitudes, and each person was rated for physical attractiveness by judges from color photos. It was therefore possible to find out whether the couples who stayed together had initially been more closely matched on various characteristics than the couples who separated. The data are shown in Table 3-1, and with striking consistency it appears that matching made for compatibility as measured by stability. "Together" couples were at the start much more alike than "broken" couples in age, SAT math, SAT verbal, physical attractiveness, and educational plans. Characteristics on which

TABLE 3-1. Initial Couple Similarity and Status Two Years Later

	All Couples (N = 231)	Together Couples (N = 117)	Breakup Couples (N = 103)
Correlation of Partners' Characteristics			
Age	.19**	.38**	.13
Highest degree planned	.28**	.31**	.17
SAT, math	.22**	.31**	.11
SAT, verbal	.24**	.33**	.15
Physical attractiveness	.24**	.32**	.16
Father's educational level	.11	.12	.12
Height	.21**	.22*	.22*
Religion (% same)	51%**	51%**	52%**
Attitudes			
Sex-role traditionalism (10-item scale)	.47**	.50**	.41**
Favorability toward women's liberation	.38**	.36**	.43**
Approval of sex among "acquaintances"	.25**	.27**	.21*
Romanticism (6-item scale)	.20*	.21*	.15
Self-report of religiosity	.37**	.39**	.37**
Number of children wanted	.51**	.43**	.57**

*Correlation significantly greater than zero with $p < .05$.
**Correlation significantly greater than zero with $p < .01$.
SOURCE: Hill, Rubin, and Peplau, 1976, Table 2, p. 154.

matching did not seem to matter included height, religion, and father's occupation. The matching principle appears, therefore, to affect not only initial pairing but also long-term compatibility.

Closely matched couples are couples in which the partners in giving themselves give each other equivalent rewards. Insofar as the two are equally attractive, equally intelligent, equally young (when youth is valued), they exchange equal rewards. Similarity or matching is one form of fair exchange in pairing, but as we know, equivalent rewards or values need not necessarily be point-for-point matches but may involve tradeoffs of equivalent value. Equity theory takes account of investments (or assets) as well as rewards, and the rule of fairness in general is a rule of equal ratios of rewards to investments, as when two employees who differ so that one has high seniority and high skill and the other has less of both are paid proportionately by a third party, the better qualified receiving more.

Intimate relations between two people are a special case of equity. To begin with, just two persons are involved. The rule of fairness is, as always, a rule of equal ratios:

$$\frac{\text{Rewards}_p}{\text{Investments}_p} = \frac{\text{Rewards}_o}{\text{Investments}_o}$$

However, with intimate pairs the investments that p brings to the relationship (e.g. some level of attractiveness, intelligence, love) are the rewards that o derives from the relationship, and vice versa. In principle, therefore, equity between intimate pairs reduces to a comparison of what p is getting from the relation with what o is getting from the relation, which makes it a matter of simple exchange or matching. However, equity research on intimate relations, to maintain theoretical consistency and also in order to elicit maximally thoughtful responses, always asks a more complicated question. For instance: "Considering what you put into your relationship [Investments$_p$], compared to what you get out of it [Rewards$_p$] and what your partner puts in [Investments$_o$] compared to what s(he) gets out of it [Rewards$_o$], how would you say your relationship 'stacks up'?" (Hatfield, Walster, and Berscheid, 1978). The parenthetical terms "Rewards" and "Investments" are not used in the question and were inserted here just to make it clear that the question is asking for comparison of the two usual ratios. If the above question were pared down to exchange terms, it would be: "Comparing what you get out of this relationship with what your partner gets out of it, how would you say the relationship 'stacks up'?"

The alternatives using the Global Measure (Hatfield, Walster, and Berscheid, 1978) are:

+ 3 I am getting a much better deal than my partner.
+ 2 I am getting a somewhat better deal.
+ 1 I am getting a slightly better deal.
  0 We are both getting an equally good ... or bad ... deal.
− 1 My partner is getting a slightly better deal.
− 2 My partner is getting a somewhat better deal.
− 3 My partner is getting a much better deal than I am.

From answers to such a scale, equity researchers are able to identify individuals who feel that their relationship is *equitable* (a scale value of 0) as well as individuals who feel that they are severely *underbenefited* (-3) and individuals who feel that they are extremely *overbenefited* ($+3$). Those are the group comparisons of primary interest in relating equity to compatibility. The equity measure described here is the simplest and most global and is called the "Hatfield 1978 Global Measure of Equity–Inequity." There are two more complicated measures: one ("Walster 1977 Global Measure") asks that overall outcomes and inputs (contributions) of both partners be separately rated, and one ("Traupmann, Utne, Hatfield 1978 Scales") asks couples to assess fairness in four different areas: (1) personal concerns, (2) emotional concerns, (3) day-to-day concerns, and (4) opportunities gained and lost.

All three equity measures are described in Hatfield, Utne, and Traupmann (1979). Since the measures are all used to identify people who feel they are in equitable relationships, people who feel underbenefited, and people who feel overbenefited, I shall not bother in what follows to identify the particular measure used. Possibly the more detailed measures are more exact, but I think the three are largely equivalent to one another and also to the simpler exchange question, which simply asks *p* to compare what he or she gets out of the relationship with what the partner gets out of it.

Hatfield, Walster, and Traupmann (1978) interviewed 537 college men and women who were dating someone either casually or steadily and asked them whether they expected to be still with their partners in one year's time and in five years' time. Those who felt their relationship was perfectly equitable were much more likely than any others to think that they would still be together in one year and in five years. Those who felt greatly underbenefited and those who felt greatly overbenefited were least likely of all respondents to think that their relationship would be intact in the future. What is most interesting here is that the overbenefited were just exactly as doubtful about future prospects as were the underbenefited, and that is what equity theory predicts. Presumably, the underbenefited expected to do better in the future and the overbenefited did not expect their luck to last. Both extremes felt the relationship was unstable, whereas the equitable relationship felt stable. There was a three-and-a-half-month followup to find which of the hundreds of couples were still together, and the facts even after that short time confirmed the expectations: The equitable relationships were the most likely to be intact and the insecure under- and overbenefited least likely to be intact.

The results using a global assessment of perceived equity confirm the results of Hill, Rubin, and Peplau (1976), who found that couples still together after two years' time were more closely matched in many specific ways (therefore equitable) than couples who had broken up after two years. It seems clear that matching or equity is associated with both expected and actual couple compatibility in the sense of stability over time.

The quality of a relationship and not only its stability is an aspect of compatibility. We think of compatible couples as more content, as happier, than incompatible couples, and there is evidence that equity (or matching) is as important to quality as to stability. Equity theory, in addition, makes the more specific prediction that the *nature* of the distress felt by the under- and overbenefited members of a couple will differ: The underbenefited should feel angry and the overbenefited guilty. Exactly those results were obtained by Hatfield, Walster, and Traupmann (1978) in their study of 537 dating men and women. Those in relationships that seemed either equitable or nearly so were the most content and also most happy. Those who felt greatly underbenefited were discontent and, in fact, angry, while those who felt greatly overbenefited felt discontent and, in fact, guilty. Identical results were obtained by Traupmann, Hatfield, and Wexler (1983). What it comes to is this: Contentment with, or happiness in, a relationship is maximal when the relationship is felt to be equitable; as equity falls off in either direction, into underbenefit or overbenefit, contentment declines and gives way in the former case to anger, in the latter case to guilt.

Bernard Murstein and his associates (e.g. Murstein and MacDonald, 1983), though they recognize that exchange and equity play a significant role in intimate relationships, hold that a very great conscious concern with exchange or equity, especially over a short time span, operates against compatibility in friendship and, especially, marriage. They have data that appear to support their claim. Forty couples married for at least three years were asked to fill out Murstein's Exchange Orientation Questionnaire (Murstein, MacDonald, and Cerreto, 1977) and also a standard measure of marital adjustment. For both husbands and wives the correlations were significantly negative: −.66 for husbands and −.62 for wives. The Exchange Attitude Questionnaire is not intended to assess equity or equivalence of exchange, but rather degree of conscious concern with fair give-and-take. Some items do seem to do just that; for instance: "1. If my spouse feels entitled to an evening out with his/her friends of either sex, then I am entitled to an evening out with my friends of either sex." However, it seems to me that ten of the nineteen items on the questionnaire go beyond concern with fair exchange in such a way as to express a feeling of underbenefit, a feeling that one is being cheated in the marriage. For instance:

11. My spouse's relationship with others sometimes makes him/her neglect me.

14. I wish my spouse would show more acknowledgement when I do or say nice things to him/her.

17. I sometimes feel that I am not fully appreciated by my spouse.

Items like those surely tap resentment at underbenefit. With half the items on the scale having that property, it is fair to suggest that the scale does not primarily test degree of exchange orientation but, rather, inequity of the underbenefit variety. If the scale measures underbenefit, then the negative correlation with marital adjustment (which includes level of happiness and contentment) is only what equity theory predicts. The original Exchange Attitude Questionnaire was being revised in 1984 to meet that and other objections, and a revision seems worthwhile, because the idea that a relentless keeping of short-term accounts in marriage may be negatively related to the quality of the relationship is a good one. It takes trust to disregard short-term imbalances and be concerned only with long-range equity. In addition, there is much to suggest that consciousness of exchange or equity in a close relation grows as sentiment declines and especially as romantic love declines.

We have seen a lot of evidence that matching, exchange, and equity are important in intimate relationships and not just in short-term casual relations. And there is still more evidence in the things people do to restore equity in a marriage that is perceived as unfair. One of the things that some people who feel "cheated" in a marriage do is to have an extramarital affair. Hatfield, Traupmann, and Walster (1978) found with two thousand married people that those who felt deprived or underbenefited had extramarital sex sooner after marriage and with more partners than did those who felt either fairly treated or overbenefited. The stabilizing effect on marriage of well-managed extramarital sexuality has not escaped the notice of sophisticated novelists, but most would

think it a bit "innocent" to suppose that stability was the goal. It is less innocent to suggest that perceived underbenefit serves nicely the need to justify infidelity.

Beyond Matching and Compatibility

If we look at the personal characteristics listed in Table 3–1, which include age,
attractiveness, intelligence, and so on and which tend to be correlated (or
roughly matched) for couples that stay together, it seems reasonable to believe
that each individual seeks selfishly to maximize what he or she obtains from the
other but settles for the best available deal, which is an approximate match in
ability to reward each other. Research with global perceived equity suggests the
same thing: The rewards of p and of o need to be equivalent for a relation to be
stable and happy. Is that all there is to intimate relations?

Something seems to be missing, something that we all know exists. The
rewards of Table 3–1, the youth, intelligence, and physical attractiveness of o,
could all be enjoyed by p quite independently of what o feels. It is not necessary
to p that o also be rewarded. But in intimate relations, at least some of the time,
p cannot be rewarded unless p feels that o is also rewarded. In romantic love
one person cannot experience rapture unless the other does so also; romantic
rapture is by definition shared. I speak of rapture, you understand, and not
simply of pleasure. More prosaically, it is often impossible for one member of a
couple to have a really good time at a party or on a vacation unless the other
does so also. In short, o may not reward p, whatever o's social value, unless o
also is rewarded. That sounds altruistic.

It is not uncommon for p's rewards to be even more strongly centered on
the other, on *alter*, or o. Some of the time in intimate relations, in romantic and
conjugal love and also in parental and filial love and even in friendship, it happens that the greatest reward p can experience is to see o rewarded. The satisfaction of the other can be more rewarding than the satisfaction of oneself. That is
not usually evident as long as a relation rolls along on an even level of mutual
contentment. It surfaces when o, the other, is seen to suffer. It then can happen
with husband and wife, parent and child, and close friends that the heartache
you feel for another's suffering is so great that you would wish to take that suffering upon yourself. How many parents with a very sick or dying child have
wished the sickness or death might pass from the child and fall upon themselves? I do not know how many, but I know there have been some.

I have known well close families that were suddenly afflicted with economic
hardship and humiliation where the response has been a competition of giving.
Nothing gave such pleasure as a sign of happiness in the others. So I am lining
up with Erich Fromm and Zick Rubin and all the other softies who hold that
there is more to intimate relations than exchange and equity. What there is is

empathy, which means feeling rewarded by the rewards of another and punished by the unhappiness of another.

Among twentieth-century social psychologists, Lauren Wispé (1978, 1983) has perhaps been most insistent on the importance of empathic processes in social life, and he has restored to us the heritage of Hume and Adam Smith, who thought of empathy as the central social sentiment. But if we acknowledge that empathy is a human sentiment which, though difficult to bring into the laboratory, still certainly exists on the evidence of everyday news and personal testimony, have we shown that psychological altruism exists? We have not, because psychological altruism was defined here as action that rewards or reinforces another, while punishing or at least not rewarding the actor, and empathy is defined as a certain kind of reinforcement or reward. The empathic actor is rewarded by evidence that he has rewarded another. The actor does not go unrewarded. It can still be said that we are all alike in that we act in the way that pleases us most. But there does seem to be something misleading about that formulation.

Does Psychological Altruism Exist?

It is not at all difficult to think of cases in which someone acts in a way that clearly rewards another but seems, superficially at least, to receive no reward himself. In very many such cases the seeming altruist is rather mindlessly conforming to a social norm. The annual, anonymous, and usually minimal donation to the United Fund or some other institutionalized charity is a clear case. It would be too much to say that such donations are rewarding or satisfying to the donor, especially the minimal donor. He does, however, *avoid feeling bad* for violating a norm that respectable, economically comfortable people conform to, and avoiding punishment or negative reinforcement counts as a reward.

The experiments on the unresponsive bystander (Latané and Darley, 1970) provide additional examples of action that clearly rewards another but does not clearly reward the actor if we look not, as we usually have, at the unresponsive people, but at the responsive ones. A helpful response to a stranger in distress was made by a majority of bystanders, often by about two-thirds of them, when they encountered the emergency all by themselves. Bystanders alone felt a clear *responsibility* to act. If they did not, no one would. The bystander who meets a clear responsibility feels fairly good about having done his duty even at some risk to himself. The reward is not obvious; it is intrinsic. Still, the reward is there, and the responsive bystander is not a clear case of psychological altruism.

Kidney donors, when they donate to kin and have been selected as the ideal available donor, are still not psychological altruists—though they are biological altruists. In some ways their behavior is quite extraordinary (Fellner and

Marshall, 1981). About 88 percent of them report that they made the decision to donate, if asked, immediately upon being notified by the doctor that the need might arise. They frequently made the decision before being informed of the costs or risks. They say that they did not engage in any cost–benefit analysis, but rather knew at once: "It was a thing I had to do."

The responsibility to donate to a relative is a moral obligation of a particularly clear sort, a moral obligation that just about anyone sees at once. It derives ultimately, perhaps, from considering the situation from John Rawls's Original Position. If it is not known which person will have no kidney and which two (the Veil of Ignorance), then a rational man, many other things being equal, must choose to divide the kidneys evenly. It may be dim awareness of the way things would look from the Original Position that tells us what the right thing to do is, though the obligation may come more immediately from religious teachings.

The "elected" donor of a kidney to a kinsman is very far from being a psychological altruist. He is likely to be rewarded both extrinsically and intrinsically (Fellner and Marshall, 1981). For a time, at least, his family will consider him something of a hero and will admire him extravagantly. In addition, he will enjoy, for a longer time, the intrinsic, self-administered reward that comes from having met a high moral obligation. He may also enjoy another sort of intrinsic reward, the empathic reward of participating in the happiness and relief of the kidney recipient and the recipient's family.

In limited degree it has proved to be possible to bring empathy into the social psychological laboratory (Archer et al., 1981; Batson et al., 1981, 1983). The paradigmatic experiment has an observer (the subject) look on at the very great distress of another person (a confederate) who is being subjected to electric shock. It seems that though the shock is not very intense, the unlucky victim has had a traumatic experience with shock earlier in life, and so for this person the shock is a terrible experience. Onlookers tend to be very upset by what they see, but there are two ways of being upset. Some people feel *distress* and describe themselves with words like *alarmed, upset, worried, distressed, disturbed*. Other people are *empathic*, and they describe themselves as *concerned, compassionate, softhearted*.

Subjects are given the opportunity simply to escape, to get out of the situation, but they are also given the opportunity, not at all required of them, to trade places with the unhappy suffering victim. They can, that is, volunteer to receive the remaining shocks themselves, thereby securing the release of the victim. What Batson and co-workers (1983) find is that *distressed* individuals mainly elect to escape the situation; only 25 percent offer to trade places with the victim. *Empathic* individuals mainly (86 percent) offer to put themselves in the victim's place and so rescue the victim. The person who is empathic in this situation seems to feel with the victim to the point where he or she will feel better, will be more rewarded, by relieving the victim and personally sustaining the shock than by simply getting away from it all.

Still, we have not found a clear case of psychological altruism. There are people who will benefit another in some obvious way in order to comply with a social norm, meet a clearly defined responsibility, fulfill a high moral obligation, or relieve their own empathic suffering. Those people seem altruistic because their rewards are not extrinsic and obvious like the rewards of those they help. However, it cannot be said that people who are satisfied by intrinsic rewards are doing without reward. They are still, basically, doing what they want to do.

Finally, there are the donors of a kidney to unrelated strangers whom they may never meet. Those people are heroes of a sort. They are like the white civil rights activists in the South in the 1960s (Rosenhan, 1970), the rescuers of anonymous Jews (London, 1970), and the people who plunge into icy waters or blazing buildings to save strangers. Those people are all clearly biological altruists, since they try to save the life of another at risk of their own. Are they also psychological altruists who act without reward or expectation of reward? In the case of the donors of kidneys to unrelated strangers, we have the information to answer that question (Sadler et al., 1971). The following quotations are typical:

a. "Deep satisfaction; my life keeps improving."
b. "Only good thing I ever did. I'm better for it."
c. "A wonderful reward. I can reach people now."
d. "Enriched, happy, deeper relationships."
e. "Very rewarding experience to me and all around me."

These people are clearly biological altruists, but they are just as clearly *not psychological altruists*, if we require that a psychological altruist do something that rewards another but does not reward himself.

It is probably correct that there are no psychological altruists in the sense defined in this chapter; probably everyone does what has been most rewarding or promises to be most rewarding, even the rescuers, the kidney donors, and Mother Teresa. The proposition is in danger of circularity in that we often do not know what the rewards are in a given case but can only guess at them, as I have often done, and that means it may reduce to the tautology that all acts are rewarded and the evidence of reward is the occurrence of the act (Rosenhan, 1978). What the proposition is generally thought to be, but emphatically is not, is cynical.

The cynical inference often drawn goes like this: "We are all the same really, in that we do what pleases us. Nobody does something for nothing." That inference overlooks something vital. Even if we all act to secure rewards, it does not follow that we are all the same—morally.

The person who donates a kidney because the recipient offers him $20,000 is not on a par morally with the person who freely elects to do it without thought even of thanks. Rewards are not all on the same moral level; we set less value on people who do helpful things for extrinsic rewards like money than on people who are rewarded by social approval and less value on people who need any sort of extrinsic reward than on those who help for intrinsic reasons, out of sympathy with the person to be helped or to conform to a norm of helpfulness. Probably we set the greatest value on those who help at personal cost just because it seems the right thing to do.

In sum, one can accept the view that people are the same in seeking what rewards them without accepting the view that they are all equally good or bad. Because it is a superior achievement to be *able* to be rewarded by acting justly, superior to being able to be rewarded by money, fame, or the good opinion of mankind. If one prefers not to accept the view that there is no such thing as psychological altruism, just for the reason that that view so strongly suggests a cynical view of human nature, then it is quite easy to define psychological altruism as help that is rewarded only intrinsically by empathy or a sense of having done one's duty or of having acted justly. In that sense psychological altruism certainly exists.

The really interesting thing is that the people who are most surprising to evolutionary biology, the donors of kidneys to kin and to strangers, are just the ones who have the happiest surprise waiting for them, the ones most richly rewarded. It is not biology that rewards them; it is not anything genetic, but rather something cultural. It feels good to have done the moral thing. Why should it? It is not the biologically sound thing to do. We must conclude that cultural evolution, not biological, has produced moral principles that can powerfully reward actions that are in accord with them.

The donor to strangers has sometimes reported an experience precipitating the decision that would seem to have facilitated taking the Original Position.

> She had no interest in kidney disease or transplantation until by chance she read in the paper that in a nearby community a 46-year-old man with two children, the ages of her own, could "have his life saved if donors with O negative blood would come forth and offer their organs." She excitingly "knew" she would volunteer. His children are the same age as mine. What if mine needed a father . . . ? [Sadler et al., p. 92]

This woman was picked up by a news story and dropped into the Original Position. What if I were he and he were me? Points of similarity seem to facilitate this kind of interchange of identities, which leads to seeing moral obligation— or opportunity.

In short, I believe, as do Lerner and Meindl (1981), that there is something like a "justice motive" in man. I think it operates much more often than these authors do. Our genetic potential has permitted us to conceive of justice in Rawls's sense, in spite of the opposition of natural selection to specific kinds of altruism. And I think cultural evolution enables us to experience great rewards for acting justly. But many things obscure the perception of justice and interfere with acting on its dictates.

Summary

An act is altruistic in the biological sense if the organism acting contributes favorably to the survival prospects and reproductive potential of another organism at some cost to its own prospects and potential. There are many examples in the social life of animals of behavior that looks altruistic. There ought not to be any biological altruism at all, however, because Darwin's theory of natural selection holds that only those genes are selected for in evolution which contribute favorably to reproductive potential, and so there ought to be selection against any genetic basis for altruism. Evolutionary biologists have succeeded in showing that all the principal kinds of seeming altruism in the life of nonhuman animals can be accounted for in Darwinian terms and so are, all of them, only seeming altruism, not real altruism in the biological sense.

In human social life all the apparent forms of altruism found in animals, kin altruism, reciprocal altruism, and equity altruism, are common. The evolutionary theories that explain those things for animals probably also explain the development of their biological substrata in humans. However, in humans kin altruism does not follow genetic lines and is not perfectly predicted by relatedness; reciprocal altruism involves money and calculations of equivalence not found in animal life; the investments in equity altruism are not fixed but endlessly disputed and revised. Human social life, shaped more by cultural evolution than by biological evolution, shows true biological altruism in which one person suffers great costs for the benefit of another. Indeed, biological altruism is idealized in human societies.

Psychological altruism can be most clearly defined in the context of a theory of behavior, reinforcement theory, which was conceived as a deliberate parallel to natural selection theory in biology. According to reinforcement theory, emitted acts (operants) are selected for, or strengthened, by contingent subsequent positive reinforcement or reward very much as genes are selected for across generations by their adaptive value. An act would be psychologically altruistic when it rewards another but negatively reinforces or punishes the actor. Is there any psychological altruism in human life and, if so, how much? Because many claim that psychological altruism is clearest and most common in intimate relations, we look for it there.

The matching hypothesis can be derived from either exchange theory or equity theory. It holds that when romantic couples are formed, each selfishly wishes for a maximally attractive partner, but the selfishness of each must accommodate to the selfishness of others and the best bargain that can usually be struck is a match. A match exists when two people have equivalent power to reward one another. In an aphorism, the matching hypothesis holds that most of us get the intimate partners we deserve.

In mundane social life, individuals do not even consider eligible others who are not good matches in terms of race, socio-economic status, and intelligence, which leaves physical attractiveness as the primary bargaining chip. The matching principle accurately explains most couple creation but, from literature and our own lives, we know that it must be qualified by the possibility of intense attraction that makes all ordinary considerations seem unimportant. Romantic love transcends exchange or equity and is usually not even explicable in conscious terms, but it is short-lived.

Once a couple has met and found itself well enough matched to continue, the question of compatibility arises, and compatibility is a matter of stability or endurance and of the quality of the relationship, the satisfaction it brings. Exchange and equity are important in compatibility.

Couples that perceive their relationship as equitable are more likely to think they will stay together in the future and more likely to stay together, in fact, than couples in which either partner feels greatly underbenefited or overbenefited. Equity is associated with stability; underbenefit with the expectation that one will do better in the future; overbenefit with the fear that one's good luck will not last. Compatible couples are relatively stable and are also relatively content or happy. The underbenefited feel angry, and the overbenefited guilty—all as equity theory predicts.

Exchange and equity seem not to include everything involved in intimate relationships. At least some of the time p's reward is evidence that o is rewarded, and p's punishment is evidence that o is suffering. That process of feeling with another is called *empathy*, and empathy sounds altruistic, or centered on the other. Nevertheless, empathy does not count as psychological altruism if altruism is defined, as it is in this chapter, as action that does not reward the actor, because the empathic actor is rewarded—by evidence that o is rewarded. Empathic reward is a special sort of reward, but it is reward still.

Rewards for action that benefits another are of many kinds. There are the extrinsic rewards of money, gratitude, and social approval and also the intrinsic, less visible rewards of empathy, conforming to an ethical norm, and fulfilling a moral obligation. Helpful action that is rewarded in some intrinsic way is likely to look altruistic, to look like action that is not rewarded at all. However, where we have data, as we do on responsive bystanders, empathic individuals who take on the suffering of another, blood donors, and kidney donors, there is always some reward. That proposition does not have the serious cynical implications it is often presumed to have. One can believe that everyone is the same in the sense of doing what either does reward him or promises to reward him or turns out to reward him without agreeing at all that this puts everyone on the same level morally. Clearly, we think it a better thing to make a sacrifice for a moral principle or an ethical norm or out of empathy than it is to do so for money or applause or gratitude.

References for Part I

ADAMS, J. S. 1965. Inequity in social exchange. In L. Berkowitz (ed.), *Advances in Experimental Social Psychology*. New York: Academic Press, 2: 267–99.

ADAMS, J. S., and P. R. JACOBSEN. 1964. Effects of wage inequities on work quality. *Journal of Abnormal and Social Psychology*, 69: 19–25.

ANDREAS, C. R. 1969. To receive from kings: An examination of government-to-government aid and its unintended consequences, *Journal of Social Issues*, 25: 167–80.

ARCHER, R. L.; R. DIAZ-LOVING; P. M. GOLLWITZER; M. H. DAVIS; and H. C. FOUSHEE. 1981. The role of dispositional empathy and social evaluation in the empathic mediation of helping, *Journal of Personality and Social Psychology*, 40: 786–96.

AUSTEN, J. *Emma*. 1972. New York: Norton (1814).

AUSTIN, W., and E. HATFIELD. 1975. Equity with the world: The trans-relational effects of equity and inequity, *Sociometry*, 38: 474–96.

BATSON, C. D.; B. D. DUNCAN; P. ACKERMAN; T. BUCKLEY; and K. BIRCH. 1981. Is empathic emotion a source of altruistic motivation? *Journal of Personality and Social Psychology*, 40: 290–302.

BATSON, C. D.; K. O'QUIN; J. FULTZ; M. VANDERPLAS; and A. M. ISEN. 1983. Influence of self-reported distress and empathy on egoistic versus altruistic motivation to help, *Journal of Personality and Social Psychology*, 45: 706–18.

BERSCHEID, E., and B. CAMPBELL. 1981. The changing longevity of heterosexual close relationships: A commentary and forecast. In M. J. Lerner and S. C. Lerner (eds.), *The Justice Motive in Social Behavior*. New York: Plenum Press.

BERSCHEID, E.; K. DION; E. HATFIELD; and G. W. WALSTER. 1971. Physical attractiveness and dating choice: A test of the matching hypothesis, *Journal of Experimental Social Psychology*, 7: 173–89.

BERSCHEID, E.; E. HATFIELD; and G. BOHRNSTETT. 1973. The body image report, *Psychology Today*, 7: 119–31.

BLAU, P. M. 1955. *The Dynamics of Bureaucracy: A Study of Interpersonal Relations in Two Government Agencies*. Chicago: University of Chicago Press.

——. 1964. *Exchange and Power in Social Life*. New York: Wiley.

BRIAR, S. 1966. Welfare from below: Recipients' views of the public welfare system, *California Law Review*, 54: 370–85.

BRICKMAN, P.; D. COATES; and R. J. BULMAN. 1978. Lottery winners and accident victims: Is happiness relative? *Journal of Personality and Social Psychology*, 36: 917–27.

BROLL, L.; A. E. GROSS; and I. PILIAVIN. 1974. Effects of offered and requested help on seeking and reactions to being helped. *Journal of Applied Social Psychology*, 4: 244–58.

BULMAN, R. J., and C. B. WORTMAN. 1977. Attributions of blame and coping in the "real world": Severe accident victims react to their lot, *Journal of Personality and Social Psychology*, 35: 351–63.

BUSS, D. M. 1985. Human mate selection. *American Scientist* (January–February): 47–51.

CUNNINGHAM, M. R. 1979. Weather, mood, and helping behavior: Quasiexperiments with the Sunshine Samaritan, *Journal of Personality and Social Psychology*, 37: 1947–56.

DARLEY, J. M., and C. D. BATSON. 1973. "From Jerusalem to Jericho": A study of situational and dispositional variables in helping behavior, *Journal of Personality and Social Psychology, 27:* 100–108.

DARWIN, C. 1859. *The Origin of Species.* London: Murray.

DAWKINS, R. 1976. *The Selfish Gene.* New York: Oxford University Press.

DEPAULO, B. M., and J. D. FISHER. 1980. The costs of asking for help, *Basic and Applied Social Psychology, 1:* 23–35.

DOUVAN, E. 1972. Changing sex roles: Some implications and constraints. Presented at symposium "Women: Resource in a Changing World," the Radcliffe Institute, April.

ELDER, G. H., JR. 1969. Appearance and education in marriage mobility, *American Sociological Review, 34:* 519–33.

FELLNER, C. H., and J. R. MARSHALL. 1981. Kidney donors revisited. In J. P. Rushton and R. M. Sorrentino (eds.), *Altruism and Helping Behavior.* Hillsdale, N.J.: Erlbaum, pp. 351–65.

FREEMAN, S.; M. R. WALKER; R. BORDEN; and B. LATANÉ. 1975. Diffusion of responsibility and restaurant tipping: Cheaper by the bunch, *Personality and Social Psychology Bulletin, 1:* 584–87.

FROMM, E. 1956. *The Art of Loving.* New York: Harper & Row.

GERGEN, K. J., and M. GERGEN. 1971. International assistance from a psychological perspective, *1971 Yearbook of World Affairs.* Vol. 25. London: Institute of World Affairs.

GERGEN, K. J.; P. ELLSWORTH; C. MASLACH; and M. SEIPEL. 1975. Obligation, donor resources, and reactions to aid in three cultures, *Journal of Personality and Social Psychology, 31:* 390–400.

GOULD, S. J. 1977. *Ever Since Darwin.* New York: Norton.

GOULDNER, A. W. 1960. The norm of reciprocity: A preliminary statement. *American Sociological Review, 25:* 161–78.

GREENBERG, M. S., and S. P. SHAPIRO. 1971. Indebtedness: An aversive aspect of asking for and receiving help, *Sociometry, 34:* 290–301.

GREGORY, C. O. 1966. The Good Samaritan and the Bad: The Anglo-American law. In J. M. Ratcliffe (ed.), *The Good Samaritan and the Law.* Garden City, N.Y.: Doubleday Anchor, pp. 23–41.

GUHL, A. M. 1953. Social behavior of the domestic fowl, *Kansas State College Agricultural Experimental Station Technical Bulletin,* No. 73.

HAMILTON, W. D. 1964. The genetical theory of social behavior, *Journal of Theoretical Biology, 7:* 1–52.

HARRIS, R. J. 1983. Pinning down the equity formula. In D. M. Messick and K. S. Cook (eds.), *Equity Theory.* New York: Praeger, pp. 207–41.

HATFIELD, E.; V. ARONSON; D. ABRAHAMS; and L. ROTTMANN. 1966. Importance of physical attractiveness in dating behavior, *Journal of Personality and Social Psychology, 4:* 508–16.

HATFIELD, E.; J. TRAUPMANN; S. SPRECHER; M. UTNE; and J. HAY. Forthcoming. Equity and intimate relations. In W. Ickes (ed.), *Compatible and Incompatible Relationships.* New York: Springer-Verlag.

HATFIELD, E.; J. TRAUPMANN; and G. W. WALSTER. 1978. Equity and extramarital sexuality, *Archives of Sexual Behavior, 7:* 127–42.

HATFIELD, E.; M. K. UTNE; and J. TRAUPMANN. 1979. Equity theory and intimate relationships. In R. L. Burgess and T. L. Huston (eds.), *Social Exchange in Developing Relationships.* New York: Academic Press, pp. 99–133.

HATFIELD, E.; G. W. WALSTER; and E. BERSCHEID. 1978. *Equity: Theory and Research.* Boston: Allyn & Bacon.

HATFIELD, E.; G. W. WALSTER; and J. TRAUPMANN. 1978. Equity and premarital sex, *Journal of Personality and Social Psychology, 37:* 82–92.

HILL, C. T.; Z. RUBIN; and A. PEPLAU. 1976. Breakups before marriage: The end of 103 affairs, *Journal of Social Issues, 32:* 147–67.

HOBHOUSE, L. T. 1951. *Morals in Evolution: A Study in Comparative Ethics.* London: Chapman & Hall.

HOMANS, G. C. 1961. *Social Behavior: Its Elementary Forms.* New York: Harcourt Brace Jovanovich.

———. 1974. *Social Behavior: Its Elementary Forms.* Rev. Ed. New York: Harcourt Brace Jovanovich.

HULL, C. L. 1943. *Principles of Behavior.* New York: D. Appleton-Century.

ISEN, A. M.; M. CLARK; and M. F. SCHWARTZ. 1976. Duration of the effect of good mood on helping: "Footprints on the sands of time," *Journal of Personality and Social Psychology, 34:* 385–93.

ISEN, A. M., and P. F. LEVIN. 1972. Effect of feeling good on helping: Cookies and kindness, *Journal of Personality and Social Psychology, 21:* 384–88.

ISEN, A. M.; T. E. SCHALKER; M. CLARK; and L. KARP. 1978. Affect, accessibility of material in memory and behavior: A cognitive loop? *Journal of Personality and Social Psychology, 36:* 1–12.

JASSO, G., and P. H. ROSSI. 1977. Distributive justice and earned income, *American Sociological Review, 42:* 639–51.

KAHN, A., and T. E. TICE. 1973. Returning a favor and retaliating harm: The effects of stated intention and actual behavior, *Journal of Experimental Social Psychology, 9:* 43–56.

KELLEY, H. H.; E. BERSCHEID; A. CHRISTENSEN; J. H. HARVEY; T. L. HUSTON; G. LEVINGER; E. McCLINTOCK; L. A. PEPLAU; and D. R. PETERSON (eds.), 1983. *Close Relationships.* San Francisco: W. H. Freeman.

KEPHART, W. 1967. Some correlates of romantic love, *Journal of Marriage and the Family, 29:* 470–74.

KIESLER, S., and R. BARAL. 1970. The search for a romantic partner: The effects of self-esteem and physical attractiveness on romantic behavior. In K. Gergen and D. Marlowe (eds.), *Personality and Social Behavior.* Reading, Mass.: Addison-Wesley.

LADIEU, G.; E. HANFMANN; and T. DEMBO. 1947. Studies in adjustment to visible injuries: Evaluation of help by the injured, *Journal of Abnormal and Social Psychology, 42:* 169–92.

LATANÉ, B., and J. M. DARLEY. 1970. *The Unresponsive Bystander: Why Doesn't He Help?* New York: Appleton-Century-Crofts.

Latané, B., and S. A. Nida. 1981. Ten years of research on group size and helping, *Psychological Bulletin, 89:* 308–24.

Latané, B.; S. A. Nida; and D. W. Wilson. 1981. The effects of group size on helping behavior. In J. P. Rushton and R. M. Sorrentino (eds.), *Altruism and Helping Behavior.* Hillsdale, N.J.: Erlbaum, 287–329.

Lerner, M. J. 1970. The desire for justice and reactions to victims. In J. Macauley and L. Berkowitz (eds.), *Altruism and Helping Behavior.* New York: Academic Press, pp. 205–29.

———. 1971. Observer's evaluation of a victim: Justice, guilt, and veridical perception, *Journal of Personality and Social Psychology, 20:* 127–35.

Lerner, M. J., and J. R. Meindl. 1981. Justice and altruism. In J. P. Rushton and R. M. Sorrentino (eds.), *Altruism and Helping Behavior.* Hillsdale, N.J.: Erlbaum, pp. 213–32.

London, P. 1970. The rescuers: Motivational hypotheses about Christians who saved Jews from the Nazis. In J. Macauley and L. Berkowitz (eds.), *Altruism and Helping Behavior.* New York: Academic Press, pp. 241–50.

Marx, K. 1963. *Economic and Philosophical Manuscripts.* In K. Marx *Early Writings.* Tran. T. B. Bottomore. London: Watts.

Mills, J., and M. S. Clark. 1980. Exchange in communal relationships. Unpublished manuscript.

Morgan, C. J. 1978. Bystander intervention: Experimental test of a formal model, *Journal of Personality and Social Psychology, 36:* 43–55.

Muir, D. E., and E. A. Weinstein. 1962. The social debt: An investigation of lower-class and middle-class norms of social obligation, *American Sociological Review, 27:* 532–39.

Murstein, B. I. 1972. Physical attractiveness and marital choice, *Journal of Personality and Social Psychology, 22:* 8–12.

———. 1978. *Exploring Intimate Lifestyles.* New York: Springer.

Murstein, B. I., and M. G. MacDonald. 1983. The relationship of "exchange-orientation" and "commitment" scales to marriage adjustment, *International Journal of Psychology, 18:* 297–311.

Murstein, B. I.; M. G. MacDonald; and M. Cerreto. 1977. A theory of the effect of exchange-orientation on marriage and friendship, *Journal of Marriage and the Family, 39:* 543–48.

Nadler, A.; J. D. Fisher; and S. Streufert. 1974. The donor's dilemma: Recipient's reaction to aid from friend or foe, *Journal of Applied Social Psychology, 4,* no. 3: 275–85.

Piliavin, I. M.; J. Rodin; and J. A. Piliavin. 1969. Good Samaritanism: An underground phenomenon? *Journal of Personality and Social Psychology, 13:* 289–99.

Piliavin, J. A.; P. L. Callero; and D. E. Evans. 1982. Addiction to altruism? Opponent-process theory and habitual blood donation, *Journal of Personality and Social Psychology, 43:* 1200–1213.

Pope, K. S. 1980. Defining and studying romantic love. In K. S. Pope (ed.), *On Love and Loving.* San Francisco: Jossey-Bass, 1–26.

PRUITT, D. G. 1968. Reciprocity and credit building in a laboratory dyad, *Journal of Personality and Social Psychology*, 8: 143–47.

PRYOR, F. L., and N. H. H. GRABURN. 1980. The myth of reciprocity. In K. J. Gergen, M. S. Greenberg, and R. H. Willis (eds.), *Social Exchange*. New York: Plenum Press, pp. 215–37.

RAE, D. 1981. *Equalities*. Cambridge, Mass.: Harvard University Press.

RATCLIFFE, J. M. (ed.). 1966. *The Good Samaritan and the Law*. Garden City, N.Y.: Doubleday Anchor.

RAWLS, J. 1972. *A Theory of Justice*. Cambridge, Mass.: Harvard University Press.

ROMER, D. 1977. Limitations on the equity-theory approval: Toward a resolution of the "negative-inputs" controversy, *Personality and Social Psychology Bulletin*, 3: 228–31.

ROSENHAN, D. L. 1970. The natural socialization of altruistic autonomy. In J. Macauley and L. Berkowitz (eds.), *Altruism and Helping Behavior*. New York: Academic Press, pp. 251–68.

ROSENHAN, D. L. 1978. Toward resolving the altruism paradox: Affect, self-reinforcement, and cognition. In L. Wispé (ed.), *Altruism, Sympathy, and Helping*. New York: Academic Press, pp. 101–13.

ROSENTHAL, A. M. 1964. *Thirty-Eight Witnesses*. New York: McGraw-Hill.

RUBIN, Z. 1973. *Liking and Loving*. New York: Holt, Rinehart & Winston.

RUBIN, Z., and L. A. PEPLAU. 1975. Who believes in a just world? *Journal of Social Issues*, 31: 65–89.

RUDZINSKI, A. W. 1966. The duty to rescue: A comparative analysis. In J. M. Ratcliffe (ed.), *The Good Samaritan and the Law*. Garden City, N.Y.: Doubleday Anchor, pp. 91–134.

SADLER, H. H.; L. DAVISON; C. CARROLL; and S. L. KOUNTZ. 1971. The living, genetically unrelated, kidney donor, *Seminars in Psychiatry*, 3: 86–101.

SCHWARTZ, S. H., and G. T. CLAUSEN. 1970. Responsibility, norms, and helping in an emergency, *Journal of Personality and Social Psychology*, 16: 299–310.

SEEDMAN, A. A., and P. HELLMAN. 1974. Why Kitty Genovese haunts New York: The untold story. *New York*, July 29, 32–41.

SIMMEL, G. 1950. *The Sociology of Georg Simmel*. Trans. and ed. by K. H. Wolff. Glencoe Ill.: Free Press.

SKINNER, B. F. 1938. *The Behavior of Organisms*. New York: D. Appleton-Century.

STERNBERG, R. J., and S. GRAJEK. 1984. The nature of love, *Journal of Personality and Social Psychology*, 47: 312–29.

TENNOV, O. 1979. *Love and Limerence*. New York: Stein and Day.

TESSER, A.; R. GATEWOOD; and M. DRIVER. 1968. Some determinants of gratitude. *Journal of Personality and Social Psychology*, 9: 233–36.

THORNDIKE, E. L. 1933. A proof of the law of effect, *Science*, 77: 173–75.

TRAUPMANN, J.; E. HATFIELD; and P. WEXLER. 1983. Equity and sexual satisfaction in dating couples, *British Journal of Social Psychology*, 22: 33–40.

TRIVERS, R. L. 1971. The evolution of reciprocal altruism, *Quarterly Review of Biology*, 46: 35–57.

TRIVERS, R., and H. HARE. 1976. Haplodiploidy and the evolution of the social insects, *Science, 191:* 249–63.

TUNC, A. 1966. The volunteer and the Good Samaritan. In J. M. Ratcliffe (ed.), *The Good Samaritan and the Law.* Garden City, N.Y.: Doubleday Anchor, pp. 43–62.

UTNE, M. K.; E. HATFIELD; J. TRAUPMANN; and D. GREENBERGER. 1981. Equity, marital satisfaction, and stability. Unpublished. Submitted to *Basic and Applied Social Psychology.*

WALLER, W. 1937. The rating and dating complex, *American Sociological Review, 2:* 727–34.

WALZER, M. 1983. *Spheres of Justice.* New York: Basic Books.

WEXLER, J. 1980. Intimacy: A critical social analysis. Unpublished manuscript.

WILKE, H., and J. T. LANZETTA. 1970. The obligation to help: The effects of amount of prior help on subsequent helping behavior, *Journal of Experimental Social Psychology, 6:* 488–93.

WILSON, E. O. 1975. *Sociobiology.* Cambridge, Mass.: Harvard University Press.

——. 1978. The genetic evolution of altruism. In L. Wispé (ed.), *Altruism, Sympathy, and Helping.* New York: Academic Press, pp. 11–37.

WISPÉ, L. 1978. Toward an integration. In L. Wispé (ed.), *Altruism, Sympathy, and Helping.* New York: Academic Press, pp. 303–28.

——. 1983. The distinction between sympathy and empathy: To call forth a concept a word is needed. Unpublished manuscript.

ZEISEL, H. 1966. An international experiment on the effects of a Good Samaritan Law. In J. Ratcliffe (ed.), *The Good Samaritan and the Law.* Garden City, N.Y.: Doubleday Anchor, pp. 209–12.

ZUCKERMAN, M. 1975. Belief in a just world and altruistic behavior, *Journal of Personality and Social Psychology, 31:* 972–76.

II

Attribution Theory

So LONG AS we agree about the causes of social action, we do not notice that causes have to be worked out by a process of induction. When there is disagreement about causes, we are more likely to notice the process. That is especially true for social actions that are both highly undesirable and highly consequential, for in such cases it is important to get causes right so as to make changes that will prevent recurrence. One such undesirable and consequential social event was the crowd crush that killed eleven at a Who concert in Cincinnati on December 3, 1979. A great many people immediately started to think about the probable causes of that event, and for some time there was disagreement on the correct conclusion. There is a public record of the conclusions reached and of much of the reasoning involved because the "Cincy Rock Fest" was a prominent newspaper story for several weeks.

One news story dated December 4, 1979, began this way:

> Eleven persons were trampled to death last night in a crowd of 8,000 concertgoers who waited for hours in near-freezing weather outside Riverfront Coliseum in Cincinnati then "lost all sense of rationality" and stormed the doors. The concert, by the rock group The Who, went on for three hours with most of the 18,000 fans inside oblivious to what one survivor called "the nightmare" outside.

How does one begin to work out the cause or causes of a complex event like this? That is a question for professional social scientists and also for laypersons of every kind, including, as especially interested parties in the present case, the members of The Who group, the mayor of Cincinnati, and also the mayors of all the other Northeastern cities The Who were scheduled to visit in December 1979. It was a question for Who fans in Cincinnati and elsewhere and for all those columnists, pundits, and savants who make a living from their opinions. In these two chapters on attribution theory we are concerned with the causal inferences of laypersons, with everyday causal inference.

The first important thing to say about everyday causal inference is that it operates with the same inductive principles as does scientific inference. Everyday lay attribution of causality is a kind of rough-and-ready, "low-tech" version of professional or scientific attribution. The same kinds of evidence are considered relevant in both cases and are weighed in the same fashion. The layman is an intuitive scientist. Chapter 4 first explains the systematic principles that are tacitly (or unconsciously) used in everyday attribution and then describes one well-documented attributional style, the style of the depressive personality.

The second important thing to say about the layman as intuitive scientist is that he has some systematic shortcomings. He is subject to three biases or errors that the professional scientist is spared. Biases and errors lead to mistakes in the determination of causes, and it is important to conceptualize such errors correctly and to be sure that the evidence for them is sound, because attribution is important in all aspects of life. Chapter 5 discusses those matters. Richard Nisbett and Lee Ross (1980) have written an excellent book on the problems of human inference, its strategies and shortcomings, which includes the subject of causal attribution.

4

The Layman as Intuitive Scientist

FOR THE CROWD CRUSH at the Who concert of 1979, possible specific causes were indefinitely numerous: drugs and alcohol, the weather, the size of the crowd, the way seats were sold, a disposition to violence in Who fans. One can make a basic cut in those possible causes by dividing them into causes *internal* to the actor and those *external* to the actor. In the present case who is the actor? In an attribution problem the actor is always simply the person or persons whose action is to be explained, and that means for the event of December 3, 1979, the crowd of eight thousand Who fans who pressed forward in such a way as to knock down and suffocate eleven of their number. Causes internal to the actors would include alcohol, drugs, a disposition to violence, and so on. Causes external to the Cincinnati actors include everything in the *situation* when and where they acted: the cold weather, a five-hour wait, the allocation of seating, the number of police present, the manner of admission to the Coliseum, and so on. When we have determined whether an action is to be attributed internally or externally, we have only determined the *locus* of causality and not the specific cause or causes. Much can be done, however, to control recurrence on the basis of knowledge of locus alone, and, furthermore, there are simple rules of induction determining internal or external locus. Those rules are known tacitly or implicitly to everyone, including quite young children (DiVitto and McArthur, 1978) and mayors of large American cities.

Within twenty-four hours of the crowd crush in Cincinnati it became evident that there was disagreement on locus of causality. It would be nice if some social psychologist had been quick enough to ask a large number of people who knew about the crush a question that has often been asked in experimental studies of attribution:

Do you think the crowd crush in Cincinnati was caused by:

a. Something about Who fans
b. Something about the situation

The question as set up calls for a choice between an internal locus of causality and an external locus. No psychologist did ask the question, but it is evident from newspaper reports of interviewers and of actions taken that the question was being asked—and answered in both ways.

Vincent A. Cianci, Jr., then mayor of Providence, Rhode Island, promptly canceled the Who's December 17 concert date in that city. And when the open date was offered to Portland, Maine, that city's manager, Jack Nicholson, said no. Why? Because it would have been a "very risky move." The cancellation and refusal imply internal attributions, because the Cincinnati *situation* would not have recurred in Providence and Portland, but there would have been, in those cities as in Cincinnati, Who fans, and if the fault lay in the fans, then there would have been some risk of recurrence.

The meaning of the Providence cancellation was apparent to everyone: The kinds of people The Who attract are bad news. For The Who themselves—John Entwistle, Kenny Jones, Roger Daltry, and Peter Townshend—the cancellation had all the force of a direct accusation. "I don't think the crowd had anything to do with it," said Roger Daltry. "When we were first told about the tragedy [after the group had finished its performance at Riverfront Coliseum] we weren't going to go on with the tour at all. But ten minutes later, I was more determined than ever to go on because it's not going to be a tragedy in vain—that just makes another tragedy out of it" (*Cincinnati Post*, December 14, 1979).

The mayor of Cincinnati, J. Kenneth Blackwell, almost immediately after the announcement of the eleven deaths issued the opinion that the primary causes were external to Who fans. For The Who concert the Riverfront Coliseum had sold 50 percent of its tickets on a reserved seat basis and 50 percent on a nonreserved first come, first served basis. Holders of reserved seats were already in the Coliseum when the crowd of eight thousand on the outside began to push forward. In addition, of the fifty doors into the Coliseum only a few had initially been opened—ostensibly because only a few ticket takers were available. There had been on duty a total security force of just twenty-five. The mayor believed that those situational factors, especially the nonreserved (or "festival" or general admission) seating were the causes.

From letters to the editors of many newspapers published some time after the event and from syndicated columns and editorials we know that many did not agree with Blackwell but believed instead in internal causes. "Unfortunately there are thousands of impatient dopeheads who are more concerned about a good seat than a human life" (*Cincinnati Post*, December 12, 1979).

"Those who would climb over people's broken bodies to reach a seat in an auditorium could be called 'the new barbarians'" (Mike Royko, *Cincinnati Post*, December 13, 1979).

Firsthand descriptions of the experience of the crush strongly suggested that there was nothing "special" about the people involved; given the situation described, it seemed as if anyone would have done what they did. For instance, there is this account by one Marty Stonely:

> "At about 6:30, you couldn't light a cigarette without burning someone, it was so tight. Then people started chanting, 'Open the doors, open the doors. . . .'
>
> "At about 7:15 a door opened. At that time we were all so packed, the crowd just swaying back and forth. . . . We were dripping with sweat, steam rising about three to four feet above us.
>
> "They let four or five people in, then shut the door and frisked them. Then they opened the door back up. . . .
>
> "The people in the back thought all the doors were open and started pushing through at a usual pace. The people at the front started falling over, getting crushed. People started to step on legs, backs. You couldn't breathe. Girls were going down near me. It was survival of the strongest.
>
> "People were down right in front of the doors screaming, 'My leg is broken, my leg is broken.' I saw a guy's arm break, heard it crack. I saw people spit up blood. Everyone was screaming for their lives. . . .
>
> "I just held my balance, tried to stay up. If you went down, you saw what happened —you got hurt damn bad." [*Columbus Dispatch*, December 5, 1979]

Apparently officials in all the cities on The Who schedule for December, except Providence, accepted the causal theory of Cincinnati mayor Blackwell, because no city but Providence canceled. There was in every case a lot of discussion; security forces were sometimes doubled; orders were given to open all doors well in advance; and, most important, all seats were reserved so that there should be no reason to come early, or push and shove, and no reason to come at all if you did not have a ticket.

Even so, there was a lot of concern over the first date after Cincinnati, the concert on December 5, just one night later in Buffalo, New York. It is clear that everyone knew how crucial whatever happened in Buffalo would be to the choice between a cause internal to Who fans (an actor locus) and a cause external to them (a situation locus). If there should be serious trouble in the new situation with another batch of Who fans, things would look bad for Who fans, if not all Rockdom. There was no trouble, and the fans made the implication of that fact explicit by displaying a banner that read "These kids are alright" (also the title of a popular Who album).

What of Providence Mayor Cianci and his cancellation of the December 17 date? There were, of course, plenty of reporters to ask him how he felt about that cancellation in view of the nonrecurrence in Buffalo. Cianci's answer shows clearly that he saw how the new evidence argued, but it also shows a certain adroitness in dealing with unaccommodating data: "They perform in Cincinnati with 11 deaths and Buffalo with no deaths. That means when they perform, their average is 5.5 deaths" (*Providence Journal-Bulletin*, December 6, 1979). The rock group continued its tour through other Northeastern cities, including Boston, and there were no more crushes or riots, but then all seating was reserved.

When there is much disagreement and contention over causes as there was in the case of the crowd crush at the Cincinnati Who concert, it is not easy to see that beneath all the fuss is a level of causal attribution on which everyone is always in agreement. Harold Kelley (1967) first systematized this level for psychology. I call that level the "causal calculus." The word "calculus" is used not in any mathematical sense (as in differential and integral calculus) but in the general sense of a systematic method of reasoning. The rules of the causal calculus do not suffice to establish specific causes, such as nonreserved seating, but only general kinds of cause: external or internal, stable or unstable. Each kind of cause is related by rule to values of three information variables called "consensus, distinctiveness, and consistency." It appears to be the case that the rules of the causal calculus are known and regularly used by all adults and also by very young children, by you and me and Roger Daltry and Mayor Cianci. That is to say that you already know the causal calculus, but you know it tacitly or implicitly rather than explicitly. You know how to use it but not yet how to conceptualize it, think about it, and talk about it.

Explicit knowledge exists when someone can formulate a rule as well as act in accordance with it. Explicit knowledge brings new powers—the power to think and talk about rules. In the domain of language it is the difference between an untutored fluent native speaker (tacit knowledge only) and a linguist, a student of the structure of language; in attribution it is the difference between any layman and a social psychologist who studies everyday attribution. Creating explicit knowledge where there was only tacit knowledge is far from an effortless process. There is something pleasurable in it but also something difficult.

The Causal Calculus

Table 4–1 represents the calculus in brief form for handy reference but is not sufficiently detailed to teach the calculus. The text follows Table 4–1 and is intended to make Table 4–1 fully intelligible. The first task is to get your intuitions working in the right domain so that you will feel the rightness of the calculus in capturing judgments you can already make, and so we return briefly to The Who story.

Attribution begins always with a behavioral event. Some person takes an action or has an experience, and that person we shall call the *actor*; the event itself we shall call an *action*. It is the event that is to be explained, and one possible locus for the cause of the event is the actor—the *internal* locus. The other

TABLE 4-1. A Pocket Calculus for Predicting Causal Attribution

I. Sample of behavioral events to be explained
   1. Mr. Brown—has trouble starting—his car. Why?
   2. John—laughs at—the comedian. Why?
   3. Sue—is afraid of—the dog. Why?

II. All events mapped as:
    Actor (A)—habitual or recurrent action—situation (S)

III. Kinds of causes (causal loci) from which a choice is to be made
   1. Something about the actor (A attribution)
   2. Something about the situation (S attribution)
   3. Something about the actor in relation to the situation, both are *necessary* (A-S interaction attribution)
   4. Something about *either* the actor *or* the situation is *sufficient* (A, S attribution)

IV. Two kinds of information governing choice among kinds of causes (with consistency high—the action or state is habitual or recurrent)
   1. Consensus (generalization across other A's)
      High (H) Most A's—action—S
      Low   (L) Few A's—action—S
   2. Distinctiveness (generalization across other S's)
      High (H) A—action—few S's
      Low   (L) A—action—most S's

V. An actor (A) attribution, or internal locus, from low consensus and low distinctiveness (LL)
   1. As a first approximation, I think of the action or state as occurring in conjunction with an actor (A) and a situation (S) and think of the goal of causal attribution as an effort to predict the action or state from either the A or the S that co-occur with it. The item of information that most strongly suggests that the action is caused by (attributable to or predictable from) A is: low distinctiveness.* Thus:

      Mr. Brown—has trouble starting—most cars.
      John—laughs at—most comedians.
      Sue—is afraid of—most dogs.

   2. In each case, one is inclined to attribute the cause to something about the person. The person seems to co-occur with the action or state and so is predictive of it. If A is the cause, then it must also be the case that consensus is low. If the action is to be predicted from A, then few other A's must co-occur with the action. Thus:

      Few people—have trouble starting—this car.
      Few people—laugh at—this comedian.
      Few people—are afraid of—this dog.

      It may be easier to think of the above in the form: "Most people do not . . . . " Thus, if the cause of the starting problem lies in Mr. Brown, most people will not (few people will) have trouble starting his car.

---

*Notice that generalization across most S's means low distinctiveness.

(Cont.)

TABLE 4–1. (*Continued*)

VI. A situation (*S*) attribution, external locus, high consensus and high distinctiveness (*HH*)

1. The item of information that most strongly suggests that the action is caused by (attributable to or predictable from) *S* is: high consensus. Thus:

> Most people—have trouble starting—this car.
> Most people—laugh at—this comedian.
> Most people—are afraid of—this dog.

2. In each case, one is inclined to attribute the cause to something about the situation. The situation seems to co-occur with the action or state and so is predictive of it. If *S* is the cause, then it must also be the case that distinctiveness is high. If the action is to be predicted from *S*, then few other *S*'s must co-occur with the action. Thus:

> Mr. Brown—has trouble starting—few cars.
> John—laughs at—few comedians.
> Sue—is afraid of—few dogs.

It may be easier to think of the above in the form: "Mr. Brown has *no* trouble starting most other cars," etc.

VII. An *A–S* interaction attribution from low consensus and high distinctiveness (*LH*)

Instead of thinking of *A* alone or *S* alone as the sole cause, one may think that both are necessary, that the action results from an interaction between *A* and *S*. This more complex attribution is suggested by low consensus together with high consistency. Thus:

> Few other people laugh at this comedian. (low consensus)
> John laughs at few other comedians. (high distinctiveness)

Apparently there is just something about this comedian that strikes John as funny.

VIII. An *A*, *S* attribution (either of two causes is sufficient) from high consensus and low distinctiveness (*HL*)

Instead of thinking of *both A* and *S* as *necessary* causes of the action, one may think that *either A* or *S* is a *sufficient* cause. This complex attribution is suggested by high consensus together with low distinctiveness. Thus:

> Most people—are afraid of—this dog. (high consensus)
> Sue—is afraid of—most dogs. (low distinctiveness)

Either this dog is especially ferocious or Sue is particularly timorous. The cause could lie in either *A* or *S*.

IX. Low consistency attributions mirroring the four high consistency attributions.

Until this point, the simplifying assumption has been made that the action or state is habitual or recurrent, but, of course, it might not be. Attribution theory adds to consensus and distinctiveness a third variable, consistency, which concerns generalization across occasions (or time). Thus:

> Consistency (across occasions or time)
> High (*H*) *A*—action—*S*—usually
> Low (*L*) *A*—action—*S*—very rarely

The event-depicting sentences we have used (e.g. "Mr. Brown has trouble starting his car") express high consistency without using the word *usually* because the grammar of English is such that the so-called (but actually misnamed) present tense of the verb (e.g. "has trouble") really carries the sense of a habitual, recurrent, or usual action or experience. In order to express low consistency, however,

TABLE 4-1. (*Continued*)

it is necessary to add the phrase "very rarely" or a nearequivalent like "seldom." Then, when we are asked to believe both: (1) Mr. Brown has trouble starting his car, and (2) Mr. Brown has trouble starting his car very rarely, we automatically understand the present tense in the first sentence to signify, not habitually, but something like today.

1. An unstable actor (A) attribution from low consensus, low distinctiveness, and low consistency (LLL)

The information pattern low distinctiveness, low consensus, when it is combined (as above) with high consistency, suggests a stable, enduring A disposition as cause. If that same pattern is combined with low consistency, it suggests an unstable or temporary A characteristic. Thus:

Mr. Brown—has trouble starting—many cars today. (low distinctiveness)
Few people—have trouble starting—this car today. (low consensus)
Mr. Brown—has trouble starting this car—very rarely. (low consistency)
John—laughs at —many things today. (low distinctiveness)
Few people—laugh at—this comedian today. (low consensus)
John—laughs at—this comedian—very rarely. (low consistency)
Sue—is afraid of—many things today. (low distinctiveness)
Few people—are afraid of—this dog today. (low consensus)
Sue—is afraid of—this dog—very rarely. (low consistency)

In the above cases, unstable (or temporary) A states (such as moods) seem to be plausible causes: Mr. Brown is impatient; John is feeling jolly; Sue is jumpy.

2. An unstable situation (S) attribution from high consensus, high distinctiveness, and low consistency (HHL)

The information pattern high consensus, high distinctiveness, when it is combined (as above) with high consistency, suggests a stable, enduring S cause. If this same pattern is combined with low consistency, it suggests an unstable S attribution. Thus:

Many people—have trouble starting—this car today. (high consensus)
Mr Brown—has trouble starting—few cars today. (high distinctiveness)
Mr. Brown—has trouble starting—this car—very rarely. (low consistency)
Many people—laugh at—this comedian today. (high consensus)
John—laughs at—few comedians today. (high distinctiveness)
John—laughs at—this comedian—very rarely. (low consistency)
Many people—are afraid of—this dog today. (high consensus)
Sue—is afraid of—few dogs today. (high distinctiveness)
Sue—is afraid of—this dog—very rarely. (low consistency)

In the above cases, unstable S states that seem to be plausible causes are: the car's battery is dead; the comedian is in peak form; the dog is rabid.

3. An unstable A-S interaction attribution from low consensus, high distinctiveness, and low consistency (LHL)

Few people—have trouble starting—this car today. (low consensus)
Mr. Brown—has trouble starting—few other cars today. (high distinctiveness)
Mr. Brown—has trouble starting—this car very rarely. (low consistency)

There is something about this car which makes trouble for just Mr. Brown just today. Some unstable interaction is called for. What could it be? Perhaps

(Cont.)

TABLE 4-1. (Continued)

Mr. Brown drove a car yesterday on which the starter and gears are laid out very differently from that in his own car and he has carried over temporarily a set of actions and reflexes that are unsuited to his car.

4. An unstable A, S attribution (either of two causes is sufficient) from high consensus, low distinctiveness, and low consistency (HLL)

Most people—have trouble starting—this car today. (high consensus)

Mr. Brown—has trouble starting—many other cars today. (low distinctiveness)

Mr. Brown—has trouble starting—this car very rarely. (low consistency)

There is something temporarily wrong with the car today since most people have trouble starting it and that is the explanation. Or else there is something temporarily amiss with Mr. Brown just today since he has trouble starting many cars. Either one will serve. The car could be out of gas or Mr. Brown could be tired.

SOURCES: Derived from Heider (1958, 1980), Kelley (1967, 1972), McArthur (1972), Orvis, Cunningham, and Kelley (1975), Weiner et al. (1971, 1972), and Wimer and Kelley (1982), but much altered by the author.

possible locus is *external*, and it includes any and all features of the *situation* external to the actor. In short, all attribution problems are to be mapped into, reduced to, just three abstract terms: actor—action—situation. In the case of the crowd at The Who concert, the relevant mapping was: Who fans—deadly crush—in Cincinnati Coliseum. In that case the primary relevant cause turned out not to be internal (some special disposition to violence in Who fans), but external (something about the Coliseum), which eventually turned out to be nonreserved, general admission seating.

What were the crucial kinds of evidence for establishing the locus of the cause of the crowd crush in Cincinnati? One was the eventual disclosure that actions of the same type as the crowd crush of December 3, 1979 (crushes and stampedes that could have caused death and injury), had previously occurred in the Cincinnati Coliseum, not just with Who fans, but with fans of Ted Nugent, Elton John, and many others. You should intuitively feel that the tendency for crowd disturbances to generalize across every sort of crowd gathered in the Cincinnati Coliseum argues that it was not something in the nature of Who fans that caused the event, but rather something about the Coliseum (eventually found to be nonreserved seating). Those who believed strongly that the cause was external (e.g. Mayor Blackwell, Who fans) were inclined to guess that practically every sort of crowd would create a disturbance in the situation the Coliseum presented; not just Who fans, not just fans of rock bands, but basketball fans, baseball fans, Pavarotti fans, and Horowitz fans. That tendency of the action to generalize across different kinds of actors (with the situation constant) is called *high consensus*.

The second type of information (first evident in Buffalo and later in cities all through the Northeast) was the failure of crowd disturbances to occur when the situation was changed, even though Who fans were in congregation. The mere crowding together of Who fans—in places that did not sell general admission seating—did not result in disturbances, not in Buffalo, not in Cleveland, not in Boston, not anywhere. You should feel that the tendency for crowd disturbances not to generalize across situations, with Who fans constant, argues it was not Who fans but something distinctive about the situation in Cincinnati that may have been sufficient to cause crowd disturbances. The failure of the action to generalize across situations with the actor constant is called *high distinctiveness*.

High consensus and high distinctiveness in conjunction strongly argue that the primary cause is in the external situation. In The Who story the telling facts were that crowd disturbances occurred in the Coliseum with every sort of fan (high consensus across actors) and did not occur when Who fans gathered in other situations (high distinctiveness of the Coliseum). The two kinds of information together established the fact that crowd disturbances co-occur with, are predictable from, the Coliseum (situation) and not Who fans (the actor). We shall see that the information pattern high consensus and high distinctiveness (or *HH*) always argues for a situational (external) attribution. The *HH* information pattern alone does *not* serve to establish a specific cause, but only the locus of the cause as external to the actor. The argument that nonreserved seating was the crucial factor draws upon more than the simple fact of high consensus and high distinctiveness (*HH*).

Suppose that consensus and distinctiveness had both been low in The Who story. That would have meant that only Who fans created disturbances in the Coliseum; no other kinds of actors did so (*low* consensus). And that Who fans wherever they congregated (in such other situations as Buffalo, Cleveland, and Boston) always created disturbances (*low* distinctiveness of the Coliseum), because the situation does not matter. We can see now, from a systematic point of view, why the first concert after Cincinnati, the Buffalo concert, was watched with such suspense. Another disturbance would have argued for low distinctiveness and suggested the *LL* pattern (low consensus, low distinctiveness) that argues for an internal attribution (these kids are *not* all right). When no disturbance occurred, that was a point scored for high distinctiveness and so for the *HH* pattern (high consensus, high distinctiveness) that argues for an external or situational attribution (therefore, Providence need not have canceled).

The calculus of Table 4–1 starts with three events (I 1, 2, 3) mapped into, or reduced to, the theoretical terms: actor—action—situation. In order to describe attribution theory, we must, of necessity, use the English language, and that necessity tends to create confusion. The essential thing to keep always in mind is that the concepts of attribution theory have no essential connection with English or any other natural language and are definitely not defined in linguistic terms. The term "actor" in attribution theory means only the internal locus of causality, the individual whose action or state is to be explained. Try to disregard the fact that the English word "actor" is not a very good word for Sue (in I 3) who is not *doing* anything, but is feeling afraid. The fact that the English word chosen for the internal factor in causality does not equally suit all examples is irrelevant to the theory. It is likewise completely irrelevant that the English word "situation" is an odd name for the comedian in I 2. "Situation," as a theoretical term in attribution theory, simply means the external factor or locus in a causal case, whether human or inanimate. It is also irrelevant that the English word "action," which seems well suited to "laughs at" in I 2 is badly suited to "is afraid of" in I 3; irrelevant because action as a theoretical term simply means the event to be explained.

Finally, the conceptual mappings of I 1, 2, and 3 in Table 4–1 look like English sentences because actor, action, and situation have been printed in declarative sentence order, but they are not to be thought of as sentences. The first mapping (I 1) could perfectly well be written:

"starting trouble; Mr. Brown; his car"

which is no sentence. I have chosen to use the terms "actor," "action," and "situation," and English sentence order because that has been the custom in the literature and because, as examples accumulate, one soon learns to abstract the theory from the words.

One last explanatory point about the conceptual mapping of Table 4–1. The action or experience is named as though it were habitual or recurrent. That is because the calculus of Table 4–1 is initially simplified so as to hold one of the three relevant information variables constant. The variable *consistency* is treated at the start of Table 4–1 as high (or *stable*) and only *consensus* and *distinctiveness* are varied. The effect of low consistency (*unstable*) is examined later in the table. Values of an information variable are simply binary: *high* or *low*. The two values serve to capture everyday causal thinking, but one of the ways in which scientific or professional causal attribution differs from the everyday variety is in the use of quantitative scales.

Probably some of you have been disturbed by the suggestion, until this point, that causes are *either* internal or external. Surely all causality is *really* an interaction; both kinds of factors are always necessary. That is absolutely correct, but in fact everyday thinking tends to simplify causality into single causes, often just external or internal, treating the cause that is more important as if it were the whole story. However, not all everyday thinking is simple in that way. Causal interactions are sometimes recognized, as when a married couple acknowledges that their difficulty arises from the way in which, for instance, his dependency violates her notion of masculinity. If "Sue—criticizes—Bill" is explained in this way, then both an internal factor (Sue's conception of masculinity) and an external factor (Bill's dependency) are necessary to produce the criticism. That kind of more complex causal thinking does fall within the scope of attribution theory and is represented in Table 4–1 by item 3 under "III. Kinds of causes."

A second form of complex causality is sometimes used in everyday thinking: the case in which either of two possible causes is seen as sufficient to account for the event. The couple we have mentioned, Sue and Bill, might acknowledge both that Sue has a critical nature and that Bill has serious faults, and *either* of those factors would alone be a *sufficient* explanation of "Sue—criticizes—Bill." This case also comes within the scope of the causal calculus and is recognized as item 4 under "III. Kinds of causes."

Attribution problems involving low consistency as well as problems involving complex causes are all covered by the full Pocket Calculus (Table 4-1). However, a large part of research and theory on attribution has involved only the contrast between internal and external locus (items 1 and 2 under III). There is some important work that also involves the contrast between stable and unstable simple causes (cases 1 and 2 under IX). It is possible to manage very nicely with just the simple attributions in Table 4-1 (four cases out of eight), because little work has been done with complex attributions. Therefore, the textual exposition as well as Table 4-1 especially concentrate on conveying understanding of the four simple attributions (internal or external, stable or unstable).

Event 1 in the Pocket Calculus sets before us Mr. Brown who has trouble (as a regular thing, which means high consistency) starting his car. Suppose that we want to know the cause of the trouble between Mr. Brown and his car. Initially we will settle for the locus only. Is the primary cause in the driver or in the car? That is well worth knowing in its own right. It would be up to the mechanic, at some later point, to say just what was wrong with the car, if that is where the problem lies, and perhaps also up to the mechanic (or a psychiatrist) to say what is wrong with Mr. Brown's performance if the problem is his.

There are two kinds of information we can easily obtain without going to a mechanic, which will determine the locus of causality: consensus information and distinctiveness information. With consensus the question is whether many (high consensus) or few (low consensus) other drivers have trouble starting the same car. With distinctiveness the question is whether Mr. Brown has trouble starting many (low distinctiveness) or few (high distinctiveness) other cars. Consensus and distinctiveness involve the same kind of information. Each asks about generalization across one factor or pole; consensus asks about generalization across actors (drivers), and distinctiveness asks about generalization across situations (cars).

A useful procedure for determining consensus values is to think of the action or experience as held constant and also the situation (his car) while the generalization question is asked about actors (many or few other actors). A useful procedure for determining distinctiveness is to think of the action or experience as held constant and also the actor (Mr. Brown) while the generalization question is asked about the situation (many or few other cars). The *only* difference between consensus and distinctiveness information is that the former concerns generalization across actors (internal locus) while the latter concerns generalization across situations (external locus). But note now, because it can be confusing, that while *many* or *most* (broad generalization) means *high consensus* and *few* means *low consensus*, the situation is reversed for distinctiveness. Wide generalization across situations (trouble with *many* or *most* cars) means that Mr. Brown's car is not distinctive, hence *low distinctiveness*; *few* (trouble with few other cars) means that *his* car is distinctive, hence *high distinctiveness*.

The information pattern that locates the cause internally, in the actor, is, as it was in The Who story, low consensus and low distinctiveness. For this pattern I will use the abbreviation *LL* in which the first place, here and always, represents the value for consensus and the second place the value for distinctiveness. In Table 4–1, see V. The *LL* pattern *always* indicates an actor attribution. Low distinctiveness means that Mr. Brown has trouble starting many or most other cars and not only his own. His car is not distinctive; Mr. Brown's trouble does not selectively co-occur with a particular car but rather indiscriminately occurs with most cars Mr. Brown attempts to start. So it is not a particular car that predicts a starting problem but perhaps a particular driver (the actor). Low consensus information unequivocally pins the tail on the driver for it says that *few* people (drivers other than Mr. Brown) have trouble starting his car.

The information pattern that locates the cause externally, in the situation, is, as it was in The Who story, high consensus and high distinctiveness (*HH*). In Table 4–1, see VI. The *HH* pattern *always* indicates an external, or situation (*S*), attribution. High consensus means that most people have trouble starting Mr. Brown's car. Therefore, one naturally thinks, the trouble probably does not stem from Mr. Brown but rather from his car. High distinctiveness settles it: Mr. Brown has trouble starting few or no other cars. The car is the problem.

It is important to be clear that the two information patterns, *LL* and *HH*, serve only to identify the locus of causality, not the specific cause. The locus of causality is, as such, well worth knowing and can alone serve to initiate corrective action. Putting it very starkly, *LL* carries the action imperative "change drivers," and *HH* the action imperative "change cars." Knowing the locus of causality serves also to narrow down the set of possible specific causes and tells us what to do to choose among them. With additional information from a mechanic it might turn out that the *S* cause (from *HH*) is a defective ignition system. An *A* cause (from *LL*) could be Mr. Brown's habit of leaving the choke out and flooding the plugs. The specific causes must be relatively enduring ones, because consistency has been fixed as high; the starting problem is habitual or recurrent.

In Table 4–1, sections V and VI parallel the discussion here of the *LL* and *HH* patterns; the information is, of course, the same, but the presentation is a little different, because saying the same thing in several ways is sometimes the best way to create understanding. In Table 4–1, in addition to the car starting problem, we have "John laughs at the comedian" and "Sue is afraid of the dog." These additional examples are derived from a study by McArthur (1972), which made a paper-and-pencil test of the attribution calculus by setting problems of the type we are considering here and obtained results consistent with the Pocket Calculus, though not so detailed. Rather than work through the two additional examples here, let us just think of specific causes that would be consistent with the outcomes. An *HH* or actor cause for John's tendency to laugh at the comedian might be John's well-developed sense of humor, and an *LL* or external (S) cause might be the comedian's comic skill. An *LL* or actor (A) cause for Sue's fear of the dog might be her timid nature and an *HH* or external cause the ferocity of this particular dog.

The fact that *LL* implies an internal locus (actor cause) and *HH* an external locus, or situation cause, is simple to memorize and can be used as a kind of uncomprehended catechism. It is perfectly all right to use it that way and, indeed, the full calculus that way, eventually, in order to speed up problem solution, but in the beginning it is important to understand it. To facilitate understanding, here are a few puzzles.

Suppose a student working on a senior honors thesis decides after consultation with his faculty adviser that it is not going well and so gives it up. Suppose the student then asks his adviser: "How are your other advisees doing?" Why would that question strike the adviser as impertinent or threatening? Because if all his advisees are doing badly, then the locus of the present failure is likely to be not the student, but his teacher. Mapped as:

Student—thesis fails—adviser

this is a high consensus outcome (most students writing theses with this adviser fail) and so calls for an external attribution. If the teacher replies, "All but you are doing splendidly," we know the response will hurt and also why.

Suppose an elderly scholar of great intelligence has always listened to your ideas with interest and even admiration but that you then overhear this scholar expressing the same admiration to a large number of other students. It will take some of the pleasure out of it. Why? Evidently the cause of the admiration is not some rare quality in yourself but rather a general benevolent style in the scholar. Clearly, locus of causality makes a difference in interpersonal relations, and not just a cognitive difference but also an affective difference, a difference in feelings.

In a criminal trial for rape the defense attorney will usually make an effort to demonstrate that the woman the accused is charged with having raped had had numerous lovers in the past. What conceivable relevance does such information have to the charge? Strictly speaking, it has none, because rape is forced intercourse and the number of consenting experiences the woman may have had is irrelevant. However, unless they are carefully instructed, jurors are not likely to think so carefully but rather use the causal calculus to reason that a large number of different male partners argues a certain indiscriminateness (low distinctiveness) and, therefore, that the woman probably consented—at least a little bit—to her rapist. The conclusion does not really follow, but that is, nevertheless, the way some people think. In many courts nowadays this kind of evidence in rape cases is inadmissible.

Section VII in the Pocket Calculus provides one example of an interaction in which two causes, one internal and one external, are necessary to produce the event. Here is another example:

Sue—criticizes—Bill

If few other people criticize Bill (low consensus), that fact alone argues that there is something specific to Sue that is necessary to produce the unhappy outcome. If, in addition, Sue criticizes few other people (high distinctiveness), then she is not just indiscriminately critical; there is something about Bill that stimulates her critical impulses. In effect, then, something in one of these two people interacts with something in the other to produce criticism. The earlier suggestion that Bill might be a dependent person and that Sue's ideal of masculinity may exclude dependence goes beyond the causal locus to suggest specific factors in each. Notice that if Sue criticized practically everybody (low distinctiveness), we could explain the event by Sue's critical nature alone (*LL* or *A*), and if Bill were criticized by just about everybody (high consensus), a sufficient explanation would be Bill's badly flawed character (*HH* or *S*).

Section VIII in the Pocket Calculus presents one example of an event for which there are two possible causes (one internal and one external) such that either one alone would be a sufficient explanation. We can provide another example of two sufficient causes, using "Sue criticizes Bill." If consensus is high, then most people criticize Bill and so there is something in Bill that gives rise to criticism, which might be his boorish nature. If distinctiveness is low, then Sue criticizes most people and so has a critical nature. Either Bill's boorishness or Sue's critical nature would alone provide a sufficient explanation for Sue's tendency to criticize Bill.

There are three information variables relevant to the calculation of causality. Besides consensus and distinctiveness, there is consistency. Until now (Part IX of Table 4-1) we have worked with the simplifying assumption that consistency is high, which means the events depicted (Mr. Brown's trouble starting his car, John's laughter at a certain comedian, and Susan's fear of a certain dog) have all been understood to be habitual or recurrent. Consensus asks about generalization across actors; distinctiveness asks about generalization across situations; consistency, let it now be said, asks about generalization across time.

For a given event we have until now considered one dimension (locus) with two values: internal or external to the actor. Consistency adds a second dimension with two values: stable or unstable. Consensus and distinctiveness determine locus of causality (internal, external, both, either). Consistency determines duration of the cause or causes: They are either stable (high consistency) or unstable (low consistency). We have distinguished four kinds of causal locus with various combinations of high and low consensus and distinctiveness when consistency was held constant. Because consistency was constant in all cases, we have not written in the value (high consistency) in characterizing the four information patterns that give rise to, respectively, A; S; A-S; and A,S attributions. Now we must do so, because we are going to allow consistency to assume the value low.

Therefore, where we wrote "LL" in V, for actor attributions, we must write "LLH" (the third position is for the consistency value); where we wrote "HH" in VI, for situation attributions, we must write "HHH"; where we wrote "LH" in VII, for actor–situation interactions, we must write "LHH"; and where we wrote "HL" in VIII, for actor and situation sufficient causes, we must write "HLH." The four information patterns are doubled if we allow the entry for consistency (third place) to be low (L) instead of high (H). This yields the pattern LLL for an unstable (or temporary) actor attribution; HHL for an unstable stimulus attribution, LHL for an unstable actor–situation interaction, and HLL for unstable actor and situation as sufficient causes. In sum, the addition of low consistency to the information patterns simply duplicates the four causal patterns already discussed with unstable replacing stable, which has been heretofore understood but not stated. It does sound pretty complicated, but a couple of examples should make it reasonably clear.

We must now understand the examples involving Mr. Brown, John, and Sue not as habitual or recurrent, but as one-time events; in effect Mr. Brown has trouble starting his car today, John laughs at the comedian today, Sue is afraid of the dog today. At the start of Part IX of Table 4-1 a small problem created by English grammar that is irrelevant to the causal calculus is explained, and so we shall ignore it here. Consider now the information pattern that gives rise, in the case of Mr. Brown, to a temporary actor attribution: LLL (Part IX, item 1 in Table 4-1).

If Mr. Brown has trouble starting many cars today (low distinctiveness), then that suggests the problem is in Mr. Brown (internal locus). If few other people have trouble starting Mr. Brown's car today (low consensus), then that also suggests an internal locus. This much is familiar. The new thing is low consistency which can be expressed as "Mr. Brown has trouble starting his car very rarely (on few occasions)." Notice that low consistency constrains the actor cause to be unstable rather than stable. What could it be? Not Mr. Brown's habit of leaving the choke out and flooding the plugs, because that is a stable characteristic. It could be that Mr. Brown is feeling a bit under the weather today and by accident tried to start the car with the gears in "Drive" position and does not notice it. Presumably an unstable aberration.

Consider now the information pattern that gives rise in the case of Mr. Brown to an unstable situation (or external attribution): HHL (Part IX, item 2 in Table 4-1). If many people have trouble starting Mr. Brown's car today, then that implicates the car (as usual). If Mr. Brown has trouble starting few other cars today, then that also implicates the car. Thus far, we have the familiar HH pattern that leads to a situation attribution. The new thing, once again, is low consistency, and that is expressed as "Mr. Brown has trouble starting his car very rarely." What now could, specifically, be wrong with the car? It cannot be a faulty ignition system since that is a stable characteristic. The car could, however, be out of gas, too cold, or something of that sort.

Part IX of Table 4–1 works out the information patterns for all three examples, and so we will not repeat here the information patterns for John and Sue, but, rather, suggest possible specific causes conforming to the temporary constraint. If John laughs at the comedian just today because of something temporary about John, one thinks of a good mood or gentle inebriation. If Sue is afraid of this dog, not usually but just today, because of something in herself, one wonders if she is nervous about a love affair or has, perhaps, just read Stephen King's *Cujo*. If John laughs today because of something temporary about the comedian, well, maybe the comedian is in rare good form, and if Sue is afraid of the dog just today because of something temporary about the dog, well maybe the dog is in rare vicious form.

Part IX, cases 3 and 4, in Table 4–1 should probably be labeled: "For Talmudic scholars only." Unstable interactions (A–S) and temporary pairs of sufficient causes (A,S) never seem to have been studied in psychological experiments and seldom seem to arise in everyday life. I include them in Table 4–1 because they are needed to fill out the set of possibilities, but I think there need be no discussion of them here.

Since we have three information variables, each of which can assume one of two values (high or low), the number of possible unique patterns of information is eight (2 × 2 × 2), and corresponding to each of these possible distinct information patterns is a distinct type of attribution. Table 4–2 reduces the full calculus to a simple table from which it is possible to read out the information pattern corresponding to each type of attribution and conversely the type of attribution corresponding to each information pattern. Table 4–3 reduces the calculus further to a table consisting of the four simple types of attribution only, since in everyday thinking about social causality that is often all that is used—in fact, sometimes just the two top lines of Table 4–3, the stable actor and situation attributions, seem to be used.

TABLE 4–2. A Reduced Pocket Calculus

Type of Attribution	Consensus	Distinctiveness	Consistency
Actor-stable	L	L	H
Situation-stable	H	H	H
Actor-unstable	L	L	L
Situation-unstable	H	H	L
Actor–situation interaction–stable	L	H	H
Actor, situation–stable	H	L	H
Actor–situation interaction–unstable	L	H	L
Actor, situation–unstable	H	L	L

TABLE 4–3. A Further Reduced Pocket Calculus

Type of Attribution	Consensus	Distinctiveness	Consistency
Actor-stable	L	L	H
Situation-stable	H	H	H
Actor-unstable	L	L	L
Situation-unstable	H	H	L

Evidence for the Psychological Reality of the Calculus

The most convincing evidence must come from your own intuitive judgments; if the calculus does not do a good job of capturing those, then it is unlikely that paper-and-pencil experiments will convince you. However, there are many such experiments, and the results conform well to the calculus in the simple cases; in the complex cases involving two causes, the results are fewer but generally confirmatory.

Experimental Evidence

Leslie McArthur did the first study in 1972. It is a very up-front and comprehensive study in which subjects were given twelve event-depicting sentences, such as "John laughs at the comedian" and "Sue is afraid of the dog" (actually used by McArthur) plus some combination of information (high or low) with respect to consensus, distinctiveness, and consistency. The information variable values were also conveyed by sentences such as, for instance, "Almost everyone who hears the comedian laughs at him" (high consensus) and "John also laughs at almost any other comedian" (low distinctiveness). Each subject had some value (high or low) for each information variable for each event-depicting sentence, and in the full design all possible combinations were realized.

The event-depicting sentence was followed by the question "Why?" and subjects were asked to choose among types of causal attributions: (a) Something about the Actor; (b) Something about the Stimulus (our situation); and so on. Not all of the eight types of cause represented in Table 4–2 were included, unfortunately. Instead, many were clumped together; for instance (d) Some combination of Actor, Stimulus, and Circumstances. Even so, there is much in the results that confirms the psychological reality of Table 4–2.

The pattern *LL* reliably led to "Something about the Actor"—an actor attribution, as predicted, and the pattern *HH* reliably led to "Something about the Stimulus"—a situation attribution, as predicted. Low consistency was reliably related to a type of cause McArthur called "Circumstances," which type is not included in Table 4–2. Upon examination of the examples, however, it is clear that "Circumstances" amounted to unstable attributions either to the actor (e.g. mood) or the situation (e.g. being in good form), and so those results also seem to confirm Table 4-2. Finally, McArthur found the pattern *LH* to be associated with *A-S* interaction and the pattern *HL* with *A* or *S* as two alternative sufficient causes. That too confirms Table 4-2. The ultimate force of McArthur's important study is to show that the information in Table 4-2 must exist as a kind of schema in subjects' minds. Table 4-2 is a good model of the tacit knowledge subjects possess, because it predicts their intuitive judgments.

McArthur's subjects made "type of attribution" judgments on the basis of complete information patterns, with values on all variables, and Table 4-2 could be generated from those data as the "latent structure" in the data. Two other investigators (Zuckerman and Mann, 1979) posed for their subjects the mirror-image task. They were asked to guess the appropriate information patterns—the values for consensus, distinctiveness, and consistency—to fit the types of causal attribution given them for particular named events. For example, a subject might read: "Nancy enjoyed the concert. Why? Something about Nancy causes her to enjoy the concert." The experiment also yielded data conforming to Table 4-2, data from which Table 4-2 could be constructed (in part).

The information patterns of Table 4-2 are such that each value for a variable that is known reduces the number of possible types of attribution. For instance, starting out knowing no value of any variable, any of the eight existing types of attribution is possible. If one knows that consensus is high (*H*), then only four types are possible, since there are only four consistent with this fact. Knowing that distinctiveness is also high (*H*) cuts the possible set in half again, since there are only two patterns that begin *HH*. Knowing finally that consistency is low (*L*) once again halves the set of possibles and, in fact, generates a unique solution: the type of attribution called "situation unstable." That is to say that there is redundancy in the information patterns, and that means a person could make reasonably good (though not certainly correct) guesses as to type of attribution on the basis of partial information. With Table 4-3 the number of alternative types of attribution is reduced, and it is possible to arrive at unique correct solutions with just two of three items of information: thus high consensus and high consistency unequivocally select the attribution type called "situation-stable." If only the first two rows of Table 4-3 are considered, as seems to be the case whenever the event to be explained is recurrent or habitual, a single item of information (e.g. high consensus) implies a "situation-stable" cause. The fact that the attribution calculus is quite redundant means that in real interaction people might draw causal inferences on the basis of very partial information, and it is clear that they do so in fact. Clear from experiment and clear from everyday observation.

In 1975 Orvis, Cunningham, and Kelley had 216 undergraduates at the University of California at Los Angeles guess various entries in Table 4-3 from incomplete information. Some were given the value for just one information variable and some the values for two. In some cases the task was to infer the values of the information variables that were not supplied, and in some cases to infer the type of attribution itself. If the subjects had had Table 4–3 in front of them, they could have easily supplied the required entries. They *did not* have Table 4–3 or any other printed calculus in front of them. However, they regularly supplied the answers the calculus yields, and so we must conclude that they had a kind of mental template, corresponding, for instance, to Table 4–3, to which they had recourse in making their inferences.

There is a large amount of paper-and-pencil evidence that Tables 4–2 and especially the simpler Table 4–3 are real mental structures. There is also evidence of a naturalistic kind, from plays, psychotherapy sessions, and everyday life. The virtue of the paper-and-pencil evidence is that it is complete, unequivocal in its meaning, and not dependent on any skill of psychological interpretation. Its shortcoming is that it is artificial and very explicit in form and might possibly not be representative of life outside the psychological laboratory. It may have left you unconvinced that the causal calculus really matters. It also promotes a catechism-like automaticity that falls short of deep understanding. The naturalistic evidence is more full blooded, convincing, and consequential, but it also requires a kind of psychological skill. You need to get the knack (not easily acquired) of mapping real speech and real events into the concepts of the calculus. Let us have one example from Eugene O'Neill's play, *A Long Day's Journey into Night* (1956).

Naturalistic Evidence

Without any question, *Long Day's Journey* is an autobiographical play; O'Neill himself has told us so. A comparison of the information disclosed in the play about the Tyrone family matches almost exactly the facts about the O'Neill family set down by his biographers (e.g. Gelb and Gelb, 1962). James Tyrone, the successful actor who was retired by 1912, the year in which the play is set, is clearly James O'Neill, Eugene's father—handsome and vigorous, a heavy drinker in a convivial Irish style, intensely penurious, though wealthy. Mary Tyrone, convent-educated, less strong than her husband, and from the time of birth of her younger son (Eugene, in life), a morphine addict, is clearly Ella O'Neill. Jamie Tyrone, the older son whose life is blasted by alcoholism and whose "adder's tongue" is turned most often against his father, is Eugene's elder brother, James O'Neill. And Edmund Tyrone, the youngest son, with the "summer cold" in 1912 that is identified as consumption in the course of the play, is Eugene himself. Carlotta O'Neill, Eugene's wife in his later years, said of her husband's state when he was writing the play: "He would come out of his study at the end of a day gaunt and sometimes weeping. His eyes would be all red and he looked ten years older than when he went in in the morning" (Peck, 1956). And what the play is about, primarily, is social causality. Who or what caused the dire events in the lives of the Tyrones (O'Neills)?

We come a long journey in the single day of O'Neill's play. When the curtain rises on Act I, it is morning. We hear laughter and then the only two speeches of the play that are unclouded by dark revelation. The third speech introduces a suspicion of something amiss, a clue that Mary, recently returned from a sanatarium, has resumed the use of morphine—though we will not know that for sure until Act II:

> TYRONE: You're a fine armful now, Mary, with those twenty pounds you've gained.
> MARY (*smiles affectionately*): I've gotten too fat you mean, dear. I really ought to reduce.
> TYRONE: None of that my lady! You're just right. We'll have no talk of reducing. Is that why you ate so little breakfast?

Next comes an exchange that reveals a calculation of social causality:

> MARY: So little? I thought I ate a lot.
> TYRONE: You didn't. Not as much as I'd like to see anyway.
> MARY (*teasingly*): Oh you! You expect everyone to eat the enormous breakfast you do. No one else could without dying of indigestion.
> TYRONE: I hope I'm not as big a glutton as that sounds. [E. O'Neill, *Long Day's Journey into Night*, Yale University Press, 1956, p. 14. Copyright © 1955 by Carlotta Monterey O'Neill]

The event for which a cause is sought in this conversation might be expressed in the sentence: "Mary ate very little breakfast." The true cause of this event is the fact that Mary has secretly resumed the use of morphine. Wanting to keep her secret, she denies the event—eating very little breakfast—and so says there is really nothing to be explained. Then comes the interesting sentence about Tyrone's enormous appetite. From that line one can, by close reading, derive a partial pattern of information: values for consensus and consistency, but not distinctiveness. However, in that sentence as in natural speech generally, there are no explicit (and awkward) statements about "few people" or "hardly anyone" and "most people" and "almost always." The information values must be inferred by indirection from other words and even from features of grammar.

Mary, by saying that no one else in the world could eat the enormous breakfast that Tyrone does, is almost paraphrasing "hardly anyone," and it is clear that this is an expression of low consensus. Consistency is also expressed, but not in words. It appears in the use of the verb "do" (eat an enormous breakfast) as opposed to "did." The difference is that "do" expresses something habitual, a usual practice, whereas "did" would express a particular completed event. If Tyrone habitually eats an enormous breakfast and Mary says "do", then consistency is high. A quick glance at Table 4–3 reveals the fact that low consensus and high consistency must imply low distinctiveness and an actor-stable attribution. There is no clear information in the play on distinctiveness, but a high value can be inferred from the partial pattern. The actor-stable attribution is also not directly asserted but only an inference. The inference is that the reason why Tyrone eats an enormous breakfast is something stable about Tyrone. And in Tyrone's prompt follow-up, we see that he has made the inference; from incomplete data, in just the same way as did the subjects of Orvis, Cunningham, and Kelley (1975).

"I hope I'm not as big a glutton as that sounds." To what does "that" refer? To Mary's speech, which does not use the word "glutton" but does contain enough information to imply a stable attribution to the actor, and glutton is one likely candidate.

For all the first two acts of Long Day's Journey and for the first part of the third, a single theme is repeated with many variations. One or another of the male Tyrones speaks of something odd in Mary's behavior, something that has recently changed. The little breakfast she ate was first, but it also appears that she has "seemed a bit high-strung in the past few days," has moved out of Tyrone's bedroom and taken to sleeping in the spare room, and also has started having some meals upstairs. All these actions of Mary's are new with respect to Mary's present stay at home (and so of low consistency) but terribly familiar in terms of her addiction (high consistency). Low consistency implies temporary attributions to actor or situation that no one need worry about, but high consistency with times of morphine-use implies a stable external attribution (morphine), which is what everyone fears. Mary knows that she has resumed the use of morphine, and the three men all suspect that she has. The talk about causality that constitutes a large part of the conversation in the first two acts represents a coordinated effort to keep the truth from becoming manifest and shared.

The causal calculus describes rules for using information that should cause everyone who uses the same information to arrive at the same conclusions and, furthermore, to do so in a way that is essentially scientific, though a bit rough-and-ready. We know that values for all three information variables (consensus, distinctiveness, and consistency) are not always present, but redundancy in the calculus makes it possible to make inferences from less than complete sets of information. Sometimes, however, values are unknown for all information variables, and yet causal interpretations are still made. The information variables define social reality, and when reality is not defined, it happens, as in the interpretation of an ink blot, that personality finds expression. There is good evidence of one sort of personality difference in causal thinking: Persons who are clinically depressed seem to favor one particular kind of attribution.

Depressive Attributions

Martin Seligman's (1975) work on depression began with a long series of experiments on animals that led him, at first, to formulate the state of depression as "learned helplessness." In a characteristic experiment, dogs in a Pavlovian hammock, which is a slinglike suspension apparatus, experienced electric shocks that could not be escaped by any response the dog was free to make. Twenty-four hours later the same dogs were placed in a shuttlebox, a two-compartment box divided by a barrier the dogs could easily learn to jump, and the dogs were exposed to shocks which could readily be escaped. Two-thirds of the dogs failed to learn the simple escape response, evidently because of their previous experience with shock from which they could not escape because control animals, spared the prior experience of helplessness, all readily learned to escape the shock in the shuttlebox. The helpless dogs looked passive and unemotional; they did not initiate enough responses to learn that shock in the box could be escaped; in fact, they looked depressed, though they could not say whether they felt sad.

Seligman proposed that the animals learned, in the Pavlovian hammock, that their responses and the delivery of shock were independent of one another, which is to say that nothing they did made any difference. They then generalized that learned helplessness to the new shuttlebox setting and failed to learn that they could now escape. A number of experiments strongly suggested that it was the uncontrollability of the bad (or aversive) event rather than its traumatizing effect that produced learned helplessness. The same sort of learned helplessness was demonstrated, with a variety of settings, in mice, cats, and eventually humans. The bad events in experiments with humans were typically shocks or loud noises that were, at first, uncontrollable by any response and afterward controllable by an easily learned response such as pressing a button or solving a simple problem. There is some reason to believe that learned helplessness is implicated in drug use (Berglas and Jones, 1978), heart attacks (Krantz, Glass, and Snyder, 1974), and other failures of adaptation, but it is best known as a model of depression.

Depression—as a mood—is familiar to everyone (with the possible exception of an elderly woman friend from Ireland who once asked me: "Dr. Brown, what do people mean when they say they are depressed?"). As a state that lasts for weeks, months, or years and is severe enough to impair work performance and drain life of all pleasure but not severe enough to require hospitalization, it is known to millions, more women than men, more older people than young, but not at all uncommon even in teenage males. Depression is more than sadness. A depressed person does usually feel sad and may be tearful, but probably "flatness" of feeling, the absence of any zest or interest, is the most common state. In severe depression there will be one or another kind of sleep disturbance—most commonly early waking in the morning. Appetites fall off, for food and especially for sex. Self-esteem is very low. Everything seems quite hopeless, and one feels quite helpless. Depression shows, even from a distance. The facial muscles droop, posture sags, movement is slow. There is no spring in the step, no sparkle in the eye, never a sign of mirth. If it gets so bad that someone really cannot meet his obligations or is a danger to himself, hospitalization is a good idea.

Manic-depressive psychosis is characterized by a relatively periodic vacillation between periods of elevated mood and hyperactivity (mania) and periods of depression. The condition is often called bipolar (two poles) affective disorder, and the best treatment for it is lithium salts (closely monitored by a physician). Unipolar depression lacks any manic component, and it was Seligman's theory that the learned helplessness formulation was relevant only to unipolar depression, not to bipolar depression, and not even to all cases of unipolar depression. He thought that learned helplessness was a sufficient condition for depression but not a necessary one. For example, *post partum psychosis*, a form of depression that some mothers experience soon after giving birth, seems to have nothing to do with learned helplessness.

As studies of learned helplessness in humans accumulated in the 1970s, the total picture became confused. Literature reviews (e.g. Miller and Norman, 1979; Wortman and Brehm, 1975) turned up so many anomalies that the validity of learned helplessness as a model of depression was in serious doubt. In 1978 Seligman and his associates (Abramson, Seligman, and Teasdale, 1978) reformulated their theory in terms of attribution. They had come to believe that it was not simply the uncontrollability of bad events that mattered but the causal attributions made for bad events, and by 1980 (Peterson and Seligman, 1980) the position was that the depressed person is characterized by a particular *attributional style*. He attributes bad events to causes that are *internal*, *stable*, and *global*.

Seligman's formulation of the depressive attributional style is consistent with the causal calculus and utilizes two of the three dimensions of the calculus: internal–external and stable–unstable. To show that this is so, here are examples from his 1978 reformulation. Suppose a student has just taken the math part of the Graduate Record Examinations (GRE) and believes he did very poorly. That is a bad event. What might have caused it? "Lack of mathematical ability" would be what the Pocket Calculus calls an "internal-stable" attribution (or "actor-stable"), and Seligman says the same. That is the kind of attribution for bad events to which depressives are thought to be disposed. What are the alternatives? "I was bored with math problems" would be an internal-unstable attribution; "ETS [Educational Testing Service] gives unfair math exams" would be an external-stable attribution; "The test was given on Friday the thirteenth, an unlucky day" would be an external-unstable attribution. Seligman conceives of and names all the above cases in just the way the Pocket Calculus does. With two dimensions of two values each (internal or external, stable or unstable), four types of attribution are possible. The internal-stable attribution (lack of mathematical ability) is clearly the most punishing of the possibilities, the one hardest on self-esteem and the one making the worst predictions for future performance. As long as there is no information whatever on consensus, distinctiveness, and consistency, the choice among the four possible types is free, and Seligman proposes that the depressive attributional style favors an internal-stable cause for bad events.

Here is an example from the domain of social inadequacy. Suppose a woman is rejected by a man she loves. (These examples are from Seligman, so please attribute any implicit sexism to him, not me.) With no information on consensus, distinctiveness, and consistency, there are four possible kinds of attribution. "I'm unattractive to him" is internal-stable, the depressive's favorite. "My conversation bored him" is internal-unstable and is punishing but correctable, after all. "He can't take intelligent women" is external-stable and not all that disagreeable. "He was in a rejecting mood" is external-unstable and leaves reason to be optimistic about the next time.

Seligman's thesis is that the depressive attributional style is not only internal and stable but also *global*. For *global* and its opposite, *specific*, there is no equivalent in our causal calculus. That simply means that Seligman has chosen to utilize a dimension of generalization that the standard calculus does not (but easily could) use. The calculus stays with a single event—an action or experience. In life, however, attributions are sometimes made over multiple events. The student who thinks he did poorly on the GRE math test might remember that he has also done poorly on verbal tests, has had low grades in all kinds of courses, and has not done well in games of skill, and this broad generalization of poor intellectual performance could lead to the attribution: "I have low intelligence." That very punishing and unpromising attribution is not only internal and stable, but also global (high generalization across events). A maximally *specific* internal-stable attribution (low generalization across events) would be: "I have low ability of whatever kind the GRE math exam tests." The rejected woman, if she elects to be depressively global, will decide that she is unattractive not just to the man who rejected her, but to men, all of them. You can see that internal, stable, and global causes for bad events represent the darkest view that can be taken since they imply that bad news is one's own fault in a way that will last and prove to be general.

Seligman's classification of attributions (Abramson, Seligman, and Teasdale, 1978) is a 2 × 2 × 2 table (internal–external, stable–unstable, global–specific), and so it yields eight cells. The causal calculus of Table 4-2 is also a 2 × 2 × 2 table that yields eight cells, and so one might have expected the two to be a perfect match. In fact, they are not. That is because Seligman utilizes global–specific, which the calculus does not, and the calculus utilizes A–S interaction and A,S (as two sufficient causes) whereas Seligman includes no account of complex causes. His causes are all single (though three-dimensional). The calculus deals with single causes (in two dimensions) plus two varieties of complex causality (in the same two dimensions). The calculus is the more basic analysis; it is intended to be exhaustive for the minimal case of a single social event. Seligman's analysis omits the not very commonly used complex patterns and allows for generalization across multiple events, which is certainly something that happens in life.

Seligman does not intend to deny the importance of the information variables—consensus, distinctiveness, and consistency—and indeed gives examples of their operation that are consistent with the calculus. Suppose a child contracts leukemia. His father marshals all his resources to save the child's life but learns that he can do nothing and also that no one else can do anything. That is a case of high consensus (the father and all relevant other people), and so, Seligman says, the attribution for the helplessness should be external. That is what the causal calculus of Table 4–3 also says: The problem is in the situation, in the disease leukemia. Suppose, by contrast, that a student does poorly in school even though he tries in every way to do well; he works endlessly, hires tutors, takes remedial courses, and so forth. It cannot be lost on the student that some, even most, people do well in the same circumstances, and so consensus is low. In those circumstances the helplessness must be attributed to an internal cause, says Seligman, and so says the calculus too. This difference between universal helplessness (leukemia) and personal helplessness (student's grades) is one of the things that led Seligman and his associates to believe that it was the way in which bad events were explained, or attributed, that produced depression, and not simply the occurrence of such events.

Assessment of Attributional Style

The distinctive claim in Seligman's work, the claim that goes beyond everyman-as-scientist and the causal calculus, is the idea that when information is constant and nothing at all is known about consensus, distinctiveness, and consistency in connection with a bad event, individuals will make causal attributions nevertheless, and there will be individual differences among these attributions such that depressives will favor internal, stable, global causes. To test for attributional style, one can use an instrument called "The Attributional Style Questionnaire" (Peterson, *et al.*, 1982). Here is a characteristic item (slightly edited):

You have been looking for a job unsuccessfully for some time.

1. Is the cause of your unsuccessful job search due to something about you or something about other people or circumstances? (Circle one number.)

   Totally due to other people or circumstances   1 2 3 4 5 6 7   Totally due to me

2. In the future when looking for a job, will this cause again be present? (Circle one number.)

   Will never again be present   1 2 3 4 5 6 7   Will always be present

3. Is the cause something that just influences looking for a job or does it also influence other areas of your life? (Circle one number.)

   Influences just this particular situation   1 2 3 4 5 6 7   Influences all situations in my life

The first question asks whether the cause is internal or external; the second whether it is stable and unstable; the third whether global or specific. There are twelve such items in the full questionnaire.

The concept of style entails personal consistency, and so if there are individual attributional styles of any sort, there should be substantial correlations between individual scores at one time and individual scores at another time. The inventors of the Attributional Style Questionnaire report correlations for one hundred subjects at two times, five weeks apart, on the scores for internality, stability, and globality and also for composite internal-stable-global scores. The correlations are all statistically significant and quite high, ranging from .57 to .69. The idea that there are individually characteristic styles in the domain of attribution meets quite well the first essential requirement: substantial consistency over time.

What evidence is there for the primary claim that depressed persons manifest an internal, stable, global style? There is quite a lot: The style is associated in college students with depression over a range of variation that does not extend to clinical severity; the style also characterizes patients hospitalized for severe depression; children as young as nine years old who have symptoms of depression also have the attributional style. To assess level of depression all studies have used as their primary instrument some form of the Beck Depression Inventory (Beck, 1967, 1976). This is a self-report inventory with such items as these:

"I feel sad all the time and I can't snap out of it."

"As I look back on my life all I can see is a lot of failures."

"I have to push very hard to do anything."

"I feel irritated all the time now."

The Beck Inventory has been validated against clinical ratings for depression.

In 1979 Seligman and his co-workers reported on the correlations between Beck Inventory scores and scores for internality, stability, and globality of attributional style obtained from 143 students at the University of Pennsylvania (Seligman et al., 1979). The results appear in Table 4-4a. All correlations are in the predicted direction and are statistically highly significant, even though they are not absolutely very high. The Beck Inventory scores of those students did not reach the high levels that are considered clinically significant, and so the next question was whether patients hospitalized for depression would show the postulated attributional style.

Raps and colleagues (1980, 1982) reported on thirty male patients who were hospitalized for unipolar depression and who also scored in the high clinical range on the Beck Inventory. With hospitalized patients it is important to know whether the attributional style hypothesized to be characteristic of depressives would in fact be distinctive of such patients in contrast with patients hospitalized for other reasons. The 1982 study compares mean style scores for depressed patients with mean scores for a group of schizophrenic patients and with mean scores for persons in hospital for somatic illness or for surgery. The results appear in Table 4-4b. The mean scores for depressives are all significantly different from other types of hospitalized patients in the predicted way.

TABLE 4-4. Relations Between Depression and Attributional Style

a. Correlations for College Students Between Beck Depression Inventory Scores and Attributional-Style Scores

Style Subscales	Beck Depression Inventory Correlations
Internality	.41
Stability	.34
Globality	.35

b. Mean Attributional-Style Scores for Patient Groups

Style Subscales	Depressives	Schizophrenics	Medical and Surgical Patients
Internality	4.90	3.51	4.30
Stability	4.89	4.01	4.06
Globality	4.84	4.10	3.65
Composite	4.88	3.87	4.00

c. Correlations Between Attributional-Style Scores and Depression Scores in Children

Style Subscales	Depression Inventory Correlations
Internality	.45
Stability	.31
Globality	.21
Composite	.51

SOURCES: a. Seligman et al., 1979. b. Raps et al., 1982. c. Peterson and Seligman, 1980.

It appears that the internal, stable, global style of mildly depressed college students is also the style of hospitalized depressives and that the style is characteristic of that particular kind of patient.

The questionnaire used to assess attributional style in adults turns out not to work with children; they have trouble making some of the ratings. Therefore, a simplified child's version was developed; it puts all questions into a choice format (Peterson and Seligman, 1980). For instance:

1. You get an A on a math test.
   a. I'm smart.
   b. I'm smart at math.

The item is an inquiry about globality with internality and stability held constant. The Child Attributional Style Questionnaire consists of forty-eight items devised to inquire equally often about each dimension of the style. The manifestations of depression in childhood seem to be essentially the same as in adult-hood, but of course a different vocabulary must be used to ask about them. Kovacs and Beck (1977) have provided the instrument. Ninety-six children in the third through the sixth grades participated, and the correlations between depression and attributional style are displayed in Table 4-4c. They are very much like the correlations for adults, all in the predicted direction and all significant.

The discovery that children as young as nine may manifest both depression and the internal, stable, attributional style (which also shows some stability over time) compels us to ask how this insidious style develops. It might, of course, be a kind of contagion from parents. If parents themselves have a con-sistent style, then it would be constantly modeled for their children, because social interaction is dense with attribution talk. Some of the parents of the ninety-six children studied themselves filled out the Adult Style Questionnaire as well as the Beck Inventory. Mothers' attribution style for bad events proved to be correlated with the styles of their children (.42), but fathers' styles were unrelated to either mothers' or children's. Not much to go on here, only a bare suggestion that mother may play a "depressogenic" role, but I would not bet on it. Seligman and his associates turned in 1982–83 to the direct study of parent–child interaction to see whether something like style transmission occurs.

There is another possibility, of course. Someone might arrive at a disposi-tion to explain bad events in terms of internal, stable, and global causes because life has taught him that that, unhappily, is the way it is. The Attribu-tion Style Questionnaire puts forward hypothetical bad events free of all con-sensus, distinctiveness, and consistency information and invites, rather com-pels, extrapolation of past experience to a new and fully ambiguous case. But suppose the hypothetical student who thinks he did poorly on the GRE and attributes it to low intelligence were a real person; what might his experience with tests and grades have been like? He might regularly (which means high consistency) have failed tests that most of his peers did not fail (low consensus), and not just one type of test but tests of all kinds (low distinctiveness). The pat-tern *LLH* compels him to make an internal, stable (also global) attribution, and it is quite reasonable to extend that attribution to cover his latest failure, the GRE math exam. Or what of the woman rejected by a particular man who depressively concludes that she is unattractive to men? What might her experience have been? Perhaps she has regularly (high consistency) gone unap-proached by men when all her girlfriends were approached (low consensus) and not just for one kind of social occasion but all kinds (low distinctiveness). If she is in touch with reality, she must make the kind of attribution an *LLH* pattern calls for: internal, stable, global; unattractive to men. In thinking about the depressive attribution style, we have probably unwittingly assumed that it was a distortion of the truth. Aaron Beck (1967, 1976), an authority on depression, definitely takes that position. He writes of the depressive "having a bias against the self" and considers "an unrealistically negative view of self" to be a prominent cause of depression. But what if, for some, there is simply a reality that is pretty grim?

Depressive Realism

None of the results set forth in Table 4–4 are the whole story on the studies in question. I have withheld one-half of the picture, beginning really with the description of the Attribution Style Questionnaire. Of the twelve hypothetical events in that questionnaire, only half, or six, were bad; the remaining events were good or desirable, for instance: "You meet a friend who compliments you on your appearance"; "You become very rich"; "You do a project which is highly praised." What kinds of attributions do depressed persons make for good events, and how do their attributions in this case compare with those of nondepressed persons? Table 4–5 is the other half, the good events half, of Table 4–4.

We return first to the 1979 study with college students (Seligman et al., 1979). For good events the correlations between depression and internality, depression and stability, depression and globality were *all negative*, and two of the three are significantly so (Table 4–5a). We return next to the study correlating attributional-style scores and depression scores for children (Table 4–5c). For good events the correlations are, as with adults, *all negative*, and in this case all significantly so. Please do not be confused and suppose that the negative correlations are simply the reverse image of the positive correlations and so devoid of new information; that would be the case if Table 4–5 reported correlations with the opposite poles (externality, instability, and specificity) for the same bad events, but that is not what Table 4–5 reports. What we have in Table 4–5 is the relation between the familiar depressive style—internal, stable, and global —with a set of six new events that are good rather than bad. The universally negative correlations demonstrate that the attributional style of depressives is *not uniform across both bad and good events* but, in fact, reverses. Depressives are consistent in that they take the darkest possible view: bad things derive from personal, unchanging, and general causes such as low ability or unattractiveness, and good things result from situational, unstable, and specific causes such as luck or another person's brief good humor.

Finally we return to the results for three kinds of hospitalized patients (Table 4–5b) to see how depressives differ from other people when the events to be explained are good. The numbers are all consistent, and many of the differences are significant. For good events depressives make attributions that are *less* internal, *less* stable, and *less* global (therefore more external, more unstable, and more global) than the attributions of hospital patients who are not depressed. What is true of the nondepressed hospital patients is even more markedly true of nondepressed persons outside of hospitals—normals, as it were. Normal per-

TABLE 4–5. Relations Between Attributional Style and Depression for Good Events

a. Correlations for College Students Between Beck Depression Inventory Scores and Attributional-Style Scores

Style Subscales	Beck Depression Inventory Correlations
Internality	−.22
Stability	−.28
Globality	−.04

b. Mean Attributional-Style Scores for Patient Groups

Style Subscales	Depressives	Schizophrenics	Medical and Surgical Patients
Internality	4.93	5.67	5.49
Stability	4.90	5.57	5.53
Globality	5.10	5.27	5.31
Composite	4.98	5.50	5.44

c. Correlations Between Attributional-Style Scores and Depression Scores in Children

Style Subscales	Depression Inventory Correlations
Internality	−.34
Stability	−.47
Globality	−.35
Composite	−.53

SOURCES: a. Seligman et al., 1979. b. Raps et al., 1982. c. Peterson and Seligman, 1980.

sons have an attributional style of their own. They take a bright view of good events and attribute them to internal, stable, global causes, such as high intelligence or great personal attractiveness. They also take a bright view of bad events, tending to attribute them to situational, unstable, specific causes such as bad luck or someone's brief bad humor.

The normal attributional style was actually discovered, in social psychology, long before the depressive style. Called the "self-serving bias," it first turned up as a tendency for actors to take credit for successes and to disclaim responsibility for failures. The self-serving bias has been demonstrated in something like one hundred experiments (e.g. Miller and Ross, 1975; Snyder, Stephan, and Rosenfield, 1978; and especially Zuckerman, 1979). Until the study of attributional style in depression began, the self-serving bias was thought to be simply a human bias, something universal. Now, however, we know that it is lacking in depression.

We have two ways of characterizing the attributional style in depression: either as the *presence* of a bias favoring internal, stable, and global causes for bad events and external, unstable, specific causes for good events or as the *absence* of a normal bias favoring internal, stable, and global causes for good events and external, unstable, specific causes for bad events. The two ways of putting it say almost the same thing, but not quite. They differ in the location of the bias. The fact that the data permit either conclusion means that the question of who is biased and who realistic is entirely up in the air. Perhaps depressives take an unrealistically dark view. It is equally possible that normals take an unrealistically bright view.

Nothing can be said about reality on the basis of the Attributional Style Questionnaire, for it is a collection of hypothetical outcomes open to any causal interpretation. Decisions about bias and realism must start with some standard of reality against which attributions can be judged, an objective standard or a consensual judgment of disinterested observers. There is some work that measures depressive and nondepressive causal thinking against a standard, and most of it so far supports the unexpected conclusion that it is the depressive who is the more realistic and the nondepressive who is under the spell of illusion.

Alloy and Abramson (1979, 1980, 1982) used an objective reality. Subjects (depressed or not, according to Beck Inventory Scores) were given the following task. At the onset of a yellow light, the subject must decide whether or not to press a given button, and if he decides to press, must do so within three seconds. If he has made the right decision (according to the experimenter's program, which is unknown to the subject), a green light will flash at the end of the three-second trial. Both pressing and not pressing are responses, and each may be correct or incorrect. There are to be forty trials in all. In fact, the experimenter's program makes the green light more or less or not at all contingent on the response the subject makes. The degree of contingency is measured by something called the "delta coefficient," which is simply the probability of a green light if the button is pressed minus the probability of a green light if it is not pressed ($[p]GL$; press $-$ $[p]GL$; no press). If the probabilities are the same, then the green light is completely unrelated to the subject's responses; he has no control whatever over the light. That is the simplest case and is the one to be considered here. This perfect absence of contingency or control is the reality. What a subject is asked to do, after all trials are over, is to estimate the degree of control he had over the light on a scale from zero to one hundred. The correct answer (reality) is zero. Insofar as his answers approach zero, he is being realistic.

In the most relevant experimental variation, subjects could either win or lose money on the forty trials. In the "Lose" condition a subject was given five dollars at the start and required to give up twenty-five cents for each trial on which the green light failed to appear. Subjects thought of such outcomes as bad events, and when they estimated the amount of control they thought they had exerted, those estimates could be considered a kind of indirect assessment of internal attribution (his personal control over bad events). Stability and globality were not assessed. Nevertheless, the depressive's supposed attributional style should lead him to make internal attributions (manifest as high estimates of control for the bad events) whereas nondepressives should make external attributions (manifest as low estimates of control), and if that should be what the two kinds of subjects did, it would also be true that nondepressives would be more *realistic* (no real control existed) than depressives.

In the "Win" condition subjects were started with no funds, and every time the green light went on, they were given twenty-five cents. The gains may be regarded as good events, and subjects' estimates of the amount of control they had exerted would, in an indirect way, be estimates of internal attributions for good events. Depressives should, according to hypothesis, take the dark view, attributing good events externally (luck on a random program), and if they did so, in this Win condition, they would be realistic, because the green light was, in fact, a matter of luck. Nondepressives should attribute good events to their own actions (internally) and so make high estimates of control which would, however, be unrealistic.

The results were very strong. Depressed subjects made estimates of control of about the same order of magnitude whether winning or losing, and those estimates were low—near zero—hence quite realistic. Nondepressive subjects made very low estimates of control when they were losing and quite high estimates when they were winning, although the reality was always a total absence of control. In short, depressed subjects were consistently realistic; they took in the actual contingencies and did so over a series of experimental variations. Nondepressed subjects were the ones who showed a bias, a departure from reality in a consistent direction, and it was the self-serving bias. They saw themselves as responsible for desirable outcomes but not responsible (in some variations unrealistically so) for undesirable outcomes. That kind of result gave impetus to the notion that depressives are realistic and can best be characterized as lacking an agreeable illusion, quite substantial in size, that nondepressives enjoy.

There is one manifestation of depressive realism that seems to me not very surprising. Lewinsohn and colleagues (1980) found that depressed patients (in treatment for depression) rated themselves low on seventeen desirable attributes such as "friendly," "assertive," "warm," "socially skilled," "humorous," and "confident," and those self-ratings, based on how they thought they had acted in an immediately preceding forty-five-minute "get acquainted" group, were realistic in that they did not significantly differ from ratings on the same traits made by trained observers who had watched the group through a one-way window. I think this "depressive realism" is not surprising because the subjects knew they were in a treatment program for depression and certainly knew that they acted and felt not very friendly, assertive, socially skilled, humorous, and so on—those undesirable deficits being a good compendium of the symptoms of depression. The observers were not told who in the group was depressed, but clinical depression shows; it is evident to almost anyone. Not uncommonly, a badly depressed person finds it impossible to speak at all in a social situation, let alone smile or be assertive. I would expect depressed patients to feel depressed and show it—it is a pretty "public" disorder.

Other findings in the Lewinsohn study are more interesting: Normal and psychiatric controls rated themselves higher on the desirable qualities than depressives did but were unrealistically high in the sense that they rated themselves significantly higher than observers did. Here, then, is a good demonstration that nondepressed persons judge themselves more kindly than they are judged. They have a self-generated warm glow of esteem that depressive patients do not have, but I think the idea of depressive realism is less interesting in patients than in nonpatients (such as Alloy and Abramson's college students), because what we should most like to know is whether there is an insidious attributional style, conceivably grounded in reality, that is an antecedent risk factor for clinical depression. In other words, is there a style that renders the individual especially vulnerable to depression in the event that many bad events occur? There is additional evidence of depressive realism (Abramson and Alloy, 1981; Alloy and Abramson, 1982; Golin et al., 1979; Ingram, Smith, and Brehm, 1982) but nothing as yet that answers the hard questions about where the style comes from and how it happens to be realistic.

The self-serving bias in the sense of attributing success, indeed desired outcomes generally (Greenwald, 1980; Taylor, 1983), to internal (actor) causes and failures and other undesired outcomes to external causes seems to me to be established beyond reasonable doubt for nondepressives. That the self-serving attributional style is a bias—that it is not realistic—is less sure but quite likely. When we know that a particular way of understanding life is biased and unrealistic, we are likely to suppose that it must necessarily be maladaptive. Good reality testing has long been considered essential to a well-adapted (healthy) personality (e.g. Erikson, 1963; Maslow, 1954; Menninger, 1963), and from a biological point of view it seems unlikely that organisms that seriously distort reality could survive. If the self-serving bias should prove to be characteristic of the entire human species (or at least the nondepressed majority), how can the genetic basis for such a cognitive tendency have evolved, given the Doctrine of Natural Selection? Several theorists (Greenwald, 1980; Lazarus, 1979; Taylor, 1983) have put forward some very interesting ideas on the possible adaptive functions of self-enhancing cognitive biases.

Taylor and her associates have for more than two years—as of 1983—been intensively interviewing seventy-eight women with breast cancer and have been impressed with the utility of various illusions in helping those women to cope. The self-serving bias, strictly defined, applies to causal attribution, and in this strict sense it seems not to be important for coping with breast cancer.

Whether a woman attributed her cancer to an external cause (some thought a blow to the breast might have been responsible or exposure to a particular environmental carcinogen) or an internal cause (bad dietary habits) did not predict the degree of success in coping with cancer. However, another sort of self-serving bias did. Every woman interviewed thought she was doing as well as, or better than, other women in coping with breast cancer, and that belief seemed to sustain them in their struggle. It is not possible that everyone be doing as well as, or better than, the others, but it is possible for everyone to think so if "the others" with whom comparison is made are picked in a strategic way. Taylor found that all the women made what are called "downward comparisons," which Wills (1981) has shown to be a general reaction to severe threat. The use of downward comparisons may be illustrated with three quotations from the women Taylor interviewed:

1. A woman whose cancer was treated with a lumpectomy (removal of the lump only) rather than a mastectomy (removal of the entire breast): "I had a comparatively small amount of surgery. How awful it must be for women who have had a mastectomy. I just can't imagine . . . "

2. A woman whose cancer was treated with a mastectomy: "It was not tragic. It's worked out okay. Now if the thing had spread all over, I would have had a whole different story for you."

3. An older woman: "The people I really feel sorry for are these young gals. I'm 73; what do I need a breast for?"

In the Taylor study the striking fact is that no woman who had had a mastectomy compared herself with a woman who had had a lumpectomy, and no younger woman compared herself with an older woman. Everyone is better off than someone if you pick the right dimension of comparison, and those women all did. Taylor and many others have suggested that the mind reacts to threat somewhat in the way that the body does to infection, with a set of automatic defensive operations, which are based largely on bias or illusion. There was a dramatic example of that kind of defensive mobilization at the 1983 meetings of the American Psychological Association. A man afflicted with the dread disease AIDS, from which no one at that date had ever recovered, asserted that he would defeat it with positive thinking. And, of course, very many people with cancer say the same thing.

It is easy to see the survival value of self-serving biases based on illusion when they occur in people whose lives are threatened. There are difficult times ahead, painful things to undergo, like radiation and chemotherapy. But some who contract terrible diseases do survive. And when cures or life-prolonging treatments are discovered, it is those who have persisted who will benefit. Greenwald (1980) suggests that self-enhancing illusions help the personality to continue to operate effectively, to persist as long as possible, and so could have survival value.

I have not, as of this date (September, 1985), had to cope with a life-threatening illness, and the main reason why I find it convincing that self-enhancing illusions have value is that I believe I see such illusions operating adaptively even in trifling everyday struggles. I have never met a college professor who did not think he was above the average (of college professors). We cannot all be above average, but we can all think we are if some care is taken in the information supplied us.

A professor's salary is an index of how good he is in the eyes of the administration, and while no one would be so foolish as to confuse that ill-informed, damn fool, Philistine opinion with objective reality, few are so self-confident as to pay it no heed. Harvard releases information on salaries with a merciful regard for the mental health of its professors. Your own salary is between you and the dean; the chairman has no say in the matter and does not even know the facts. When averages are reluctantly given to the press, they are calculated across all ages and departments, so that it is really not possible to make pairwise equity assessments. Some universities, however, provide their professors with exact information on salaries, broken down by department, age, seniority, and so on. That information forces a professor receiving a salary below average for his rank either to get mad or to feel inferior. By my observation, the effects of rubbing in this particular reality are universally deleterious. Half the members of a faculty are deprived of an illusion that is quite important in sustaining commitment and morale. Of course, "grading on the curve" does the same for students, but I feel it less.

We have also to survive student evaluations. At Harvard they are voluntary. You need not have your course and yourself evaluated unless you wish to do so, but few dare say no. Each student gives numerical ratings and also has a large white space, quite like a bathroom wall, which he is invited to fill with comments. My practice has always been to look at the average numerical ratings; one might as well, since they are published for all to read. However, I have never asked the administration to send me the individual student comments to read—though they are ever so keen on doing so. My self-esteem is not so firm that I can discount the possibility of deflation by a well-aimed student barb.

Summary

In everyday life the causes of social action are worked out by a set of inductive principles, and insofar as the layman follows those principles he operates as a kind of intuitive scientist. The principles relate three kinds of information (consensus, distinctiveness, and consistency) to three dimensions of causality. Is the cause internal to the actor or is it external? Is the cause stable or unstable? Is causality simple or complex?

For the most part we do operate with the same inductive principles (the calculus of causality). When people have the same information, they agree about causality. When new information is introduced, people agree about its bearing on causality. In ordinary conversation people understand much more about causality than is expressed in words, because the mental calculus common to all develops the implications in what is given. In that respect causal thinking is like all thinking, and talk about causality is like all talk.

The causal calculus is the bedrock level on which everyone thinks the same way and, furthermore, thinks like an intuitive scientist. It is not the whole story of attribution. Individuals with a depressive outlook seem to have a characteristic attributional style whereby they attribute their own successes (or desirable outcomes in general) to causes that are external, unstable, and specific, and their own failures (or undesirable outcomes in general) to causes that are internal, stable, and global. That style exactly reverses the attributional predilection of most people (normals), which is to attribute their successes to causes that are internal, stable, and global and their failures to causes that are external, unstable, and specific.

The "bright outlook" that is normal has been called the "self-enhancing bias," and the "dark view" of the depressive has been called a "bias against the self." The term "bias" suggests a departure from realism, and the conventional presumption has been that the self-enhancing person is the more realistic person, but recent findings suggest that it may be the depressive who is the more realistic and so the less biased. It may be that normal persons have an unrealistic positive bias and that it helps them to cope with adversity. Depressives may be best characterized as deficient in a bias that is normal and life-sustaining.

5

Systematic Biases in Attribution

FOR ABOUT A DECADE (in 1984) social psychologists have been hot on the trail of three systematic shortcomings of the intuitive scientist. They are not conceived of as shortcomings resulting from individual differences of personality, as is the depressive attributional style, but rather shortcomings thought to characterize laymen in general; not, in effect, individual differences, but characteristics of the generalized human mind. One such shortcoming, the *self-serving bias* (a preference in the actor for attributing desirable actions to internal psychological causes—dispositions in himself—and undesirable actions to the external situation), is already familiar to us.

In 1971 Edward Jones and Richard Nisbett conceptualized the *actor-observer divergence*, which is a tendency in actors to attribute their actions to external situational causes, whereas observers, by contrast, tend to attribute the *same actions* to causes internal to the actors (dispositions such as personality traits). If actors and observers disagree on causes, it is natural to suppose that one or the other is in error. In 1977 Lee Ross proposed that the error lay in the observer's tendency "to underestimate the impact of situational factors and to overestimate the importance of internal dispositional factors." He called that tendency "the fundamental attribution error."

A natural alliance developed between social psychologists studying attribution and personality theorists of what is called the "situationist" school. Mischel (1968), the prototypical situationist, had shown that the faith personality psychology had in global traits, conceived to be stable over time and general over situations, was not justified by the facts then available, which showed mainly instability and specificity; personality assessment correlations were, Mischel showed, characteristically very low, in the vicinity of .30. Attribution theorists, by identifying a general tendency in observers who were laymen to overestimate the importance of internal dispositional causes, had explained how it could happen that personality psychologists would continue to believe in the reality of stable global traits in the face of massive contradictory evidence. It seemed that personality psychologists were making the same fundamental error as laymen.

The systematic shortcomings were at first conceptualized as completely general—human universals. In the case of the self-serving bias, we already know that reasons have appeared for exempting from that very common bias humans who are depressed. Depressed actors appear to lack the bias and show a preference, possibly realistic, for attributing successes externally and failures internally. With time and extensive research, exceptions to the operation of the actor–observer divergence and the fundamental attribution error have also appeared. However, the exceptions in these cases seem to be a matter not of individual differences or of personality, but rather of certain variables in the attribution problem such as perceptual salience, direction of empathy, and differences of knowledge and experience. In effect, the originally monolithic actor–observer divergence and fundamental attribution error have been shattered into a set of more specific factors causing them sometimes to appear and sometimes not. Of course, we do not yet know the end of the story, but the story to date (1984) has incidentally unearthed discoveries of great interest in their own right. First, however, a look at divergence, error, and bias on familiar terrain: obedience to malevolent authority (Chapter 1) and the unresponsive bystander (Chapter 2).

Obedience to Authority and the Unresponsive Bystander

There is one aspect of obedience to authority and the unresponsive bystander that we have not explored. The approach in Chapters 1 and 2 was to attempt as social psychologists, using the best evidence and theory available, to identify the true causes of those phenomena and develop scientific understanding of them. The time has now come to speak of the causes intuitively arrived at by persons involved in the events as either actors or observers. Those intuitive causes are interesting because there is a disagreement—a cleavage or divergence—between actors and observers, which is extremely common when laymen assign causes to social events. Since actor and observer disagree, one must be incorrect, and from the full pattern of evidence on obedience to authority and the unresponsive bystander, it appears to be the observer who is in error.

The actor is, as always, the person performing the action or having the experience to be explained. The observer is a new character in our minimal social script (Abelson, 1981) since he is not someone who might himself be a cause of the action or experience, not someone interacting with the actor; this familiar character is subsumed by us, for reasons previously explained in Chapter 4, under the term "situation." The new character is an onlooker, not an interactant, a person who observes the event or reads of it or knows about it by hearsay and who seeks an intuitive cause for it. The actor and the observer both form causal explanations for *the same event*—an action or experience of the actor. It seems very generally to be the case that actors favor external causes (something in the situation) whereas observers favor (for the same event) internal psychological causes (dispositions in the actor).

In Chapters 1 and 2 we had a liberal advance sampling of actor and observer attributions, but the systematic divergence was not pointed out. Eichmann, the enactor of monstrous deeds, attributed his deeds to orders from above, an external attribution. His judges in Jerusalem and the prosecuting attorney and most of the world attributed just the same deeds to the monstrous character of Eichmann; to fanatic anti-Semitism or sadism—all internal attributions. In Milgram's experiments (1974) on obedience to authority, we know that psychiatrists and behavioral scientists and others who read about the experiment (and so were observers) judged that anyone who delivered 450 volts to an innocent victim must be a psychopath, and that is an internal attribution. We know also that these same observers guessed that fewer than 1 percent of subjects actually would deliver a shock of 450 volts. We can identify that low estimate now as a judgment of low consensus, and because low consensus strictly implies an internal attribution when only simple stable causes are considered (see Table 4-3) and that is the only kind of cause involved in the actor–observer divergence, the guess that very few people would deliver the shock is another way of saying that the cause when the shock is delivered must lie in a queer disposition in the actor.

The most complete and direct demonstration of the divergence in the case of obedience to authority comes from a 1975 experiment (Harvey, Harris, and Barnes, 1975), which used a scenario similar to, but not identical with, Milgram's and added an observer. Both actors (the teachers who delivered shocks) and the observers, who watched the whole thing, were asked to rate the responsibility for what was done of, respectively, the teacher and the experimenter who gave the orders. Actors attributed more responsibility (or causal force) to the experimenters than to themselves (8.4 versus 4.0 on an eleven-point scale). Observers (simply onlookers) reversed that pattern and rated the teachers as primarily responsible, the experimenters less so.

When Kitty Genovese was murdered, while thirty-eight neighbors did nothing to rescue her, people who read about it (observers, therefore) were outraged at the unresponsiveness. At whom or at what were they outraged? The thirty-eight neighbors, not the killer, not the New York police, not anything situational. A. M. Rosenthal, then metropolitan editor of *The New*

York Times, wrote a book called *Thirty-Eight Witnesses* which included the causal explanations of various kinds of "expert" observers—psychiatrists, sociologists, the usual array of savants. The large number of unresponsive neighbors created a certain difficulty for the observer's preference for internal causes; one could hardly call the witnesses all sadists, not thirty-eight in one Kew Gardens apartment. But the human mind is adept at surmounting such impediments to prejudice, and so the experts simply moved to a larger unit in assigning internal causes. "Urban apathy" was the favorite, even though it was obvious that the witnesses had not been apathetic, because they had *watched* for half an hour. The fact is, they were interested. New Yorkers generally thought the thirty-eight ought to be punished somehow, perhaps by having their names listed in the newspaper. The thirty-eight witnesses themselves (the actors) saw the whole thing very differently. The reasons they gave for not responding had nothing to do with their own characters. There was a maniac at large out there. As for calling the police, the New York police were so routinely abusive that no sane person wanted to get involved with them.

Evidence collected incidental to other purposes by two research teams pins down the observer's preference for internal causes when it comes to explaining unresponsive bystanders. In one case (Wells and Harvey, 1977), subjects read an accurate account of one of the Latané and Darley (1970) experimental scenarios inspired by the Genovese case, the "epileptic seizure" scenario with four bystanders, and were told that a certain person named "Greg" had not gone to the rescue. In what degree did these observers (they read about the events) consider Greg's personality (internal attribution) responsible for his unresponsiveness? They thought it was the main factor, and they went on to characterize this hypothetical Greg. They thought he must be extremely "indecisive," "undependable," and, of course, "not helpful." In the second case (Nisbett and Borgida, 1975), readers of the same scenario were asked to guess what percentage of persons would not help the epileptic and guessed 30 percent, a minority. We can now (see Chapter 4) recognize that guess as a judgment of low consensus, and when, as here, only simple stable causes are involved, low consensus strictly entails an internal attribution.

For obedience to authority and the unresponsive bystander, actor and observer attributions clearly diverge. Who is in error? To establish error in the observer it is necessary to have more than attributions. One must have some kind of standard or norm that establishes correctness—from which the observer can be shown to depart. As an ultimate philosophical conception, such norms are difficult to define (Funder, 1982; Harvey, Town, and Yarkin, 1981; Harvey and McGlynn, 1982; Reeder, 1982), but in a rough-and-ready but fairly satisfactory way it is sometimes possible to bring forward evidence that observer attributions are wrong. It is so in the case of obedience to authority and the unresponsive bystander.

The psychiatrists, behavior scientists and others who guessed that fewer than 1 percent of Milgram's subjects would deliver 450 volts and that the 1 percent would be psychopathic were demonstrably in error. We know that, because actually two-thirds of Milgram's subjects delivered 450 volts, and when Elms and Milgram (1966) gave personality tests to the maximally obedient subjects, they proved not to be psychopathic and, in fact, to be almost indistinguishable from maximally rebellious subjects.

The subjects who read the Latané and Darley epileptic seizure scenario (Wells and Harvey, 1977) and guessed that only 30 percent of bystanders would fail to help were in error, because Latané and Darley actually found that 69 percent failed to help in the case described. The subjects might also be said to have been in error in characterizing a hypothetical "Greg," who did not help, as "undependable," "indecisive," and so on, because Latané and Darley found that those who helped were not, on a battery of personality tests, different from those who failed to help.

For obedience and the unresponsive bystander, then, the actor–observer divergence and the fundamental attribution error are substantiated by data. Is there not, however, a more obvious explanation than either: the self-serving bias? Eichmann was, after all, on trial for his life, and Genovese's neighbors were undergoing a kind of trial by public opinion. Simple self-preservation required that they deny responsibility and blame the situation. Milgram's "teachers" and the unresponsive bystanders of Latané and Darley were not under overt attack, but both had done things their own consciences could not approve, and so simple maintenance of self-esteem dictated external attribution. In effect, it looks as if the self-serving bias, with which we are already familiar, offers a sufficient explanation.

The self-serving bias when carefully formulated, as it was in Miron Zuckerman's 1979 review, does not as such account for the *difference* between observer and actor. In fact, the self-serving bias has nothing to say about observers and nothing to say about the fundamental attribution error. Its domain is limited to actors, and the generalization it makes is that actors will favor internal attributions for desirable actions (whether judged against standards of achievement or morality) and external attributions for undesirable actions (failures of achievement or character). The self-serving bias makes the same prediction as the actor–observer divergence for actor attributions in the case of undesirable actions, which is the case that fits obedience and the unresponsive bystander, and it is likely that in such cases motivational (self-serving) and positional considerations combine to overdetermine the actor's denial of responsibility. However, for successes (desirable outcomes) the self-serving bias makes a prediction (internal attribution) contrary to that of the actor–observer divergence (external attribution by the actor), and it is the many studies demonstrating that actors take credit for successes that most strongly support the self-serving bias.

What kinds of evidence will argue for the actor–observer divergence and the fundamental attribution error and yet not be subject to an alternative explanation by the self-serving bias? Essentially attributions for any actions except undesirable actions or failures. In the case of neutral actions, the self-serving bias makes no predictions at all, and so that is a domain specific to the divergence and the error—their unique domain, as it were. Actions that are desirable pose especially strong tests, because the self-serving bias predicts internal attributions and that prediction is contrary to the external attribution always predicted for the actor by the divergence. Studies finding external attributions in those circumstances argue forcefully for the divergence.

The Actor–Observer Divergence

Quite a few studies confirm the actor–observer divergence with respect to either neutral actions or successes. Cunningham, Starr, and Kanouse (1979); Funder (1980); Goldberg (1978); Jones et al. (1968); McArthur (1972); Nisbett et al. (1973); and Storms (1973), among others, all found actors preferring external attributions for their actions and observers preferring internal attributions for the same actions. Unfortunately for simplicity, there are also a few studies that fail to find the predicted divergence (e.g. Funder and Van Ness, 1981; Miller and Norman, 1975; Miller and Porter, 1980). The failure of the divergence to be invariably confirmed has led to the study of specific determinants that can account for both confirmations and disconfirmations. Before turning to that interesting matter, however, we should have a few examples of confirmations. I have chosen three that point clearly to the various determinants of divergence.

One very straightforward prediction from the actor–observer divergence is that if an actor having a conversation with a stranger ("situation" in our mapping) and someone observing the actor are both asked to explain the actor's behavior in the conversation, they will disagree. Storms (1973) created just such a setup. The conversation lasted five minutes, and then both the actor and his observer were asked to rate the actor's friendliness, talkativeness, nervousness, and dominance in the conversation just completed. Each was also asked to say in what degree the actor's behavior in the conversation was probably determined by his personal characteristics—traits, style, attitudes—and in what degree by the situation—the behavior of the external person, the requirement to get acquainted. Actors placed greater importance on situational factors than did observers, and observers placed greater importance on personal characteristics than actors did. That is the predicted divergence.

Notice in the Storms experiment the ways in which the actor's informational position differs from the observer's. The actor's gaze is turned outward at the external person, but the observer was told to watch the actor, so there was a sharp difference in what they attended to. Actors knew about their own past and their own behavior outside the present situation: how friendly, talkative, nervous, and dominant they were generally and on past occasions. Observers knew nothing of that. Finally, actors knew not only how they had behaved but what they had thought and felt, their inner mental life. Observers could know of this only if it were very clear from the actor's facial expression and vocal quality, which it probably was not. Those three differences—orientation of the gaze or visual salience, knowledge of behavior in the past and in other situations, and access to private experience—were all mentioned by Jones and Nisbett in 1971 as possible causes for an actor–observer divergence.

Another straightforward prediction from the actor–observer divergence is that persons describing themselves (which puts them in the role of actors) should be less willing to use unqualified general global trait names (such as *honest, fierce, trustworthy, smart*) than they would be to use such names for people they know, since in the latter case they would be acting as observers. For themselves, persons ought to prefer to say something like: "The word is only occasionally descriptive—in other words, it depends on the situation." Goldberg (1978) made a really massive test of that prediction. He asked fourteen samples of one hundred persons each (half males and half females) to apply (in all) 2,800 trait terms—or else the situational alternative—to themselves as well as to three others they knew well, and also to such public figures as Barbara Walters and Walter Cronkite. The results strongly confirmed the actor–observer divergence. More than 92 percent of the trait terms were more often applied to others than to the self, and 2,800 trait terms just about exhausts the English lexicon in that domain. In this study we notice especially that actors must know more about variations in their own behavior from one situation to another than they could possibly know about variations in anyone else. Barbara Walters and Walter Cronkite, in particular, must be known to them only as roles—interviewer and anchor man—and not really as persons at all.

Finally, we have a prediction that clearly follows from the actor–observer divergence but is less obvious than the predictions tested by Storms (1973) and by Goldberg (1978). College women (the actors) were asked to volunteer some time to entertain potential donors to a university institute that was concerned with learning disabilities in disadvantaged children. Other college women (the observers) were asked to watch the actors, one observer for each actor, as the project was described, and the actor either volunteered or did not. The question then put to the actor and observer was not the obvious attributional one: Did personal characteristics (internal) or the project (external) determine the decision? Instead, both were asked to rate the likelihood that the same woman would volunteer to help in another good cause, the United Fund. In the degree that the single sample of behavior—volunteering or not for the first project—was taken to be a manifestation of a personal characteristic (call it "volunteerism"), the prediction should be that women who had volunteered for one project would volunteer for another. That is what observers thought. It is not what the actors themselves thought, however. Their predictions about themselves, whether they would or would not volunteer to help with the United Fund, were unrelated to what they had done in the first case (no general trait). Notice, once again, that the actors knew how they felt about each project but observers did not, and actors knew, as observers did not, whether they were in the habit of volunteering (Nisbett et al., 1973).

The Fundamental Attribution Error

There are a good many studies that confirm the fundamental attribution error (all those on what is called "correspondent inference" from Jones and Harris [1967] to Miller, Jones and Hinkle [1981], plus Ross, Greene, and House [1977]) but, again unfortunately for simplicity, some that do not (e.g. Ajzen, Dalto, and Blyth, 1979; Quattrone, 1982). In view of the mixed evidence, it is regrettable that when Ross (1977) named the beast, he embedded an evaluation in the title. Now we are stuck with "the fundamental attribution error" and with evidence suggesting that it is not *the* error, but one of several, and also not fundamental in the sense of unanalyzable (Harvey, Town, and Yarkin, 1981, but see Reeder, 1982). Before going into possible determinants causing the error to be sometimes found and sometimes not, we shall deal with the two principal confirmations.

CORRESPONDENT INFERENCE

A series of experiments extending over more than a decade demonstrates the fundamental attribution error in the special case called "correspondent inference." Correspondent inference refers to the tendency we all have to take someone's statement of opinion as a sign of what he believes, to infer from talk (an action) a corresponding attitude (internal attribution). Edward Jones and his associates have been able to show again and again that corresponding attitudes are inferred from statements even when the speaker has been assigned the position to argue (as in a debate) and so would seem to have exercised no choice. In a no-choice situation, the investigators contend, any inference that true opinions are in line with what has been said is an example of the fundamental attribution error, because the situational factor, assignment to a position, is alone a fully sufficient explanation of the actor's performance. To treat that performance as reflective of his private attitude is to underestimate external causes (the situation) and overestimate internal causes (real attitude).

In some studies of correspondent inference (especially Snyder and Jones, 1974), data have been reported that give evidence of attribution *error* that is more direct than the fact of correspondent inference itself in the no-choice situation. Subjects who wrote statements taking an assigned position were also asked to report their true attitudes, and a comparison of those with attitudes inferred from the statements demonstrates that the inferences are in error in that they depart from the true attitudes in the direction of correspondent inference. In correspondent inference experiments the subject, the one asked to infer attitudes, is always in the role of observer; he is explaining another person's action. The question asked the observer is not the brute inquiry: "What do you think caused this person to argue as he did?" Probably observers would answer: "The position he was assigned to take." However, such an accurate answer does not necessarily exclude the possibility that the fundamental attribution error is operating on a subtler level. To get at that subtler possibility subjects are not simply asked to attribute the performance internally or externally but are asked to guess at the real underlying attitude to see whether they infer something internal and dispositional where nothing should be inferred. Note that a test of the fundamental attribution error does not require soliciting attributions from actors (authors of the essays) but only from observers (readers of the essays). It does, however, require that the observers' attributions be shown to be erroneous.

The first experiment (Jones and Harris, 1967) created a design model for all that followed. Subjects (in the observer role) read an essay either for or against Castro's Cuba, and on the basis of just that single short essay (about two hundred words) were asked to guess the writer's true opinion on Castro's Cuba on a scale from 10 (maximum anti) to 70 (maximum pro). The short essay was alleged to have been written under one of three conditions: as an answer to a question on a political science exam asking for (1) *criticism* of Castro's Cuba, (2) a *defense* of Castro's Cuba, or (3) either a defense or a criticism. In short, subjects were led to believe that the essay they read had been either an "assigned" position or a freely chosen position. In the first experiment all the essays were actually written by the investigators, Jones and Harris, and so attribution error could not be demonstrated by comparing the true attitudes of authors with attitudes inferred from their essays.

The results created a pattern that has been repeated again and again; they appear in Table 5–1 in abstract form. It was determined in this first experiment that the subjects themselves (the readers of essays) held clear anti-Castro attitudes. For that reason they would have expected the writers of the essays who were said to be students like themselves also to have anti-Castro attitudes. Therefore, the anti-Castro essays can be said to have had a high "prior probability." They were the expected, the not-surprising thing. The pro-Castro essays, on the other hand, would have been surprising; their prior probability was low. In this first experiment very pro inferred attitudes (cell *a*) had the value of 59.62 on a scale with 70 as maximally pro. Mildly pro inferred attitudes (cell *c*) were 44.10. Mildly anti inferred attitudes were 17.38 in cell *b* and 22.87 in cell *d*. The last two values were not significantly different from each other, and so there is no basis for a distinction between very and mildly anti.

In Table 5–1 correspondent inference is represented by the fact that writers of pro-Castro essays (cells *a* and *c*) were credited with more favorable (pro) attitudes than were writers of anti-Castro essays (cells *b* and *d*). Comparing *a* with *b*, and *c* with *d*, one sees that the attitudes attributed to essay authors were always in line with the essays themselves; that is, the actions (essays) were at-

TABLE 5-1. The Classical Correspondent Inference Effect

	Prior Probability	
	Low (Pro-Castro)	High (Anti-Castro)
Choice	$^{++}(a)$	$^-(b)$
No choice (position assigned)	$^+(c)$	$^-(d)$

Notes: $^{++}$ means very pro; $^+$ means mildly pro; $^-$ means anti. Correspondent inference: $a > b$; $c > d$. Fundamental attribution error: $c > d$

tributed to personal dispositions. The presumed fundamental attribution error appears in Table 5-1 as the occurrence of correspondent inference in a situation of "no choice," a situation in which the position was assigned. The fact that cell c is very different from cell d seems to mean that subjects, essay readers who knew that the positions taken in the essays they read were assigned positions, were underestimating the causal efficacy of the situation (the assignments) and overestimating the importance of personal dispositions, since they inferred correspondent attitudes.

Research subsequent to the first Jones and Harris experiment has definitively shown that the effects of Table 5-1 are not specific to the particular issue of Castro's Cuba but are seemingly completely general across issues. The same effects have been demonstrated, for instance, with respect to pro- and antisegregation attitudes (Jones and Harris, 1967); attitudes on the legalization of marijuana (Jones et al., 1971); attitudes toward free medical care paid by the federal government (Snyder and Jones, 1974); and attitudes on affirmative action (Miller, Baer, and Schonberg, 1979). In 1981 Miller, Jones, and Hinkle showed that correspondent inference was not limited to attitudes at all but could also be obtained for supposedly stable personality traits.

There are two ways in which correspondent inference studies have undertaken to demonstrate that observers (subjects reading essays or listening to taped speeches) commit an error, the fundamental attribution error, when they infer attitudes from essays written under no-choice conditions. The simpler way is to have subjects first report their own attitudes on the issue in question and then themselves write essays on positions assigned to them. The subject-authored essays are then exchanged among subjects so that each reads one written by another, and the reader (the subjects now in the observer role) is asked to infer from the essay the attitude of its author. For each essay, then, one has both the author's attitude and the attitude attributed to the author on the basis of his essay, and a comparison of the two can be considered a test of accuracy or error in the attribution. That was the approach taken by Snyder and Jones (1974) in a series of experiments. They found that readers (observers) persistently misjudged the author's attitude in the direction of the essays they had been constrained to write, the direction of correspondent inference, and the effect was not small but usually amounted to something like one-quarter of the full range on the attitude scale. In short, subjects who have themselves written essays under constraint, when they read essays written by others under the same constraint, draw attitude inferences, incorrect ones, from the essays. This demonstration by itself is enough to establish the existence of some error of the fundamental attribution variety in the case of correspondent inference. It does not show that it is totally erroneous to draw any attitude inferences at all from essays written on assignment.

The second way of establishing error in correspondent inference is a lot trickier, but it is also more instructive. It does not involve any use of true author attitudes; in fact, the essays might be written by the investigators, as they were in Jones and Harris (1967). The argument for error is simply that since the essays are believed to have been written under conditions of no choice, it is totally erroneous to interpret them as expressions of attitude. However, the conditions labeled "no choice" by Jones and Harris (1967) seem to have been too strongly labeled. An observer reading an essay that takes a position alleged to have been assigned on an exam might not see this as a no-choice situation. He might quite reasonably take account of the fact that there is more to an essay than the position taken. There are the quality of the argument used, the artfulness of construction, and persuasiveness of phrasing; if the argument is listened to rather than read, there is the amount of conviction in the voice. From any of those expressive channels an observer might expect to learn something about an author's attitude even though the position taken is known to have been assigned. And it would not be an error, therefore, to think that the argument in its full dimensionality was influenced by the attitude of its author and so to infer attitude from essay.

The Jones and Harris essays had been written by the investigators, and they may simply have been too good, both pro and anti Castro's Cuba, for an observer to believe that they could have been composed without a correspondent conviction. For that reason Snyder and Jones (1974) used essays actually written by subjects on assigned positions. Presumably those essays were not as excellent as those of Jones and Harris, but nevertheless the pattern of data of Table 5-1 was reproduced. However, there is more to an essay than the quality of its arguments.

Miller (1976) had subjects (as observers) guess the real attitudes of persons who read aloud essays that the observers knew had been written by someone else. In other words, the person whose attitude was to be guessed contributed nothing to its construction; not the arguments, not their ordering, not their phrasing. But he did contribute a reading, and that could be more or less convincing. The familiar correspondent inference result was obtained, but one could not say that the observer was in error since a potentially expressive channel, the reading, was uncontrolled.

What all the experiments on correspondent inference come to is this: Observers will draw internal inferences from an actor's behavior unless the actor's behavior is so fully controlled as to be robotlike. Snyder and Jones (1974) had someone (the actor) simply copy in his own hand an essay supplied by someone else, and observers were asked to guess the real attitude of the copyist on the topic treated in the essay. In that condition correspondent inference finally disappeared. Jones considers that last demonstration to be trivial; of course observers do not make internal attributions (or attitude inferences) for an actor who is as externally controlled as a marionette. To do so would be so irrational as to border on insanity. Still, one might argue it is only in that absurdly extreme case that correspondent inference can be said to be, for sure, totally erroneous. Jones and many others believe it is reasonable to speak of error—in fact, of the fundamental attribution error, overestimation of the importance of dispositions and underestimation of the situation—well short of the absurd extreme.

Whether it be error or only a bias (as Harvey, Town, and Yarkin, 1981, and others prefer), correspondent inference is a strong phenomenon, stronger than most of us realized before the experiments were done. Now that they have been done, we can understand a number of mildly odd things. For instance, moviegoers are strongly inclined to attribute to movie actors, especially typecast actors, beliefs, attitudes, and even character traits that correspond with the kinds of lines they read on the screen. But those lines were written for them by others, and they were assigned their parts—perhaps exercising little or no choice. Still, we believe that each is the kind of person he or she habitually plays. And we believe it very strongly. If you do not think so, ask yourself whether George Sanders or Vincent Price would have made as promising a candidate for the Presidency as Ronald Reagan. The American people want a white hat in the White House.

The interesting thing is that the movie example is plagued by the same problem as the research tradition: It is not quite clear that observers (moviegoers) are altogether mistaken. Movie actors are sometimes cast to a particular type not just because they look right for the type, but because someone at the studio senses a good characterological fit. And movie actors are not totally powerless. There are parts they will not play. Probably there is a more than trivial basis for valid inference, and that makes it difficult to convict moviegoers of the fundamental attribution error. A bias there certainly is, and it is most clearly revealed where we know it has gone wrong. Boris Karloff, who played Frankenstein's monster and countless other magnificent horrors, was a cultivated, soft-spoken English gentleman. He would have made a very imposing President, but who wants to vote for the Mummy?

THE INVISIBLE ADVANTAGE

A graduate student once told me that his favorite experiment in all of social psychology was that of Ross, Amabile, and Steinmetz (1977), and it is easy to see why. It exposes the self-presentation advantage that teachers always have over students. In any sort of examination, written or oral, it is the teacher who enjoys the prerogative of making up the questions. Of course, he asks questions to which he himself knows the answer but believes may stump the student. With roles assigned in that way, the teacher is bound to seem more generally knowledgeable than the student. The teacher can select his own areas of expertise and skirt his areas of ignorance, but the student must follow where he leads. The experiment is also a favorite of mine but for a different reason. It always works. We replicate it every year as a laboratory exercise.

Ross and colleagues devised a quiz game in which half of their Stanford University students were randomly assigned the role of quizmaster and half the role of contestant. The person assigned the role of quizmaster was given fifteen minutes in which to compose ten challenging but not unfair or impossible questions. He was encouraged to ask about things he knew well; music or sports or geography or history, but not, of course, to ask about private matters (What is my brother's first name?), which the contestant could not conceivably know. The contestant heard those directions and awaited the quizmaster's questions. The quizmasters made a good job of it and contestants on the average answered only four of the ten questions correctly. When the game was over, both participants were asked to rate their own and their partner's level of general knowledge compared to other Stanford students on a scale from zero to one hundred.

Quizmasters and contestants reacted very differently to the quiz game. Quizmasters saw little difference between themselves and their yoked contestants in general knowledge; they saw themselves and contestants as approximately average (a rating of 50) Stanford students. Contestants took a very different view; they saw their quizmasters as far above average and themselves as well below average.

What happens in this lovely experiment is that contestants treat the brief samples of knowledge displayed in the game as equally representative of the general knowledge of the two participants. Of course, quizmasters in these samples look more knowledgeable; they know ten answers where contestants know only four or so. In truth, of course, the behavior samples are not equally representative. The quizmaster enjoys the great invisible advantage of controlling the topic and question.

Contestants, since they infer differential general knowledge from performances, may be said to attribute the performances to a knowledge differential, to personal dispositions. In doing so, there is no doubt that contestants commit the fundamental attribution error of underestimating the power of the situation. We know, for sure, that it is an error, in this experiment, because Ross and co-workers administered a fair objective test of general knowledge, and quizmasters and contestants were not different from one another.

Why are quizmasters not subject to the same error as are contestants? It should even be agreeable to them to attribute their success in stumping the contestants to their own greater knowledge (self-serving bias), but they do not do it. The reason seems to be that the quizmasters are on the inside of the process of question composition and know they have bypassed many areas of personal ignorance in favor of areas where they know they are better informed than most. They can guess that the contestant would be able to do the same, but he, not having gone through the process, does not realize how selective it has to be. The advantage that is invisible to the contestant is very salient for the quizmaster. That difference of salience, which causes subjects in the contestant role to overlook a situational factor not overlooked by subjects in the quizmaster role, appears to be a leading factor causing the error and the divergence to be found only some of the time.

Salience as an Explanation

In his 1979 review of all the studies demonstrating the fundamental attribution error in the form of correspondent inference, Jones (1979) argues that humans are probably inclined to think that verbal behavior (speech or writing) is caused by psychological factors in the actor, because the actor and his actions are both perceptually salient. Persons are interesting to us. Behavior is vivid and novel and characterized by movement and so is likely to capture attention. In perceptual terms the actor and his actions will usually be figure, whereas the situation will be ground. We tend to make a causal unit of percepts that are salient and contiguous in space and time. Jones sums up this claim in Fritz Heider's (1958) picturesque phrase: "Behavior engulfs the field."

In visual perception, whether of persons or of things, there is an almost irresistible tendency to make a causal unit of two events, both salient to attention and close together in space and time (Koffka, 1935; Nisbett and Ross, 1980). We do it even when we have knowledge that there is no true causality. I used to demonstrate perceived causality in a laboratory course taught in the evening by clapping my hands together just before a flashbulb was set off outside the window. It looks like magic; that is, it looks like cause and effect, though we know it is not. And, of course, the technique of magicians is largely a matter of distracting attention from true mundane causes by making salient causally irrelevant waves and flourishes or magic words. By analogy, we might argue that the actor and his actions exert a kind of natural magic in that they attract attention away from contextual factors that may be causal, such as the fact that a speech was produced under "no-choice" instructions.

Differential salience has been invoked to explain the fact that the contestants of Ross, Amabile, and Steinmetz failed to notice the advantage enjoyed by quizmasters, whereas the latter took full account of it. It has also, we shall see, been invoked to account for the actor–observer divergence in the Storms experiment. With respect to correspondent inference and the fundamental attribution error, the salience explanation predicts that if a situational cause of behavior were somehow made salient, there should be overestimation of the power of the situation and underestimation of dispositional causes (attitudes) in the person. George Quattrone, who studied with Jones, has shown that that is indeed what happens (1982).

A REVERSAL OF CORRESPONDENT INFERENCE

Once again observers read essays (pro or anti nuclear energy) and drew inferences from them, but with certain important changes. This time the observers were given the self-report attitudes (ratings on a scale) of the persons who had actually written the essays in free-choice circumstances, and the essays were entirely congruent with the authors' attitudes and, therefore, fully explained by the attitudes. Because the readers knew the actual attitudes, they were not asked to infer author attitudes from essays but, rather, to say how much they thought the content of the essays might have been influenced by the situation in which they had been written. There ought to have been no reason to attribute any influence at all to the situation since the essays could be entirely accounted for by the known corresponding attitudes of their authors. However, the situation in which the essays were written was made especially salient.

Before reading any essays, observers read a two-page description of the problem of "experimenter bias" in psychological research. This is a real problem, demonstrated in depth by Robert Rosenthal (1966). Experimenters are seldom indifferent to the outcomes of the experiments they run. Quite usually they hope to see one or another favored theory confirmed. Subjects in psychological experiments are sometimes concerned about the experimenter's evaluation of their performance; they sometimes want to do a good job for the experimenter. The result, observers were told, is that careless experimenters may, by unwitting subtle signals, convey to subjects what kind of outcome they hope for, and when subjects are anxious to please, they may, also unwittingly, perform in such a way as to produce the hoped-for result. Bias in the experimenter and "evaluation anxiety" in subjects can combine to produce a biased result. All that is quite true (see Chapter 14).

The report to essay readers actually much understated the dangers of experimenter bias—stressing the fact that such bias was far from inevitable and occurred only from time to time. Still, the possibility was made clear to observers before they read the essays and were told the true attitudes (on nuclear energy) of the authors. What the observers were asked to infer from the essays was the extent to which essay content seemed to have been determined by the situation in which they had been written. How important did readers think experimenter bias had been in determining the essays? Observers had not been present when the essays were written, so they had to guess at the force of the situation from the essay itself.

In fact, no experimenter bias had existed. All essays were written and all attitudes reported in the same session run by the same female experimenter, who expected only to find a range of opinion on nuclear energy. The writers of the essays were naive subjects arguing the position of their choice. The essays of six extremely pro–nuclear energy authors were given to observers and also the essays of six extremely anti–nuclear energy authors. The authors of the essays themselves were told about the possibility of bias and asked whether they had experienced any, and they were sure they had not. Furthermore, their essays were entirely in line with their self-reported attitudes. In those circumstances, Quattrone reasoned, if readers of the essays were to infer situational biases congruent with the essays they read—a pro bias, in the situation, for pro essays and an anti bias, in the situation, for anti essays—they would be reversing the fundamental attribution error. It would be a reversal because they would be overestimating the importance of the situation and underestimating the importance of the disposition (the truly reported attitude). The result would clearly be an error, because the attitude was fully sufficient to account for its corresponding essay and because there had really been no bias in the situation and the authors had felt none.

The fundamental attribution error *was* reversed. The extent of the inferred situational cause was indicated on a thirteen-point scale from $+6$ (maximally pro) to -6 (maximally anti). The overall result went like this: For pro essays the *situational* determinant was estimated as $+4.16$ whereas for anti essays the *situational* determinant was estimated as -5.84. In other words, from the essays, strongly correspondent inferences were made, not to attitudes now, but to the salient situation.

Quattrone's experiment, if his explanation of it is correct, changes "the fundamental attribution error" into an error that is ultimately dependent on the relative salience of actor and situation. Quattrone's own position, and also that of Edward Jones, is that "the error" is *actuarily* entitled to its special status. That is to say it is usually the case that situations are less salient and persons more salient and so usually the case that the causal efficacy of situations is underestimated and the efficacy of actor dispositions overestimated. Just why that is so, what the selection value of such a bias might be in the evolution of the species, is a deep and difficult question that will not be discussed here.

When Jones and Nisbett introduced the actor–observer divergence in 1971, they suggested that one of its causes might be that "different aspects of the available information are salient for actors and observers" (p. 85). The actor is bound to look outward to the external world, which can include another person ("situation" focus) interacting with him. The observer, tuned to explain the actor's behavior, will turn his visual regard on the actor. Michael Storms asked the fascinating question: What would happen if, by some technical means, actors were put in the position of looking at themselves and observers were given the outward view the actor normally has? Could actors be turned into observers and observers into actors, thereby reversing the normal divergence?

A REVERSAL OF THE ACTOR-OBSERVER DIVERGENCE

Storms (1973), you may recall, confirmed the usual actor–observer divergence by having both rate the actor's friendliness, talkativeness, nervousness, and dominance in an immediately preceding get-acquainted conversation and then having both say how responsible personal traits were for the behavior and how responsible the situation (including the person the actor faced, who is not, please recall, the observer). There was more than that to the Storms experiment, and we need to know more about his experimental situation. The description here preserves the essentials but is somewhat simplified for expository purposes.

Two strangers are introduced and seated opposite each other at a table. They are to have a five-minute get-acquainted conversation. We designate them $actor_1$ and $actor_2$, but it is necessary to remember that from the standpoint of either actor the other, his interactant, is, by our definition, part of the situation. In this case each actor's situation is another person. Present at the conversation are two nonspeakers who will function as passive observers. Each is asked to direct his gaze at just one actor and to devote all his attention to that actor: the one seated diagonally across from him. $Observer_1$ is the observer of $actor_1$, and $observer_2$ is the observer of $actor_2$. Figure 5–1a maps the situation, in which lines of regard are normal: The actor looks out at the external situation, and the observer looks at the actor. In this situation (attributing the friendliness, talkativeness, nervousness, and dominance of the actors) the actor–observer divergence was confirmed; for instance, $actor_1$ made external attributions (mainly to $actor_2$) whereas $observer_1$, the observer of $actor_1$, attributed expressed friendliness, talkativeness, and so forth to dispositions internal to $actor_1$.

In addition to actors and observers, Storms had video cameras trained on $actor_1$ and $actor_2$. Under a cover story he then exposed all participants to a replay of the conversation on videotape with the tapes being assigned in such a way as to cause some participants to see again what they had seen the first time (same orientation) and others to see the reverse of what they had originally seen (Figure 5–1b).

For the sake of simplicity consider only $actor_1$ and his observer ($observer_1$). In the actual conversation $actor_1$ looked outward, but in reversed orientation he looked at a videotape of himself, which, as far as visual regard is concerned, put him in the position of $observer_2$. The reversed tape turned an actor into an observer. $Observer_1$ had initially looked at $actor_1$, but in reversed orientation he looked where $actor_1$ would normally look—outward at the situation, or $actor_2$. The essential question was whether reversing visual lines of regard could cause actors to make the internal (to themselves) orientations normally made by observers and also cause observers to make the external (to the actor) attributions normally made by actors. That is what happened.

What exactly has Storms shown? Someone has participated in a conversa-

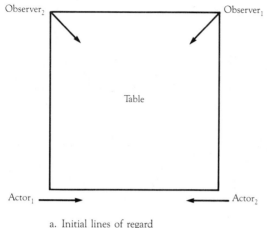

a. Initial lines of regard

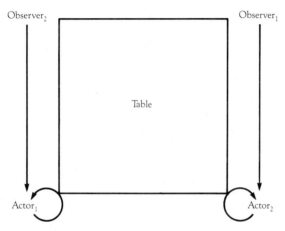

b. Reversed orientation lines of regard

Figure 5–1. Normal and reversed orientations in the Storms experiment

tion and been more or less friendly, talkative, nervous, and dominant. Usually he would think he has acted as he has on this occasion mainly because of the nature of the conversation and the way his partner "came on." In short, his own manner has been drawn out of him by external factors. But now, in this extraordinary case, he has just been shown a videotape of the way he himself looked and acted in the conversation. Probably he is quite surprised to see what he looked like, and as an observer of himself he is inclined to think that he must have acted the way he did in part because he is a certain sort of person and has certain internal dispositions.

To see yourself as others see you and assume personal responsibility for your actions is sometimes a goal of psychotherapy. It is a goal not easily achieved by means of talk. The reversed orientation videotape does very directly and powerfully cause you to see yourself as one other saw you on a particular occasion, and it also increases dispositional attributions (personal responsibility). It is not surprising, therefore, that videotape confrontation has often been tried in therapy. In marital therapy, Kagan, Krathwohl, and Miller (1963) have reported that one or more partners in a bad relationship are more willing to assume personal blame after seeing themselves on videotape.

If you have seen yourself in a candid home movie, you will know that it can be a powerful experience, and you might guess that its effects are not always benign. And that has proved to be the case with self-confrontation by videotape. An alcoholic who fancies that he successfully conceals his drinking or perhaps that he is attractively ebullient when deeply in liquor may have his self-esteem brutally damaged by videotape (Paredes et al., 1969) and may, as a consequence, drink more rather than less. A depressed person who is perhaps already all too inclined to blame himself for everything untoward that happens may have his morbidity increased by self-confrontation. In general, self-image feedback by means of videotape appears to be a potentially very powerful experience that cannot be casually used in psychotherapy.

What the Storms experiment accomplished was the separation of two things that in normal life are invariably conjoined: (1) the role of actor, the person who produces the behavior to be explained, and (2) an outward-aimed, away from the actor, visual perspective. When those two variables were disentangled, it turned out that the causal perspective conformed to the visual perspective; that is, actors made to look at themselves made attributions not normally associated with actors (situations) but, rather, attributions usually made by observers (dispositional). The role of observer was similarly separated from the usual visual orientation, and attributions were in accord with visual orientation rather than role.

Visual orientation is an index of perceptual salience, and we can count the Storms experiment as another demonstration that salience is a determinant of perceived causality. Since the actor's orientation is normally outward and the observer's is normally aimed at the actor, it would seem to follow that the actor–observer divergence merits special status for the same reason that the fundamental attribution error does; both are more usual than their alternatives and so have an actuarial claim on importance.

SALIENCE GENERALLY

Shelley Taylor and Susan Fiske (1978) have put forward a general claim that perceptual salience determines perceived causality not just in the case of a single actor and a single observer, but also where there are multiple actors and/or observers, and the salience of any one is not *a priori* likely to be greater than the salience of any other. Taylor and Fiske have arbitrarily manipulated salience to see whether causality follows its lead. We need examples.

Six observers were watching a dialogue, and the experimenters had seated them so that for two observers one actor was salient; for two other observers the second actor; and for the remaining observers two actors were equally salient. Observers were asked to say how important each actor had been for setting the tone of the conversation, determining the information exchange, and how much talking each participant did. The observers assigned greater causal responsibility to the actors who had been made salient for them.

Perceptual salience was more interestingly manipulated (Taylor et al., 1978) by creating groups in which one person would stand out by reason of race or sex. It has been demonstrated many times with nonsocial stimuli (Berlyne, 1960) that novelty attracts selective attention. If one contrasts groups with a solo black with groups having all black members, then the novel person should be disproportionately salient and so credited with greater causal efficacy than other group members. The same prediction can be made for a group consisting of one woman and a number of men as opposed to groups in which all members are of the same sex. And when many other things are held constant, that is the way it goes; the novel person in a given context is perceived as an especially important cause of what happens in the group. Taylor and Fiske (1978; also Duval and Hensley, 1977; Duval and Wicklund, 1973) have amassed a great weight of evidence that attentional salience predicts perceived causality.

Psychological Perspective as an Explanation

The Storms experiment holds great fascination for me. I keep trying to check its findings against my own experience. There is one sort of experience in which the findings of the experiment seem to point to the wrong conclusion, and that is what happens at the movies. Any movie would probably demonstrate the point, but it first occurred to me in connection with the movie *Tess*, based on Thomas Hardy's *Tess of the D'Urbervilles*. In that film Roman Polanski's camera certainly spends a disproportionate amount of time focused on the radiant face of Nastassia Kinski (Tess). The division of camera closeup time between, for instance, Tess and the blackguard who seduces her must be on the order of ten to one. The observer (here the moviegoer) strongly identifies with Tess and adopts her causal point of view. The man acts as he does because he is a blackguard, whereas poor Tess is bullied and frightened into submission. Of course, one says, Tess is, after all, the heroine. Yes, but the perceived causality outcome is not the one predicted by the Storms experiment. Polanski's camera does not consistently give us Tess's visual perspective or line of regard. On the contrary, it gives us the perspective of her vile seducer (we look at Tess), and so the

Storms outcome says that we ought to see her dispositionally and the man situationally; we ought to see his actions drawn out of him by her.

Watching the film a second time, I developed a hunch about how it is that Polanski's camera angles serve to give us Tess's causal perspective. We do not look always and only at Tess, nor do we observe from a distance, as in the Storms experiment. What happens instead is that we look often but briefly and at a distance at her seducer and then lingeringly at Tess, usually in closeup, and on Tess's face we read her reaction to the man. It gives us the seducer not as he objectively is but as he is perceived by Tess. The back-and-forth movement of the camera gives us not Tess's visual perspective but rather her psychological perspective. Perhaps when two persons are involved it is ultimately the psychological perspective we receive that determines the causal view we take rather than something so mechanical as the visual line of regard.

One experiment (Regan and Totten, 1975) suggests that psychological perspective is what matters and that psychological perspective can even be manipulated by instructions (see also Gould and Sigall, 1977). The basic situation was much like that of the Storms experiments. Subjects were all in the observer role, and what they looked at was a videotape of a real get-acquainted conversation between two women. Some subjects were only observers and were instructed to watch either the woman on the left or the woman on the right. Other subjects were not directed to look at only one woman but were given instructions designed to create in them the psychological perspective of one woman or the other:

> While you are watching this "get-acquainted" conversation, please try to empathize with Margaret, the girl on the left side of the screen. Imagine how Margaret feels as she engages in the conversation. . . . Think about her reaction to the information she is receiving from the conversation. In your mind's eye, you are to visualize how it feels to Margaret to be in this conversation. [Regan and Totten, 1975, pp. 852–53]

After watching the conversation, all observers, empathizers as well as mere viewers, were asked, as in the Storms experiment, to rate the target person's behavior with respect to friendliness, talkativeness, nervousness, and dominance and then to indicate the degree to which they thought this behavior had been caused by situational factors as opposed to dispositional factors. Observers who were only viewers, comparable to the observers in the Storms experiment, showed the expected tendency to think of dispositional factors as more important than situational factors. Observers given instructions selectively to empathize ought, if the instructions served to give them the psychological perspective of the person empathized with—the target person—to have assigned the greater causal efficacy to the situation. And that is what they did.

The selective empathy instructions did not direct an observer to look only at one person and did not even suggest any particular division of viewing time between the two participants. And, in fact, empathizers varied considerably in how much of the time they devoted to the empathic target. What is particularly interesting, in view of the problem that cinematic technique poses for the visual perspective results of Storms, is the fact that those who gave situational factors (the external person) greater weight tended to spend more time looking at the empathic target. Remember that the actor's bias is to overestimate situational factors. It looks as if, in the Regan and Totten experiment as in movie closeups, one is most likely to adopt the psychological perspective of the actor and so participate in the actor's bias if one looks not at the external situation, as the actor does, but at the actor's face, which is the situation—as experienced by the actor.

To summarize what we know about visual orientation and psychological perspective: In the everyday case, in which the usual actor–observer divergence appears actors look outward at the situation and attribute their actions to the situation, whereas observers look at the actor and attribute the actions to dispositions internal to the actor. In the Storms experiment with reversed orientations, actors look at themselves and attribute to themselves, whereas observers look at the situation (an interactant other) and attribute to the situation. In the Taylor and Fiske experiments, in which observers are caused to look mainly at one actor rather than another, they attribute causality to the one they look at. Thus far all results follow the same rule: Attributors locate primary causality in whomever they look at. This rule is broken by the movie *Tess*, because Tess is the person looked at most, but primary causality is attributed externally—not to Tess, but to her seducer, which is the way Tess herself sees things. The Regan and Totten experiment, for persons instructed to empathize selectively, is like the movie *Tess* in that the person looked at most is the person with whom one empathizes and empathizers do not attribute causality *to* the one looked at but, rather, attribute causality *in the way that* that person does—externally.

What the full set of results suggests is that there are two ways of *looking at* someone. If you look simply at action or behavior, large muscle movement, you attribute causality to the actor. If you look closely, at expressive behavior, not gross actions, you are in effect looking at the mental state of the actor, and you attribute his actions not *to him*, but *in the way that he does*, and that is to the situation. It is an implication of this view that the actuarial dominance of the usual actor–observer divergence is caused by the fact that most looking-at is of the first type, looking at gross behavior rather than the finer expressive behavior which usually requires close examination and, of course, unguardedness in the actor—no reason to conceal the expression of feeling. It is also an implication of this position that the usual actor–observer divergence should be eliminated if the observer is able to see fine physiognomic and gestural expressions, and these are not deliberately falsified by the actor.

Recall, if you will, the experiment confirming the actor–observer divergence in which college women, under observation, either did or did not volunteer to help in one good cause (entertaining potential donors to an institute). The question then asked of both actor and observer was: Would you (this woman) volunteer to help also with the United Fund? Actors' predictions were unrelated to what they did the first time. Observers' predictions were that those who had volunteered once would volunteer again, and those who had not volunteered the first time would not the second time. What did actors know that observers did not? They knew their minds. They knew what was or was not attractive about the first cause and how much the United Fund resembled, in their view, the first cause.

Instructions to empathize and that special way of "looking at" that takes in expressive movements are presumably just two ways in which the observer can tune in to the actor's psychological perspective, two ways of many. In criminal trials it is the primary goal of the prosecution to bring the jury to adopt the psychological perspective of the victim and so attribute what was done to traits internal to the accused: lust, viciousness, criminality, whatever it takes to make the accused deserving of punishment. The reciprocal task of the defense is to bring the jury to take the perspective of the accused (the person being defended) and so attribute what he did externally to a come-on from the defendant, a scam, an entrapment. Each attorney works at his goal in many ways, including sympathetic biographical information and careful attention to the appearance and expressive behavior of his client.

The Divergence in A Long Day's Journey into Night

Each member of the Tyrone family in O'Neill's play believes that his or her behavior is externally caused, drawn out or forced by the environment. However, each Tyrone usually sees the behavior of other Tyrones as rising out of character. Father is a "dirty miser" to his sons; son James is a blackguard to his father; son Edmund a weakling to his father; and Mary a "dope fiend" to Edmund. The accusations may be directly made, but more often they are made by the information latent in a sentence that does not explicitly call names. Father Tyrone, for instance, says of son James: "He's forever making sneering fun of somebody, that one" (O'Neill, 1956, p. 18). The event to be explained may be expressed as "James—makes sneering fun of—somebody." "Forever" clearly asserts high consistency. But high consistency in Table 4-3 is associated with both a situation attribution and an actor attribution. How can we tell that it is the latter Tyrone has in mind? From the word "somebody." This indefinite form says that nobody in particular elicits sneering fun from James, but just anybody, and so the situation is low on distinctiveness, and the attribution (Table 4-3) must be to the actor. James himself, however, does not see his sneering fun as internally caused, and he also does not see it as low on distinctiveness. It is drawn from him by deserving others, most frequently and especially his "dirty miser" of a father.

Some of the most powerful scenes of the play are ones in which one Tyrone brings another Tyrone to his own point of view. Father's "miserliness" (a personality trait) is, in the sons' eyes, the evident cause of the family's wretched state. Years ago that trait led him to hire a cheap quack doctor to treat Mary when she was ill, and that doctor prescribed the morphine that initiated Mary's addiction. In the course of the long day that contains the action of the play, Tyrone plans, when Edmund is discovered to have consumption, to send him to some "cheap dump" of a state sanatorium where, the boys believe, he will surely die. In Act IV Tyrone moves Edmund out of his judgmental observer's role and puts him inside the "miser's" own skin. Learning for the first time of the harrowing poverty of Tyrone's childhood, Edmund must feel as Tyrone does that his compulsive penuriousness was created by his life circumstances.

In fact, however, something happens in this encounter between Edmund and his father that goes deeper than the actor–observer divergence. It is not quite enough, in my opinion, to say that Edmund is brought to take the actor's view of the causes of his father's behavior. The changed perspective involves more than causality; it involves responsibility. An actor who is responsible for his action is the cause of it, to be sure, but he can, in addition, be held *accountable* for it. If the consequences have been bad, he is guilty and may be blamed. In the law a person is not automatically held to be accountable or responsible for everything that he causes. If, in washing a window, you could not have foreseen that the window would break and so cannot be thought to have intended it, you are not responsible for the "accident." Responsibility entails, in addition to causality, some notion of *intent*, and it is generally held that any consequences that can be foreseen may be regarded as intended even if not consciously planned. What Tyrone ultimately convinces Edmund of concerns responsibility more than causality.

One consequence of Tyrone's penuriousness proves more important than anything else in changing Edmund's view. The compulsive fear of poverty caused young Tyrone, the most promising classical actor of his day, to forswear Shakespeare in order to tour year after year in the sure-fire melodrama, *The Count of Monte Cristo*, with the ultimate consequence that his talent decayed and his youthful ideals were not realized. Why should that fact above all have brought Edmund to believe that his father was not responsible for Mary's addiction and the myriad other results of penny-pinching? It is overwhelmingly persuasive because Tyrone cannot be supposed to have intended to destroy his own life and cannot have foreseen that he was doing so. And if that consequence was not intended, the others also were not.

In the end, when we know everything about the Tyrones, we must take the view of causality and, more exactly, of responsibility in this family that Mary expresses:

> None of us can help the things life has done to us. They're done before you realize it, and once they're done they make you do other things until at last everything comes

between you and what you'd like to be, and you've lost your true self forever. [Act II, p. 61]

Long Day's Journey demonstrates that the causal calculus of Table 4–3 is in the minds of all the characters in O'Neill's profoundly psychological play. Speech after speech requires that we impute the laws of causal induction to the Tyrones and to the O'Neills. *Long Day's Journey* also draws us into psychological matters that are not captured by the causal calculus nor as yet by any systematic psychological theory. There is no surprise in that. Of course, a great work of literature *implicitly* utilizes a human psychology that is deeper than the principles of psychology *explicitly* known to us today. What is encouraging for psychology is the fact that so good a play is always consistent with the principles we know and suggestive of new principles not far beyond our present reach.

Summary

Attributors may disagree with one another in a systematic way that is not a function of personality or motivation but of role in the minimal social script. In the minimal script the actor is the one producing the action or having the experience to be explained, and the observer is an onlooker, not himself a causal factor, who offers a causal explanation of the actor's behavior or experience. The attributions of actor and observer commonly diverge in such a way that the actor favors external causes and the observer favors causes internal to the actor (psychological dispositions). Since actor and observer commonly disagree in their explanations of the same event, one or the other is likely to be in error. When a criterion for error is available, it is the observer who is typically in error, and the observer's tendency to overestimate dispositional causes and underestimate situational causes has been called "the fundamental attribution error."

Neither the actor–observer divergence nor the fundamental attribution error occurs invariably, so there is an ongoing effort to discover more basic determinants causing them sometimes to occur and sometimes not. One such determinant appears to be perceptual salience, which for the actor usually favors the situation as cause and for the observer favors the actor. When those usual relative saliences are reversed, it appears that both the actor–observer divergence and the fundamental attribution error can also be reversed. Probably the actor–observer divergence and the fundamental attribution error have a special status that is only actuarial; they are the common systematic tendencies. The perceptually salient factor in the minimal social script is more generally the factor assigned the larger causal role.

While the attributions made by observers of an actor and an interacting other can generally be predicted from perceptual salience, it seems likely that this is not the ultimate determinant. Probably perceptual salience is only one factor among many that influence the psychological perspective taken by the observer. If he is made to share the perspective of the actor, he will attribute causality not *to the actor,* but *as the actor does,* and if he is made to share the perspective of the interacting other, he will attribute causality as the other does.

Since there are several powerful factors that can cause individuals to disagree about the causes of social action, factors of motivation and outlook, it is not surprising that social life is thick with argument about causes. In the courts, in marriages, in therapy sessions, and in the General Assembly of the United Nations, attributional squabbling is incessant and entrenched positions painfully familiar. The causal calculus, the shared rules of induction, represents the hope of rationality.

References for Part II

ABELSON, R. P. 1981. Psychological status of the script concept, *American Psychologist*, 36: 715-29.

ABRAMSON, L. Y., and L. B. ALLOY. 1981. Depression, nondepression, and cognitive illusions: Reply to Schwartz, *Journal of Experimental Psychology: General*, 110: 436-47.

ABRAMSON, L. Y.; M. E. P. SELIGMAN; and J. D. TEASDALE. 1978. Learned helplessness in humans: Critique and reformulation, *Journal of Abnormal Psychology*, 87: 49-74.

AJZEN, I.; C. A. DALTO; and D. P. BLYTH. 1979. Consistency and bias in the attribution of attitudes, *Journal of Personality and Social Psychology*, 37: 1871-76.

ALLOY, L. B., and L. Y. ABRAMSON. 1979. Judgment of contingency in depressed and nondepressed students: Sadder but wiser? *Journal of Experimental Psychology: General*, 108: 441-85.

——. 1980. The cognitive component of human helplessness and depression: A critical analysis. In J. Garber and M. E. P. Seligman (eds.), *Human Helplessness: Theory and Application*. New York: Academic Press, pp. 59-70.

——. 1982. Learned helplessness, depression, and the illusion of control, *Journal of Personality and Social Psychology*, 42: 1114-26.

BECK, A. T. 1967. *Depression: Clinical, Experimental, and Theoretical Aspects*. New York: Harper & Row.

——. 1976. *Cognitive Therapy and the Emotional Disorders*. New York: International Universities Press.

BERGLAS, S., and E. E. JONES. 1978. Drug choice as a self-handicapping strategy in response to noncontingent success, *Journal of Personality and Social Psychology*, 36: 405-17.

BERLYNE, D. E. 1960. *Conflict, Arousal, and Curiosity*. New York: McGraw-Hill.

CUNNINGHAM, J. D.; P. A. STARR; and D. E. KANOUSE. 1979. Self as actor, active observer, and passive observer: Implications for causal attributions, *Journal of Personality and Social Psychology*, 37: 1146-52.

DIVITTO, B., and L. Z. McARTHUR. 1978. Developmental differences in the use of distinctiveness, consensus, and consistency information for making causal attributions, *Developmental Psychology*, 14: 474-82.

DUVAL, S., and V. HENSLEY. 1977. Extensions of objective self-awareness theory: The focus of attention-causal attribution hypothesis. In J. H. Harvey, W. J. Ickes, and R. F. Kidd (eds.), *New Directions in Attribution Research*. Hillsdale, N.J.: Lawrence Erlbaum Associates, 1: 165-98.

DUVAL, S., and R. A. WICKLUND. 1973. Effects of objective self-awareness on attribution of causality, *Journal of Experimental Social Psychology*, 9: 17-31.

ELMS, A. C., and S. MILGRAM. 1966. Personality characteristics associated with obedience and defiance toward authoritative command, *Journal of Experimental Research in Personality*, 1: 282-89.

ERIKSON, E. H. 1963. *Childhood and Society*. New York: W. W. Norton (1950).

FUNDER, D. C. 1980. The "trait" of ascribing traits: Individual differences in the tendency to trait ascription, *Journal of Research in Personality*, 14: 376-85.

FUNDER, D. C. 1982. On the accuracy of dispositional versus situational attributions, *Social Cognition*, 1: 205–22.

FUNDER, D. C., and M. J. VAN NESS. 1981. On the nature and accuracy of attributions that change over time. In B. Moore (chair), *Attributions Over Time.* Symposium presented at the annual meeting of the American Psychological Association, Los Angeles, August.

GELB, A., and B. GELB. 1962. *O'Neill.* New York: Harper.

GOLDBERG, L. R. 1978. The differential attribution of trait-descriptive terms to oneself as compared to well-liked, neutral, or disliked others: A psychometric analysis, *Journal of Personality and Social Psychology*, 36: 1012–28.

GOLIN, S.; F. TERRELL; J. WEITZ; and P. L. DROST. 1979. The illusion of control among depressed patients, *Journal of Abnormal Psychology*, 88: 454–57.

GOULD, R., and H. SIGALL. 1977. The effects of empathy and outcome on attribution: An examination of the divergent perspectives hypothesis, *Journal of Experimental Social Psychology*, 13: 480–91.

GREENWALD, A. G. 1980. The totalitarian ego: Fabrication and revision of personal history, *American Psychologist*, 35: 603–18.

HARVEY, J. H.; B. HARRIS; and R. D. BARNES. 1975. Actor–observer differences in the perceptions of responsibility and freedom, *Journal of Personality and Social Psychology*, 32: 22–28.

HARVEY, J. H., and R. P. McGLYNN. 1982. Matching words to phenomena: The case of the fundamental attribution error, *Journal of Personality and Social Psychology*, 43: 345–46.

HARVEY, J. H.; J. P. TOWN; and K. L. YARKIN. 1981. How fundamental is "the fundamental attribution error?" *Journal of Personality and Social Psychology*, 40: 346–49.

HEIDER, F. 1958. *The Psychology of Interpersonal Relations.* New York: Wiley.

———. 1980. On balance and attribution. In D. GÖRLITZ (ed.), *Perspectives on Attribution Research and Theory.* Cambridge, Mass.: Bellinger.

INGRAM, R. E.; T. W. SMITH; and S. S. BREHM. 1982. Depression and information processing, *Journal of Personality and Social Psychology*, 45: 412–20.

JONES, E. E. 1979. The rocky road from acts to dispositions, *American Psychologist*, 34: 107–17.

JONES, E. E., and V. A. HARRIS. 1967. The attribution of attitudes, *Journal of Experimental Social Psychology*, 3: 1–24.

JONES, E. E., and R. E. NISBETT. 1971. The actor and the observer: Divergent perceptions of the causes of behavior. In E. E. Jones, D. E. Kanouse, H. H. Kelley, R. E. Nisbett, S. Valins, and B. Weiner (eds.), *Attribution: Perceiving the Causes of Behavior.* Morristown, N.J.: General Learning Press, pp. 79–94.

JONES, E. E.; L. Rock; K. G. SHAVER; G. R. GOETHALS; and L. M. WARD. 1968. Pattern of performance and ability attribution: An unexpected primacy effect, *Journal of Personality and Social Psychology*, 10: 317–40.

JONES, E. E.; S. WORCHEL; G. R. GOETHALS; and J. GRUMET. 1971. Prior expectancy and behavioral extremity as determinants of attitude attribution, *Journal of Experimental Social Psychology*, 7: 59–80.

KAGAN, N.; D. R. KRATHWOHL; and R. MILLER. 1963. Stimulated recall in therapy using videotape: A case study, *Journal of Counseling Psychology*, 10: 237–43.

KELLEY, H. H. 1967. Attribution theory in social psychology. In D. Levine (ed.), *Nebraska Symposium on Motivation*. Lincoln: University of Nebraska Press, 15: 192–240.

KELLEY, H. H. (1972). Attribution in social interaction. In E. E. Jones, D. E. Kanouse, H. H. Kelley, R. E. Nisbett, S. Valins, and B. Weiner (eds.), *Attribution: Perceiving the Causes of Behavior*. Morristown, N.J.: General Learning Press, pp. 1–26.

KOFFKA, K. 1935. *Principles of Gestalt Psychology*. New York: Harcourt Brace.

KOVACS, M., and A. T. BECK. 1977. An empirical-clinical approach toward a definition of childhood depression. In J. G. Schulterbrandt and A. Raskin (eds.), *Depression in Childhood: Diagnosis, Treatment, and Conceptual Models*. New York: Raven.

KRANTZ, D. S.; D. C. GLASS; and M. L. SNYDER. 1974. Helplessness, stress, and the coronary-prone behavior pattern, *Journal of Experimental Social Psychology*, 10: 284–300.

LATANÉ, B., and J. M. DARLEY. 1970. *The Unresponsive Bystander: Why Doesn't He Help?* New York: Appleton-Century-Crofts.

LAZARUS, R. S. 1979. Positive denial: The case of not facing reality, *Psychology Today*, 12: 44–60.

LEWINSOHN, P. M.; W. MISCHEL; W. CHAPLIN; and R. BARTON. 1980. Social competence and depression: The role of illusory self-perceptions, *Journal of Abnormal Psychology*, 89: 203–12.

MASLOW, A. H. 1954. *Motivation and Personality*. New York: Harper & Row.

MENNINGER, K. 1963. *The Vital Balance*. New York: Viking.

McARTHUR, L. A. 1972. The how and what of why: Some determinants and consequences of causal attribution, *Journal of Personality and Social Psychology*, 22: 171–93.

MILGRAM, S. 1974. *Obedience to Authority*. New York: Harper & Row.

MILLER, A. G. 1976. Constraint and target effects in the attribution of attitudes, *Journal of Experimental Social Psychology*, 12: 325–39.

MILLER, A. G.; R. BAER; and P. SCHONBERG. 1979. The bias phenomenon in attitude attribution: Actor and observer perspectives, *Journal of Personality and Social Psychology*, 37: 1421–31.

MILLER, A. G.; E. E. JONES; and S. HINKLE. 1981. A robust attribution error in the personality domain, *Journal of Experimental Social Psychology*, 17: 587–600.

MILLER, D. T., and S. A. NORMAN. 1975. Actor–observer differences in perceptions of effective control, *Journal of Personality and Social Psychology*, 31: 503–15.

MILLER, D. T., and C. A. PORTER. 1980. Effects of temporal perspective on the attribution process, *Journal of Personality and Social Psychology*, 40: 532–41.

MILLER, D. T., and M. ROSS. 1975. Self-serving biases in the attribution of causality: Fact or fiction? *Psychological Bulletin*, 82: 213–25.

MILLER, I. W., and W. H. NORMAN. 1979. Learned helplessness in humans: A review and attribution theory model, *Psychological Bulletin*, 86: 93–118.

MISCHEL, W. 1968. *Personality and Assessment*. New York: Wiley.

NISBETT, R. E., and E. BORGIDA. 1975. Attribution and the psychology of prediction, *Journal of Personality and Social Psychology*, 32: 932–43.

NISBETT, R. E.; C. CAPUTO; P. LEGANT; and J. MARECEK. 1973. Behavior as seen by the actor and as seen by the observer, *Journal of Personality and Social Psychology, 27:* 154–64.

NISBETT, R., and L. ROSS. 1980. *Human Inference: Strategies and Shortcomings of Social Judgment.* Englewood Cliffs, N.J.: Prentice-Hall.

O'NEILL, E. 1956. *A Long Day's Journey into Night.* New Haven: Yale University Press.

ORVIS, B. R.; J. D. CUNNINGHAM; and H. H. KELLEY. 1975. A closer examination of causal inference: The roles of consensus, distinctiveness, and consistency information, *Journal of Personality and Social Psychology, 32:* 605–16.

PAREDES, A.; K. D. LUDWIG; I. N. HASSENFELD; and F. S. CORNELISON. 1969. A clinical study of alcoholics using audio-visual self-image feedback, *Journal of Nervous and Mental Disease, 148:* 449–56.

PECK, S. 1956. A talk with Mrs. O'Neill, *New York Times,* November 4.

PETERSON, C., and M. E. P. SELIGMAN. 1980. Helplessness and attributional style in depression. Symposium on the Development of Metacognition, the Formation of Attributional Styles, and the Formation of Self-Instruction.

PETERSON, C.; A. SEMMEL; C. VON BAEYER; L. Y. ABRAMSON; G. I. METALSKY; and M. E. P. SELIGMAN. 1982. The attributional style questionnaire, *Cognitive Therapy and Research, 6:* 287–300.

QUATTRONE, G. A. 1982. Overattribution and unit formation: When behavior engulfs the person, *Journal of Personality and Social Psychology, 42:* 593–607.

RAPS, C. S.; C. PETERSON; K. E. REINHARD; L. Y. ABRAMSON; and M. E. P. SELIGMAN. 1982. Attributional style among depressed patients. *Journal of Abnormal Psychology, 91:* 102–8.

RAPS, C. S.; K. E. REINHARD; and M. E. P. SELIGMAN. 1980. Reversal of cognitive and affective deficits associated with depression and learned helplessness by mood elevation in patients, *Journal of Abnormal Psychology, 89:* 342–49.

REEDER, G. D. 1982. Let's give the fundamental attribution error another chance, *Journal of Personality and Social Psychology, 43:* 341–44.

REGAN, D., and J. TOTTEN. 1975. Empathy and attribution: Turning observers into actors, *Journal of Personality and Social Psychology, 32:* 850–56.

ROSENTHAL, A. M. 1964. *Thirty-eight Witnesses.* New York: McGraw-Hill.

ROSENTHAL, R. 1966. *Experimenter Effects in Behavioral Research.* New York: Appleton.

ROSS, L. 1977. The intuitive psychologist and his shortcomings: Distortions in the attribution process. In L. Berkowitz (ed.), *Advances in Experimental Social Psychology.* New York: Academic Press, *10:* 173–220.

ROSS, L. D.; T. M. AMABILE; and J. L. STEINMETZ. 1977. Social roles, social control, and biases in social perception processes, *Journal of Personality and Social Psychology, 35:* 485–94.

ROSS, L.; D. GREENE; and P. HOUSE. 1977. The "false consensus effect": An egocentric bias in social perception and attribution processes, *Journal of Experimental Social Psychology, 13:* 279–301.

SELIGMAN, M. E. P. 1975. *Helplessness: On Depression, Development and Death.* San Francisco: Freeman.

SELIGMAN, M. E. P.; L. Y. ABRAMSON; A. SEMMEL; and C. VON BAEYER. 1979. Depressive attributional style, *Journal of Abnormal Psychology*, 88: 242–47.

SNYDER, M., and E. E. JONES. 1974. Attitude attribution when behavior is constrained, *Journal of Experimental Social Psychology*, 10: 585–600.

SNYDER, M. L.; W. G. STEPHAN; and D. ROSENFIELD. 1978. Attributional egotism. In J. H. Harvey, W. J. Ickes, and R. F. Kidd (eds.), *New Directions in Attribution Research.* Hillsdale, N.J.: Erlbaum, 2: 91–117.

STORMS, M. D. 1973. Videotape and the attribution process. Reversing actors' and observers' point of view, *Journal of Personality and Social Psychology*, 27: 165–75.

TAYLOR, S. E. 1983. Adjustment to threatening events: A theory of cognitive adaptation. The tenth Katz-Newcomb Lecture, delivered at the University of Michigan.

TAYLOR, S. E., and S. T. FISKE. 1978. Salience, attention, and attribution: Top of the head phenomena. In L. Berkowitz (ed.), *Advances in Experimental Social Psychology.* New York: Academic Press, 11: 249–88.

TAYLOR, S. E.; S. T. FISKE; N. L. ETCOFF; and A. J. RUDERMAN. 1978. The categorical and contextual bases of personal memory and stereotyping, *Journal of Personality and Social Psychology*, 36: 778–93.

WEINER, B.; I. FRIEZE; A. KUKLA; L. REED; S. REST; and R. M. ROSENBAUM. 1971. Perceiving the causes of success and failure. In E. E. Jones, D. E. Kanouse, H. H. Kelley, R. E. Nisbett, S. Valins, and B. Weiner (eds.), *Attribution: Perceiving the Causes of Behavior.* Morristown, N.J.: General Learning Press, pp. 95–120.

WEINER, B.; H. HECKHAUSEN; W. MEYER; and R. E. COOK. 1972. Causal ascriptions and achievement behavior: A conceptual analysis of effort and reanalysis of locus of control, *Journal of Personality and Social Psychology*, 21: 239–48.

WELLS, G. L., and J. H. HARVEY. 1977. Do people use consensus information in making causal attributions? *Journal of Personality and Social Psychology*, 35: 279–93.

WILLS, T. A. 1981. Downward comparison principles in social psychology, *Psychological Bulletin*, 90: 245–71.

WIMER, S., and H. H. KELLEY. 1982. An investigation of the dimensions of causal attribution, *Journal of Personality and Social Psychology*, 43: 1142–62.

WORTMAN, C. B., and J. W. BREHM. 1975. Response to uncontrollable outcomes: An integration of reactance theory and the learned helplessness model. In L. Berkowitz (ed.), *Advances in Experimental Social Psychology.* New York: Academic Press, 8: 278–336.

ZUCKERMAN, M. 1979. Attribution of success and failure revisited or the motivational bias is alive and well in attribution theory, *Journal of Personality*, 47: 245–87.

ZUCKERMAN, M., and R. W. MANN. 1979. The other way around: Effects of causal attributions on estimates of consensus, distinctiveness, and consistency, *Journal of Experimental Social Psychology*, 15: 582–97.

6

Group Polarization

THE WELL-KNOWN TELEVISION PLAY and movie *Twelve Angry Men* (Rose, 1955) dramatizes the situation in which a single juror favors acquittal in a trial for first-degree murder and so faces a majority of eleven favoring conviction. The play opens with the judge's instructions to the jury in which he tells them that they are required to return a unanimous verdict. If, he stresses, there is "any reasonable doubt," the verdict must be "not guilty," but if there is no doubt, it is their duty to bring back a verdict of "guilty." The jury then moves into the jury room, and the whole action of the play is the deliberation that takes place there. An initial ballot is taken almost at once: Eleven vote "guilty"; one votes "not guilty." When the play ends, the majority has been converted to the minority position, and the unanimous verdict is "not guilty." Audiences at the movie version know from the very start that "not guilty" is the correct verdict, because the lone holdout is played by Henry Fonda. At the end, they also know it because what transpires in the jury room has convinced them.

Twelve Angry Men is treated as something of a joke in books on jury process (Saks and Hastie, 1978) because it is known from records of real trials (Kalven and Zeisel, 1966) and also from laboratory and computer simulations (Tanford and Penrod, 1983) that a switch from 11–1 in one direction to 12–0 in the other is an extreme statistical rarity, in fact, assigned zero probability in most prediction models. *Twelve Angry Men* is therefore, some think, an absurdly unrealistic play. The trouble with that conclusion is that audiences always find the play totally convincing and so most presumably judge it to be psychologically realistic. On what basis can they do so?

Psychological realism in fiction, or truth in fiction, cannot mean typicality in life. It would be hard to make a drama of a jury process that moved from an initial ballot of 11–1 in one direction to a final verdict of 12–0 in the same direction. It would be true in the sense of typical, but would it make a play, especially a three-act play? Some surprise somewhere, something not typical, is essential to the arousal of interest. Perhaps the movie of *Twelve Angry Men* is atypical yet convincing because the lone holdout is Henry Fonda, from whom prodigies of heroic accomplishment are credible. In fact, however, that is not what makes the play "work." And it does work; it works like a perfectly designed mechanical toy. It works because the jury deliberations conform to known principles of group dynamics, which would in fact produce the decision reversal represented.

In general, I think realism in fiction must be judged against the implicit or tacit psychology that we all know. We must know a lot of psychology on the implicit level, because humans have from the beginning worked steadily, if informally, at figuring one another out, guessing at thoughts and feelings so as to anticipate actions. The routine of life could not proceed as smoothly as it does without a large amount of shared psychological knowledge, and I think we probably judge the truth of fiction against this criterion rather than the simple criterion of event probability. Sometimes when the events are very improbable, writers assure us, "This is a true story," but that assurance has become the very hallmark of a story writers have failed to make credible, as witness *The Amityville Horror*—a true story.

The unusual thing about *Twelve Angry Men*, and it may even be unique in this respect, is that we can judge it to be psychologically realistic against explicitly formulated psychological principles. It is written as if its author, Reginald Rose, had studied the topic of group polarization and tailored his play to the principles that explain it—which he could not have done since the play antedates the discovery of the principles. It will be my goal in this chapter to prove the realism of *Twelve Angry Men* by telling the story of group polarization.

The Risky Shift

We must begin at a point remote from the play and from jury deliberations or anything to do with the law, so it may be well first to expose the essential structure of *Twelve Angry Men*; on that level of abstraction we shall always be discussing the same thing. What happens in the play is, very abstractly, this. At time 1, designated individuals (in the play it is the jurors) arrive individually, in advance of any discussion among themselves, at decisions on a problem that has been presented to all (the trial proceedings in the play). At time 2, the individuals convene as a group and discuss the problem with the intention of reaching a collective decision. At time 3, the group decision is reached (the verdict in the play). In *Twelve Angry Men* interest focuses on the relation between the individual decisions at time 1 (the initial ballot), which were 11–1 in favor of guilty, and the group decision at time 3, the 12–0 verdict "not guilty." The theory of group polarization describes a regular relationship between the distribution of initial decisions and the eventual group decision and identifies two processes in the intervening discussion that are responsible for the relationship. Therefore, the remarkable reversal in the play is an instance of the kind of thing the theory must explain.

Prediscussion individual decisions on a problem and postdiscussion group decisions characterize the operations of every sort of board and committee. The decision may involve admission of an applicant to a medical school, approval of an application for a research grant, or, for that matter, the decision of President John Kennedy's advisers to make the Bay of Pigs invasion of Cuba or the decision of President Reagan's advisers to go ahead with the 1985 income tax revisions. If there is a law in this domain, it is likely to be consequential.

There are many dimensions on which decisions can vary and, therefore, many dimensions on which group decisions might consistently differ from individual decisions. One such dimension, one that was important in the decision about the Bay of Pigs, is *riskiness*. Committees and boards in business and government have been generally thought to favor the pussyfooting compromise rather than the bold action. Whyte (1956), for example, has argued that the team approach in business enterprises leads inexorably to an inhibition of daring and risk-taking, a preference for the conservative course when a choice must be made between more and less risky courses of action. The academic committees on which one has served, committees to decide on appointments, course offerings, and degree recommendations, do not leave one breathless at their daring. Consequently, the discovery by Stoner (1961) that group decisions following discussion were, on certain problems, consistently riskier than individual decisions immediately awakened great interest.

Stoner first reported the effect in a dissertation submitted to the School of Industrial Management at MIT. Stoner used problems that were devised by Wallach and Kogan (1959, 1961) and first used by them for the investigation of individual differences in risk-taking. Each problem describes a situation in which the central person is faced with a choice between two actions whose outcomes differ in their attractiveness and their probability. The respondent is to act as an adviser to the central person in the story and is asked to indicate the minimum probability of success that he would demand before recommending the alternative that might have the more desirable outcome. Here is an example of the problems used by Stoner:

1. Mr A, an electrical engineer who is married and has one child, has been working for a large electronics corporation since graduating from college five years ago. He is

assured of a lifetime job with a modest, though adequate, salary, and liberal pension benefits upon retirement. On the other hand, it is very unlikely that his salary will increase much before he retires. While attending a convention, Mr. A is offered a job with a small, newly founded company with a highly uncertain future. The new job would pay more to start and would offer the possibility of a share in the ownership if the company survived the competition of the larger firms.

Imagine that you are advising Mr. A. Listed below are several probabilities or odds of the new company's proving financially sound. Please check the *lowest* probability that you would consider acceptable to make it worthwhile for Mr. A to take the new job.

[   ] The chances are 1 in 10 that the company will prove financially sound.

[   ] The chances are 3 in 10 that the company will prove financially sound.

[   ] The chances are 5 in 10 that the company will prove financially sound.

[   ] The chances are 7 in 10 that the company will prove financially sound.

[   ] The chances are 9 in 10 that the company will prove financially sound.

[   ] Place a check here if you think Mr. A should *not* take the new job, no matter what the probabilities.

Brief résumés of several of the other problems, numbered as they were by Stoner, will suggest their range:

3. A man of moderate means may invest some money he inherited in secure "blue-chip" low-return securities or in more risky securities that offer the possibility of large gains.

4. A captain of a college football team, in the final seconds of a game with the college's traditional rival, may choose a play that is almost certain to produce a tie score, or a more risky play that would lead to sure victory if successful, sure defeat if not.

6. A college senior planning graduate work in chemistry may enter University X where, because of rigorous standards, only a fraction of the graduate students manage to receive the Ph.D., or he may enter University Y which has a poorer reputation but where almost every graduate student receives the Ph.D.

In this chapter I shall call the problems Stoner used by the name they came to be known by in social psychology: "Choice Dilemmas."

What is a "risky" decision, and how is the amount of risk determined? A person in a state of risk must have something to lose, a stake. For Mr. A in the first story above it is an assured lifetime job with an adequate salary. To take a risk is voluntarily to endanger that stake. Presumably neither Mr. A nor anyone else would do such a thing unless there were also a prize; the prize in the present case is a superior job in a new firm. If the individual is to have a problem of decision-making, the prize must exceed the value of the stake but be less certainly available than the stake. If the prize and stake were equally valuable and yet the probability of attaining the prize varied, as it does in problem 1 above, then Mr. A would not consider risking his stake. Would he give up his present job in order to take a new job exactly like the one he has in a company that might fail? Probably not.

Stoner's subjects were male graduate students of industrial management. They first studied the problems, twelve problems in all, and made individual decisions on each problem. Subsequently, they were assembled in groups of six and instructed to discuss each problem and to arrive at a unanimous group decision. Twenty-three other subjects did not meet as groups but did study the problems a second time, after a lapse of a few weeks. Stoner put together thirteen groups, and for twelve of them the predominant direction of shift on the problems between the means of the initial individual decisions and the later group decisions was toward greater risk. The twenty-three control subjects showed no systematic shift in either direction.

Stoner also asked his subjects to record their private judgments after the group decision had been made; it was understood that a man's private opinion might or might not agree with the group consensus. Those private opinions, subsequent to discussion, were compared with the private opinions expressed in advance of discussion. About 45 percent of the subjects did not change their private views; of the remainder, however, 39 percent changed toward greater risk and only 16 percent toward greater caution. Something in the group discussion appears to have influenced private opinions, as well as the group decision, in the direction of greater riskiness. The change came to be called (grammar be damned) the "risky shift."

Stoner's finding proved not to be a one-time outcome; it was promptly replicated with several kinds of subject. Wallach, Kogan, and Bem (1962) repeated the procedure with more than two hundred undergraduate students in the liberal arts curriculum at the University of Colorado. Groups were either all male or all female. Fourteen out of fourteen male groups shifted in a risky direction, and twelve out of fourteen female groups did the same. In this experiment, as in Stoner's, subjects were asked to record their individual decisions following the discussion, and while their decisions often did not agree with those reached by the group, they ran to greater risk than the decisions made prior to the group discussion.

In 1971 a special issue of *The Journal of Personality and Social Psychology*, under the editorship of Dean Pruitt (1971a, 1971b), was devoted to papers on the risky shift. By that date, one decade after Stoner wrote his thesis, the effects he obtained with the Choice Dilemmas had been replicated so many times that people had stopped counting. One decade further along (Myers, 1982) it was estimated that more than a hundred studies in a dozen countries had been done with the Choice Dilemmas, and the original effects had always been obtained.

It is important to define precisely the risky shift that is so robust a result. It is not the case that every group that discusses a Choice Dilemma shifts to greater risk, and it is still less the case that every individual does. It is not the case that groups must be of the same size, six members, as those Stoner used; the risky shift has been reliably obtained with groups of two to seven members, and probably larger groups would also work. It is not the case that the group convened to hold a discussion must be required to reach a consensus decision, because the risky shift occurs between initial individual opinions and final post-discussion opinions as well as between initial opinions and the group's consensual decision. The exact definition of the risky shift, the one that can be replicated at will, is: The mean risk scores on the Choice Dilemmas obtained from individuals prior to a group discussion are less risky than the mean of group scores (across groups) obtained after discussion.

A Sample Discussion

In our introductory social psychology course, we have for many years used the Choice Dilemmas and the full risky shift design (initial individual decisions—group discussion—group decision—final individual decisions) as a laboratory exercise. The exercise works beautifully, but one must be careful to forewarn a class that the risky shift does not occur with every group, but only as the mean across several groups, and that the effect is not large, but usually on the order of one unit.

From many discussions of problem 1 (Mr. A, the electronic engineer) I have created a composite discussion and imagined a characteristic risky shift outcome.

The participants are six men whom we shall identify by the letters A to F.

A: Let's see where we stand. I favor taking the job if the odds are one in ten.

B: Only if they are five in ten.

C: Right, five in ten.

D: I say seven in ten.

E: My judgment is three in ten.

F: Also three in ten.

A: (to D) Where do you get that seven in ten?

D: This guy is not on his own; he's not free to do whatever he—. He has a wife and child to support.

C: He will have the expense and trouble of moving, and he will lose his retirement benefits, which means something after all.

B: Why should he leave a sure thing, a perfectly secure job? Only greed could lead him to—.

A: What's the matter with you guys? Security! Retirement! What're you, half dead? Be dynamic! Go forward, have a spirit of adventure. Nothing ventured, nothing gained!

E: My reasoning is this: The man is out of school almost five years; he is a relatively young man, school-wise or experience-wise. I feel he has nothing to lose by taking the chance of going with a new, young company and possibly going much farther than he will as an organization man in some huge outfit.

C: You're all talking as if this is the only chance he's ever going to get to move. Just because he turns down this job doesn't mean he has to stay put the rest of his life. Within two years or so he will get another offer, so why should he go with a company that only has one chance in ten of making it? Statistics on the failure and success of new businesses show that the large majority actually succeed.

F: Yes, but the most he can lose on this change is moving expenses. I read in *The New York Times* or somewhere that there is a big demand for electrical engineers. Even if this company should fall through, he can always get a job, probably at the same salary. I figure even if the company goes broke, he can still claim valuable experience in looking for another job later on. That's why I'd say three in ten.

C: That's true; if the company fails, it isn't a personal failure. I propose a compromise on three in ten.

D: I can go along with that.

B: O.K.

E: O.K.

A: Why not?

The initial individual decisions of the persons constituting this group were: 1 in 10, 3 in 10, 3 in 10, 5 in 10, 5 in 10, and 7 in 10. The mean of these values is 4 in 10, and the unanimous group decision is represented to be 3 in 10. Let us imagine that the subjects were also asked to record their personal decisions following the discussion and that it was pointed out to them that these might not agree in every case with the group consensus. In Figure 6-1, we have an imaginary but typical set of final positions compared with the initial positions. The two effects common to all the experiments we have cited can be observed in these data: The unanimous group decision is riskier than the mean of initial individual decisions; the mean of the final individual positions (3 in 10) is also riskier than the mean of initial positions. Notice, however, that it is not the case (see Figure 6-1) that every individual changes to a riskier decision; what happens is that those initially near the middle of the scale become more extreme in the risky direction.

The phenomenon called the "risky shift" was thought of as a surprising fact about the difference between individual decisions and group decisions. The effect has held up for twenty years, but the nature of the effect has turned out to be incorrectly conceptualized as a shift to greater risk; it must be more abstractly defined. However, the idea of the risky shift lasted long enough for people to propose two explanations for it, conformity or leadership, and for those explanations to fail (Brown, 1965). It is worth reviewing the usefulness of conformity and leadership, because they fail also to explain the reconceptualized phenomenon that replaced the risky shift.

Explanations That Fail

Because in the risky shift (see Figure 6-1) individual initial positions converge after discussion, the social force of conformity (Chapter 1) seems a likely explanatory principle. Certainly the individual judgments do converge after discussion, as Figure 6-1 shows. The convergence on a unanimous group decision is fully accounted for by the experimenter's instructions to reach such a decision, and one need not invoke conformity to explain that outcome; it looks more like simple obedience to authority. However, there is also substantial convergence in the individual final positions (the mean is, like the group decision, 3 in 10), and that individual convergence is explicitly *not* required by the experimenter. It probably represents genuine changes of opinion consequent to discussion. However, there is more to the risky shift than convergence or conformity.

If the individual decisions in Figure 6-1 converged to the exact mean of their initial positions (4 in 10), that would be a simple conformity effect. Or if very many groups were to discuss the problem of Mr. A and if some converged to the mean of their original position, some to positions somewhat riskier than

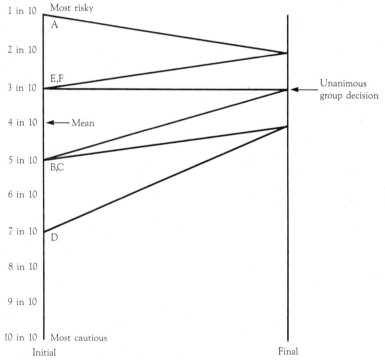

Figure 6-1. Initial positions, final positions, and the unanimous group decision on a problem involving risk

the mean, and some to positions somewhat more cautious, such that the overall mean of the final positions was the same as the mean of the initial positions, that too would be a simple conformity effect. However, the risky shift is not convergence to the mean of initial positions, but, rather, to points on one side of the mean, the riskier side. Therefore, conformity cannot account for the effect.

The decision of a group will settle on a position that is not the mean of the group if some members are disproportionately influential. When one member is notably more influential than the others, he is a leader. Like the leader of a group of nomadic anthropoids, he is the one "out front," the one who seems to select the way that all will go. Perhaps the shift to risk in group decisions on the Stoner problems is a phenomenon of leadership.

There is clear evidence that qualities of leadership do not account for the risky shift. In one study (Burnstein and Vinokur, 1973), after individuals had recorded their initial decisions, they were required to go into the group discussion and defend a position that was the mirror image of their real preference; e.g. if someone chose a risky 2 in 10, he had to argue for a cautious 8 in 10. If it were the case that general qualities of leadership (charisma?) characterized high risk takers, then those qualities should enable them to cause any position they defended to prevail. Since persons really disposed to high risk were defending cautious positions, one looked for a shift to caution, but it did not happen. On normally risky Choice Dilemmas, no shifts at all occurred. The influentiality of high risk takers does not export.

Several other kinds of result rule out leadership as the explanatory principle. It was shown many times in the 1970s that choice shifts could be produced without group discussion by simply having group members announce aloud their individual decisions, and there would seem to be no way to exercise leadership in such circumstances. In addition, it was discovered that shifts on the Choice Dilemmas were not always in the direction of greater risk but were sometimes in the direction of greater caution. That rules out an explanation of high risk-takers as leaders. However, it also rules out the risky shift as the phenomenon to be explained and is, in fact, the critical discovery that moved the entire discussion up one notch in generality.

Risky Shift or Cautious Shift

The fact is that the Choice Dilemmas had produced some cautious shifts from the very first (Stoner, 1961). A cautious shift is defined in exact parallel with a risky shift as a change in the mean of groups or of final individual postdiscussion decisions by contrast with the mean of initial individual decisions. For a short time it was possible to overlook the cautious shifts (they occurred on Stoner's problems No. 5 and No. 12), because results were summed across the full set of twelve Choice Dilemmas, and in the full set risky shifts swamped cautious shifts. When attention was first paid to the fact that some shifts were to greater caution on the Choice Dilemmas, there was a moment of discomfort in which we thought we had lost our phenomenon. If collective decisions are sometimes riskier than individual decisions and sometimes more cautious and (it eventually was noticed) sometimes not significantly different, then there is no generalization at all, because all logical possibilities occur.

The concern was short-lived. What dispelled it was the realization that it was always the same problems (No. 5 and No. 12) on which cautious shifts occurred. With many studies of the Choice Dilemmas on record, it was possible to see that individual dilemmas tended to breed true; that is, always to produce the same sort of shift, either to risk or to caution. That meant there was a general phenomenon, there was a regularity, though it was more complex than had originally been thought. It took some years and a lot of work to find the best way to conceptualize the new regularity.

What kind of problem produces a shift after discussion to increased caution? Here is the first one that consistently did so, Stoner's No. 12.

> Mr. M is contemplating marriage to Miss T, a girl whom he has known for a little more than a year. Recently, however, a number of arguments have occurred between them, suggesting some sharp differences of opinion in the way each views certain matters. Indeed, they decide to seek professional advice from a marriage counselor as to whether it would be wise for them to marry. On the basis of these meetings with a marriage counselor, they realize that a happy marriage, while possible, could not be assured. Listed below are several probabilities or odds that their marriage could prove to be a happy and successful one.
>
> Imagine that you are advising Mr. M and Miss T. Please check the *lowest* possibility that you would consider acceptable for advising Mr. M and Miss T to get married.

Nordhøy (1962), who was the first to take a serious interest in cautious shifts, succeeded in writing some new choice dilemmas that consistently produced a shift to increased caution, as did David Myers, Colin Fraser, and others, and soon there was a good-sized stock of problems known to have as a reliable property the power to produce either the risky shift or the cautious shift. Here is a problem that was not included in Stoner's original set that produces a strong cautious shift:

> A good friend of yours, call him Sam, is about to board a plane at the airport to begin his overseas vacation. He has been looking forward to this trip very much, but he is troubled because he awoke in the morning with a quite severe abdominal pain. Because Sam has never flown before, he thinks that the pain may simply be an upset stomach brought on by anticipation of the flight. Although he is not far from a hospital where he knows he could obtain quick attention, he realizes that a visit to the hospital would cause him to miss his flight which, in turn, would seriously disrupt his vacation plans. The pain seems to have grown more severe in the last few minutes. Listed below are several probabilities or odds that Sam's stomach trouble will go away.
>
> Imagine that you are advising Sam. Please check the *lowest* probability or odds

that you would consider acceptable for Sam to go ahead with his trip. [Stoner, 1968, p. 446]

While no one has quite worked out a formula for writing the two kinds of problem to order, it is possible to identify one property of a story problem that makes caution likely: a very large stake. If someone's life or marriage is at stake, the cautious shift is likely. Another usual property of cautious shift problems is the involvement in the decision of others besides the protagonist. Caution is likely when a risky decision threatens a fiancée, a family, or parents, and not only the protagonist. As for what makes people disdain to be cautious, a small stake and very large prize help. Here, for instance, is a dilemma (Myers, 1982) with those qualities:

> Henry is a writer who is said to have considerable creative talent but who so far has been earning a comfortable living by writing cheap Westerns. Recently he has come up with an idea for a potentially significant novel. If it could be written and accepted, it might have considerable literary impact and be a big boost to his career. On the other hand, if he was not able to work out his idea or if the novel was a flop, he would have expended considerable time and energy without remuneration.
> Imagine that you are advising Henry. Please check the *lowest* probability that you would consider acceptable for Henry to attempt to write the novel.

The fact that some choice dilemmas reliably produce risky shifts and that other choice dilemmas reliably produce cautious shifts is a regularity, to be sure, but not a very useful one. What is wanted is a general characterization of the kinds of problem that will produce each effect so that one can predict beyond those that have been tried out and found to work. One sort of characterization is suggested by the "hints" listed above for writing items that make people cautious, but those are just hints and have not led to any interesting results. A shift predictor of a completely general kind has been found, and though it may at first seem less interesting than a content formula would be, its discovery has, in fact, helped to unlock the deeper reasons why shifts occur.

A Predictor of the Shifts

Teger and Pruitt (1967) were, I think, the first to identify the shift predictor. They used the twelve original Choice Dilemmas and the full standard design, defining the shift as the difference between the mean of initial decisions and the mean of final postdiscussion decisions. The new question they asked of their data was whether or not any general relationship existed between the mean of the initial decision and the size of the shifts that occurred. Looking first at just the ten problems that usually produced risky shifts (exclusive, that is, of Stoner's No. 5 and No. 12), it was apparent that there was considerable variation from item to item in the size of risky shift produced, from a tiny shift of .16 to a sizable shift of 1.48. The shift of .16 is not actually large enough to be significant and so counts as no shift at all, and that was true of a couple of other items, though most of the shifts were large enough to be significant. We know today, when so much work has been done with the Choice Dilemmas, that the tendency of items to "breed true" is not limited to the gross division between risky shift types and cautious shift types, but holds true on the level of the individual item. That is to say that among risky shift items and among cautious shift items, each one tends to hold a characteristic place in terms of both the direction and the size of the shift produced.

Returning to the item that produced no significant risky shift (.16) and the item that produced a healthy shift of 1.48, it turned out that there was a surprising difference in the mean of the initial decisions. The item that shifted a lot had a quite extreme risky initial position whereas the item that shifted a little or not at all started out near the middle of the scale. Across the ten risky shift items there was a significant correlation of −.64 between mean initial preference and mean shift. The correlation is negative because high risk means low odds, and the relationship was such that the riskier the initial disposition an item evoked (across all subjects), the larger the shift to increased risk. The two items that produced cautious shifts (No. 5 and No. 12) had initial positions that were less risky and so more cautious (odds of about 8 in 10 were the minimum acceptable), and the cautious shifts they produced may be thought of as negative risky shifts, and so the correlation can be computed across all twelve items, and it rises to −.78. The meaning of that correlation is the same for both risky and cautious items: a group discussion moves decisions to more extreme points *in the direction of the original inclination.* Group discussion produces polarization, which means shift to either risk or caution in the direction of the original disposition, and the size of shift increases with the degree of initial polarization.

There are many studies demonstrating that initial decisions on choice dilemmas predict sizes of shift on the same items, but the sharpest and clearest is that of Myers and Arenson (1972). They worked with six of the original Stoner problems, all of which reliably produced risky shifts, and with six new items written (successfully) to produce cautious shifts. Subjects were all females, and groups ranged in size from two to seven. The correlation between mean initial positions on items and shifts on the same items was −.89, which is very high indeed. The plot of initial means against mean shifts (Figure 6–2) is especially instructive. Notice first that shifts to greater caution are represented on the ordinate as negative risky shifts. There are just four cautious shifts, and they occur where the initial minimal odds acceptable are 7 in 10 or greater. If you follow the 0.0 shift line across, you will see that there is a region of neutrality on the odds scale which seems to extend (roughly) from about 5.5 to about 7. We can think of these data as indicating that items that initially dispose individuals to risk (defined as odds of 5.5 in 10 or lower) elicit more risky decisions after discussion whereas items that initially dispose to caution (defined as odds of 7 in 10 or greater) elicit more cautious decisions after discussion, and items occupying a psychologically neutral region (5.5 in 10 to 7 in 10) show no signifi-

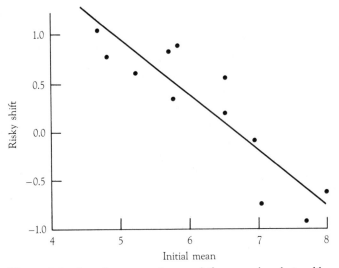

Figure 6–2. Initial means and mean shifts on twelve choice dilemmas

(Reprinted with permission of authors and publisher from D. G. Myers and S. J. Arenson, Enhancement of dominant risk tendencies in group discussion, *Psychological Reports* [1972], 30:615–23, Fig. 1)

cant shift. The psychologically neutral region does not, as it happens, exactly coincide with the midpoint of the scale. These findings are very representative of the whole set of similar studies.

One aspect of the relationship pictured in Figure 6–2 can be puzzling. The relationship is such that the more extreme the original preference, the greater the shift in the same direction. One might think that extremity to begin with would limit or put a ceiling on further extremity. Notice, however, that the riskiest initial position in Figure 6–2 is not even as risky as odds of 4 in 10, whereas odds of 1 in 10 are possible; so for those data there is plenty of room for further polarization to be produced by discussion. There is also quite a bit of room at the cautious extreme for further polarization. The other relevant consideration, and it is very important to keep this in mind, is that the initial mean for an item is a *property of that item* across multiple groups. This means that a problem that averages odds of 4 in 10 across groups may, for any particular group, yield a less risky mean, such as 5 in 10 or 6 in 10. That is a fact that has a future in this discussion, because it might be taken to mean that the overall initial mean of an item is its real position on a risk–caution scale and a group scoring nearer the midpoint on that item may have a lot of room for change.

Explanation of the Shifts

There are two processes—"social comparison" and "persuasive arguments"— that account for the shifts in risk. In the original group discussions, the two act together and reinforce each other. I think it is now clear that either process alone is sufficient to produce a significant shift (whether to increased risk or to increased caution). I also think it likely that the two processes are about equally powerful. In this evaluation of two decades of research, I believe I am in agreement with Fraser (1971), Myers and Lamm (1976), Lamm and Myers (1978), Pruitt (1971a, 1971b), Sanders and Baron (1977), and others. However, Eugene Burnstein (1982) and others believe that one of the two processes, "persuasive arguments," is alone necessary and sufficient to explain all findings.

The evidence supporting each process is by now quite massive and must be accorded proper respect. I myself, however, respond to something in addition to the evidence, which is a little click of intuitive rightness. Just what produces the click is hard to say; it has something to do with simplicity, something to do with introspective recognition, and something to do with tightness of fit among the several component parts of each process.

The phenomenon we have come to know as shifts in risk, that is shifts to either risk or caution, was for some years thought of as the risky shift, or shifts to increased risk only, and both the social comparison explanation and the persuasive arguments explanation date, in nascent form, from the risky shift period. That is to say that the two processes, especially social comparison, were originally devised to explain the risky shift. Later on it proved possible to generalize both processes so as to explain all shifts in risk, whether risky or cautious. However, a certain amount of early experimental evidence was collected to test explanations of the risky shift only, and so some individual studies are asymmetrical from our present vantage point. Eventually, however, completely parallel sets of data were collected for both cautious shifts and risky shifts.

SOCIAL COMPARISON

Stoner's subjects were graduate students in the School of Industrial Management at MIT, and when members of the school first heard about the outcome of Stoner's experiment (then thought of as risky shift), they argued that it could be explained by the fact that the field of industrial management sets a positive value on the ability to take risks. It is a part of the role of an industrial management student to favor risky decisions, they held. Of course the risky shift was soon produced with liberal arts students, both male and female, and by 1982 had been produced with many kinds of persons in many countries, so nothing specific to students of management could possibly matter. If a value on taking risks were involved, it would have to be a very widely held value. Such a value might exist, but even if it did, how would it help to explain the shift that is the phenomenon? If someone thinks risk-taking is admirable, he thinks it when he is alone making the initial individual decision just as much as when he assents to the group consensus or, also again, makes the final postdiscussion decision. That line of thought looked profitless.

An accidental observation of an atypical group suggested a way in which a value on risk might cause a risky shift to be produced by discussion. Group discussions of the Choice Dilemmas practically always begin with an "initial ballot" in which each participant states the odds he favors. On one occasion a group I was observing neglected to do that. One member of the group made extravagant use in the discussion of what can be called the "rhetoric of risk." "Life is not static; it's dynamic. You have to take chances. Nothing ventured, nothing gained!" When the group was ready to try for a consensual decision, they finally thought to take a poll of initial opinions. The rhetorician turned out to have selected odds of 7 in 10, the second most conservative position in the group. He had clearly conceived of his position as daring, but until all decisions were made public he had no way of knowing whether 7 in 10 was risky or cautious for the problem being discussed.

What if everyone wanted to take a moderately risky position on Stoner's Choice Dilemmas, and what if everyone thought he *was* taking such a position when he wrote down his initial private preference? It would not be possible for everyone in the group to be on the risky side of the mean of the preferences of the group. Really, no one could tell what a risky position would be on novel problems before the distribution became known. Once the real location of the mean was known, should it not be the case, granting that everyone wanted to see himself as reasonably audacious, that those who were really below the mean would be motivated to adopt riskier positions and so change the mean and produce the risky shift? It would all be a process of self-presentation and social comparison (Festinger, 1954), and the effective function of the group discussion would simply be to teach each person how to present himself (to himself and to others) in the way he wished.

The paragraph above states the kernel of the social comparison theory, but it was formulated before all the facts were known. Shifts were as likely to be cautious as risky, so no general value on risk-taking could explain all shifts *in* risk. But the idea of an unqualified value on risk-taking was always silly—one sees in retrospect. No one wants to see himself or have others see him as a big risk-taker when a life is in danger and the welfare of dependent children and elderly parents is part of the stake. In such circumstances caution is a virtue. In fact, a social comparison theory adequate to the phenomenon of shifts in risk as we now know it must hold that the value engaged, the relevant virtue, is a function of the particular choice dilemma. For some problems one wants to be like everybody else, to conform to the central tendency; for others one wants to be on the risky side of the central tendency, though not so far out as to seem foolhardy; on some problems one wants to be on the cautious side, though not so far out as to seem cowardly.

The theory of social comparison can be stated in three interlocked propositions.

1. Any given choice dilemma evokes in most people the desire to be risky or cautious or average.

2. In advance of information as to the distribution of positions on the

choice dilemma, each person imagines that he does, in fact, occupy the kind of position he considers desirable.

3. When the actual distribution of positions on the choice dilemma of all individuals in a group becomes known, those who are not where they want to be, and thought they were, will be motivated to change, thereby producing group mean decisions that represent, according to the individual dilemma, a risky shift, a cautious shift, or no shift at all.

What kinds of evidence support the theory? One claim the theory makes is that people think a more-than-average ability to take risks is an admirable quality for those problems on which a risky shift occurs. Why should they do so in, for instance, the case of Mr. A, the electrical engineer? Whether or not he can afford to take the chance of going with a new company that has a low probability of success but promises a terrific payoff if it does succeed, should, by anyone's reasoning, depend on how good an electrical engineer Mr. A is. If he is exceptionally intelligent, well-trained, and creative, he really need not worry about the company's chancy future, because there will always be a good position for a really top engineer. If his competence is marginal and he considers himself lucky to have the job he has, then he probably would be wiser to hang onto it and move only if a very sure thing is offered. The experimental subject in the role of adviser to Mr. A has to imagine A's competence, and that he does by projecting his own, as he sees it, and so a recommendation of high risk will suggest high competence. That line of thought has been very directly tested in several clever ways (Jellison and Riskind, 1970, 1971; Jellison, Riskind, and Broll, 1972).

Using just those ten of the twelve original Choice Dilemmas which reliably produced risky shifts, subjects read through booklets purportedly filled out by individuals of whom the subjects were to form general impressions. One set of booklets contained ten very low-risk answers (a mean of 8.0), and one contained very high-risk answers (a mean of 2.4). After reading his booklet, each subject was given a rating form on which to record his impression of the person who had filled out the booklet. The form included the adjectives "clever," "creative," "ingenious," "innovative," "intelligent." The high risk-taker was rated as significantly higher on all those aspects of ability than was the low risk-taker. The ten items of the original twelve are all items on which individual ability ought to affect willingness to take risks, and high risk-takers were, accordingly, credited with higher ability than low risk-takers.

The social comparison theory holds not only that risk-taking will be admired with respect to items that show risky shifts, but also that caution will be admired on items that show cautious shifts. That claim has been tested by having subjects first answer a set of choice dilemmas (both risky shift and cautious shift dilemmas) and then go through the same dilemmas answering in the way "they would most admire." Many laboratories have carried out this exercise with largely uniform results (Levinger and Schneider, 1969; Myers, 1982).

For items that reliably produce risky shifts (e.g. in Stoner's Choice Dilemmas, all but No. 5 and No. 12), the most admired answer is consistently riskier than a subject's own answer, and that result strengthens the conclusion that risk is valued on those dilemmas. For items that produce cautious shifts (No. 5 and No. 12 in Stoner's set and numerous dilemmas written by others) the most admired answer is often more cautious than the subject's own answer, but it is sometimes simply not significantly different. The evidence that caution is valued on cautious shift items is not so strong as the evidence that risk is valued on risky shift items, but that fact actually supports the social comparison theory. It does so because one finds in the literature (e.g. Fraser, 1971; Fraser, Gouge, and Billig, 1971) reports that cautious shifts are not so large as risky shifts and not so regularly obtained, on the items where they should be obtained, and Fraser has speculated that risk has a certain attractive daring quality in some cultures even when it entails irresponsibility.

Another claim of the social comparison theory is that most people think they are superior to the average in ability to take risks when risks should be taken and in ability to be cautious when one should be cautious. The claim is tested by asking people first to answer a set of choice dilemmas (both risky and cautious) and then to go through a second time, answering as they think the average person would do. The test has been made many times (e.g. Hinds, 1962; Levinger and Schneider, 1969; Myers, 1982; Wallach and Wing, 1968), and the claim seems always to be confirmed; in advance of discussion almost everyone thinks his decision better realizes the ideal the item engages than does the answer of the average person. Since not everybody can be better than the average person, there is something to be learned when positions are made known.

The credibility of social comparison theory is strengthened by the fact that the tendency to think oneself somewhat better than the average of a reference group is extremely general. Jean-Paul Codol (1975) of the Université de Provence has provided a massive demonstration (some twenty studies) of the phenomenon he calls the "superior conformity of the self" or the "PIP effect" (for *primus inter pares* or "first among equals"). Codol's view is that with respect to behavior or traits expected of a reference group and valued by the group, each person tends to see himself as like the others, only a bit better. Codol has demonstrated the PIP effect in children at various grade levels; in adults who are legal, medical, and academic professionals; and in trade unionists. He has, in addition, put together groups of strangers and created a premium on accuracy or on cooperativeness or on competitiveness, and, sure enough, each individual saw himself as closer than the others to the ideal created.

The final claim of social comparison theory is that when the actual distribution of decisions is made known in group discussion, it is that information which serves to produce a shift either to increased risk or to increased caution. It was Teger and Pruitt (1967) who first thought of the best way to test the claim. If it is the information on others' positions that causes shifts, then that information alone, with no discussion whatever, should be sufficient to produce the effects. With all discussion forbidden, subjects simply held up cards on which appeared the odds each favored. That position information alone was sufficient to produce significant risky shifts on the usual ten Stoner problems and also to produce cautious shifts (just short of significance) for No. 5 and No. 12. The size of the shifts was, however, only half that produced by discussion, so it is clear that position information is not the only important product of free discussion.

The Teger and Pruitt findings have been very often replicated (e.g. Myers and Bishop, 1971; Myers, 1978; Stokes, 1971), but there have also been attempts at replication that failed (Pruitt, 1971a, 1971b). Most of the failures occurred in the 1960s and early 1970s, prior to the discovery of two factors that may have caused the social comparison effect to appear to be less robust than it is. It occurred to Myers that the initial decision a subject makes, before he learns the decision of others (in the standard experimental design), may function as a kind of commitment causing the individual to resist change, especially as his only reason to change would seem to be information about what others think. Therefore Myers, Bach, and Schreiber (1974) tried a different experimental design (called a "between-groups" design) in which all subjects simply made decisions once, but some (randomly selected) did so with information about the decisions of others and some without such information. With that design, the ability of positional information to produce shifts was greater than usual, and Myers (1982) thinks it is clear that the initial commitment decision dampens the social comparison effect.

PERSUASIVE ARGUMENTS

Suppose a problem has an objectively correct answer that is not known to all the subjects available for group discussions but is known to some of them. Here is such a question: "If you were to go due south from Detroit, Michigan, what would be the first foreign country you would reach? Brazil? Cuba? Mexico?" The answer is Canada; the city of Windsor, Ontario, because of a twist in the United States-Canadian border, lies south of Detroit. If each member of a population of subjects answered independently, then those who knew the correct answer would give it and the rest would not. If the subjects were then convened as small groups to discuss the question, there would be some groups in which one or two members knew the answer and the rest did not. The correct answer would prevail more often than the various incorrect answers. This answer—Canada—would usually not represent the most common prior response of the members, and so its victory could not be attributed to majority pressures. Neither is "Canada" the mean or central tendency of the initial opinions, and so the simple impulse to converge will not account for the agreement on "Canada." "Canada" is a minority answer, on one side of the mean, which happens to be correct. If the decision to take a high risk on the Stoner problems could be considered objectively correct, then the shift to risk would be explained.

Surely it is pointless to compare choice dilemmas to questions of fact concerning geography, history, politics, and the like, because choice dilemmas have no right answers in the sense that the question about Detroit has a right answer. Notice, however, that a group of persons asked to identify the first foreign country south of Detroit would have no way, while in discussion, of checking on the correctness of the unexpected suggestion: "Canada." Probably, however, all would be persuaded to adopt that answer. Why should they be? It is likely that the person who made the suggestion, knowing that it can be checked on a map, would make his suggestion with great confidence, and confidence is a powerful persuader. The Canada answer would also be persuasive by virtue of its paradoxical quality. Since Canada, in general, lies north of the United States, and everyone knows that, anyone who asserts that a part of Canada lies south of a part of the United States must be presumed to have good reason for his assertion. Evidently information can be persuasive even when it is not known to be factual.

Look once again at the sample discussion of the problem of Mr. A, the electrical engineer, attending now to the content. Participant F says: "I read in *The New York Times* or somewhere that there is a big demand for electrical engineers. Even if this company should fall through, he can always get a job, probably at the same salary. I figure even if the company goes broke, he can still claim valuable experience in looking for another job later on." Nothing in this contribution identifies the correct answer to the problem of Mr. A, the minimal odds that he should accept. However, if you had not thought of F's argument—that engineers are in short supply and can easily find jobs as good as the one A now has—then this argument should operate as a *correction* on whatever odds you initially chose. The argument exercises a force toward greater risk, and if it has not figured in your thinking and you find it persuasive (citing *The New York Times* would help make it so), then the argument should move you toward the acceptance of lower odds, whatever your initial thought.

That much of the persuasive arguments theory was worked out when the phenomenon to be explained was still the risky shift. Group discussions of the dilemmas were not altogether different from discussions aimed at solving problems of fact or logic, because while it was true that the dilemmas had no objective correct answers, there were always relevant arguments that were more or less persuasive. It seemed reasonable to suppose that each individual prior to discussion would think of some relevant arguments, but not all, and that the arguments one thought of would not be identical with those another thought of. In group discussion each would tell all he knew, and that would shift group opinion.

From these beginnings a really beautiful set of ideas dawned (Bishop and Myers, 1974; Vinokur and Burnstein, 1974). Decision shifts, we knew, could be either to risk or to caution and could be large or small, depending on the item.

Suppose any given item could be said to have a pool of possible arguments, a latent population of relevant arguments, a below-ground bulb structure of relevant arguments. And suppose the total pool for a given item favored risk or caution in a given degree. A tendentious pool of that kind would be analogous to the correct answer that an objective question has. Suppose, further, that each individual who ruminates on an item draws a sample of relevant arguments from that item's pool. Insofar as the pool favors risk, weakly or strongly, his sample will do the same, and insofar as the pool favors caution, weakly or strongly, so will each sample. The samples drawn from the pool will determine the initial individual decisions, and so the mean of these should be more or less risky or cautious according to the character of the total pool.

Assuming that individual samples of arguments are not identical, that arguments are only partially shared, in group discussion all samples will be combined and all samples together will better represent the character of the total pool than individual samples. The mean of individual initial decisions correlates highly with the size of the shift after discussion simply because extreme initial means must be drawn from extreme pools and moderate initial means from moderate pools. And so discussion will shift the mean of individual initial positions farther out in the direction of initial inclination.

1. For each choice dilemma there exists a pool of arguments favoring risk or caution, and the number and persuasiveness of the arguments varies from item to item. The character of the pool for a given item must be presumed to be culturally and historically relative even though for twenty years in many countries there is little evidence of variation.
2. Each person who considers a given dilemma thinks of some sample of the arguments in the total pool, but not all. The arguments he thinks of determine his initial individual decision. The arguments considered by any set of individuals will be only partially shared prior to discussion.
3. The important thing that happens in discussion is that individual arguments are expressed and become fully shared. Because the choice dilemmas have total argument pools in which the balance favors either risk or caution, the larger sample of the pool made available to all in discussion will produce either a risky shift or a cautious shift according to the direction of prediscussion inclinations as revealed in the means of initial decisions.

What sorts of evidence support the persuasive arguments theory? The theory claims that each Choice Dilemma is associated with a distinctive pool of relevant arguments, which may favor risk or caution strongly or moderately, and that the means of the initial decisions (because they are based on samples from the pool) should reflect the character of the pool. Vinokur and Burnstein (1974) asked subjects first to respond individually to each of five dilemmas (two risky, two cautious, and one neutral) in the usual way. Subjects were then asked, without benefit of any discussion, to list all the arguments they could think of relevant to each item, indicating whether an argument favored risk or caution. Those combined complete argument lists can be thought of as an approximation to the total pool characteristic of each item. Choice dilemmas known to shift to risk had item pools in which the proportion of risky arguments was greater than it was in the pools for cautious shift items, and the pool for the neutral items was almost exactly evenly balanced between risky and cautious arguments. In addition, the means of the individual decisions on the items were correlated with the proportion of risky to cautious arguments in the item pools.

The persuasive arguments theory further predicts that the persuasive arguments constituting the pool for a given item will be only partially shared among persons prior to group discussion of the item. Vinokur and Burnstein had judges classify together arguments that were essentially identical and so obtained lists for each item of distinct arguments. They were then able to determine how widely each argument was shared. If all arguments for any given item were known to all those convened for a discussion, no sharing would be created by the discussion and so no shift should occur. In fact, sharing was only partial for each item; indeed, no argument was shared by more than one-third of the subjects. So partial sharing in advance of discussion, which is a *sine qua non* of discussion-induced shifts, was, in fact, the case.

Finally, the ratio of risky to cautious arguments in an item's pool should predict the size of shift produced in discussion, since each participant will increase his sample from the total pool, and that sample will be biased toward risk or caution as the pool is. This discussion necessarily had to involve subjects other than those who produced the complete lists of arguments, as the listing process would be expected to make shifts unlikely. The discussions of the items were created by Vinokur (1971) for another experiment, and the mean shifts for each item were taken from that experiment. The size of the shift on an item was predicted by the proportion of risky to cautious arguments in its pool— exactly as the theory requires.

The acid test of the persuasive arguments explanation parallels that for social comparison: Is the one critical variable sufficient in the absence of the other? Are arguments alone sufficient to produce decision shifts? It has been repeatedly and consistently shown that they are. Clark, Crockett, and Archer (1971) had groups discuss choice dilemmas (a subset of six) with the restriction that no one was on any account to say what recommendation he favored. That arguments-only discussion produced as large a risky shift as did full discussion with individuals stating the odds they favored. Myers, Bach, and Schreiber (1974) and Burnstein and Vinokur (1973) have shown in several different clever ways that exposure to arguments alone is enough to produce significant shifts.

One study (Ebbesen and Bowers, 1974) stands out for me, because it is especially elegant and also because it will help us to explain *Twelve Angry Men*. This experiment pulls apart the natural risk position of a dilemma, as determined by its pool of relevant arguments and the ratio of risky to cautious arguments actually generated in a discussion. Five of Stoner's problems were used, chosen so as to sample the range from high risky shift to high cautious shift. For each of the items the experimenters created five different scripted discussions, contrived so as to vary the risky-to-cautious argument proportion. In each scripted, rehearsed, and tape-recorded discussion just ten relevant arguments were used. For each item there was a discussion in which the risky-to-cautious proportion was .90, which meant nine arguments favoring risk and one favoring caution. For the same items there were discussions in which the proportions were: .70, .50, .30, and .10. Discussions with arguments in just the same five proportions, then, were created for each item in spite of the fact that the items had quite different natural "bents." Subjects were passive auditors who first answered an item for themselves, then listened to one of the five discussions of that item, and finally answered again for themselves. The question was whether the contrived argument proportions would predict the direction and size of the shift. Figure 6–3 shows how well they did so.

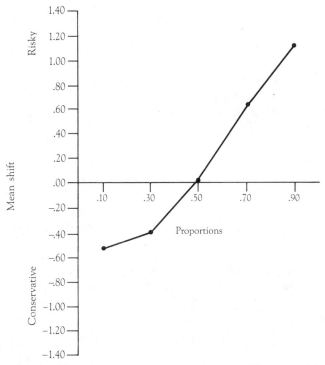

Figure 6–3. Average shift in risk estimates as a function of the proportion of risky arguments that subjects heard

(From E. B. Ebbesen and R. J. Bowers, Proportion of risky to conservative arguments in a group discussion and choice shift, *Journal of Personality and Social Psychology*, 29 [1974]. Copyright 1974 by the American Psychological Association. Reprinted by permission of the publisher and author)

When half the arguments favored risk and half caution, the shift was exactly .00. As the proportion of arguments favoring risk increased, so did the shift to increased risk, and as the proportion of arguments favoring caution ("conservative") increased, so did the size of the shift to increased caution. As you can see in Figure 6-3, however, shifts to caution were not as large as shifts to risk. I take that to be yet another manifestation—and there are many running through the study of group polarization—that the value on risk is in some general way more powerful than the value on caution.

Decision shifts were produced by arguments actually heard and not by the natural bent of an item, not by the total pool of arguments associated with an item. That is very interesting, because it shows that if we think of the pool of relevant arguments as something like the correct answer for that item, it is possible for an odd, unrepresentative discussion to produce an incorrect answer. I shall want to argue that precisely this must be supposed to have happened in the trial that precedes the jury deliberations in *Twelve Angry Men*. We have to suppose that, because Henry Fonda, the lone juror voting "not guilty," is in the course of the play able to produce powerful evidence and arguments, not brought out in the trial, in favor of that verdict, arguments so powerful that the audience is convinced that the correct verdict is "not guilty." For some reason the pool of arguments that defines the right answer for the young defendant accused of murder was not properly sampled in the trial itself. There are several remarks in the play to the effect that the defense did a poor job, which in our terms must mean a failure to penetrate to the pool of evidence and arguments that establishes "not guilty" as the correct verdict. The inadequate defense leaves the way open for Henry Fonda to re-try the case and come up with the right answer.

Polarization in General

It is odd really that most of the work using choice dilemmas (Stoner's or others) has also presented subjects with choice options in the awkward form of odds ranging from 1 in 10 to 10 in 10. The form is awkward because low odds represent high risk, and so an unnecessary though simple mental transformation must be made. More important, there is no printed option that is clearly intended to represent psychological neutrality. For those reasons I am happy to introduce work done at the University of Bristol by Colin Fraser and his associates (Fraser, Gouge, and Billig, 1971). They used eight dilemmas, four risky and four cautious, some of them Stoner problems and some new problems written by the authors. They first used the familiar odds options (1 in 10, 2 in 10, etc.) and replicated all the usual shifts and correlations. With new subjects they used the same problems, but response options were a simple seven-point scale. For Mr. A, the electrical engineer, the riskiest choice was "1. Strongly recommend Mr. A take the new job," and the most cautious was "7. Strongly recommend Mr. A remain in present job." Positions 2 and 3 were labeled so as to represent, respectively, moderate and little risk, and positions 5 and 6, little and moderate caution. Position 4 was labeled "Neutral, i.e., the two alternatives appear equally balanced."

The seven-point scale with a labeled position of neutrality produced results exactly comparable with those produced using the odds alternatives. It was easier to answer, and the neutral point on the scale functioned as the psychologically neutral position: Dilemmas that scored between 3.5 and 4.5 on the initial individual means showed no significant shift as a result of discussion. The odds options and the seven-point scale were proved to be essentially equivalent instruments for the study of problems involving risk. However, the seven-point scale has a wider range of usefulness not shared by the odds options. A seven-point scale of the kind Fraser used is called a Likert-type scale (named for Rensis Likert, a pioneer in opinion survey work), usually used to measure attitudes, not risk options. The use of the seven-point scale clears the way for a new reformulation of our decision choice phenomenon, a reformulation having nothing to do with risk and, indeed, not linked to any one kind of content. A seven-point scale can even be used with the meaning: "1. Very definitely guilty"; "4. Equally likely to be guilty or not guilty"; "7. Very definitely not guilty." We shall shortly see it used in that way and so draw near to *Twelve Angry Men.*

It was Moscovici and Zavalloni (1969) of the Laboratoire de Psychologie Sociale in Paris who first suggested that the much-studied shifts in risk might be an instance of a completely general group polarization effect. Perhaps it is the case with every sort of attitude, belief, and decision that group discussion moves the mean of initial individual decisions farther out, away from the mean, in the direction of the initial inclination. The Paris group used Likert scales running from +3 to −3, rather than from 1 to 7, which was Fraser's choice; it makes no difference, and since most work since has adopted the Paris form, we shall do the same. A scale item reads like this:

− 3: strongly disagree
− 2: disagree
− 1: slightly disagree
  0: incapable of expressing an opinion
+ 1: slightly agree
+ 2: agree
+ 3: strongly agree

With items in this form the group polarization hypothesis can be very simply stated: On whichever side of zero the initial mean falls, it will, after discussion, move farther away from the mean toward the nearer pole.

The first experiments were done with secondary school students (eighteen or nineteen years old) in Paris using discussion groups of four members each. Attitudes were initially assessed toward General de Gaulle and toward "the

Americans." A typical item on de Gaulle reads: "He is too old for his important political task" (agree or disagree on a scale from +3 to −3). A typical item on "les Américains": "American economic aid is always used for political purposes." The average initial attitude toward de Gaulle was mildly favorable (+.90); after discussion both the group consensus and the mean of final individual decisions became more favorable (+1.18), which is to say that discussion moved opinion farther in the direction of the nearer pole. Initial attitudes toward Americans were mildly negative (−.60) at first and became more so (−1.09) after discussion, which is to say that they moved farther out from zero in the direction of the original departure from zero. While we are in Paris, we should add the study by Doise (1969), which showed group polarization in the case of attitudes of students at a school of architecture toward their school; initially negative, they became more so after discussion.

The work we have considered until this point all concerns problems or objects of attitudes that elicit the same initial inclination from all the groups studied, and that leaves us wondering how group polarization would work with social issues that arouse a range of opinion, including opposed polarizations. For instance: racial prejudices. Myers and Bishop (1971) had high school students respond to a 100-item prejudice inventory, and they then created two sorts of homogeneous populations: the more prejudiced and the less prejudiced. The mean scores of the two populations fell on either side of zero. What would happen to individual attitudes if like-minded persons were formed into small groups and given some statements relevant to prejudice to discuss? The theory of group polarization holds that because of social comparison and the sharing of relevant arguments, the initially divergent groups should move toward their individual poles and, therefore, end up farther apart than they were before discussion.

The groups were given eight propositions to discuss, for instance: "Some people recently have been saying that 'white racism' is basically responsible for conditions in which Negroes live in American cities. Do you agree or disagree?" However, everyone was first asked to respond for himself to each item on a Likert-type scale. After discussion, they were asked to respond again. Both homogeneous groups moved toward their respective extreme poles, and so they were farther apart after discussion than before. Notice that these discussions did not put the prejudiced and unprejudiced together, the kind likely to take place when, for instance, a neighborhood action related to prejudice is to be voted on. The discussions in the experiment were the kind that would take place in advance of any official representative meeting, discussions in which, for the most part, like-minded individuals get together and exchange views. It is perhaps the first principle of social psychology that people associate with people who are similar to themselves, and so most informal discussion of issues goes on in homogeneous groups. Such discussions should, the theory holds, *amplify* initial disagreements between opposed groups.

When we are interested in "cooling off" an issue, in depolarizing extreme factions, and that is certainly something we are often interested in doing (the middle East, relations between the United States and the U.S.S.R., prison riots, Italians and blacks in Boston), the cry that always goes up is "keep them talking." Evidently the layman's theory is that if extreme factions are brought to talk together, there will be a net depolarization, a movement away from both extremes toward a moderate position. Eugene Burnstein (1982) of the Research Center for Group Dynamics at the University of Michigan has recently reported some results on depolarization that are so suggestive they are sure to be followed up in many experiments.

Burnstein has been the principal champion of the persuasive arguments explanation of shifts in risk, and his studies on depolarization were done with four standard risky shift choice dilemmas, one standard cautious shift dilemma, and two standard neutral (or no shift) dilemmas. He created six-member groups to discuss the items, but those groups, unlike those put together to demonstrate group polarization, were not homogeneous. They were made up of two sets of opposed extremes (three members each). What happened? The principal effect was depolarization or convergence to the central tendency, and it was a big effect—two or more units on the odds scale. So the layman's prescription for damping contention seems to be right. However, even the first experiments indicate that two qualifications must be entered.

Neutral items are items that have argument pools evenly balanced between risk and caution. When polarized factions are put together, the only thing that happens on those items is depolarization or convergence. Risky items are items having pools in which arguments for risk are more numerous and persuasive than arguments for caution, and for cautious items the balance of arguments in the total pools is just the reverse. In a certain sense, remember, risky and cautious dilemmas can be said to have "correct answers"; the correct answer is just the total pool of relevant persuasive arguments. What happens when problems like these are discussed by opposed extremes with equal numbers representing each extreme? Depolarization is still the largest effect—the extremes move toward one another—but it is not the only significant effect. The naturally risky items also all show a risky shift and the naturally cautious items a cautious shift. This is to say that the new, converged-upon moderate position is for the risky items closer to the initial position of the risky extreme than to the initial position of the cautious extreme, and for the cautious items it is nearer the initial cautious extreme.

Here is an example: On dilemma A, a risky shift dilemma, the two extremes were 5.09 points apart initially and only 2.00 points apart after discussion. They closed 3.09 points of difference. However, they did not evenly split the difference. The cautious faction moved more than the risky faction, with the result that the final mean position (3.50) was riskier than the initial mean position by 1.21 points. For cautious item E it was the risky factor that did the greater part of the moving. What that means is that the final outcome is a kind of compromise between depolarization or convergence and the right answer, so that the final position is more moderate than either extreme but is nearer the extreme that argued for the correct answer or, more exactly, the extreme that had the better pool of arguments to draw from. The action implication would seem to be: Bring extreme factions together if you want a decision more moderate than either extreme, but if one extreme is more nearly correct or has a better stock of arguments, the final common position will suit them better than the opposition.

Of course, depolarization on long-standing real social issues involving race, gender, capital punishment, and the like is not so easily accomplished as it is with story problems involving risk. Burnstein has identified one reason why not (we know there are many others). He compared the amount of depolarization produced when extremes discussed long-familiar, much-debated issues (including capital punishment) with the amount produced for new problems. On unfamiliar problems massive depolarization occurred, but on familiar social issues, little or none. That tells us what we know; that getting three Israelis and three members of the PLO to talk together will not produce sweet harmony. We knew that already, but persuasive arguments theory tells us one general reason why familiar and long-debated issues do not depolarize easily. It must be, in part, because the total pool of arguments has long been familiar to all. There is nothing new to be learned in group discussion.

Group Polarization in Jury Deliberations

A jury must deal with a choice dilemma for which the response options are verdicts of "guilty" or "not guilty." The problem a jury faces is not a one-paragraph story or a one-sentence statement of opinion. It is nothing less than the trying of a case: evidence, testimony, argument, and rebuttal, extending sometimes over many days. The trial each juror hears disposes him more or less strongly to one or the other of the two verdicts, and each goes into the jury room with an initial prediscussion opinion, which is often promptly disclosed on a first ballot. The discussion that then takes place is designed to produce the level of consensus the judge has instructed them to reach; for six-member juries it must be unanimous, and for twelve-member juries it is often the same, but majority decisions are also sometimes legal. In jury discussions both persuasive arguments and social comparison processes occur. Jury deliberations are therefore the sort of situation in which group polarization should occur, and Myers and Kaplan (1976) have shown that it does—at least in an experiment.

The law requires that jury deliberations be private, and so they may not be directly studied. The research approach, therefore, is to simulate the real thing. Myers and Kaplan did not attempt a very realistic simulation: Juries were ten groups of six undergraduate subjects each, and the cases were printed adaptations taken from the *California Law Reviews*. In Chapter 8 some extremely realistic simulations are described in which jurors were actually drawn from the juror rolls, and cases were carefully reenacted in courtrooms with real judges and attorneys. In order to see whether group polarization occurred in jurylike deliberations, Myers and Kaplan judged that elaborate efforts at realistic simulation were not necessary.

Four traffic felony cases abstracted from the *California Law Reviews* were used. Each case was written in two forms: High incrimination or low incrimination. Here is one case in the high incrimination form; it created a very strong presumption of guilt:

> L., a bakery truck driver, was charged with negligent death in the fatal injury of a 2-year-old child, C. The defendant was engaged in driving a bakery truck which made both home deliveries and "on the street" sales. Purchasers "on the street" were generally children. The truck had made regular visits to this particular street and was well known to local children. On the day in question, L. parked parallel to the curb. No other vehicles were parked in the vicinity of the truck. L. noted a group of children playing in a nearby backyard and rang some chimes, the customary means of attracting customers. The children approached the truck, on the street side, and made several purchases. While selling the children the bakery products the driver's back was turned to the front of the truck. In this period, C., who had been playing with the others, approached the truck and began playing in the street, in front of the left front wheel.
>
> Due to his position while serving the children, and the size of the truck, it was impossible for the defendant to see the child, unless he walked around to the front.
>
> After serving, the defendant returned to his seat in the truck. The truck was deemed by safety officials to have adequate windshield area and mirrors to assure good visibility on all sides. The driver looked into the side mirror to ascertain that the children he had served were standing on the sidewalk, but in testimony, couldn't remember whether he had looked in front of the truck for children. C. was 3 feet tall, and would have required a downward glance from the front seat to be seen.
>
> Since children were the primary customers of the truck, police officers had instructed the driver on several occasions to blow his horn when leaving a parking space. Adult witnesses testified that the defendant did not, on this occasion, blow his horn. The driver started the truck, checked his rear view mirror, and pulled out into the street. While pulling out, his head was turned to the rear, watching for traffic. He stopped when he heard the child's screams. Front and rear wheels had passed over the child. [Kaplan and Kemmerick, 1974]

In the low incrimination version of this case the driver blew his horn several times, checked his rear view mirror, and also looked through his windshield in front of the truck but failed to allow for a blind spot just forward of the front wheels that resulted from a peculiar driving position. "Jurors" read one or the other version of a case and then rated the degree of guilt of driver "L." from "0 (Definitely not guilty)" to "20 (Definitely guilty)." In addition, they were asked to assume that L. had been found guilty and to recommend a level of punishment from the minimum the law allowed for the charge (1) to the maximum (7). Those judgments, made for both versions of four cases, were the individual prediscussion opinions. The cases were then discussed for a few minutes by a "jury," and jurors individually made the two sets of ratings a second time. A control always used in group polarization studies was used also here: Some subjects simply rated the cases twice without intervening discussion so that any possible effect of familiarization with the materials could be checked.

Initial mean guilt ratings across high incrimination (or high-guilt) cases were about 12.5 (on the "Definitely guilty" side of the midpoint 10), and means after discussion moved toward the extreme to a mean value of about 15.0. Low-guilt cases were eventually rated at about 6.0 (on the "Definitely not guilty" side of the midpoint) and after discussion had moved out to about 4.0. In short, a polarization effect of substantial size occurred, with the "initial ballots" turning into group verdicts more extreme in the original directions. Comparable polarization effects occurred for the levels of punishment recommended, and the controls for familiarization showed no significant effects at all. All results are pictured in Figure 6–4.

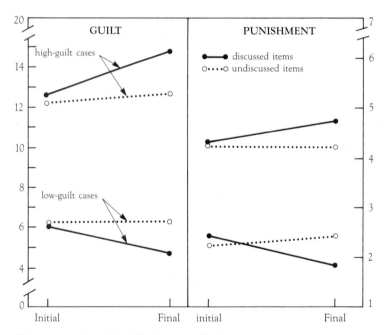

Figure 6–4. Initial and final ratings for discussed and undiscussed cases

(D. G. Myers and M. F. Kaplan, Group-induced polarization in simulated juries, *Personality and Social Psychology Bulletin, 2* [1976], pp. 63–66. Copyright © 1976 by the Society for Personality and Social Psychology, Inc. Reprinted by permission of Sage Publications, Inc.)

The Myers and Kaplan study seems to be the only jury simulation study that was set up to test group polarization, but just about all mock jury studies have incidentally collected data that make possible a check on group polarization: individual predeliberation opinions and a postdeliberation group verdict, often also individual postdeliberation opinions. In every instance where the report of data makes it possible to check, group polarization occurs (e.g. Davis et al., 1975; Hastie, Penrod, and Pennington, 1983; Kerr and MacCoun, 1985; Padawer-Singer, Singer, and Singer, 1977; Saks, 1977; Valenti and Downing, 1975).

Of course, even the most realistic simulation is not a real jury-of-record, making a decision with consequences for a real defendant, but we can be sure that group polarization occurs also in real juries because of a very telling statistic on their outcome. While it is unlawful to "tamper" with real juries by studying them when they are doing their work, it is entirely lawful to question jurors after they have discharged their obligations, and that was done on a massive scale by Kalven and Zeisel (1966). The vital statistic is that for 90 percent of juries that must reach unanimous agreement and do not hang, the final verdict is consistent in direction with the majority on the initial ballot. It is very rare for an initial ballot to yield a unanimous outcome; initial ballots are less extreme than that. Therefore, to know that the predeliberation majority, whether for conviction or for acquittal, predicts the final verdict 90 percent of the time is powerful presumptive evidence that group polarization occurs in real juries.

Twelve Angry Men

The vital statistic from Kalven and Zeisel that 90 percent of real juries finally vote in the direction of their initial majorities restores in full the apparent absurdity of the vote switch in Reginald Rose's play. So, apparently, does the entire story of group polarization, since Rose's twelve-man jury precisely *does not polarize*. It does not become more extreme in the direction of original inclination but reverses an original inclination that was initially almost unanimous. What then can be the purpose of linking a silly piece of fiction with a tradition of good cumulative research, and how is it possible that the research should prove the verisimilitude of *Twelve Angry Men*? The congruence is on the level not of surface outcomes but of causal processes. Persuasive arguments and social comparison operate in the play in such a way as to make the vote switch the correct outcome. And the play is more than an illustration of the two principles of group dynamics; it expands our understanding of them.

A trial has just ended as the curtain rises; a trial of murder in the first degree, premeditated homicide, the most serious charge in our criminal courts. "If there is reasonable doubt in your minds," the judge instructs the jury, "as to the guilt of the accused—then you must declare him not guilty. If—however—

there is no reasonable doubt, then he must be found guilty" (Rose, 1956, p. 9). The verdict must be unanimous.

What are the principal facts in the case? A man has been stabbed to death, and his nineteen-year-old son is the accused. They are members of some unspecified ethnic minority, living in a poor section of a large city in an apartment that is periodically shaken by the rush past its windows of an elevated train. What pieces of evidence connect the son with the crime? There are several small circumstantial items but only three weighty ones.

The murder weapon is a switchblade knife. Everyone agrees that it is an unusual knife, and a storekeeper has testified that he sold just such a knife to the son, arguably just this knife, it being the only one of its kind he had in stock, and everyone thinks it unique. The son, however, testifies that he bought the knife for a friend and lost it through a hole in his pocket before the murder took place.

In the apartment just beneath the scene of the murder lives an old man who has suffered two strokes and walks, with difficulty, with the help of two canes. The old man has testified that on the night of the murder he heard a quarrel overhead and heard the son scream, "I'm going to kill you," and then a body fell to the floor. He heard someone running down the stairs and, hurrying to the door of his own apartment, looked out and saw the son.

Just at the time the murder occurred, an elevated train thundered past the windows of the father's apartment. In the apartment across the tracks a woman lay in bed unable to sleep, her head beside a window looking directly toward the scene of the murder with the passing train between. At the trial she testified that she saw the murder and identified the son as murderer. The prosecutor demonstrated to the jury that it was, in fact, possible to look through the windows of a moving train and identify someone on the opposite side. That eyewitness testimony weighed very heavily with the jurors who voted "guilty."

Persuasive Arguments

The play does not ask us to accept on faith the credibility of the vote switch that occurs between the initial ballot and the final verdict; that is the event the playwright undertakes to make credible. However, the play does require us to accept something quite improbable, to "suspend disbelief" on one point, which is, in fact, the point that makes it possible for persuasive arguments to operate in the jury room in such a way as to make "not guilty" the correct verdict. We must believe that even though the trial has been long and complex, the defense attorney has done a very poor job; only if a poor job was done in the trial would it be possible for the holdout juror, Henry Fonda, to come up with new evidence and new arguments so persuasive as to convince both jurors and audience. There is passing reference to that improbably bad defense:

JUROR NO. 8: I had a peculiar feeling about this trial. Somehow I felt that the defense counsel never really conducted a thorough cross-examination. Too many questions were left unasked.

JUROR NO. 4: While it doesn't change my opinion about the guilt of the kid, still, I agree with you that the defense counsel was bad. [p. 22]

From the point of view of persuasive arguments theory, the case on trial is a problem for which the total pool of arguments and evidence favors "not guilty." That verdict is, in the persuasive arguments sense, the "correct answer." The trial that has taken place before the play begins should be regarded as strictly analogous to one of the contrived discussions, using a total of ten arguments, divided one way or another between risky and cautious, used by Ebbesen and Bowers (1974) with five problems, some of which had correct answers that were risky and some of which had correct answers that were cautious. The trial that took place is like a discussion contrived to go against the natural bent of a problem. The initial ballot is congruent with the balance of arguments heard, as in the Ebbesen and Bowers experiment, but the way is open for a new trial to be carried on in the jury room, and that trial unfolds in a way that is consistent with the total pool of arguments. In effect, the play asks us to entertain as a premise the possibility of a seriously unrepresentative trial so that the playwright can show us what interesting things follow from such a premise.

The holdout juror (Henry Fonda) systematically destroys the three principal pieces of evidence, in the order of their listing here, which puts the most important piece, the eyewitness testimony, in final position. This is, after all, a play, and a play should build to a climax. If it were within the province of this book to include an explicit mathematical model of the persuasive arguments theory, it would be possible to describe more exactly what Fonda accomplishes. In terms of an information integration analysis (Anderson and Graesser, 1976), each piece of evidence would have both a value (for guilty or not guilty) and a weight. The three pieces of evidence retain their value (if accepted, they argue guilty), but Fonda systematically reduces the weight of each to zero.

First—the unique knife. Fonda (Juror No. 8) asks that the guard bring in the knife so that it may be examined again.

JUROR NO. 4 (holding up knife): Everyone connected with the case identified this knife. Now are you trying to tell me that someone picked it up off the street and went up to the boy's house and stabbed his father with it just to be amusing?

JUROR NO. 8: No. I'm saying that it's possible that the boy lost the knife, and that someone else stabbed his father with a similar knife. It's possible. (Juror No. 4 flips knife open and jams it into wall just downstage of door L.)

JUROR NO. 4 (standing back to allow others to see): Take a look at that knife. It's a very strange knife. I've never seen one like it before in my life.

Neither had the storekeeper who sold it to him. (*Juror No. 8 reaches casually into his pocket and withdraws an object. No one notices him. He stands up.*) Aren't you trying to make us accept a pretty incredible coincidence?
JUROR NO. 8 (*moving toward Juror No. 4*): I'm not trying to make anyone accept it. I'm just saying it's possible.
JUROR NO. 3 (*rising, shouting*): And I'm saying it's not possible!" (*Juror No. 8 swiftly flicks open blade of a switchknife, jams it into wall next to first knife, and steps back. They are exactly alike. There are several gasps and EVERYONE stares at knife. There is a long silence.*) [pp. 23–24]

It turns out that No. 8 found an exact replica of the murder weapon in a junk shop just around the corner. So much for the unique knife. The weight of the evidence connecting the murder weapon to the knife the son bought is now zero. Of course, it is reduced to zero in a dramatic way. I have not said that there was nothing to Rose's play except persuasive arguments and social comparison. He uses them (intuitively), but he is also a dramatist.

The second item of evidence is the testimony of the old man downstairs. Whether or not he could have heard the son scream, "I'm going to kill you" with a train going past, and whether such a statement should be taken as a statement of serious intent in any case, is left moot. Much more serious is his testimony that he identified the son running down the stairs. He said he saw him just fifteen seconds after the body hit the floor overhead. The question is raised by the holdout juror whether an old man who has had two strokes and who walks with two canes could in fifteen seconds rise from his bed, take hold of his canes, and walk 12 feet to his bedroom door and 43 feet more down a hallway to his apartment door. Those numbers let us in for one of those tiresome reenactments favored in courtroom drama, with one juror holding a stopwatch and Henry Fonda acting the old man. His time is thirty-nine seconds, not fifteen.

The reenactment raises reasonable doubt about the old man's testimony. What remains is the testimony of an eyewitness, and eyewitness testimony always counts for more with juries than does circumstantial evidence. A woman across the tracks from the father's apartment has said she saw the son commit the murder through the windows of a passing el train.

Juror No. 4, who is the most intelligent and temperate of those convinced the son is guilty, grants that reasonable doubt has been created about much of the evidence, but he himself remains convinced the verdict should be "guilty" precisely because of the eyewitness testimony. He reviews what the woman said and concludes: "As far as I can see, this is unshakable testimony" (p. 60). At this point—late in Act III—it had begun to look as if a verdict of "not guilty" might be brought in; a majority of nine had come round to that view. However, No. 4's obviously fair and well-reasoned summary, together with his impressive appearance, has shaken all the unsteady voters. There is a long silence, and then No. 4 suggests that the time may have come to admit that they are a hung jury.

JUROR NO. 2: What time is it?

JUROR NO. 8: Can't you see the clock without your glasses?

JUROR NO. 2 Not clearly.

JUROR NO. 8: Oh.

JUROR NO. 4: Glasses are a nuisance, aren't they?

JUROR NO. 8 (an edge of excitement in his tone): Well, what do you all do when you wake up at night and want to know what time it is?

JUROR NO. 2: I put my glasses on and look at the clock.

JUROR NO. 8: (to Juror No. 2): Do you wear your glasses to bed?

JUROR NO. 2: Of course not. No one wears eyeglasses to bed.

JUROR NO. 8: The woman who testified that she saw the killing wears glasses. What about her? [p. 61]

The jury takes a few minutes to digest the new information. The woman had worn bifocals in court and had never taken them off. Henry Fonda wraps it all up by saying the eyewitness probably was not wearing her eyeglasses in bed. "Maybe she honestly thought she saw the boy kill his father. I say that she only saw a blur" (p. 62).

In the end, reasonable doubt has been created about every single piece of evidence, and so "not guilty" must be the verdict. If the premise is accepted that the trial that preceded the jury deliberations was unrepresentative of the total pool of arguments, then it is credible that a new sample from that pool, drawn in the jury room, might be more representative and lead to the correct answer. Perhaps it is unrealistic to have one juror think of most of the new arguments, but that one juror is the star of the show, the hero, Henry Fonda. For once the heroism on view is largely cognitive or intellectual in nature. The most extraordinary thing about No. 8 is that he comes from the trial which all twelve have attended with something like a full set of the persuasive arguments that make "not guilty" the correct answer whereas the eleven others do not. However, No. 8 is heroic in character as well as intellect and so a second process of group dynamics operates in the play.

Social Comparison

Social comparison operates in *Twelve Angry Men* in a way that is more subtle and more general than its mode of operation in problems involving risk or in discussions of social issues. Indeed, I think the play reveals better than any experiment the real domain of social comparison in group decisions. Imagine that you are a member of some decision-making body, a board or a committee, and that you are expected to vote on every issue that comes before the group even though you privately know that you are not always well qualified to do so. That happens. It has happened to me fairly often. One can be elected or appointed to a position on the basis of presumed qualifications and yet not necessarily have all the qualifications. I have voted to accept dissertations when I did not fully understand some technical matter controversial among the readers. I have voted for or against the award of fellowships in areas entirely outside my knowledge: theoretical physics or the pronominal system of Vietnamese. Such votes are not necessarily "incorrect," though they may be morally dubious. But let us imagine a worse case than any of those.

The city of Cambridge, Massachusetts, as of the fall of 1983, did not yet have cable television, nor had it made any contract for the installation of cable TV. I have somewhere read that there is disagreement as to whether Cambridge should itself undertake the installation or whether it should contract with an outside company. That is as much as I know. Suppose that by some Satanic maladvertence I were appointed to the group charged with making the decision. Suppose further that all members of the group were unknown to me, that I could not evaluate their professional credentials, that when the discussion took place the arguments made were all completely beyond my comprehension, and that the group, quite unaware of my total incompetence, expected me to cast a vote for either city control of cable or outside control. I ought, of course, to excuse myself and go home, but maybe I do not want to admit to my full ignorance. Would there be any way that I could, listening to a discussion of which I understood nothing, guess at the correct answer? In fact, there would be.

In a good expressive discussion, such as the deliberations in *Twelve Angry Men*, information is transmitted that is not part of any relevant argument. Each participant in some degree expresses his individuality: assertiveness, intelligence, education, fair-mindedness, compassion, prejudice, cowardice, and so on. Each participant also reveals which side of the issue he supports and how strongly. In such circumstances, positions on the issue *take on meanings* even if the issue itself is not understood at all. In the imaginary case of Cambridge cable, I might learn that the position labeled "city control" is championed by people who seem to be authoritarian, not highly educated, distrustful of others, and identified with wealth, whereas the position "outside control" is championed by people who seem to me to be fair-minded, highly educated, and equally concerned for the welfare of all citizens. The casting of my ignorant vote becomes a pure act of self-presentation. What sort of person do I myself want to be, and what sort of person do I want to appear to be? Not knowing the cognitively correct answer, there is still an answer correct for me; it is the answer championed by the kind of people I admire and wish to resemble. (Remember, please, that the suggested linkage between position and personality is entirely imaginary. I really do not know anything about the issue.)

In an important way the extreme case imagined is like social comparison as it operates in risk problems: The individual has certain values he wishes to realize, to express in his decision, but he cannot know how to realize his values until he finds out the distribution of positions in the group. In another way the case imagined is unlike decisions on risk or attitudes on race or gender: The individual knows nothing about the positions and so cannot make an initial pre-discussion decision except by tossing a coin. The choice dilemmas offering various odds options or seven-point-scale positions, and also the scale on prejudice, contain some information, enough to give the individual the strong impression that he knows in advance of discussion how to make a decision congruent with his values. If he wants to be a risk-taker or unprejudiced, he at least thinks he knows on which side of the middle of the scale he ought to place himself. The group polarization phenomenon, setting aside persuasive arguments, indicates that people do not know everything they need to know in order to express the values they hold until a real distribution of positions becomes public.

The jurymen in Rose's play have as their decision options "guilty" and "not guilty." In advance of the trial and of the jury deliberations, those options have no meaning at all, either cognitive or expressive. Then comes a trial that the judge says has been long and complex. Now, assembled in the juryroom, each individual has information on which to base a decision, and each has made a decision. However, there is disagreement within the group. Originally, only one member dissents, but after some discussion, he is joined by another and later another, and by the time they take a second formal ballot, opinions are evenly divided: Six vote not guilty and six vote guilty. How is an individual juryman to know what to do? He ought, of course, to attend to the relevant arguments coming from either side and let his decision be determined by the weight of argument. However, the arguments are many and complex, and so it is possible that some attention would be paid to social comparison as an alternative route to the right decision, a route less demanding than the purely intellectual one.

How would a conscientious juror wish to present himself to himself and to others? Presumably as a person able intellectually to evaluate the evidence, as disinterested and conscientious, as strong enough to convict if necessary but compassionate enough to acquit if there is reasonable doubt. How can he act so as to seem to have all those virtues? The hard way is, in fact, to have them all, but not everyone can manage that. There is an easier way, and that is to vote as those vote who seem to be intellectually capable, disinterested, conscientious, strong, and compassionate. How can one find out who these people are? By the way they conduct themselves in the discussion, by all their expressive behavior, by the great residue of action that goes beyond statement of relevant arguments.

The published form of Rose's play has an odd feature. Each juryman, named only by number, is characterized by the author, before the play starts, in a single-paragraph vignette. Here are the full vignettes for Juror No. 8 (Henry Fonda) and his opposite number, the juror most strongly attached to conviction, Juror No. 3 (Lee J. Cobb in the movie):

Juror No. Eight: He is a quiet, thoughtful, gentle man—a man who sees all sides of every question and constantly seeks the truth. He is a man of strength tempered with compassion. Above all, he is a man who wants justice to be done, and will fight to see that it is. [p. 5]

Juror No. Three: He is a very strong, very forceful, extremely opinionated man within whom can be detected a streak of sadism. Also he is a humorless man who is intolerant of opinions other than his own, and accustomed to forcing his wishes and views upon others. [p. 4]

When you read the two character vignettes and know that No. 8 is the juror most attached to "not guilty" and No. 3 the juror most attached to "guilty," the response options take on a meaning. It is a meaning independent of any relevant arguments, for none has been heard when one reads the vignettes. It is a meaning that results from the implicit question: "Who would I prefer to agree with?"

As it happens, the author has built into his play, not deliberately I would guess, but intuitively, an almost perfect correlation between the social desirability of each juror and the degree to which each juror is attached to conviction or acquittal. Here are the full vignettes for, respectively, the juror next to No. 8 in his attachment to acquittal (No. 9, the old man) and the juror next to No. 3 in his attachment to conviction (No. 10):

Juror No. Nine: He is a mild, gentle old man, long since defeated by life, and now merely waiting to die. He recognizes himself for what he is, and mourns the days when it would have been possible to be courageous without shielding himself behind his many years. [p. 5]

Juror No. Ten: He is an angry, bitter man—a man who antagonizes almost at sight. He is also a bigot who places no value on any human life save his own. Here is a man who has been nowhere and is going nowhere and knows it deep within him. [p. 5]

It becomes increasingly clear that "not guilty" is the good guys' ticket, as it were, and "guilty," the bad guys'. The little vignettes written as guides to the actors suggest no great characterological complexity, but then this is not a play of character; it is a play almost purely about group dynamics.

How can one determine from the action of the play the degree of adherence of each character to the alternative verdicts? There are two ways. The main way is the order in which jurymen switch from their initial vote for "guilty" to an eventual vote for "not guilty." Some of these changes of heart occur in one person at a time and some occur in two or three at once—as on the second formal ballot. Because they do not all move one at a time, there are some ties in adherence to a verdict, and so only a partial ordering is possible. Using hyphens to link jurors who switch at the same time and semicolons to separate jurors who switch at different points, the partial ordering by vote change from "not guilty" (anchored by Henry Fonda, No. 8, who votes that way from the start) is:

8; 9; 5; 2–6–11; 7–12–Foreman; 10–4; 3.

Adherence to one verdict or the other is also revealed, rather astonishingly, by the order in which the author directs that hands be raised on the initial ballot, voting "guilty." Using hyphens to connect simultaneous votes and semicolons to separate votes that can be ordered, the order of adherence from "guilty" now to "not guilty" (the reverse of the vote switches) is: 3-10-7-12; 4-Foreman-2-6-5; 11; 9; 8. It is, again, the case that No. 8 is distinctive because he never does vote "guilty"; he, therefore, anchors, as on the vote switches, the "not-guilty" extreme. Arraying the two orders from "not guilty" to "guilty," it becomes clear that we have two indices of the same thing:

Verdict switches: N.G. 8; 9; 5; 2-6-11; 7-12-Foreman; 10-4; 3
Voting order: N.G. 8; 9; 11; 2-6-5-Foreman-4; 3-10-12-7

In Figure 6-5 the jurors (identified by number) are arrayed from left to right in the more differentiated order, the order of verdict switches. I take it for granted that you will agree that social desirability declines from left to right.

The vignettes are advance guidelines for actors, but the jurors do not hold up cards describing their characteristics. How are the characteristics revealed? In dialogue and action strewn across three acts but generally extremely unambiguous fairly early on. Here are some characterizing speeches:

JUROR NO. 8: I want to talk for a while. Look—this kid's been kicked around all his life. You know—living in a slum—his mother dead since he was nine. That's not a very good head start . . . [p. 5]

Register "compassionate." Here is an early speech of his opposite number:

JUROR NO. 3: You're right. It's the kids. The way they are—you know? They don't listen (*Bitterly*). I've got a kid. When he was eight years old he ran away from a fight. I saw him. I was *so* ashamed. I told him right out, "I'm gonna make a man out of you or I'm gonna bust you up into little pieces trying." When he was fifteen he hit me in the face. He's big, you know? I haven't seen him in three years. Rotten kid! I hate tough kids! [p. 5]

Not exactly disinterested and certainly disposed to force his ways on others.

The jurors do not hold up cards on which their characters are written, but imagine a Theater of the Absurd in which they would (Figure 6-5). It would certainly make social comparison easy. And, given that one must choose between just two options, "guilty" and "not guilty," can there be any doubt which is the "right" answer? Once the correlation between virtue and verdict emerges, any doubtful juror, having trouble weighing the relevant arguments, would know how to vote.

The near-perfect correlation between attraction to acquittal and social desirability is the second unlikely premise the playwright asks us to entertain. Juror No. 4 is the only person seriously out of line, and he has to be—for a reason of dramaturgy. The vignette reads as follows.

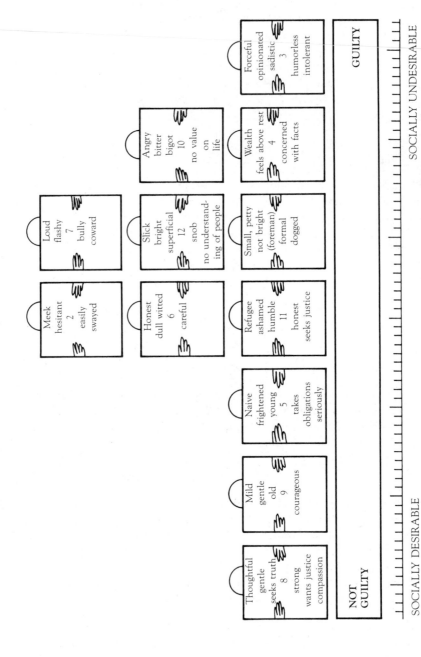

Figure 6-5. *Twelve Angry Men* display their characters and their verdict preferences (by order of vote switch)

SOCIALLY DESIRABLE

SOCIALLY UNDESIRABLE

NOT GUILTY

GUILTY

Thoughtful
gentle
seeks truth
8
strong
wants justice
compassion

Mild
gentle
old
9
courageous

Naive
frightened
young
5
takes
obligations
seriously

Meek
hesitant
2
easily
swayed

Honest
dull witted
6
careful

Refugee
ashamed
humble
11
honest
seeks justice

Loud
flashy
7
bully
coward

Slick
bright
superficial
12
snob
no understand-
ing of people

Small, petty
not bright
(foreman)
formal
dogged

Angry
bitter
bigot
10
no value
on
life

Wealth
feels above rest
4
concerned
with facts

Forceful
opinionated
sadistic
3
humorless
intolerant

Juror No. Four: He seems to be a man of wealth and position and a practiced speaker who presents himself well at all times. He seems to feel a little bit above the rest of the jurors. His only concern is with the facts in this case and he is appalled with the behavior of the others. [p. 4]

Juror No. 4 is especially appalled by his closest neighbors in Figure 6-5: a sadistic swine (12) and a bitter bigot (10). Those two are not equipped to keep the play going by making persuasive arguments in a temperate tone, designed to counter the arguments of No. 8. Gentlemanly, reasonable No. 4, however, is able to sustain some uncertainty, and it is only when he is persuaded—on the evidence of the eyeglasses—that the far right collapses.

The first premise the playwright implicitly asks us to entertain is the possibility that a person accused of murder could be so inadequately defended at his trial as to yield a near unanimous verdict that is incorrect as a representation of the total pool of arguments. Granted, the premise the "improbable" vote switch in the course of the play follows quite strictly from the theory of persuasive arguments. The second premise is the high correlation between attraction to acquittal and social desirability. Granted that premise, the vote switch follows quite strictly from the theory of social comparison. The author has proved *his* case in two ways, just the two that the theory of group polarization provides. He cleverly leaves implicit and barely detectable the two improbabilities he does not attempt to make credible—the unrepresentative case and the virtue–verdict correlation. The improbability that cannot be missed, the improbability that gives the play its punch, is the vote switch, and that improbability is rendered fully credible. While the play's construction is not exactly a proof in geometry, it has some of the elegance of such a proof.

Scientific Jury Selection

If group polarization operates in the jury room, it would seem to follow that selection of the jury is an all-important process. That must be so, because except in the improbable case of an unrepresentative trial, like the one in *Twelve Angry Men*, the initial inclination of the jury simply becomes more extreme in group discussion. The trick, then, from an attorney's point of view, whether prosecuting or defending, is to get jurors with the "right" initial inclination. There is nothing new in this, and books on trial tactics are filled with guides to juror selection. What is new and is sometimes regarded as a strong threat to our judicial system and, less often, as a major advance in attaining justice, is the use since 1972 of a technology that promises greatly to improve upon intuitive guides for selecting juries—even those of such eminent attorneys as F. Lee Bailey and Melvin Belli.

The idea is simply to do an opinion survey of the community from which jurors will be drawn, asking respondents how they would be inclined to vote, for example, in the case of a particular defendant X accused of murdering a particular Y. Those pretrial inclinations are then related to age, sex, political affiliation, marital status, and every sort of personality characteristic. From the correlations between opinions on the trial and juror characteristics, it is possible to work out profiles of the "good" juror and the "bad" juror from the point of view of the side that commissioned the survey. Then in the *voir dire* (Old French: to speak the truth) procedure, in which prospective jurors are interrogated, an attorney can use what are called his peremptory challenges (free dismissals made without having to show cause) to eliminate the "bad" jurors and so incline the jury his way.

The process of jury selection begins with some kind of list of membership in a community, most often voter registration rolls, but because young people, minorities, and the poor are underrepresented on those rolls, they are sometimes supplemented with welfare lists or lists of persons holding driver's licenses. The Supreme Court has, in a series of decisions, taken the position that a jury must be a representative cross-section of the community in which the offense was committed. The reasons for doing so are, from a group problem-solving point of view, excellent. "Representative" has, in practice, generally meant heterogeneous, and problems are in general more likely to be solved if a variety of perspectives and experiences are brought to bear upon them.

From the source list of members of a community the jury commissioner's staff selects (usually at random) a pool of potential jurors, who are sent a questionnaire. Some are disqualified (not knowing English is a clear disqualification), and some are exempted (doctors, nurses, mothers of infants, and so on), but eventually a pool of prospective jurors, called the venire, is selected to serve for a given period, usually about a month. Then comes the *voir dire* procedure in which defense and prosecuting attorney and/or the judge question members of the venire to ascertain whether or not they can serve without bias. A panel member, a potential juror, may be excused in either of two ways. A "challenge for cause" occurs when the judge is persuaded that a panel member cannot be impartial. In addition, both defense and prosecution are allowed some number (e.g. six to twelve) of "peremptory challenges," for which it is not necessary to give any reason. The number of peremptory challenges varies with the jurisdiction, the seriousness of the charge, and the number of defendants.

In trials with political implications, such as the trials on conspiracy charges in the late 1960s and 1970s of Angela Davis, Black Panther Huey Newton, the Berrigan brothers and, in the post-Watergate period, of John Mitchell and Maurice Stans, the probability of bias was very great, and the *voir dire* was lengthy and searching. The number of peremptory challenges allowed the defense was also unusually large. Lawyers have for centuries tried to select jurors favorable to their side of a case, and they quite naturally and inevitably have developed generalizations about how to do so. It is equally natural and inevitable that those generalizations have never been impartially tested and that most of them simply traffic in stereotypes. Bailey and Rothblatt, in their *Successful Techniques for Criminal Trials* (1971), advise defense lawyers to choose women if the principal witness against the defendant is female, because women are "somewhat distrustful" of other women. On the question of wealth and status, Clarence Darrow (1936) warns that the wealthy will convict unless the defendant is accused of a white-collar crime. Goldstein (1935) has ranked ethnic groups on emotionalism, from high to low: Irish, Jewish, Italian, French, Spanish, Slavic, and Nordic. The last (including English, Scandinavians, and Germans) are to be preferred if it will be necessary to combat emotional appeals.

The examples just given probably do not inspire much confidence in the juror selection tactics that lawyers have developed by unsystematic trial and error, but of course there are also some more prepossessing examples. It would be extremely interesting to know how much truth there is in each generalization that has been put forward, but no one is ever going to carry out that research program.

In the winter of 1971-72, the Harrisburg Seven, including the Berrigan brothers, were tried for conspiracy to raid draft boards and destroy records; blow up the heating tunnels in Washington, D.C.; and kidnap Secretary of State Henry Kissinger. The trial was held in Harrisburg, Pennsylvania, a very conservative and pro-government community, and so a group of sympathetic social scientists joined the defense team, headed by former Attorney General Ramsey Clark. That group made the first methodologically sound use of the technique called "scientific jury selection."

They carried out surveys of samples in Harrisburg, asking about attitudes toward the defendants and their case, administering various sorts of possibly relevant personality scales and collecting such demographic data as age, sex, occupation, race, education, media contacts, and hobbies. There is really no telling what might be significantly related to attitudes toward a case. One might find young, egalitarian females who read *The New York Times* well disposed to the defense and older, authoritarian males who read the *New York Daily News* on the side of the prosecution. Those data were combined (nowadays it would be by computer) to yield profiles of the good juror and the bad juror. Then, in the *voir dire*, defense attorneys asked such seemingly "innocent" questions as, "What newspapers do you read regularly?" and used their peremptory challenges (several hundred were granted) to excuse bad jurors. The trial ended in a hung jury, 10-2 favoring the defense. A clear victory for the defense. Is it also clear proof that scientific jury selection works? Not quite.

For one thing, the Harrisburg defense did not rely entirely on its surveys and profiles; in fact, the social scientists, not knowing whether they would work well or not, advised against such total reliance, so the lawyers also exercised their own judgment. The story is that the computer had vetoed one juror that Ramsey Clark decided to keep, and that juror was one of the two who held out for conviction—that too, however, is not serious evidence. In addition to the informed intuition of the lawyers, the defense made use of an old technique used to some extent also by prosecution. While it is illegal directly to approach a venireman, it is not illegal to ask around about him; in short, you can ask someone who knows someone on the venire. That is a rather tricky thing to do, because if the target gets wind of your inquiries, he may develop a strong bias against you (Berman and Sales, 1977; Bonora and Krauss, 1979; Kairys, Schulman, and Harring, 1975; McConahay, Mullin, and Frederick, 1977).

Scientific jury selection has created a great stir; there are commercial firms that will do the whole job for a rather large fee. And here lies a possible danger to our justice system since only wealthy defendants (usually corporations) may be able to afford scientific jury selection. The curious thing is that the faith in the method is not supported by the best research on the topic (Berman and Sales, 1977; Hastie, Penrod, and Pennington, 1983; Penrod, 1979; Saks, 1977). What convinces many is the very high batting average. Almost no cases have been lost by a defense that used the method. However, until recently (the John DeLorean drug case and the Agent Orange class action suit) these cases have usually been highly political cases where the charge was conspiracy, and conspiracy is a difficult charge to prove. As it turns out (Hans and Vidmar, 1982; Saks and Hastie, 1978), the records of cases that did not use scientific jury selection but are comparable to those that did are equally good. So the high batting average is just no evidence at all—which does not necessarily mean that defendants with plenty of money will neglect to use it.

The work that has been done to assess the value of scientific jury selection is actually heavily loaded in favor of the method. The practice has been to determine many individual characteristics of actual jurors (always in simulated juries) and to find out how well those characteristics predict verdict preferences on a first, posttrial predeliberation verdict. This problem is, in two ways, easier than the problem that confronts any actual practitioner. In the first place, he is not allowed to approach actual jurors but must generalize to them from the study of samples of populations to which jurors belong. A more serious difficulty is that no survey can present respondents with the real problem jurors will face, which is forming verdict preferences *after* hearing a trial. A trial includes evidence, testimony, and argument that may last some days, and everything indicates (Hans and Vidmar, 1982; Hastie, Penrod, and Pennington, 1983; Saks, 1976) that the content of the trial is much the most important determinant of initial verdict preferences. The respondent to a survey cannot be put in the juror's posttrial position. All the survey can do is try to find a question highly relevant to or predictive of verdict preferences, and such questions are hard to find.

The problem that has been posed in research designed to evaluate scientific jury selection is much easier than the field problem, and so if it were solved, we should not really know whether the field problem can be solved. However, if even the much-simplified procedure of predicting posttrial verdict preferences from individual characteristics of jurors does not work, then we can be sure that the more difficult field procedure will not work. A single example will serve to represent a strikingly unanimous research outcome (Berman and Sales, 1977; Hastie, Penrod, and Pennington, 1983; Penrod, 1979; Saks, 1977).

In the highly realistic simulation study of Hastie, Penrod, and Pennington (1983), the 828 participating jurors provided information, including age, gender, occupation, residence, education, political party, marital status, race, income, and number of previous cases heard as a juror. That information was entered into a multiple regression equation designed to combine predictors in the most powerful way with posttrial, predeliberation verdict preferences as the dependent variable. The result: Only four predictors had any significant relation to verdict preferences, and the total R was .179, which is no use at all. A subsample of 269 jurors completed a more extensive questionnaire that included information about reading habits, attitude toward the death penalty, and other characteristics. Just five items had any relation to verdict preferences. Those were optimally combined, and verdict preferences simply dichotomized into votes favoring conviction for murder and votes favoring acquittal. In this form the votes of 61 percent of the jurors were correctly predicted. The result is a bit better than chance, but it hardly suggests a powerful technique. Furthermore, it must be a considerable overestimate of what can be accomplished in a real situation.

Even though the weight of the experimental evidence is that scientific jury selection is not of much use (at least in felony trials), I would not expect the market for the service to disappear, mainly because the idea seems too good. How can it fail eventually to work to some degree? In 1984 some "decision research" companies, as they call themselves, do not simply sample attitudes in advance of the real trial. They conduct advance mock trials, many times, before juries that are representative of the juror pools, and instead of simply trying to predict final votes from demographic characteristics they interview jurors on the main aspects of the trial.

If scientific jury selection ever attains substantial demonstrated power, there are many ways in which that power could be and probably would be checked. There is, in the first place, considerable risk in carrying out a prolonged *voir dire* with many questions not clearly relevant to the detection of bias; the attorney may prejudice the jury against his case if he seems to be trying to do what he may be trying to do, select a jury partial to his client. There are some attorneys even today who think the best strategy to use in the *voir dire* is unconcerned acceptance of the first twelve possible jurors, because the expressive meaning of this stance is roughly that of having so clear a case that it can safely be entrusted to anyone at all, and that expressive meaning is more important than the detection of bias (Blunk and Sales, 1977). In the second place, all questions in the *voir dire* are supposed to be designed to detect bias, and the judge can rule out any questions that do not seem to him to have this purpose. Finally, of course, the judge can, and in Massachusetts often does, simply relieve the attorneys of the interrogation task and take it entirely upon himself. What then would be the use of profiles of good jurors and bad jurors?

Summary

In the play *Twelve Angry Men* an initial juror ballot of 11–1 in favor of "guilty" becomes changed by jury discussion to a final verdict unanimously favoring "not guilty." Such an outcome would be an extreme statistical rarity, and yet in the play it seems entirely credible. That is because the play makes the outcome credible by means of the expert deployment of two processes of group dynamics: persuasive arguments and social comparison. The audience is led to believe that an extremely unrepresentative trial has taken place, with a completely inadequate defense, and that makes it possible for persuasive arguments to lead to a correct verdict in what amounts to a new and more representative trial held in the jury room. The audience accepts, without noticing it, an almost perfect correlation between the character and competence of twelve jurymen and their degree of attraction to a "not guilty" verdict. This makes it possible for social comparison processes to explain the "unrealistic" vote switch of the play.

Conceptualization of the two basic group processes—persuasive arguments and social comparison—was developed over a period of two decades, beginning in 1962. Development was consistently in the direction of increased generality and abstraction. The processes were first thought of as explanations of the risky shift, then as explanations of shifts either to increased risk *or* increased caution, then as processes explanatory of group polarization with respect to any content whatever—including trials at law. Group polarization is the following phenomenon: The means of individual decisions or attitudes, if they fall to one side of psychological neutrality, will, following group discussion by like-minded persons, become more extreme or polarized in the direction of the original inclination.

The theory of persuasive arguments (one of two sufficient explanations of group polarization) has the following essential features:

1. For each decision or judgment or attitude position, there exists a (culturally and historically relative) pool of arguments pro and con, with the balance varying from item to item.
2. Each person who individually takes a position draws upon some sample of the total pool of arguments; that sample determines the position he takes; and the character of the pool determines the mean of the individual positions. Prior to discussion, the arguments considered by any set of individuals are only partially shared.
3. In discussion, arguments are expressed and shared, and so each individual takes account of a larger and more representative portion of the total pool, and decisions shift toward the position anchored by the total

pool, which will be away from psychological neutrality in the same direction as the mean of the initial decisions, but more extreme or polarized.

The theory of social comparison (a second sufficient explanation of group polarization) has the following essential features:

1. Any given problem, decision, or dilemma engages in most people the desire to express certain values or virtues.
2. In advance of information as to the distribution of positions taken by other persons, each imagines that his own position does, in fact, express the relevant values or virtues.
3. When, in discussion, the actual distribution of positions is made known, those whose positions do not express the relevant values will be motivated to shift.

There is reason to think that group polarization operates in the deliberations of real juries; 90 percent of juries that do not hang reach verdicts consistent with the original ballot and, by definition, more extreme than that ballot. Because jury deliberation primarily amplifies initial jury inclination, it would seem to be very important for the winning of a case to have the right jury. A method of scientific jury selection has been invented which, in essence, tries to predict juror inclinations on a case from individual characteristics shown by empirical survey methods to be related in the general community. There are two deep difficulties. The problem a real jury considers is nothing less than the total hearing of a case plus their own group deliberations upon it. That problem cannot be presented by survey methods to a community sample, and the surrogate problem (a questionnaire) may not realistically represent what the people surveyed would do if required to serve. Furthermore, it seems not to be the case that jurors' predeliberation verdict preferences are determined by demographic characteristics or prior attitudes. It looks very much as if jurors try to carry out their solemn duty as impartial fact finders and so establish verdict preferences based mainly on the trial evidence.

References

ANDERSON, N. H., and C. C. GRAESSER. 1976. An information integration analysis of attitude change in group discussion, *Journal of Personality and Social Psychology*, 34: 210–22.

BAILEY, F. L., and H. B. ROTHBLATT. 1981. *Successful Techniques for Criminal Trials*. New York: Lawyers Cooperative.

BERMAN, J., and J. B. SALES. 1977. A critical evaluation of the systematic approach to jury selection, *Criminal Justice and Behavior*, 4: 219–40.

BISHOP, G. D., and D. G. MYERS. 1974. Informational influence in group discussion, *Organizational Behavior and Human Performance*, 12:902–1104.

BLUNK, R. A., and B. D. SALES. 1977. Persuasion during the *voir dire*. In B. D. Sales (ed.), *Psychology in the Legal Process*. New York: Spectrum, pp. 39–58.

BONORA, B., and E. KRAUSS. 1979. *Jury Work: Systematic Techniques*. National Jury Project.

BROWN, R. 1965. *Social Psychology*. New York: Free Press.

BURNSTEIN, E. 1982. Persuasion as argument processing. In H. Brändstetter, J. H. Davis, and G. Stocker-Kreichgauer (eds.), *Group Decision Making*. London: Academic Press, pp. 103–24.

BURNSTEIN, E., and A. VINOKUR. 1973. Testing two classes of theories about group induced shifts in individual choice, *Journal of Experimental Social Psychology*, 9:123–37.

———. 1975. What a person thinks upon learning he has chosen differently from others: Nice evidence for the persuasive arguments explanation of choice shifts, *Journal of Experimental Social Psychology*, 11:412–26.

CLARK, R.; W. H. CROCKETT; and R. L. ARCHER. 1971. Risk as value hypothesis: The relationship between perception of self, others, and the risky shift, *Journal of Personality and Social Psychology*, 20: 425–29.

CODOL, J.-P. 1975. On the so called "superior conformity of the self" behavior: Twenty experimental investigations, *European Journal of Social Psychology*, 5: 457–501.

DARROW, C. 1936. Attorney for the defense, *Esquire Magazine*, May.

DAVIS, J. H.; N. L. KERR; R. S. ATKIN; R. HOLT; and D. MEEK. 1975. The decision processes of 6- and 12-person mock juries assigned unanimous and two-thirds majority rules, *Journal of Personality and Social Psychology*, 32: 1–14.

DOISE, W. 1969. Intergroup relations and polarization of individual and collective judgments, *Journal of Personality and Social Psychology*, 12: 136–43.

EBBESEN, E. B., and R. J. BOWERS. 1974. Proportion of risky to conservative arguments in a group discussion and choice shift, *Journal of Personality and Social Psychology*, 29: 316–27.

FESTINGER, L. 1954. A theory of social comparison processes, *Human Relations*, 7: 117–40.

FRASER, C. 1971. Group risk-taking and group polarization, *European Journal of Social Psychology*, 1: 493–510.

FRASER, C.; C. GOUGE; and M. BILLIG. 1971. Risky shifts, cautious shifts, and group polarization, *European Journal of Social Psychology*, 1: 7–30.

GOLDSTEIN, I. 1935. *Trial Technique*. Chicago: Callaghan.

HANS, V. P., and N. VIDMAR. 1982. Jury selection. In N. L. Kerr and R. M. Bray (eds.), *The Psychology of the Courtroom*. New York: Academic Press, pp. 39–82.

HASTIE, R.; S. PENROD; and N. PENNINGTON. 1983. *Inside the Jury*. Cambridge, Mass.: Harvard University Press.

HINDS, W. C. 1962. Individual and group decisions in gambling situations. Unpublished master's thesis, School of Industrial Management, Massachusetts Institute of Technology.

JELLISON, J. M., and J. RISKIND. 1970. A social comparison of abilities interpretation of risk-taking behavior, *Journal of Personality and Social Psychology*, 15: 375–90.

———. 1971. Attribution of risk to others as a function of their ability, *Journal of Personality and Social Psychology*, 20: 413–15.

JELLISON, J. M.; J. RISKIND; and L. BROLL. 1972. Attribution of ability to others on skill and chance tasks as a function of level of risk, *Journal of Personality and Social Psychology*, 22: 135–38.

KAIRYS, D.; J. SCHULMAN; and S. HARRING (eds.). 1975. *The Jury System: New Methods for Reducing Prejudice*. Philadelphia: National Jury Project and National Lawyers Guild.

KALVEN, H., JR., and H. ZEISEL. 1966. *The American Jury*. Boston: Little, Brown.

KAPLAN, M., and G. D. KEMMERICK. 1974. Juror judgment as information integration: Combining evidential and nonevidential information, *Journal of Personality and Social Psychology*, 30: 493–99.

KERR, N. L., and R. J. MACCOUN. 1985. The effects of jury size and polling method on the process and product of jury deliberation, *Journal of Personality and Social Psychology*, 48: 349–63.

LAMM, H., and D. G. MYERS. 1978. Group-induced polarization of attitudes and behavior. In L. Berkowitz (ed.), *Advances in Experimental Social Psychology*. New York: Academic Press, 11: 145–95.

LEVINGER, G., and D. J. SCHNEIDER. 1969. Test of the "risk is a value" hypothesis, *Journal of Personality and Social Psychology*, 11: 165–69.

MCCONAHAY, J.; C. MULLIN; and J. FREDERICK. 1977. The uses of social science in trials with political and racial overtones: The trial of Joan Little, *Law and Contemporary Problems*, 41: 205–29.

MOSCOVICI, S., and M. ZAVALLONI. 1969. The group as a polarizer of attitudes, *Journal of Personality and Social Psychology*, 12: 125–35.

MYERS, D. G. 1978. Polarizing effects of social comparison, *Journal of Experimental Social Psychology*, 14: 554–63.

———. 1982. Polarizing effects of social interaction. In M. Brandstätter, J. H. Davis, and G. Stocker-Kreichgauer (eds.), *Group Decision Making*. London: Academic Press, pp. 125–61.

MYERS, D. G., and S. J. ARENSON. 1972. Enhancement of dominant risk tendencies in group discussion, *Psychological Reports*, 30: 615–23.

MYERS, D. G.; P. J. BACH; and F. B. SCHREIBER. 1974. Normative and informational effects of group interaction, *Sociometry*, 37: 275–86.

MYERS, D. G., and G. D. BISHOP. 1971. The enhancement of dominant attitudes in group discussion, *Journal of Personality and Social Psychology*, 20: 386–91.

MYERS, D. G., and M. F. KAPLAN. 1976. Group-induced polarization in simulated juries, *Personality and Social Psychology Bulletin*, 2: 63–66.

MYERS, D. G., and H. LAMM. 1976. The group polarization phenomenon, *Psychological Bulletin*, 83: 602–27.

NORDHØY, F. 1962. Group interaction in decision-making under risk. Unpublished master's thesis, School of Industrial Management, Massachusetts Institute of Technology.

PADAWER-SINGER, A.; A. N. SINGER; and R. L. J. SINGER. 1977. An experimental study of twelve vs. six member juries under unanimous vs. nonunanimous decisions. In B. D. Sales (ed.), *Psychology in the Legal Process*. New York: Spectrum, pp. 77–81.

PENROD, S. D. 1979. Study of attorney and "scientific" jury selection models. Unpublished doctoral dissertation, Harvard University.

PRUITT, D. G. 1971a. Choice shifts in group discussion: An introductory review, *Journal of Personality and Social Psychology*, 20: 339–60.

———. 1971b. Conclusions: Toward an understanding of choice shifts in group discussion, *Journal of Personality and Social Psychology*, 20: 494–510.

ROSE, R. 1955. *Twelve Angry Men*. Chicago: Dramatic Publishing Co.

SAKS, M. J. 1976. The limits of scientific jury selection: Ethical and empirical, *Jurimetrics Journal*, 17: 3–22.

———. 1977. *Jury Verdicts*. Lexington, Mass.: Heath.

SAKS, M. J., and R. HASTIE. 1978. *Social Psychology in Court*. New York: Van Nostrand Reinhold.

SANDERS, G. S., and R. S. BARON. 1977. Is social comparison irrelevant for producing choice shifts? *Journal of Experimental Social Psychology*, 13: 303–14.

STOKES, J. P. 1971. Effects of familiarization and knowledge of others' odds choices on shifts to risk and caution, *Journal of Personality and Social Psychology*, 20: 407–12.

STONER, J. A. F. 1961. A comparison of individual and group decisions including risk. Unpublished master's thesis, School of Management, Massachusetts Institute of Technology.

———. 1968. Risky and cautious shifts in group decisions: The influence of widely held values, *Journal of Experimental Social Psychology*, 4: 442–59.

TANFORD, S., and S. PENROD. 1983. Computer modeling of influence in the jury: The role of the consistent juror, *Social Psychology Quarterly*, 46: 200–12.

TEGER, A. I., and D. G. PRUITT. 1967. Components of group risk taking, *Journal of Experimental Social Psychology*, 3: 189–205.

VALENTI, A. C., and L. L. DOWNING. 1975. Differential effects of jury size on verdicts following deliberation as a function of the apparent guilt of a defendant, *Journal of Personality and Social Psychology*, 32: 655–63.

VINOKUR, A. 1971. Cognitive and affective processes in influencing risk taking in groups: An expected utility approach, *Journal of Personality and Social Psychology*, 20: 472–86.

VINOKUR, A., and E. BURNSTEIN. 1974. Effects of partially shared persuasive arguments on group-induced shifts: A group-problem-solving approach, *Journal of Personality and Social Psychology*, 29: 305–15.

WALLACH, M. A., and N. KOGAN. 1959. Sex differences and judgment processes, *Journal of Personality*, 27: 555–64.

———. 1961. Aspects of judgment and decision making: Interrelationships and changes with age, *Behavioral Science*, 6: 23–36.

WALLACH, M. A.; N. KOGAN; and D. J. BEM. 1962. Group influence on individual risk taking, *Journal of Abnormal and Social Psychology*, 65: 75–86.

WALLACH, M., and C. W. WING, JR. 1968. Is risk a value? *Journal of Personality and Social Psychology*, 9: 101–6.

WHYTE, W. H., JR. 1956. *The Organization Man*. New York: Simon & Schuster.

III

Some Psycholegal Issues

AMERICAN LAW TODAY enjoys the invigorating impact of a social psychology that questions its every assumption and promises eventually to motivate reforms. Social psychology, in turn, benefits from a sharp cross-examination, from the legal perspective, of its methods and findings and gains the gratification of feeling relevant to the good of society. The law at first made the mistake of citing the conclusions of studies without evaluation of research design, very much as if psychological studies were legal precedents. Social psychologists at first made the mistake of thinking that lawyers, judges, and jurors would be as ready as we are to believe that results obtained from college undergraduates will hold true for humans everywhere. The law has been sensitized to research design or internal validity: Is it clear that variation in dependent variables is caused by independent variables? Social psychology has been sensitized to external validity: Is it clear that findings obtained in one setting—the laboratory—will hold true in another—the arraignment to set bail or the jury room (Carlsmith, Ellsworth, and Aronson, 1976)?

It took a while for the law to take notice of social psychology, but it cannot disregard the field today, because every year brings some result that threatens to dynamite a foundation. In 1979, for instance, Kassin and Wrightsman found that while the judge's instructions to the jury are typically given at the end of the trial, when the evidence has all been heard, they might better be given at the start, before the evidence is heard. In 1980 Grisso and Manoogian found that the majority of "juveniles" are not able to understand the *Miranda* warn-

249

ing advising them of their rights in a police interrogation. In 1981 Thompson, Fong, and Rosenhan found that jurors do not do what the judge directs them to do with respect to inadmissible evidence, which is to strike it from their memories as it is stricken from the written record. In 1982 Wissler and Saks found that although jurors are supposed to disregard a defendant's prior criminal record in assessing the likelihood of guilt, they are very far from doing so. In 1983–84 Phoebe Ellsworth and her associates (1984) put together massive evidence that jurors willing to impose a death penalty and so "death-qualified" in capital cases are more prone to agree with the prosecution and convict than are potential jurors opposed to the death penalty and so "excludable" from juries in capital cases (Cowan, Thompson, and Ellsworth, 1984; Fitzgerald and Ellsworth, 1984). This means that those willing to impose the ultimate penalty in addition tend to be biased against the defendant.

We are social psychologists, not law students, and so the problems that researchers have chosen to study most deeply, and the problems that I have chosen to examine here, have been selected not because they are the most frequent events in the justice system nor even because they are the most consequential. Eyewitness identification (Chapter 7) and jury selection (Chapter 8) have been given special attention because they are applied instances of classic topics in social psychology, instances, respectively, of person perception and of group dynamics. It is essential, however, to know where the topics fit in the justice system if we are to form sound judgments as to the relevance of what social psychologists have done, and so Chapter 7 begins with an overview of the system.

7

Eyewitness Identification

THE LAW HAS TWO BRANCHES: civil and criminal. Criminal law is designed to regulate behavior in the interests of society and defines certain actions as crimes. The initiating party in criminal cases is a prosecutor, state or federal, who acts on behalf of the public. Conviction for serious crimes, "felonies" as opposed to "misdemeanors," carries such punishments as prison sentences and heavy fines. Civil law is designed to settle disputes between individuals or among individuals, organizations, and branches of government. If someone sues you, that is a matter of civil law. Typically, there is an accusation of wrongful injury (a tort) or else a claim that a contract or agreement has been broken. Most cases in the courts involve civil rather than criminal law, but almost all social psychological research has concerned the criminal justice system.

The operation of the American justice system has one overwhelming problem: case overload and, therefore, case delay. We are a rather litigious people who initiate about five thousand new civil lawsuits a year for every 100,000 population, as opposed to the 300–500 per 100,000 population in the Scandinavian countries. One result of the heavy court load is that civil suits, for instance personal injury cases, often take more than four years to process in cities like New York, Chicago, Boston, and Philadelphia. There are also substantial delays in the criminal courts (as long as some months to a year between arrest and trial), but they are less extreme, thanks to the speedy trial acts, than the delays in civil law. Another serious problem with the civil law is that the poor are disadvantaged by it, because going to court is usually expensive.

In response to the problems of our legal system, various alternative extralegal mechanisms for the settlement of disputes, mainly civil disputes but also certain kinds of criminal cases, have been proposed. They include mediation, arbitration, and negotiation and range from completely voluntary to somewhat coercive. Their common property is that they are conducted by ordinary citizens, not by lawyers and judges. Some of them resemble and have been modeled on community and tribal mechanisms in societies where people seldom or never go to law. The American Bar Association, the United States Senate, and the United States Justice Department are all, in their varying ways, active in the search for alternative means of resolving social conflicts. In the early 1980s projects of this kind were operating and under evaluation in Boston, Columbus, Miami, New York, Rochester, San Francisco, and elsewhere.

Daniel McGillis (1980) has been in the forefront of social psychologists helping to design and evaluate the new procedures. He argues that there are many family disputes, fallings-out between neighbors, and landlord–tenant conflicts that are probably better suited to a no-fault mediation or arbitration process than to the adversarial processes of the law. In terms of attribution theory (Part II) the new extralegal procedures encourage thinking in terms of complex causal interaction, whereas the courts are bound to attribute fault to one party or the other. Social psychological theory is relevant to the planning of new mechanisms for resolving conflict, and the methods of social psychology are the best methods for evaluating them. Therefore, we may see in the future less emphasis on existing criminal justice procedures and more emphasis on new extralegal mechanisms for handling what would otherwise have been civil law cases.

The Criminal Justice System

Figure 7-1 is a diagram of the American criminal justice system prepared by Vladimir Konečni and Ebbe Ebbesen (1982) which reflects the distinctive approach those investigators take to psycholegal research. The boxes represent classes of decision-makers ordered sequentially from the top of the page to the bottom, from deciding to commit a crime to being sentenced after conviction. Each box is to be thought of as containing 100 percent of the people who make decisions of that type, and the vertical line exiting downward from each box represents the percentage (of the 100 percent in the box) progressing to the next ordered stage in the criminal system.

Some percentages are completely unknown. For instance, it is known that not all crimes committed are reported, so there should be some percentage, probably very large, on the horizontal line labeled "Unreported" (Greenberg,

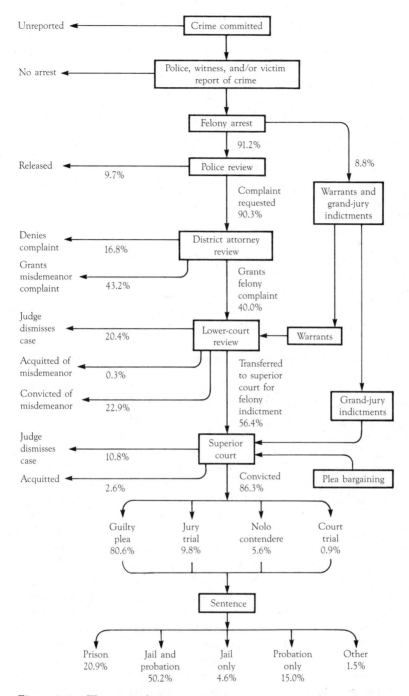

Figure 7-1. The criminal justice system

(From *The Criminal Justice System*, by V. J. Konečni and E. B. Ebbesen. Copyright © 1982 by W. H. Freeman. P. 15, Fig. 1-2)

Wilson, and Mills, 1982). Horizontal lines, generally, represent exits from the criminal justice system, instances that do not go on to the next stage. Of arrests for felony (serious crimes), a minority (8.8 percent) go to the local grand jury (of about twenty-five citizens), and the grand jury decides whether there is enough evidence to justify holding the arrested person. The majority arrested for felony (91.2 percent) proceed directly to a police interrogation. Note that the two percentages (91.2 percent and 8.8 percent) sum to 100 percent, which holds true for the percentages on all the lines leaving a given box. It follows that the 4.6 percent, at the very bottom, who go to jail are not 4.6 percent of persons committing crimes (very far from it), but 4.6 percent of persons convicted of felony and sentenced.

The percentages in Figure 7-1 are from the more than 145,500 felony arrests made in California in 1977, and the percentages are probably fairly representative of other states, though the absolute numbers would not be. What most people find startling in the diagram of Figure 7-1 is the very large number of points of exit from progression through the full criminal justice system and the high percentages that pass through some of those exits. The probability that a person who commits a crime will go to jail is evidently extremely small.

There are interesting social psychological findings concerning almost every box (or decision-making node) and every line of progression or exit. For instance, what could cause a victim of a crime to leave it unreported? The crime of rape is the one we know most about (Borgida, 1980). Rape is defined as an act of sexual intercourse forcibly accomplished by a man with a woman not his wife or, following recent decisions, with his wife. While exact figures are not known, it is known that many victims of rape do not report the crime, and the reason why is also known. Under common law rules of evidence, still in effect in eleven states in 1980, it is permissible to admit evidence of the victim's prior sexual history with third parties. This means that in pressing a rape charge, under common law, a woman exposes herself to humiliation and abasement. She often feels more "on trial" than the accused. It is also known that juries are influenced by evidence of sexual freedom, presumably on the attributional principle of high consistency (Chapter 4) or, still more grossly, a kind of base rate calculation (Chapter 16). Neither way of thinking is appropriate in a trial for rape: The problem is to find the facts in a given case, as always in a trial, and not to estimate probabilities. As a result of legal and social psychological criticism, forty states as of 1980 had reformed their laws of evidence so as to exclude third-party instances either altogether or in some circumstances.

At the police review or interrogation, the person suspected or accused of a felony is read his "Miranda rights," and then the police try hard to get him to answer questions and perhaps reveal incriminating information or even confess. If the person under arrest does not cooperate, there is a substantial probability that the police will have to release him for lack of sufficient evidence. The next interesting point of decision is the arraignment before a judge of the lower court, who makes sure that the accused understands the charge against him and is represented by counsel. At that point the question of bail arises.

The due process assumption that a defendant is innocent until proved guilty raises the question, in these days of crowded court calendars, of what to do with him in the months that may intervene between arrest and trial. To hold him in jail when he is supposed to be presumed innocent and may, upon trial, in fact be proved innocent can hardly be right, but if he is released, he may leave the area or commit further crimes. The bail system is an effort to deal with that dilemma. Bail is a monetary guarantee of appearance. Some defendants are not required to pay bail but are released on their own "recognizance" (acknowledged obligation to appear). If a defendant is too poor to pay either the bail set, or the 10–30 percent of it required by a professional bondsman who acts as surety for the bond, then he goes to jail.

What are supposed to be the determinants of release on recognizance or bail and, if bail, the amount set? In rough summary, the factors most often recommended for consideration are these: (1) the nature and severity of the crime; (2) the defendant's past record; (3) the defendant's community ties; and (4) the character and dangerousness of the defendant. It is the judge who decides, but the district attorney (prosecution) and defense counsel are also present at the arraignment along with the defendant. The prosecution and defense attorneys will both make recommendations of dollar amounts to the judge.

What factors actually determine the decisions made by judges? Ebbesen and Konečni (1975, 1982) undertook to find out in a study that is extraordinary because it uses both the method of experimental simulation and the method of naturalistic, real-world observation. The investigators found that the two methods yielded somewhat different results, different conceptions of the causes of the judges' decisions. That has led Ebbesen and Konečni to oppose the common social psychological research strategy, which is to design experimental simulations for reasons of internal validity (that is, because they make it possible to manipulate and control variables) while, at the same time, striving for external validity by making the simulations as realistic as possible. In brief, Ebbesen and Konečni take the radical stand that simulations never can be realistic enough and that one must study the real process, in its natural setting, relying on various statistical techniques to separate out causal factors.

In the simulation study Ebbesen and Konečni had eighteen judges in San Diego County read case reports on imaginary defendants and asked the judges to make the bail recommendations they would, in fact, make if they were acting on the cases. There were four independent variables: the dollar amount recommended by the prosecuting attorney; the dollar amount recommended by the defense attorney; the nature of the prior criminal record (none, as opposed to several felony convictions); the extent of community ties (employed with family in San Diego, as opposed to unemployed with family in northern California). The values of the independent variables were combined in all possible ways across cases, and so it was possible to determine the independent effect of each. From the judges' bail recommendations in the simulation study, it appeared that community ties, prior record, and prosecutor recommendation all exerted significant independent causal effects, of which community ties was the strongest. The decision-making procedure here accords quite well with procedures that have conventionally been recommended.

With five of the eighteen judges a naturalistic study was also done. Those judges were unobtrusively observed making actual bail decisions in court on cases for which the investigators had all relevant data. Of course, the problem with the naturalistic case always is that variables are confounded, whereas they can be separated in experiments (Carlsmith, Ellsworth, and Aronson, 1976); examples are prosecutor's recommendation and extent of community ties. There are statistical techniques that can be used to disentangle confounded variables, but the techniques make very strong assumptions. Making the assumptions, Ebbesen and Konečni find a model of the judges' bail-setting that is very different from the model suggested by the results of the simulation. In brief, the real-life data suggest that judges, in making bail decisions, are responding to social influences, primarily to the recommendation of the prosecution and, in lesser degree, to the recommendation of the defense attorney. They do not respond to community ties directly at all, and that had seemed to be the single most important determinant in the simulation study. The case history facts were influential only indirectly, only insofar as they influenced the recommendations of the two attorneys. The difference in the two decision schemes is important. The social influence model (from the real-life data) suggests that the bail arraignment is, like the trial itself, a kind of adversarial procedure, a contest between attorneys, in which the judge favors the prosecution. The simulation data suggest that the bail hearing is what it is supposed to be, a weighing by the judge of many facts about the defendant that will affect the likelihood of his appearing for trial.

The overall strategy for studying the criminal justice system recommended by Konečni and Ebbesen (1982) is to make naturalistic studies of the class of decision-makers represented by the boxes or nodes in Figure 7-1. The goal is to find the decision scheme or implicit rule operating in each case. It is to be expected from the study of such other kinds of expert decision-makers as medical diagnosticians, stockbrokers, admissions officers, and clinical psychologists (Slovic and Lichtenstein, 1971) that this rule will be considerably simpler than the experts themselves think it is. The operations of the criminal justice system will be fully predictable when the sequential decision-making schemes have all been worked out.

Konečni and Ebbesen (1982) forcefully condemn approaches alternative to their own:

Concepts are borrowed from social-psychological theories and then empirically tested under conditions that attempt to simulate a few impoverished aspects of the legal system. Often the role that the decision under study plays in the system is completely ignored so as to make it appear that the theoretical concepts are important and apply to "relevant" and "meaningful" settings. [p. 5]

The discovery in the case of bail-setting that experimental simulation produces a different outcome from real-life study must be worrisome to all experimental psychologists. However, the cure is not obvious. There is always a residual problem of external validity, even when you study the so-called real-life process—unless, of course, you do not intend to generalize beyond five judges in certain courts in San Diego County in the 1970s. There is no guarantee that other judges in other places with other kinds of cases will follow the same decision rules. In fact, you have to select your real-life case to be as representative as possible of the population of real-life cases to which you mean to generalize. The problem is usually said to be one of representativeness rather than external validity, but they are the same kind of problem.

Returning to Figure 7-1, the person indicted for a felony will spend some months awaiting trial, either freed on bail or on his own recognizance or else in jail. In that period the process of plea bargaining occurs. The defendant has pleaded not guilty to the felony indictment. His attorney and the prosecution engage in negotiations designed to avoid a trial, and about 80 percent of the time they succeed. In effect, the prosecution offers to lower the charge or drop some charges or perhaps recommend a light sentence if the defendant will plead guilty and so make sentencing possible without trial. In general judges go along with the plea bargain struck by the two attorneys; sometimes they participate in the process. If plea bargaining did not succeed, as it does, in the vast majority of cases, the courts could not handle the case burden that would ensue. As the system now works, plea bargaining is not just allowable; it is essential. The process has certainly not been studied as much as it should be, partly because it is not entirely open.

If plea bargaining fails and the charges are not dismissed at any of several points, a trial will eventually be held. The prosecution (having the burden of proof) must make its case first. Witnesses testify and are cross-examined. Eyewitness testimony, we shall see, is especially influential with jurors. The judge acts as a kind of referee preserving due process by ruling out inadmissible evidence and the like. When the evidence is all in, the judge's role becomes even more important, for he must instruct the jury as to its role—explain relevant points of law, the definition of relevant verdicts, and the decision rule under which the jury is to operate (whether unanimity or some kind of quorum rule). The jury adjourns to the jury room, elects a foreman (sometimes chosen by the judge or by a drawing), and deliberation begins. Jury size, decision rule, and deliberation process are the topics of Chapter 8.

If, after a time, jury members think they are deadlocked, they are read the "dynamite charge," which directs them to try again. In the end they either declare themselves hung or deliver a verdict, and if the verdict is guilty, the judge, after about a week, sentences the defendant.

The law sets maximum and minimum limits on sentences, but those allow wide latitude for the judge's discretion to operate. For example, in Massachusetts a conviction for armed robbery can carry a sentence from five years to life in prison. Simulation studies which present real judges with imaginary defendants (e.g. Partridge and Eldridge, 1974; Clancy et al., 1981) generally find that some judges are characteristically lenient, some characteristically severe, and, above all, that there is wide variation in the sentences proposed for identical cases. For instance, where the most severe sentence given a particular bank robber was eighteen years in prison and a $5,000 fine, the most lenient was five years in prison and no fine.

Konečni and Ebbesen (1982, pp. 293–332) have been able to study the real sentencing decisions of judges, and they find that while there is considerable individual disparity in, for instance, the proportion of prison sentences imposed, all judges used the same decision strategy. The strategy is very simple, especially as compared with what judges say they do. So simple is the decision-making that Konečni and Ebbesen suggest that there is little reason to keep the judge in the process at all. He or she might be replaced by a very simple computer program that would take into account just severity of the crime, prior record, and jail/bail status. Computer-based decisions would eliminate disparity, increase the speed of decision-making, and, probably, to quote Dickens, "decrease the surplus population."

Eyewitness Identification

The paradox of eyewitness identification is that judges, defense attorneys, and psychologists believe it to be just about the least trustworthy kind of evidence of guilt under the criminal law, whereas jurors have always found it more persuasive than any other sort of evidence. The legal theorists and psychologists are right, but the jurors bring in the verdicts, and in the United States, England, and Wales (though not Scotland) a person accused under the criminal law can be convicted on eyewitness identification in the absence of any corroborative evidence. It follows that there must be a substantial number of miscarriages of justice, more than is generally realized. The disagreement between laymen and psychologists and legal theorists, and the fact that the latter two are right, means that psychologists and legal theorists know something that laymen do not. To prevent miscarriages of justice, surely laymen should be told what they need to know. They could be told by defense attorneys or judges without straining usual courtroom procedure. They could be told by psychologists testifying as expert witnesses, but such testimony is often not allowed. Should it be? I think so.

Some people just do not believe that mistakes occur under American criminal law, and all of us would prefer not to dwell on it. However, nowadays it occasionally happens that a person imprisoned for many years is proved to be innocent, and that person sues for a few million dollars in damages, thereby creating a "story" that the newspapers feature, and so it is difficult not to know that some mistakes occur. In October 1983 an unfortunate man who had been in prison for thirty years won his millions and very shortly thereafter died of a heart attack. It was difficult not to notice that miscarriage of justice, and it is not easy to forget it.

To prove that some mistakes occur is easy; all you need is one. To prove that more mistakes occur than most people think is impossible. What most people think is unknown but could be found out. What cannot be found out is the number of mistakes that occur. My guess that there have been more mistaken convictions based on mistaken identifications than most people think is pure projection. All I know is that I was surprised by what I learned when I studied the problem; because I think I am neither more idealistic nor more out of touch than average, I guess that most people would be surprised. You will judge that for yourselves at the end of this section, but just to open your mind to the possibility here are a few items from the juridical literature that shook me.

Borchard's *Convicting the Innocent: Errors of Criminal Justice* (1932) discusses sixty-five certain cases; of those sixty-five errors, twenty-nine resulted from mistakes of eyewitness identification. Rattner (1983) was able to identify 205 "pure" cases of wrongful conviction (*innocent* beyond doubt), and 52 percent involved errors of eyewitness identification. Are those numbers large or small? Impossible to say, but they are larger than I would have guessed, and Rattner and others express the belief that the "pure" cases are just the tip of the iceberg.

When you learn how bad the evidence has been in some cases that nevertheless resulted in conviction because there was a mistaken identification, you must guess that less extreme cases of undiscovered error are more numerous than you had supposed. Perhaps Harry Cashin (Wall, 1965) is close to a worst case, but still he was convicted. The case asks us: "How many have there been that were not so bad but were still mistakes?"

In a speakeasy in New York City on February 19, 1931, a robbery and a gun battle took place. One policeman was killed and also one of two robbers; the other escaped. Almost two months later Harry Cashin, an acquaintance of the dead bandit, was picked up by the police and identified by one witness to the robbery. That identification—two months after the robbery—was the only evidence against Cashin. Yet the single identification prevailed against the following points arguing his innocence: (1) The identifying witness had previously sworn she could not identify him; (2) all other witnesses of the robbery refused to identify him; (3) he did not fit the description of the robber originally given to the police; (4) the second robber was thought to have been wounded, but Cashin was without injury just three hours after the crime; (5) a cab driver who drove the two robbers to the speakeasy swore that Cashin was not one of them; (6) he had an alibi supported by his fiancée and aunt. Nevertheless, Harry Cashin was convicted of murder in the first degree. The conviction was eventually reversed. How many cases in which the evidence against eyewitness identification was less overwhelming have gone uncorrected?

Patrick Wall's book, *Eyewitness Identification in Criminal Cases* (1965), is something like the standard reference work on the subject for attorneys. Wall convinces me that errors based on eyewitness identification have been more common than I thought, not with a case but with a set of conclusions from the record of known errors, which argue that errors have been more numerous than I supposed because they contradict ideas I had uncritically held. The agreement of a large number of witnesses has proved to be no guarantee of accuracy; in English and American legal history, twelve, thirteen, fourteen, seventeen, twenty-one, and thirty witnesses have agreed in sworn testimony and yet been shown to be mistaken. Friends and acquaintances of the person identified have sometimes (rarely) made errors. Trained observers (the police) have been in error. No amount of confidence on the eyewitness's part precludes error. "That's the man. I'll always remember to my dying day the faces of the guys who pulled guns on me" (Wall, p. 15). But he remembered wrongly. "I should know him among a thousand. I recognized him at once; I am quite sure he is the man" (Wall, p. 15). But, once again, quite wrong. Finally, errors have been made in capital cases (the death penalty), when one would have thought an eyewitness would feel some obligation to be cautious. Wall cites a number of cases in which the mistake was discovered before execution and a similar number in which it was discovered after execution. If many witnesses, close acquaintance, trained observation, fierce conviction, and capital punishment have not invariably prevented mistakes, what must be true in the more usual case of one untrained stranger who hesitantly identifies a thief or mugger?

In Britain concern about eyewitness testimony became intense in the 1970s, when in close succession two individuals convicted on the basis of such testimony were found to be innocent. The Home Secretary appointed a committee to look into the subject under the chairmanship of Lord Patrick Devlin (1976). The Devlin Report recommends that the trial judge be required to instruct the jury that it is not safe to convict upon eyewitness testimony alone except in exceptional circumstances (a close friend or relative) or when there is substantial corroborative evidence. The thrust of the report is that prosecutions based on nothing but eyewitness identification should fail. The safeguards recommended by the Devlin Report are much stronger than those created by the United States Supreme Court but are closely similar to those recommended by such American legal authorities as Wall (1965) and Woocher (1977). The fact that American Constitutional safeguards are much weaker than those recommended by excellent legal authorities suggests the possibility that our legal safeguards have been too weak and so have permitted the occurrence of a substantial number of erroneous convictions based on eyewitness identification.

Finally, there is the testimony of many distinguished jurists that errors of eyewitness identification are the chief cause of mistaken convictions in the

United States and that, as Felix Frankfurter noted while still a professor of law at the Harvard Law School, there are a "formidable number" of such mistakes. Of all that I have read, the most haunting statement is this: "It must also be remembered that while these cases were selected because truth eventually came out, there are countless others where it never does, and there are doubtless now behind bars, deprived of their liberty and undergoing unmerited disgrace and punishment, many innocent men, convicted upon the uncertain testimony of slight recognition" (Wilder and Wentworth, 1918, p. 40). Of course, we have often heard that almost every person in prison claims to be innocent and, of course, they cannot all be, nor even most. But it does not follow, as we have sometimes carelessly supposed, that none is.

The Paradox

The paradox lies in the fact that psychologists and many jurists (Brigham and Wolfskeil, 1983) think eyewitness identification is untrustworthy, whereas jurors place great trust in that kind of evidence, probably more than in any sort of circumstantial evidence. The paradox, once it is shown to be real, must raise a question: "Why should laymen and psychologists be so far apart in their evaluation of eyewitness identification since, after all, everyone every day recognizes people or fails to do so, and it does not seem as though it should be necessary to do experiments to determine (roughly) how accurate recognition is?" The answer is of great practical importance, because it speaks to one of the conditions that must be met by "expert" testimony if it is to be admissible in a trial. The judge must be convinced that the putative expert can offer knowledge that goes beyond that of the jury. It must be knowledge that will aid the "trier of fact" (juror) more than it will prejudice him, as the testimony of a pseudo-expert may do. Therefore, the paradox and its understanding lead directly into an ongoing dispute about expert testimony on eyewitness identification (e.g. Loftus, 1983; McCloskey and Egeth, 1983). First, however, it is necessary to demonstrate that a paradox exists.

JURY RELIANCE ON EYEWITNESS IDENTIFICATION

We shall often want to talk about cases in which the only evidence against an accused person is eyewitness identification, and it may be a good idea to have in mind what such cases are like, because detective fiction, bearing still the stamp of Sherlock Holmes, has made us more familiar with complex webs of evidence. Elizabeth Loftus in her book *Eyewitness Testimony* (1979) has done us all the great favor of describing a real case (with names changed) of this type in which she herself gave expert testimony. On October 12, 1977, two men robbed a liquor store in Watsonville, California. There were two clerks in the store; the elder was shot dead, but the younger, Joseph Melville, hit the floor and then looked up as the robbers left the store and caught a glimpse of one of them. Joseph Melville's eventual identification of one José Garcia as the robber he had seen was *the only evidence* of Garcia's guilt. Note that the witness was a stranger to the accused, that his view of the accused was brief, that the "witnessing" occurred in a condition of high fear—all rather typical circumstances for such cases.

Here is a brief history of the identification process in Melville's case. On October 13 (the next day) Melville described the thief to the police as well as he could, and a composite drawing was made. It had the blank generic quality of most such composites. On October 15 (three days after the robbery) Melville went to a lineup in the jail in Santa Cruz and picked no one. On October 26 (two weeks after) he went to another lineup in Salinas and again picked no one. That same day the Watsonville police showed Melville a large set of black-and-white photographs, and he picked out one that he said looked very much like the robber; the photograph was of José Garcia. Actually, the complete set of photos included two of Garcia, but Melville passed over the first. On October 31 (nineteen days after the robbery) Melville was shown six color photos, including one of Garcia, and after some deliberation he picked it out, saying: "This is the guy. I wouldn't forget the face." That was about it, except that, asked to pick out Garcia's voice, Melville mistakenly picked an Oakland police officer, but he decided he was more confident of the photo. Garcia was arrested in November and tried in March 1978. Notice that two weeks passed between the robbery and the first identification and that all subsequent identifications might be regarded as efforts to be consistent with the first.

We will come back to José Garcia, to the outcome of his trial, and to the testimony given by Elizabeth Loftus, but the immediate problem is to establish the fact that juries rely heavily on eyewitness identifications. The Devlin Report (1976) to the Home Secretary in Great Britain includes the following telling statistics. In England and Wales in the year 1973, the total number of persons accused of and prosecuted for a crime who were identified by an eyewitness was 850. Of those 850 accused persons, there were 347 for whom *the only evidence* of guilt was the identification. Seventy-four percent of the 347 were convicted. That is an important figure. It says that when there was no evidence of crime other than eyewitness identification, that evidence was judged to be sufficient for conviction in 74 percent of all cases. Evidently English and Welsh juries in the year 1973 found eyewitness identification powerfully persuasive evidence.

It is good to have real conviction outcomes such as the Devlin Report supplies, but a controlled experiment is also valuable, because it makes it possible to study cases involving circumstantial evidence as well as eyewitness identification. In life, of course, there are never two cases identical with respect to circumstantial evidence and differing only in that one includes an eyewitness while the other does not. However, such matched cases can be invented. They must be presented to mock juries, and that is an artificiality. Loftus (1974) did just that, devising a robbery case with much circumstantial evidence and so quite unlike that of José Garcia, and varying only in the presence/absence of a witness. Without a witness identification, only 18 percent of the jurors judged the defendant in the case to be guilty, but with a witness the vote was 72 percent guilty. That is heavy reliance indeed on eyewitness testimony.

One might suppose that jurors trust eyewitness identifications, much as the Devlin Report and the Loftus experiment indicate that they do, for a very good reason: Perhaps they are able to distinguish accurate witness identifications from inaccurate ones (McCloskey and Egeth, 1983). How might they do so? The best guess is that the accurate witness will feel confident and will manifest confidence in a way the jury can pick up. In other words, accuracy may lead to confidence and confidence to juror belief. There seems to be nothing or next to nothing in the idea that accuracy produces confidence, but a great deal in the idea that perceived confidence is a (probably *the*) principal determinant of belief. On the first point we have Deffenbacher's (1980) review of forty-three studies; he found the relation between witness accuracy and witness confidence to be, on the average, very weak. On the second point, the reliance of juries on perceived confidence, we have some very nice evidence from Gary Wells and his associates (Wells, Leippe, and Ostrom, 1979; Wells, Ferguson, and Lindsay, 1981; Lindsay, Wells, and Rumpel, 1981) at the University of Alberta.

A theft is staged in a highly credible way. Someone has left a calculator behind in an experimental cubicle, and a newly arrived subject (actually a confederate) pops it in her purse under the eyes of a witness (real subject) and quickly exits. The experimenter asks what has become of the calculator; the witness tells the story, and the experimenter asks the witness to pick out the thief in a set of six pictures. At this point deception ends and the witness is interrogated before a set of mock jurors.

In Wells, Leippe, and Ostrom (1979) only 58 percent of the eyewitnesses to the theft of a calculator made correct identifications, but jurors believed 80 percent of them. It was the perceived confidence of the witness that chiefly determined whether he would be believed or not; the correlation between jurors' ratings of witness confidence and their tendency to believe witnesses was .706, but as this and many other studies have shown, confidence is not a very trustworthy index of accuracy. In a related study (Lindsay, Wells, and Rumpel, 1981) the conditions in which a calculator was stolen were varied in such a way as to make accurate identification very improbable, moderately probable, or highly probable. Jurors, in deciding whether to believe witnesses, showed some sensitivity to the varying circumstances, but the main effect was a simple tendency to be credulous. Even when the situation made accuracy improbable and, in fact, only 30 percent of witnesses were accurate, jurors still believed 60 percent.

The Devlin Report and the 1974 Loftus experiment show that juries rely heavily on eyewitness identifications in arriving at verdicts. Gary Wells's studies show, in addition, that juries are strongly disposed to believe eyewitnesses, especially those who appear confident. Of course, lawyers do not need experiments to inform them of those facts, and the prosecution always places great value on an eyewitness. Perceived confidence is usually helped along with some pretrial briefing on the questions the witness is likely to be asked. Wells, Ferguson, and Lindsey (1981) showed experimentally that such briefing really works and can make an inaccurate witness highly credible.

PSYCHOLOGISTS' DISTRUST OF EYEWITNESS IDENTIFICATION

We can safely conclude that eyewitness identifications have considerable impact on juries, and we already know one reason why psychologists might think they should not: Juries use confidence as an index of accuracy, but confidence is a very poor index of accuracy. However, the principal kind of evidence that convinces psychologists and many others that eyewitnesses are not to be trusted is more direct and dramatic.

Street muggings are crimes in which identification is often the most important item of evidence. Statistics on muggings in New York City show that it is a fast-moving crime that leaves witnesses and victim little time in which to register the culprit's face. Robert Buckhout (1980), a strong advocate of expert psychological testimony on eyewitness identification, supervised the professional filming of a highly representative purse-snatching that took just thirteen seconds. He was given permission to include the film in a news show on WNBC-TV in New York and then to show a lineup film of six men, identified by number, standing against a wall, and invite viewers to phone in the guilty number. Some 2,145 viewers made identifications, and they picked the actual mugger 14.1 percent of the time, which is slightly worse than a random guess; with six possibilities, 16.7 percent should be correct by chance. The film has also been used in situations such that witnesses did not select themselves (by choosing to telephone), and the results were about the same. With various other staged crimes, Buckhout (1974) has put together a consistent picture of eyewitness unreliability. In some variations he has found that an innocent bystander to a crime is almost as likely to be picked as the actual perpetrator.

In Tallahassee, Florida, a police survey indicated that 43 percent of all business robberies occurred at convenience stores, and so John Brigham and his associates (1982) undertook to find out just how good convenience store clerks were at recognizing customer faces. The investigators did not stage crimes but simply had two male customers, one white and one black, make purchases at all sixty-three convenience stores in Tallahassee; then, just two hours later, the investigators asked the clerks to look at photo lineups and say whether any of the men pictured had been in the store within the past twenty-four hours.

The external validity of the Tallahassee study is exceptionally high. The settings (sixty-three convenience stores) and the witnesses (clerks) were just those most likely to turn up in court and be asked to identify culprits. In addition, the two photo lineups used were constructed by the Tallahassee Police

Department in accordance with what has come to be considered good police procedure. The "distraction" photos were all of males matching the targets in age and race and resembling the targets in hairstyle and general appearance. In addition, all photos were head-and-shoulder color prints taken at a fixed distance, from a fixed angle, and with uniform facial expressions. The general principle guiding the construction of a good lineup, whether of photos or live persons, is: A person without any knowledge of the crime should be equally likely to pick any person in the lineup (Wells, Leippe, and Ostrom, 1979).

In 1967 the United States Supreme Court ruled against identification procedures "so unnecessarily suggestive as to be conducive to a mistaken identification," and this ruling has helped to make fair lineups routine in American police work (long after they had become so in Britain). The "showup" in which a witness is confronted with a single suspect and knows that he faces a suspect is certainly "unnecessarily suggestive" (Levine and Tapp, 1982). So also is any lineup in which a suspect is salient by reason of race, age, sex, facial expression, or anything else unconnected with guilt, because research has shown (Buckhout, 1974) that a salient face will tend to be overchosen by persons knowing nothing of the crime, as well as by witnesses. Figure 7-2 is a good lineup except for the deviation in No. 5, which is enough to cause that person to be picked much more frequently than is the case when his pose matches the others.

With a photograph layout or a live lineup it makes a difference whether the identification question is posed in such a way as to suggest that a serious suspect is included in the array or may or may not be included. The better procedure is that which leaves the witness uncertain as to whether the array does or does not include a suspect. Ideally the interrogating officer would also be "blind" as to the inclusion of a suspect since there are so many ways, both verbal and nonverbal, in which a knowledgeable questioner can influence answers (Rosenthal, 1966). That last refinement and others under investigation are still not usually realized in police practice.

The Tallahassee convenience store study was in almost all ways representative of the real circumstances in which store clerks might be asked after a robbery to make an identification, but in one way the study was unrepresentative. There had been no theft and so, one might think, nothing to cause two customers in particular to be noticed. In fact, though, Brigham had made the two targets unusual. Each engaged the clerk in conversation for three or four minutes by paying for his purchase in pennies, which it took some time to count out, and by asking for directions to the nearest airport and maintaining eye contact while they were given. So those were not speedy, routine transactions. The clerks had unusually good opportunities to study the customers' faces, and in view of that fact the outcome is rather astonishing. A pilot study showed that if twenty-four hours passed between initial encounter and the photo identification, selections were not better than chance; that is, there was no evidence of any recognition at all. With only the very short interval of two

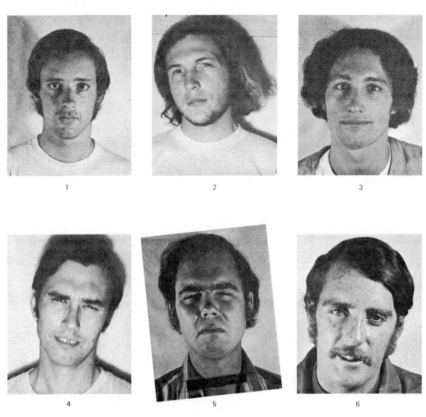

Figure 7–2. A biased photograph layout
(Courtesy Dr. Robert Buckhout, 1985)

hours, there was some recognition. The overall rate of accurate recognition was 34.2 percent. That is not very high in view of the fact that the chance level is 16.7 percent. In a followup of the convenience store study, Brigham and Bothwell (1983) showed that 83.7 percent of prospective jurors substantially *overestimated* the accuracy of eyewitness identification in this situation.

Staged crimes and field studies will impress a juror more than the evidence of the psychology laboratory, because they more closely resemble the case of mugging or robbery he has to deal with, but the laboratory study of face recognition is sufficient on its own to establish eyewitnesses as highly fallible. In fact, the most radical recommendation I have read for reforming the use of eyewitness identification in the legal process comes from Alvin Goldstein (1977), an experimental psychologist specializing in the laboratory study of face recognition. Goldstein proposes that eyewitness identification testimony *not even be admissible as evidence* if it is the only kind of evidence available in a criminal trial. In fact, he goes still further and proposes that no official police action of any kind be permitted on the basis of eyewitness identification alone—since it is a serious thing even to be accused of a crime.

In the laboratory study of face recognition there are typically two steps: (1) a single exposure to one or more target faces for some short period of time, and (2) exposure to a set of faces with instructions to say of each one whether or not it has been seen before. Many experiments, varying the parameters of the task, permit such generalizations as: The larger the number of target faces, the more difficult the task; the shorter the initial exposure time, the more difficult the task; the longer the interval between exposure and recognition, the more difficult the task; the closer the resemblance between target faces and distractor faces in the recognition array, the more difficult the task; and so on. Letting those variables fall as they may, in one study and another, Goldstein discredits eyewitness testimony with this simple conclusion:

> How often in laboratory studies will an observer commit errors in face recognition for a face seen only once for a short period of time? The evidence to answer that question is clear and remarkably consistent: an average error of about 30 per cent can be expected to occur and only rarely will the average error fall below 15 per cent. This conclusion is based on data from many experiments, using a variety of faces and a broad sample of observers. [1977, p. 228]

(As a sample of laboratory studies, see Bower and Karlin, 1974; Chance, Goldstein, and McBride, 1975; Cross, Cross, and Daly, 1971; Ellis, Davies, and Shepherd, 1977; Goldstein, Stephenson, and Chance, 1977; Hochberg and Galper, 1967; Malpass and Kravitz, 1969; Patterson and Baddeley, 1977; Shepherd, Deregowski, and Ellis, 1974; Yin, 1969.)

Someone might agree with Goldstein that an average error of 30 percent was too large to justify the faith juries have in eyewitness identification but agree that laboratory studies (usually involving black-and-white photos) overestimate the amount of error to be expected in real life when faces are seen in three dimensions, with movement and color. However, Goldstein says the laboratory-based estimate of 30 percent error is probably a minimal estimate. In the first place, the subject in the laboratory usually knows at step 1, when he first sees the face, that he is going to be asked to recognize it; witnesses are not so forewarned. In the second place, the step 1 exposure in the laboratory is usually to a photo identical with the photo later to be recognized. A living face is not a single still photo but is, rather, an enormous set of potential appearances, of possible still photos. To convince yourself of that you need only think of your varying reactions to multiple photos of yourself taken on a given occasion. "That doesn't look like me" is what we say when confronted with a possible appearance we would rather forget. There is one other important way in which the laboratory task is easier than the culprit identification task: Laboratory studies usually employ recognition arrays that are a random set of faces, not a closely matched set like the photo layout used by the police. Finally, a direct comparison between error levels in field studies with staged crimes and Goldstein's 30 percent average for the laboratory supports his contention that 30 percent is probably a minimal estimate.

How can Goldstein justify using an *average* figure, across very many studies, to demonstrate the fallibility of face recognition when every parameter of a study will affect the level of accuracy? Citation of an average is appropriate to his general argument and recommendation. The average shows that the witness is not a videocamera recording everything unselectively and accurately. The witness is a fallible human being who perceives, encodes, stores, and retrieves—with error, interpretation, and intrusion possible at every point. Consequently, his testimony cannot be taken as *direct evidence*, involving no inferential processes, as the law has tended to take it. In fact, it needs expert interpretation just as much as the evidence of fingerprints does, or voiceprints, or rifling patterns on a bullet, or the tracings of a polygraph (lie detection). However, Goldstein does not favor admitting expert testimony, because he thinks both prosecution and defense could find experts who would argue for a given case that the probability of accuracy was either high or low, and the result would be another unseemly battle of experts. His proposal is radical; it aims at the root difficulty. In general, recognition of faces seen once and for a short time is so poor that it should not be admissible evidence or grounds for police action unless there is also evidence of some other kind.

WHY THE DIFFERENCE BETWEEN LAYMAN AND PSYCHOLOGIST?

The most interesting question raised by the issue of eyewitness identification is why laymen and psychologists evaluate it so differently. Face recognition is not a rare and esoteric process but is, rather, something everyone engages in every day from quite early infancy (Fagan, 1972). How does it happen that the layman and the psychologist are so far apart in their opinions, with the layman thinking one very seldom makes a mistake in recognizing a face (though names are easily forgotten) and the psychologist thinking face recognition is very likely to be erroneous? I think of three possibilities.

Familiar faces or unfamiliar. It seems very likely that when the layman thinks of face recognition, he thinks of the recognition of faces seen not once but innumerable times, faces of family, friends, classmates, fellow workers. For the case he is thinking of—if it is this case—he is right; accurate recognition over very long times is the rule. Bahrick, Bahrick, and Wittlinger (1975) addressed the fascinating question: How long, for how many years after graduation from high school, is a person able to recognize photos taken at the time of graduation, and published in the yearbook, as faces he has seen before, faces he knows? The study also asked for how long a time faces and names can be matched, but that is not the problem of the witness to a crime; he need only recognize a face as seen before at some place and time. With high school classes numbering about 150, one can, at the time of graduation, identify class members in a large array that includes many nonmembers with about 90 percent accuracy. That accuracy is *virtually unimpaired* for thirty-five years.

No wonder the juryman thinks face recognition can be trusted. It is no wonder, that is, if he is thinking of faces seen many times. But the eyewitness to a crime is almost never reporting on familiar faces; he is reporting on faces seen just once. The two are not the same. It is even very likely that the two processes have, as Arthur Benton's work (1980) argues, distinct neuropsychological mechanisms. Defects in the two kinds of face recognition (familiar faces and unfamiliar faces seen once) have different anatomical correlates. Facial agnosia is a rare defect resulting from brain injury in which the faces of family members (parents, spouse, children) are not recognized, and yet performance is normal on a test requiring discrimination between strangers' faces seen just once and strangers' faces never seen. It has been suggested that the recognition of strangers' faces is a relatively slow process of feature detection and the recognition of familiar faces a relatively rapid process of figural perception (Carey and Diamond, 1977; Yin, 1969).

High emotion and accuracy. No one has shown that jurors, when they believe an eyewitness, are confusing the recognition of familiar faces with the recognition of strange faces. Perhaps they are not, or at any rate not always, but are clear that the eyewitness is testifying to recognition of a face seen but once before. It could still be the case that jurors have in mind recognition circumstances unlike those of the laboratory, circumstances in which jurors believe that accuracy can be high and retention perfect over very long time periods. There is a kind of statement witnesses sometimes make that probably reminds jurors of episodes in their own lives for which they retain vivid memories even after many years: "That's the man. I'll always remember to my dying day the faces of the guys who pulled guns on me" (Wall, 1965, p. 15). Is it not the case that at times of extreme emotion memories are created that have an almost perceptual clarity, memories that may last many years, even though the episode happened just once?

Probably every juror has vivid memories that have not faded with time: unexpected news of the death of a close relative or friend; the birth of a younger brother or sister; the letter of admission to college; first experience of sexual intercourse; first menstruation; and so on. Then there are the unfaded memories that are shared by a generation: For almost everyone over twenty-nine years old the news of the assassination of John F. Kennedy; for many young people, the assassination of John Lennon; for some, the resignation of Richard Nixon; the first moon landing; and so on. Whether or not a juror reasons it out consciously, may he not think that a murder, a mugging, or a robbery would be more like the emotional landmarks of a lifetime than it would be like the calm, even boring exposure to a stranger face in the experimental laboratory?

Because of psychology's devotion to laboratory methods, vivid autobiographical memories were but little studied before 1977. In that year Brown and

Kulik published "Flashbulb Memories" (1977), a study inspired by the prototypical example of the memories people have for the circumstances in which they learned of the assassination of President Kennedy on November 22, 1963. Just about everyone (over twenty-nine years old) remembers where he was when he heard, what he was doing, and who told him the news, plus one or more idiosyncratic trivial details, such as: "I can still feel the tread on the steps of Emerson Hall." "I was carrying a carton of Viceroy cigarettes, which I dropped." "The weather was cloudy and gray." (p. 30). The flashbulb memory is not the *fact* of Kennedy's assassination; there is nothing extraordinary in remembering that, since it has been rehearsed in conversation, print, and film countless times since it occurred. The extraordinary thing, the flashbulb effect, is the retention of details that happened just once—where you were, what doing, and who told you.

Brown and Kulik suggest that the highly emotional central event issues to the nervous system a kind of "Now print!" order (Livingston, 1967), which results in the vivid retention over many years, perhaps a lifetime, of some of the incidental concomitant circumstances. If the assassination of a president can produce such vivid memories of one-time events, why should not a murder or an assault or a holdup stamp in accurately and forever the face of a culprit seen but once? Laboratory experiments conducted in calm circumstances show that strange faces are not well recognized after a single exposure, but surely all such experiments are just irrelevant to eyewitness identifications, which probably derive from flashbulb memories.

Many things of considerable interest have been learned about flashbulb memories. Brown and Kulik showed that emotional importance is what matters by comparing, for seven important news events having relevance to race, the percentages of black Americans having flashbulb memories with the percentages of white Americans. Just about everyone (99 percent), black or white, had such memories for the assassination of JFK (see also Yarmey and Bull, 1978), but while 75 percent of blacks had flashbulbs for the assassination of Martin Luther King, Jr., only 32 percent of whites did. Results for the shooting of George Wallace showed that it really was emotional consequentiality that mattered and not just a matching of race between victim and subjects; 50 percent of blacks had flashbulbs for Wallace and only 27 percent of whites. Ninety-one percent of all subjects had vivid flashbulbs for at least one personal shock in their individual lives. Pillemer (1984) showed that the 1981 attempt on President Reagan's life elicited elaborate memories from just those people who reported a strong emotional reaction to the news, and Pillemer also discovered that repeated telling of one's story to others was not necessary to preservation of the memory. Winograd and Killinger (1983) found that flashbulb memories in the JFK case were not often produced in informants who had been under seven years of age in 1963 (hence under twenty-nine in 1985), but for persons older than that the effect almost always occurred. So much interest in the assassination of one President led Neisser (1982) to the discovery of an article published in 1899 (Colegrove, 1899) in the *American Journal of Psychology* reporting just the same sort of memory for incidental details for the circumstances in which people learned of the assassination of President Lincoln, reports made thirty-three years after the event.

It is worth a paragraph of digression to point out a connection between flashbulb memories and Latané's (1981) Law of Social Impact. One of the uses of the law (Chapter 1) is the prediction of the magnitude of news stories (as assessed by column inches of newsprint). News impact has been shown by Latané to increase with the importance of the person(s) involved, their number, and their psychological immediacy. The news coverage of the JFK assassination was as extensive as for any event in my lifetime, and it was great all over the world. The flashbulb memories in individual minds were produced by the same factors that produced the mammoth headlines, extra editions of newspapers, and continuing television coverage. Just one person had been killed, but that one person was of such importance and such psychological immediacy as to produce a powerful emotional arousal. The extraordinary thing, of course, is that the reaction was worldwide—I have been told flashbulb memory stories for the event not just by Americans and Europeans, but by Barbadians, Moroccans, Japanese, and Egyptians. The reaction of each person's memory system was like that to be expected from the sudden death of a brother, parent, or child. In a sense that is positively neurophysiological, JFK's death made the whole world kin.

No one has as yet made a formal study of flashbulb memories created by the assassination of John Lennon, but I take informal polls of flashbulb memory every year in teaching social psychology, and my impression is that now that college students are too young to remember Kennedy's assassination, it is John Lennon's that elicits the largest number of flashbulb memories— though not from all students by any means, and not only from college students. What seems to matter is the degree of identification with Lennon's gentle, libertarian philosophy of life, which was to do what you want as long as you do not hurt others—that and the intensity of response to the music of the Beatles.

Of course, most vivid memories are not collective but private. Rubin and Kozin (1984) found that a majority of their subjects had vivid memories for serious car accidents, for early romantic experiences, and for college admission letters. Sheingold and Tenney (1982) found that even in their college years students had vivid memories of the birth of a younger sibling—provided the informant was at least three years old at the time—and that they often included such information as who told you when your mother went to the hospital, what time of day it was, who took care of you, and so on. If personal emotional events can cause the long-term retention of concomitant detail of all kinds, why should a mugging or a shooting not result in long-term accurate retention of a face seen but once?

The hitch is the word "accurate." So far, all studies of flashbulb memories have been retrospective, often years after the event, and while there is much to suggest that the material recounted is accurate—informants are convinced it is, and it does not change much from one telling to another—in fact, we do not know that any of the material "recalled" actually happened. Ulric Neisser (1982), commenting on flashbulb memories, thinks there is good reason to be skeptical about accuracy and reports that he himself vividly recalls that the announcement of the attack on Pearl Harbor interrupted a broadcast of a baseball game, but there was no such broadcast on December 7, 1941. Neisser's anecdote is not serious evidence, and as yet there is no serious evidence on the accuracy of flashbulb memories, but there is evidence (Loftus, 1982; Loftus and Marburger, 1983) that people fairly often do not recall at all events known to have taken place that ought to have been suffcient to produce flashbulb memories. The National Crime Survey, for instance, does periodic surveys of known crime victims and has found that twelve months after the event about 25 percent of those victimized by assault, robbery, or burglary in the previous year fail to recall the fact. From those survey data, however, it is not possible to tell how vivid the original experience was or whether the event is really not recalled or for various reasons not reported (Greenberg, Wilson, and Mills, 1982).

Surely the experimental study of face recognition has worked out the relation between emotion (or stress or arousal) and accuracy? One might think it had since several authorities (Loftus, 1979; Penrod, Loftus, and Winkler, 1982) say that stress and recognition accuracy are related in such a way that accuracy is optimal at intermediate levels and falls off with either very low stress or very high stress. If very high stress can be taken as equivalent to the high emotionality that produces flashbulb memories, then there is an apparent conflict between the principle and the facts of flashbulb memory. However, the research sources cited on stress and accuracy (Clifford and Scott, 1978; Johnson and Scott, 1978; Krafka and Penrod, 1981; Yerkes and Dodson, 1908) do not establish the principle they are sometimes said to establish.

The shortcomings of the evidence are egregious. The 1908 research of Yerkes and Dodson is sometimes inflated into the "Yerkes–Dodson Law," relating stress and information processing in organisms generally. The work on which this "Law" is based was done with white mice trying to learn to enter one compartment rather than another and nudged along with electric shocks of weak, moderate, or strong intensity. Moderate shock worked best. The work had nothing to do with face recognition, emotion, or even humans.

The recent studies were done with humans and do involve face recognition and other points of eyewitness testimony, but they do not clearly establish a Yerkes–Dodson kind of relation between stress and recognition such that accuracy is best at moderate stress levels and less good at very high or very low levels. Clifford and Scott (1978), for instance, varied stress levels by having witnesses view either a nonviolent crime or a violent crime and found that details of the nonviolent crime were better remembered than were details of the violent crime. However, the supposed high stress produced by the violent crime cannot have been at the high level associated with flashbulb memories since subjects (witnesses) simply looked at a videotape in which there was an altercation involving an exchange of blows between police and another person.

Johnson and Scott (1978), however, may have produced a really high level of stress (or emotion). Subjects (who were to be witnesses) overheard a staged violent fight, with the sound of breaking bottles and falling chairs. Then a confederate (in the role of culprit) bolted through the room carrying a bloodied letter opener and with blood on one hand. In the low-stress case the culprit simply ran through the room with a pen in his hand and grease on his arms. It does seem possible, if subjects took seriously all they saw, that the bloodied culprit may have aroused emotion at something like a flashbulb level. However, as Wells (1978) has emphasized, in this case the total results were mixed, with high arousal facilitating recognition for some subjects but not for others. In connection with the Johnson and Scott study, Wells comments that it may be beyond the ethical and practical bounds of experimental psychology to carry stress levels any higher.

The argument, in full, is this: Jurors who believe eyewitness identifications to be highly accurate may be thinking of personal episodes of high emotion in their own lives for which they retain, over long periods, vivid and detailed memories. Vivid and detailed memories can, in fact, be produced by high emotion and have been called "flashbulb memories." The picturesque name may be misleading, however, because it suggests accurate recording, as on a film, and no study of flashbulb memories to date can say whether such memories are accurate or not—vividness and detail are not the same thing as accuracy. In particular, there is nothing in flashbulb memory studies to date that bears on the recognition of faces seen but once. As for experimental studies of stress and face recognition, there seems to be just one (Johnson and Scott, 1978) that may have created stress at the high levels associated with flashbulb memories, and that one study produced mixed, uninterpretable results.

The consequence of developing the possibility that jurors may be trustful of eyewitness testimony because they assimilate it to highly emotional experiences of their own for which they retain vivid memories is to identify a kind of research, not easily done, that badly needs to be done: research on the identification of unfamiliar faces under conditions of really high emotion. It is easy to conceive of such research in raw terms that committees watching over research on human subjects would not approve. Let there be more bloodied culprits and, just to raise the level a bit higher, let the seeming victim be a close friend of the witness. Alternatively or additionally, let a stranger (unfamiliar face) pop his head into a room and shout: "The President has been assassinated!" Then, a few hours later, show the people who heard the shout a photo lineup and ask them to identify the face. Of course, one of them may have suffered a heart attack in the interim. It will take considerable ingenuity to transform such raw scenarios into ethically defensible experiments, but if it can be done, the outcome will be important.

No feedback on unfamiliar faces. There is a third possible reason why laymen jurors and psychologists are so far apart in their estimation of the accuracy of eyewitness identification. The juror may be perfectly clear that the witness is testifying on recognition of a stranger's face seen but once, and though he has great experience of that kind of recognition himself, he has very little feedback by which to gauge its accuracy—unless the psychologist in expert testimony tells him how it works out in the laboratory. An experimental study differs from everyday experience in that "hits" and "misses" are regularly recorded.

What is our everyday experience of stranger recognition like? Imagine taking a walk on a busy street in your town or attending a concert, movie, or play in a crowd. One continually scans faces. How many that are scanned on this one occasion have been seen before and so may be said to be recognized? The question is not the same as how many you know by name. Recalling names is more difficult than simple recognition, but recognition is all that is required in eyewitness identification. Think of a long line at a box office or store as a *lineup,* and think of trying to say which, if any, of these people you have seen before. If you live in a large city, you can go to a well-attended event and see no one you are sure you have seen before or perhaps only one or two. Are you right or are you wrong?

It is perfectly possible that in any large crowd of strangers you have seen quite a large number at least once before—not very recently, perhaps, not regularly, but somewhere not too long ago. In fact, you may be completely wrong in thinking you have seen none before; there could be a large number of "false negatives" (people you think you have not seen but actually have seen). Suppose the experience goes the other way and you think you recognize quite a few—not by name and not even with enough confidence to lead you to nod. You could again be wrong; they could be mostly "false positives"—people you think you have seen whom you actually have never seen. In neither case does one ever find out the facts. Everyday life provides no baseline data on the recognition of strangers' faces. How could the layperson possibly learn whether recognition of strangers' faces tends to be accurate or not?

When do you get recognition feedback in ordinary social life? When you know the name, you can, of course, speak, make introductions, and so on. But if you can recall the name, the face is usually a familiar one in the technical sense that you have seen it many, many times. We are seldom wrong on a face when we can recall a name, and so most of the feedback we get will be positive, suggesting that face recognition is a highly accurate process. Very, very rarely does one go wrong.

For the most part the layman gets no feedback on recognitions and nonrecognitions of strangers and so has, in spite of his familiarity with the process, little evidence as to its accuracy. The feedback he gets will mostly come in cases of recognition accompanied by name recall, and feedback will be almost always positive, because name recall is more difficult than face recognition. Therefore, it is not surprising that the juror tends to trust eyewitness identification; what information he has on the recognition of unfamiliar faces suggests that it is quite accurate.

Do We Want Expert Testimony?

In 1908 Professor Hugo Münsterberg, in his book *On the Witness Stand: Essays in Psychology and Crime*, wrote: "It seems astonishing that the work of justice is ever carried out in the courts without consulting the psychologist" (1908, p. 194). He meant the experimental psychologist, not the clinical psychologist or psychiatrist, and he thought eyewitness testimony was one of the subjects on which expert psychological opinion was needed. Münsterberg drew a very sarcastic answer in the *Illinois Law Review* from J. H. Wigmore (1909), who doubted very much that the science of psychology (represented in his article by a "Mr. X. Perry Ment") had rigorously demonstrated any facts not known to the average juryman. Today in the United States expert psychological testimony is sometimes admitted as evidence but more often is not; in some European countries it is readily admitted as evidence. When the exclusion of such testimony has served as the basis of an appeal to a higher court, the higher court has upheld the discretionary power of the judge to admit such evidence or to rule it inadmissible, and judges do not agree with one another on this matter. Neither do psychologists, not even those psychologists best qualified to serve as experts on eyewitness identification. Most of the arguments on both sides were brought out in a 1983 exchange in *American Psychologist* (Loftus, 1983; McCloskey and Egeth, 1983).

The first recorded case in which an experimental psychologist was permitted to testify on eyewitness identification occurred in Belgium in 1910 (Yarmey, 1979). A nine-year-old child named Cecile had been murdered, and the primary evidence against the accused was the identification testimony of two playmates of Cecile, aged eight and ten. The psychologist, J. Varendonck, both reviewed existing evidence on the reliability of testimony by small children and carried out new experiments, maximally germane to the case at hand. What role Varendonck's evidence played in the jury's deliberations is not known, but the verdict was for acquittal.

Several court decisions (especially *United States* v. *Amaral*, 1973) and commentaries on court decisions (especially Woocher, 1977) have led to the formulation of criteria that should govern a judge's decision to admit or not to admit expert psychological testimony as evidence. Expertise is not to be defined in terms of academic degrees alone but must be manifest in research published in the field of eyewitness identification. In addition, the judge must be persuaded that the expert possesses knowledge (not opinion) beyond the ken of the average juryman and that the value of such knowledge exceeds any prejudicial effect an expert might exert. The most common ground for ruling expert testimony inadmissible is that it invades the province of the jury; it is the jury's responsibility to weigh the value of a witness's testimony. When an expert is allowed to testify, the court will warn him not to violate jury prerogatives by confining himself to statements about general factors affecting the reliability of witnesses insofar as those factors are known from research.

Elizabeth Loftus, who has described an actual case (*People* v. *Garcia*, in 1978) in her book *Eyewitness Testimony* (1979), has also published the testimony given by the psychologist expert (herself) in that case. The verbatim record helps those of us who are not experts and have never testified to think realistically about the issues. José Garcia, you may remember, was accused of robbing a liquor store in Watsonville, California, and of murdering one of two clerks. The only evidence of Garcia's guilt was an identification made by the surviving clerk, Joseph Melville. A positive identification (from a lineup in Salinas) was not made until two weeks after the robbery.

In the absence of the jury, the court made it very clear that the only relevant evidence for the jury to hear concerned the general factors that go into identification. The court very explicitly prohibited the expression of any opinion as to whether Mr. Melville had in this case made a good identification or a bad identification, because the judge did not think *anyone* could qualify as an expert on that other than Melville himself. The court asked Elizabeth Loftus about the kinds of evidence in existence ("And have any of these studies actually involved human beings being observed as well as just movies?") and about her qualifications ("Have you yourself conducted experiments which, in your opinion, would entitle you to discuss the kind of factors I'm talking about?") (p. 220). The court was satisfied that relevant evidence beyond the knowledge of the average juror existed and that Dr. Loftus was an expert on that evidence, and the jury was called in.

The defense attorney carried out the direct examination, with the court asking a few questions and with cross-examination by the prosecution. Because Joseph Melville's identification of José Garcia was made two weeks after the crime, Dr. Loftus was asked to testify on the relation between memory and retention interval. Because Joseph Melville had just seen his fellow clerk shot and so was undoubtedly in a state of high stress, Dr. Loftus also testified on the relationship between stress and memory. Because José Garcia was a Mexican-American and Joseph Melville was not, Dr. Loftus testified on "cross-racial" identification. She testified on much more, but those three points will serve well to illustrate the value of expert testimony as well as the problems with it. In each instance I shall quote the core of the testimony given by Dr. Loftus and then play the role of an expert hired by the prosecution to counter her testimony, keeping my remarks as brief as hers, because the need to be brief strongly affects how good a scientist one can be.

Elizabeth Loftus is a psychologist I particularly like and admire, so I would not play this little joke on her without her consent, which she cheerfully gave. She did notice, however, that "Dr. Brown gets to sound very articulate and scientific, since he has written his testimony. Dr. Loftus, whose testimony is transcribed from spoken speech, sounds less smooth, and certainly doesn't have the extensive citations. Fair?" We agreed that publishing this brief forewarning would make it almost fair.

RETENTION AND MEMORY

DR. LOFTUS: If you look at—this is the conclusion that psychologists have reached about the relationship between memory and the retention interval. The function between these two is a negatively decelerating function. That means it drops off quite rapidly at first and then the decay is much more gradual. And this was first discovered by Ebbinghaus in 1885. It's called the forgetting curve and it's been replicated in laboratories across the country with different kinds of material and different kinds of witnesses. [p. 222]

DR. BROWN: The Ebbinghaus memory curve was originally derived exclusively from one kind of learning material and one subject. The subject was Ebbinghaus himself and the materials learned were all consonant-vowel-consonant nonsense syllables like *wug* and *bik*. While it is true generally that memory falls off with time—and everyone has always known that—for some materials of high significance, such as human faces, memory has been shown to remain unimpaired for as long as thirty-five years (Bahrick, Bahrick, and Wittlinger, 1975).

STRESS AND MEMORY

DR. LOFTUS: Again, while the relationship between memory and stress is somewhat more complex, this is memory or any sort of cognitive performance, and this is stress or fear or arousal, the relationship is an inverted U-shaped function, and this is called the Yerkes-Dodson law, named after the two psychologists who discovered it in 1908. What this is saying is that under very high stress, or fear or arousal and also under very, very low stress, such as when you are just waking up in the morning, we are less good rememberers and perceivers than we are under ordinary optimal moderate levels of stress. [pp. 222-23]

DR. BROWN: The research done by Yerkes and Dodson was on white mice trying to learn to go through one door rather than another while being prodded by low, moderate, or high electric shock. The subjects were not human, facial identification was not the task, and the stressor was electric shock. Brown and Kulik (1977) have shown—what everyone has long known—that extremely high stress, fear, or arousal, as in a major automobile accident or the unexpected death of a child or parent or news of the assassination of President John F. Kennedy, can produce memories, called "flashbulb memories," that last a lifetime.

CROSS-RACIAL IDENTIFICATION

DR. LOFTUS: A cross-racial identification is one in which a member of one race attempts to identify a member of a different race . . . . The repeated finding in studies of cross-racial identification is that we are less good, less accurate at identifying a member of another race than we are at identifying members of our own race . . . . The experiments—quite a few experiments that have been done in cross-racial identification have involved whites, blacks, Japanese-Americans, and Chinese-Americans. And the conclusion that is reached in the studies is based upon subject populations involving those races. Mexican-Americans have not been studied as a group . . . . In my opinion, the cross-racial problem that exists with these other groups would extend into a cross-racial identification with whites and Mexican-Americans, yes. [p. 225]

DR. BROWN: It is certainly true that there have been many studies of cross-racial identification. For instance: Barkowitz and Brigham (in press); Brigham and Williamson (1979); Brigham and Barkowitz (1978); Brigham et al. (1982); Chance, Goldstein, and McBride (1975); Cross, Cross, and Daly (1971); Ellis, Deregowski, and Shepherd (1975); Ellis, Davies, and Shepherd (1977); Malpass and Kravitz (1969); Malpass, Lavigeur, and Weldon (1973); and Shepherd, Deregowski, and Ellis (1974). Just about all of these studies have used college undergraduates as subjects, and the most popular stimulus material has been high school yearbook photos. A single field study (Brigham et al., 1982) using as subjects clerks in convenience stores and as stimulus material live customers, may be more germane than all the laboratory studies. The field study found whites to be as accurate in identifying black customers (32.3 percent correct) as in identifying white customers (31.3 percent). This study also found that the accuracy of the white clerks in identifying black customers increased with increasing interracial contact.

Ceasefire and Conclusions

Playing the role of expert under the adversarial conditions of American criminal law and accepting a limit on length and complexity of testimony is very instructive. It satisfies the combative debater but frustrates the impartial truth seeker. Accepting the assignment to impeach the expert testimony of the defense, I find myself citing evidence very selectively, omitting essential qualifications, and ordering information and picking words for dramatic impact. I should not like to be stuck with my expert testimony as representing all I know on the subjects in question, any more than Elizabeth Loftus would like to be stuck with just the parts of her total testimony that I have quoted.

In her full testimony Dr. Loftus says that the Ebbinghaus curve of forgetting cannot be fitted to particular time values, because when forgetting will occur depends "completely on the kind of material." Given a chance to respond to my testimony, she would never let me get away with citing the unimpaired retention for thirty-five years of faces in high school yearbooks (Bahrick, Bahrick, and Wittlinger, 1975) as if it were relevant to the case of Joseph Melville's identification of José Garcia but would, with gentle sarcasm, point out that the yearbook faces were familiar faces seen innumerable times.

In her full testimony, Dr. Loftus says that the Yerkes–Dodson inverted U-shaped function relating stress and memory cannot be fitted to particular kinds of stress at particular measured levels and grants that if an event is significant to someone, "the person's probably going to be able to remember that that event happened." If she were given a chance to respond to my reference to lifelong flashbulb memories, she would certainly point out that there is no evidence of such memories for unfamiliar faces and no evidence that the memories are accurate.

On cross-racial identification, what Elizabeth Loftus said is certainly what most research shows and what most authorities (e.g. Brigham and Williamson, 1979; Levine and Tapp, 1982; Penrod, Loftus, and Winkler, 1982; Wells, 1978) have concluded: "We are less good at identifying members of another race than we are at identifying members of our own race." In her full testimony she also speaks to the hypothesis that accuracy should increase with experience with members of another race and correctly says that on the whole that hypothesis has not held up. My rejoinder that most studies have not been field studies is also accurate (and Dr. Loftus would accept it), and if I choose to repose more confidence in one field study than in the many laboratory studies, I am free to do so, but she would not overlook the fact that I reported correct identifications only; she would certainly point out that the false alarm rate (incorrect identifications) was higher for white clerks identifying black customers than it was for white customers. The difference was small (about 5 percent), but it is in the usual direction (cross-racial identification is less accurate than same-race identification), and false identification is the practically significant rate, not correct identification.

The point of the exercise was not to question the testimony Dr. Loftus gave but to feel in myself and reveal to you what the effects are of playing the expert for one side or the other. In fact, the role led me to lop off the very qualifications and details about longtime memory for familiar faces and accuracy in flashbulb memories which I have taken pains to make clear in the role of trustworthy author of a text. It does look as though the admission as evidence of expert testimony from experimental social psychologists would turn us all into debaters and create an unseemly spectacle that would discredit serious psychology. Nevertheless, the admission of such testimony is what I favor.

The decision on expert testimony is not a decision on whether or not to debate but, rather, a decision on how public the debate should be and who should be invited to participate. I, myself, think it is okay for experimental social psychologists to be called as experts and do their debating in public. I think so because I believe the debate is a good one. There is evidence of the kind that can support really interesting arguments. Hardly anyone would be bored, and just about everyone would learn. The jury that paid attention would be likely to know more of the pool of relevant arguments (Chapter 6) implicit in the case they were trying than they would be if no experts were heard. Which is a way of saying that they would be more likely to reach a just verdict with experts than without.

Psychologists shrink from the expert role and the prospect of an unseemly battle of experts because we have in mind one long-running, really bad debate, the debate between psychiatrists called to testify on the insanity plea. The trouble with that debate is that it has almost no content; there are never any new facts to refresh it, but only endless wriggling to resolve the unresolvable. The law assumes freedom of choice and responsibility, whereas psychiatry assumes determinism, which is the same for all and does not admit of any distinction between the responsible sane and the not responsible insane. It takes a very subtle philosopher to say anything that even sounds interesting on the subject. Our debate would not be so dull and so hopeless. We agree on our axioms, and so a battle of the experts can be an instructive discussion of evidence and inference.

Of course, debating in court means admitting to the debate defense and prosecution attorneys, the judge, and also the jurors (since they can ask questions through the judges). Fine. I have a lot of respect for all those people and in general believe that the questions asked by outsiders tend to be salutary. It probably will be good for psychology if psychologists are called as experts and good also for criminal justice.

And—oh yes—the jury that tried José Garcia, with almost nothing to go on but the eyewitness identification and Elizabeth Loftus's expert testimony, was unable to reach a verdict. From interviews afterward it was determined that the final count was nine for acquittal and three for conviction. The chief investigator wrote Dr. Loftus: "There seems to have been a consensus within the jury that your testimony was not only valuable but also a useful tool" (Loftus, 1979, p. 215).

Summary

Just about every step in the criminal justice system, from the decision to report a crime to the sentencing of a convicted person, may be viewed as a problem in applied social psychology. In recent years, since about 1970, social psychological research on legal issues has increased at a rapid rate. There is significant knowledge on reluctance to report crimes, comprehension of Miranda rights, timing of judge's instructions, the ability of jurors to disregard inadmissible evidence, bail-setting, sentencing, and much besides. Civil law has thus far proved less attractive to social psychologists than criminal law, but there is much contemporary interest in community mediation and arbitration procedures that have been created as extralegal alternatives to the greatly overburdened civil justice system.

Utilization of social psychological research by the legal professions was slow at first but is now growing rapidly. The tension between the demands of internal validity (research design) and external validity (research realism) presents problems for those in the law who try to use the findings of social psychology and also divides psychological opinion on optimal research strategy. Law schools as yet provide no training in the evaluation of behavioral research, and so long as that is true lawyers are likely to be more sensitive to external validity, the degree to which research represents the reality they know, than to internal validity—the clarity of the causal analysis. Most social psychologists doing research related to legal issues have chosen to maximize internal validity by using the experimental method and are only gradually becoming equally concerned about external validity. Ebbe Ebbesen and Vladimir Konečni are the two most prominent exceptions. Their work has led them to conclude that all simulations of legal processes are untrustworthy and that there is no alternative, for relevant research, to the study of the real-life process of interest.

Two psycholegal issues have been more intensively studied than any others: eyewitness identification and jury process. On eyewitness identification there is a difference of opinion between the laymen who become jurors and the psychologists who have studied identification of faces. Jurors typically give great weight to an eyewitness identification, sometimes convicting on such evidence alone. Psychologists (and many legal authorities) believe that eyewitness identification in the case of a stranger's face seen briefly at one time and identification at a later time from an array of similar faces is a very inaccurate process that should be given little weight as evidence. It seems probable that the layman overestimates the accuracy of eyewitness identification because he is thinking either of his experience in successfully recognizing highly familiar faces or else of certain vivid flashbulb memories that remain fresh for years because of their great emotional significance. Psychologists who specialize in face recognition research are quite often called nowadays as expert witnesses. In the present state of knowledge it is possible to find experts who disagree. However, the disagreements are substantive and ultimately resolvable, so it seems a healthy thing for society, the law, and psychology to continue and to expand the use of expert witnesses.

8

Jury Size and Decision Rule

OF ALL THE THINGS that might be studied in American law, it is the jury trial that has been the most studied. There is a case for finding that strange and a reason for thinking it deplorable. In the flow chart of the criminal law process (Figure 7–1), which begins with the many decisions to commit crime, very few starters, amazingly few, wind up in a jury trial. Most are not reported, not arrested, or not prosecuted or are plea-bargained out. Why concentrate research on what is relatively rare: trial by jury?

The name, "trial by jury," frozen in form as sacred sayings tend to be, answers the question. It is not frequency of occurrence that makes trial by jury important, but the fact that it is a "right" designated in the American Constitution. The right is specified in the Constitution in several places (Article Three; the Seventh Amendment) but most importantly in the Sixth Amendment: "In all criminal prosecutions, the accused shall enjoy the right to a speedy and public trial, by an impartial jury . . . ." The existence of that right, as a possibility that may be realized, is a powerful force affecting all the cases that exit from the flow chart prior to the possible terminus; the decisions to arrest, prosecute, and plea-bargain operate in its shadow. It is even possible to argue that, as a social institution, trial by jury is more diagnostic of the real state of freedom and justice in a nation than is democratic election of political leaders.

There must, of course, be another reason why jury trials attract research, because, after all, they also attract dramatists—far more than plea bargaining or bail decisions. Indeed, almost every layman has a rough idea how trials and juries work, an idea derived from plays and movies. Criminal trials in American law are adversarial; it is the prosecution against the defense, and the jury is in the position of the audience, trying to decide between combatants, pulling for one side or the other. That is dramatic stuff, and it appeals to social psychologists as much as it does to playwrights and audiences.

There is, finally, a serious theoretical reason why jury deliberation should be a central problem in social psychology. In the jury, individual psychology and social process come together in serial order. The individual jurors function first as individuals, hearing a trial, weighing evidence, feeling sentiments, and then they come together and become a new organism—a small group. The process by which individual beliefs, ideas, attitudes, and feelings become integrated into a collective decision is, as Reid Hastie (Hastie, Penrod, and Pennington, 1983) has said, as fascinating as anything in science.

When we think of the jury, we think of one form of jury, the prototypical form: twelve persons required to come to a unanimous decision. In fact, that was the form the jury took in English and American law from something like the fourteenth century until 1966 in England and 1970 in the United States. Where that form came from originally is unknown. Why the mystic number twelve? It has no obvious functional superiority to neighboring numbers. Some have speculated that the origin really is mystical: the twelve apostles or the twelve tribes of Israel or the twelve months of the year. No one knows. But even today when other numbers operate as juries there is something that cannot quite be made rational, because the other number seems almost always to be six, half of twelve. Why it should not be four or eight or whatever, I cannot say.

In 1966 English law changed so as to make acceptable a new decision rule, a majority rule: ten of twelve. At the same time in the United States there were forces operating against the prototypical jury in favor of smaller numbers of jurors and rules short of unanimity. Saks (1977) has guessed that the important factors were a rising crime rate, the underfunding of the courts, and, you may be surprised to learn, doubt that juries were really good at making correct decisions. A few states (e.g. Oregon, Georgia, Florida, Louisiana) had begun to use six-member juries for some kinds of cases and to let twelve-member juries render verdicts when they reached majorities of nine, ten, or eleven. The question was whether those departures were constitutional, and some individuals convicted by a jury of less than twelve or a rule less demanding than unanimity made appeals that they carried to the Supreme Court.

Beginning in 1970 with *Williams* v. *Florida*, the Supreme Court made a series of decisions on jury size and verdict rule. Quite early on the Court not only noted that the Constitution itself was completely silent on the numbers and decision rules entailed in trial by jury but also decided that it would not be useful to try to figure out what James Madison and the other framers had in mind. Instead, the Court undertook to say whether juries with fewer than twelve members and rules less demanding than unanimity might be considered "functionally equivalent" to the prototypical twelve–unanimous type. Were six as likely to arrive at correct verdicts as twelve? If ten out of twelve were the decision rule, would that mean that minority opinions would not be given full consideration? Such questions are, of course, empirical questions, in the domain of social psychology. It occurred to a number of social psychologists about the same time that those questions ought not to be settled by the unsupported "opinions" of Supreme Court Justices and need not be if the right research were done. And so it came to pass that of all the research on trial by jury, it is the number of jurors and the decision rule under which they operate that have been most studied.

The Court on Jury Size

Florida was one of the states using six-person juries in certain cases, but when a man named Williams was convicted by such a jury, he felt that he had a constitutional right to trial by a twelve-member jury, and Williams appealed the case to the level of the Supreme Court. In *Williams* v. *Florida* (1970) the Supreme Court (by a close decision of five to four) ruled that a jury of six is not too small to be constitutional. Justice White in the majority opinion wrote that the specific number "twelve" was without significance except to mystics and "that there is no discernible difference between the results reached by the two different sized juries" (six and twelve). The Court did not in *Williams* v. *Florida* specify a constitutionally acceptable minimum size but said only that six was *not below the minimum.*

The opinion written in the case of *Williams* v. *Florida* is replete with strong generalizations about the behavior of people in groups, and the Court showed some awareness of the existence of possibly relevant empirical evidence. On page 101 it cites six "studies"; four are no more than reports of unsystematic observation, but the remaining two, Kalven and Zeisel's *The American Jury* (1966) and Asch's work on conformity (1952a, 1956), do indeed present important evidence. The problem with the two serious citations, we shall see, is that the Court got the conclusions wrong. For its bold and unsupported assertion that group size was of no discernible importance in jury deliberations, the Court drew some sharp criticism (e.g. Zeisel, 1971; Saks, 1977), which had at least one consequence: The Court's most recent opinion concerning jury size, *Ballew* v. *Georgia*, 1978, reads like a review of research in a psychological journal.

Ballew had been convicted by a five-member jury, and *Ballew* v. *Georgia* tested whether juries of that size were too small to satisfy constitutional guarantees. The Court ruled that juries of five *were* too small and at the same time restated its faith in juries of six. In spite of the copious citation of social science evidence and reasonably sophisticated evaluation of that evidence, one must wonder just what role it played, since that evidence does not clearly reject the number five and approve the number six. When, eight years earlier, in *Williams* v. *Florida*, the court ruled that juries with as few as six members, and possibly fewer, were permissible, both federal and state courts all over the country moved quickly to adopt smaller juries for certain kinds of cases, because smaller juries have two undoubted advantages: They take less time to deliberate and they cost less money. It would have been extremely disruptive for the Supreme Court in 1978 to have ruled against six-member juries, but at the same time to have permitted a minimum below six would have been to disregard completely all the juridical opinion and social science evidence arguing that smaller juries in general posed certain problems. It is not surprising, therefore, that five seemed too few and six just enough.

Smaller juries, juries with as few as six members, would seem to pose two threats to the justice process: (1) How representative can a smaller jury be of the community from which it is drawn? (2) How strong, in a smaller jury, will be the ability to resist conformity pressures? The Court was aware that jury size might affect representativeness and conformity pressures, and the Court was aware in 1970 that social science theory and research relevant to those matters existed. However, the utilization of social science in the 1970 opinion was minimal and, in part, erroneous. In fact, in 1970 it would have been possible clearly to predict the effects of a reduction in jury size on both representativeness and conformity, and those predictions are described in the sections that immediately follow.

Representativeness

The Court has repeatedly held that in the interests of the impartiality that the Sixth Amendment prescribes, a jury should be as nearly as possible a representative cross-section of the community from which members are drawn. Jurors are drawn from the total community by an approximately random process, and so the problem of attaining representativeness is essentially the same as it is in drawing a random sample from some population for a survey of opinion, political or otherwise. Just how large a sample must be to be considered representative depends most importantly on how heterogeneous the population is. One thing is clear, however: Other things being equal, the larger the random sample, the more representative it will be. For instance, to take an example from Saks (1977), if there were 10 percent blacks in a community and if we repeatedly drew samples of twelve from that community, 72 percent of the juries so constituted would have one or more blacks in their membership. If, on the other hand, we repeatedly drew samples of six, only 47 percent of the resultant juries would include one or more blacks.

What sampling theory says should be true of the relation between representativeness and jury size has been shown to be true. Saks carried out a highly realistic jury simulation study (1977) using persons drawn from real juror pools (in Ohio) with twenty-nine juries of twelve and twenty-nine juries of six. Blacks constituted 10 percent of the community population. Of six-member juries only 41 percent included at least one black, whereas 80 percent of twelve-member juries did so. Another minority, extreme conservatives, constituted 9 percent of the population and were represented on only 40 percent of six-member juries but on 75 percent of twelve-member juries. Notice that the obtained values are close to the values predicted for very large numbers of juries of the two sizes: 47 percent and 72 percent. There is no doubt that smaller juries, other things being equal, must constitute less representative cross-sections of a community than larger juries.

The Supreme Court was aware at the time of *Williams* v. *Florida*, that a smaller sample meant a less representative jury, though the Court chose not to inform itself on the details of sampling theory. More information would not in any case have answered the question on which the Court had to take a position. Would the decreased representativeness inevitably associated with the change from twelve-member to six-member juries be great enough to threaten the right to impartial jury trial? The Court had to decide and did: The difference would be "negligible." Saying so does not, of course, make it so, but demonstrating that the difference is not negligible is a hard thing to do. At any rate the Court must have realized that further reductions could not forever be "negligible," and it has made no further reductions.

The Supreme Court's faith in the representativeness of a sample of six is not surprising in the light of research showing that belief in "the law of small numbers" characterizes not only laymen but also psychologists and mathematicians in unguarded moments (Tversky and Kahneman, 1971). All these groups have been shown to be subject to a kind of illusion that a very small sample, if it is drawn at random, will preserve all the essential characteristics of the population from which it is drawn. The faith in small numbers is excessive by the standards of sampling theory.

Conformity Pressures

The first ballot in the jury room will ordinarily identify the existence of two factions: a majority and a minority. In an ideally fair and rational deliberation process, all the arguments of both factions will be weighed before coming to a decision, which may be required to be explicitly unanimous. The majority, we know, has some power to influence the perceptual judgments of the minority by the force of conformity (Chapter 1), which has nothing to do with rational argument, and it is also known that small minorities in juries sometimes agree to "go along" with a unanimous verdict although they have not been persuaded that it is correct (Simon, 1967). That is something the Constitution, the Court, and all who believe in the value of trial by jury would like to avoid. When jury size is reduced from twelve to six, is there any reason to fear that the ability of a minority to hold out will be diminished? The Court thought not, which is odd, because they cite Asch's (1952a) studies of conformity as supportive of their view.

Suppose that the random process by which a jury of twelve is selected yields two people who, by virtue of politics, sensibilities, intelligence, race, sex, or whatever, find themselves to be the minority on the first ballot. A minority of two in a jury of twelve has some ability x to resist the conformity force exerted by a majority of ten. How would that power of resistance compare with a parallel case in a jury of six? The answer depends on what you take the parallel case to be. If we hold the absolute number in the minority constant and so have two against four instead of two against ten, the power of resistance in the smaller group would be greater than in the larger, since two of six is almost half. However, the parallel is wrong. If a random process yields a minority of two in a set of twelve, that process is most likely to yield a minority of *one* in a set of six. The essential question is whether the power to resist conformity pressure of one against six is equal, greater than, or less than the power of two against ten. On that point the Court chose to make a very definite statement—of the "foot in mouth" type.

"Studies of the operative factors contributing to small group deliberation and decisionmaking suggest that jurors in the minority on the first ballot are likely to be influenced by the proportional size of the majority aligned against them" (*Williams* v. *Florida*, 1970, n. 49, p. 101). If it is the "proportional size" of the majority to the minority that determines the strength of the force exerted, then the force of ten-to-two would equal the force of five-to-one. In the very article by Asch (1952a) that is cited in the *Williams* opinion, data are reported that refute any such equation. In Asch's basic experiments (Chapter 1) a minority of one confronted a unanimous majority (varying in size), and in about one-third of the trials (objectively clear visual judgments) the minority person reported falsely in agreement with the majority. When, however, Asch changed the situation so as to provide the lone naive subject with one ally (confederate) who consistently reported truthfully, the social situation was completely transformed. "With one person at their side most subjects were able to face the majority with independence and the weakest were spared the extremes of yielding" (Asch, 1952b, p. 479). The conformity force of the majority on the minority was, in Asch's experiments, quite definitely not a matter of the proportional size of the majority; one person against five is not in the same situation as two persons against ten, but in a distinctly weaker position. From Asch's work (1952a, 1952b, 1956) in conjunction with sampling theory, the Court ought to have concluded that the six-person jury risked creating more cases in which a minority would yield to a majority because of the force of conformity than did the twelve-person jury.

From the social psychology that was known in 1970, when the Supreme Court decided that six-person juries were permissible in criminal cases, it is possible to say that the smaller juries would be less representative than the larger and also would run greater risk of conformity effects. It is not, however, possible to say that six-person juries would be less *just* than twelve-member juries either in the verdicts they returned or in the quality of the deliberation process, and the verdicts and process are what really matter. There were in 1970 some good social psychological reasons for thinking the smaller juries might tend to be less just and very little reason for the Court's majority "opinion" that there would be no important difference between the two. However, reduced representativeness and increased risk of conformity cannot be guaranteed to degrade either the process of jury deliberation or the verdicts that are its product. It is always possible that jurors called to do a solemn duty and render an impartial decision would rise above all the considerations of special interest and sympathy that make representativeness look important and would also stiffen their backbones to resist conformity pressures. As you may imagine, quite a few social psychologists got busy after 1970 trying to find out whether jury size did in fact make a difference in jury verdicts.

The Court on Decision Rules

In 1972 the Supreme Court heard cases of people who had been convicted by twelve-member juries operating under majority rules rather than the ancient rule of unanimity, and the Court found that majorities as small as nine of twelve satisfied constitutional guarantees in state but not federal criminal trials. The State of Oregon had been using a majority rule of ten of twelve for certain kinds of cases, and the defendants in *Apodaca, Cooper, and Madden* v. *Oregon* (1972) appealed their convictions under that rule. The State of Louisiana had used a nine-of-twelve rule, and Johnson (*Johnson* v. *Louisiana*, 1972) appealed conviction under that rule. All petitioners lost their cases, and majorities as low as nine of twelve (and conceivably lower since no minimum was made explicit) became constitutional.

The majority and minority opinions in *Apodaca* and in *Johnson* are extremely interesting, because they make sharply distinct assumptions about juror behavior. The majority opinion was based on the Theory of the Conscientious Juror. The Conscientious Juror would not terminate discussion with a dissenting minority of one, two, or three persons just because he operated under an explicit rule that permitted him to do so. Serious discussion, fair consideration, would continue so long as dissenters presented arguments, even though they might do so well after the time when there was a majority large enough to bring in a verdict. The Conscientious Juror's dominant concern is with justice and not simply the rendering of a verdict, so easing the explicit rule would not affect either the quantity or the quality of debate.

The minority opinion in *Apodaca* was written by Justice William O. Douglas. In essence, it said that since a majority rule meant that jurors need not deliberate beyond the point where the requisite majority was reached, there was no guarantee that they would do so. A unanimous decision rule *obliged* the jury to deal with dissent, any dissent at all, but a majority rule lifted that obligation. Even if jurors were to go on talking beyond the point where they could vote and reach a majority-rule verdict, the minority opinion held that this talk would be merely "polite and academic conversation," not the kind of "robust and earnest argument necessary to reach unanimity."

The division of opinion in those cases translates very neatly into two empirical questions, a question of quantity and a question of quality. The quantity question is: Will a majority-rule jury, when it has attained the requisite majority (e.g. nine-of-twelve), continue to deliberate as long as a unanimous-rule jury will do, after reaching that same point (e.g. nine-of-twelve), which for that kind of jury is not sufficient to produce a verdict? The quality question is: If both kinds of jury deliberate for equally long periods beyond the point that could mean a verdict for the majority-rule jury but not the unanimous-rule jury, will the deliberation beyond the critical point be equally "robust and earnest" in the two cases?

The fascinating thing about the two ways of thinking about juror behavior is that they seem equally plausible, and in 1972, when the cases were heard, there was no substantial evidence at all as to which might be correct. Yet the matter was clearly of the highest consequence, and so once again social psychologists launched an effort to find the answer.

The Court having approved juries as small as six and decision rules less demanding than unanimity, it is natural to wonder whether it would relax both historic requirements at once. So far the answer is no. In *Burch v. Louisiana* (1979) the Court ruled a majority of five out of six unconstitutional, and in all states six-member juries are required to reach unanimity.

Internal Validity and External Validity

Internal validity and external validity are two standards by which all psychological research is evaluated (Carlsmith, Ellsworth, and Aronson, 1976), but in research on juries it is more than ordinarily difficult to satisfy both standards at once. The internal validity of a research design is the degree to which variations in dependent variables are caused by variations in independent variables. External validity is the degree to which effects obtained in one sort of situation (typically a laboratory situation) will hold true in another sort of situation (e.g. real-life juries).

The sure way to satisfy external validity, of course, is to study the matter of interest directly. The deliberation processes of real-life juries are, we know, secret and may not be directly studied, but the products of real juries, for instance the verdicts they render, are not secret. It seems then as though it would be quite easy to learn something about the effects of jury size by doing archival research on the verdicts rendered by six-member and twelve-member juries. As soon as the comparison is proposed, you feel the tug of internal validity. If differences in distributions of verdicts are to be attributed to differences of jury size, the juries ought ideally to be in all other conceivably relevant ways equal, and that is not going to be true of real-life juries. However, if it can be shown that the decision between juries of six and juries of twelve is random, that fact, randomness of the decision between six and twelve, will satisfy the requirements of internal validity. Several such comparisons were undertaken after 1970, and one (Bermant and Coppock, 1973) will serve to illustrate the difficulties.

In the State of Washington there was a one-year period—1970—when attorneys in workmen's compensation disputes could choose between juries of six and juries of twelve. There were just 128 cases of this type, and Bermant and Coppock compared the percentages of verdicts favoring the plaintiff when juries had six members with the percentages for juries of twelve. The percentages were essentially identical: 54.5 percent for the smaller juries and 53.7 percent for the larger. Can we conclude that jury size had no effect on finding for the plaintiff? The problem is, of course, that attorneys *chose* the size of jury for each case and not, we may be sure, by the toss of a coin. Zeisel and Diamond (1974) argue that the attorneys probably opted for the larger jury in complex and expensive cases and for the smaller in simple and inexpensive cases and that the comparison therefore is probably between six-member juries hearing one kind of case and twelve-member juries hearing quite a different kind. If so, it is not a pure study of jury size at all.

The internal validity problem of Bermant and Coppock (1973) is a completely general one for nonexperimental studies comparing small juries and large, with respect to some outcome on the public record. They are never known to be otherwise identical, and the choice between them is never really random. Therefore, the possibility always exists that some third variable confounded with jury size is affecting the outcomes. Three archival studies of the type of Bermant and Coppock were published in years immediately following *Williams* v. *Florida* (1970), and none of them found any important difference in the products of six- and twelve-member juries. The Supreme Court has cited the studies (*Colgrove* v. *Battin*, 1973) as convincing empirical evidence that jury size has no effect on jury decision-making, but Saks (1977) has shown that all were seriously flawed with respect to internal validity.

Studies of real-life outcomes, which satisfy external validity at serious cost to internal validity, create an appetite for experiments, for studies that put internal validity first. An elegant experiment was designed by Davis and co-workers (1975) that promised to answer not only the questions raised by jury size but also those connected with decision rule. They created four kinds of juries: juries of six and juries of twelve operating either under a rule of unanimous decision or of two-thirds majority (eight of twelve; four of six). They created eighteen juries of each type.

In an experiment you can introduce a control that real life never permits:

All juries can deliberate and render verdicts on just the same case. Davis and colleagues chose the trial on a charge of rape of one C. T. Haney. In an experiment you can, and the Davis group did, ask for private individual opinions prior to deliberation as well as opinions after deliberation. Indeed, after deliberation, when it would not affect verdicts, an extensive questionnaire was administered that asked about all kinds of possibly relevant matters. Of course, created juries are not real juries of record; they are simulated or mock juries. That means one must worry about the external validity of anything discovered. Would the findings from the mock juries be true also in real cases?

Social psychologists have clearly chosen the experimental method, the path of internal validity, using mock or simulated juries as their way of learning about the effects of group size and decision rule. At the same time they have striven for a high level of external validity by creating simulations as near the real thing as possible. In three cases they have come very near indeed: Hastie, Penrod, and Pennington (1983); Padawer-Singer, Singer, and Singer (1977); and Saks (1977). The 1975 study of Davis and his associates also paid some attention to external validity (e.g. the trial used was an abbreviated version of the transcript of a real trial, and it was played on audiotape), but it is interesting today primarily for several things it did not do which it seems a good jury simulation must do.

The jurors of Davis and his co-workers were university undergraduates. Are university undergraduates serving as subjects in a simulation experiment different from persons drawn from actual jury rolls? Saks (1977) made the comparison by doing one not very realistic simulation study using Ohio State undergraduates and one extremely realistic simulation study using former jurors from Ohio's Franklin County. The typical undergraduate juror was "an eighteen-year-old white, single male, with some college education, [who] considers himself to be a liberal Democrat" (Saks, 1977, p. 62). The typical former juror was "a forty-six-year old, white, married, female, high school graduate, [who] considers herself to be a conservative Republican" (Saks, 1977, p. 62).

The undergraduate experimental subject is very different indeed from real jurors. Saks's study was not designed to compare the decision-making of the two kinds of juror (they were given different cases), but other studies have done so and found systematic differences (Kerr and Bray, 1982). The vast majority of jury simulation studies (about 80 percent of them) have used students as jurors, and the external validity of all such studies must be considered doubtful.

The case used by Davis and associates turned out to have an unexpected property, which subsequent investigators have taken care to avoid. It was a trial on a charge of rape, and of seventy-two juries exactly none found the accused, C. T. Haney, guilty. About 87 percent found him not guilty, and the remaining juries were all hung. Since there was very little variation in the dependent variable, there was very little for the independent variables of group size and decision rule to explain. As Saks says, the trial was simply too extreme a stimulus and so constituted a highly insensitive test. Kalven and Zeisel (1966) in their large-scale study of real trial outcomes found that judges agreed with jury verdicts 86 percent of the time. If we suppose that such cases are so clear-cut as to preclude the possibility of much jury-to-jury variation, it follows that only about 14 percent of real criminal trial cases are uncertain enough in outcome to constitute sensitive tests of variables like group size and decision rule. Anyone today who undertakes the enormous task of a realistic simulation study must be sure that he selects a case that he knows will yield high variability.

There is another problem involving case selection that is not easily solved. The three best simulation studies (Hastie, Penrod, and Pennington, 1983; Padawer-Singer, Singer, and Singer, 1977; Saks, 1977) all use a single case each. The reason for doing so is that even a 2 × 2 design, with two jury sizes and two decision rules, has four cells in each of which the n for statistical purposes is number of juries, not number of persons. With at least fifteen to twenty-five juries needed per cell, or experimental condition, the investigator is in for a lot of work with just one case. The studies done so far have assigned a higher priority (time and money) to the collection and analysis of detailed data on the decision-making process than to the multiplication of cases. Eventually, however, the fact must be faced that there is a large population of heterogeneous real-life cases to be sampled, and a single case cannot be very representative of that population. External validity requires a larger and so more representative sample of cases.

Davis and his colleagues set an upper limit on deliberation time of thirty minutes. That was probably too short a time and may be partly responsible for the large number of hung juries in the study (ten of seventy-two). How long a deliberation time should be allowed? Kalven and Zeisel (1966) report that for criminal trials lasting two days or less, 74 percent of deliberation times are under two hours, so perhaps a two-hour limit after which a jury is declared hung, such as Saks (1977) used, is sufficient. However, real juries operate under no stated time limit though there is always some effective limit beyond which they would be compelled to give up. It may be important in the deliberation process to feel that there is no time limit, and that is the condition created by Padawer-Singer, Singer, and Singer (1977) and Hastie, Penrod, and Pennington (1983).

Juror selection, case selection, and deliberation time are the dimensions of external validity that raise the most interesting questions, but the dimensions in which a simulation can be more or less realistic are many more than three: the form in which the trial is presented to the jurors, the places in which trial and deliberation occur, the persons in the roles of judge, defense attorney, prosecution, and so on. There are very many jury simulations, with one study realistic in certain ways, another in different ways, but three studies stand out from all the rest in their external validity: Hastie, Penrod, and Pennington (1983); Padawer-Singer, Singer, and Singer (1977); and Saks (1977). The most recent (Hastie) is the one that has attained the highest external validity and also the one that has given greatest attention to the fascinating problem that the Court had to confront when deciding on majority decision rules: Would jurors prove conscientious and engage in serious discussion with dissenters when a majority sufficient to bring in a verdict had been attained? That is the problem with which the present section concludes.

Most recent simulation studies have manipulated both jury size and decision rule, pretty much in the manner of Davis and associates (1975), but the most recent of all drops the jury size variable. A great deal of work was done on jury size between the 1970 *Williams* decision and 1980. There are archival studies (Beisser and Varrin, 1975; Bermant and Coppock, 1973; Institute of Judicial Administration, 1972; Mills, 1973) as well as experimental jury simulation studies (Buckhout et al., 1977; Kessler, 1973; Padawer-Singer, Singer, and Singer, 1977; Saks, 1977; Valenti and Downing, 1975). None of this work is entirely free of methodological flaw, and Saks (1977) has done a masterful critique of the total evidence. Still, it must be granted that Hastie and his collaborators were correct when they said that significant differences between six-person and twelve-person juries in either trial outcome or the quality of deliberation had not, as of 1983, been demonstrated. In 1985, despite some evidence (Kerr and MacCoun) that as group size increases the probability of a hung jury also increases, it is still the case that juries of six persons and of twelve persons have not been shown to differ in quality of deliberation or in verdict distribution. That is quite surprising since, as we have seen, the smaller juries must be less representative and must run greater risks of conformity effects. But, again as we have seen, neither possibility *need* affect juror verdicts or discussion. Hastie, Penrod, and Pennington apparently decided that the jury size variable was not promising enough to include in their design.

It seems to me that we ought manfully to acknowledge that when the Supreme Court, operating without evidence or with evidence misinterpreted, decided that the differences between large and small juries were "negligible," it may have been right. It did not deserve to be, but I have noticed before that some people do everything wrong and yet have things turn out well for them; Winston Churchill was such a one. Strictly speaking, of course, research has not proved that jury size (twelve versus six) has *no* significant effects; that is the null hypothesis, which never can be proved. The correct statement is that research thus far has failed to show significant effects, except—I almost forgot—the smaller jury takes less time to deliberate. The Supreme Court thought that too obvious to speculate about. The Court was more troubled by decision rules than by jury size, however, and on that topic its majority may not have been so wise (or lucky).

Inside the Jury

The heading is the title of the book by Hastie, Penrod, and Pennington, and it is a title well chosen, because the research reported exploits, as no other research has done, the opportunity the experimental method creates to study in fine detail those deliberation processes which are secret in juries of record. This study truly takes us *inside*.

The design of the study is very simple as far as the independent variable is concerned. Three explicit decision rules were used for twelve-person juries: unanimity, or twelve of twelve; majority of ten of twelve; majority of eight of twelve. Twenty-three juries of each type were created, sixty-nine juries in all. Each jury saw and heard (on videotape) the same trial. On the dependent variable side the study was exceedingly fine-grained, and a full description here is not possible. Predeliberation individual verdict preferences were asked for, as were postdeliberation individual preferences. There was an elaborate postdeliberation questionnaire asking about personal characteristics. In addition, the entire deliberation process of each jury was filmed by an unobtrusive camera and the resultant videotapes were coded for forty-three fact categories (trial evidence, testimony, and so on); thirty-nine issue categories (exact definitions of verdicts, witness credibility, and so on); eighteen types of utterance categories (questions, statements, directions); and more besides, stopping just this side of the movements of molecules in the air. Two coders did the whole job and were shown to be highly reliable with one another and with themselves from time to time.

The chief dependent variable was verdict rendered. Possible verdicts were not simply "guilty" and "not guilty" but rather first degree murder; second degree murder; manslaughter; and self-defense (not guilty of murder). Those must be at least roughly defined. First degree murder is unlawful killing with malice and premeditation; evidence of premeditation includes intent to kill, having a plan, and so on. Second degree murder is unlawful killing with malice but without premeditation. Manslaughter is unlawful killing in the absence of malice, and self-defense is killing in response to an attack. The prosecution charged Frank C. Johnson with the first degree murder of Alan Caldwell on the night of May 9, 1976. The defense pleaded not guilty because the defendant acted in self-defense. The "correct" verdict, the right answer as defined by legal experts and also by the judgment of the actual jury of record, was second degree murder. However, the trial was a complex one that could and did produce a variety of verdicts.

The pains taken to achieve external validity, to make the simulation realistic, were extraordinary, and I shall only mention a few. The stimulus trial was based on a complete transcript of an actual murder trial. It was reenacted by professional actors, university faculty, a police officer, a Superior Court judge, and two attorneys, filmed, and then edited down to a three-hour videotape. Jurors were drawn from trial jury pools in Massachusetts. The filmed trial was viewed in a courtroom, and jury deliberations were held in a jury room. Everything was done on regular working days, and there was no limit on deliberation time; one jury kept at it for four consecutive days. Indications that all those attempts to achieve realism succeeded include the fact that the modal (most frequent) verdict was the same as the verdict reached by the jury of record (second degree murder), and the modal deliberation time was within ten minutes of the time taken by the actual jury. Legal experts of various kinds rated the whole proceedings very high on seriousness and realism.

Of course, a simulation remains a simulation, and the one serious ineradicable difference from the real-life case is that mock jurors know their verdicts will not have consequences for an accused person. They also know they are being studied, but the researchers were not present during the deliberations and were represented only by a camera. The videotaped trial was shorter than the original, but much of the time in the original was taken up by recesses. Probably the fact that verdicts have no consequences is the most worrisome feature of the mock trial, and that is not terribly worrisome because jurors in the present study gave every indication .that they took the whole process seriously. There was none of the bemused detachment that can occur with student juries and a classroom court.

When the Supreme Court decided in *Apodaca, Cooper, and Madden* v. *Oregon* (1972) and in *Johnson* v. *Louisiana* (1972) that twelve-person juries in state criminal courts need not reach unanimous agreement in order to render a verdict, but could do so with majorities as small as nine in twelve (and perhaps smaller), the great question was what effect would a majority rule have on the deliberation process. The answer provided by *Inside the Jury* is very much more subtle than the Justices or anyone else imagined in advance of the study. The majority and minority opinions of the Supreme Court came to a sharp focus in the differential predictions made about what would happen in the deliberations of a majority-rule jury once the requisite majority had been attained. Would the jury promptly halt discussion and take a formal vote, leaving dissenters with arguments unanswered and (perhaps) some dissatisfaction with the American jury process? That is a question of quantity, but there is also a question of quality. Even if the majority-rule jury did continue discussion well beyond the point when a verdict had become possible, would the discussion be "robust and earnest" or nothing but a "polite and academic conversation" aimed at soothing the defeated minority? In discussing what *Inside the Jury* discovered on that point, I shall contrast just the extreme cases of the unanimity rule (hereafter the 12/12 jury) and the smallest majority (hereafter the 8/12 jury), leaving out the intermediate majority (10/12), because it will make the discussion easier to follow without misrepresenting anything essential.

The question of quantity can be answered without ambiguity. The twenty-three 8/12 juries kept talking for only a few minutes, typically under five minutes, after the point at which the largest faction first became eight or more (hereafter post-8). Since the average total deliberation time for 8/12 juries was seventy-five minutes, their post-8 time was less than 6 percent of the total. The quality of those few minutes of post-8 talk was not such as to be called "robust and serious." There was little reference to either trial evidence or legal issues. Thus far, it looks like a clear defeat for the Court majority's conception of the

Conscientious Juror and a clear victory for the more skeptical views stated in the minority opinion written by Justice Douglas.

Knowing that little of importance happened post-8 in the 8/12 jury makes one wonder what happened in the 12/12 juries after they reached that same point when a majority of eight or more first came into existence. In other words, what happened post-8 in juries for which a majority of eight was not enough to make a verdict possible? On the average, 12/12 juries had longer total deliberation times; their average was 138 minutes. This still means that a very substantial amount of their total deliberation (20 percent) occurred beyond the point when they might have reached a verdict if they had been operating on an 8/12 rule.

Was the deliberation of those last twenty-seven minutes of the sort that might be called "robust and earnest"? It clearly was. In that last period, there occurred 27 percent of the requests for additional instructions from the trial judge; 25 percent of the oral corrections of errors made in discussion; 34 percent of the discussion of the "beyond a reasonable doubt" standard of proof; and so forth. In addition, for seven juries of twenty-three the verdict favored by the largest faction, when that faction first became as large as eight, was not the verdict finally rendered. That is to say that seven juries, 30 percent of the total, had not attained their final position by the time they reached the point when they could have rendered a verdict if they had been operating on an 8/12 rule.

Everything we have learned until now seems clearly to favor the Court's minority opinion, to contradict the idea of the Conscientious Juror, and to damn the majority-rule jury as an inadequate instrument of justice. It would appear that the 8/12 jury is simply a 12/12 jury cut off prematurely, cut off before it can deliberate fully and reach the verdict that full deliberation requires. However, there are some other facts, and they force us to think of a subtler conclusion.

Analyses of the content of discussion over the total course of discussion refute the idea that an 8/12 jury is simply a prematurely cut-off or truncated 12/12. We start with the fact that total deliberation time for 8/12 juries averages seventy-five minutes, whereas for 12/12 juries it averages 138 minutes. In both cases we divide total time into equal one-fifth portions or quintiles. Of course, this means that a quintile for an 8/12 jury will take up about fifteen minutes whereas a quintile of a 12/12 jury will last about twenty-seven minutes.

Comparing the content of discussion, quintile by quintile, for the two sorts of jury, something very important appears. The quintiles, matched in serial order (first, second, third, and so on), also match quite well in terms of content. For both sorts of jury, early quintiles contain much discussion of evidence and testimony, many questions and answers, whereas the content of late quintiles concerns the definition of verdict categories (first degree murder, second degree murder) and the matching of the facts of the present case to the appropriate verdict category. Both kinds of jury progress through the same sort of phase sequence, from determining the facts to fitting the facts to a verdict. In terms of content or process, the 8/12 jury appears definitely not to be simply a cut-off 12/12. It seems nearer the truth to say that it is a *compressed* (in time) 12/12.

If you compare the two sorts of jury for what happens in any given interval of time, say the first forty minutes, they are unlike. But the first forty minutes will catch the average 8/12 jury past the middle of its third quintile, halfway through its total deliberation, whereas the 12/12 jury will be in only its second quintile, not yet one-third of the way through its total deliberation. Compared quintile for quintile, the two sorts of jury will be at similar points in the decision task. If, as this analysis suggests, the 8/12 jury is a compressed 12/12 jury, the next question, a very critical question, is how do they compare in the quality of the job they do? The information most pertinent to that question is the distribution of verdicts reached by the twenty-three juries of each type.

Here are the distributions:

	Decision Rule	
Jury Verdicts	12/12	8/12
First degree murder	0	1
Second degree murder	13	13
Manslaughter	7	8
Not guilty	0	0
Hung	3	1

The two distributions are practically indistinguishable. Certainly they are not different at a statistically significant level. For both juries the most common verdict (the modal verdict) is the correct verdict, as defined by legal experts and by the decision of the real-life jury. What is more, exactly thirteen of twenty-three juries of both types attain this correct answer, and for both types of jury (seven of the 12/12 and eight of the 8/12) manslaughter is the next most common verdict.

My omission of the 10/12 juries is slightly misleading here, because while thirteen of twenty-three of those juries also rendered the correct second degree murder verdict, there were five first degree murder verdicts, and the authors of *Inside the Jury* consider it possible, though not clearly demonstrated, that majority-rule juries exert less of a moderating or damping influence on jurors with inclinations to extreme verdicts. The discussion is complicated and in-conclusive and may be omitted here, because it is not essential to the main argument.

A startling conclusion must now be entertained. We have two sorts of jury, 12/12 and 8/12, and the deliberation time for the average 12/12 jury is nearly twice as long as the time for the 8/12 jury (138 minutes versus seventy-five minutes). A quintile-by-quintile analysis suggests that the two sorts of jury go through much the same phase sequence in the decision-making process, and their products, if verdicts are products, are indistinguishable. The one is as likely to reach the correct decision as the other. Why not prefer the one that takes less time, the majority-rule jury, the kind of jury authorized by the 1972 Court decisions? A straightforward, very American efficiency analysis seems to require that conclusion.

Notice how the new facts, the quintile analysis and the verdict distributions, change the meaning of the first findings, which were that the 8/12 jury does not deliberate long after reaching its verdict minimum of a majority of eight, whereas the 12/12 jury deliberates for twenty-seven minutes beyond that point and deliberates seriously and makes important decision changes in that final period. When we first looked at those facts, we took them to mean that the 8/12 jury was cut off before it could complete its fact-finding task. Certainly the 12/12 juries needed that post-8 period; those juries had not completed their tasks when they reached a majority of eight. However, we can now see that it does not necessarily follow that the 8/12 juries needed a similar period. It does not follow because the 8/12 juries had attained the last phase in their decision-making process and, furthermore, had, in the modal case, thirteen of twenty-three, reached the correct answer.

If it is fair to say that the 8/12 jury solved the problem faster than the 12/12 jury, what enabled it to do so? Presumably, it must be the fact that those juries were instructed to reach an eight-or-more-out-of-twelve outcome rather than a twelve-of-twelve outcome. It is tempting to invoke Parkinson's Law: "Work expands to fill the time allowed for it." All juries were allowed unlimited time, of course, but perhaps there is a variation on Parkinson's Law that goes: "Group decision processes expand with the number of people who are required to agree." That line of thought suggests not that the 8/12 jury is compressed, but that the 12/12 is inflated. However, there are some further data.

It is surprising in the Hastie, Penrod, and Pennington study to find exactly thirteen of twenty-three for each of the three decision rules reaching the correct verdict, second degree murder, and so uniform an outcome reminds us that just one case was used, after all. May not the case have been simply too clear for significant differences in verdict distribution across decision rules to be found? That is certainly possible but seems unlikely because of the results on verdict distribution and decision rule found in the two other studies having very high external validity. Saks (1977) and Padawer-Singer and co-workers (1977) both compared juries operating on unanimous and nonunanimous rules, and both studies found no significant differences in verdict distributions. Those two studies used two additional cases, and percentages of juries voting for conviction and for acquittal were close enough to indicate that the cases were fairly ambiguous. I am inclined to conclude with respect to the three best studies to date that it has not been demonstrated that decision rules affect verdict distributions. However, Hastie and his colleagues conclude, with respect to the finding in their own study that first degree murder convictions (a mistake) occurred only in majority-rule juries (six of forty-six), that "there is convincing evidence that a part of this result is due to decision rule influence on performance. Even quantitatively small effects such as those observed are of great significance in the context of the legal commitment to a trial process that is not biased against the defendant" (1983, p. 238).

Verdicts—correct ones—are the most important product of jury deliberations, but they are not the only important product. Jurors themselves say that while their main goal was fact-finding, the goal next in importance was "doing a good job." What does doing a good job mean to them beyond fact-finding? It means having a fair-minded, thoughtful, and thorough discussion. Whether or not a given verdict is "correct" is never, strictly speaking, knowable, and a jury will not ordinarily learn even the expert legal opinion on their verdict. That means the quality of the discussion as they perceive it is the main criterion of the quality of the job done. If enough jurors feel that their jury has not done a good job, general confidence in the institution itself will be weakened. It has long been supposed that the experience of serving on a jury enhances a citizen's respect for legal institutions. I think Hastie, Penrod, and Pennington have clear evidence that in this respect the 12/12 jury is more successful than the majority-rule jury.

On a questionnaire given out after deliberation and verdict, individual jurors rated the quality of the discussion in which they had participated. "Thoroughness of deliberation" and "seriousness of deliberation" are, perhaps, the two most important scales. It is important to distinguish the ratings of majority members from the ratings of holdout members since the former prevailed and the latter did not. Common sense suggests that holdouts, since they also lost out, will be less impressed with the quality of the discussion than will the majority, and common sense is correct: For all decision rules, holdout jurors rated the deliberation as less thorough and serious than did the majority. The difference is a socially important one, even though its occurrence is simple common sense. Unanimous rule juries had no holdouts except in the three juries that hung. Juries following the 10/12 rule had an average of 1.61 holdouts per jury, and those following the 8/12 rule had an average of 2.89 holdouts. It is of incidental interest that those averages show that some majority-rule juries rendered verdicts with larger numbers in the majority than the minimum required. The socially important fact is that majority-rule juries regularly have two or three members who rate the seriousness and thoroughness of deliberation one full scale point (on a 0–9 scale) lower than do the members of unanimous-rule juries.

In both unanimous-rule juries and majority-rule juries we have jurors who prevailed; in the former case the prevailing jurors had no holdouts to consider, whereas in the latter case they did have holdouts to think about. How did prevailing jurors in the two sets of circumstances evaluate the quality of the deliberation process? The differences are not large, but they are consistent. What they show is that even those jurors who belong to the prevailing majority are less favorably impressed with the deliberation process when it leaves a dissenting faction of two or three members than when it leaves no dissenters (unanimous-rule).

Without going into detail, it is fair to say that most other relevant ratings are consistent with a conclusion that the unanimous-rule jury leaves jurors with the best impression of the deliberation process. Majority-rule jurors agreed with one another less well on the key issues in the trial and were less impressed with one another's open-mindedness. Decision difficulty was rated highest in unanimous-rule juries, and if deliberation times are an index of difficulty, that was an accurate perception. Of course, a more thorough and serious discussion should also feel more difficult.

Jurors think of the right decision as their main objective and doing a good job in the sense of having a fair and thorough discussion as second in importance. In the law justice does not mean the right decision; it means observance of "due process," which entails the kind of fair and thorough discussion jurors had in mind. It would be seriously wrongheaded from the legal standpoint to evaluate decision rules in terms of the efficiency or speed with which they lead to the production of correct verdicts. Verdicts are not cars, and the social mechanisms for producing them should not be evaluated by Detroit standards. The process is everything, and Hastie and his colleagues have considerable evidence that the process is better in unanimous-rule juries.

Perhaps the single most telling thing to look at in evaluating the real quality of the process is the behavior of small factions of one or two persons. In unanimous-rule juries, small factions of one or two jurors were extremely likely to speak relative to jurors in large factions. This makes sense, of course, since the minority of one or two would, in such juries, have been blocking a verdict and so would have had to explain themselves. In 10/12 juries such minorities were much less likely to speak and in 8/12 juries still less likely. In such juries their votes were not ultimately needed in order to reach a verdict, and the authors' impression is that group pressure tended to keep them quiet. That is strong evidence against the functional equivalence of juries operating under the three rules, and the evidence argues that the unanimous-rule jury best realizes due process.

There are other outcomes that argue the superiority of the unanimous-rule jury in terms of due process. A reversal of a first-ballot verdict (as in *Twelve Angry Men*, though none so extreme occurred) is a sign of serious and robust discussion, and seven reversals occurred out of twenty-three unanimous-rule juries, but only six of forty-six in majority-rule juries. Some discussions were categorized as "verdict-driven" (jurors took sides and argued consistently one way or the other) and some discussions as "evidence-driven" (individual jurors seemed to consider both sides). The verdict-driven discussion, which is remote from the ideal of jury process, was more common in majority-rule juries (33 percent) than in unanimous-rule juries (17 percent). Finally, more unanimous-rule juries hung (three of twenty-three) than did majority-rule juries (one of forty-six), and while one does not want a decision rule that results in a large number of hung juries, it is certainly important for the perceived justice of deliberation that the possibility should clearly exist.

Inside the Jury does not shy away from policy implications: "The proper decision rule is thus the unanimous rule" (1983, p. 238). I do not think that the unanimous rule has been shown to be the best for efficiently producing correct verdicts. However, I also do not think that that is the right criterion to apply. In terms of perceived justice and observance of due process, which are the right criteria, Inside the Jury has, I think, established the superiority of the unanimous rule.

Summary

From about the fourteenth century in common law until 1970 in the American law a jury was understood to comprise twelve persons who were required to be in unanimous agreement to reach a verdict. From 1970 on the United States Supreme Court made decisions that made it possible in some cases to use juries with as few as six members, but the smaller jury was still required to reach a unanimous decision. In the case of the twelve-member jury, however, majorities as small as nine of twelve (and possibly smaller) were ruled constitutional. The Court in its decisions enunciated various propositions concerning the effects of group size and decision rule on the quality of decision-making which seemed to belong to the province of empirical social psychology. Subsequent research comparing six-member and twelve-member juries has not discovered any consistent effects on the quality of deliberation or verdict and so does not challenge the Supreme Court's intuition that any difference would be "negligible." The results on the effect of decision rules are still complex and arguable. On the evidence of the best study to date (Hastie, Penrod, and Pennington, Inside the Jury, 1983) it appears that unanimous-rule juries and majority-rule juries do not differ in the verdicts they render and are, in fact, exactly equally likely to render correct verdicts, with the majority-rule jury doing so in less time. However, the unanimous-rule jury is superior to the majority-rule jury in the quality of its deliberation, in its satisfaction of due process, and in the respect for the process felt by jurors after they have served.

References for Part III

Apodaca, Cooper, and Madden, v. Oregon. 1972. 406 U.S. 404.

ASCH, S. E. 1952a. Effects of group pressure upon the modification and distortion of judgments. In G. E. Swanson, T. M. Newcomb, and E. L. Hartley (eds.), *Readings in Social Psychology.* New York: Holt, pp. 2–11.

———. 1952b. *Social Psychology.* Englewood Cliffs, N.J.: Prentice-Hall.

———. 1956. Studies of independence and conformity: I. A minority of one against a unanimous majority, *Psychological Monographs* No. 146, vol. *70,* no. 9.

BAHRICK, H. P.; P. O. BAHRICK; and R. P. WITTLINGER. 1975. Fifty years of memory for names and faces: A cross-sectional approach, *Journal of Experimental Psychology: General, 104,* no. 1: 54–75.

BARKOWITZ, P., and J. C. BRIGHAM. In press. Recognition of faces: Own-race bias, incentive, and time delay, *Journal of Applied Social Psychology.*

BEISSER, E., and R. VARRIN. 1975. Six-member juries in the federal courts, *Judicature, 58:* 425–33.

Ballew v. Georgia. 1978. 435 U.S. 223.

BENTON, A. L. 1980. The neuropsychology of facial recognition, *American Psychologist, 35:* 176–86.

BERMANT, G., and R. COPPOCK. 1973. Outcomes of six- and twelve-member jury trials: An analysis of 128 civil cases in the State of Washington, *Washington Law Review, 43:* 593.

BORCHARD, E. M. 1932. *Convicting the Innocent: Errors of Criminal Justice.* New Haven: Yale University Press.

BORGIDA, E. 1980. Evidentiary reform of rape laws: A psycholegal approach. In P. D. Lipsett and B. D. Sales (eds.), *New Directions in Psycholegal Research.* New York: Van Nostrand Reinhold, pp. 171–97.

BOWER, G. H., and M. M. KARLIN. 1974. Depth of processing pictures of faces and recognition memory, *Journal of Experimental Psychology, 103:* 751–57.

BRAY, R. M., and N. L. KERR. 1982. Methodological considerations in the study of the psychology of the courtroom. In N. L. Kerr and R. M. Bray (eds.), *The Psychology of the Courtroom.* New York: Academic Press.

BRIGHAM, J. C., and P. BARKOWITZ. 1978. Do "they all look alike"? The effect of race, sex, experience, and attitudes on the ability to recognize faces, *Journal of Applied Social Psychology, 8:* 306–18.

BRIGHAM, J. C., and R. K. BOTHWELL. 1983. The ability of prospective jurors to estimate the accuracy of eyewitness identifications, *Law and Human Behavior, 7:* 19–30.

BRIGHAM, J. C., and N. L. WILLIAMSON. 1979. Cross-racial recognition and age: When you're over 60, do they still all look alike? *Personality and Social Psychology Bulletin, 5:* 218–22.

BRIGHAM, J. C., and M. P. WOLFSKEIL. 1983. Opinions of attorneys and law enforcement personnel on the accuracy of eyewitness identifications, *Law and Human Behavior, 7:* 337–49.

BRIGHAM, J. C.; A. MAAS; L. D. SNYDER; and K. SPAULDING. 1982. Accuracy of eyewitness identifications in a field setting, *Journal of Personality and Social Psychology*, 42: 673–81.

BROWN, R., and J. KULIK. 1977. Flashbulb memories, *Cognition*, 5: 73–99.

BUCKHOUT, R. 1974. Eyewitness testimony, *Scientific American*, 231: 23–31.

——. 1980. Nearly 2000 witnesses can be wrong, *Bulletin of the Psychonomic Society*, 16: 307–10.

BUCKHOUT, R.; S. WEG; F. REILLY; and R. FROHBOESE. 1977. Jury verdicts: Comparison of 6- vs. 12-person juries and unanimous vs. majority decision rule in a murder trial, *Bulletin of the Psychonomic Society*, 10: 175–78.

Burch v. Louisiana. 1979. 99 S. Ct. 1623.

CAREY, S., and R. DIAMOND. 1977. From piecemeal to configurational representation of faces, *Science*, 195: 312–14.

CARLSMITH, J. M.; P. C. ELLSWORTH; and E. ARONSON. 1976. *Methods of Research in Social Psychology.* Reading, Mass.: Addison-Wesley.

CHANCE, J.; A. J. GOLDSTEIN; and L. MCBRIDE. 1975. Differential experience and recognition memory for faces, *Journal of Social Psychology*, 97: 243–53.

CLANCY, K.; J. BARTOLOMEO; D. RICHARDSON; and C. WELLFORD. 1981. Sentence decision-making: The logic of sentence decisions and the extent and sources of sentence disparity, *The Journal of Criminal Law and Criminology*, 72: 524–54.

CLIFFORD, B. R., and J. SCOTT. 1978. Individual and situational factors in eyewitness testimony, *Journal of Applied Psychology*, 63: 352–59.

COLEGROVE, F. W. 1889. Individual memories, *American Journal of Psychology*, 10: 228–55.

Colegrove v. Battin. 1973. 413 U.S. 149.

COWAN, C. L.; W. C. THOMPSON; and P. C. ELLSWORTH. 1984. The effects of death qualification on jurors' predisposition to convict and on the quality of deliberation, *Law and Human Behavior*, 8, nos. 1/2: 53–79.

CROSS, I. F.; J. CROSS; and J. DALY. 1971. Sex, race, age, and beauty as factors in recognition of faces, *Perception and Psychophysics*, 10: 393–96.

DAVIS, J. H.; N. L. KERR; R. S. ATKIN; R. HOLT; and D. MEEK. 1975. The decision processes of 6- and 12-person mock juries assigned unanimous and 2/3 majority rules, *Journal of Personality and Social Psychology*, 32: 1–14.

DEFFENBACHER, K. 1980. Eyewitness accuracy and confidence: Can we infer anything about their relationship? *Law and Human Behavior*, 4: 243–60.

DEVLIN, HONORABLE LORD PATRICK (chair). 1976. *Report to the Secretary of State for the Home Department of the Departmental Committee on Evidence of Identification in Criminal Cases.* London: Her Majesty's Stationery Office.

EBBESEN, E. B., and V. J. KONEČNI. 1975. Decision making and information integration in the courts: The setting of bail, *Journal of Personality and Social Psychology*, 32: 805–21.

——. 1982. An analysis of the bail system. In V. J. Konečni and E. B. Ebbesen (eds.), *The Criminal Justice System: A Social-Psychological Analysis.* San Francisco: W. H. Freeman, pp. 191–229.

ELLIS, H. D.; G. M. DAVIES; and J. W. SHEPHERD. 1977. Experimental studies of face identification, *Journal of Criminal Defense*, 3: 219–34.

ELLIS, H. D.; J. B. DEREGOWSKI; and J. W. SHEPHERD. 1975. Descriptions of white and black faces by white and black subjects, *International Journal of Psychology, 10:* 119–23.

ELLSWORTH, P. C.; R. M. BUKATY; C. L. COWAN; and W. C. THOMPSON. 1984. The death-qualified jury and the defense of insanity, *Law and Human Behavior, 8*, nos. 1/2: 81–93.

FAGAN, J. F. 1972. Infants' recognition memory for faces, *Journal of Experimental Child Psychology, 14:* 453–76.

FITZGERALD, R., and P. C. ELLSWORTH. 1984. Due process vs. crime control, *Law and Human Behavior, 8*, nos. 1/2: 31–51.

GOLDSTEIN, A. G. 1977. The fallibility of the eyewitness: Psychological evidence. In B. D. Sales (ed.), *Psychology in the Legal Process.* New York: Spectrum, pp. 223–47.

GOLDSTEIN, A. G.; B. STEPHENSON; and J. CHANCE. 1977. Face recognition memory: Distribution of false alarms, *Bulletin of the Psychonomic Society, 9:* 416–18.

GREENBERG, M. S.; C. E. WILSON; and M. K. MILLS. 1982. Victim decision-making: An experimental approach. In V. J. Konečni and E. B. Ebbesen (eds.), *The Criminal Justice System; A Social-Psychological Analysis.* San Francisco: W. H. Freeman, pp. 73–94.

GRISSO, T., and S. MANOOGIAN. 1980. Juveniles' comprehension of Miranda warnings. In P. D. Lipsitt and B. D. Sales (eds.), *New Directions in Psycholegal Research.* New York: Van Nostrand Reinhold, pp. 127–48.

HASTIE, R.; S. PENROD; and N. PENNINGTON. 1983. *Inside the Jury.* Cambridge, Mass.: Harvard University Press.

HOCHBERG, J., and R. GALPER. 1967. Recognition of faces: I. An exploratory study, *Psychonomic Science, 9:* 619–20.

INSTITUTE OF JUDICIAL ADMINISTRATION (IJA). 1972. *A Comparison of Six- and Twelve-Member Juries in New Jersey Superior and County Courts.* New York: IJA.

JOHNSON, C., and B. SCOTT. 1978. Eyewitness testimony and suspect identification as a function of arousal, sex of witness, and scheduling of interrogation. Paper presented at the meeting of the American Psychological Association, Washington, D.C.

Johnson v. Louisiana. 1972. 406 U.S. 356.

KALVEN, H., JR., and H. ZEISEL. 1966. *The American Jury.* Boston: Little, Brown.

KASSIN, S. M., and L. S. WRIGHTSMAN. 1979. On the requirements of proof: The timing of instruction and mock juror verdicts, *Journal of Personality and Social Psychology, 37:* 1877–87.

KERR, N. L., and R. M. BRAY (eds.). 1982. *The Psychology of the Courtroom.* New York: Academic Press.

KERR, N. L., and R. J. MACCOUN. 1985. The effects of jury size and polling method in the process and product of jury deliberation, *Journal of Personality and Social Psychology, 48,* 349–63.

KESSLER, J. 1973. An empirical study of six- and twelve-member jury decision-making processes, *University of Michigan Journal of Law Reform, 6:* 712–34.

KONEČNI, V. J., and E. B. EBBESEN. 1982. *The Criminal Justice System: A Social-Psychological Analysis.* San Francisco: W. H. Freeman.

KRAFKA, C., and S. PENROD. 1981. The effects of witness and stimulus factors on eyewitness performance. American Psychology–Law Society Biennial Convention, October.

LATANÉ, B. 1981. The psychology of social impact, *American Psychologist, 36*: 343–56.

LEVINE, F. J., and J. L. TAPP. 1982. Eyewitness identification: Problems and pitfalls. In V. J. Konečni and E. B. Ebbesen (eds.), *The Criminal Justice System: A Social-Psychological Analysis.* San Francisco: W. H. Freeman, pp. 99–127.

LINDSEY, R. C. L.; G. L. WELLS; and C. M. RUMPEL. 1981. Can people detect eyewitness-identification accuracy within and across situations? *Journal of Applied Psychology, 66*: 79–89.

LIVINGSTON, R. B. 1967. Reinforcement. In G. C. Quarton, T. Melnechuck, and F. O. Schmitt (eds.), *The Neurosciences: A Study Program.* New York: Rockefeller University Press, pp. 568–76.

LOFTUS, E. F. 1974. Reconstructing memory: The incredible eyewitness, *Psychology Today, 8*: 116–19.

——. 1979. *Eyewitness Testimony.* Cambridge, Mass.: Harvard University Press.

——. 1983. Silence is not golden, *American Psychologist, 38*: 564–72.

LOFTUS, E. F., and W. MARBURGER. 1983. Since the eruption of Mt. St. Helens, has anyone beaten you up? Improving the accuracy of retrospective reports with landmark events, *Memory and Cognition, 11*: 114–20.

MALPASS, R. S., and J. KRAVITZ. 1969. Recognition for faces of own and other race, *Journal of Personality and Social Psychology, 13*: 330–34.

MALPASS, R. S.; H. LAVIGEUR; and D. E. WELDON. 1973. Verbal and visual training in face recognition, *Perception and Psychophysics, 14*: 286–92.

McCLOSKEY, M., and H. E. EGETH. 1983. Eyewitness identification: What can a psychologist tell a jury? *American Psychologist, 38*: 550–63.

McGILLIS, D. 1980. Neighborhood justice centers as mechanisms for dispute resolution. In P. D. Lipsitt and B. D. Sales (eds.), *New Directions in Psycholegal Research.* New York: Van Nostrand Reinhold, pp. 198–233.

MILLS, L. R. 1973. Six- and twelve-member juries: An empirical study of trial results, *University of Michigan Journal of Law Reform, 6*: 671–711.

MUNSTERBERG, H. 1908. *On the Witness Stand: Essays on Psychology and Crime.* New York: Clark, Boardman.

NEISSER, U. 1982. Snapshots or benchmarks? In U. Neisser (ed.), *Memory Observed.* San Francisco: W. H. Freeman, pp. 43–58.

PADAWER-SINGER, A. M.; A. N. SINGER; and R. L. J. SINGER. 1977. An experimental study of twelve vs. six member juries under unanimous vs. nonunanimous decisions. In B. D. Sales (ed.), *Psychology in the Legal Process.* New York: Spectrum, pp. 77–86.

PARTRIDGE, A., and C. ELDRIDGE. 1974. *The Second Circuit Sentencing Study: A Report to the Judges of the Second Circuit.* Washington, D.C.: Federal Judicial Center.

PATTERSON, K. E., and A. D. BADDELEY. 1977. When face recognition fails, *Journal of Experimental Psychology: Human Learning and Memory, 3*: 406–17.

PENROD, S.; E. LOFTUS; and J. WINKLER. 1982. The reliability of eyewitness testimony: A psychological perspective. In N. L. Kerr and R. M. Bray (eds.), *The Psychology of the Courtroom.* New York: Academic Press, pp. 119–68.

Pillemer, D. B. 1984. Flashbulb memories of the assassination attempt on President Reagan, *Cognition, 14*: 63–80.

Rattner, A. 1983. *Convicting the Innocent: When Justice Goes Wrong.* Unpublished doctoral dissertation, Ohio State University.

Rosenthal, R. 1966. *Experimenter Effects in Behavioral Research.* New York: Appleton-Century-Crofts.

Rubin, D. C., and M. Kozin. 1984. Vivid memories, *Cognition, 16*: 81–95.

Saks, M. J. 1977. *Jury Verdicts.* Lexington, Mass.: Heath.

Sheingold, K., and Y. J. Tenney. 1982. Memory for a salient childhood event. In U. Neisser (ed.), *Memory Observed.* San Francisco: W. H. Freeman, pp. 201–12.

Shepherd, J. W.; J. B. Deregowski; and H. D. Ellis. 1974. A cross-cultural study of memory for faces, *International Journal of Psychology, 9*: 205–11.

Simon, R. J. 1967. *The Jury and the Defense of Insanity.* Boston: Little, Brown.

Slovic, P., and S. Lichtenstein. 1971. Comparison of Bayesian and regression approaches to the study of information processing in judgment, *Organizational Behavior and Human Performance, 6*: 649–744.

Thompson, W. C.; G. T. Fong; and D. L. Rosenhan. 1981. Inadmissible evidence and juror verdicts, *Journal of Personality and Social Psychology, 40*: 453–63.

Tversky, A., and D. Kahneman. 1971. Belief in the law of small numbers, *Psychological Bulletin, 76*: 105–10.

Valenti, A. C., and L. L. Downing. 1975. Differential effects of jury size on verdicts following deliberation as a function of apparent guilt of the defendant, *Journal of Personality and Social Psychology, 32*: 655–63.

United States v. Amaral. 1973. 488 F 2A 1148 (9th Cir.).

Wall, P. M. 1965. *Eyewitness Identification of Criminal Cases.* Springfield, Ill.: Charles C Thomas.

Wells, G. L. 1978. Applied eyewitness-testimony research: System variables and estimator variables, *Journal of Personality and Social Psychology, 36*: 1546–57.

Wells, G. L.; T. J. Ferguson; and R. C. L. Lindsay. 1981. The tractability of eyewitness confidence and its implications for triers of fact, *Journal of Applied Psychology, 66*: 688–96.

Wells, G. L.; M. R. Leippe; and T. M. Ostrom. 1979. Guidelines for empirically assessing the fairness of a lineup, *Law and Human Behavior, 3*: 285–93.

Wigmore, J. H. 1909. Professor Münsterberg and the psychology of evidence, *Illinois Law Review, 3*: 399–445.

Wilder, H. H., and P. Wentworth. 1918. *Personal Identification: Methods for the Identification of Individuals, Living or Dead.* Boston: R. G. Badger.

Williams v. Florida. 1970. 399 U. S. 78.

Winograd, E., and W. A. Killinger, Jr. 1983. Relating age at encoding in early childhood to adult recall: Development of flashbulb memories, *Journal of Experimental Psychology: General, 112*: 413–22.

Wissler, R. L., and M. J. Saks. 1982. On the inefficacy of limiting instructions: When jurors use prior conviction evidence to decide on guilt. Paper presented at the Convention of the American Psychological Association in Washington, D.C.

WOOCHER, F. D. 1977. Did your eyes deceive you? Expert psychological testimony on the unreliability of eyewitness identification, *Stanford Law Review*, 29: 969–1030.

YARMEY, A. D. 1979. *The Psychology of Eyewitness Testimony*. New York: Free Press.

YARMEY, A. D., and M. P. BULL, III. 1978. Where were you when President Kennedy was assassinated? *Bulletin of the Psychonomic Society*, 11: 133–35.

YERKES, R. M., and J. D. DODSON. 1908. The relation of strength of stimulus to rapidity of habit-formation, *Journal of Comparative and Neurological Psychology*, 18: 459–82.

YIN, R. K. 1969. Looking at upside-down faces, *Journal of Experimental Psychology*, 81: 141–45.

ZEISEL, H. 1971. ". . . And then there were none": The diminution of the federal jury, *The University of Chicago Law Review*, 38: 710–24.

ZEISEL, H., and S. S. DIAMOND. 1975. Convincing empirical evidence on the six-member jury, *University of Chicago Law Review*, 41: 181.

IV

Some Issues of Sexual Liberation

W HO OR WHAT has been liberated? Women? Gay men? Lesbians? Bisexuals? Androgynes? Perhaps even men, who have been supposed to be free all along, but now find out otherwise. We're all trying—but the basic liberation is not one of persons at all. It is the liberation of coitus—the male-female thing done in the traditional way—from procreation (the production of offspring), and that liberation follows from a few changes of technology. Above all, it follows from the invention of reliable methods of contraception: the pill, the diaphragm, the condom, the intrauterine device, the vasectomy. What follows when sex is not necessarily linked with procreation, when the recreational aspects, which evolution built in to guarantee reproduction of the species, are set free? We are still finding out.

The irreducible sex functions, which cannot be changed without changing the meaning of sex, are for the female menstruation, gestation (carrying a fetus in pregnancy), and lactation, and for the male impregnation. The male function is distinctly less time-consuming. All over the world, for almost all the time humanity has been on earth, those distinct irreducible functions have produced a rough division of labor between the sexes. The female has had to be sedentary for much of her life, because pregnancy and nursing take more than a year, and one pregnancy has often followed directly upon another. Being necessarily sedentary, she devoted herself to child care, housekeeping, and a little agriculture. The male's sex role has always enabled him to venture abroad to gather food, hunt, combat enemies, argue with Socrates, or just go to the office.

As far as we know (Barry, Bacon, and Child, 1957), most or all cultures for most or all of history have believed that the sex-based division of labor between males and females is made convenient and adaptive by biologically sex-linked differences of physique (strength, size, speed, endurance), of ability (abstract, mathematical, and spatial versus concrete and verbal), and of temperament (instrumental, assertive, dominant versus expressive, warm, and nurturant). Most measurement and assessment of sex differences has confirmed those beliefs as true today, and there have always been social theorists (Bakan, 1966; Parsons and Bales, 1955) who could develop arguments that it all was natural and necessary.

What potential consequences do contraceptive devices have for this right little, tight little world? They mean that sex can be enjoyed without the intention (or fear) of childbearing. Women can find out whether they like being sedentary, whether they are keen on housekeeping, whether they lack mathematical ability and are temperamentally unable to be assertive. The contemporaneous invention of machines that make muscles unimportant and housework a speedy business and of infant feeding formulas that men can administer make it *possible* for the sex-linked division of labor to disappear altogether. The more recent invention of artificial insemination and fetal transplantation make it possible for a woman to do without any intimate contact with a man whatever and so deprive him of his previously necessary procreative function, though not herself of hers. Coitus can be bypassed; pregnancy continues to be necessary (so far) for reproduction of the species.

How can the changes in the main sex functions change life for male and female homosexuals and bisexuals? The word *homo*, incidentally, is from the Greek for *same* (not the Latin for *man*) and so *homosexual* is etymologically appropriate for both males and females. There have always been homosexuals and bisexuals in human societies: in hunting-and-gathering tribes, in Periclean Athens, in Victorian London and twentieth-century San Francisco, and even in the Soviet Union. They have sometimes been considered an everyday natural variant (ancient Greece and Rome), sometimes assigned high status roles (the North American Plains Indians), and sometimes treated with extreme intolerance (the Inquisition, Nazi Germany, nineteenth- and early twentieth-century Britain and United States, the U.S.S.R. today). Because they have survived even the most punishing social treatment and antagonistic attitudes, it would appear that they are not simply life-styles, picked from a closet like a too-loud plaid jacket.

So long as procreation passed as the putative point of sex, homosexuals were bound to be thought of as less than ideal human specimens. It is sometimes suggested that this has been the dominant view in Western civilization since ancient Judaic times and that both the Old and the New Testament of the Christian Bible repeatedly denounce homosexual acts. In fact, however, only Leviticus 18:22 unequivocally condemns homosexuality: "Thou shalt not lie with mankind as with womankind: it is abomination," and even that passage was more concerned with ritual purity than with intrinsic wrongdoing.

Insofar as the Gospels accurately represent the teachings of Jesus, He never referred to homosexuality and generally did not represent sexual practices as morally important. In the Hellenic and Roman worlds, in urban centers, at least, homosexual interest and practice were regarded as part of the ordinary range of human eroticism. Hostility to gay people and to their sexuality first became noticeable in the West during the period of the decline of the Roman state, and homosexuality did not become illegal in Rome until the sixth century A.D. The most authoritative history of homosexuality in the Christian era (Boswell, 1980) attributes the hostility of the late Roman Empire and the more virulent hostility beginning in the twelfth century to a general intolerance of deviation, which was also leveled against Jews, witches, and sorcerers. The intolerance of the High Middle Ages resulted in legal and moral rules that were largely unchallenged until the nineteenth century, when a few people began to think of homosexuality as a sickness, biological or mental, rather than as a crime or sin.

In the second half of the twentieth century a new tolerance developed in some, without displacing any of the old kinds of intolerance; the criminal view, the mortal-sin view, and the sickness view are all still very popular. Perhaps the most common view of homosexuality taken by heterosexuals today is that it is "queer," weird, unnatural. But then all sex acts are, for anyone not excited by them, either slightly comical or else distasteful. Sex is not for the disinterested bystander. Before the technological changes occurred that made sexual liberation possible, not many, in modern times, thought of homosexuality and bisexuality (which are sexual "orientations") as unrelated to morality and mental or physical health. Exclusively heterosexual orientation has in modern times been considered an essential feature of virtue or mental health or both. But the effects of the basic technological changes had a potential for changing those views.

By definition, homosexuals and bisexuals (on their left-handed nights) are not interested in performing the sex act in the traditional way and turn instead to oral-genital and anal-genital possibilities. When sex ceases to be primarily procreative and becomes recreational, two important changes of thought become possible vis-à-vis homosexuals. What is wicked or unhealthy about them ceases to be obvious since sex is for them, as for the folks in Iowa, mainly for fun. A heterosexual population—bent on recreation—seems bound to wonder whether homosexual practices would provide an agreeable variation for themselves. Not, of course, that heterosexuals had not tried oral-genital and anal-genital modes and everything else anatomy permits, from the beginning; of course, some had. But more now do, and, more important, oral-genital sex has become respectable and a regular feature of daytime serials and family movies.

All this dizzying fluidity in the domain of sex has made people wonder what, if anything, necessarily follows from chromosomal sex (forty-six XX chromosomes for females and forty-six XY for males). And that has led to a certain playfulness about sex, which in 1984 is manifest in androgynous styles. To look androgynous a man or woman must have fairly delicate features and combine in just the right balance masculine-typed and feminine-typed clothing and mannerisms and voice. The intent is to be attractive—in a slightly unsettling way. And attractive is what the androgynous rock singers seem to be. Of course, the word *androgyny* refers not only to appearance, mannerisms, and temperament, but also to bisexuality, sleeping with both sexes, and there is much speculation about the sexual orientation of the androgynous star. My guess is that the millions of young women and young men who, respectively, squeal or howl admiration at androgynous performers are not destined for life-long bisexuality. That is my guess even though I know that bisexual "trials" are often made by high school and college students on the principle that one should experience everything at least once.

I think androgyny in the 1980s represents a fluid, playful (but not anxiety-free) attempt to cope with sexual liberation on the part of young people. Often it is manifestly secondary to narcissism, a pleasure in being admired and desired by whichever sex. Not many people over thirty seem to be caught up in this movement, presumably because they have settled on exclusive orientations. Any notion that the young people are going bisexual must cope with a complete sex orientation survey (anonymous responses) of the student population at San Francisco State University in 1978 (Shively and DeCecco). Less than 1 percent of either males or females characterized themselves as equally attracted to males and females, and less than 9 percent as *at all significantly* attracted to both. And San Francisco State is not a "square" school.

In surveying the implications of a few technological changes for conventional sex roles and less conventional ones, I have deliberately always spoken of potential or possible changes. Of course, the possibilities are not automatically or inevitably ever realized. Some threaten the economy; more threaten persons. Social change is stressful, especially at its peak of fluidity. Women continue, as of early 1984, to earn on the average only sixty-one cents to the man's dollar. Homosexual acts between consenting adults are still illegal in some states. ERA has not passed. People got up to look androgynous are likely to be insulted or harassed if they stray from their sympathetic milieu.

In addition, it should not be assumed that all possible changes in the domain of sex are desirable. Young people say they have trouble committing themselves to one person; about 50 percent of the marriages taking place in 1984 will end in divorce. The increased permissiveness seems to have led many to a promiscuity that is apparently associated with the herpes epidemic and, in gay men, the terrible disease AIDS (though not, I would guess, God's punishment for promiscuity in either case).

In this part something is said about all the topics now passed in preview.

Chapter 9 focuses on the study in social psychology, for nearly a decade, of what is called the "androgynous personality," a study independently initiated in just the same year, 1974, by Sandra Bem and Janet Taylor Spence. The contemporaneity of the two approaches argues that the concept of the androgynous personality was a response to deep and general cultural influences, which I have tried to identify. Chapter 10 focuses on the determinants of erotic orientation: heterosexual, homosexual, and bisexual. First we need a little terminology.

I think we can manage with just three terms: *sex, erotic orientation,* and *gender.* My definitions for the three probably do not exactly correspond with those of anyone else, and so it will not do simply to carry over your present understandings. I think two out of three of the terms are reasonably clear. To find out what sex you are, you need only look between your legs—to speak crudely but operationally. The external genitals (not the internal and not the sex chromosomes) are the ultimate criterion of sex used by the self and by others. To find out your erotic or sexual orientation, you need only note your principal sexual "turn ons" (John Money's apt term) and whether in phantasy and in action your sex life is mainly with persons of the other sex or the same sex. I use the word *gender* for masculinity–femininity, and this concept is the real puzzler.

The word *sex* is best reserved for the following set of male–female contrasts having to do with reproduction:

1. Chromosomes: XX for females and XY for males
2. Gonads or sex glands: ovaries for females; testes for males
3. Major hormone levels: more estrogens and progesterone in females; more androgens in males
4. Internal sex organs: uterus or womb for females; prostate gland and seminal vesicles for males
5. External genitals: vagina and clitoris for females; penis and scrotum for males
6. Erotic and reproductive capacities: menstruation, gestation, and lactation for females; impregnation for males

All of the above ordinarily co-occur in a binary way so as to produce individuals who are either 100 percent male or 100 percent female. Sex determination is ordinarily unambiguous. The qualifier "ordinarily" is necessary because it is not invariably true that all primary sexual characteristics in an individual are either male or female. Several kinds of sex scramblings naturally occur in hermaphroditism and something called the "adrenogenital syndrome," and several kinds of sex scramblings are artificially produced nowadays by transsexual surgery. Those scramblings have proved highly informative in the scientific study of sexuality, but the layman disregards them and thinks of sex as necessarily binary or two-valued; everyone is either male or female.

The term *sexual orientation* or *erotic orientation* refers to sexual stimuli (or objects or turn-ons), and the chief distinction is that between *homosexual* and *heterosexual*. The word *lesbian*, derived from the sexual history of Sappho who lived on the island of Lesbos, is sometimes used for female homosexual. The word *gay*, largely restricted to males, is like the name *black*—a term chosen by an oppressed group to designate itself.

Simple politeness makes *gay* the preferred term, and I will use it as much as possible. However, it usually cannot be used because there is no derived abstract nominal in common use (*gayness* has not displaced *homosexuality*) and because *gay* suggests a contemporary social consciousness that makes it anachronistic for other historical periods and inaccurate for research that investigates sexual acts without reference to consciousness.

While the general semantic domain marked off by the term sexual orientation is clear, there are several kinds of semantic dispute. Some (e.g. Bem, 1976; Kinsey, Pomeroy, Martin, and Gebhard, 1953) advocate using *homosexual* and *heterosexual* to name only acts, never persons. That modern scientific preference coincides with what seems to have been the linguistic practice in ancient literature. Terms equivalent to *heterosexual* and *homosexual* used as names for categories are very rare, though accounts of heterosexual and homosexual activities are abundant, and the probability is that the majority of persons in the ancient world did not think in terms of those categories. Boswell (1980) is probably correct in saying that minority categories in sex as in race ("black," "colored," "mulatto," "octoroon," and so on) are created by intolerant majorities. The fact that it may be intolerance that creates the categories does not make them less of a social reality, and the terms *homosexual* (or *gay*) and *heterosexual* as names for persons have become realities to the point where they are widely used even in self-characterization.

I use the dreary term *gender* to refer to masculine and feminine, or masculinity–femininity. In this domain everything is disputed. Is there one dimension or many? Are masculinity and femininity necessarily negatively correlated, or can someone be high on both or low on both? What counts in the calculation of masculinity–femininity? Secondary sexual characteristics? Hobbies and occupations? Color preference? How does sexual orientation relate to gender? Does a primarily homosexual orientation in a woman necessarily exclude femininity? The disputes about gender constitute much of the substance of Chapter 10, and so it is enough here to take note of their existence.

9

The Androgynous Personality

SANDRA BEM MUST HAVE BEEN feeling exuberant on the day that she set down these words:

> I consider myself an empirical scientist, and yet my interest in sex roles is and has always been frankly political. My hypotheses have derived from no formal theory, but rather from a set of strong intuitions about the debilitating effects of sex-role stereotyping, and my major purpose has always been a feminist one: to help free the human personality from the restricting prison of sex-role stereotyping and to develop a conception of mental health which is free from culturally imposed definitions of masculinity and femininity.
>
> But political passion does not persuade and, unless one is a novelist or a poet, one's intuitions are not typically compelling to others. Thus, because I *am* an empirical scientist, I have chosen to utilize the only legitimated medium of persuasion which is available to me: the medium of empirical data. [1976, p. 49]

When Sandra Bem announced her intention of using empirical science as a medium of persuasion for the political purposes of feminism, she did not mean that she was prepared to "cook" her data, but only that she would, and indeed had, picked her research problems with an eye to political relevance. There is nothing unusual in that beyond the self-knowledge and candor.

Sandra Bem's remarks are the opening paragraphs of an article called "Probing the Promise of Androgyny," which appeared in a book called *Beyond Sex-Role Stereotypes; Readings Toward a Psychology of Androgyny* (Kaplan and Bean, 1976). In that same book Kaplan and Bean (as editors and authors of articles) propose that the androgynous personality constitutes a good modern model of mental health, a better model for psychotherapy than either *machismo* masculinity or helpless femininity. Bem seems to have agreed in 1976, for she expressed the wish "to develop a conception of mental health which is free from culturally imposed definitions of masculinity and femininity." In 1981, reflecting on her work in the late 1970s, she was even clearer: "Politically, of course, androgyny was a concept whose time had come, a concept that appeared to provide a liberated and more humane alternative to the traditional sex-biased standards of mental health" (1981b, p. 362).

The word "androgyny" has three principal senses. In one sense, probably the most usual, it means combining masculine and feminine features, looking both male and female, without being a hermaphrodite. A second sense is psychological: the androgynous person is, in terms of tastes, abilities, and especially temperament, both masculine and feminine and in about equal degree. Finally, "androgyny" is also used as a synonym for bisexual erotic orientation. It was and still is fairly radical to propose that androgyny constitutes the ideal of mental health, more radical if androgyny is understood as bisexuality than if it is understood as psychological masculinity and femininity.

The psychologists who have studied androgyny have clearly intended the word to be understood in its psychological sense, indeed to be understood specifically as the combination of two temperaments, the masculine and feminine. Nevertheless, the word "androgyny" does also mean bisexuality, and the researchers who chose the word were at the least willing to risk a misunderstanding. None of them ever explicitly disavowed the bisexual meaning, and in her candid 1976 paper Bem suggests that we entertain the possibility that "compulsive exclusivity in one's sexual preference, whether homosexual or heterosexual, may be the product of a repressive society" (p. 49). Of course, exclusivity of sexual preference (never characterized with the pejorative word "compulsive") was an essential feature of traditional concepts of mental health, whether psychiatric or nonprofessional.

For the androgynous personality to appear in academic American psychology, a cultural path had to be cleared. One obstacle lay in the fact that masculinity and femininity were traditionally conceived of as opposite poles on a single dimension, and many widely used psychological tests had that conception literally built into them. As such tests had been designed and were scored, it was simply impossible for an individual to register as both highly masculine and highly feminine and so impossible ever to find any psychologically androgynous people. The masculinity–femininity tests did not allow for their existence. To "discover" androgyny it was necessary to conceive of masculinity and femininity in a new way, not as mutually exclusive psychological characteristics, not as opposite ends of one dimension, but as two independent dimensions. It was further necessary to incorporate that conception in the design of a new sort of test that would yield two scores, logically independent of each other: a score for psychological femininity and a score for psychological masculinity. That is what Bem did.

The Women's Liberation Movement was very ready for Bem's psychometric innovation. The Equal Pay Act had been passed in 1963 to remedy a gross inequity: Women were earning sixty cents to every dollar earned by men. (In February 1984 it was sixty-one cents to a dollar.) In 1964 the Civil Rights Act was passed, which included an article prohibiting sex discrimination in employment. Alert women had no use for the idea that an expressive, sensitive, unassertive, passive temperament rendered them unfit for the best jobs and no use for tests that had that idea built into their design. They were ready for the refreshing idea that one could perfectly well be both assertive and sensitive, whether male or female.

Bem's conception of the androgynous personality included the stimulating idea that it constituted a good model of ideal mental health for both men and women. Until 1974 clinicians tended to define mental health for men and women according to a double standard, which held, in accordance with stereotypes of temperament, that the healthy man would be assertive and dominant and the healthy woman nurturant and passive (Broverman et al., 1972). Women were ready for the idea that mental health in both sexes meant the same thing, an "androgynous" combination of assertiveness and sensitivity. There was, however, a subtle obstacle in the path of that idea. It lay in the double sense of "androgyny." In the erotic sense, bisexuality, it ran strongly counter to the common wisdom, which held that only exclusive heterosexuality was healthy, whereas any degree of bisexuality was rare, perverse, and unnatural. A "single drop" of bisexuality, by analogy with the parallel belief about Negro blood, rendered you less than ideal. That subtle obstacle was blasted out of the way in 1948 and 1953 by the Kinsey reports on, respectively, the human male and the human female, which demonstrated that very large numbers of people had at least a touch of bisexuality.

There were many social changes in the United States in the decades just preceding 1970, and so some choice exists in the ones to be considered as setting the stage for the androgynous personality. I have chosen (1) the assessment of masculinity–femininity and its vicissitudes; (2) the Women's Liberation Movement; and (3) the documentation of actual sex behavior in American males and females by Alfred Kinsey's Institute for Sex Research. One should at least add the meticulous study of sex differences in ability (e.g. Maccoby and Jacklin, 1974), which demonstrated that such differences were slight and probably a result of rearing patterns.

Traditional Assessment of Masculinity–Femininity

Masculinity–femininity is, in the first place, a conception of everyday psychology. It is, in popular thinking, like sex in being bipolar: The more feminine one is, the less masculine one is. It is unlike sex, as the layman conceives it, in not being binary or dichotomous or two-valued. Masculinity–femininity is conceived of as a single continuous dimension whereon individuals may be more or less masculine–feminine. What no one can be, in the popular conception, is *both* highly masculine *and* highly feminine. Bem's concept of the androgynous personality makes a radical break with the everyday line of thought in holding that masculinity is one dimension and femininity another and that the two are mutually independent, so that it is possible to be both highly masculine and highly feminine. Indeed, that is how the androgynous personality is defined.

The lay conception of masculinity–femininity embraces everything in which the sexes tend to differ. It includes such secondary sexual characteristics as growth of breasts or a beard, baldness, and voice quality. It includes the division of labor by which the female takes on child care, housekeeping, and agriculture and the male ventures forth to earn the family living. The lay conception of masculinity–femininity also includes the differences of temperament that are widely believed to suit men and women to their respective roles: Men are supposed to be instrumentally competent and dominant by nature, and women are supposed to be warm and expressive.

Finally, the lay conception of masculinity and femininity includes the endless list of opinions, preferences, and habits that are linked to sex only arbitrarily, locally, and transiently: wearing skirts or trousers; wearing two earrings, none, or one; hair long or short; smoking cigarettes or not; knowing how to cook or not, and so on. It is difficult to realize today that when the Beatles first made long hair popular with young men, horrified parents took it for a sign of effeminacy, of which beards were, paradoxically, supposed to be another. The resolution of the paradox is that any evidence of high concern with grooming was considered (absurdly, of course) to be a feminine characteristic.

When professional psychologists became interested in assessing masculinity –femininity, they took up the lay concept. The paper-and-pencil self-report inventories developed from the 1930s until the 1960s all operated with the same basic assumptions. For instance, Terman and Miles (1936) thought of masculinity–femininity as a single bipolar dimension, the core of personality, rooted somehow in sexual anatomy and physiology, relatively fixed and resistant to change. What they, as psychometricians or test-makers, undertook to create was an instrument that would assign to individuals numerical scores and so make it possible to study the relation between masculinity–femininity and such interesting matters as childrearing, hormone levels, and sexual preference —including especially what they called "sexual inversion."

The method of test creation was very simple. From every sort of source they collected items that might be expected to produce responses from women significantly different from those of men. Candidate items were tried out with samples of both sexes differing in age, education, occupation, and familial background, and those items were retained that best differentiated males from females. With no great difficulty they composed two equivalent forms, A and B, with 456 items to a form. The items were classified under seven headings; for instance, Word Association, Information, Interests. Among the more obvious (and arbitrary) items we have these: Males were more interested in football than were females and less interested in hopscotch, more interested in wrestling and less in sewing. As a response to the stimulus word "gentle," men liked "horse" whereas women favored "mother," as a response to "flesh," men liked "meat" and women liked "pink." Differences like those are pretty obviously not universal either historically or across cultures.

A male response to any item of any type was scored $+1$ and a female response -1. Every response had to be one or the other, and an individual's total score on the "M–F Test" was the algebraic sum (addition, taking account of plus and minus signs) of all items. The rule for scoring the test made it impossible to obtain high scores on both masculinity and femininity (or low scores on both). The design of the test incorporated the assumptions that masculinity-femininity was (1) a single dimension (2) with masculine and feminine as opposite poles. The overall average male score (many different samples) was $+52$ and the overall average female score was -70. The Terman-Miles M–F Test was designed so that the zero point should distinguish the sexual male from the sexual female, and for the most part it did so.

There are numerous other masculinity–femininity scales (e.g. Gough, 1952; Guilford and Guilford, 1936; Hathaway and McKinley, 1943; Strong, 1943), and they are all the same in assuming that masculinity–femininity was a single bipolar dimension. What results in the traditional assessment of masculinity versus femininity suggested that it might be worthwhile to think about gender as something other than a one-dimensional bipolar scale? Constantinople (1973) summarized several kinds of evidence which demonstrate that masculinity–femininity is definitely not one dimension, but several, even many. In the first place intercorrelations of scores on one test with scores on other tests, though almost always positive, were often quite low (around $+.40$), and that is not surprising since the content of the tests ranged very widely. Factor analyses of scores on single tests or several tests always yielded multiple factors, from three to eleven, but seemingly never just one.

Among the factors discovered were two factors of temperament that, though variously named, appeared to have rather consistent meaning: independent, assertive, dominant instrumentality as masculine; interpersonal sensitivity, compassion, and warmth as feminine. Those two dimensions, because they kept turning up in analyses of one test after another and because they corresponded closely with sociological (Parsons and Bales, 1955) and anthropological (Barry, Bacon, and Child, 1957) ideas of what might be universally masculine and feminine, seemed by the early 1970s to be the dimensions most worth measuring. In addition, it was not difficult to see that independence and assertiveness, sensitivity and warmth could all be desirable qualities if they were not gender-typed and so to wonder if they really needed to be. There was really no way to tell from the traditional tests, because opposition or bipolarity was built into the scoring. *Neither the tests nor the assumption was ever shown to be factually wrong.* It is important to remember that. What gradually became clear (Constantinople, 1973) was that one could make a different assumption, that a person could have both a masculine and a feminine temperament, and then design a new sort of test that would yield two independent scores.

The Women's Movement

In the 1950s, the Eisenhower years, disadvantaged Americans seemed to acquiesce in their own disadvantage, to accept the conventional view that in the calculation of equity (Chapter 2) Negro was less good than Caucasian, female than male, homosexual than heterosexual, Mexican-American than American, deaf than hearing, Indian than American. (See Part VI, "Ethnic Relations," for a full discussion.) If the disadvantaged brought intrinsically less valuable investments to their jobs, their schools, their marriages, and all their interactions, then, in equity or fairness, they *deserved* lower rewards, and gross inequalities of outcome were consistent with justice or equity. With varying lag times, all of those groups reassessed their investments in the 1960s and 1970s, decided they were not by definition inferior, and undertook to persuade the larger society that discrimination must end because it was morally wrong, and laws must be enacted to guarantee the revised calculation of equity. The easiest reform accomplished was a lexical one. Negroes became blacks in little more than a year's time, homosexuals quickly became gays, Mexican-Americans became Hispanic Americans, Indians became native Americans, the deaf became the hearing-impaired. Women did not reject their name, but their linguistic problems were as numerous, deep, and subtle ("man" for both men and women; "he" as the generic pronoun for "he or she") as their social and economic disadvantages.

There was a rough synchrony in all those liberation movements and also some tendency toward uniformity of ideology in that people tended, at least verbally, to be in favor of them all or opposed to them all. There was also considerable independent selfishness in action. Jo Freeman, who organized the first women's consciousness-raising group in Chicago in 1967, became a feminist when she found out that her male comrades in the Civil Rights Movement expected her to make the coffee and run the Xerox machine and to be liberated only in the sense of sleeping around. And gay men and lesbian women found out that in what came to be called the "Rainbow Coalition" politicians would prefer that their particular colors not shine too brightly.

In the 1960s there was a deep and general change in social thinking in the United States. One facet of it was attributional. The college-educated but somehow unfulfilled and depressed housewife began to balk at attributing her problems to herself and looking to psychiatry to help her "adapt." She became more inclined to attribute her unhappiness to prevailing social arrangements, and so did the black who could not get a job and the gay man who was arrested for committing a homosexual act.

The actor's natural tendency to look outward to the situation in seeking causes for his or her problems had long been inhibited by a vast consensus convinced that depression, unemployment, and criminal acts were the responsibility of the individual (Part II, "Attribution Theory"). Both psychiatry and the law were of that opinion and, of course, found employment in altering individuals. What made it possible for the individual woman especially, but also for the individual black and homosexual, to revert to the more normal external attribution was the discovery that they were not alone, that many others of their kind had the same problems. Backed by new special-interest consensuses, they could make external attributions. However, a change of attribution alone, while it would have made an intrapsychic difference, need not have produced social action.

Coincident with the shift in attributional balance was a shift in the degree of inertia, inevitability, and sacredness thought to characterize social arrangements. *Rearrangement* came to seem quite possible, and it no longer seemed hopeless to question the desirability of things as they are. I vividly remember that change in thinking, because in the 1950s I was a new instructor at Harvard and, very much in the spirit of the times, never thought to question any rule or tradition of the institution to which I had come but, with complete docility, learned and complied. In the late 1960s I was for a few years chairman of our department, and the young faculty of that period amazed me by holding up every little rule, practice, and cozy arrangement to the tests of reason and justice. Was it not permitted that an undergraduate teach a course on something of which he had expert knowledge? Why should that be so? I could never think at first of any answer better than "Because that is the way it has always been." After some time, I realized that I was not really required to defend every facet of the *status quo.*

What caused us to come to see social arrangements as less than immutable, as subject to planned revision even in one generation? One possibility is that the principal cause was the experience everyone now had of unplanned but substantial changes brought about in our own lifetime by technology—the automobile, the airplane, television, and so on. Technology had, we have seen, by the 1960s changed the necessities or inevitabilities of sex roles through the automatic washing machine and other labor-saving devices, infant feeding formulas, and, above all, new means of contraception.

In the 1960s there was no clear reason why women should not aspire to any occupation for which their training suited them and no clear reason why they should not seek any training for which their talents suited them. As far as anyone knew, female talents might run the same range as male talents since every sort of existing difference in occupations and tested abilities (e.g. lower scores in math and in visual-spatial tests) could be explained by socialization pressures and lack of opportunity (Maccoby and Jacklin, 1974). In those circumstances would women be deterred from pursuing the kinds of education and kinds of job they wanted by a set of tests of masculinity–femininity that represented them as temperamentally unsuited to the world of affairs, as lacking in instrumental competence and oversupplied with sensitivity and nurturance? Not bloody likely!

The possibilities for change in the lives of women created by technology were not such as to be automatically and immediately realized. There were established ways of thinking and acting that could have simply continued as before, in spite of the new possibilities, if awareness and outrage had not developed. It is interesting to recall now some of the landmarks.

President Kennedy in his inaugural address called on Americans, especially young Americans, to participate in social adventures, in the conquering of social problems, and thereby contributed mightily to the growing belief that social systems might really be improved by deliberate design. He also created a Commission on the Status of Women, and its report, issued in 1963, confirmed what feminists already knew: Americans discriminated against women. The professions did not admit them, graduate schools discriminated against them, and even in elementary school girls were encouraged to prepare themselves for marriage, not the professions.

President Kennedy's Commission recommended more flexible admissions requirements to colleges, government-sponsored day care centers, and an end to discrimination in employment practices within the federal government. The changes produced by the report were mostly trifling, but in 1963 something happened that promised to be really important: The Equal Pay Act was passed. This act made it illegal to pay unequal wages to men and women doing exactly the same work. The act was certainly needed, but it has not accomplished even today what it seemed to promise to accomplish. While the percentage of women in the work force has markedly increased since the 1960s (from 33 percent in 1960 to 43 percent in 1983), the annual earnings of women are still only about 60 percent of the earnings of men. How is it possible that such inequality should still exist in view of the Equal Pay Act?

When it became illegal to have unequal female and male wage rates, Westinghouse Electric, to take one example, kept female grades 1–5 in place and made the corresponding male grades into 6–10. That left women earning less than men in comparable, but *not exactly equal,* jobs, and the inequality was not considered illegal even though newly hired men were regularly assigned to grades 6–10 and women were placed in the lower grades. That is only a most obvious case. More typical was the practice in the State of Oregon of paying "prison matrons" who guard female prisoners $200 a month less than "deputy sheriffs" who guard male prisoners. In short, if highly comparable male and female jobs are named differently and even slightly differentiated in definition, the Equal Pay Act does not apply.

In the end it may be that the 1964 Civil Rights Act passed under President Lyndon Johnson will do more to win equality of pay for women than the Equal Pay Act did. The Oregon prison matrons brought suit against the state not on the identical-job principle but on a principle of "comparable worth" of jobs, and in 1981 the Supreme Court ruled that comparable worth claims were legitimate under the Civil Rights Act of 1964, which, in article 7, prohibits sex discrimination in employment. The calculation of "comparable worth" was fairly easily done in the case of "prison matrons" and "deputy sheriffs," but once recognized, one saw that it could in theory be applied very broadly.

Are "engineering layout clerks" (women at Michigan Bell, a unit of AT and T) doing jobs of comparable worth to those of draftsmen (men) in the same company? The women are paid $120 a week less, but they claim they are classified as "clerks" because they are women, and they have brought suit under the principle of comparable worth for $10 million in back pay. Are a nurse and a plumber of comparable worth? How about a rock star and a brain surgeon? Traditionally, the market place decides those difficult questions, but there is precedent now for comparing jobs not in terms of supply and demand but in terms of skills, responsibilities, hazards, mental and physical effort (see Figure 9–1). This is clearly a job for equity theory (Part I), but is equity theory up to it?

Skills, responsibilities, hazards, mental and physical effort are all classifiable as rewards or costs or investments. Consider the problem of the prison matrons and the deputy sheriffs. In order to satisfy equity (or fairness), there must be equality of ratios:

$$\frac{\text{Matrons: Rewards-Costs}}{\text{Investments}} = \frac{\text{Sheriffs: Rewards-Costs}}{\text{Investments}}$$

The matrons claimed inequity because the "rewards-cost" for sheriffs were $200 a month greater than for matrons. This *inequality* would not constitute an *ineq-*

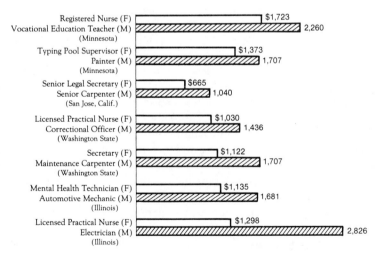

Figure 9–1. Men's and women's pay for jobs of comparable worth

(*New York Times*, Jan. 1, 1984; sources: Council on the Economic Status of Women, State of Minnesota; Hay Associates; Norman D. Willis & Associates. Copyright © 1984 by The New York Times Company. Reprinted by permission)

uity if it were permissible to count "male" as a superior investment to "female." It is precisely that which the Equal Payment Act and Civil Rights Law forbid and precisely that which the matrons accused Oregon of doing.

To defend against the charge, Oregon would have had to show that sheriffs have either higher investments (exclusive of sex, which it is illegal to count as an investment) or higher costs than matrons and therefore are entitled to higher rewards. I have no idea how they may have tried to do so and no knowledge of the jobs in question, but it is easy to imagine how the argument might go. If deputy sheriffs were required to take a twelve-month training course and matrons only a six-month course, that could count as a higher investment satisfying greater rewards. If sheriffs were more often injured by their prisoners than matrons were by theirs, that additional hazard could count as a higher cost justifying higher rewards. It is very clear how to think about the problem in equity theory terms, but it is equally clear that the theory itself provides no method for making an inventory of rewards, costs, and investments, let alone a method for assigning numerical values to them.

The principle of comparable worth can, however, be invoked. In Washington State, the American Federation of State, County, and Municipal Employees, which has one million members, 400,000 of them women, brought suit against the state for nearly $1 billion on behalf of its women members, and a federal judge ruled in December 1983 that the state had practiced discrimination and must pay. Because of the possible implications of that ruling for every sort of employer, the case is likely to be appealed to the Supreme Court. How did the judge decide that different jobs were of comparable worth? He relied on a job evaluation study that had been done by an outside consulting firm prior to the suit. AT and T has done a job evaluation study for its entire system, employing some fourteen factors, all of them rewards, costs, or investments. In short, the assessment of relative worth and so of equity and inequity can be done—though in an *ad hoc*, unprincipled but knowledgeable way. Of course, the worth of a job will not be static but will change with new technology and other factors. It would be extremely interesting to have some social psychologists interested in equity theory tackle this applied problem and try to find general principled ways of inventorying rewards, costs, and investments.

When women win a comparable worth suit it costs an employer money, possibly a lot of money, because the Civil Rights Act explicitly forbids the employer to solve his inequity problem by *lowering* the pay of the advantaged group. The disadvantaged must be raised to the level of equity. Employers and their attorneys are already claiming that society cannot afford to see the principle of comparable worth prevail. That, if so, means that the system depends upon the existence of a lower-paid female work force, which is morally intolerable.

The goals of the Women's Liberation Movement extend far beyond equal pay for comparable work. Equal opportunity for admission to higher education and equal opportunity employment are ultimately more important. Discrimination, especially in employment, is still very widespread, but U.S. Census figures released in 1984 showed that women have substantially increased their representation in the professions and in the managerial levels of business.

Stereotypes about women's abilities are changing fast in American universities in the 1980s, even faster, I think, than the increase in the number of women who work in mathematically and formally developed sciences. In thinking about female intelligence, we seem to follow what Tversky and Kahneman (1973) call the "availability heuristic." A person is said to operate with the availability heuristic whenever he estimates the frequency of a class of events by the ease with which an example can be brought to mind. Almost every male psychologist today can think at once of a female colleague whose formal-analytic ability is higher than his own, and that seems to change opinions about the sex-typing of abilities very fast.

It has taken organized political effort to accomplish what has been accomplished. In 1966 a group of educated women led by Betty Friedan (author of the influential book *The Feminine Mystique*, 1963) organized the National Organization for Women (NOW), which attacked sex discrimination in employment and pushed for equal benefits in Social Security and equal opportunities in employment. By 1969 the NOW platform included a statement of woman's right to an abortion, and in 1973 the Supreme Court ruled that all state laws restricting a woman's right to an abortion in the first trimester of pregnancy are unconstitutional.

The radical Redstockings Manifesto published in 1969 expressed the full range of anger that some women (far from all) had come to feel: "Women are an oppressed class. Our oppression is total, affecting every facet of our lives. We are exploited as sex objects, breeders, domestic servants and cheap labor. We are considered inferior beings, whose only purpose is to enhance men's lives. Our humanity is denied."

In the face of statements like the Redstocking Manifesto and books like Kate Millett's *Sexual Politics* (1970), psychology's masculinity–femininity scales looked like ugly Victorian mementos. Woman as warm, nurturant, sensitive, unassertive, and unaggressive *by nature* seemed to many women to be a kind of psychological sell. The definition of male temperament as instrumental-competent and female as expressive-nurturant seemed to be little more than an excuse for the traditional and now dated sex roles in which man was the provider and woman the homemaker. It was time for new thoughts on masculinity and femininity.

The Kinsey Reports

The Institute for Sex Research at the University of Indiana published in 1948 (Kinsey, Pomeroy, and Martin) a report on sexual behavior in the human male and in 1953 (Kinsey et al.) a report on sexual behavior in the human female.

The reports concern *sexual*, not psychological, androgyny; they concern behavior, often defined by the attainment of orgasm; they have nothing direct to say about masculinity–femininity or gender androgyny, which was the focus of psychological assessment between the 1930s and 1970. Alfred Kinsey was a zoologist, and the tone in the books is quite consistently zoological, stressing the continuity of the human animal with all other mammals, and yet the books are not "objective" in the foolish sense of pretending to say nothing evaluative. The numbers reported are implicitly evaluative, so clearly and powerfully so that the authors were wise to make the implications explicit.

With respect to behavioral or sexual androgyny, the numbers reported are implicitly evaluative because so many males and females turned out to have had some homosexual experience, in addition to heterosexual experience, as to make it impossible to continue to define everyone who had committed even one homosexual act as sick or criminal. All the jails and consulting rooms in the country could not begin to contain them.

Some implications of the numbers were expressed in these passages:

> In view of the data which we now have on the incidence and frequency of the homosexual, and in particular on its co-existence with the heterosexual in the lives of a considerable portion of the male population, it is difficult to sustain the view that psychosexual relations between individuals of the same sex are rare and therefore abnormal or unnatural, or that they constitute within themselves evidence of neuroses or even psychoses. [Kinsey, Pomeroy, and Martin, 1948, p. 659]

> The police force and court officials who attempt to enforce the sex laws, the clergymen and business men and every other group in the city which periodically calls for enforcement of the laws—particularly the laws against sexual "perversion"—have given a record of incidences and frequencies in the homosexual which are as high as the rest of the social level to which they belong. [p. 665]

When the first Kinsey report came out, the report on males, there were many social scientists, psychoanalysts, religionists, and legal authorities who made the point that mere frequency did not make an action right. Of course, that is true. Still, large numbers from every station in life do put a certain strain on any rule that would assign the lot to extreme and expensive "treatment." While neither Kinsey report ever says or implies that sexual androgyny, or a mix of heterosexuality and homosexuality, is desirable, let alone more desirable than exclusive heterosexuality, they made it difficult to think of such mixtures as reprehensible or deplorable and impossible to think of them as unnatural.

The Kinsey reports provided data never before available in human history: highly detailed confidential histories of the sexual practices of large numbers of clinically normal people; nearly 6,000 white American females and 5,300 white males. The limitation of the first two reports to data on whites only has been repaired in later volumes (Bell and Weinberg, 1978; Bell, Weinberg, and Hammersmith, 1981), which include data on blacks, male and female. The large numbers of respondents do not serve to make the figures in the report *represen-*

tative of American males and females. No one yet has figured out how to get a representative sample for the intimate domain of sexual behavior. What can be said is that respondents ranged in age from childhood to ninety years; geographic dispersal was wide, as was occupational diversity; and there was rural and urban representation, religious representation, and marital status representation. In sum, the institute had a far better empirical base than anyone else had ever had, but just how good it was for the years in question and how much things may have changed since then, no one can say. For males and females we have in Table 9-1 the percentage of persons exclusively heterosexual over the lifetime, the percentage exclusively homosexual always, and the percentage having at least one homosexual experience and up to a definite homosexual preference. The criterion of experience is a narrow one— response to orgasm.

Large majorities of both males and females report only heterosexual experience and small minorities of both (smaller for females) report only homosexual experiences. That leaves a substantial percentage of males (37 percent) *technically* androgynous in the erotic sense and a substantial but much smaller percentage of females (13 percent) the same. The percentages for homosexual experience are always more likely to be too low than too high, since social pressures operate against admitting them. Spokesmen for gay/lesbian movements in 1984 estimate that about 10 percent of males are exclusively homosexual and something more than 5 percent of females, but no one really knows. In any case the technically androgynous are far too numerous to be considered an extreme deviation.

The lower incidence of female than male homosexuality certainly cannot be explained by a difference in the strength of social prohibitions. In fact, the Kinsey reports determined that attitudes were more tolerant in the case of females, and a search through legal records from 1696 until 1952 turned up no convictions at all of women for homosexual acts, by contrast with many thousands of convictions of men.

The difference in legal convictions represents something more basic than a difference in social tolerance. In the 1953 Kinsey report only 4 percent of

TABLE 9-1. Lifetime Incidence Figures for Exclusive Heterosexuality, Exclusive Homosexuality, and Some Mixture of Homosexuality and Heterosexuality, in Males and Females

	Lifetime Incidence (%)		
	Exclusive Heterosexuality	Mixture of Heterosexuality and Homosexuality	Exclusive Homosexuality
Males	63	37	4
Females	87	13	1-3

SOURCE: Based on Kinsey, Pomeroy, and Martin (1948), and Kinsey et al. (1953).

women reported having had more than ten homosexual partners, as compared with 22 percent of men (1948). In 1978 the Institute for Sex Research (Bell and Weinberg, 1978) reported a study on the "homosexualities" based on 879 case studies of males and females, whites and blacks. From that report it is clear that females do not seek promiscuous anonymous sex on the street, in bathhouses, and in other public places as some males do. Fifteen percent of the males reported having had between five hundred and a thousand partners, and 28 percent had had a thousand or more. Only 3 percent of females reported having more than a hundred different partners. The authors speculate that those differences reflect, perhaps more clearly than the study of heterosexuals can, a basic difference in male and female sexuality. The male may be biologically programmed to seek many partners, since that would maximize reproductive potential, and the homosexual male, unconstrained by females, perhaps acts out what most heterosexual males only dream about. The female, because of the long gestation period in the species, would have more need for an enduring relationship and little to gain in reproductive potential from multiple partners. Whatever the reason, it does seem to be the case that gays and lesbians, though alike in having a homosexual orientation, are unlike in that they remain, respectively, male and female.

The authors of the Kinsey reports were persuaded by their data that homosexual and heterosexual experience constituted a continuum with many millions of individuals, more males than females, falling somewhere between the exclusive extremes, and those reports strengthened a growing impression among educated people that a mixed experience was, if not desirable, at least not so rare as to be considered unnatural. The Kinsey reports also strengthened the notion that androgyny was natural by stressing its cultural and historical universality in human societies and by stressing something less well known, the seeming universality in mammalian species of some homosexual behavior, always less common than heterosexual.

The mammalian facts, the facts discovered in their own survey, and the facts of anthropology and human history taken together led to this strong statement:

> The inherent physiologic capacity of an animal to respond to any sufficient stimulus seems, then, the basic explanation of the fact that some individuals respond to stimuli originating in other individuals of their own sex—and it appears to indicate that every individual could so respond if the opportunity offered and one were not conditioned against such responses. [Kinsey et al., 1953, p. 447]

Sandra Bem in the 1976 article already quoted issued a challenge that follows naturally from the Kinsey data: We ought to consider the "possibility that compulsive exclusivity in one's sexual responsiveness, whether homosexual or heterosexual, may be the product of a repressive society which forces us to label ourselves as one or the other" (1976, p. 49).

A Test for Androgyny

The androgynous personality was more an invention than a discovery. It emerges from the traditional masculinity–femininity tests not as a novel empirical finding but as a novel method of test design and scoring. In order to see how that comes about, we shall consider five temperamental characteristics that have always turned out to be masculine and five that have always turned out to be feminine and show how they would be handled in a test of individual masculinity *as opposed* to femininity, a test of masculine and feminine stereotypes, and a test of individual masculinity *and* femininity *and* androgyny. The important thing to bear in mind is that the conception of masculinity and femininity as two independent dimensions rather than as a single bipolar dimension and of androgyny as a combination of high masculinity with high femininity preceded their assessment. The idea that a two-dimensional conception of masculinity and femininity might be more reasonable than the old one-dimensional bipolar way was the result of the social forces described above, and the tests are simply operations for assessing the conceptions. The five masculinity characteristics and the five femininity characteristics and the three ways of using them appear in Table 9–2.

In this chapter just one of the many masculinity–femininity tests (Constantinople, 1973) has been described: the Terman–Miles M–F Test. However, all such tests include items that assess personal *temperament*, the only kind of item in Table 9–2, but they also include items of other kinds. In the assessment of the androgynous personality only temperament has been considered, for the reason that the characterization of masculine and feminine temperament has a very high consistency across both cultures and historical eras. No such consistency exists for preferences in occupation, hobby, dress, and so on—those are the culturally and historically relative aspects of masculinity and femininity. Their relativity is manifest in the fact that very many items that distinguished men from women in the United States in 1940–60 do not do so today (Lunneborg, 1970).

The stability of temperament characterizations is so great that some authors (e.g. Tiger and Fox, 1971) believe they must be rooted in genetics or else derivative from basic reproductive roles. Sex role differentiation is universal in human societies, and it is usually, perhaps always, such that women have primary responsibility for caring for children and the family dwelling, while men have the responsibility for the family's economic wellbeing. Parsons and Bales (1955) characterize that division of labor as a distinction between instrumental and expressive roles, with men operating as the family's representative to the outside world and women charged with satisfying both the physical and emotional needs of family members and maintaining harmonious interaction among them. Paralleling that role distinction, men are expected either naturally to be independent, active, and so on or else to be socialized into that instru-

TABLE 9–2. Methods of Deriving Test Items for Three Kinds of Scale

Test Items	Masculinity–Femininity Scale	Masculinity–Femininity Stereotypes	Masculinity and Femininity and Androgyny
Masculine			
Aggressive	True (M) - False (F)	More characteristic of men	More ideal for men
Independent	True (M) - False (F)	More characteristic of men	More ideal for men
Dominant	True (M) - False (F)	More characteristic of men	More ideal for men
Self-confident	True (M) - False (F)	More characteristic of men	More ideal for men
Active	True (M) - False (F)	More characteristic of men	More ideal for men
Feminine			
Emotional	True (F) - False (M)	More characteristic of women	More ideal for women
Kind	True (F) - False (M)	More characteristic of women	More ideal for women
Warm	True (F) - False (M)	More characteristic of women	More ideal for women
Sympathetic	True (F) - False (M)	More characteristic of women	More ideal for women
Altruistic	True (F) - False (M)	More characteristic of women	More ideal for women

mental temperament, whereas women are expected either to be or to become warm, sympathetic, and the rest. Bakan (1966) calls the role and temperament distinction by the names "agency" and "communion," but the conceptions are essentially the same as those of Parsons and Bales and many others.

While there are no data that clearly speak to the possibility of a genetic base for masculine and feminine temperaments, there is no doubt that in both preliterate and postindustrial societies boys and girls are differentially reared so as to produce or reinforce the appropriate temperaments (Barry, Bacon, and Child, 1957; Maccoby and Jacklin, 1974). The traits listed in Table 9-2 and all the temperamental traits that ultimately figure in the individual assessment of masculinity and femininity and androgyny divide into the clusters: masculine instrumentality and feminine expressiveness.

For any of the traditional masculinity–femininity tests the ten traits of Table 9-2 would have been selected from some much larger set of traits (perhaps also tastes, interests, hobbies, and so on), because for some large sample of males and females those traits significantly differentiated between the sexes. The typical task (Lunneborg, 1970) is to ask each person to check a trait as "true" if he or she "usually" or "nearly always" manifests it and "false" if she or he "never" or "hardly ever" manifests it. The five instrumental characteristics and the five feminine characteristics having met the criterion of sex differentiation could be included in a test of masculinity versus femininity. The individual taking that test, and so having his or her degree of masculinity–femininity assessed, would mark each item as true or false for himself. One masculinity point would be scored for each instrumental trait marked "true" and also for each expressive trait marked "false." Each item response is scored as either masculine or feminine, with the necessary result that one score is the reciprocal of the other, and so the test yields a single number, which is some score on a one-dimensional masculinity–femininity scale.

To determine masculine and feminine stereotypes, one changes the instructions. For instance, Broverman and colleagues (1972) started with a collection of 122 traits they thought might have something to do with stereotyped conceptions of masculinity and femininity. They then asked about a thousand subjects to say, with respect to each trait, the extent to which it characterized an adult man or else to say the extent to which it characterized an adult woman. Traits significantly more often assigned to men than to women were judged to belong to the stereotype of masculinity and traits significantly more often assigned to women, to the feminine stereotype. The outcome of the procedure is not an assessment of an individual's masculinity–femininity but rather the characterization of two shared social stereotypes. Notice that the procedure for determining the content of stereotypes is similar to the procedure for selecting items to use in a masculinity–femininity scale, so naturally one finds much the same content in both. It follows that if a subject responds to the items on a masculinity–femininity scale for "self," he or she might answer with exclusive attention to the self or might describe the self so as to conform more or less well to the sex-appropriate stereotype. Broverman and associates (1972) did have subjects respond "true" or "false" for the self and found that most described themselves in ways that fitted the sex-appropriate stereotype, but generally the selves were less extreme in consistency than the stereotypes.

We come at last to Bem's conception of the androgynous personality:

> The concept of psychological androgyny implies that it is possible for an individual to be both assertive and compassionate, both instrumental and expressive, both masculine and feminine, depending upon the situational appropriateness of these various modalities; and it further implies that an individual may even blend these complementary modalities in a single act, being able, for example, to fire an employee if the circumstances warrant it but with sensitivity for the human emotion that such an act inevitably produces. [Bem, 1974, p. 196]

Notice that the conception does not deny the reality of masculinity and femininity, but only the notion that they must be negatively related. In effect, it conjures up the possibility of someone's being both at once, a psychological guy/girl more ideal in Bem's mind than the all-guy or all-girl. How is this androgynous ideal to be identified using a paper-and-pencil test and the traits in Table 9-2?

Bem and her students put together two hundred traits, all positive or socially desirable, but seeming to be either masculine or feminine in tone. Then, to select items for the Bem Sex-Role Inventory (BSRI), they used a new question. For each item, some judges were asked: "In American society how desirable is it for a man to be 'X' (e.g. aggressive or emotional or whatever)?" Other judges were asked for all items how desirable it was for a woman to be 'X' (aggressive or emotional or whatever). Not, please notice, how characteristic of a man (or woman) is 'X', but how desirable. The judgments were made on a seven-point scale ranging from (1) extremely desirable to (7) not at all desirable.

The items selected for the BSRI were all judged to be *desirable for both men and women* (ratings 1–3). However, twenty items were considered to be masculinity items, because they were judged to be significantly *more desirable* for men than for women, and twenty items were considered to be femininity items because they were judged to be more desirable for women than for men. In short, what we have in the BSRI are forty traits, all socially desirable, but half of them more so in men and half more so in women. Masculinity items (desirable for all but more for men) include: assertive, dominant, individualistic, and willing to take risks. Femininity items (desirable for all but more for women) include: affectionate, cheerful, loyal, and sensitive to the needs of others.

It is not now a question of the traits that respectively characterize men and women but a question of the traits desirable for both but more so for one sex than the other. Some items that would turn up on a traditional masculinity-femininity scale could not turn up on either the masculinity or the femininity scale of the BSRI. For instance, *conceited* is a trait that might be judged more characteristic of men than of women and so might turn up on a traditional masculinity–femininity test, but because it is not desirable for both sexes, or for either, it could not appear on the scales of the BSRI.

We know how the items for the BSRI were selected but not yet how a test-taker responds to them. Each trait is judged on a seven-point scale with respect to self: (1) never or almost never true to (7) always or almost always true. An individual's masculinity score is the sum of his ratings for masculinity items and the femininity score is the sum of ratings for femininity items; he or she gets two scores. Accepting a masculinity item as true of the self does not entail denying a femininity item and vice versa. Consequently, masculinity and femininity scores are logically independent in the test. For both dimensions the possible range in scores is from twenty (twenty items at a rating of 1) to 140 (twenty items at a rating of 7), and all combinations of masculinity and femininity scores are possible: both can be high, both can be low, and so on.

For large samples that include both males and females, the mean score on masculinity is higher for males and the mean score on femininity is higher for females, which means that the two scales do differentiate the sexes. For samples in which all subjects are of the same sex, individual masculinity and femininity scores are uncorrelated, and that means that the two dimensions are empirically or factually, and not only logically, independent. Bem's measure has the properties she wanted it to have: Masculinity and femininity function as two independent dimensions and not as opposite extremes of one dimension.

That leaves the scoring for androgyny. In her earlier work Bem conceptualized individuals as masculine-sex-typed if their masculinity score were much higher than their femininity score and as feminine-sex-typed if the converse were the case. An individual was considered androgynous if he or she obtained masculinity and femininity scores that were not significantly different. However, Spence, Helmreich, and Stapp (1975) found a better way to define androgyny.

Janet Taylor Spence and her collaborators, Robert Helmreich and Joy Stapp (1974), developed a measure of masculinity and femininity, as independent dimensions, and of androgyny in the very same year that Bem developed the BSRI and in complete independence of her work. Furthermore, with minor qualifications, the two methods of test design were the same, and recent work (Lubinski, Tellegen, and Butcher, 1983) indicates that they may now (the BSRI has been revised) be considered equivalent measures. Evidently the idea of the androgynous personality was in the *Zeitgeist* of 1974. The Spence–Helmreich (1978) test is called the "Personal Attributes Questionnaire"(PAQ) and is composed of instrumental (masculine) and expressive (feminine) trait terms largely derived from the stereotypes described by Broverman and associates (1972). The PAQ yields two essentially independent scores, one for masculinity and one for femininity, and they are calculated in the same way as the parallel scores on the BSRI. However, Spence and her collaborators did not assess androgyny in the way that Bem did in 1974.

There is a problem with defining the androgynous personality as anyone whose masculinity and femininity scores do not significantly differ. The scores might not differ either because both were high (*HH*) or because both were low (*LL*), and it seems likely the *HH* folks might be quite different from *LL* folks. Spence and Helmreich used the PAQ to identify four categories of person. The masculine person is, as for Bem, the person who scores high on masculinity and low on femininity (*HL*), and the feminine person is the reverse (*LH*). It is the *HH* scorer, the person with many ideal masculine traits and also many ideal feminine traits, whom they identify as androgynous; the *LL* scorer, the person with few socially desirable traits of either kind, they call "undifferentiated." To create the four categories, the distributions of scores on masculinity and femininity from a large number of male and female subjects are split at the medians. See Table 9–3 for the percentages of individuals found in each of the four cells, for males and females, in a large sample of Stanford students.

Bem (1977) compared the results she had collected using her original "no-difference" definition of androgyny with results for the same data using the median-split method of Spence and Helmreich, and she concluded that the four-cell method, defining androgyny as *HH*, was superior and used it after 1977. In discussing Bem's basic ideas about androgyny and the kinds of results she at first obtained, I shall write as if the androgynous personality had always been defined as the *HH* scorer. I shall also describe the research in a slightly idealized way, ignoring some unaccommodating details, because the important thing is the idea, and the fine points in the data scarcely matter in retrospect. A problem lay ahead that makes the little hitches in the early results insignificant.

Bem's Conception of the Androgynous Personality and First Findings

The idea was certainly an interesting one, and I want to quote from Bem when confirming research was at its high-water mark:

> Over the last few years, the Women's Liberation Movement has made us all aware of the many ways that we, both men and women, have become locked into our sex roles. As women, we have become aware of the fact that we are afraid to express our anger, to assert our preferences, to trust our own judgment, to take control of situations. As men, we have become aware of the fact that we are afraid to cry, to touch one another, to own up to our fears and weaknesses. [1976, p. 50]

> In a modern complex society like ours, an adult clearly has to be able to look out for himself and to get things done. But an adult also has to be able to relate to other human beings as people, to be sensitive to their needs and to be concerned about their welfare, as well as to be able to depend on them for emotional support. Limiting a person's ability to respond in one or the other of those two complementary domains thus seems tragically and unnecessarily destructive of human potential. [p. 50]

In terms of experimental research using the Bem Sex Role Inventory (BSRI) these ideas translated into the following kind of design (Bem, 1976, 1978; Bem,

TABLE 9–3. Percentages of Males and Females in Each of Four Cells on the PAQ

a. Males

	Masculinity	
Femininity	High	Low
High	Andro. 32%	Fem. 8%
Low	Masc. 34%	Undiff. 25%

b. Females

	Masculinity	
Femininity	High	Low
High	Andro. 27%	Fem. 32%
Low	Masc. 14%	Undiff. 28%

SOURCE: Derived from Spence and Helmreich (1978) p. 53.

Martyna, and Watson, 1976). You start with some kind of action or manifestation of temperament that is, in our society today, supposed to be more characteristic of one sex than of the other. For instance, ironing napkins is woman's work, fondling a kitten is a woman's diversion, and being dependent and conforming is an aspect of the female temperament—or so they say. Baiting fish hooks and hammering nails are a man's work, and independence is an aspect of his temperament—or so they say. You use the BSRI to identify persons who are masculine (HL), persons who are feminine (LH), and persons who are androgynous (HH) and then give them all the opportunity to engage in sex-typed activities or to manifest sex-typed traits. The general prediction is that sex-typed persons will be able to engage in congruently sex-typed tasks and to manifest congruently sex-typed traits but relatively unable to do anything cross-sex-typed or to manifest cross-sex-typed traits. Masculine and feminine persons are expected to have their respective areas of easy competence and also their areas of incompetence or aversion. Androgynous persons are expected to be competent and relaxed with the tasks and traits of either sex; therefore, more flexible or adaptable; therefore, more nearly ideal psychologically. The early experiments generally confirmed those ideas.

Bem and Lenney (1976) asked subjects to choose between pairs of tasks such that one was sex-typed in the same way as the subject and the other was cross-sex-typed; the latter carried more financial reward than the former and so should have been preferred if sex-typing were not a problem for the subject. For example, feminine subjects (LH) could choose between mixing a baby formula for two cents or oiling hinges for four cents. All tasks came with instructions and were at such a low skill level as to pose no challenge to anyone. The performance of the task was for a photography session. As expected, sex-typed subjects were more likely than androgynous subjects to choose sex-congruent tasks and reject cross-sex tasks. Sex-typed subjects who did perform cross-sex tasks also felt more "nervous" and "peculiar" about being photographed in such circumstances than did androgynous subjects. ("Catch me mixing a baby formula! That'll be the day!")

In another experiment (Bem, 1975) masculine, feminine, and androgynous subjects (on the BSRI) were given the opportunity to play with and fondle a kitten or not to do so, and feminine and androgynous subjects proved more likely to do so than masculine subjects. A third experiment (Bem, 1975) created an Asch-type conformity situation (see Chapter 1), though with a task different from that used by Asch. Masculine and androgynous subjects were equally independent and more so than feminine subjects, who tended to conform to the majority.

Androgyny and Mental Health

From the notion that the androgynous personality is more flexible and adaptable, it is no great distance to the notion that androgyny best defines the ideal of mental health. When Broverman and collaborators (1972) had documented the stereotypes of masculine and feminine temperament, they went on to find out how those stereotypes were related to conceptions of mental health. They asked a large number of practicing mental health clinicians, both male and female, to characterize "the mature, healthy, socially competent *adult*" or else "the mature, healthy," etc. *man* or "the mature, healthy," etc. *woman*. The characterization was to be made in terms of just those traits of temperament, instrumental or expressive, that had constituted the content of the sex stereotypes. The results have infuriated feminists from the day they appeared.

The ideally healthy man was described as high on all the traits that constitute the instrumental cluster and also on a few of the more desirable expressive traits. The mature adult, sex unspecified, was described in the same way as the man, which probably means that the genderless English word was understood as if it referred to males. That gave some cause for annoyance, but it was not the worst.

The ideal of mental health in women, for both male and female practitioners, was different from the ideal for men and adults. In effect, the healthy woman was not expected to be high on the instrumental traits. As compared with the healthy man, she ought to be more submissive, more easily influenced, excitable in minor crises, concerned with her appearance, and disposed to have her feelings hurt, but less independent, dominant, aggressive, objective, and adventurous. She was expected to have most of the expressive feminine traits. Mental health practitioners appeared to hold a double standard. Men should ideally be high on the stereotypically masculine instrumental traits and also on the more desirable feminine traits (e.g. tactful). The ideal of health for a woman was to be a traditional stereotyped feminine woman, not just high on expressive traits but also low on masculine instrumentality.

Perhaps the strongest reaction against the double-standard clinical conceptions of mental health came from Alexander Kaplan and Joan Bean (Kaplan, 1976; Kaplan and Bean, 1976), who proposed that androgyny was a good model of mental health for both sexes. Bem, we know, was of much the same opinion. Spence and Helmreich have never claimed that androgyny (assessed by the PAQ) represents mental health, though their 1978 finding that androgynous subjects had higher self-esteem than any of the other types defined by the PAQ has been cited by others as evidence that androgyny is healthy.

The items on both the PAQ and the BSRI are all traits of temperament, and the androgyny, defined by the conjunction of high masculinity and high femininity, an *HH* scoring pattern, can only be understood as a psychological androgyny, not as a sexual androgyny, not as bisexuality. Bem (1976, 1981a) and Kaplan and Bean (1976) explicitly propose only temperamental androgyny, only the kind of androgyny the BSRI assesses, as a model of mental health.

In fact, there was just one important result using the BSRI and PAQ arguing that temperamental androgyny was healthy. With respect to self-esteem, Spence and Helmreich (1978) found that the order from lowest to highest was: undifferentiated, feminine, masculine, androgynous, as assessed by the PAQ.

Bem (1977), using the BSRI to identify the four types, found exactly the same order for self-esteem. The androgynous personality evidently has very high self-esteem, and that would seem to be an important aspect of mental health.

What Do the Tests Really Measure?

The fact that high self-esteem is the aspect of mental health consistently related to HH scores on the BSRI and the PAQ creates a problem of interpretation, because such a relationship could exist for reasons having nothing to do with masculinity and femininity. Suppose we forget the word "androgynous" and think in terms of the scale items. What they all are is socially desirable traits, desirable for both sexes, but more desirable for one sex than the other. The way to get an "androgynous" score is to rate yourself high on very many desirable traits, both masculine and feminine. Is it surprising that people who think very well of themselves in terms of traits also think well of themselves in a direct measure of self-esteem? We must begin to wonder how appropriate it is to call these people *androgynous* and, therefore, how appropriate the terms *masculinity* and *femininity* are for the component scales.

The possibility that it is the social desirability of all the traits on the PAQ and the BSRI that causes the HH pattern to be associated with high self-esteem, rather than the desirability of combining masculinity and femininity, is made stronger by study (Spence, Helmreich, and Holahan, 1979) of instrumental (masculine) and expressive (feminine) traits that are socially undesirable. The undesirable masculine traits included *arrogant, egotistical, dictatorial,* and *boastful;* the undesirable feminine traits included *spineless, servile, whining,* and *nagging.* It was first demonstrated that those traits, like the socially desirable traits, were more often assigned to one sex than the other and so might be considered undesirable aspects of the stereotypes of masculinity and femininity. Scores on those undesirable masculine and feminine traits and their "androgynous" combination were correlated with self-esteem. Of course, the correlations were either negative or zero. Seeming-"androgyny" (endorsing both masculine and feminine traits) does not go with high self-esteem if the traits are undesirable. What this work shows is that androgyny in the unqualified sense of combined high levels in masculine and feminine traits cannot be a model of mental health. For undesirable traits it does not work.

There are, then, problems with thinking of the scores on the BSRI and the PAQ simply as measures of masculinity, femininity, and androgyny. Nevertheless, both tests do always distinguish male test-takers from female test-takers (e.g. Bem, 1974, 1977; Spence and Helmreich, 1978; Storms, 1979). The differences in the means are usually not large, and there is always substantial overlap in male and female distributions, but the mean differences are always significant and that suggests that the scales have something to do with masculinity and femininity. And other results suggest the same. For instance, Spence and

Helmreich (1978) report results on the PAQ for samples of gay men and lesbian women at the University of Texas that accord with popular notions about homosexuality. The gay men, compared with unselected male student samples, were significantly lower on masculine instrumentality and higher on feminine expressiveness. The lesbian women, contrasted with unselected female samples, were more masculine and less feminine. Larson (1981) obtained similar results using the BSRI. However, Storms (1980) found that while the PAQ differences between homosexuals and heterosexuals in his sample were in the expected direction, they fell short of statistical significance. The BSRI and PAQ instrumental and expressive scales do have something to do with masculinity and femininity. The question is, how much?

The full list of items for Bem's BSRI includes two that are entirely different from the rest: *masculine* and *feminine*. In 1979 Pedhazur and Tetenbaum did a large-scale factor analysis of scores on the BSRI and discovered something very important about the terms *masculine* and *feminine*. The two main factors in the test proved to be pretty much what Bem's conceptualization would predict: (1) a factor including *assertive, forceful, dominant, aggressive*, and so on, which is close to instrumentality, and (2) a factor including *sensitive, sympathetic, compassionate, understanding*, and so on, which is close to expressive. The surprising thing is that there was an additional factor composed of just the two terms, *masculine* and *feminine*. What that means is that the most direct inquiry in the test about masculinity and femininity, the items with the highest face validity, did not belong to the instrumental and expressive factors. Self-assigned masculinity and femininity were only slightly related to the temperamental clusters; they were nearly independent of them. From this analysis it appears that the relation between the two temperaments and popular understanding of masculine and feminine is slight. As a consequence of this analysis, Bem dropped the traits *masculine–feminine* from a revised shorter form of the BSRI. The PAQ never included among its items *masculine–feminine*. The question, then, is: In the absence of the terms *masculine* and *feminine*, what do the BSRI and PAQ really measure?

Michael Storms (1979) came through with a good, clear answer. He used only the PAQ, but it has been shown (Lubinski, Tellegen, and Butcher, 1983) that the revised BSRI, which omits the traits *masculine–feminine*, is equivalent to the PAQ. Storms asked his subjects about their masculinity and femininity in a completely straightforward way, with the following questions:

1. How masculine (feminine) is your personality?
2. How masculine (feminine) do you act, appear, and come across to others?
3. In general, how masculine (feminine) do you think you are?

Answers ranged from "0, not at all" to "30, extremely," and the questions were asked in both forms; i.e. with respect to "masculine" and with respect to "feminine." Subjects had no trouble making such ratings, and answers to the questions in the masculine form were highly correlated (above $+.66$) as were answers to the questions in the feminine form (above $+.70$). Furthermore, the direct questions very sharply distinguished males from females; the male mean score (with high scores masculine) was 24.4, and the female mean score was 7.9. How did scores on this clear index of self-assessed masculinity and femininity relate to scores on the PAQ?

For males, the correlation between self-assessed masculinity and PAQ assessed masculine instrumentality was a significant $+.43$ while the correlation for males on the two indices of femininity was $-.05$, which is in the right direction but not significant. For females, self-assessed femininity correlated with PAQ assessed femininity significantly and in the right direction (.41) while the correlation for the two indices of masculinity was in the right direction but not significant (.07). For both sexes, then, there were significant correlations on the sex-appropriate psychological dimension, but not on the sex-inappropriate dimension. There seems to be no doubt that the instrumentality cluster and the expressiveness cluster on the PAQ and the BSRI are linked to sex, but the linkage is not strong, not perhaps strong enough to think of these two temperaments as the essential core of masculinity and femininity.

Considering all the results, Janet Spence wrote in 1983 that "the PAQ and BSRI primarily measure only what their manifest content indicates and (as the already available evidence suggests) have, at best, weak relations with other gender-related phenomena that are not quite directly influenced by instrumental and expressive traits" (p. 442). Spence has decided that the tests primarily measure instrumentality and expressiveness and can no longer legitimately be characterized by the all-encompassing terms *masculinity* and *femininity*. It follows that *androgyny* is also inappropriate and that any evidence seeming to link mental health with androgyny should be more conservatively interpreted as linking socially desirable instrumentality and socially desirable expressiveness with, mainly, high self-esteem. Spence (1983) regrets the use of the original labels and the fuss caused by the "surplus meanings" they carried.

Bem (1984) has chosen to reformulate rather than write off: She calls her reformulation "gender schema" theory. Bem does not agree with Spence that the BSRI and PAQ measure only the personality traits of instrumentality and expressiveness but thinks the tests are adequate measures of sex-typing and androgyny when these concepts are properly understood. The essence of sex-typing is a spontaneous tendency to think of things in sex-typed terms, whereas androgyny is a disposition to process information in accordance with relevant non-sex principles. In deciding whether a particular attribute on the BSRI is or is not self-descriptive, the sex-typed person does not take the time to recollect individual behavior but, instead, quickly "looks up" the attribute in his or her gender schemas and responds "yes" if it is sex-appropriate and "no" if it is not. The essential difference between the sex-typed and the androgynous person is one of cognitive style. It no longer seems reasonable to expect androgynous *behavior* in a sex-typed culture to be a model of mental health, but Bem still believes that information processing freed of the tyranny of sex-typing, and in that sense androgynous, is desirable. Gender schema theory, as developed in Bem's 1984 contribution to the *Nebraska Symposium on Motivation*, may deepen understanding of masculinity, femininity, and androgyny.

In summary, two tests, the BSRI and PAQ, were designed to correct or at least improve upon traditional masculinity–femininity tests, which were so designed as to incorporate a one-dimensional bipolar conception of masculinity and femininity. The BSRI and the PAQ were constructed on a different assumption, an assumption that masculinity and femininity were two logically independent dimensions. The scales constructed were, however, limited entirely to socially desirable aspects of temperament. Three patterns of scores were labeled, respectively, *masculine (HL)*, *feminine (LH)*, and *androgynous (HH)*, and Sandra Bem and others claimed that the androgynous personality constituted an ideal of mental health for both sexes. The principal evidence supporting this claim was the repeated finding that the "androgynous" person had higher self-esteem than either the "masculine" or the "feminine" person. However, that finding is most conservatively explained by thinking of the so-called masculinity scale as socially desirable instrumentality and the so-called femininity scale as socially desirable expressiveness because it then follows as a necessary or tautological result that the so-called androgynous person—high on both kinds of socially desirable traits—will have the highest self-esteem. That way of looking at the BSRI and PAQ suggests that the main patterns of scores are not well-labeled as "masculine," "feminine," and "androgynous." Factor analyses of the scales, the study of undesirable instrumental and expressive traits, and other findings strongly suggest that the new tests of masculinity and femininity do not capture the essentials of those ideas and, indeed, are so far from doing so that Spence (the principal author of the PAQ) recommends dropping the old labels and simply thinking of the scales as measures of instrumental and expressive temperamental traits.

It is perfectly certain that the layman's conception of masculinity and femininity continues as always to agree with the traditional psychometric conception: a single dimension with two opposed poles. This is demonstrated very clearly by Storms's (1979) results using a direct measure. The questions Storms asked did not, in the manner of the traditional tests, *guarantee* that bipolar conception by building it into the design and scoring of the measure. Essentially his six questions reduce to these two:

1. In general, how masculine do you think you are?
2. In general, how feminine do you think you are?

Responses to each could range from "0, not at all" to "30, extremely." Nothing whatever prevented subjects from adopting the Bem–Spence conception and making their answers to the two questions independent of one another. They could perfectly well have represented themselves as both highly masculine and highly feminine, or as low on both, or as any combination. What they did, however, was treat masculine and feminine as opposed poles. The correlation between scores for masculinity and femininity was − .74 for women and − .64 for men. In addition, the male mean score was a very high 24.4 and the female mean a very low 7.9. What this means is that the layperson finds it completely natural to place himself or herself somewhere on a straight line between masculine and feminine. The bipolar linear conception is still in our minds and has not been shaken by all the rhetoric and research arguing against it.

The fact that the layman conceives of masculinity–femininity as one dimension with two poles and furthermore (Pedhazur and Tetenbaum, 1979), thinks of that one dimension as only very slightly related to instrumental and expressive temperament does not mean that there may not be scientific purposes for which it should be conceived differently. Physics and chemistry started with lay concepts but, as they matured, moved light-years away. There is, however, a difference. It is the layman's mind and behavior that psychology seeks to explain, and so the layman's self-description carries great authority initially. In order to show that there is a better way of conceiving of masculinity and femininity than the global, bipolar, one-dimensional way, it is necessary to show that the new way improves prediction and understanding in the domain of gender, and that has not been accomplished as yet by the undeniably interesting idea of the Androgynous Personality.

Erotic or sexual orientation is not the same thing as gender, but one word— androgyny—has been used in both domains. Chapter 10 discusses the determinants of erotic orientation and concludes that androgyny of orientation, equivalent to bisexuality, is not simply a position intermediate on a continuum between the poles of exclusively same-sex and other-sex orientations, but is in some respects qualitatively different and, indeed, like both extremes at once.

Summary

The androgynous personality simply meant anyone who was by temperament both highly masculine and highly feminine, and therefore free flexibly to adopt male-typed or female-typed tastes, skills, hobbies, and occupations, as circumstances might dictate. Adaptive flexibility is a kind of ideal, and the claim was made that androgyny represented a single standard of mental health for both males and females.

Three things prepared the way for the invention of tests (the BSRI and the PAQ) that would identify androgyny. There seemed to be something wrong with traditional tests of masculinity–femininity, which were so designed that as one became more masculine, he or she by definition became less feminine. The Women's Liberation Movement in striving for equality of opportunity could not accept the idea that a mentally healthy woman must be feminine in the sense of submissive and nurturant. The Kinsey studies reported the surprising news that large percentages of both males and females had at least a touch of bisexuality and so, in a sense, of androgyny.

Androgyny of temperament could not be shown even to exist until tests were designed that measured masculinity and femininity independently and so made it possible to score high on both. Once the androgynous personality could be identified, it became possible to find out how ideal that personality was. The principal evidence that androgyny was good was the high self-esteem associated with it. However, this high self-esteem was an artifact of test design; both the masculinity scale and the femininity scale (of the BSRI and PAQ) had used only socially desirable traits. That raised the question whether high scores on both scales were aptly labeled "androgynous" and, indeed, the question whether the composite scales were aptly named "masculinity" and "femininity." Direct self-ratings on masculinity and femininity (permitting high scores on both) indicated that the scales of the BSRI and PAQ were only slightly related to self-assessed masculinity and femininity and might better be conservatively identified as tests of the traits of instrumental and expressive temperament. In this way the tests designed to assess sexual temperaments and androgyny were compelled to retreat from their original goal.

10

Sources of Erotic Orientation

THE TOPIC IS a delicate one. Very few people can feel emotionally indifferent to the causes of sexual orientation, and that is because one of the two major outcomes, a same-sex or homosexual outcome, if acted upon, is considered a sin in most churches in Western civilization; a crime in some states in this country, in the U.S.S.R., and in other nations; a sickness by many mental health professionals; and a personal disaster by many who subscribe to none of those definitions. There is probably nothing psychology can discover about homosexuality that will change the minds of those who think that acting on this orientation is a sin. There is information that can influence those who think a same-sex orientation is an illness, but the information is ironic. Officially a homosexual orientation does not *ipso facto* constitute mental illness for the reason that the newest *Diagnostic and Statistical Manual of Psychiatry* (*DSM III*) says it is not. However, *DSM III* adds: unless it is a serious problem for the client. And what can best make it a serious problem if not thinking it is a sin or a crime or a mental illness? That is the irony.

Would homosexuality be a psychological problem even if majority social attitudes were less punishing? There are some facts that bear on this question. They come primarily from two studies done by the Kinsey Sex Research Institute, the Institute founded by the late Alfred Kinsey, and they are reported in *Homosexualities* (Bell and Weinberg, 1978) and *Sexual Preference* (Bell, Weinberg, and Hammersmith, 1981). The two studies were surveys reporting on the same sample of respondents, a sample (with slight variations in numbers) made up as follows: white homosexual males, 546; white heterosexual males, 261; white homosexual females, 220; white heterosexual females, 65; black homosexual males, 105; black heterosexual males, 99; black homosexual females, 58; black heterosexual females, 30. All respondents came from the San Francisco Bay Area which was at the time (1970) a relatively benign "scene" for homosexuals (little police harassment, some political power). The Kinsey Institute Researchers made extraordinary efforts to attain a representative sample, but there is finally no way of being sure that a sample of respondents to questions on erotic orientation is representative—even of the city from which all were drawn. There is no doubt, however, that the data in the two institute reports (based on a 125-page interview schedule) constitute the most trustworthy comparative data available on sexual orientation in the United States in recent times.

Data analyses in *Homosexualities* and *Sexual Preference* make use of the categories homosexual and heterosexual, and so it is important to know how those were defined. They were not defined by the self-characterizations of interviewees, but by criterion scores on the Kinsey Heterosexual–Homosexual Scale (Figure 10-1). The scale ranges from "0, entirely heterosexual" to "6, entirely homosexual" and exists in two forms, one for behavior and one for feelings. Each interviewee characterized himself or herself on both scales, and the two scores were averaged with a resultant range from 0 to 6. Anyone scoring two or more was categorized as homosexual, which means that some number of technical bisexuals was included. Not many, however, since the authors say that 90 percent of those in this category scored five or more. Anyone who scored less than two was categorized as heterosexual, and 90 percent of those in this category had a score of zero.

What can survey studies tell us about the comparative mental *wellbeing* (a less prejudicial term than *mental health*) of persons with same-sex versus other-sex erotic orientations? Nothing subtly psychodynamic. What they can do, however, and it is something immensely important, is provide relatively trustworthy answers, given in complete assurance of confidentiality, to flat-out questions that bear on mental health. These are mostly questions to which mental health professionals are likely to think they already know the answers—from clinical experience—but, with the biasing effect of the clinic removed, the answers are sometimes surprising. As to whether or not homosexuals in the San Francisco Bay area in 1970 greatly regret that they are homosexuals, the answer for males and females, blacks and whites, is clearly negative. Only tiny percentages (0–6) report such regret, and the regret felt is furthermore attributed not to sexual orientation, but to society's attitude toward that orientation. There is one stereotype eliminated, and here goes another. The job stability of homosexuals is, on the whole, about equal to that of heterosexuals in matched categories. The frequency of moving from one job to another is not a function of sexual orientation. The same is true of job satisfaction. Finally, with respect to employment, large majorities (61–89 percent) in all homosexual

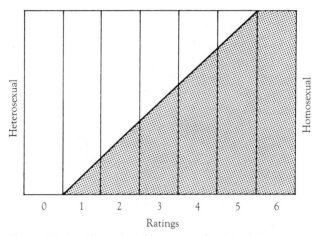

Figure 10-1. Heterosexual-homosexual rating scale

Definitions of the ratings are as follows: 0 = entirely heterosexual. 1 = largely heterosexual, but with incidental homosexual history. 2 = largely heterosexual, but with a distinct homosexual history. 3 = equally heterosexual and homosexual. 4 = largely homosexual, but with distinct heterosexual history. 5 = largely homosexual, but with incidental heterosexual history. 6 = entirely homosexual. The light and shaded areas are intended to represent varying balances of orientation—not percentages of persons or data of any kind. (Based on A. C. Kinsey, W. B. Pomeroy, C. E. Martin, and P. H. Gebhard, *Sexual Behavior in the Human Female* [Philadelphia: Saunders, 1953], p. 470, Fig. 93. Reproduced by permission of The Kinsey Institute for Research in Sex, Gender & Reproduction, Inc.)

categories thought that their orientation had had little effect, whether for better or worse, on their careers. That result, of course, is especially likely to reflect San Francisco's tolerant 1970 social climate.

With the questions that ask about traditionally psychiatric matters, aspects of adjustment and wellbeing, the picture changes. Homosexuals in just about all categories turn out to be less happy, more tense, more depressed, and more likely to describe themselves as "great worriers" than heterosexuals in matched categories. In no case does one find as many as 50 percent of the homosexuals answering in the more maladjusted way; something like 25 percent is the average, but that is quite significantly greater than the average for heterosexuals. One particularly telling question asks about behavior and not just feelings, and so probably those answers are quite accurate. Asked if they had attempted suicide one or more times, slightly more than 20 percent of homosexuals (varying by subcategory) said yes. Heterosexuals, varying radically across categories, had attempted suicide in only 7 percent of all cases. For both orientations, females, especially black females, were more likely to have attempted suicide than males. In general, then, it must be said that homosexuals reported more problems of adjustment than heterosexuals, and so as a first approximation, at least, one concludes that mental wellbeing is not independent of sexual orientation but, rather, that the two are rather strongly related. That is, however, a first approximation.

The authors of *Homosexualities*, having arrived at this point in their own thinking, write: "These data confirm our conviction that studies which compare homosexual men and women with their heterosexual counterparts in terms of their psychological adjustment are more informative when homosexual types are delineated" (1978, p. 215). The title of their book, after all, is in the plural and so signals that homosexuality will not be treated as a single phenomenon. The typology used is one of sexual life-style and goes, essentially, like this:

"Close-Coupled": The title says it; a quasi-marriage, largely though not entirely monogamous.

"Open-Coupled": Living together in a marital way but with quite a lot of outside activity.

"Functional": In effect, single and "swinging," with many contacts.

"Dysfunctional": Single, but with a very disturbed sex life.

"Asexual": Inactive or infrequent and covert, often in a heterosexual marriage.

Female homosexuals were much more likely to be living as couples than were men, but about 40 percent of the men were coupled, and that figure undermines the stereotype of the male homosexual invariably going it on his own.

When the figures relevant to mental wellbeing and adjustment are broken down in terms of the five life-styles, it turns out that the Close-Coupled and Functionals are scarcely distinguishable from heterosexuals; in fact the homosexual Close-Coupled rated themselves happier than did their married heterosexual counterparts. The psychiatric symptoms and suicide attempts were largely limited to the remaining three life-styles, especially the Dysfunctional and Asexual. The authors conclude that if they had not made the typological breakdown, "we would have been forced to conclude that homosexual adults in general tend to be less well adjusted than heterosexual men and women" (1978, p. 216).

The life-style results do not alter the fact that homosexuals as such are at greater risk for symptoms of maladjustment, especially depression and suicide attempts, than are heterosexuals. The question is, What are the mental health implications? One implication is very clear and is well stated in *Homosexualities*: "Surely the time has come for psychiatry to give up the archaic practice of classifying the millions of men and women who prefer homosexual object choices as being, by virtue of that fact alone, mentally ill." Psychiatry has come to agree. The Close-Coupleds and Functionals are not more likely to be mentally ill than are heterosexuals. In fact, however, the statement is also true of the Open-Coupled, Dysfunctional, and Asexual. It is true of all homosexuals that they should not be considered mentally ill, "by virtue of that fact alone," since even for those following the life-style with the most problems the probability of illness is low.

While erotic orientation as such does not guarantee mental illness, a minority orientation, disapproved more or less strongly by the majority, is probabilistically related to illness. Is it the social disapproval that causes the illness, as minority respondents think, or is there something the matter that is more intrinsic to the orientation? Male sexuality, for instance, probably makes the Close-Coupled style difficult to attain (Harry, 1984; McWhirter and Mattison, 1984; Peplau, 1982) and the Functional style, as opposed to the Dysfunctional, is probably attainable only by those judged to be very attractive. We shall never know whether social attitudes are the entire cause of the existing connection between homosexuality and symptoms of maladjustment until social attitudes become more benevolent.

Suppe (1981), reviewing the Bell and Weinberg report on data collected in 1970 in San Francisco, thought the results were out of date, because San Francisco between 1970 and 1981 had become a more tolerant city. It seemed as if the homosexual, metamorphosed into the gay person, had at last graduated out of abnormal psychology and into social psychology. In late 1984 the new identity is threatened by a selective plague, AIDS (acquired immune-deficiency syndrome) which has stricken 750 gay men in San Francisco and threatens, besides lives, mental health and individual pride. It operates subtly on meanings and has already added a sordid connotation to the word *gay* and even to the name of the city of San Francisco.

The Etiology of Orientations

While the word "etiology" may be properly applied to any theory of causal determinants, in practice it is largely limited to theories of the determinants of disease. There is therefore some offense in those studies of orientation etiology which confine themselves largely or entirely to the etiology of homosexuality. Such work conveys an unspoken assumption that the heterosexual orientation is "natural" and requires no explanation. More than one gay rights activist has asked in connection with one kind of research or another: "Why is this study being done at all?" The question seems to me proper in that it warns of a real danger in the eventual interpretation of results. Lynda Birke (1981) has convincingly shown that the medical or disease model of some research on hormonal determinants has very directly contributed to mistakes of interpretation. The deepest thinkers (Sigmund Freud, John Money, some of the learning theorists) seem always to have understood that what we want is a general theory of sexual orientation in which paths are traced for all existent outcomes.

We do not yet have the theory of sexual orientation we should like to have, but we can identify quite a few theories, believed by significant numbers of people, as definitely false, and it certainly helps to get those out of the way. We also know that both learning and constitution at birth are important. That knowledge comes to more than the truism that sexual orientation, like all other behavior, is a function of both nature and nurture, for it specifies some of the things that matter in both nature and nurture and also tentatively specifies a kind of homosexuality in which constitutional factors are more important and a kind in which learning is more important.

Our inquiry into etiology can be directed only at sexual orientations as they exist in the contemporary United States. For other times and places there are no serious data, but there is a serious possibility that the orientations have not always been the same phenomena. The most dramatic contrast is with the ancient Hellenic and Roman worlds (Boswell, 1980). For those periods, as for all history until the very recent past, information about homosexuality is information about male homosexuality. That is because the primary documents are written expressions of love, and men did all the writing that was done. If homosexual, they wrote about male lovers; if not, about female lovers—a combination of factors that leaves lesbian love largely unrecorded.

What we today can hardly grasp is the extreme *ordinariness*, then, of same-sex attraction. It was regarded as a ubiquitous natural aspect of human life, which called for no person categories, like homosexual and heterosexual, and, indeed, was almost never the important thing to say about a relationship. It was not merely sensual but often idealized and poetic. It was not limited to older men and boys. It was not limited to the upper classes or to decadent Roman emperors, though of the first fifteen emperors all but Claudius had a homosexual lover—and Claudius was a moron (Gibbon, 1898). It was not considered effeminate; Hercules was said to have had more than fourteen male lovers. It did not preclude marriage and fatherhood; Socrates loved Alcibiades but also had a wife and children. It did not cause the decline of the Roman Empire; it would be more accurate to say that only in decline did Rome become intolerant of homosexuality. The classical world seems another world, and homosexuality then another phenomenon than homosexuality today. And yet Aristotle said it was always a minority *preference*, and both he and Plato thought it, as a *preference*, a congenital physical condition.

Classical and Operant Conditioning

There are many forms of learning and many theories about how they work, and so I have had to be very selective. Classical and operant conditioning are the two kinds of learning that have been most clearly defined, most studied, and demonstrated to exist across the greatest range of human behavior as well as the greatest range of organisms in the animal kingdom (Hilgard and Marquis, 1940). In classical conditioning (e.g. Pavlov's dog learning to salivate in response to a metronome), the response is originally *elicited* by an unconditioned stimulus (e.g. food powder in the mouth) and comes to be elicited by a previously neutral stimulus (e.g. the metronome) after a series of trials in which the conditioned stimulus preceded the unconditioned by a short interval. The response in classical conditioning is usually autonomic.

In operant (or instrumental) conditioning, the response is skeletal (a rat pressing a bar) and is not elicited by any known stimulus, but rather *emitted* for reasons unknown. Learning involves increasing the frequency of response emission and is produced by providing positive reinforcement, or reward, following the response (e.g. the bar press is followed by delivery of a food pellet). There are several forms of operant conditioning, including aversive training and avoidance, in which the reinforcement is negative, escape from or avoidance of some noxious stimulus. With both classical and operant conditioning, one can obtain stimulus generalization, extinction, spontaneous recovery, response inhibition, and numerous other reliable effects. There is every reason to expect that sexual responses, both autonomic and skeletal, will be subject to conditioning and related effects in all the ways that are familiar in psychology.

Rachman (1966) provided an interesting demonstration of sexual arousal becoming attached to previously neutral stimulation by the process of classical conditioning. He undertook to create in the laboratory a model of the development of a sexual fetish. A sexual fetish is an inanimate object that causes strong sexual arousal. Fetishism is a variety of what are nowadays called "paraphilias" ("unlikely loves" is not a bad translation), and while those "orientations" were sometimes grouped with homosexuality and bisexuality in nineteenth-century lists of "perversions," there is a fundamental distinction. A paraphilia (as for women's underwear) interferes with, or rather narrowly restricts, the possibilities of falling in love, because there is not likely to be available a partner who has the reciprocal "turn on." Homosexuality and bisexuality can be ways of falling in love. See Table 10–1 for a list of popular paraphilias.

As fetish-to-be, Rachman picked a pair of black, knee-length woman's boots. Such boots are one of the more frequent fetishes found in nature, but the three young psychologists who participated in Rachman's experiment could

TABLE 10–1. A List of Popular Paraphilias

Acrotomophilia (amputee partner)	Kleptophilia (stealing)	Rapism or raptophilia (violent assault)
Apotemnophilia (self-amputee)	Klismaphilia (enema)	Sadism
Asphyxiophilia (self-strangulation)	Lust Murderism	Scoptophilia (watching coitus)
Autoassassinatophilia	Masochism	Somnophilia (sleeper)
Coprophilia (feces)	Mysophilia (filth)	Telephone scatophilia (lewdness)
Ephebophilia (youth)	Narratophilia (erotic talk)	Troilism (couple + one)
Exhibitionism	Necrophilia (corpse)	Urophilia or undinism (urine)
Fetishism	Pedophilia (child)	Voyeurism or peeping-Tomism
Frotteurism (rubbing)	Pictophilia (pictures)	Zoophilia (animal)
Gerontophilia (elder)		

SOURCE: J. Money, *Love and Love Sickness: The Science of Sex, Gender Difference and Pair-Bonding* (Baltimore: The Johns Hopkins University Press, 1980), p. 82.

view them with indifference prior to conditioning. The response to be conditioned was penile erection, and that response was measured by a phallic plethysmograph, which electronically records increases of volume in the penis. Don't laugh; in the early days of sexual conditioning psychologists had a lot of trouble inventing an apparatus that did not cause an erection when attached. Initially, a colored slide of the black boots produced no trace of an erection, so that slide became the conditioned stimulus (CS). Slides of attractive naked girls produced arousal responses from the start, so those slides were the unconditioned stimulus (UCS). Classical conditioning involves repeated pairing of the CS and the UCS, with the CS preceding the UCS by a short interval (one second in this case). Conditioning has occurred when the CS on its own reliably produces the arousal response.

All three subjects conditioned after about twenty to sixty trials. Stimulus generalization (the same response to other originally neutral stimuli that resemble, more or less closely, the CS) occurred for high-heeled black shoes, but not gold sandals. To extinguish (or eliminate) a conditioned response, the classical procedure is to present repeatedly the newly conditioned stimulus (the boots) in the absence of the UCS (the naked girls). Extinction was produced rapidly in all subjects—about twenty trials (Rachman and Hodgson, 1968). In general, Rachman and others (e.g. McConaghy, 1970) showed that sexual arousal followed the laws of classical conditioning.

McGuire, Carlisle, and Young (1965) studied the case histories of forty-five "sexual deviants" whose individual turn-ons ranged widely (e.g. four-year-old little girls, elderly gentlemen, women undressing in front of a window) and came up with a theory of deviation based on operant conditioning. In operant conditioning a response becomes more frequent when it is directly followed by positive reinforcement (reward). Each deviant seemed to have had an accidental initial experience of arousal-and-ejaculation, produced in association with what became his obsessive turn-on. The "response" that became frequent was deliberate rehearsal of the stimulating image or fantasy, and that, being reinforced by masturbation to ejaculation, grew stronger and eventually led to action in the world that got the man in trouble.

If you reflect for a few minutes on the implications of the discovery that neutral stimuli can be made erotic by classical conditioning and that sexually instrumental behavior can be made more frequent by primary sexual reinforcement, you will be able to guess at the theories of sexual orientation they suggested. You will also see how the early work led quite directly to techniques of behavior modification in the domain of sex, which from 1960 until the present have been much used. Almost all behavior modification work in connection with sex, incidentally, has been done with males, and that is apparently because it is chiefly males whose sexuality gets them in trouble with the law and causes them to be referred for therapy, and it is also mainly males who refer themselves because they are unhappy about their sex lives.

If neutral boots can become erotic stimuli by association with naked girls, perhaps it is the case that naked girls (or naked boys or whatever) first become erotic stimuli by association with a more ultimate unconditioned stimulus, direct tactile stimulation of the genitals. That would make the first genuine sexual encounter terribly consequential since it might result in either a hetero-orientation or a homo-orientation. If rehearsal of imagery in masturbation is important, then it would still be the case that the first experience on which the imagery is modeled would be extremely important.

Responses that can be conditioned can be extinguished. Suppose a man is unhappy about being aroused by his own sex (or gets in trouble with the law because he is); extinction becomes a therapy. One might try simply satiation with male nudes in the absence of any unconditioned stimulus to arousal, but sex is a drive as well as a response, so a better thought would be to pair male nudes with an unconditioned stimulus that gives rise to a response incompatible with arousal. A still better thought would seem to be to work at the same time on building arousal to female stimuli. Those things have all been tried.

Barker (1965) describes a series of treatments using drug-induced nausea. The patient was a male transvestite, or cross-dresser. A projector was mounted behind the head of his bed, and he looked at a large screen. He was injected with apomorphine, and as soon as he developed a headache and nausea, slides were flashed on the screen of himself in woman's clothing, and a tape began playing his own voice describing his dressing up. All this was continued until he vomited, for a total of sixty-six "emetic" trials over six days and six nights.

Barker reports that the method was both messy and time-consuming. For those and other reasons, electric shock displaced drugs in aversion therapy (the soles of the feet, rather like what one reads of Turkish prisons). Yates (1970) reviewed aversion therapies and the evidence of success and failure. The only reliable outcome seems to be a reduction of the punished deviant arousal, which can be objectively demonstrated in the laboratory. As far as life outside the laboratory is concerned (the only stimulus generalization that really matters), improvements have been often reported, but usually only on the former patient's say-so, and the follow-up period has rarely exceeded six months.

Behavior modification techniques of many kinds have been used in an effort to change a homosexual orientation to a heterosexual one (see Craighead, Kazdin, and Mahoney, 1981; Rimm and Masters, 1979). These techniques rely more heavily on positive reinforcement or reward than on aversion or punishment, though aversion is not seldom a part of a "broad-spectrum" approach. Because homosexual activity between consenting adults is becoming legal in more and more states, cases in which a therapy is mandated by a court are becoming less frequent.

It is always extremely difficult to evaluate the results of any putative therapy, whether medical and somatic, that is not clearly and obviously successful. A few things seem to be clear. Behavior modification (if it makes sense to use one term for an enormous variety of techniques) is more effective with self-referrals than with persons referred by the courts or by relatives. Behavior modification is more effective by far with persons in the technically bisexual range on the Kinsey scale than with exclusively homosexual persons. Exactly what is accomplished when success is claimed is usually unclear but seems most often to be the ability to engage in heterosexual intercourse. Follow-up periods seldom exceed six months, and I have found no account that claimed effectiveness for more than two years. There are many cases in which a man initially bisexual on the Kinsey scale and very powerfully motivated to become heterosexual has been "modified" to the point of marriage and then, after five and even ten years, becomes exclusively homosexual and loses all interest in changing.

The Kinsey Institute study, Sexual Preference (Bell, Weinberg, and Hammersmith, 1981) asked questions designed to test etiological theories. The questions ask about life-history events and on the whole ought to be answered one way by eventual homosexuals and another way by eventual heterosexuals, if a given theory of orientation is even roughly right. It seems to me that the answers obtained are mostly bad news for conditioning theories of sexual preference. Consider first the simplest sort of theory, a theory explicit in McGuire, Carlisle, and Young (1965), and implicit in many others, the theory that the first encounter is highly determinative.

First Encounter Theory

The First Encounter theory, in simplest form, holds that both sexes are initially equally able to respond with pleasure to direct stimulation of the genitalia—whatever the sex of the stimulating person. The potential for pleasure exists before adolescence but is much intensified at that time. Everything then depends on what is essentially an accident—the sex of the person who first gives pleasure. The one who first gives pleasure will usually be opposite in sex to the one pleasured, because that is the way the world works, and so the majority turns out heterosexual in orientation, but a significant minority, because of bad luck in first encounters, turns out homosexual. The Kinsey Institute group asked just the right question of their homosexual and heterosexual interviewees: Was the first sexual encounter with a person of the same sex or the other sex? Granting that there can be mistakes of memory and granting that later learning ought also to be allowed considerable determinative power, still—on the whole—homosexuals' first encounters should be more often reported to be with a person of the same sex than should heterosexuals' first encounters. For white females there was no difference; for white males many more heterosexuals (62 percent) reported homosexual first encounters than did homosexuals (39 percent). In the whole study, reports of early homosexual seductions were trivially infrequent. So much for the theory of first encounters.

Early Onset Theory

In 1981 Michael Storms developed the interesting theory that for both males and females early sex drive onset should predispose the individual to homosexuality. It should do so because at the earlier ages boys associate mostly with boys, and girls with girls, and so the predominant stimuli likely to be conditioned to produce sexual arousal are stimuli from the same sex. At later ages peer association is less "homosocial" and more "heterosocial," and so for those who reach adolescence late, stimuli from the other sex would have a greater opportunity to be erotized. There are many subtleties in Storms's (1981) theory involving the role of sexual fantasy, classical conditioning as well as social learning, but everything really hinges on there being large, reliable differences between the ages of adolescence of homosexuals and heterosexuals, both male and female. The data on that point are decidedly mixed.

The strongest evidence that early adolescence is linked with homosexual activity comes from the Kinsey volume on the human male (1948):

> Homosexual activities occur in a much higher percentage of the males who became adolescent at an early age; and in a definitely smaller percentage of those who became adolescent at later ages (Tables 77, 78, Figure 94). For instance, at the college level, during early adolescence about 28 per cent of the early-adolescent boys are involved and only 14 per cent of the boys who were late in becoming adolescent. This difference is narrowed in successive age periods, but the boys who became adolescent first are more often involved even ten and fifteen years later.

This verbal summary certainly seems to support the age of adolescence theory, but there is a problem. The tables and the figure referred to do not report on the percentages of males who are exclusively or mainly homosexual in orientation; in fact, there is no analysis in the book that relates homosexuality as a preferred orientation to age at adolescence. The homosexual activity that is slightly higher in early-adolescence males constitutes only a small percentage of the total sexual activity of those males. The same early-onset men also have more heterosexual activity, far more than do the late-onset men. They masturbate more and they are sexually active until a later age. Therefore it is possible that the early-onset males are simply those having the greatest sex drive. In fact, Kinsey and his collaborators wrote: "There is some reason for thinking that these early-adolescent males are more often the more alert, energetic, vivacious, spontaneous, physically active, socially extrovert and/or aggressive individuals in the population" (1948, p. 325).

The evidence in Kinsey, Pomeroy, and Martin (1948) of an association between early onset of sex drive and homosexuality is actually equivocal. However, Storms cites several small-scale studies (e.g. Saghir and Robins, 1973) that do report earlier adolescence in homosexuals than in heterosexuals, but, on the other hand, the Kinsey volume on the human female finds no consistent relation at all between homosexual activity and age of adolescence (1953, Table 137). Finally, the *Sexual Preference* volume, which probably has the best data, reports of the males that there was no difference between heterosexuals and homosexuals in reported age of first ejaculation, first masturbation, or first nocturnal emission. Of the heterosexual and homosexual females, it says there was no difference in age at which they began to menstruate. In sum, there is not much support for the theory of early sex drive onset.

It is only the simplest and most clearly stated conditioning theories of sexual orientation that can be rather decisively disconfirmed by survey data of the kind supplied by the Kinsey Institute of Sex Research. To show that the simple and clear theories do not bear up well against survey data is not, of course, to question that sexual arousal and sexually instrumental responses can be conditioned. That has been demonstrated beyond all possible doubt. It is also not possible to doubt that learning of some sort, including conditioning, plays an important role in determining sexual orientation. The popular paraphilias listed in Table 10-1 could hardly be constitutionally determined. Learning must also play an important role in determining the principal orientations—homosexuality and heterosexuality. What is lacking is a theory of just how it does so.

Psychodynamic Ideas

Psychodynamic theories of a vaguely Freudian kind do not stand up to the survey data any better than conditioning theories do. There is the added extreme difficulty of making out just what the psychoanalytic predictions should be. Freud himself portrayed the heterosexual orientation in males as deriving from a positive resolution of the Oedipus complex. The young male is, like Oedipus in the Greek legend and in Sophocles' play, supposed to desire his mother and fear the rivalry of his powerful father. In a "positive resolution" the young male identifies with his father, wishes to be like him, and relinquishes his mother as a love object in favor of other women. All or most of that is supposed to occur in the unconscious, so many psychoanalytic theorists would not consider the answers to any questions posed in a single superficial interview acceptable as tests of their theories. As to the determinants of male homosexual orientation and either sort of orientation in females, Freud was both vague at times and self-contradictory at times, except in seeing all sexual orientation and sexual identifications as outcomes of the Oedipal (or female equivalent) drama. When we look at post-Freudian psychoanalytic writings, we find just about every sort of maternal and paternal relationship represented as highly determinative.

It will be enough to sample the clearer findings in the survey results. Between white homosexual males and their heterosexual counterparts, there was no difference in the frequency with which they said that when growing up they had wanted to be like their mothers or felt similar to their mothers. So much for the "common wisdom" about homosexual boys and their mothers. On the other hand, the two groups of males did make very different reports of their relationships with their fathers. About 60 percent of eventual heterosexual males had wanted to be like their fathers and had felt similar to them, whereas only about 30 percent of homosexual males gave such father-identification answers. In addition, about twice as many heterosexuals as homosexuals said that father had been the dominant parent in their homes. Those results are roughly consistent with the positive resolution of the Oedipus complex, which pictures the boy as identifying with his dominant father. For the "negative resolution," which should be the path to homosexuality, the responses simply suggest an absence of identification with father, without suggesting an iden-tification with mother. The results with homosexual and heterosexual women are most confusing. There was no indication that eventually homosexual females were like heterosexual males in having lived in father-dominated households and in wanting to grow up to be like father. The single most consis-tent result for both males and females was that their relationships to father more often differentiated eventual homosexuals from heterosexuals than did relationships to mother, and that is a result contrary to the general tendency of psychoanalytic theory to ascribe more importance to the maternal relationship than to the paternal.

The failure of survey studies to confirm any specific learning or experiential theories cannot mean that life history factors play no role in determining sexual orientations. It is logically necessary and empirically obvious that they do. However, the familiar theories are much more explicit and detailed (though mutually contradictory) than can be justified by existent evidence. It seems to me far wiser at this time to put forward a loose formulation that fits the facts but, just because the facts are complicated, the formulation cannot be highly explicit. For instance: Homosexuality is "a response to diffusely mixed covert and overt signals that seem to indicate that by being a girl with a penis, or a boy with a vulva, the child can be retained in or restored to an intact family unit and their continued allegiance to one another mutually ensured" (Money, 1984, p. 78). Any such formulation of experiential, family-life factors must, however, be qualified by saying that they are only necessary and not sufficient conditions because it is clear that there is also some kind of constitutional "risk" factor.

Hormone Levels in Adulthood

In the 1920s and 1930s the sex hormones were first isolated and then tech-niques were invented for synthesizing them (creating them artificially in the laboratory) as well as techniques for assaying hormonal levels in living in-dividuals from either the bloodstream or the urine. By the 1940s a hormonal conception had developed of the immediate (rather than life-history) determinants of sexual orientation and a concomitant theory of treatment (for homosexuals, of course, not heterosexuals).

In the names given the sex hormones, one can, as John Money (1980) points out, see the oversimplicity of the theory. The *androgens* (from *andros*, meaning man) and *testosterone* (the main androgen, which is produced in the adult *testes*) were considered to be male hormones. *Estrogen* (from the *estrus* cycle) and *progesterone* (from *gestation*, or carrying a child in pregnancy) were considered to be female hormones. Males, the theory went, were erotically oriented to females because they had in their bloodstreams the male hormones, and females reciprocated the desire because they had in their bloodstreams the female hormones. You could say that this conception of hormonal operation was one-dimensional and bipolar. Given that conception of the normal orientation, it was inevitable that homosexual adult males should be thought to be undersupplied with male hormones and homosexual adult females undersupplied with female hormones. That being the nature of their illness, the remedy was obvious: corrective injections.

The problems with the simple hormonal theory begin with the fact that none of the four hormones is *exclusive* to either sex; both occur in both sexes in uneven and varying ratios. Females do have more estrogen than males, but just how much more depends on the point in the estrus cycle, so that males may have from 2 percent to 30 percent of the female level. Males will have from 6 percent to 100 percent as much progesterone as females. Females may have up to 20 percent of the male level of androgens and apparently even some testosterone (from the adrenal gland) is important to create in the female an "appetite" for sex. The nonexclusivity of the hormones does not, obviously, mean that male levels and female levels are indistinguishable. Neither does it rule out the possibility that homosexuals may be characterized by *relatively* low levels of the relevant sex hormones. A test of the hypothesis would seem easy to make, but it has not proved so.

One difficulty with determining heterosexual and homosexual levels of the hormones is that those levels are responsive to many things other than sexual orientation. They vary from day to day and respond to stress, alcohol, drugs, recent sleeplessness, and so on. The early methods of bioassay were crude and so added unreliability. In many studies the definitions of homosexual and heterosexual went unstated or were very approximate. Still, of course, one study could improve on another, and many studies were done. Swyer summarized this work in 1954 as follows: "[T]here is no convincing evidence that human homosexuality is dependent upon hormonal aberrations" (1954, p. 377). In the 1960s precision radioimmunassay was invented, and a new and still continuing set of studies began. John Money, who is director of the Psychohormonal Research Unit at The Johns Hopkins University, exhaustively reviewed the work in 1980 and concluded: "Attempts to prove the hypothesis gave inconsistent, inconclusive, or contradictory results" (1980, 128). He says of the gonadal hormones: "Their levels in homosexuals as compared with heterosexual controls have been found to be the same, lower, or higher" (p. 130). Masters and Johnson (1979), reviewing much the same work, conclude that secure information is lacking and that an "intellectually open stance" is the right one (p. 411). So far then, though the sex hormones play important roles in human sexual development and behavior, the hypothesis that adult heterosexuals are distinguished from adult homosexuals by hormonal levels has failed to be confirmed.

If research proceeded in strict logical sequence, one would expect trials of the hormonal therapies to have waited upon clear demonstration of hormonal differences. If they had done so, they would still be waiting, but of course they did not. The one neat idea seemed so certain eventually to be proved true that the second neat idea was tried at once. The first discovery was that raising the level of androgens in male homosexuals either had no effect on sexual behavior or else elevated the level of drive without affecting direction and so made them more homosexually active. That was decidedly not a neat outcome. Injection of males with progesterone resulted in impotence and enlargement of the breasts. John Money's (1980) conclusion is that injecting humans in their adult years with hormones as a treatment for homosexuality is valueless. The results seem to be very clear, and there is a consensus among the best scholars (e.g. Birke, 1981) that hormone therapy is without value, but, as you may by now anticipate, evidence seldom stops a therapy, and such injections are still sometimes given to clients who request them.

Hormone Levels in Prenatal Life

While sex hormone levels in adult life seem not to affect sexual orientation, levels in prenatal life, in the uterus before birth, are another matter (Dörner, 1976; Money, 1984; Reinisch and Karow, 1977). Two kinds of evidence indicate that the amount of androgenization (bathing in androgens) of the fetus can affect the level of masculinity of the individual long after birth. One sort of evidence is experimental and therefore for ethical reasons has been obtained only with subhuman animal species. The second sort of evidence derives from humans whose prenatal environments have been abnormal in such a way as to make them into natural experiments which are, like most natural experiments, imperfect in design.

In humans (and also in the other primates) the primordial (or original) gonads of the fetus are hermaphroditic, which is to say that they have the potential for developing into either male or female genitals. If the fetus is a genetic female, that is, has XX chromosomes rather than XY, the genitals and the brain will become female. If the fetus is a genetic male, that is, has XY chromosomes, androgens will be produced in the womb and the effect of androgenization of the fetus is to masculinize the genitals and also the brain (most importantly the hypothalamus). It has been established, in short, that prenatal hormones are, in primates and indeed in all mammals, crucial for the sexual differentiation of the external genitalia and the brain (Birke, 1981). Normally, a chromosomal (XX) female fetus will not be androgenized and will develop as a female anatomically, physiologically, and behaviorally, and a normal chromosomal male (XY) fetus will be androgenized and will develop as a male. The question that can be answered by experiments on animals is: What will happen if a female fetus is artificially androgenized by injecting the pregnant mother with androgens? The XX chromosomes guarantee genetic femininity, but what will androgenization do as an added foreign element?

In a typical experiment a pregnant monkey is injected with testosterone (the major androgen) for several weeks beginning with early pregnancy. When the fetus is a chromosomal female, the effect of androgenization is to cause the infant to be born with ambiguous genitalia (for instance, a penis and empty scrotum or a vagina and much enlarged clitoris). The inner genitalia (uterus and so on) remain female, and the female role in reproduction is the only possible role, whatever the external genitals look like. Mother monkeys are said to inspect the genitals of such ambiguous daughters with evident puzzlement. The most suggestive finding is that in life after birth the behavior of the ambiguous daughters may be described as masculinized.

The androgenized female monkey, as it grows up, does not behave exactly like a male, but it behaves much more like a male than the normal female does. It engages in more rough-and-tumble play than the normal female; it does more threatening; and it mounts other monkeys as if it were a male. In one case intromission (penetration) occurred, but not ejaculation, since the internal genitals were female. Money and Ehrhardt (1972) and Money (1980) describe the young androgenized female monkey as an extreme sort of tomboy. Comparable results, indeed more extreme results, have been obtained with other mammals. There is a general principle, formulated by Beach (1948), that the sexual behavior of mammals is more tightly controlled by the sex hormones the lower the species in the phyletic scale. Therefore the androgenized female rat, guinea pig and sheep are more masculinized in anatomy, physiology, and behavior than is the androgenized monkey. The human is higher in the phyletic scale than the monkey, and so one wonders what effect, if any, artificial androgenization would have on the behavior of chromosomally female humans. It is an experiment that cannot be done for obvious ethical reasons, but it is an experiment that nature, indifferent to ethics, occasionally carries out in what is called the "adrenogenital syndrome" in girls.

In the adrenogenital syndrome something is wrong with the adrenocortical glands of the female fetus, with the result that androgens are produced and therefore an abnormal, but naturally created, androgenized infant girl. The newborn girl has ambiguous external genitals, looking more or less like a male, and also a male-differentiated brain, which at puberty produces male secondary sexual characteristics, and so a tragically virile female is the outcome—or rather, used to be the outcome. Nowadays, when the adrenogenital syndrome is recognized at birth (before birth it cannot be), it is possible by surgery to "correct" the external genitals so as to make them female (in line with chromosomal sex and the internal genitals). It has also been possible since 1950 to prevent the development of additional male anatomical characteristics, using injections of cortisol (like cortisone). The fetally androgenized female today who is properly treated is in all anatomical respects female. She was so chromosomally from the first; the internal genitals needed no correction; the external genitals have been made feminine by surgery; cortisol prevents virilization and produces secondary sexual characteristics that are female. The only thing that cannot be undone is the androgenization that occurred in the womb before birth. Does that prenatal androgenization have any effect?

John Money in 1980, reviewing all cases to date (thirty) of the adrenogenital syndrome in girls, says that they all in childhood exhibited what he calls "tomboyism." They regarded themselves, with pride, as tomboys and were so regarded by others. They liked outdoor athletic play, including competitive team sports like football and baseball, and they liked to be permitted to play on the boys' teams. They preferred functional jeans or shorts to dresses. They neglected or gave away their dolls and had no interest in rehearsing parentalism by playing house. Later on they were averse to babysitting and had no taste for stereotypically female interests generally.

In young adulthood the fetally androgenized girls reported on their erotic imagery in spontaneous fantasy or dreams and on their erotic experience (Money, Schwartz, and Lewis, 1984). Five of thirty (17 percent) rated themselves as homosexual and six of thirty (20 percent) as bisexual; 37 percent then considered themselves to be either bisexual or homosexual, and of these 17 percent had had erotic partner experience by the age of twenty. Entirely by coincidence, rather comparable questions were asked of adult homosexual women in the *Sexual Preference* study. Some 44 percent said that before the age of nineteen their sexual feelings had been predominantly homosexual. No heterosexual women at all made this response in the *Sexual Preference* study. The questions asked in the two studies were not identical, and the percentages in the survey study for black women homosexuals were slightly different from those for white women. No doubt the nearly identical reports on early adulthood made by fetally androgenized girls and (retrospectively) by adult women homosexuals are in part coincidental. There is, however, one important point: In order to count as a factor in adult homosexuality, fetal androgenization need not be associated with a homosexual orientation in 100 percent of cases in early adulthood or even with such an orientation in a majority of cases.

The parents of the androgenized girls, of course, knew of the androgenization, the initially ambiguous genitalia and the need for corrective surgery, and so one might think that the tomboyism of those girls appeared because their parents expected it. Nature's experiment cannot be "blind" in the experimental design sense. However, the idea that parental expectancies produced tomboyism seems unlikely to be correct. As Money (1980) has pointed out, it seems more likely that the parents would have been worried about any manifestations of masculinity in their daughters and inclined to discourage them as far as possible but, finally, we simply do not know.

It has sometimes happened that an androgenized chromosomal female has been given masculinizing surgery and hormone treatment and raised as a boy. The assigned sex corresponding with the external genitals easily prevails over chromosomal sex. Those chromosomal females grow up as boys, and the characteristics that would be called "tomboyism" in a girl simply make them "real boys" as males.

The adrenogenital syndrome is not the only condition that can result in ambiguous genitalia. The term "hermaphrodite" (half Hermes, half Aphrodite) is used to name all such cases, whatever the cause of the condition. From studies of the development of hermaphrodites (e.g. Hampson and Hampson, 1961; Imperato-McGinley, Peterson, and Gautier, 1976; Money and Ehrhardt, 1972) something extremely important has been learned. The sex of social assignment, with only rare exceptions, dominates chromosomal sex. The sex of social assignment is the sex that parents initially, as everyone eventually, believe the child to be. The physician in normal cases announces it as the child is delivered, basing his announcement on the clear evidence of a penis or a vagina. In borderline cases (hermaphrodites) the physician makes the decision on the basis of the predominant character of the genitals; that decision is accepted by the social world and determines how the child is treated and what the child's own sex identification will be. It has even been shown with pairs of hermaphrodites matched in terms of the male-to-female balance in the appearance of the genitals that when one member has been assigned to the male sex and the other to the female sex, that assignment prevails. There is, of course, a limit to the flexibility of sex assignment. No one has yet shown that a child with an unmistakable penis or an unmistakable vagina can be successfully assigned to the sex that its genitals contradict. The external genitals are the criterion of social assignment. They prevail over chromosomal sex. If the criterion is somewhat ambiguous, parents will accept the authority of the doctor's decision, but presumably they could not believe in an assignment clearly contradicted by the anatomical criterion.

While sex determination (or assignment, if there is any ambiguity) ordinarily occurs at birth and is never changed thereafter, it has sometimes happened that a change of assignment, a reassignment, has for some reason been attempted. Money and Ehrhardt (1972) say that eighteen months is about the upper age limit for successfully imposing reassignment on a child. They believe that the first eighteen months of life constitute a "critical period" in which the child learns its sex and that such learning cannot be reversed later on. However, sex identity has nothing to do with homosexuality. Gay males know they are males and lesbians know they are females.

What the adrenogenital syndrome suggests about the etiology of homosexuality is the possibility that male homosexuality derives from a lower level of fetal androgenization than is normal for males and that female homosexuality derives from a higher level of fetal androgenization than is normal for females. In both cases one would have to add that the departure from normal is not great enough or not timed so as to affect sexual anatomy. The hypothesis seems to be implicit in much that John Money has written, for example: "No one knows how many genetic females born with normal female genitalia might, in fact, have been subject to prenatal androgen excess insufficient to influence the external anatomy, though perhaps sufficient to influence the brain" (Money and Ehrhardt, 1972, p. 17). Money also points out, however, that there is no way to know prenatal hormonal history in retrospect. Nevertheless, the prenatal androgenization hypothesis is an idea interesting enough to check against other data, especially the survey data of the *Sexual Preference* volume.

Genetic Evidence

John Money, writing on the genesis of homosexuality in 1984, says: "Historically, gender transposition of the complete type was explained as hereditary. However, the hereditary attribution has proved too simple and is now anachronistic. The current explanation is hormonal. Like its hereditary predecessor, the hormonal explanation applies to development that takes place before birth. This development is governed not by the genetic code directly but by sex hormones that program the sexual differentiation of the brain" (p. 78). Abnormal levels of fetal androgenization *can* be genetically determined; the adrenogenital sydnrome, for example, originates in a genetically recessive defect (Money, Schwartz, and Lewis, 1984). However, variation in levels of fetal androgenization need not be genetically based, but can be caused by substances breathed, swallowed, or otherwise absorbed by the mother. For instance, it is known that barbiturates may have a demasculinizing effect on a fetus. In sum, genetic factors may have an indirect effect on sexual orientation by way of a direct effect that is hormonal, but hormonal effects need not be genetically based. It follows that genetic studies of sexual orientation are potentially instructive but, if such studies did not give evidence of a significant genetic factor, that would not eliminate the possibility of a significant constitutional factor. All of this is at present rather "academic" since there are only two published genetic studies (Kallmann, 1952; Heston and Shields, 1968) and, though both have been sometimes interpreted as evidence of a significant genetic factor, neither one is actually good enough to count as evidence of anything.

Franz Kallmann, who did the earlier study (1952), had seriously flawed data and has himself admitted that the 1952 study greatly overestimated the genetic factor. That is clear enough to anyone, because he reported that of thirty-seven pairs of identical twins, if one was homosexual, the other always was also, and if one was heterosexual, the other always was also. This result is called 100 percent concordance, and if we believed the sample of twins to have been representative and the determination of their monozygotic status well established, as well as their sexual orientations, the concordance would mean that homosexuality *and also heterosexuality* were under complete genetic control. In fact, we cannot believe that any of the necessary research conditions was satisfied, and it has become well known that there are identical twins who are not concordant for sexual orientation.

Heston and Shields, both eminent in behavioral genetics, also did a twin study. They worked from the Twin Register of Maudsley Hospital in London, which has been the research archive for much important work. Every mental patient admitted to the Maudsley Hospital since 1948 has been asked if she or he is a twin, and the answer recorded. For research purposes, one selects a sample of Maudsley twin patients with the characteristic of interest (usually it has been a mental illness), and those patients are called the "index" cases. It is then necessary to locate the co-twins of the index cases, and that can take years in a large study, as twins sometimes lose track of each other. It then remains to determine accurately whether the twins are identical or fraternal, a technical business involving blood tests, fingerprints, and so forth. The final question is whether the co-twin has the characteristic that the index case had, in which case the two are concordant, and if not, discordant.

Heston and Shields found for the entire period 1948–66 only four pairs of identical twins in which one, the index case, had been recorded as homosexual. All cases were, for some reason, males. Probably homosexuality was only entered in a record in cases of self-characterization as such. Of the four index cases (all homosexual by definition of index case), two had homosexual co-twins and two had heterosexual co-twins. That is a concordance of 50 percent. It is far below Kallmann's 100 percent but well above the concordance for the seven pairs of fraternal twins the researchers found, which was 14 percent (of seven homosexual index cases, six, or all but one, had heterosexual co-twins).

The Heston and Shields 14 percent concordance for fraternal twins is interesting to compare with certain results from the Kinsey Institute study of sexual preference (Bell, Weinberg, and Hammersmith, 1981). Their homosexual subjects, male and female, were asked if any of their siblings, brothers or sisters, were bisexual or homosexual. Between 11 percent and 12 percent thought at least one was. Genetic theory predicts the same concordance for fraternal twins as for siblings, and though the numbers are not exactly comparable for the fraternal twins and the Kinsey Institute siblings, because of differences of procedure, it is interesting to see that they are close together and larger than the percentages obtained in the institute study for siblings of heterosexual males and females. When the index cases, or starting points, are heterosexual, the percentages of homosexual siblings should be close to prevalence in the population as a whole, and the range obtained was 0–4 percent, which is the right order of magnitude. The Kinsey Institute finding that homosexual respondents reported more homosexual or bisexual siblings than did heterosexual respondents can stand on its own, without comparison with the Heston and Shields twins, as possible evidence for a genetic factor, but it is evidence that cannot count for much, because, of course, shared family experience could account for it just about as well as genetic theory.

The two studies that have been done are fascinating, but neither really *proves* anything. The numbers are so small and the circumstances so special that Heston and Shields adds up to little more than a case study. In addition, both of the studies are ultimately open to the logical objection as genetic evidence that the twins or siblings who turned out to be concordant may have been treated in the same way at some critical time in their lives. The way out of the dilemma that has been found for some mental illnesses is to study siblings adopted away from their biological families shortly after birth. No such studies have been made with respect to homosexuality.

Leading authorities like Money (1980) and Masters and Johnson (1979) assert that there is no evidence that any kind of homosexuality is seriously influenced by genetics, but for some reason they do not discuss the studies that were available. The sociobiologist E. O. Wilson (1978), on the other hand, does cite the studies and judges that they are "suggestive enough to justify further study" (p. 145). One thing that the homosexual twins in the Heston–Shields study told the people who interviewed them is interesting because it seems to fit the hypothesis that variations of fetal androgenization might be associated with homosexuality and because it can be checked against the data of the large-scale Kinsey Institute study of sexual preference. All twins reported that they had felt sexually attracted to other males and had thought of themselves as "different" in that respect—long before they had had any sexual experience, long before they had done anything homosexual. Notice that the private, and indeed concealed, mental state of homosexual arousal prior to any homosexual encounters fits the theory of fetal androgenization but does not fit theories that would make sexual conditioning the primary factor.

Survey Data Relevant to Learning and Constitutional Theories

The sexual preference study of Bell, Weinberg, and Hammersmith (1981) aimed at evaluating theories of the development of homosexuality and heterosexuality, and so a number of questions were asked (of adult interviewees) about their preadult, childhood, and adolescent feelings and experiences. The most crucial questions pertaining to the fetal androgenization and conditioning theories are those asking about first sexual feelings and first sexual encounters. A majority of both heterosexual and homosexual males reported preadult encounters of both kinds; there was little difference in what *happened* behaviorally to the two groups. There was, however, a large difference in early sexual *feelings*. I shall just cite the percentages for the 546 white homosexual males and the 261 white heterosexual males; findings for black males were similar (with an exception not relevant here), but the samples were smaller. Fifty-nine percent of white homosexual males reported that their feelings in childhood and adolescence were predominantly homosexual, whereas only 1 percent of white heterosexual males said so. Seventy-two percent of white heterosexual males reported that their feelings in childhood and adolescence were predominantly heterosexual, whereas only 5 percent of white homosexual males said so.

The results for females are very similar; I shall cite only those for the 220 white homosexual females and the 85 white heterosexual females, because, again, the findings for blacks are similar but the samples smaller. Forty-four percent of white homosexual females said that their feelings in childhood and adolescence were predominantly homosexual, whereas zero percent of white heterosexual females said so. Eighty-one percent of white heterosexual females reported that their feelings in childhood and adolescence had been predominantly heterosexual, whereas only 11 percent of white homosexual females said so.

The evidence that sexual orientations were established early and that feelings of arousal, predicting eventual dominant orientation, preceded homosexual or heterosexual activities argue that there is a predisposition to homosexuality or heterosexuality. That predisposition could be a delayed effect of the level of androgenization of the fetal brain, but of course there are many alternative possibilities. The evidence for predisposition is, however, important in any case since it rules out explanations in terms of the conditioning effects of essentially accidental early encounters. In addition, however, the strongest single developmental predictor of adult orientation discovered by the Kinsey Institute study is what was called "Childhood Gender Nonconformity." For boys that means the kind of behavior our culture punishes with the term "sissified." For girls it means the kind of behavior labeled, much less punishingly, "tomboyish." And tomboyism is, we recall, Money's term for the childhood behavior of all thirty of the fetally androgenized girls.

It is important, I think, to have some *verbatim* statements to give meaning to Gender Nonconformity. First, homosexual women, responding to the question: "In what ways do you think you were different from other girls your age?":

"I was a tomboy . . . . I thought I'd grow up to be a boy . . . . I had streaks of being feminine, but not very often." [p. 148]

"I was more masculine, more independent, more aggressive, more outdoorish." [p. 148]

"I didn't cry a lot. The other girls seemed to cry a lot." [p. 148]

"I didn't like girls' things such as sewing parties or paper dolls." [p. 145]

"I liked playing outdoors, football and baseball, and sort of ended up with the boys because of that." [p. 145]

"I didn't play with my dolls. I'd rather be out climbing trees and shooting marbles or playing soldier." [p. 145]

The replies quoted make it very clear, I think, that Childhood Gender Nonconformity for women means exactly the same thing as Money's tomboyism. Bell, Weinberg, and Hammersmith asked their women respondents, both homosexual and heterosexual, to say whether they enjoyed typical girls' activities, whether they enjoyed typical boys' activities, and also to rate themselves, when growing up, on a masculine–feminine scale. On all those variables the differences between heterosexual and homosexual women were enormous. Childhood Gender Nonconformity is a composite index that strongly predicts adult sexual orientation (Holeman and Winokur, 1965).

The ratings on the masculine–feminine scale must interest us, of course, because Chapter 9 deals with the assessment of masculinity–femininity. The women in the study done by the Kinsey Institute had no problem placing themselves on a one-dimensional bipolar scale explicitly labeled "masculine–feminine," and Storms (1979) found the same, using a direct explicit scale. Sixty-two percent of the white homosexual females rated themselves as having been "very masculine" when growing up and only 10 percent of the white heterosexual women reported this. It is especially interesting that the two groups did not differ at all in ascribing to themselves such undesirable but stereotypically feminine traits of temperament as *weak, passive, submissive,* and so on. In addition they differed very little on such desirable features of male temperament as *dominance.* Those results confirm the correctness of Spence's (1983) conclusion that instrumental and expressive traits of temperament are only weakly related to masculinity and femininity. The direction of early sexual arousal and childhood feelings about boys' and girls' activities and tastes are much nearer the essence of masculinity and femininity.

Here now are some homosexual men's answers to the question: "In what ways do you think you were different from other boys your age?":

"I didn't like baseball and that automatically makes you 'gay'." [p. 75]

"I wanted no involvement in sports where you have to prove your strength. I hated phys. ed. and sports." [p. 75]

"I was never a real boy. I was afraid of fighting." [p. 78]

"I was indifferent to boys' games, like cops and robbers. I was more interested in watching insects and reflecting on certain things." [p. 75]

Bell and co-workers asked their male respondents, both homosexual and heterosexual, to say whether they had enjoyed typical boys' activities; as the quotations suggest, the difference between the groups was enormous (70 percent of white heterosexual males said they had, and only 11 percent of white homosexual males said so). However, while the homosexual respondents were more likely than the heterosexual males to say they had liked girls activities, the majority of homosexual males did not say so. The majority reported most enjoying activities not closely linked stereotypically with sex, such as drawing, reading, and music. On the masculinity–femininity scale, few homosexual men said they had been "feminine" when growing up, but few also said they had been "very masculine" whereas 67 percent of white heterosexual males said the latter. The composite index called Childhood Gender Nonconformity is, as with the females, the single strongest developmental predictor of eventual sexual orientation. Traits of temperament like *submissive, passive,* and so forth were only slightly related to either masculinity–femininity or adult sexual orientation.

Everyone tends to think of the less common outcome as the only outcome to be explained, and with respect to sexual orientation the homosexual is less common than the heterosexual. Of course, both outcomes, all outcomes, are equally in need of explanation. It is important to reiterate that fact, because a too relentless attention to one outcome easily slides into an assumption that other outcomes are just "natural," and "natural" easily turns into "more desirable." If we ask what is the etiology of heterosexuality and review the results we have just described, we find the following: 72 percent of white heterosexual males said their feelings had been predominantly heterosexual from childhood on, and 81 percent of white heterosexual females said the same. Heterosexual males and females showed a high degree of what may be properly called Childhood Gender Conformity. Only 11 percent of white heterosexual males reported liking girls' activities even "somewhat." Sixty-seven percent had been "very masculine" in childhood and adolescence. Of white heterosexual females, only 28 percent reported liking boys' activities when growing up and only 21 percent said they had been "dominant." In short, the survey data for heterosexuals suggest that there is a biological predisposition for heterosexuality even as there may be for homosexuality.

The findings for male and female homosexuals are, in one respect, not parallel. The women characterized themselves as "masculine" and said they had in childhood disliked typical girls' activities and liked boys' activities. The men did not characterize themselves as "feminine" (only not "very masculine"), and while most had disliked boys' activities, the majority had not liked girls' activities. The asymmetry surely represents the basic inequality in our society of men and women. It is understandable that a girl might like boys' activities and characterize herself as masculine, because she is thereby manifesting something the society values—striving to "better herself," in an odd sense. For a boy to describe himself as feminine and liking girls' activities is doubly deviant and incomprehensible. He is not only departing from his sex role; he is striving after downward mobility. It is for that reason probably that the male homosexuals expressed aversion to stereotypic masculinity, but not attraction to stereotypic femininity. Male–female inequality is, by the same reasoning, the reason why "sissy" is a much more punishing term than "tomboy."

The Fetal Androgenization Theory

The results for Childhood Gender Nonconformity are in line with the hypothesis that the level of fetal androgenization of the brain is a determinant of adult sexual orientation. One important connecting link is Money's (1980) finding that females afflicted with the adrenogenital syndrome and known to have had high fetal androgenization to the point where the external genitals were not normal before surgery were, in childhood, all tomboys. The second important link is the 1984 report that 37 percent of the adrenogenital women rated themselves in young adulthood as either bisexual or homosexual. This is about all there is to go on, and a complete theory, for both males and females, would entail assuming much that is undemonstrated.

Even if all the assumptions are made, the theory has a considerable element of mystery. Stereotypical boys' activities are surely largely cultural and open to change; there can be no direct inevitable connection between baseball and level of fetal androgenization. The androgenization theory implies that somehow prenatal hormones determine attraction and aversion to whatever activities a given society regards as typically boys' activities and typically girls' activities. No one can say how that might work in detail. Still, it seems to work somehow in the known case of the adrenogenital-syndrome girls who become tomboys. It would be interesting to know what such girls are like in societies that do not have baseball, football, doll play, and so on. Perhaps outdoor, physical competitive sports are universally considered male activities even though baseball is not, and perhaps indoor rehearsals of parentalism are universally considered girls' activities though sewing may not be.

In view of the importance of his findings to the androgenization theory, it is important to know what Money himself said about the theory:

> There is a possibility that heterosexualism, bisexualism, and homosexualism—maybe transsexualism and transvestism also—are to some degree determined in a rather direct way by the amount of androgenic influence on the brain in prenatal life. If so, then there is no known way of specifying this degree, and the hypothesis itself, though scientifically legitimate, is still largely science-fictional with respect to proof. It is equally feasible to hypothesize that all people are potentially bisexual when born, and that some become postnatally differentiated to become exclusively heterosexual or homosexual, whereas others always retain their original bisexuality. [1980, p. 32]

The parallel between the Childhood Gender Nonconformity results and Money's finding of tomboyism in androgenized females seems to make the fetal androgenic influence theory slightly less science-fictional.

A Third Orientation?

The results we have so far seen all treat homosexual respondents as a single group, but we know that that group was defined by a range of scores on the Kinsey Scale (Figure 10-1) running from 2 to 6. Bell, Weinberg, and Hammersmith report some analyses that contrast the technical bisexuals, defined as rating themselves 2–4 on the Kinsey Scale, from the exclusive homosexuals, defined as 6. For bisexuals, male and female, early homosexual genital *activities* are important predictors of eventual orientation, but *activities* are not important for exclusive 6's. For 6's, you may recall, it is early developmental *feelings* of homosexual arousal, typically preceding any activities, that are important; for bisexuals, early feelings of arousal are not significantly different from the feelings of heterosexuals. That difference in the relative importance of activities or encounters, as opposed to feelings that precede encounters, suggests that some theory of social conditioning may fit the bisexual case better than the theory of fetal androgenization does.

Bisexuals are also unlike exclusive 6's in not reporting Childhood Gender Nonconformity, and that fact is consistent with the findings on arousal and activity. The bisexuals did not describe themselves as having been, in childhood, tomboys and sissies. This strongly tells against fetal androgenization in their case. Bell and co-workers conclude: "These findings seem to suggest that *exclusive homosexuality tends to emerge from a deep-seated predisposition, while bisexuality is more subject to influence by social and sexual learning*" (1981, italics all in original, p. 201). Concerning exclusive 6's, they say that *"our findings are not inconsistent with what one would expect to find if, indeed, there were a biological basis for sexual preference"* (p. 216). But: *"If there is a biological basis for homosexuality, it probably operates more powerfully for exclusive homosexuals than for bisexuals"* (p. 216).

If conditioning and learning are especially important in the etiology of bisexuality, we would expect the conditioning "therapies" to be more effective with bisexuals than with homosexuals. That is, you may recall, one of the few clear generalizations to emerge from the literature on behavior therapy. It is interesting to find Bell, Weinberg, and Hammersmith coming to the same conclusion by a different route:

> The biological basis would also be consistent with the study of homosexuality recently published by Masters and Johnson (1979). They claim to have had a high rate of success in "converting" or "reverting" homosexual men and women into heterosexuals. It should be noted, however, that 60 per cent of the men and women they "cured" were, at the time of treatment, heterosexually married! Thus, presumably, they were already bisexual rather than exclusively homosexual. (We are not told how many of the remaining 40 per cent were bisexual.) Indeed, our analysis of bisexuals on the one hand, and exclusive homosexuals, on the other, suggests that bisexuals are probably more susceptible to having their sexual responses altered by behavior "therapy." Exclusive homosexuality, we suspect, is probably more resistant to change because it seems more deeply ingrained. [1981, p. 217]

I want finally to set down a wild guess about bisexuality, or learned homosexuality, versus exclusive homosexuality in men and in women. The guess is wild because it is contrary to all the important surveys (especially Kinsey et al., 1953; Bell, Weinberg, and Hammersmith, 1981) in proposing that bisexuality, or acquired homosexuality, is more common, much more common, in women than in men. There are two principal reasons why that should be so. The first is that the social taboo on male homosexuality or bisexuality is today, and in Western civilization always has been, much more severe than the taboo on female homosexuality or bisexuality (Boswell, 1980). We see it most clearly in the asymmetries of the law, which have always made the male case criminal and said nothing about the female case.

The second cause is the inequality of the sexes in the United States and Western civilization generally. There are many kinds of evidence of it, but most relevant is the fact that male homosexual respondents in the Kinsey Institute survey, while they reported having disliked boys' activities in childhood, did not report having liked girls' activities, whereas female homosexual respondents freely reported preferring boys' games and finding girls' activities silly. They may have been gender-deviant, but they were upwardly mobile.

Since it is thought to be better to be male than to be female, worse to be a sissy than a tomboy, a crime to be a male homosexual but not to be a female homosexual, males have more and better reasons than females to learn to suppress any homosexual impulses they may have—if they can do so. Females have less reason to do so. It follows that the males who are homosexual at all are more likely to be so for unalterable biological reasons than are the females. The females not yet having been subjected to society's maximum force are more likely to be bisexual or experimentally homosexual when they need not be, as far as biological predisposition is concerned.

There is a third reason for suspecting acquired and alterable homosexuality to be more common in women than in men. It was suggested to me by a thoughtful leader of the Women's Movement. Awareness of male oppression, in her opinion, has in recent years moved many women toward lesbianism. The wish to be loved but not dominated, she thinks, may have caused 20–30 percent of women to experiment with female homosexuality. That is, of course, an estimate far higher than any the published surveys provide, but then it is not possible to do a really representative survey on the subject.

The Dimensionality of Orientation

We launched this section with the strong intuitions of Bem, Constantinople, Spence, and others (Chapter 9) that there was something about human sexuality not captured by the conception of one dimension and two poles. Of course, their intuitions led them into the study of temperament, not sexual orientation, but they did give the name "androgynous" to the new sort of personality that interested them, and *androgyny* means, among other things, bisexuality. And now in the end it seems there is something about human sexuality that is not captured by one dimension and two poles, and the condition that escapes this formulation is well-named "androgyny"—but in the sense of bisexuality. If we take as our starting point not masculinity–femininity but, rather, for each sex, the bipolar orientations homosexual–heterosexual, it appears that positions intermediate between the poles do not simply differ quantitatively from the extremes, but rather qualitatively.

Exclusive heterosexuality and exclusive homosexuality are both associated with predisposing feelings that generally precede encounters. There is no great difference in the nature of the encounters themselves; the early opportunities are similar, but exclusive heterosexuals find their heterosexual encounters most arousing and pleasurable, and exclusive homosexuals find their homosexual encounters most arousing and pleasurable. The extremes are alike in that it is feelings and not accidental events that matter. The extremes are also alike in that exclusive homosexuals manifest a high degree of Childhood Gender Nonconformity whereas the heterosexuals manifest a high degree of Childhood Gender Conformity. The extremes consider themselves to have been either very masculine or very feminine when growing up. All these things suggest that both exclusive heterosexuality and exclusive homosexuality are deeply rooted in biology. The bisexuals, those in the middle, seem to be different.

A bisexual orientation is apparently more related to early sexual activities than to early predisposing feelings. What happens, or the nature of their early encounters, is apparently significant for eventual adult orientation. The bisexuals in childhood apparently manifest neither extreme gender conformity nor extreme gender nonconformity. Those things suggest that social learning is more important and biological predisposition less important for bisexuals than for either sort of exclusive orientation. In addition, we know that behavior "therapy," some kind of learning procedure, is more effective with bisexuals than with exclusive homosexuals. No one has tried by behavior "therapy" to change the orientation of exclusive heterosexuals, so far as I know, but presumably they would be at least as refractory to change as are exclusive homosexuals. Again, a strong suggestion that the relative significance of biological predisposition as opposed to learning is greater at the extremes than in the middle.

Storms (1980) had 185 subjects (recruited so as to get sizable numbers with all orientations) rate themselves on the Kinsey Scale (Figure 10-1) and also categorize themselves on the threefold scheme: "straight, gay, or bisexual." He found that the Kinsey ratings and the self-categorizations agreed perfectly in .that those who rated themselves at 0 or 1 categorized themselves as "straight"; those who rated themselves at the opposite extreme, 5 or 6, all categorized themselves as "gay"; and those who rated themselves in the middle, positions 2, 3, or 4, rated themselves as "bisexual." The investigator devised a paper-and-pencil test to inquire about erotic fantasies involving males or females. He thought it possible that bisexuals would, with respect to erotic fantasy, not simply fall between the extremes, but, rather, match both. He tested the hypothesis that bisexuals would have as much homosexual fantasy as homosexuals and also as much heterosexual fantasy as heterosexuals. That is the way the results came out. If those results stand up to further testing and critical analysis, then it will have turned out, after all, that there is a way of being both highly masculine and highly feminine—not, as originally thought, in temperament, but in sexual or erotic orientation.

Clearly the domain of sexuality is fluid today, and I trust it is also clear that all the ideas put forth are still highly speculative. They have been set down for their interest, not their certainty. Among those ideas, one of the most interesting surely is the fetal androgenization, biological theory of homosexuality. I think it is important if such a theory is expressed to make clear that its consequences ought to be helpful to gay men and women and not damaging. Bell and colleagues have eloquently said why this is so:

> Should it ever be discovered with more certainty that homosexuality is derived primarily from physiological origins what might be the implications for society? First, those who argue that homosexuality is "unnatural" will be forced to reconsider their belief because something that is biologically innate must certainly be natural for a particular person, regardless of how unusual it may be. People might ultimately come to the conclusion that everyone is unique, biologically and socially, and that natural physiological factors will make it inevitable that a certain percentage of people in any society will be fundamentally homosexual regardless of whether they are momentarily (or even continuously) engaged in heterosexual behaviors. This conclusion would make the moral condemnation of homosexuality even more indefensible, and it would reaffirm that discrimination against homosexuals is clearly no more justified than discrimination against redheads or blue-eyed persons. [Bell, Weinberg, and Hammersmith, 1981, p. 219]

Summary

Sexual orientations concern objects of desire who may be *homo* (same sex), *hetero* (other sex), or bisexual. The traditional belief has been that mental health was in part defined by an exclusively heterosexual orientation. The Kinsey Institute volumes called *Homosexualities* and *Sexual Preference* have shown that there are various homosexual life-styles and that mental health is more closely associated with life-style than with homosexuality itself.

The etiologies of the heterosexualities and homosexualities are undoubtedly multiple and undoubtedly combine learning of several types with constitutional factors. It has been demonstrated beyond all doubt that autonomic sexual arousal can be classically conditioned and that sexually instrumental operant responses can be made more and less probable by positive and negative reinforcement. Sexual conditioned responses also operate like other responses in stimulus and response generalization, extinction, spontaneous recovery, and so on. However, explicit clear theories of etiology in terms of conditioning (e.g. first encounters and age of adolescence) are not supported by answers to relevant questions asked in Kinsey Institute surveys. Behavior therapy, a family of modification methods loosely derived from conditioning phenomena, when used to change sexual orientation or eliminate paraphilias, is limited in what it can accomplish. Arousal to "inappropriate" stimuli can be temporarily eliminated, and in bisexual self-referred men heterosexual coitus can be made primary, but the evidence is that exclusive homosexuality cannot be reversed by behavior modification. Some techniques of modification, especially the aversive therapies, are so much like severe corporal punishment that they surely ought not to be mandated by courts for harmless sex offenses.

With respect to the sex hormones, it has not been demonstrated that adult homosexuals, male or female, differ from adult heterosexuals in any consistent way. There is, however, some reason to think that prenatal exposure to various levels of the sex hormones, especially the androgens, could constitute a biological predisposition to heterosexuality or homosexuality. There is also a very small amount of evidence from twin studies that one or more kinds of homosexuality might have a genetic basis—possibly the primary cause of the prenatal hormonal differences.

The most significant evidence supporting the idea that levels of *in utero* androgenization predispose sexual orientation is Money's report of tomboyism in thirty girls who had the adrenogenital syndrome with surgical and hormonal treatments to feminize them. That evidence seems to be in accord with the fact that Childhood Gender Nonconformity (tomboy and sissy behavior and feelings) was the strongest developmental predictor of adult homosexuality in the Kinsey Institute study. It also agrees well with the finding in the same study that feelings of same-sex attraction in childhood and adolescence were more important than same-sex encounters in predicting adult homosexuality and also typically antedated such encounters. Those Kinsey Institute findings offer more support for some biological predisposition in sexual orientation than they do for a pure learning theory.

In the Kinsey Institute population, homosexuals were defined by a range of scores on the Kinsey Scale, from 2 to 6. When bisexuals (2–4) and exclusive homosexuals (6) are separately analyzed, the former seem to have had their sexual orientations more determined by learning whereas, for the latter, biological predisposition seems to have been more important.

It appears that human erotic orientation is not well described with one dimension and two poles. There is a group, properly called *androgynous*, that is not simply intermediate but qualitatively distinct. The distinctiveness seems to be in the nature, etiology, and modifiability of sexual orientation, and the group is *androgynous* not in the sense of temperamental androgyny but in the sense of bisexuality.

References for Part IV

BAKAN, D. 1966. *The Duality of Human Existence*. Chicago: Rand McNally.

BARKER, J. 1965. Behavior therapy for transvestitism: A comparison of pharmacological and electric aversion techniques, *British Journal of Psychiatry*, 111: 268–76.

BARRY, H.; M. K. BACON; and I. L. CHILD. 1957. A cross-cultural survey of some sex differences in socialization, *Journal of Abnormal and Social Psychology*, 55: 327–32.

BEACH, F. A. 1948. *Hormones and Behavior: A Survey of Interrelationships Between Endocrine Secretion and Patterns of Overt Response*. New York: Hoeber.

BELL, A. P., and M. S. WEINBERG. 1978. *Homosexualities*. New York: Simon & Schuster.

BELL, A. P.; M. S. WEINBERG; S. F. HAMMERSMITH. 1981. *Sexual Preference*. Bloomington: Indiana University Press.

BEM, S. L. 1974. The measurement of psychological androgyny, *Journal of Consulting and Clinical Psychology*, 42: 155–62.

———. 1975. Sex role adaptability: One consequence of psychological androgyny, *Journal of Personality and Social Psychology*, 31: 634–43.

———. 1976. Probing the promise of androgyny. In A. G. Kaplan and J. P. Bean (eds.), *Beyond Sex-Role Stereotypes: Readings Toward a Psychology of Androgyny*. Boston: Little, Brown, pp. 48–62.

———. 1977. On the utility of alternative procedures for assessing psychological androgyny, *Journal of Consulting and Clinical Psychology*, 45: 196–205.

———. 1978. Beyond androgyny: Some presumptuous prescriptions for a liberated sexual identity. In J. Sherman and F. Denmark (eds.), *Psychology of Women: Future Directions in Research*. New York: Psychological Dimensions, pp. 3–23.

———. 1981a. The BSRI and gender schema theory: A reply to Spence and Helmreich, *Psychological Review*, 88: 369–71.

———. 1981b. Gender schema theory: A cognitive account of sex typing, *Psychological Review*, 88: 354–64.

———. 1984. Androgyny and gender schema theory: A conceptual and empirical integration. In R. A. Dienstbier (ed.), *Nebraska Symposium on Motivation*. Lincoln: University of Nebraska Press, pp. 179–226.

BEM, S. L., and E. LENNEY. 1976. Sex-typing and the avoidance of cross-sex behavior, *Journal of Personality and Social Psychology*, 33: 48–54.

BEM, S. L.; W. MARTYNA; and C. WATSON. 1976. Sex-typing and androgyny: Further exploration of the expressive domain, *Journal of Personality and Social Psychology*, 34: 1016–23.

BIRKE, L. I. A. 1981. Is homosexuality hormonally determined? *Journal of Homosexuality*, 6: 35–49.

BOSWELL, J. 1980. *Christianity, Social Tolerance, and Homosexuality*. Chicago: University of Chicago Press.

BROVERMAN, I. K.; S. R. VOGEL; D. M. BROVERMAN; F. E. CLARKSON; and P. S. ROSENKRANTZ. 1972. Sex-role stereotypes: A current appraisal, *Journal of Social Issues*, 28: 59–78.

CONSTANTINOPLE, A. 1973. Masculinity–femininity: An exception to a famous dictum? *Psychological Bulletin, 80:* 389–407.

CRAIGHEAD, W. E.; A. E. KAZDIN; and M. J. MAHONEY. 1981. *Behavior Modification, Principles, Issues, and Applications.* 2d ed. Boston: Houghton Mifflin.

DÖRNER, G. 1976. *Hormones and Brain Differentiation.* Amsterdam: Elsevier.

FRIEDAN, B. 1963. *The Feminine Mystique.* New York: Dell.

GIBBON, E. 1898. *The History of the Decline and Fall of the Roman Empire.* D. Milman, M. Guizot, and W. Smith (eds.). London.

GOUGH, H. G. 1952. Identifying psychological femininity, *Educational and Psychological Measurement, 12:* 427–39.

GUILFORD, J. P., and R. B. GUILFORD. 1936. Personality factors, S, E, and M and their measurement, *Journal of Psychology, 2:* 109–27.

HAMPSON, J. L., and J. G. HAMPSON. 1961. The ontogenesis of sexual behavior in man. In W. C. Young (ed.), *Sex and Internal Secretions.* Baltimore: Williams and Wilkins, II: 1401–32.

HARRY, J. 1984. *Gay Couples.* New York: Praeger.

HATHAWAY, S. R., and J. C. MCKINLEY. 1943. *The Minnesota Multiphasic Personality Inventory.* New York: Psychological Corporation.

HESTON, L. L., and J. SHIELDS. 1968. Homosexuality in twins, *Archives of General Psychiatry, 18:* 149–60.

HILGARD, E. R., and D. G. MARQUIS. 1940. *Conditioning and Learning.* New York: D. Appleton-Century.

HOLEMAN, R. E., and G. WINOKUR. 1965. Effeminate homosexuality: A disease of childhood, *American Journal of Orthopsychiatry, 35:* 48–56.

IMPERATO–MCGINLEY, J.; R. E. PETERSON; and T. GAUTIER. 1976. Gender identity and hermaphroditism, *Science, 191:* 872.

KALLMANN, F. J. 1952. Comparative twin study on the genetic aspects of male homosexuality, *Journal of Nervous and Mental Diseases, 115:* 283–98.

KAPLAN, A. G. 1976. Androgyny as a model of mental health for women: From theory to therapy. In A. G. Kaplan and J. P. Bean (eds.), *Beyond Sex-Role Stereotypes: Readings Toward a Psychology of Androgyny.* Boston: Little, Brown, pp. 353–62.

KAPLAN, A. G., and J. P. BEAN (eds.). 1976. *Beyond Sex-Role Stereotypes: Readings Toward a Psychology of Androgyny.* Boston: Little, Brown.

KINSEY, A. C.; W. B. POMEROY; and C. E. MARTIN. 1948. *Sexual Behavior in the Human Male.* Philadelphia: Saunders.

KINSEY, A. C.; W. B. POMEROY; C. E. MARTIN; and P. H. GEBHARD. 1953. *Sexual Behavior in the Human Female.* Philadelphia: Saunders.

LARSON, P. C. 1981. Sexual identity and self-concept, *Journal of Homosexuality, 7:* 15–32.

LUBINSKI, D.; A. TELLEGEN; and J. N. BUTCHER. 1983. Masculinity, Femininity, and Androgyny. *Journal of Personality and Social Psychology, 44:* 428–39.

LUNNEBORG, P. W. 1970. Stereotypic aspects in masculinity–femininity measurement, *Journal of Consulting and Clinical Psychology, 34:* 113–18.

MACCOBY, E. E., and C. N. JACKLIN. 1974. *The Psychology of Sex Differences.* Stanford, Calif.: Stanford University Press.

MASTERS, W. H., and V. E. JOHNSON. 1979. *Homosexuality in Perspective*. Boston: Little, Brown.

McCONAGHY, N. 1967. Penile volume changes to moving pictures of male and female nudes in heterosexual and homosexual males, *Behaviour Research and Therapy*, 5: 43–48.

———. 1970. Penile response conditioning and its relationship to aversion therapy in homosexuals, *Behavior Therapy*, 1: 213–21.

McGUIRE, R. J.; J. M. CARLISLE; and B. G. YOUNG. 1965. Sexual deviations as conditioned behavior: A hypothesis, *Behavior Research and Therapy*, 2: 185–90.

McWHIRTER, D. P., and A. M. MATTISON. 1984. *The Male Couple: How Relationships Develop*. Englewood Cliffs, N.J.: Prentice-Hall.

MILLETT, K. 1970. *Sexual Politics*. New York: Doubleday.

MONEY, J. 1980. *Love and Love Sickness: The Science of Sex, Gender Difference and Pair-Bonding*. Baltimore: Johns Hopkins Press.

———. 1984. Gender-transposition theory and homosexual genesis, *Journal of Sex and Marital Therapy*, 10: 75–82.

MONEY, J., and A. A. EHRHARDT. 1972. *Man and Woman; Boy and Girl*. Baltimore: Johns Hopkins Press.

MONEY, J.; M. SCHWARTZ; and V. G. LEWIS. 1984. Adult erotosexual status and fetal hormonal masculinization and demasculinization: 46,XX congenital virilizing adrenal hyperplasia and 46,XY androgen-insensitivity syndrome compared, *Psychoneuroendocrinology*, 9: 405–14.

PARSONS, T., and R. F. BALES. 1955. *Family Socialization and Interaction Process*. Glencoe, Ill.: Free Press.

PEDHAZUR, E. J., and T. J. TETENBAUM. 1979. Bem Sex Role Inventory: A theoretical and methodological critique, *Journal of Personality and Social Psychology*, 37: 996–1016.

PEPLAU, L. A. 1982. Research on homosexual couples: An overview, *Journal of Homosexuality*, 8: 3–8.

RACHMAN, S. 1966. Sexual fetishism: An experimental analogue, *Psychological Record*, 16: 293–96.

RACHMAN, S., and R. HODGSON. 1968. Experimentally-induced "sexual fetishism": Replication and development, *Psychological Record*, 18: 25–27.

REINISCH, J. M., and W. G. KAROW. 1977. Prenatal exposure to synthetic progestins and estrogens: Effects on human development, *Archives of Sexual Behavior*, 6: 257–88.

RIMM, D. C., and J. C. MASTERS. 1979. *Behavior Therapy: Techniques and Empirical Findings*. New York: Academic Press.

SAGHIR, M. T., and E. ROBINS. 1973. *Male and Female Homosexuality*. Baltimore: Williams & Wilkins.

SHIVELY, M. G., and J. P. DeCECCO. 1978. Sexual orientation survey of students on the San Francisco State University campus, *Journal of Homosexuality*, 4: 29–40.

SPENCE, J. T. 1983. Comment on Lubinski, Tellegen, and Butcher's "Masculinity, femininity, and androgyny viewed and assessed as distinct concepts," *Journal of Personality and Social Psychology*, 44: 440–46.

SPENCE, J. T., and R. L. HELMREICH. 1978. *Masculinity and Femininity*. Austin: University of Texas Press.

——. 1981. Androgyny versus gender schema: A comment on Bem's gender schema theory, *Psychological Review*, 88: 365–68.

Spence, J. T.; R. L. HELMREICH; and C. K. HOLAHAN. 1979. Negative and positive components of psychological masculinity and femininity and their relationships to self-reports of neurotic and acting out behaviors, *Journal of Personality and Social Psychology*, 37: 1673–82.

SPENCE, J. T.; R. L. HELMREICH; and J. STAPP. 1974. The Personal Attributes Questionnaire: A measure of sex-role stereotypes and masculinity–femininity, *JSAS Catalog of Selected Documents in Psychology*, 4: 43.

——. 1975. Ratings of self and peers on sex role attributes and their relation to self-esteem and conceptions of masculinity and femininity, *Journal of Personality and Social Psychology*, 32: 29–39.

STORMS, M. D. 1979. Sex role identity and its relationships to sex role attributes and sex role stereotypes, *Journal of Personality and Social Psychology*, 37: 1779–89.

——. 1980. Theories of sexual orientation, *Journal of Personality and Social Psychology*, 38: 783–92.

——. 1981. A theory of erotic orientation development, *Psychological Review*, 88: 340–53.

STRONG, E. K. 1943. *Vocational Interests of Men and Women.* Stanford, Calif.: Stanford University Press.

SUPPE, F. 1981. The Bell and Weinberg study: Future priorities for research on homosexuality, *Journal of Homosexuality*, 6: 69–97.

SWYER, G. I. 1954. Homosexuality: The endocrine aspects, *Practitioner*, 172: 374.

TERMAN, L. M., and C. C. MILES. 1936. *Sex and Personality.* New York: McGraw-Hill.

TIGER, L., and R. FOX. 1971. *The Imperial Animal.* New York: Holt, Rinehart & Winston.

TVERSKY, A., and D. KAHNEMAN. 1973. Availability: A heuristic for judging frequency and probability, *Cognitive Psychology*, 5: 207–32.

WILSON, E. O. 1978. *On Human Nature.* Cambridge: Mass.: Harvard University Press.

YATES, A. J. 1970. *Behavior Therapy.* New York: Wiley.

11

Impressions of Personality

IN SOME WAYS the field of impression formation or person perception is more advanced than any other in social psychology. The people studying impression formation are able to ask questions on a level of detail that is extraordinary. For instance, suppose someone knows that another person has engaged in particular actions (doing a certain favor, telling a difficult truth) that suggest certain traits (e.g. kindness, honesty) and both the behavioral facts and the inferred traits have been stored in memory. Are the facts and the inferred traits stored separately, and do both affect later judgments of the person perceived, or do the trait implications take over, leaving the stimulus information about actions without any influence, or can both kinds of information be retrieved (Allen and Ebbesen, 1981; Carlston, 1980; Lingle, Dukerich, and Ostrom, 1983; Ostrom et al., 1980; Wyer and Gordon, 1982; Wyer, Srull, and Gordon, 1984)?

Research that poses questions on the level illustrated clearly aims high; it aims, in fact, at nothing less than completely explicit information-processing models of mental operations (Wyer and Srull, 1984). The high aim entails a cost for the nonspecialist. In order to study very detailed cognitive processes, a certain *impoverishment* of stimulus materials seems inevitable, and so what we have are mostly experiments on trait names (adjectives), verbal descriptions of action (sentences), occasionally still photos, and, very rarely, videotapes. For the new student that impoverishment is a serious barrier. We cannot easily grasp what it is that led the cognitive-processing people to *care* about the questions they ask; the original lure is lost. Therefore, indulge me, please, in an anecdote that serves, I think, to show how juicy and consequential a topic impression formation ultimately is, even though its contemporary embrace is a bit dry.

It happened on a spring break, the year I went to Nassau in the Bahamas. I remember that from the air everything looked even better than advertised. You've seen the pictures: pale green water turning emerald and then deep blue, with a fringe of froth around each island. The bus ride from the airport to the Paradise Beach Hotel was less idyllic, but then no brochure ever includes the bus ride. The tweed suit that one wore in Boston in March and never noticed there took on weight and a scratchy texture under the Caribbean sun. The roadside hibiscus blooms were dusty, the azaleas scraggly, and it was hard to penetrate the driver's Bahamian accent when he called out the stops.

At the registration desk of the Paradise Hotel, impression formation began. The clerk there was the first person in the Bahamas whom I could expect to see multiple times and so learn to recognize. There are various ways of conceptualizing the initiation in the mind of a personality impression. John Anderson (1977), thinking in terms of a model of memory called "HAM" (for "Human Associative Memory"), thinks of impression formation, or person perception, as beginning with an individual "node" that will eventually become connected by "pathways" to many other nodes. We can just as well think of it as starting with the creation of a new file or dossier into which information of many kinds will eventually be placed.

It is not known just what the minimal conditions are for starting a new individual node. It is not sufficient to see a person in a crowd with no expectation of future contact, and it is too much to require an introduction. We have many nodes in memory not labeled with proper names: people who work in the same building or who catch the same subway, people we recognize and nod to but who are anonymous for us. The information at those minimal nodes probably does not go much beyond sex, age, an attractiveness rating, possibly race, and a guess at socioeconomic status.

The registration clerk would not make eye contact but, looking just past my left ear, said something I could not make out, though it was certainly English. On the third repeat it came through as "Wel-kum to the Paradise Ho'-tel." The sentence stresses were syncopated in the Bahamian manner, but the intonation was very flat. In fact the whole manner seemed unfriendly or truculent, and some such trait entries were made along with male, Bahamian, desk clerk.

The bellmahn, definitely not a bellboy, became my second Bahamian node. He was a long time arriving—by American standards at least—and a short time leaving. His interest in showing me how things worked in the room was minimal. A personality entry encoding his expressive style would have to read "unfriendly." I rushed out to the beach and found it narrow and crowded. No new nodes started there that day. Back in the room I found out that Bahamian television was black and white, British-controlled, relentlessly educational, and not on after nine P.M. Every little Bahamian house triumphantly sported a tall aerial to bring in, twenty-four hours a day, the many splendored vulgarities of American TV, but not the Paradise Hotel.

At breakfast next morning I met my third Bahamian, a waitress. Waitresses in the United States understand that at breakfast they are supposed to be nurturant, to wean us from sleep and gradually reconcile us to the day. If the Bahamian waitress knew the role, she chose not to play it. The menu was slapped down, no substitutes were possible, and the coffee would come when it came. A third node labeled "unfriendly, rude," and the like.

Besides forming impressions at the individual level, my mind was forming impressions at the categorical level—not at my direction, but just because it would. The three individual nodes were connected to a Bahamian node, and all the unfavorable impressions entered at the individual level were being automatically "copied" at the categorical level. The creation of a Bahamian node was impossible to prevent. Never mind the shared dialect and the service positions; the important thing was that Bahamians are black. Not American Negro black, but a blackness that suggested no interbreeding since the days of slavery. And so there was growing in my brain a node labeled: "Bahamian, Black, Unfriendly, Truculent, Rude." In fact it was a racial stereotype, and not even a stereotype anyone had ever heard of before. I was making a contribution to bigotry!

However, the new growth in my brain conflicted with an old growth, my self-concept or self-schema. It cannot be said that psychological understanding of the self-schema is very advanced. It is clear that it has to be constructed and is not simply given from within. Daryl Bem (1972) has shown that in making this construction we draw inferences from our own behavior just as we draw inferences from the behavior of another in making ordinary person schemas or nodes. In part we are in the position of another vis-à-vis the self but in part, of course, not. We have, as Bem puts it, some 3 or 4 feet of potential stimuli inside us that are available for inferences and unavailable to others, and we have knowledge of our past as well as unspoken feelings and thoughts.

There is one method for studying the self-schema that I have always mistrusted: the self-descriptive trait inventory of the sort that asks you to indicate in what degree you are "sociable" or "unsociable," "dominant" or "submissive," "conscientious" or otherwise. My usual reaction is that I have never thought about it, that I do not conceive of myself as a bundle of traits (see Chapter 5).

Hazel Markus (1977; Markus et al., 1982) has solved for me the problem of the intuitively unrealistic self-descriptive inventory with the simple idea of distinguishing with regard to any trait, not just those who are high and low but also those for whom the trait is "aschematic." If you are aschematic with respect to any particular trait, then that trait does not figure in your self-concept, because you do not believe that your behavior is consistent across situations on that dimension.

Working with the trait "dependent-independent" in women, Markus has shown the difference between being one or the other and being aschematic in this dimension. Women who were dependent or independent rated themselves as extreme one way or the other on the dimension and, in addition, rated the trait itself as an important one. They were furthermore able, on request, to give numerous examples of specific actions they had taken or would take in which the trait was expressed, and when an effort was made to get them to believe information that ran counter to their self-schemas (as dependent or independent), they resisted it. The woman for whom "dependent–independent" was aschematic, if forced to rate herself on that dimension, chose a moderate position but felt that it would be more accurate to say that she was dependent in some situations and independent in others. She was slow to think of actions expressing the trait and did not resist counterschematic information.

With respect to dependence–independence, friendly–unfriendly, dominant–submissive, and many other standards of the self-descriptive inventory, I think I am aschematic but not with respect to all and especially not with respect to a characteristic that forbids the development of ethnic stereotypes. I think of myself as extremely nonracist and would unhesitatingly check that position on a self-descriptive inventory. Furthermore, I can pass all the Markus tests. The trait called "nonracist" is an important one to me. Illustrative incidents? A good friend once said wonderingly, "Roger never knows whether or not someone is Jewish; it doesn't occur to him to think about it." At the University Health Serivce if I am assigned to a Pakistani woman physician, with a diamond in her nostril, I do not flinch. Resistance to counterschematic information? That is what you are about to see.

The belief that Bahamians in general have certain undesirable qualities does not count as an ethnic stereotype unless you think the qualities are caused by the ethnicity, arise inevitably from the nationality. Attribution is everything. We have plenty of beliefs about groups and cannot help having them, especially when they are perceptually based, as with the Bahamians. The critical thing is: What do you think causes those qualities you believe in? I never even entertained the idea that Bahamian unfriendliness was an innate ethnic quality. I attributed Bahamian unfriendliness to the way they were treated by others. What others? Tourists, of course. Year after year, all year long, Bahamians had to accommodate to spoiled, critical foreigners. It would be enough to turn anyone unfriendly.

After two days in which my conception of Bahamians did not change, I recollected that I was supposed to be a social psychologist and an empiricist and so that I really ought not to leave the island without finding out the facts. As informant, I chose a taxi driver who was an irrepressible talker and so easy to question. My tactful beginning was: "I guess the Bahamian people are pretty fed up with tourists." He looked at me incredulously, then beamed and said: "They don't mind the tourists. You got to smile at them, mahn."

And then I realized what had been going on. Not tourists generally, but this tourist, myself, was the cause. Confronted with my unrelaxed wintry Boston face, they had assumed I had no interest in them and had responded non-committally, inexpressively. I had created the Bahamian national character. Everywhere I took my face it sprang into being. So I began smiling a lot, and the Bahamians changed their national character. In fact, they lost any national character and differentiated into individuals.

The story makes some general points. We do quite often feed several nodes (or dossiers or files) with data from just one individual and almost always do so when we think of the individual as the first of some type. The individual will have membership in some city or nation, some occupation and age group, and, of course, gender, though dossiers on gender are likely to be pretty full and sometimes seem to be sealed. We do not use each individual as a source of data on all the groups to which he belongs and can even fall into the habit of disregarding some with the occasional result that what are really group charac-teristics are mistaken for personality. If you go to one of the Big Ten universities from a city in the Midwest, as I did, the first girl you meet from New York City is likely to seem to have the most extraordinarily original personality you have ever encountered. Until you meet half a dozen other girls from New York and learn that the "personality" is 99 percent New York generic. She, in turn, will learn that you are 99 percent Indiana standard.

The story makes two points with respect to the contrast, discussed in Part II, of personal and situational causality. The conception you form of another person is partly a function of yourself as stimulus. It should follow that you see the other as more consistent than he sees himself since you have little knowl-edge of his interaction with third parties. Any person's self-concept ought to be less simply consistent than the corresponding conception of that person formed by others, simply because any single other will depend upon a sample of behavior biased by his presence (see the actor–observer divergence in Chap-ter 5).

The distinction Hazel Markus has made between persons who are self-schematic with respect to a given trait and persons who are aschematic with respect to that same trait should, perhaps, always be taken into account in stu-dying the consistency of personality, but, since the distinction is fairly new, it seldom has been. There are many studies showing very low personal con-sistency in traits across situations, but perhaps consistency with respect to a standard grid of traits imposed from without on everyone alike is not to be expected. Perhaps there is high personality consistency in everyone with respect to those traits that are self-schematic for each one. I conceive of myself as nonracist, and I would be surprised if I am not consistent on this dimension. Perhaps those of Milgram's subjects (Chapter 1) who did not obey the teacher and those of Asch's subjects (Chapter 1) who did not conform were persons for whom independence was a trait in the self-schema.

Not all of the phenomena alluded to in the Bahamian anecdote have been studied by social psychologists, and not all that have been studied can be discussed here. The first important thing to say about impressions of persons is that they are unified: Traits, actions, facts, and appearance are all closely connected in memory even though the information about a person is not ordinarily received as a continuous block but is interspersed in a rather random way among other kinds of information, including information about other persons. The process of person unification was long taken for granted by students of impression formation, as it was taken for granted in the Bahamian anecdote, which made one node of the registration clerk, another of the bellmahn, and another of the waitress. However, Thomas Ostrom and John Pryor and their associates (Ostrom et al., 1980; Ostrom, Pryor, and Simpson, 1981; Pryor and Ostrom, 1981; Pryor et al., 1982) have shown that social information, information involving persons, is not necessarily organized in terms of persons. Other kinds of preintegrative organization are possible.

The second important thing to say about person impression, probably the most important thing of all, is that such impressions are *integrated*. That was the main point of the very first research, published in 1946 by Solomon Asch and reiterated and clarified by him (Asch and Zukier) in 1984. Integration means, in the first place, that impressions of persons always go beyond the information given; they strain toward completeness even when the data base is very small. Integration means, in the second place, that each item of information is interpreted in the light of all the others, that each part takes its character from the whole. What is it that guides us in going beyond what we know and in adjusting the parts to one another? It is some kind of implicit personality theory, some unconscious notion, often very simple, of how persons are constituted, how they hang together. In the integration process not all information carries equal weight; a principle of primacy operates, and also a principle of centrality. This is the terrain to be covered: preintegrative organization of unification, integration in terms of implicit personality theories, and primacy and centrality.

Preintegrative Organization (Unification of Persons)

The process works so well and seems so natural that it is necessary first to realize that there is a problem. Conceive of a cocktail party where the quests are mostly strangers, which has reached that advanced stage when conversations become quite fragmentary. One might be told by Bill that he is divorced, notice that Susan is attractive, overhear someone say that she is a stewardess, be told by Bill that his work is mining and by Abe that he is a surgeon with four kids, note that Bill drinks beer, and so on (Ostrom, Pryor, and Simpson, 1981). The important thing to notice about that stream of information is that it is not blocked by person. That is, we do not learn all the facts about Bill before learning anything about Susan nor all about Susan before learning anything about Abe. That is the way we usually build person impressions; information extends over time and is interspersed rather than blocked, though sometimes blocking does occur, as when one reads a set of application folders, one folder after another.

Very many experiments (e.g. Puff, 1973) have shown that temporal blocking of information input facilitates memory organization in accordance with blocks, and that is true of information about persons. While interspersed input on persons is more common than blocked input in life, blocked input has been more common in research, probably because Asch started things off that way, so the unification process largely escaped notice until the 1980s. In order to make it clear that there could be preintegrative organization that was not in terms of persons, Pryor and Ostrom have in their experiments usually used an interspersed format.

How might social information be organized in terms other than person impression? A dinner party is a sustained stretch of social information that can be organized in more than one way. If all the guests know one another, person organization is most probable, but suppose most are strangers and do not expect to meet soon again. In such circumstances one might remember the evening in terms that are spatial and temporal: drinks in the living room, dinner in the dining room, partings in the hall. Or one might pay little heed either to persons or places and organize by conversational themes, recalling first an argument against legalized abortion, then a rejoinder, and a further rejoinder before recalling any part of another discussion. It is also quite clear from experience that more than one organization can be imposed upon a given flow of information by the same person.

The question not yet answered is how can the mode of memory organization be discovered when multiple modes are possible? Of the several methods that have been used (Pryor and Ostrom, 1981) the best is the assessment of clustering in free recall. Clustering has been used to study memory organization of verbal materials ever since Bousfield (1953) gave subjects a list of words to memorize which interspersed names of animals with names of flowers and then asked subjects to recall as many names as they could, in any order they liked. They tended to list animals sequentially together at one point and flowers together at another. That kind of temporal clustering of output has been shown in several ways to be a valid reflection of memory organization.

We need, I think a situation that is realistic and familiar but not too different from the paradigms that have been used in real experiments. Imagine a small section meeting directed by a teaching fellow, the first meeting of a section arbitrarily constituted from among the hundreds of students taking some introductory course of very general interest, like Economics I. Imagine that no one recognizes anyone or knows anyone's name, and so the instructor suggests that the members take turns giving their names, fields of concentration, home towns, and vocations or hobbies. Everyone then hears social information of this kind:

Timothy Clark, classics, Detroit, guitar
Joseph Williams, economics, New York, rowing

Humphrey Turnbull, psychology, Los Angeles, Gilbert and Sullivan society
Richard Lennon, political science, Boston, school paper
Lawrence Stouffer, folklore, Reno, bird watching
William Winthrop, sociology, Atlanta, writing poetry

Everyone in the room has heard the same social information: A set of new proper names and with each name what may be called three "descriptors," or items of information. Everyone will be able to recall some of this information, but probably not all. The question is, How has the recallable information been stored in memory? Until Pryor and Ostrom thought to question it, students of impression formation assumed, as does the layman, that social information is automatically and always stored in terms of persons. In the present case that would mean the three descriptors attached to the same name would cluster together.

Breaking with the lifelike situation, suppose now that all class members are asked to recall as much information as possible about the characteristics of members of the group—exclusive of the proper names. The organization in memory of the information recalled is to be inferred from the way in which the items recalled in succession are clustered. For instance, a perfect recall, in terms of persons, might look like this:

classics, guitar, Detroit/school paper, political science Boston/Reno, bird watching, folklore/Gilbert and Sullivan society, psychology, Los Angeles/Atlanta, sociology, writing poetry/economics, rowing, New York

What is significant about this pattern of recall (which is highly idealized) is that all the facts about each person are exhausted before any facts about another person are presented, and so the recalled facts cluster *in terms of persons* and presumably are so organized in memory. It is as if six person nodes had been started and the descriptions attached to the appropriate nodes. In effect, this idealized subject has recalled: Timothy Clark, Richard Lennon, Lawrence Stouffer, Humphrey Turnbull, William Winthrop, Joseph Williams. Except that he has not given their names since he was not asked to, nor would he have provided the slash marks, which I have added to make the clustering-by-person more obvious. The order of the names was also not preserved, and so that seems not to have been a principle of organization. Real data are never so perfect but require quantitative measures to reveal the amount of clustering. The important point is that mere succession in recall, or clustering, can reveal mental organization.

Imagine now another member of the classroom group who has total recall but brings back the descriptors in a different order:

New York, Detroit, Atlanta, Los Angeles, Boston, Reno/economics, classics, political science, sociology, folklore, psychology/rowing, guitar, school paper, Gilbert and Sullivan society, bird watching, writing poetry.

This subject has not stored the facts in memory by person but, rather (note the added slash marks), by descriptive category.

The imaginary classroom differs from an experimental situation used by Pryor and Associates (1982) in one important way. In the classroom, in the interests of verisimilitude, the input information was blocked by person with the descriptors of one exhausted before any descriptors of another were started. In the experiments the information was randomly interspersed in units of one person with one descriptor. However, a certain force toward person organization was introduced by "tuning" (Zajonc, 1960) subjects to try to assess from all they learned the probable compatibility as a roommate of each person for themselves. In spite of the tuning, with information interspersed, the recall clusters indicated that organization was in terms of type of descriptor. The unfamiliar persons had not been unified in memory. If input information has been blocked by persons, probably the information recalled would have been organized in terms of persons.

When the persons connected with descriptors are familiar, organization (as evidenced by clustering) is likely to be in terms of persons. Reproducing a portion of the information used, in interspersed not block form, by Ostrom, Pryor, and Simpson (1981) will convince you of that:

Abraham Lincoln, tall, honest, self-taught, leader, bearded
Bob Hope, golfer, old, conservative, comedian, hard-working
Muhammed Ali, religious, athlete, champion, black, opinionated

As you can imagine, the recall clusters tended to exhaust the attributes of one famous person (e.g. tall, honest, self-taught, leader, bearded) before going on to another (e.g. religious, athlete, champion, black, opinionated). When the familiar names were replaced, for other subjects, by such unfamiliar names as Stephen Falcon, Don Carr, and Alexander Cox, with the descriptors kept the same, the clustering by persons was greatly reduced but not quite eliminated. The residual person-clustering was caused by another sort of familiarity in the materials. While subjects rarely recognized from the five descriptors the famous people they knew, the descriptors could not be said to be related to one another in a random way. An athlete would not be likely, for instance, to be old. There was a low level of implication from some descriptors to others, and that is a kind of familiarity, a familiarity of types or of trait associations rather than proper names. It could easily be made very strong and then, no doubt, the familiarity of descriptor associations would lead to a strong unification or organization of persons. This is to say that stereotypes, even with unknown names and interspersed input, would unify in memory.

Preintegrative organization has been shown to be not necessarily in terms of persons. A little is known about the determinants of fusion in person perception: Familiarity of the persons strongly favors fusion, and so do some kinds of relevant tuning or set (e.g. being told that you will be asked to make favorability ratings on individuals), and information about the self is organized together and enjoys an advantage in recall (Rogers, Kuiper, and Kirker, 1977).

Beyond those few points it seems clear that persons have a general priority for the organization of social information and that more than one kind of organization can go on at the same time.

Integration as Going Beyond the Information Given

Solomon Asch's classic 1946 article on impression formation begins:

> We look at a person and immediately a certain impression of his character forms itself in us. A glance, a few spoken words are suffcient to tell us a story about a highly complex matter. We know that such impressions form with remarkable rapidity and with great ease. [p. 258]

The quoted paragraph describes integration in the sense of going beyond what is given, and Asch's way of studying that effect was in all his early experiments the same. He told his subjects that they would hear a list of discrete qualities that belonged to a particular person and that they should try to form an impression of the character in question. With respect to the present discussion[1] his most basic demonstration is the one that presented the following qualitites: *intelligent–skillful–industrious–warm–determined–practical–cautious.*

The task to form a total character impression from such a short list is not familiar to us in ordinary life. The nearest thing to it that frequently occurs is the reading of a letter of recommendation. For instance:

> I am writing to recommend for graduate work in your department Ms. Mary Jones. Ms. Jones has taken a large lecture course with me ("Introduction to Personality"), and I served as principal adviser for her senior honors thesis.
>
> Mary Jones is one of the most *intelligent* students I have ever had in my lecture course. Her thesis research showed that she is a *skillful* experimenter and an *industrious* worker. She is also the kind of *warm* person who easily recruits subjects and elicits their best efforts. When difficulties arose, as they always do in research, she proved *determined* to overcome those that could be overcome and showed good *practical* judgment. In interpreting her findings, she was admirably *cautious*.
>
> I recommend Mary Jones with much enthusiasm.

This good, strong letter of recommendation was written around the seven trait terms that served as Asch's stimulus list, using them all in the order he used, but embedding them in typically colorless letter-of-recommendation prose.

The task as Asch set it without any letter is unfamiliar but not, to use his perfect word, *lebensfremd*—not, that is, make-believe or foreign to real life. In

---

[1] Instructors should note that this presentation departs from the most familiar one, Asch's own, in order to highlight certain points.

order to determine the kinds of impressions subjects formed on the narrow base of seven traits, Asch had subjects write character sketches. Those yielded only qualitative data since each sketch was unique, and so he also obtained quantitative data. Subjects were given a list of eighteen trait contrasts (e.g. *generous-ungenerous; shrewd-wise*), not including any of the seven terms on the stimulus list, and asked to select that member of a pair they thought would best apply to the person imagined. The results appear in Table 11-1.

Please take the time to absorb those results, because, if you think about it, they are quite bizarre. The qualities on the left are all good qualities, socially desirable qualities, while those on the right are all bad or undesirable, and the stimulus list, comprising good qualities only, would apparently expand into an altogether, in every respect, good person. The nearest thing to an exception is No. 15, with *imaginative* and *hard-headed* judged almost equally probable for this projected person, but then *hard-headed* is unique in the right column in being something of a virtue. What is there in that stimulus list that could justify 98 percent of the subjects in thinking *honesty* was implied, or 88 percent in thinking the person must be *important*, and 90 percent *happy*? Is that the way the world goes? Is every good quality combined in real persons with every other good quality and every bad quality with every other bad quality. Are people totally free of moral and evaluative contradiction? And what about No. 11? Are the virtuous and wise reliably *good-looking* and the wicked and foolish *unattractive*?

TABLE 11-1. Traits Inferred from: *intelligent-skillful-industrious-warm-determined-practical-cautious* (percentages)

1. generous	91	1.* ungenerous	9
2. wise	65	2.* shrewd	35
3. happy	90	3.* unhappy	10
4. good natured	94	4.* irritable	6
5. humorous	77	5.* humorless	23
6. sociable	91	6.* unsociable	9
7. popular	84	7.* unpopular	16
8. reliable	94	8.* unreliable	6
9. important	88	9.* insignificant	12
10. humane	86	10.* ruthless	14
11. good-looking	77	11.* unattractive	23
12. persistent	100	12.* unstable	0
13. serious	100	13.* frivolous	0
14. restrained	77	14.* talkative	23
15. altruistic	69	15.* self-centered	31
16. imaginative	51	16.* hard-headed	49
17. strong	98	17.* weak	2
18. honest	98	18.* dishonest	2

SOURCE: S. Asch in the *Journal of Abnormal and Social Psychology, 41,* 1946, Table 2, p. 263.

The Simplest Implicit Personality Theory

Beyond Asch's results on impression formation there is abundant general evidence that people use the nontechnical "natural language of personality" as if all good things tended to occur together in persons and all bad things likewise, as if mixtures of the good and the bad were rare. For instance, Bruner, Shapiro, and Tagiuri (1958) asked subjects to make direct trait-to-trait inferences. A typical question was: "Suppose that a person is *intelligent*, how likely is it that he will be *reliable* (on a numeral scales)"? The results consistently showed that one good trait was inferred from another and one bad trait from another. Evaluative consistency was the main principle of inference. Osgood and Ware (Osgood, 1962) set out to develop what they called a "Personality Differential," which was to be an instrument for differentiating individuals using the natural language of personality. It was necessary, however, to reduce the huge population of trait terms in English which numbers more than seventeen thousand (Allport and Odbert, 1936), and that was to be done by subjecting trait-to-trait inference judgments to factor analysis, a mathematic procedure for discovering the underlying dimensionality or structure of a set of data. Osgood and Ware drew two independent samples of thirty-four traits each from the full Allport–Odbert list and asked subjects to make such inferences as: "A person who is mature (not immature) is likely to be: logical __ __ __ __ __ __ __ inquisitive." The investigators report what they found in these words: "The factor analyses of these two samples . . . yielded such large evaluative factors . . . that little else could be determined." (Osgood, 1962, p. 25).

The idea that one good thing can be inferred from another and one bad from another, the idea of evaluative consistency in persons, seems a pretty stupid simplification of reality, but that might just be because the task is stupid. Social psychologists do sometimes ask subjects to draw unjustified inferences, and it could be the case that evaluative consistency is nothing more than a way of obliging an experimenter. I think we would agree that it would not be a silly or unreasonable task to ask subjects to rate others, especially others whom they knew well, on trait terms like those used in the inference study. Ratings of real persons can actually be analyzed just as if they were trait inferences; you simply see what traits go together or co-occur as assigned to individuals. The startling fact is that evaluative consistency is almost as strong in ratings of real persons as in pure inference. Furthermore, it makes little difference whether the raters are laypeople or professional clinicians, whether the persons rated are known well or hardly at all (Passini and Norman, 1966), whether the structure in the data is found by cluster analysis, factor analysis, or multi-dimensional scaling (Powell and Juhnke, 1983). Using more traits yields a more complex structure, usually a structure of five traits (Digman and Takemoto-Chock, 1981), but the most general factor is always evaluation.

Asch's task is a task of pure inference, not for people generally, but for a particular person. What could guide such inference but some notion of how traits tend to be associated in people, some notion of what goes with what—as discovered, for instance, by Osgood and Ware. Cronbach (1955) called such conceptions "implicit personality theories," and that seems to be what we have here. It is a theory of evaluative consistency. Why we should think this way is a deep question. Perhaps the implicit personality theory is basically an accurate reflection of reality that is, in cognition, exaggerated or sharpened. Perhaps we just want to believe in consistency because ambivalence is difficult to deal with.

In social psychology evaluative consistency was formulated as an axiom of human thought by Fritz Heider (1946). It is fundamental to several social psychological theories: congruity theory (Osgood and Tannenbaum, 1955) and symbolic psycho-logic (Abelson and Rosenberg, 1958) for example. Brown (1965) has discussed the principle of evaluative consistency, also called the principle of "balance," in theories of attitude change.

What is clear about evaluative consistency is that people act as if they believed in it. What is not known at all is how much truth there is in it. Yet it goes so deep as to guide even certain language choices that seem automatic.

In English there is a class of words that we regularly use to code relations of negative implication between two propositions: the class of contrastive conjunctions, of which *but* is the most frequently used member. The class includes *nevertheless*, *although*, *even so*, and *yet*, among others. Just now, in late October of 1984, a commonly heard case of negative implication is: "I agree with Mondale on everything *but* I am going to vote for Reagan." Another is: "I am a registered Democrat *but* I plan to vote for Reagan." Sentences like those take *but* rather than *and* because the first proposition would not ordinarily imply or lead you to expect the second. The *but*, in effect, warns you that what is to come is not usual. We employ *and* to connect sentences expressing conventional implications: "He is a registered Democrat *and* he will vote for Mondale," not: "He is a registered Democrat *but* he will vote for Mondale." In speaking or writing complex sentences, we evidently think ahead, note relations of positive or negative implication, and choose conjunctions accordingly, even before the subsequent proposition has been expressed.

The relations of negative implication that call for a contrastive conjunction need not be at all illogical, but simply unconventional or unexpected. For example:

> Canada is north of the United States but Detroit is south of Windsor.
> The whale is not a fish but is sure looks like one.
> He was born in poverty but he died a rich man.
> Sally Green is beautiful but dumb.

The last example was designed to introduce the fact that evaluative inconsistency is also expressed by *but*, and that strongly suggests that we assume evaluative consistency according to which one good proposition about a person implies another good proposition about that person and does not imply a bad proposition. It is necessary first to notice that there *are* two propositions in the sentence about Sally Green. There seem not to be, because English grammar permits abbreviation so that we need not repeat subject and verb and say: "Sally Green is beautiful but Sally Green is dumb."

The trait terms of Table 11–1 can be put together as two propositions about a single person in very few words by just using the form: "a _____ and/but _____ person." Thus: "a generous *but* unhappy person." Is *but* the right conjunction to use? Try "a generous *and* unhappy person." Only your own intuition will convince you that *and* seems semantically odd. Most English speakers think it is. There is nothing wrong grammatically with using *and*; as far as grammar is concerned *and* and *but* are equally acceptable conjuctions in the frame: "a _____ and/but _____ person."

My intuitive sense of English usage finds the combinations in Table 11–2a semantically well formed or ordinary and the combinations in Table 11–2b odd. The ordinary combinations follow the rule of evaluative consistency: good traits are taken to imply one another and bad traits likewise, so combinations from within a single column of Table 11–1 are linked with *and* whereas trait combinations in which one is drawn from each column are taken to be affectively inconsistent and are linked with *but*. The odd or anomalous combinations use *but* with traits of the same affective value (whether good or bad) and *and* with traits of contrasting or opposed value.

If it is a fact, as I take it to be, that evaluative consistency affects our use of contrastive and coordinating conjunctions, which more generally are governed by relations of positive and negative implication, then it does seem certain that evaluative consistency is a deeply rooted implicit theory of personality. However, at this point, I feel like saying with Eliza Doolittle in *My Fair Lady*: "Words! Words! Words!" There is more to impression formation than words, and indeed words may be the least important thing. Let us take up adjectives 11 and 11* from Table 11–1, *good-looking* and *unattractive*, and ask not whether those words are linked, respectively, with other good words and bad, as they are, but whether photographs of attractive and unattractive faces are so linked.

Physical Attractiveness

What kinds of inferences are drawn from looks alone? The title of the article reporting the research tells the whole story: "What Is Beautiful Is Good" (Dion, Berscheid, and Walster, 1972). A subject received three envelopes with one yearbook-type photo in each. The photos had been rated in advance for physical attractiveness by one hundred undergraduates. Each subject received one photo high on attractiveness, one low, and one average. The pictures were alleged to be of young people enrolled in a long-term study of personal development scheduled to continue into their adult years. A photo provided a subject judge with a "first impression" from which twenty-seven personality traits were to be judged as well as the prospects for marital happiness, occupational suc-

TABLE 11-2. Trait Pairs in Evaluatively Consistent or Inconsistent Constructions

a. Constructions Manifesting Evaluative Consistency

Good with Good: *and*	Bad with Bad: *and*	Good with Bad: *but*
a generous and happy person	an ungenerous and unhappy person	a generous but unhappy person
a humorous and popular person	a humorless and unpopular person	a humorous but unpopular person
an important and good-looking person	an insignificant and unattractive person	an important but unattractive person
a serious and altruistic person	a frivolous and self-centered person	a serious but self-centered person
a strong and honest person	a weak and dishonest person	a strong but dishonest person

b. Constructions Violating Evaluative Consistency

Good with Good: *but*	Bad with Bad: *but*	Good with Bad: *and*
*a wise but happy person	*a shrewd but unhappy person	*a wise and unhappy person
*a sociable but popular person	*an unsociable but unpopular person	*a sociable and unpopular person
*a humane but good-looking person	*a ruthless but unattractive person	*a humane and unattractive person
*a restrained but altruistic person	*a talkative but self-centered person	*a restrained and self-centered person
*a strong but honest person	*a weak but dishonest person	*a strong and dishonest person

*Semantically odd or anomalous.

cess, and happiness as a parent. Subjects were led to believe that the developmental study would eventually produce the true answers to all the questions and so they should strive for accuracy so that psychology might eventually know just how much could be foreseen from first impressions.

There was no suggestion that inferences and predictions should be based on attractiveness, but they evidently were. The more attractive photos suggested personalities generally higher on social desirability. In addition, the persons pictured in photos rated high on attractiveness were expected ultimately to take up occupations of higher status, to have happier marriages and happier lives generally than the persons pictured in photos rated lower on attractiveness.

Ray Bull in London (1983) has extended the study of physical attractiveness beyond low attractiveness to facial disfigurement and found that moderately disfigured faces suggest to the general public characters that range from unsavory to distinctly nasty. In one particularly well-conceived study his stimulus materials were adult facial photographs taken before and after cosmetic oral surgery, and his subjects were children (five to twelve years of age) who were, quite sensibly, *not* asked to judge attractiveness. They were asked to imagine that some new teachers came to their school (the photos) and to say "which one would help you a lot" (positive) or "which one would be cross with you" (negative) and to make similar good or bad predictions from the faces. By the age of twelve almost all positive responses were made to "after" photos, the ones adults thought more attractive.

It is easy to overestimate the significance for everyday life of a set of beliefs of the kind documented by Asch, by Dion and collaborators, and by Bull. Requested to choose between trait terms, to rate photos for personality traits, or to guess positive or negative actions, subjects had no easy way to say: "You cannot judge these things from appearance alone." Of course, they could always have just said it and dropped out of the experiment, but subjects seldom do that; they tend to go along with the researcher's whim. The forced choices in "What Is Beautiful Is Good" leave open the possibility that subjects made a lot of wild inferences under constraint that they would by no means make in ordinary life.

In the case of physical attractiveness we do have evidence, as it happens, not simply of verbal stereotypes but of genuine unfair discrimination. Landy and Sigall (1974) gave male college students the task of evaluating the quality of essays, each of which they understood to have been written by the female college student whose photograph was in the same file with the essay. The essays were independently demonstrated to be of either good or poor quality and the photos of the young women as either highly attractive or unattractive. All this was managed credibly. A control group of male judges simply evaluated the essays without any knowledge of authorship. With nothing to affect judgment but the essay itself, control judgments should represent fair, uncontaminated assessments. Evaluation was on a nine-point scale, with 1 being "poor" and 9 "good."

Essays supposedly written by attractive women were more highly rated overall (6.0) than *the same essays* when supposedly written by unattractive women (4.3). The male judges were asked to estimate the general ability of each author as well as the specific quality of the essays read, and those estimates also showed the effect of physical attractiveness (6.5 and 4.7).

The Landy and Sigall results seem to be a clear demonstration of discrimination. The essays themselves are completely sufficient grounds for essay evaluation, and yet author attractiveness exerted a strong bias. Still, one might hold out for something a little stronger before granting that discrimination occurs. The behavior affected by attractiveness was only a rating, an evaluative rating to be sure, but not one that had any clear consequences for the attractive and unattractive persons concerned. Benson, Karabenick, and Lerner (1976) have supplied a case in which nonverbal actions are involved and where consequentiality is not only real but downright poignant.

The study made use of application folders, applications for graduate school with photos attached. The dependent variable was not evaluation but helping, a kind of low-cost altruism (see Chapter 3). Application folders were discovered in telephone booths in a large Midwestern airport, as if left behind by someone rushing to catch a plane. The folders were complete with stamped addressed envelopes and with photos attached in such a way as to make it impossible not to see them. By various ingenious devices, it was also made clear that if the person finding the folder wanted to help the person who had filled it out and whose photo was attached, the only thing to do was to mail the application; nothing else would be of any use. However, the finder might simply not care to take the very small trouble involved and would in that case just leave the folder where he found it. Some photos were male, some female; some were of blacks and some of caucasians; some rated in advance as attractive and some as unattractive. More than six hundred white adults, male and female, served as subjects in the experiment—without every knowing it.

The overall helping rate was just 41 percent, which may shock you but will not if you have read Chapter 2, since this was a situation in which the potential helper would be anonymous and had no well-defined responsibility. "Why me? Let someone else do it." The biasing effect of attractiveness was highly significant and greater than the biasing effect of race. Attractive persons were helped, overall, 47 percent of the time and unattractive, 35 percent. Whites were helped 45 percent of the time and blacks, only 37 percent (a statistically significant difference). The effects of attractiveness were the same in direction whether helper and applicant were of the same or different sex, but in the cross-sex case the attractiveness variable exerted a somewhat larger effect.

Bull's work in London on the effects of mild facial disfigurement confirm the American work showing that appearance has consequential effects on the way someone is treated. Women soliciting door to door for a children's charity sometimes appeared normal and sometimes with what is called a facial "port wine stain" (actually created by makeup), which made them look mildly disfigured (Bull and Stevens, 1981). They collected quite a lot more money, a sort of low-cost altruism, when not disfigured. In a study of pedestrians on a busy London street (Rumsey, Bull and Gahagan, 1982) it was shown that when confederates had a birthmark under one eye (makeup), people stood at a greater distance from them than when they appeared without birthmark. Those and other studies showing that disfigurement is a kind of disadvantage have caused some enlightened prison systems, especially in the United States, to make available corrective plastic surgery to selected inmates. The possible effects of improving the stimulus value of former prisoners on rates of recidivism (repeated arrests) are being studied (Bull, 1982).

We now know that physical appearance, from attractive to disfigured, can lead to the inference of personality traits and guesses about future happiness, can affect the evaluation of a person's work (essays) and general ability, can affect the likelihood of being helped and even how closely others will approach. We also know that effects occur the other way, from information about personality or behavior to guesses about appearance. Asch's subjects thought that someone who was *intelligent–skillfull–industrious–warm–determined–practical–cautious* would also be "good-looking." In addition, Nisbett and Wilson (1977) had college students rate the physical attractiveness of an instructor from a seven-minute interview; though the instructor was always the same person, he sometimes endeavored to be likable and sometimes rather cold. He was guessed to be much more *physically* attractive when likeable. All of this work documents the same implicit personality theory: evaluative consistency. Good things go together in real people and bad things likewise. It is truly a simple primitive theory, but it is seriously held. It is not just talk; it is a theory with action consequences.

Evaluative Consistency Evaluated

I think a theory of evaluative consistency if unqualified is grotesque. The necessary qualification I call the "Anything Goes Rule." This is the rule that absolutely anything *can* go with anything. That is not to say that personalities are random collections of traits, skills, talents, and opinions. There are some usual, more probable than not, co-occurrences, including some that are affective or evaluative. But if you think all personalities must be, in all respects, thus evaluatively unified, then you will find that *any* personality you know really well, which is to say across time and situations, is "enigmatic"—including and especially, your own.

There are people, experienced well-read people, who nevertheless seem to believe in an unqualified evaluative consistency. If there were not, why would there be 22,000 books on, for instance, the "enigma" of Richard Wagner? The supposed enigma is that a man who wrote some music that is sublime (*Parsifal*), some that is noble and romantic (*Lohengrin*), and some that is wise and gently humorous (*Meistersinger*) should have been an active anti-Semite, the seducer of a loyal friend's wife (Cosima Von Bülow), and at various times a liar, cheat, politician, egomaniac, and sybarite. Why on earth not? There is no enigma in Wagner if you remember the Anything Goes Rule. The real enigma is that experienced people who must know that traits of character and talent have complex, shifting causes, can believe, or pretend to believe, that a personality must be all of a piece morally.

Wagner is not an enigma, and neither is Mozart with his silly jokes and bathroom preoccupations; nor Martin Luther King, said to have been something of a "womanizer"; nor John Cheever, revealed by his daughter to have been alcoholic; nor Robert Frost, the unworldly poet who worked tirelessly at promoting his literary standing. I sometimes think the only famous people who are not "enigmatic" are the people whose biographies have not yet been written. There is something amazingly strong about the theory of evaluative consistency, and it applies to the largely disapproved person with an "enigmatic" good quality as strongly as it does to the good person with an "enigmatic" flaw. In spite of all the people who profess to be mystified, there is no real enigma in the fact that the Nazis who executed millions in concentration camps loved their own small children and pet dogs and that mafia Godfathers cherish their own families.

The real enigma is that we can still be astonished by evaluative inconsistency and can still find it inexplicable when we know that traits have complex genetic bases and are affected by many different kinds of learning. I think the explanation must lie in Asch's discovery that personality impressions can be started by very minimal data but then always strain toward completeness and are completed in accordance with the simple implicit theory of evaluative consistency. When something inconsistent is discovered, we will have quite forgotten that we never had any good data on that point and will mistake the imagined lineaments of the full figure for things we knew.

Primacy and Integration as Semantic Interaction

Primacy is the name for the fact that the first information about a person is more influential in shaping the total impression than is the same information when received later on. The popular belief that first impressions count heavily is true. Primacy has been demonstrated for many kinds of information: trait names, verbal descriptions of behavior, test performance, and appearance. There are several theories as to the cause of primacy, theories that contend over the explanation of one sort of data only. No single general explantion of primacy has yet been found.

Trait Names

Asch (1946) discovered primacy in impressions formed from lists of trait names by using, with different subjects, the following two lists.

    I. *intelligent–industrious–impulsive–critical–stubborn–envious*
    II. *envious–stubborn–critical–impulsive–industrious–intelligent*

Series I begins with two strongly positive qualities (*intelligent* and *industrious*), proceeds to qualities that could be interpreted as either good or bad qualities (*impulsive-critical-stubborn*), and ends with an unequivocally bad quality. That order is reversed in Series II, and the comparison of impressions derived from reversed-order lists is the primacy paradigm in research, often called the High–Low, Low–High, or HL–LH paradigm.

Subjects were told, as usual in these 1946 studies, that they would hear a set of discrete qualities that belonged to a particular person and that they should try to form an impression of the character in question. Lists I and II are quite different from the first list we looked at in that all the traits on the first list were socially desirable, whereas on List I the first two traits are highly desirable, the middle three can be interpreted as desirable or undesirable, and the last trait is strongly undesirable; List II just reverses the order. The first list we saw was evaluatively consistent within itself and gave rise to a full impression, manifest in the inferred traits of Table 11-1, that was as a whole consistently good. The first list we saw conformed to the implicit personality theory of evaluative consistency; everything to be integrated was good. Lists I and II both violate the theory of evaluative consistency with List I being high–low (HL) and List II low–high (LH). This violation of evaluative consistency did not cause subjects to say that such characters were impossible or did not exist or violated the theory of personality. On the contrary, as long as subjects received all six traits, one after another, they experienced no difficulty in integrating them. How were they able to do so in view of the fact that personalities are expected to be evaluatively consistent? Roughly speaking, they were able to integrate the traits because of the effect of primacy, which caused the first two on List I (*intelligent* and *industrious*) to color the understanding of the middle three and the first one on List II (*envious*) to color the same three.

One thing Asch's subjects did after hearing either List I or List II was write a short character sketch that fitted the traits heard in the order given. Here is one sketch written in response to List I (*HL*):

> The person is intelligent and fortunately he puts his intelligence to work. That he is stubborn and impulsive may be due to the fact that he knows what he is saying and what he means and will not therefore give in easily to someone else's idea which he disagrees with. [1946, p. 270]

In this freely improvised character sketch, notice that the traits *impulsive* and *stubborn* have been favorably interpreted as justified by the person's intelligence. They seem to mean something like "decisive" or "resolute." For subjects who wrote character sketches on the basis of List II, which begins with *envious*, a very undesirable trait, the middle traits took on a negative quality, so that *stubborn* meant something like "obstinate" and *impulsive* something like "reckless" and *critical* something like "fault-finding."

Quantitative data were collected as before by giving subjects the check list of eighteen trait contrasts (e.g. *generous–ungenerous; wise–shrewd*) and asking them to select that member of a pair they thought would best apply to the person they had imagined. The results appear in Table 11-3. For the sake of brevity, percentages for the positive member only of each pair are listed; percentages for the contrasting member may be obtained by subtracting from 100, and the contrasting terms are listed in Table 11-1.

The patterns of inferred traits, from the two lists differing only in order, are quite unlike each other and are consistent with the character sketches in showing that the trait(s) that came first carried the greater weight. The pattern inferred from List I (*intelligent . . . envious*) is very generally, though not quite invariably, more favorable or socially desirable than the pattern inferred from List II (*envious . . . intelligent*). Asch's explanation of the effect obtained is that

> . . . the first terms set up in most subjects a *direction* which then exerts a continuous effect on the later terms. When the subject hears the first term, a broad, uncrystal-

TABLE 11–3. Traits Inferred from Lists Differing Only in Order (percentages)

	Intelligent → Envious (N = 34)	Envious → Intelligent (N = 24)
1. generous	24	10
2. wise	18	17
3. happy	32	5
4. good natured	18	0
5. humorous	52	21
6. sociable	56	27
7. popular	35	14
8. reliable	84	91
9. important	85	90
10. humane	36	21
11. good-looking	74	35
12. persistent	82	87
13. serious	97	100
14. restrained	64	9
15. altruistic	6	5
16. imaginative	26	14
17. strong	94	73
18. honest	80	79

SOURCE: S. Asch in the *Journal of Abnormal and Social Psychology, 41*, 1946, Table 7, p. 271.

ized but directed impression is born. The next characteristic comes not as a separate item, but is related to the established direction. Quickly, the view formed acquires a certain stability, so that later characteristics are fitted—if conditions permit—to the given direction. [1945, pp. 271–72]

Asch's concept of direction does not really explain primacy; it simply restates it. That becomes clear if we ask the following question: Why should the direction be from earlier to later, for trait terms spoken aloud, or from left to right for trait terms read on a page? Why should not the "direction" come from the last three terms, *envious–stubborn–critical*, with those terms selecting, as consistent additional terms: *ungenerous, unhappy, humorless, weak?* I think there is an answer to the question and that Professor Asch probably had it tacitly in mind. The answer is that the first adjectives describing a person are completely unpredictable. That means they carry a disproportionate amount of information, in the technical sense of information, which is unpredictability. As we shall see, it is a general principle of cognitive psychology that high information gets more attention and carries more weight than low information—which is redundant or predictable.

How does Asch conceive of the *effect* (as opposed to the *cause*) of primacy? On that he is very clear. The fundamental point in his explanation is that the trait adjectives used in the stimulus list, and indeed almost all words, are capable of expressing a number of different meanings. When subjects are asked to integrate a list of traits so as to form an impression of personality, what they integrate is *meanings*. Since the six adjectives on the stimulus list, as words, as forms on the page, all have more than one possible meaning, it must somehow happen that when subjects are asked to integrate the traits, they select from among the possible meanings of the words those that best fit together. In short, the parts (the individual traits) do not enter into combination as fixed semantic elements but, rather, take on individual senses dictated by the whole. That is a "holistic" or Gestalt interpretation of impression formation, and Asch, as a *Gestalt* psychologist, was and is (Asch and Zukier, 1984) much concerned to show that, in person perception as in perception generally, the whole is not just the sum of its parts.

To make his basic point that the meaning of a term depended on the terms with which it was integrated, Asch carried out several incidental demonstrations using as "target terms" English trait adjectives that are strongly susceptible of meaning change: *calm, aggressive,* and *strong.* Each of those words was to be integrated with two or three preceding words. The preceding words were for some subjects uniformly good or desirable qualities and for comparison subjects uniformly bad or undesirable qualities. The task of the subject was to provide one or more synonyms or paraphrases for the target words in context, and the point of interest is the sharp differences of meaning for the *same words* (as shapes on a page) induced by context. In Table 11-4 we have illustrative results.

TABLE 11-4. Meanings Induced by Contrasting Antecedent Contexts

Target Words:	CALM		STRONG		AGGRESSIVE	
	+	–	+	–	+	–
Positive and negative contexts	kind wise honest	cruel shrewd unscrupulous	kind wise honest	cruel shrewd unscrupulous	active helpful	strong self-centered
Synonyms	Calm = serene, poised, reserved	Calm = calculating, emotionless	Strong = fearless, forceful, courageous	Strong = ruthless, overbearing, hard	Aggressive = determined forceful	Aggressive = combative

The word *calm* coming after the evaluatively good words *kind*, *wise*, and *honest* seemed to express the good meaning of "serenity," but the same word coming after the unfavorable *cruel*, *shrewd*, and *unscrupulous* expressed the unfavorable meanings "calculating" and "emotionless." *Strong* coming after *kind*, *wise*, and *honest* took on the senses of "forceful" and "courageous," but in the context of *cruel*, *shrewd*, and *unscrupulous* it meant "hard" and "ruthless." The sense of *aggressive* in conjunction with *active* and *helpful* was, essentially, "resolute" or "determined," but *aggressive* with *strong* and *self-centered* meant "combative." In short, the meanings of the trait adjectives shifted radically with changes in context and, furthermore, shifted so as to make the integrated impression evaluatively consistent.

Contemporary researchers sympathetic to Asch's position on impression formation (Hamilton and Zanna, 1974; Wyer, 1974; Higgins and Rholes, 1976; Zanna and Hamilton, 1977), using various ingenious methods, have provided many more examples of meaning change resulting from preceeding context. For instance, the word *proud* in a favorable context means "confident," and in an unfavorable context "conceited." How do the various demonstrations that the meaning of a trait adjective can be shifted by context between something desirable and something undesirable explain the results of the original primacy experiment?

It is necessary to look once more at the two lists:

I. *intelligent–industrious–impulsive–critical–stubborn–envious*
II. *envious–stubborn–critical–impulsive–industrious–intelligent*

The words at either end (*intelligent*, *industrious*, and *envious*) are somewhat different from the three in the middle (*impulsive*, *critical*, *stubborn*). Asch intuitively grasped the difference; he described *intelligent* and *industrious* as qualities of "high merit" and *envious* as of very "dubious" merit, but *impulsive*, *critical*, and *stubborn* as permitting of a "better or poorer evaluation." Today that difference has been objectively demonstrated in the insightful work of Dean Peabody (1967, 1970, 1984), though Peabody was not directly concerned with explaining primacy. He and his students searched dictionaries, Roget's Thesaurus, and books of synonyms and antonyms to find the meanings of seven hundred common trait terms. Work on impression formation had dwelt so much on evaluative meaning that Peabody was concerned to bring forward the fact that there is much more to word meaning than evaluation. After all, evaluatively similar words (e.g. *intelligent* and *industrious*), though they may seem to imply one another, are very far from being synonymous. Peabody suggested the term "descriptive meaning" for the dimension in which evaluatively close terms differed. He and his students found that most of the seven hundred trait terms fell into sets of four, describable in terms of two levels of descriptive meaning (high and low) and two of evaluative meaning (positive and negative, or + and −). As his first example Peabody (1967) suggests that the descriptive meaning that might be generally called "risk taking," at its low level yields the terms *cautious* and *timid* and, at its high level, *bold* and *rash*, and while *cautious* and *bold* are evaluatively positive, *timid* and *rash* are negative, so a 2 × 2 table will yield unique values for each word in this domain.

In Table 11–5a we have the meaning sets that are relevant to the middle terms on the stimulus list in the primary experiment: *impulsive, critical,* and *stubborn.* The descriptive meanings relevant to those terms are, respectively, control of impulse, inclination to critize, and mental changeability. For each there are high-level meanings and also low-level meanings, and for the highs there is always both an evaluatively positive and a negative term; likewise for the lows. The result is that there are four meanings to each set. In the first case control of impulse, the high-control meanings are "resolute" and "determined," and the low-control meanings are "spontaneous" and "reckless." Of the two high-control meanings, "resolute" is good and "obstinate" is bad, and of the two low-control meanings, "spontaneous" is good and "reckless" is bad. How does the word *impulsive* fit into this semantic field? It always means low control of impulse, but it may take on either the positive sense "spontaneous" or negative sense "reckless." The other two words that fell in the middle of the stimulus list (*critical* and *stubborn*) have the same properties as *impulsive*: the descriptive meaning is stable, but positive and negative senses are both possible. Remember what Asch said of the three middle terms: They permit of a "better or poorer evaluation." That is what the representations in Table 11–5 say in a more systematic way.

Peabody found that some domains of descriptive meaning yielded incomplete sets, and three of those imcomplete sets are relevant to the end terms in the stimulus list used by Asch in the primary experiment: *intelligent, industrious,* and *envious.* The sets appear in Table 11–5b. In the domain of intellectual capacity, for instance, we have the meaning "intelligent" for a high level and the meaning "stupid" for a low level. Those terms contrast in descriptive meaning but also in evaluative meaning. What is lacking is an evaluatively negative sense of high intellectual capacity and an evaluatively positive sense of low intellectual capacity. It seems not to be just words that are missing, but the very meanings themselves. It is difficult to think of low intellectual capacity as desirable. The other two sets in Table 11–5b are incomplete in just the same way. "Industrious" and "lazy" are meanings opposite one another both descriptively and evaluatively, and so are "altruistic" and "envious." How do the words *intelligent, industrious,* and *envious* fit into the three semantic domains? Each one is stable in descriptive meaning but also in evaluative meaning. *Intelligent* and *industrious* are good terms and *envious* bad, and they cannot be otherwise, and that is what Asch said about them.

We are now in position to understand the results of the primacy experiment in terms somewhat more explicit than Asch's but essentially the same. According to Table 11–5a, *impulsive* can mean either "spontaneous" (good) or "reckless" (bad). *Critical* can mean either "fault-finding" (bad) or "discriminating" (good). *Stubborn* can mean either "obstinate" (bad) or "resolute" (good).

TABLE 11–5. Meanings in Two Dimensions: Descriptive and Evaluative
a. Full Sets with Four Meanings

	1. Descriptive Meaning: Control of Impulse	
	High	**Low**
Evaluative meaning	+ "resolute" – "inhibited"	"spontaneous" "reckless" Word: *impulsive*

	2. Descriptive Meaning: Inclination to Criticize	
	High	**Low**
Evaluative meaning	+ "discriminating" – "fault finding" Word: *critical*	"tolerant" "undiscriminating"

	3. Descriptive Meaning: Mental Changeability	
	High	**Low**
Evaluative meaning	+ "flexible" – "vacillating"	"resolute" "obstinate" Word: *stubborn*

b. Incomplete Sets with Two Meanings

	1. Descriptive Meaning: Intellectual Capacity	
	High	**Low**
Evaluative meaning	+ "intelligent" – Word: *intelligent*	"stupid"

	2. Descriptive Meaning: Habitual Work Level	
	High	**Low**
Evaluative meaning	+ "industrious" – Word: *industrious*	"lazy"

	3. Descriptive Meaning: Attitude Toward Others	
	High	**Low**
Evaluative meaning	+ "altruistic" –	"envious" Word: *envious*

	4. Descriptive Meaning: Temperament	
	High	**Low**
Evaluative meaning	+ "warm" –	"cold"

SOURCE: After Peabody (1967, 1984) but with examples modified.

Suppose now that the end terms (*intelligent, industrious,* or *envious*) with their firm, uninfluenceable good or bad evaluations operate on the subsequent influenceable terms by selecting that meaning of the two possible meanings which has a congruent evaluative sign. The result would be an impression that was largely (but not perfectly) evaluatively consistent, whether the bad term had primacy or the good terms. The two lists of words would become two lists of meanings as follows:

I. *"intelligent"*–*"industrious"*–*"spontaneous"*–*"discriminating"*–*"resolute"*–*"envious"*

II. *"envious"* – *"obstinate"* – *"fault-finding"* – *"reckless"* – *"industrious"* – *"intelligent"*

The two sets of integrated meanings are quite unlike, with I being more generally favorable than II. The integrated impressions do not show perfect evaluative consistency, and what prevents that is the appearance in both impressions of the unalterably bad "envious" and the unalterably good "intelligent" and "industrious." Please look again at Table 11–3, and this time notice that while List I (*intelligent . . . envious*) is quite consistently more favorable than List II (*envious . . . intelligent*), it is far from being the case, as it was in Table 11–1, that all the positive traits, the ones listed in Table 11–3, are higher than 50 percent. If the integrated favorable impressions were perfectly consistent, the percentages for I, *intelligent . . . envious* should all be over 50 percent and the percentages for II, *envious . . . intelligent* should all be under 50 percent, which would mean perfect negative consistency. What is instead the case in Table 11–3 is that the two lists, for almost every trait, give percentages on the same side of 50 percent. This means that both impressions must integrate the meanings of *intelligent, industrious,* and *envious.*.

Looking down the list of Table 11–3 comparing percentages, adjective-by-adjective, you will find that everything makes sense if we suppose that the two sets of meanings listed just above represent the two integrated impressions. Such amiable social qualities as *generous, happy, good-natured, humorous, sociable, popular,* and *good-looking* are in implicit personality theory more congruent with "spontaneous," "discriminating," and "resolute" than with "obstinate," "fault-finding," and "reckless." Probably *altruistic* is low in both impressions because the rooted quality *envious* in both stimulus lists is a near antonym. Probably *persistent* and *serious* are high on both because of the rooted quality—*industrious.*

In Asch's primacy experiment two kinds of integration go on. One is inference or going beyond the information given by using the stimulus list as a basis for making choices on the checklist. That is the kind of integration that was involved in producing Table 11–1, where seven evaluatively good traits guided the inference to eighteen additional good traits. The second kind of integration occurs within the stimulus lists and involves the selection of evaluative meanings for influenceable adjectives by the first (primacy) evaluatively firm traits.

Both kinds of integration—going beyond and fitting together—are guided by the same primitive implicit personality theory: evaluative consistency.

Subjects in the primacy experiment, whether asked to integrate List I or List II, reported no difficulty in doing so, and that would seem odd in view of evaluative consistency, since the end words, in their most familiar senses, were far apart in social desirability. From what we now know, we can see why the two halves of the list did not seem to contradict each other: The words that came first selected evaluatively consistent senses for those that came later. In a nice variation on the experiment Asch gave subjects just half the list (words) and asked them to write character sketches and make selections on the check-list; then he gave them the three words constituting the other half of the list, as applying to a new person, and asked for character sketches and checklist choices. The two "impressions," based on three traits each, were sharply different: those based on the three good terms were highly positive and those based on the three bad terms, largely negative. To the surprise of his subjects, Asch then told them the two lists described a single person and asked for a new impression.

Subjects' comments reveal their amazement:

> "I had seen the two sets of characteristics as opposing each other. It was hard to envision all these contradictory traits in one person."

> "The person seemed to be a mass of contradictions."

> "He seemed a dual personality. There are two directions in this person." [Asch, 1946, p. 274]

The comments strongly confirm the theory that in the basic primacy experiment the early terms selected meanings for the later terms in accordance with the implicit personality theory of evaluative consistency. The full set of six traits was difficult to integrate after its constituent subsets of three each had been integrated, because the first integration manifest in the sketches and checklists served to fix the meanings of the words in either a good or a bad sense, and so they were not free to assume new senses in a new list.

Algebraic Integration

Norman Anderson has, like Asch, used trait names presented in serial order as stimulus material for impression formation. Anderson's goal was the creation of a mathematical model of impression formation, and his model of algebraic integration has worked well not only for impressions derived from serially ordered adjectives but for several other problems in social psychology. In attaining a mathematical model, there has been some concomitant loss in realism, and even Asch's version of impression formation is not very realistic. It is true, as Anderson stresses, that we do in life get to know a person serially, a bit at a time, but not from the peeling off of packaged traits, let alone adjectives. The letter of recommendation remains the nearest thing to a natural parallel.

Over about a decade, in very many experiments, Anderson has worked with a list of 555 trait adjectives, which he had rated for likableness on a seven-point scale by one hundred judges (Anderson, 1968a). Very often those adjectives are characterized in terms of four rating ranges: High (H) adjectives like *truthful* and *reasonable* range from 5.0 to 5.45; Moderate Plus (M+) adjectives like *painstaking* and *persuasive* range from 3.45 to 3.74; Moderate Minus (M-) adjectives like *unpopular* and *dependent* range from 2.22 to 2.54; Low (L) adjectives like *spiteful* and *abusive* range from .72 to 1.00. In a typical experiment subjects (who were not judges in the normative rating task) read or hear six adjectives in order, are told to think of them as all *equally important* traits of the same single person, and at the end are asked to rate the person described in just one respect: likableness (often on an eight-point scale).

With impressions made one-dimensional (likableness) and normative ratings on a large set of trait adjectives, it is possible to ask some very precise questions about the process. For instance, how exactly are the final ratings related to the individual ratings? Is the value on likableness of the total person perhaps the simple average of the values of the adjectives being integrated? Before asking and answering that question, however, the primacy paradigm (HL–LH) was used in many experiments (e.g. Anderson, 1965a; Anderson and Barrios, 1961; Anderson and Norman, 1964), and so long as the task has been, like Asch's, formation of a final impression from serially ordered adjectives, a primacy effect has always been obtained, usually large and in accordance with the implicit personality theory of evaluative consistency.

With known scale values for the component trait terms we can draw from the fact that HL does not equal LH in likableness (and, in fact, is higher than LH) a conclusion more powerful than the simple proposition that primacy exists. If HL is greater than LH, then the adjectives are not integrated into a personality by simple averaging (e.g. $5+5+5+2+2+2$ does not turn out to equal $2+2+2+5+5+5$, as simple averaging requires). Instead we must think of the early traits as somehow carrying greater weights than the later traits, as if the first three fives were multiplied by values greater than one, or the last three twos by values less than one, causing them to be discounted.

There is a question prior to the weighting question: Do the values of the traits combine by averaging at all? Perhaps they are not averaged but added. For the writer of letters of recommendation the question of whether favorable terms are averaged or added by the reader in forming a total impression has clear strategic implications. Suppose you are prepared to say of someone three very good things (high likableness ratings) such as *intelligent, trustworthy,* and *considerate*; would you further enhance the person's value by adding three true moderately good traits such as *prudent, perceptive,* and *convincing?* That real question translates very neatly into an experiment contrasting HHH (*intelligent, trustworthy, considerate*) with HHHM + M + M + *intelligent, trustworthy, consider-ate, prudent, perceptive, convincing*.

Remember that the person forming the impression in an experiment knows only the trait names, not their numerical values, and provides as data a single number on a rating scale for his total impression. The subject, in short, does not have the information that would enable him *explicitly* either to add or to average; only the experimenter has that information. The question is whether the data the subject produces are such as to indicate implicit adding or implicit averaging. The answer, from a very large amount of data (e.g. Anderson, 1965b, 1968b), is quite clear. The process is one of averaging, not adding. So, in writing your letters, confine yourself to the most favorable things you are prepared to say and omit the lukewarm things—if, that is, you are simply con-cerned with conveying the most favorable, likable portrait possible, rather than the most accurate. Accuracy involves descriptive meaning, and so while *trust-worthy* and *intelligent* might be equally favorable, they are quite different in descriptive meaning.

Likableness values of traits are averaged rather than added to arrive at a final impression, but the average cannot be a simple one since the information received early is more influential than the information received later (the prim-acy effect). The average must weight earlier traits more heavily than later ones. Anderson thought that might well be so and might perhaps be caused by diminishing attention as the series progressed. The first traits would perhaps be strongly attended to but, the subject having a general impression, might then attend less closely to the later traits. An ingenious way to test that hypothesis would be to instruct subjects not only to form an impression of personality, but also to be prepared to recall all the traits (e.g. six or eight) at the end of the trial (Anderson and Hubert, 1963). The instruction to be prepared to recall ought to force a subject to give the equal attention that he is instructed to give to each trait. In fact the recall requirement did eliminate the primacy effect and so sup-ported the differential attention explanation (see also Stewart, 1965). Still more refined experiments led Anderson (1968b) ultimately to favor a *discounting* explanation, which holds that later traits simply are not worth much for a total impression.

Asch (1946) did not explicitly explain primacy in terms of diminishing attention, but his concept of "direction" suggests that the first information about a person, since it is least likely to be predictable, will be given most atten-tion. Asch's subjects gave their impressions of personality not in terms of lik-ableness ratings but as character sketches or as inferred additional trait terms such as *generous, happy, humourous, strong*, and so on. The primacy *effect* in Asch's data is a difference in the traits inferred from a good–bad list contrasted with a bad–good list. His explanation of the effect is, we know, that the first terms in a set select certain additional meanings as consistent and reject others as inconsistent.

While Asch's view that primacy results in the selection of meanings for subsequent words by preceding words makes good sense and is supported by quite
a lot of evidence, not everyone believes that this is the correct understanding of
what primacy does. Certainly, Anderson and his associates do not, nor does
Kaplan (1971, 1974), who has found evidence that questions meaning-change
in at least some cases.

Anderson's experimental paradigm does not permit meaning change to
appear, as his dependent variable is simply a rating of likableness for the person
described by adjectives that have been normatively scaled in that respect. The
likableness or favorableness of stimulus adjectives creates (in a lawful way) the
overall favorableness of the person described. Primacy appears in that early
adjectives are weighted more heavily than later; the later adjectives are discounted.

I do not thing that the effect of primacy in impression formation from
adjective sets will ever be shown to be *either* meaning change *or* a weighted average of evaluative ratings. I do not think a crucial experiment will ever be
invented that decides between them, because it seems clear that both are true.
If you look for meaning change by asking for synonyms for one word in different contexts, one good and one bad, you will find it as Asch did with *calm*
meaning either "serene" or "calculating." But those meaning changes seem
always to be of the same kind, changes on the same semantic dimension, and
that is the dimension of evaluation (or likableness). Suppose you used the same
sets of antecedent adjectives that Asch used as contexts (*kind, wise, honest* versus *cruel, shrewd, unscrupulous*) and simply looked up their normative likableness
ratings. You would, of course, find them far apart; the former very high and the
latter very low. Suppose you now ask a subject to rate the likableness of the
total impression in each case: The former will be high and the latter low.
Anderson's weighted average model enables you to predict how high and how
low, while Asch's method does not. However, Anderson's method does not
admit of the possibility of discovering meaning changes. Meaning change and
evaluative averaging should both be true effects.

Primacy in Behavior Itself

Happily, not all research on impression formation has worked from verbal
materials. From Jones and co-workers (1968) we have a live person actually trying to solve multiple-choice problems and being evaluated for intelligence by an
observer. The problems were analogies and progessions, much like those on the
SAT, and were difficult enough so that an observer would find it quite credible
for a proffered solution to be called either "correct" or "incorrect." One that I
like, because I was able to solve it, is: *Tam, tan; rib, rid; rat, raw; hap*—(1) *hat*,
(2) *hit*, (3) *his*, (4) *him*.

The problem-solvers all solved just fifteen problems out of thirty, but they did so in one of two patterns: ascending or descending. The "ascender" solved more later in the series, whereas the "descender" started out doing extremely well (primacy) and then did somewhat less well. When thirty problems had been attempted and fifteen solved, the observer was told there would be thirty more problems of the same level of difficulty and was asked to predict how well the person he was watching (an ascender or a descender) would do. The result was striking, because either of two sorts of prediction makes a kind of sense. One might quite reasonably extrapolate the curve of the ascender, reasoning that whatever had galvanized him into improving would continue to do so and, therefore, predict a high proportion of correct solutions. But that is not what observers did. In four different experiments they predicted that the solver who started off well and then declined would do better on the second thirty problems than the solver who had shown an ascending pattern. In addition, observers were, at the end, asked to estimate the intelligence of those they had watched, and the descenders, those who started well, were rated as the more intelligent. That is, of course, a primacy effect; the first information (many correct answers for the descenders; few for the ascenders) was given the greater weight.

The results of the experiment by Jones and collaborators (1968) are likely to strike teachers as the right way to think, simply because we ourselves are prone to it. We do tend to take the first performance as diagnostic of a stable general level of ability and to think of later fallings off, if they occur, as attributable to temporary circumstances: mood, motivation, or external situation. The "student who improves" is also familiar to us. We think of his early, not so high, level of performance as indicative of his stable ability and his improvement as the result of extraordinary effort. Don't mistake me, however. Teachers tend to like the student who improves and to reward him for the direction of his movement with a high grade. We respect, for his high ability, the student who starts high and then declines, but if the later falling off is attributed to laziness we may deplore his character. It would be interesting to have an experiment in which ascending and descending orders with the same absolute level of performance were manipulated over an entire semester in a course to see how teachers would assign grades.

For the first information to be taken as most diagnostic is, once again, just the phenomenon of primacy. The differential attention explanation picks up some independent support in the Jones (1968) study, for observers were asked, when all was over, to recall how many problems of the first thirty had been correctly solved by the person they had observed. In all four experiments, descenders were remembered as having solved more problems than ascenders although all alike had always solved just fifteen. In the most extreme case, descenders were actually thought to have solved 20.6 problems (on the average) and ascenders only 12.5.

How do the recall differences support the theory of heightened attention at the start, the very start, as a determinant of primacy? In the first *fifteen* of the thirty problems, descenders would, in fact, have solved more problems than ascenders. If the high or low frequency of solutions were closely attended to and then rather inattentively extrapolated to the second fifteen problems, the difference in recall would result.

Centrality and a Two-Dimensional Implicit Personality Theory

Traits are not all equally potent in shaping impressions of personality; some seem to be central and some peripheral. Once again, it is Solomon Asch (1946) who created the classic experiment. As in the experiments on primacy, he worked with sets of adjectives. This time there were seven adjectives in each of two sets, and the sets were identical except for the middle word, which was *warm* in one and *cold* in the other. One set or the other was read to a subject who was instructed, as before, to let a general impression grow in his mind of the person being described. He was then to write a brief character sketch.

In the sketches produced, the nature of the contrast was not the same as it was in the primacy experiments. In that case words from the stimulus list tended to be assigned positive or negative meanings ("spontaneous," "discriminating," "resolute," versus "reckless," "fault-finding," "obstinate") so as to make them evaluatively consistent with the first traits on the list. In the present case, the words on the stimulus list seem not to shift in meaning with *warm* and *cold*. Except for *warm* and *cold* the words all have to do with intrapersonal, task-oriented, more or less intellectual traits of character and, in this respect, contrast markedly with *warm* and *cold*, which are interpersonal, social qualities. The intellectual traits on the stimulus list are all evaluatively good, whereas *warm* and *cold* are at opposite poles with respect to evaluation. What the contrasting sketches suggest is that the good intellectual qualities are stable but that the *warm–cold* contrast led subjects to form impressions in a new dimension, a dimension of interpersonal, social qualities. The integration that occurs in this experiment is going beyond the information given even as it was on the first list of consistently good traits, but now we have two varieties of evaluation.

Once again, quantitative data were collected by asking subjects to select that term in a pair (the same eighteen pairs used in the primacy experiments) most consistent with the impression created by the seven stimulus traits. The results appear in Table 11-6 for the favorable members only.

It is worthwhile looking closely at the checklist. When the original set of traits (the stimulus list) included *warm*, most subjects thought the person involved would also be *generous, humorous, sociable,* and *popular*. When the stimulus list included *cold*, most subjects thought the person would not have those agreeable traits. Some other traits on the list seemed about equally likely to be checked whether the person was *warm* or *cold*. In either case, subjects thought he would be *persistent, serious,* and *restrained*.

TABLE 11–6. Traits Inferred from Lists Differing
Only With Respect to *Warm* and *Cold* (percentages)

	Warm (N = 90)	Cold (N = 76)
1. generous	91	8
2. wise	65	25
3. happy	90	34
4. good natured	94	17
5. humorous	77	13
6. sociable	91	38
7. popular	84	28
8. reliable	94	99
9. important	88	99
10. humane	86	31
11. good-looking	77	69
12. persistent	100	97
13. serious	100	99
14. restrained	77	89
15. altruistic	69	18
16. imaginative	51	19
17. strong	98	95
18. honest	98	94

SOURCE: S. Asch in the *Journal of Abnormal and Social Psychology, 41*, 1946,
Table 2, p. 263.

The full portrait projected from a list of seven traits is markedly changed by the substitution of *cold* for *warm*, and so *warm* and *cold* are highly "central" terms. They are central to their list *not because they occupied a middle position* but because they proved strongly determinative of the impressions derived from the list. Asch, in another study (1946), replaced *warm* and *cold* in the preceding series with *polite* and *blunt*. The differences then obtained in the projected list were markedly weaker. Within this stimulus list the traits *polite* and *blunt* are a less central pair than *warm* and *cold*. The centrality of the terms *warm* and *cold* does not seem to be absolute, however, for Asch obtained evidence that in other lists the same pair had less power.

What causes a trait to be central (highly potent) or peripheral (slightly potent) in impression formation? Today that question can be answered and the effects Asch discovered explained. The explanation involves implicit personality theory, as did did the explanation of the semantic integration produced by primacy, but the implicit personality theory that explains the centrality effect has two dimensions, not one. Rosenberg, Nelson, and Vivekananthan (1968) handed subjects sixty slips of paper with a trait on each list and asked for implicit personality theory in just about the most direct way possible:

> We are interested in finding out which traits you think are likely to go together in the same individual and which traits seldom, if ever, go together in the same individ-

ual. Your task is to put those traits which tend to go together in the same individual into the same category. One way to make these judgments is to think of a number of people that you know (for example, friends, relatives, public figures, etc.) that are quite different from one another. A category will then correspond to a person. Each trait may be used in one and only one category. You may use as many categories as you wish but try to use no more than 10 categories. [1968, p. 285]

The sixty traits were selected so as to sample evenly the full range of likableness as used by Anderson, while including the traits Asch used in studying centrality. There were more than a hundred subjects, and each trait was correlated with each other so as to determine the closeness of association. The resulting large matrix of correlations was subjected to a procedure called multidimensional scaling, which identifies the principal dimensions underlying the correlations. As it turned out, there were just two, both evaluative, but evaluative in different domains of descriptive meaning: (1) Good-Intellectual versus Bad-Intellectual and (2) Good-Social versus Bad-Social. A two-dimensional solution can be graphically displayed, and it appears as Figure 11–1.

The sense of Figure 11–1 is conveyed by noticing that while *sincere, helpful, tolerant* fall near the Good-Social pole and *unpopular, unhappy,* and *vain* at the Bad-Social pole, the traits *impulsive* and *reserved* are relatively neutral. *Scientific, persistent, determined* fall at the Good-Intellectual pole; *foolish, frivolous,* and *unintelligent* at the Bad-Intellectual pole, and the traits *impulsive* and *reserved* are relatively neutral on the Intellectual Scale as well as on the Social Scale. The two axes are not quite at right angles (not orthogonal), and that is not the artist's whim but a representation of something in the pattern of correlations. The axes are drawn as they are because the two kinds of good evaluation are somewhat associated, and so are the two kinds of bad evaluation. In short, there is some evidence of a completely general evaluative consistency, but it is not so strong as to collapse the two dimensions into one.

Using Figure 11–1, we can explain Asch's results with *warm–cold* and also provide a general definition of centrality. The six adjectives in Asch's stimulus set that were unchanged when *warm* and *cold* displaced one another are: *intelligent, skillful, industrious, determined, practical,* and *cautious.* In Figure 11–1 those adjectives (marked with the letter A) are all located on the Good-Intellectual side of neutrality, and four of them are clustered close together at the polar extreme. All of those six adjectives lie close to the midline between Good-Social and Bad-Social, which means they are neutral with respect to social desirability. In short, the six adjectives that constitute the unchanging context for either

Figure 11–1. Two-dimensional configuration of sixty traits on the axes of intellectual desirability and social desirability

Letter "A" marks Asch's stimulus straits. (From S. Rosenberg, C. Nelson, and P. S. Vivekananthan, A multidimensional approach to the structure of personality impressions, *Journal of Personality and Social Psychology,* 9 [1968], p. 290, Fig. 3. Copyright 1968 by the American Psychological Association. Reprinted by permission of the publisher and author)

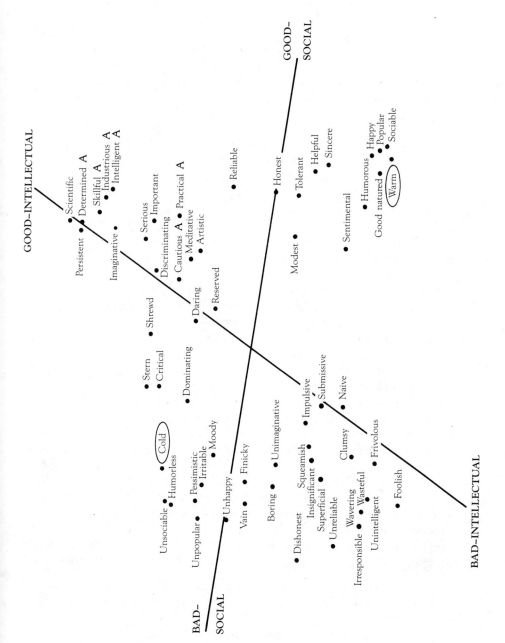

GOOD-INTELLECTUAL

GOOD-SOCIAL

BAD-SOCIAL

BAD-INTELLECTUAL

Scientific
Determined A
Skillful A
Industrious A
Intelligent A
Persistent
Imaginative
Serious
Important
Discriminating
Cautious A Practical A
Meditative
Artistic
Reliable
Honest
Tolerant
Helpful
Sincere
Humorous Happy
Popular
Sociable
Good natured
Warm
Sentimental
Modest
Daring
Reserved
Shrewd
Stern
Critical
Dominating
Submissive
Naive
Impulsive
Cold
Humorless
Moody
Pessimistic
Irritable
Unsociable
Unhappy
Unimaginative
Finicky
Frivolous
Clumsy
Squeamish
Unpopular
Vain
Boring
Insignificant
Superficial
Foolish
Dishonest
Unreliable
Wavering
Wasteful
Irresponsible
Unintelligent

413

warm or *cold* express, very redundantly, the meaning "Good-Intellectual" while saying nothing about the Social axis.

Warm and *cold*, the alternatives for the middle slot in the stimulus list, can be located in Figure 11-1 (encircled) at opposite ends of the Social scale. Why should *warm* and *cold* have a potent influence on the personality impression created by just this set of seven traits? They should have such an effect for two reasons: (1) The central or potent terms provide almost the only information on one basic dimension of personality, the social evaluation dimension, and (2) The information supplied by *warm* and *cold* is contrasting and extreme, which is to say that they fall near opposite poles. This definition of centrality is not specific to *warm* and *cold* but is completely general, and it should be possible using it to create new stimulus lists in which different traits would be central. For example, in the list *cold-unsociable-unhappy-vain-irritable-humorless* one would expect *intelligent* versus *foolish* to be central traits. Why?

Centrality was manifested quantitatively in Asch's data by changes in the traits on the checklist that seemed to go with the personality impression depending on whether *cold* or *warm* appeared (Table 11-6). The checklist traits were presented to subjects as antonym pairs, such as *happy-unhappy*, *popular-unpopular*, though Table 11-6, for reasons of brevity, records results for the favorable member alone. Rosenberg, Nelson, and Vivekananthan included nine of Asch's eighteen pairs, and in Figure 11-2 those are plotted (both poles) along with the fixed stimulus list plus *warm* and *cold*. For the following pairs Asch found the favorable pole much more likely to be inferred when *warm* was in the list and the unfavorable when *cold*: *happy-unhappy*; *popular-unpopular*; *sociable-unsociable*; *humorous-humorless*; *good-natured-irritable*. In Figure 11-2 you can see that those pairs line up in implicit personality theory close to one another and all close to *warm-cold*. Rosenberg and colleagues found that their subjects thought those Socially Good and Socially Bad traits clustered together in persons as the figure indicates. Asch's subjects inferred from the word *warm*, which is one member of the Socially Good set, all the rest of the set and from the word *cold*, which is one member of the Socially Bad set, all the rest of the set. It is as if Asch's subjects made their inferences in accordance with the implicit personality theory held by the subjects of Rosenberg, Nelson, and Vivekananthan (1968).

Not all antonym pairs on the checklist were responsive to *warm-cold*. Some were about equally likely to be inferred whichever of the two terms was

---

Figure 11-2. Two-dimensional configuration of Asch's stimulus traits and nine of the antonym pairs in his checklist

Stimulus traits are in capitals; checklist pairs in lower case; encircled are *Warm* and traits inferred from *Warm* and *Cold* and traits inferred from *Cold*. (From S. Rosenberg, C. Nelson, and P. S. Vivekananthan, A multidimensional approach to the structure of personality impressions, *Journal of Personality and Social Psychology*, 9 [1968], p. 290, Fig. 3. Copyright 1968 by the American Psychological Association. Reprinted by permission of the publisher and author)

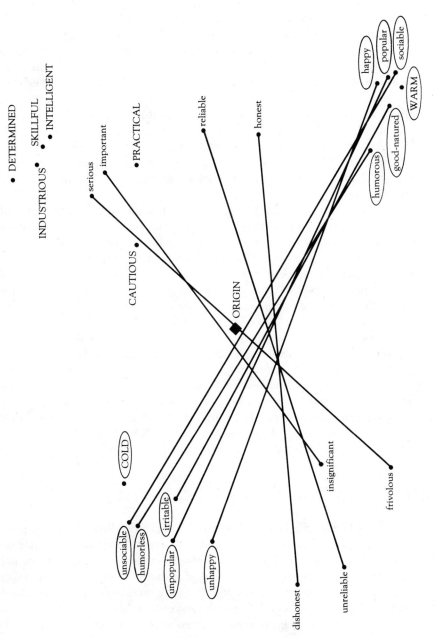

DETERMINED

INDUSTRIOUS • • SKILLFUL
• INTELLIGENT

• PRACTICAL

important

serious

reliable

honest

CAUTIOUS

ORIGIN

COLD

insignificant

frivolous

unsociable
humorless

irritable

WARM

humorous

good-natured

unpopular

unhappy

dishonest

unreliable

happy
popular
sociable

used. Four of those pairs appear in Figure 11–2: *serious–frivolous; important–insignificant; reliable–unreliable; honest–dishonest.* None of those lines up with the social axis, and so none is affected by *warm–cold.* All of them line up fairly well with the intellectual axis. What should follow from that fact? The six unchanging traits are all on the Intellectual-Good side and so should lead to the inference of the Intellectual-Good member of the pairs, to *serious, important, reliable,* and *honest.* That should happen whether *warm* is in the list or *cold,* because *serious, reliable,* and so on are traits that have much to do with intellectual evaluation and little to do with social evaluation. If you look back at Table 11–6, at traits 8, 9, 12, and 13, you will see that the favorable word is inferred with great frequency (88–100 percent) and with equal frequency in the *warm* and *cold* conditions. So this result of Asch's is also explained by implicit personality theory.

For the reader of academic letters of recommendation, the discovery that sixty different trait terms mainly express two kinds of evaluation, intellectual and social, explains the almost canonical form of such letters. The first paragraph usually describes the duration and character of the author's contacts with the person being recommended; its goal is to define the credibility of the source. The main part of the letter, short or long, one paragraph or many, is devoted to the precise calibration of the intellectual goodness of the candidate and includes words like *intelligent, persistent, skillfull.* The main question is how far out on the scale (or limb) will the author go? Some wag has suggested that you could write a very simple computer program for reading such letters: "(1) Search for the word *brilliant;* (2) Discount it if misspelled." The last paragraph almost always reads as if the author had recollected, late in his composition, the Social-Good versus Social-Bad dimension and realized that saying nothing on that dimension risked conveying a cool impression. So the writer swoops into a final paean roughly equivalent to: "Oh, I almost forgot, *warm, happy, humorous, sociable,* and will make a good colleague."

How Different Are Primacy and Centrality?

Because Asch treated primacy and centrality as distinct phenomena, the principal phenomena of impressions formed from trait lists, they have been treated so ever since. However, they have numerous similarities. The experimental operations are the same: Subjects are read a small number of trait terms in serial order, told to think of all as describing the same person, to let a general personality impression form, to write a brief sketch of that personality, to check that member of each of eighteen pairs of new terms that seems to fit best with the impression generated by the stimulus list.

The phenomena discovered, primacy and centrality, when viewed abstractly are the same kind of thing. In both cases certain trait terms (whether the first one or two or *warm–cold*) are discovered to carry more weight, to be more influential in the creation of the impression than other terms. Further-more, the weighting or influence is manifest in just the same ways in both cases. If the heavily weighted terms are evaluatively very favorable, socially desirable, the qualitative sketches and the additional terms selected will also be favorable; if the heavily weighted terms are less favorable or unfavorable, the sketch as a whole will be less favorable, and more of the unfavorable poles will be checked for the additional eighteen antonyms. That is how weighting effects are assessed for both primacy and centrality, even though the question for primacy is whether *intelligent–industrious–impulsive* have come first or *envious–stubborn–critical*, whereas for centrality the question is whether the stimulus set has included, in whatever position, the word *warm* or, alternatively, the word *cold*.

Turning to the explanations that have been put forward for primacy and centrality, the two seem farther apart. Asch explained primacy by "direction," which seems to reduce to heightened attention to the first terms in a list. Anderson, using a different experimental paradigm, also explained primacy as heightened attention, and Anderson and Hubert (1963) provided substantiat-ing evidence by giving instructions that equalized attention across the series. Centrality never was explained by Asch, though he showed that the centrality, or heavy weighting, of a given pair of antonyms like *warm–cold* was not abso-lute but relative to the other terms in the stimulus set. Rosenberg and co-workers (1968) were able to explain the centrality of *warm–cold* in Asch's list and to provide a general definition of centrality. Terms are central to, or heav-ily weighted in, a list when they provide the only information on a dimension (intellectual evaluation or social evaluation) and are extreme on that dimen-sion. Centrality does not enter into Anderson's experimental paradigm and so is not explained by him.

The attentional explanation of primacy and the explanation of centrality by Rosenberg and colleagues can both be reduced to a single explanation, which has, furthermore, the advantage of being a completely general principle of cognitive psychology. The more *information* an item conveys, the more closely it will be attended to. Information is to be understood as the opposite of predictability or redundancy. An item that carries high information is an item that could not have been guessed, an item that tells you something new. That is most clearly the case with *warm* or *cold* in an Intellectual-Good list of *intelligent–skillful–industrious–determined–practical–cautious*. Neither *warm* nor *cold* is predictable from the fixed set of adjectives since this set falls on the intel-lectual evaluation axis, so whichever occurs, *warm* or *cold*, is highly informa-tive. First or primary information in any set is also disproportionately informa-tive, because nothing precedes it that can be used as a basis for prediction. Early words in English sentences are, other things equal, less predictable than later words. As the sentence is developed, grammatical and semantic con-straints tighten and so later words become more predictable. One might expect that tendency to attend closely to the beginnings of series of words to transfer from English sentences and phrases to adjective sets of the sorts used by Asch and Anderson, and, of course, Anderson's explanation of primacy is in terms of high attention at the start (though he does not propose a high information explanation).

There is an apparent problem with the theory that high information produces heightened attention and heavy weighting and in that way accounts for both primacy and centrality. The problem arises with the lists Asch used (sometimes also Anderson) to study primacy; those lists were of the types HL and LH with evaluatively good (H) words at the start and evaluatively bad (L) words at the end or vice versa. The evaluation was not, in those lists, specific to intellectual or social, but a mixture of the two. However, if one has heard the H set, *intelligent–industrious–impulsive,* and then hears the first of the L set (*critical*), why should one not attend especially closely to that first negative word and to those that follow since they must be very unexpected and so highly informative coming after three good words? The same question applies for the LH set.

The answer lies in the mechanism by which primacy operates. Asch and many others have shown that *the same word* takes on different senses to suit the evaluative quality of its prior verbal context. In Asch's primacy list we have seen that *impulsive* can be understood as "spontaneous" or "reckless"; *critical,* as "discriminating" or "fault-finding"; *stubborn,* as "resolute" or "obstinate." In fact, most trait words have, we know, both an evaluatively positive sense and an evaluatively negative sense. A consistently positive (*intelligent–industrious–impulsive*) context need not register the printed form *critical* as unexpectedly negative and highly informative, because it can instead be understood as meaning "discriminating," which is its evaluatively consistent meaning. A consistently negative (*envious, stubborn, critical*) context need not register the printed form *impulsive* as positive, unexpected, and a signal to attention; it can simply select the meaning "reckless," which is negative and evaluatively consistent with what has gone before. In sum, the existence of both positive and negative meanings for trait terms means that potentially startling evaluative shifts need never come to mind. Semantic selection by context should be as automatic here as in ordinary sentences.

But something seems to be wrong with the idea that meaning selection is an alternative to the registration of an unexpected word, because *warm–cold* are in exactly the position of *critical* or *impulsive:* All are the fourth words in a set where the first three have been evaluatively consistent with one another. I do not think the cases really are the same, though at first they seem so. Neither *warm* nor *cold* contradicts the Intellectual-Good set (*intelligent–skillful–industrious*) that has preceded it. The intellectual evaluation axis is approximately (not exactly) at right angles to the social evaluation axis, which means the two kinds of evaluation are roughly independent of each other. That means a very intelligent person might be *either warm or cold,* and so the Intellectual-Good adjectives if followed by *cold* need not search for an evaluatively consistent sense of *cold.* Instead, *cold* is unconstrained by its prior context and so is understood in its most frequent sense, which is "unemotional" and "forbidding." Similarly, *warm* is free to assume its most common sense, which is "genial" or "agreeable." *Warm* and *cold* do then register as new information, not predictable from prior context, and so will be attended to and will carry great weight in the toal impression when in a set composed entirely of Social-Good words or Social-Bad words.

Warm and *cold* are unlike *impulsive*, *critical*, and *stubborn* in that they belong to an incomplete semantic set in Peabody's sense. If you will look back at Table 11–5, you will find that if the descriptive meaning is "temperament," then *warm* is high and *cold* is low and *warm* is positive and *cold* is negative. What is lacking, however, is an evaluatively negative sense of "warm" and an evaluatively positive sense of "cold." That means the pair *warm–cold* is, in semantic structure, like *intelligent–stupid*, *industrious–lazy*, and *altruistic–envious*. There is no bad sense of "warm" and there is no good sense of "cold." Consequently it is not clear that semantic selection could occur if the rest of the list called for it. In a weak way the Intellectual-Good words do call for selection when *cold* is on the list, because that extreme word on the Social-Bad side is somewhat contradictory to the rest with respect to general evaluation. *Warm* as an extreme on the Social-Good side is not at all contradictory. One would say "an intelligent *and* warm person"; "an intelligent *but* cold person." However, semantic selection is presumably blocked by the absense of a good sense of "cold."

One way to test the idea that *warm* and *cold* belong to incomplete sets would be to place them in sharply contradictory contexts such that semantic selection should occur and centrality disappear if the words have evaluative alternatives. Asch (1946), as so often, has done a relevant experiment. He puts *warm* in the middle of a list preceded by *vain*, *shrewd*, *unscrupulous*, and followed by *shallow*, *envious*—all Social-Bad words. *Warm* in this list ceases to be central or heavily weighted and, in fact, is reported by subjects to be one of the least important words on the list. The conditions for semantic selection were there, but the word *warm* did seem to present a problem for Asch's subjects in that they failed to come up with a Social-Bad alternative. Does the human mind blow a fuse? Not at all. One subject said: "I assumed the person only to appear warm rather than really to be warm" (p. 267). Another said: "He was warm only when it worked in with his scheme to get others over to his side. His warmth is not sincere" (p. 267). Asch also put *cold* in the middle of a contradictory list, preceded by *intelligent*, *skillful*, *sincere*, and followed by *conscientious*, *helpful*, *modest*. How is *cold* to be integrated with the rest? One said: "[He] is cold only superficially." Another said the quality "would disappear after you came to know him" (Asch, 1946, p. 268).

What shall we make of the responses that do not interpret *warm* in a bad way and *cold* in a good way when their contexts and the implicit personality theories we know seem to require it? Presumably the problem is that the required senses are not available and yet the integration process goes forward with no sign of strain. Perhaps the answer is that contradictory lists like this call into operation an implicit personality theory with a third dimension, a dimension of appearance versus reality, of seeming as opposed to being. That is hardly an unfamiliar or subtle dimension: "For one can smile and smile yet be a villain"; she is "laughing on the outside but crying on the inside." When almost every trait is bad and only *warm* is good, then the *warmth* is only external or seeming; the real person is bad. When almost every trait is good and only *cold* is bad, then the *cold* is understood to be superficial or only apparent; the real person is good.

Primacy and centrality are the same, then, in that both name cases in which certain trait terms are discovered to carry great weight in a total impression, to be more influential than the other terms. They are also the same in that the special weight could result from heightened attention, which in turn results from high information. Terms can be especially informative either because they are the first information received about a person or because they are the first information *on a new dimension*. The apparent problem with that formulation is that the special weighting afforded *warm–cold* as the first items on a new dimension is not also afforded the first terms that are evaluatively inconsistent in the *HL, LH* primacy paradigm. That problem disappears if we distinguish between contradictory information (primacy) and information that is only independent or unpredictable and if we distinquish between words that have both good and bad senses (*impulsive, critical, stubborn*) and words that have only one evaluative sense (*warm, cold*).

Integration of Acts into Traits

Asch started the impression formation process in the laboratory with trait names (e.g. *intelligent, industrious*) but it is hard to think of a real-life case of which this is representative; the letter of recommendation is the best we could do. It is much more usual to know first (whether from observation or report) specific actions someone has carried out and to integrate actions into traits. The work that has been done on the integration of traits shows that unexpected, or highly informative, traits are especially heavily weighted in a total impression, and the work that has been done on the integration of actions suggests that the same principle is at work.

Generalizing far beyond what we know, I suggest that we form impressions of persons so that we may predict what each is likely to do and so interact effectively with them. When our expectancies are wrong, when a person is discovered to have a trait that is inconsistent with their other traits or when a person acts in a way that is incongruent with some trait we had supposed them to possess, we must, in order to continue to be well-adapted to interpersonal reality, revise our impressions. It is perhaps to the adaptive purpose of updating our expectancies that we give heavy weight to unexpected information, recall it especially well, and are especially likely to proccess it for causality (Schank, 1982).

The experimental paradigm for the integration of acts was created by Hastie and Kumar (1979) and has been used by many others (e.g. Hamilton, Katz, and Leirer, 1980; Wyer and Gordon, 1982). The essentials are these. Specific actions or events are presented to the subject who has been asked to form an integrated impression of the person acting, an impression that takes account of all information. The actions might be described in sentences ("He won a chess tournament," "She enjoyed the new symphony") or might be enacted by confederates, in person or on video (e.g. someone cheating at cards).

Suppose there were (as there sometimes have been) nine actions of the same person. The majority of these will have been selected so as to suggest a particular trait (e.g. *intelligent* or *honest* or *friendly*) and an action consistent with the majority of the evidence is considered congruent, whereas an action inconsistent with the dominant impression is considered incongruent. After receiving all this information subjects are, to their surprise, asked to recall as many as possible of the specific actions (some of which will have been incongruent with the total impression and some of which will have been congruent). Sometimes (e.g. Hastie, 1984) subjects are asked to follow up each sentence describing an action (or each depicted action) with a short sentence. Subjects would have been given some cover story for the task (e.g. "This is a psycholinguistic study of sentence construction") concealing the actual interest in causally attributive sentence continuations such as: "He cheated at cards . . . because he was desperately short of money."

The method for identifying congruent and incongruent acts is elegant. You begin with a small set of adjective pairs of opposite meaning such as *intelligent–unintelligent, friendly–hostile, honest–dishonest*. A dozen or so pretest subjects are given instructions of the form, "Consider a person who is very intelligent; you would expect him (her) to . . . "and in this way actions suggestive of, and so congruent with, the target trait are elicited. To obtain actions incongruent with the target trait, you simply draw upon those offered as exemplary of its antonym. An honest person might be expected to "call a cashier's attention to a mistake from which he would have profited"; "refuse to tell a convenient lie"; "turn down a bribe." All these acts would be congruent but "cheating at cards" would be sharply incongruent. Subjects are instructed to read over the full list of descriptive sentences (or to view all relevant acts), first of all, and so the dominant direction of the impression, which separates the congruent from the incongruent, is the same throughout the experimental procedures.

In a characteristic procedure (e.g. Hastie, 1984) subjects first formed impressions (from lists of acts) of six persons, then wrote sentence continuations for each act, and finally recalled for each person (identified by a common American name) as many acts as possible. One result obtained by Hastie (1984) and very many others is that *incongruent* acts are recalled much more often than congruent acts, about twice as often in fact. This is true whether the total set of acts is large (nine) or small (three) so long as the ratio of congruent to incongruent acts is constant (e.g. two to one).

A second important result is a stronger tendency—about two times stronger—to compose sentences that are causal in content as continuations of incongruent acts than as continuations of congruent acts. Continuation sentences that are not causal explanations are all categorizable either as "elaborations" or as "temporal" successions. If a person whose acts mostly suggested that he was *intelligent* were said to "have won a chess tournament," the continuation might be a laconic "elaboration" such as, "that lasted an entire week," or a reasonable temporal succession such as, "and so carried off the trophy." But if the dominant impression were *unintelligent*, the continuation might be a causal attribution for the unexpected victory, such as, "since he had been coached for years" or "only because his opponent was ill."

In our discussion of causal attribution in Part II of this book nothing is said about the circumstances necessary to initiate processing for causality, but quite a bit is known about these circumstances. The tendency to seek causes for events which are actions of persons is clearly very general (Schank and Abelson, 1977; Zajonc, 1980) but not inevitable. Introspection, at least, suggests that the detached contemplation of strangers doing familiar things like crossing the street or buying subway tokens does not raise *why* questions. Four conditions that do lead to causal inference have been identified (Hastie, 1984). The least interesting, because the most obvious, is the explicit asking of a *why* question. Berscheid et al. (1976) found that men and women expecting to date one another engage in causal reasoning, and the general formulation has been proposed "dependence on another person for desired outcomes" (Hastie, 1984, p. 45). Harvey et al. (1980) have shown that observers who take an empathic, involved attitude toward others being observed engage in more causal inference than do detached observers. Finally, many studies (e.g. Lau and Russell, 1980; Wong and Weiner, 1981) have shown that unexpected events as opposed to expected events inspire causal reasoning, and it is precisely here that we must place the result for incongruent acts in impression formation.

Incongruent acts are by definition unexpected and so, again by definition, highly informative. Experiments on trait integration would lead us to expect incongruent acts to receive high selective attention and to be heavily weighted in consequent impressions. We do not know that this is true of incongruent acts but only that recall of them is superior and that they are especially likely to initiate causal inference. However, both recall and attribution are likely to depend on heightened attention.

I suggest that the act that does not conform to our present expectancies with respect to a person must be attended to, held in memory and thought about because it challenges the impression we have. It poses a problem of mental integration, but there would seem to be several possible outcomes: (1) The incongruent act might simply be held in memory as the piece that does not fit against the time when it will be seen to fit; (2) the incongruent act might be directly added into the present impression, lowering the evaluation of intelligence perhaps; (3) the incongruent act might be explained away by imagining such special circumstances as to leave the personality impression unchanged; or (4) the incongruent act might be integrated into the personality by giving a new qualitative tint to some present trait (e.g. *unintelligent* only in everyday matters).

The transition from act integration to trait integration will, when it has been worked out, go a long way to synthesize the field of impression formation. Quite powerful and explicit syntheses seem likely to be attained even in the 1980's.

Semantics, Implicit Personality Theory, and the Real Structure of Personality

A large portion of the research on impression formation has been done with words—trait names—and one explanatory principle—semantic selection—is similar to a general psycholinguistic principle. That concentration on the natural language of personality with insufficient attention to nonverbal acts (but see Buss and Craik, 1983, for a promising exception) is something to worry about. However, it does not necessarily follow that the work done is seriously artificial or that the principles discovered apply only to verbal materials. The semantics of trait terms, implicit personality theory derived from judgments of co-occurrence in persons, and the real structure of personality all closely correspond with one another, and just why they should do so is a deep and important question to which Richard Shweder (1982) and Jack Block and his associates (Block, Weiss, and Thorne, 1979) have offered different answers.

Consider the sixty trait terms of Figure 11–1, since that is the data set we know best. There are three distinct operations that can be performed on those traits that will all yield the same two-dimensional analysis: intellectual evaluation and social evaluation. Judges can be asked to group together those traits that tend to occur together in persons and to separate widely those traits that seldom occur together. That is what Rosenberg and colleagues (1968) did ask judges to do, and the underlying structure in the data, discovered by multidimensional scaling, was called an implicit theory of personality, a *conception* of the structure of personality—not necessarily the real structure. Judges could, alternatively, be asked to do a personality assessment task, to rate individuals they know well on all sixty traits, and the underlying structure, we may be confident, would be just the same two dimensions of evaluation. For many years such ratings of real persons were interpreted as unequivocally yielding the real structure of personality in terms of factors or dimensions (e.g. Cattell, 1946, 1950, 1957; Guilford, 1959; Tupes and Christal, 1961). Mulaik (1964) was one of the first to point out that the structure extracted from such ratings might equally well be thought of as a revelation of real structure or as a reflection of the beliefs of the raters as, in fact, implicit personality theory. Mulaik provided relevant evidence, as did Passini and Norman (1966), Powell and Juhnke (1983), and many others. Block and associates (1979) expressed the view of most students of personality that implicit theory and real structure tend to coincide because the beliefs are an "Accurate Reflection" of the facts.

A third interesting operation could be performed with the sixty trait terms of Figure 11-1, and it was performed on a subset of them by Gara and Rosenberg (1981). The terms, now explicitly thought of as English adjectives, are combined in all possible pairs, and judges are instructed, for each pair, to rate the two words for *similarity of meaning* on a scale from 7 (very similar in meaning) to 1 (completely opposite in meaning). Roy D'Andrade (1974) and Richard Shweder (1975) created the model for this method of studying semantic structure (not either implicit or real personality structure).

How would the judgments of meaning similarity go? *Intelligent* and *unintelligent*, *warm* and *cold* would anchor opposite poles, just as they do in Figure 11-1, which was, however, derived from co-occurrence judgments. *Popular* and *sociable* would probably be rated very similar in meaning and very different from *humorless* and *pessimistic*—exactly as they appear in Figure 11-1. The Gara and Rosenberg (1981) study of the structure of meaning in a subset of the full sixty traits yielded exactly the same structure as did the study of co-occurrence judgments. As of 1982 Shweder reports this kind of similarity-in-meaning task has been superimposed on eleven major factor-analytic studies of earlier years, which had originally asked subjects to rate persons on the trait terms, and in all cases the original structure was closely duplicated.

How has it come about that judgments of meaning similarity have the same structure as judgments of co-occurrence in persons and ratings of real persons? Block and associates (1979) argue that the meaning structure must be an Accurate Reflection of real personality structure even as they think that implicit personality theory is. D'Andrade (1974) and Shweder (1975, 1982) have made an interesting case for a possibility that language systematically distorts personality ratings, but while the issue is not settled, I think the better case can be made for Accurate Reflection. Consider the terms *popular* and *sociable*. They can be distinguished in descriptive meaning by glossing the first as "well-liked" and the second as "gregarious." Why should those two be rated similar in meaning and remote from *pessimistic* and *humorless*? The most plausible explanation is, I think, that pessimistic and humorless people tend not to be well-liked and also, for all those reasons, not gregarious. That is to suggest that the actual structure of personality affects judgments of similarity in meaning.

Summary

Impressions of persons are unified and integrated in memory. Ordinarily the information we receive about persons does not come in unbroken blocks such that everything about one person is learned before anything is learned about another. Instead, bits of information about one person arrive randomly interspersed over time with bits of information about other persons and about everything else, and still, in memory, everything about one individual is stored together or unified. When social information as input is not blocked by person, it is not necessarily organized (as revealed by clustering in free recall) in terms of persons but may be organized in terms of events, arguments, ethnic groups, or otherwise. Organization in terms of persons is more likely with acquaintances than strangers and with traits in stereotypical combination rather than unpredictable combination. Person organization is also facilitated by tuning the perceiver to make person-relevant judgments. When the person is the self, unification and superior recall occur.

Integration of an impression of a person means (1) going beyond the information given, inferring the unknown in an effort to achieve a full impression, and (2) fitting together the parts of an impression so that they are accommodated to one another and subordinate to the whole. The two kinds of integration were the focus of the first experimental studies of impression formation (Asch, 1946). In all of those studies subjects were asked to think of a presented short list of traits as belonging to one person, and so the process of unifying information was bypassed. Integration of the traits in the sense of going beyond the information given was evidenced in qualitative personality sketches and in choices between pairs of contrasting adjectives (usually eighteen). In order to infer unknown traits from a short list of given traits, a person must have some impression of how traits generally go together in persons, must have what is called an "implicit personality theory."

The most basic experimental demonstration is that a short list of traits, all evaluatively good, will lead to strong inferences of other good traits. Those inferences are guided by the simplest of all implicit personality theories, the theory of evaluative consistency. There is abundant general evidence that humans do believe in that theory. Not all of the evidence is entirely verbal and inferential. It has been shown that physical attractiveness, as evident in a photo, leads to the inference of every kind of good quality and success and also to discriminatory action. Evaluatively negative inferences and actions have been shown to be associated with facial disfigurement.

Integration means, in addition to going beyond the information given, fitting together the parts of an impression so that they constitute a well-formed whole. Asch demonstrated this second sort of integration in conjunction with the phenomenon of primacy, which is the disproportionate weight in a total impression given to the information first received. A list of six adjectives was used such that the terms on one end named unequivocally good qualities and the terms on the other end unequivocally bad, while the middle three terms were open to either an evaluatively good or bad interpretation. Primacy is demonstrated by showing that the total impression (in character sketches or choices on a checklist) is more dependent on the first terms than the last, and the experimental paradigm simply involves reversing a single list.

Asch's explanation of integration in the primacy paradigm is essentially that the words in the middle of the list, having both good and bad possible senses, are influenced by the evaluative "direction" of the first words so as to be interpreted or understood in an evaluatively consistent way. Peabody's analysis of the meanings of trait terms in two dimensions (descriptive meaning and evaluative meaning) makes a more explicit explanation possible, because the end terms turn out to have fixed evaluative meanings whereas the middle terms have both good and bad meanings. In psycholinguistic terms one would say that a set of adjectives modifying a single noun are "in construction," and the words processed first (primacy) select consistent meanings for those processed afterward. The principle of semantic composition has nothing to do with linguistics, however, but is the implicit personality theory of evaluative consistency.

Norman Anderson has also worked with the integration of trait meanings with the difference that he has "likability" ratings on the more than five hundred adjectives used in his work, and subjects are asked only to rate the integrated impression on one dimension: likability. It has been possible to develop a mathematical model of algebraic averaging for the process, a model that takes account of primacy. In Anderson's experiments, primacy appears to result from heightened attention. Primacy has also been demonstrated for the case in which an impression is based on problem-solving behavior, and the explanation seems again to be heightened attention.

Centrality of a trait refers not to position in a list but to heavy weighting in an impression, and was demonstrated by Asch using *warm* or *cold* in a list of terms all meaning Intellectual-Good qualities. With *warm* in the list many Social-Good qualities are chosen on the checklist, and with *cold* many Social-Bad qualities. The explanation lies with a more complex implicit personality theory, one having a dimension of evaluation in the intellectual sphere and a not-quite-orthogonal dimension of evaluation in the social sphere. The integration that occurs is going beyond the information given—on two dimensions.

Primacy and centrality are the same phenomenon: Both name disproportionately high weighting due to heightened attention due to high information (low predictability). The difference is that first information is highly informative because it is the first information of any kind about the person, whereas "central" information is simply the first on a given dimension. There is an apparent difficulty with this formulation in the fact that the central words in the *HL–LH* primacy paradigm, being inconsistent with what has gone before, should, like *warm* or *cold*, attract heightened attention. The difficulty disappears when we distinguish (1) between the inconsistency of negative implication, which applies in the primacy paradigm and strongly calls for meaning selection, and the inconsistency of *warm–cold*, which is simply the unpredictability of values on a new dimension, and (2) between words that have both positive and negative evaluative senses like those in the middle of the primacy list and words that have only a single evaluative sense, like *warm* and *cold*.

Three experimental operations involving trait terms yield very similar underlying situations: (1) judgments of co-occurrence in persons; (2) ratings of real individuals; (3) ratings of the words for similarity of meaning. Probably the three coincide because implicit personality theory and semantic structure are both reflections of the real structure of personality.

References

ABELSON, R. P., and M. G. ROSENBERG. 1958. Symbolic psycho-logic: A model of attitudinal cognition, *Behavioral Science*, 3: 1–13.

ALLEN, R. B., and E. B. EBBESEN. 1981. Cognitive processes in person perception, *Journal of Experimental Social Psychology*, 17: 119–41.

ALLPORT, G. W. and H. S. ODBERT. 1936. Trait names: A psycho-lexical study, *Psychological Monographs*, vol. XLVII, whole No. 211.

ANDERSON, J. R. 1977. Memory for information about individuals, *Memory and Cognition*, 5: 430–42.

ANDERSON, N. H. 1965a. Primacy effects in personality impression formation using a generalized order effect paradigm, *Journal of Personality and Social Psychology*, 2: 1–9.

———. 1965b. Averaging versus adding as a stimulus-combination rule in impression formation, *Journal of Experimental Psychology*, 70: 394–400.

———. 1968a. Likableness ratings of 555 personality-trait words, *Journal of Personality and Social Psychology*, 9: 272–79.

———. 1968b. Application of a linear-serial model to a personality-impression task using serial presentation, *Journal of Personality and Social Psychology*, 10: 354–62.

ANDERSON, N. H., and A. A. BARRIOS. 1961. Primacy effects in personality impression formation, *Journal of Abnormal and Social Psychology*, 63: 346–50.

ANDERSON, N. H., and S. HUBERT. 1963. Effects of concomitant verbal recall on order effects in personality impression formation, *Journal of Verbal Learning and Verbal Behavior*, 2: 379–91.

ANDERSON, N. H., and A. NORMAN. 1964. Order effects in impression formation in four classes of stimuli, *Journal of Abnormal and Social Psychology*, 69: 467–71.

ASCH, S. E. 1946. Forming impressions of personality, *Journal of Abnormal and Social Psychology*, 41: 258–90.

ASCH, S. E., and H. ZUKIER. 1984. Thinking about persons, *Journal of Personality and Social Psychology*, 46: 1230–40.

BEM, D. J. 1972. Self-perception theory. In L. Berkowitz (ed.), *Advances in Experimental Social Psychology*, 6: 1–62.

BENSON, P. L.; S. A. KARABENICK; and R. M. LERNER. 1976. Pretty pleases: The effects of physical attractiveness, race, and sex on receiving help, *Journal of Experimental Social Psychology*, 12: 409–15.

BERSCHEID, E.; W. GRAZIANO; T. MONSON; and M. DERMER. 1976. Outcome dependency: Attention, attribution, and attraction, *Journal of Personality and Social Psychology*, 34: 978–89.

Block, J; D. S. Weiss, and A. Thorne. 1979. How relevant is a semantic similarity interpretation of personality ratings? *Journal of Personality and Social Psychology, 37:* 1055-74.

Bousfield, W. A. 1953. The occurrence of clustering in the recall of randomly arranged associates, *Journal of General Psychology, 49:* 229-40.

Brown, R. 1965. *Social Psychology.* New York: Free Press.

Bruner, J. S.; D. Shapiro; and R. Tagiuri. 1958. The meaning of traits in isolation and in combination. In R. Tagiuri and L. Petrullo (eds.), *Person Perception and Interpersonal Behavior.* Stanford, Calif.: Stanford University Press, pp. 227-88.

Bull, R. 1982. Physical appearance and criminality, *Current Psychological Reviews, 2:* 269-82.

———. 1983. The general public's reactions to facial disfigurement. Conference on the Psychology of Cosmetic Treatments, University of Pennsylvania, September 19-20.

Bull, R., and J. Stevens. 1981. The effects of facial disfigurement on helping behaviour, *The Italian Journal of Psychology, VIII:* 26-33.

Buss, D. M., and K. H. Craik. 1983. The act frequency approach to personality, *Psychological Review, 90:* 105-26.

Carlston, D. E. 1980. The recall and use of traits and events in social information processing, *Journal of Experimental Social Psychology, 16:* 303-28.

Cattell, R. B. 1946. *Description and Measurement of Personality.* Yonkers N.Y.: World Book.

———. 1950. *Personality: A Systemic, Theoretical, and Factual Study.* New York: McGraw-Hill.

———. 1957. *Personality and Motivation.* Yonkers, N.Y.: World Book.

Cronbach, L. J. 1955. Processes affecting scores on "understanding of others" and "assumed similarity," *Psychological Bulletin, 52:* 177-93.

D'Andrade, R. G. 1974. Memory and the assessment of behavior. In T. Blalock (ed.), *Social Measurement.* Chicago: Aldine-Atherton.

Digman, J. M., and N. E. Takemoto-Chock. 1981. Factors in the national language of personality: Re-analysis, comprehension, and interpretation of six major studies, *Multivariate Behavioral Research, 17:* 149-70.

Dion, K.; E. Berscheid; and E. Walster. 1972. What is beautiful is good, *Journal of Personality and Social Psychology, 24:* 285-90.

Gara, M. A., and S. Rosenberg. 1981. Linguistic factors in implicit personality theory, *Journal of Personality and Social Psychology, 41:* 450-57.

Guilford, J. P. 1959. *Personality.* New York: McGraw-Hill.

Hamilton, D. L.; L. B. Katz; and V. O. Leirer. 1980. Organizational processes in impression formation. In R. Hastie, T. M. Ostrom, E. B. Ebbesen, R. S. Wyer, Jr., D. L. Hamilton, and D. E. Carlston (eds.), *Person Memory: The Cognitive Basis of Social Perception.* Hillsdale, N. J.: Erlbaum, pp. 121-53.

Hamilton, D. L., and M. P. Zanna. 1974. Context effects in impression formation: Changes in connotative meaning, *Journal of Personality and Social Psychology, 29:* 649-54.

Harvey, J. H.; K. L. Yarkin; J. M. Lightner; and J. P. Town. 1980. Unsolicited interpretation and recall of interpersonal events, *Journal of Personality and Social Psychology*, *38*: 551–68.

HASTIE, R. 1984. Causes and effects of causal attribution, *Journal of Personality and Social Psychology*, *46*: 44–56.

HASTIE, R., and P. A. KUMAR. 1979. Person memory: Personality traits as organizing principles in memory for behavior, *Journal of Personality and Social Psychology*, *37*: 25–38.

HEIDER, F. 1946. Attitudes and cognitive organization, *Journal of Psychology*, *21*: 107–12.

HIGGINS, E. T., and W. S. RHOLES. 1976. Impression formation and role fulfillment: A "holistic reference" approach, *Journal of Experimental Social Psychology*, *12*: 422–35.

JONES, E. E.; L. ROCK; K. G. SHAVER; G. R. GOETHALS; and L. M. WARD. 1968. Pattern of performance and ability attribution: An unexpected primacy effect, *Journal of Personality and Social Psychology*, *10*: 317–40.

KAPLAN, M. F. 1971. Context effects in impression formation: The weighted average versus the meaning-change formulation, *Journal of Personality and Social Psychology*, *19*: 92–99.

——. 1974. Context-induced shifts in personality trait evaluation: A comment on the evaluative halo effect and the meaning change interpretations, *Psychological Bulletin*, *81*: 891–95.

LANDY, D., and H. SIGALL. 1974. Beauty is talent: Task evaluation as a function of the performer's physical attractiveness, *Journal of Personality and Social Psychology*, *29*: 299–304.

LAU, R. R., and D. RUSSELL. 1980. Attributions in the sports pages: A field test of some current hypotheses in attribution research, *Journal of Personality and Social Psychology*, *37*: 25–38.

LINGLE, J. H.; J. M. DUKERICH; and T. M. OSTROM. 1983. Accessing information in memory-based impression judgments: Incongruity vs. negativity in retrieval selectivity, *Journal of Personality and Social Psychology*, *44*: 262–72.

MARKUS, M. 1977. Self-schemata and processing information about the self, *Journal of Personality and Social Psychology*, *35*: 63–78.

MARKUS, H.; M. CRANE; S. BERNSTEIN; and M. SILADI. 1982. Self-schemes and gender. *Journal of Personality and Social Psychology*, *42*: 38–50.

MULAIK, S. 1964. Are personality factors raters' conceptual factors? *Journal of Consulting Psychology*, *28*: 506–11.

NISBETT, R. E., and T. D. WILSON. 1977. The halo effect: Evidence for unconscious alteration of judgments, *Journal of Personality and Social Psychology*, *35*: 250–56.

OSGOOD, C. E. 1962. Studies on the generality of affective meaning systems, *American Psychologist*, *17*: 10–28.

OSGOOD, C. E., and P. H. TANNENBAUM. 1955. The principle of congruity in the prediction of attitude change, *Psychological Review*, *62*: 42–55.

OSTROM, T. M.; J. H. LINGLE; J. B. PRYOR; and N. GEVA. 1980. Cognitive organization of person and impressions. In R. Hastie, T. M. Ostrom, E. B. Ebbesen, R. S. Wyer, Jr., D. L. Hamilton, and D. E. Carlston (eds.), *Person Memory: The Cognitive Basis of Social Perception*. Hillsdale, N.J.: Erlbaum Associates, pp. 55–88.

OSTROM, T. M.; J. B. PRYOR; and D. D. SIMPSON. 1981. The organization of social information. In E. T. Higgins, C. P. Herman, and M. P. Zanna (eds.), *Social Cognition: The Ontario Symposium*. Vol. *1*. Hillsdale, N.J.: Erlbaum Associates.

PASSINI, F. T., and W. T. NORMAN. 1966. A universal conception of personality structure? *Journal of Personality and Social Psychology, 4:* 44–49.

PEABODY, D. 1967. Trait inferences: Evaluative and descriptive aspects, *Journal of Personality and Social Psychology,* vol. *7:* whole No. 644.

———. 1970. Evaluative and descriptive aspects in personality perception: A reappraisal, *Journal of Personality and Social Psychology, 16:* 639–46.

———. 1984. Personality dimensions through trait inferences, *Journal of Personality and Social Psychology, 46:* 384–403.

POWELL, S. R., and R. G. JUHNKE. 1983. Statistical models of implicit personality theory: A comparison, *Journal of Personality and Social Psychology, 44:* 911–22.

PRYOR, J. B., and T. M. OSTROM. 1981. The organization of social information: A converging-operations approach, *Journal of Personality and Social Psychology, 41:* 628–41.

PRYOR, J. B.; D. D. SIMPSON; M. MITCHELL; T. M. OSTROM; and J. LYDON. 1982. Structural selectivity in the retrieval of social information, *Social Cognition, 4:* 336–57.

PUFF, C. R. 1973. Effects of types of input structure upon recall and different clustering scores, *Bulletin of the Psychonomic Society, 2:* 271–72.

ROGERS, T. B.; N. A. KUIPER; and W. S. KIRKER. 1977. Self-reference and the encoding of personal information, *Journal of Personality and Social Psychology, 35:* 677–88.

ROSENBERG, S.; C. NELSON; and P. S. VIVEKANANTHAN. 1968. A multidimensional approach to the structure of personality impressions, *Journal of Personality and Social Psychology, 9:* 283–94.

RUMSEY, N.; R. BULL; and D. GAHAGAN. 1982. The effect of facial disfigurement on the proxemic behavior of the general public, *Journal of Applied Social Psychology, 12:* 137–50.

SCHANK, R. C., 1982. *Dynamic Memory*. New York: Cambridge University Press.

SCHANK, R. C., and R. P. ABELSON. 1977. *Scripts, Plans, Goals, and Understanding*. Hillsdale, N.J.: Erlbaum.

SHWEDER, R. A. 1982. Fact and artifact in trait perception. The systematic distortion hypothesis, In B. A. Maher (ed.), *Progress in Experimental Personality Research*. Vol. *11*. New York: Academic Press, pp. 65–100.

SHWEDER, R. A. 1975. How relevant is an individual difference theory of personality? *Journal of Personality, 43:* 455–83.

STEWART, R. H. 1965. Effect of continuous responding on the order effect in personality impression formation, *Journal of Personality and Social Psychology, 1:* 161–65.

TUPES, E. C., and R. E. CHRISTAL. 1961. Recurrent personality factors based on trait ratings. Lackland Air Force Base: Personnel Laboratory, Aeronautical Systems Division, Air Force Systems Command, United States Air Force, Technical Report ASD-TR-61-97.

WONG, P. T. P., and B. WEINER. 1981. When people ask "why" questions and the heuristics of attributional search, *Journal of Personality and Social Psychology, 40:* 650–63.

Wyer, R. S. 1974. Changes in meaning and halo effects in personality impression formation, *Journal of Personality and Social Psychology*, 29: 829–35.

Wyer, R. S., and S. Gordon, 1982. The recall of information about persons and groups, *Journal of Experimental Social Psychology*, 18: 128–64.

Wyer, R. S., and T. K. Srull (eds.). 1984. *Handbook of Social Cognition*. Hillsdale, N.J.: Erlbaum Associates.

Wyer, R. S.; T. K. Srull; and S. Gordon. 1984. The effects of predicting a person's behavior on subsequent trait judgments, *Journal of Experimental Social Psychology*, 20: 29–46.

Zajonc, R. B. 1960. The process of cognitive tuning in communication, *Journal of Abnormal and Social Psychology*, 61: 159–67.

——. 1980. Feeling and thinking: Preferences need no inferences, *American Psychologist*, 35: 131–75.

Zanna, M. P., and D. L. Hamilton. 1977. Further evidence for meaning change in impression formation, *Journal of Experimental Social Psychology*, 13: 224–38.

V

Language
and Communication

WHY NOT, JUST ONCE, dear author, begin at the beginning rather than at some livelier point, brought forward from its logical position in a tacky effort to engage interest? And from the beginning, proceed in straightforward fashion to the most closely related next topic and from that to the next until you reach a conclusion, feeling the satisfaction an honest man must feel at simple linear exposition. I am willing to try, but that is probably because the topic at the beginning is the origins of language, which is just the craziest topic of all.

12

The Origins of Language

WRITING SYSTEMS WERE INVENTED only about six thousand years ago. The most recent date for the origin of language that I have seen postulated by a modern scientist is about 40,000 years ago (Jaynes, 1976). Most students of human prehistory would push the date back by 1 million to 3 million years (Holloway, 1976). There is no written record of the event of origination, and there are no fossilized phonemes or shards of ancient grammar. This has left the way open to speculation.

Most early "contributions" to the origins question were transparently motivated by a desire to establish the essential nature of man as either Godlike or animal-like by, as it were, starting him off on the right foot. In 1866 the Linguistic Society of Paris, grown weary of this stuff, expressly prohibited discussions on the topic, but in 1975, the New York Academy of Sciences held a four-day conference on "Origins and Evolution of Language and Speech," which captured the interest of scientists everywhere. The new respectability of the topic seems to me to be due to three new kinds of information: (1) evidence of some linguistic capacity in nonhuman primates, especially chimpanzees; (2) instances of something like language invention occurring in the present day; and (3) new thoughts and findings from archaeology, paleoneurology, and paleoanthropology.

Linguistic Capacities of Chimpanzees

While there has been some work with an orangutan and some with a gorilla (Patterson and Linden, 1981), most of the contemporary research on language-like behavior in nonhuman primates has been done with chimpanzees (*Pan troglodytes*). It will soon be twenty years since the chimpanzee Washoe arrived at the University of Nevada in Reno to be reared as a child by Allen and Beatrice Gardner and taught the language of the deaf in North America, the American Sign Language (ASL). Washoe was just short of one year old when she arrived in 1966, and she lived with the Gardners (having her own little trailer in their back yard) until she was five, when the onset of puberty made her less manageable and she had to be returned to the primate research center at the University of Oklahoma. There Roger Fouts, a former student of the Gardners, continued to work with Washoe. Fouts also initiated a parallel sort of study with six other chimps. The Gardners meanwhile began work with a second generation of four: Moja, Pili (now deceased), Tatu, and Dar by name. For the second generation the Gardners were able significantly to improve their methods: The chimps came to them soon after birth; the human signers of ASL were highly fluent (some of them deaf); and comparisons were to be made with a published developmental study (Collins-Ahlgren, 1975) of the acquisition of ASL by a human child. The Gardners in all their work have reared chimps like children and used ASL as the target language. Roger Fouts has done the same, and so has Penny Patterson with Koko, a lowland gorilla. A quite different approach, shortly to be described, has been taken at the primate research center in Georgia by Duane Rumbaugh and E. Sue Savage-Rumbaugh.

It has always made good sense to look for linguistic capacities of some sort in chimpanzees simply because *Pan troglodytes* and *Homo sapiens* have genotypes that are 99 percent the same. It did not make good sense to look for chimpanzee linguistic abilities in chimpanzee vocalizations, but that was done by five investigating teams (e.g. Hayes and Hayes, 1951; Kellogg and Kellogg, 1933) before 1960. Of course, we can see why vocalizations seemed the right thing to study. Speech is the primary form of language, and speech is vocalized. However, no one would want to call vocalization the *essence* of language, as that would deny linguistic status to writing and signing and every sort of code. The chimpanzee vocal anatomy and neurology are, however, quite different from the human (Lieberman, 1973; Myers, 1976) and are not much exercised beyond a few emotionally expressive calls, which cannot be shaped to resemble vowels and consonants. Chimpanzees do, however, have manual dexterity of a very high order, and they can by several methods, especially "molding," which means shaping by a human of the passive chimpanzee hand, be taught to produce fairly good approximations to most of the signs of ASL. These signs are transcribable in terms of the parameters of configuration, location, orientation, and movement.

The full linguistic status of ASL is not doubted today by any informed person, though it would have been as recently as twenty years ago, when even some linguists thought of the manual signing of the deaf as a set of pantomimic gestures severely limited in communicative power. The layman then, as now, was likely to think of deaf signs as a universal system used by the deaf everywhere—probably because most of us have heard (correctly) that the North American Plains Indians (West, 1960) shared a set of signs that could be used for limited communication between speakers of different languages. Today we know that there are many sign languages, probably as many as there are distinct deaf communities, and the Chinese, Japanese, Israeli, British, and Italian systems are all being studied, but far more is known about the American Sign Language than any other. It is not related to spoken English and is very unlike English in its grammatical structure, but that structure includes declaratives, interrogatives, negatives, and imperatives; it includes pronouns, parts of speech, subject and object, and markers for number, tense, aspect, and so on. ASL is able to express any meaning whatsoever, and so one can only say that ASL is language in another modality: manual-visual instead of vocal-auditory.

The work of producing an explicit description of how ASL works has mostly been done at the Salk Institute for Biological Research by Ursula Bellugi, Edward Klima, and their collaborators (Klima and Bellugi, 1979) over a period of about fifteen years. At no point, so far as I know, has the Salk group attempted to define the essense of language or entered into any disputes about definition. They have simply described it piece by piece, system by system, and in the end everyone has felt compelled to accommodate his or her definition of language to include ASL. Equally painstaking descriptions of chimp signing have not led to a similar consensus.

In *human hands*, as it were, ASL is undoubtedly a language, but to suppose that the signs of ASL in chimpanzee hands must necessarily constitute language use is to mistake response topography, muscles moved, for the essentials. It is the same mistake that led early investigators of language-like behavior to concentrate on vocalization (similar to speech in superficial response topography), and it is as great a mistake as supposing that the amazing imitations of speech produced by a mynah bird qualify as language. What must be shown, if chimps are to be credited with a given linguistic capacity, is that they are able to use the signs of ASL in just those ways that would convince us that a human had the capacity in question.

What is not fair, if the comparative psychological question is to be seriously posed, is to exclude chimp signing from the domain of language just because it is chimps and not humans who are moving their hands. While hardly anyone would make that logical mistake in an explicit way, there are many who make it in an implicit, disguised way by asserting that chimp signing is not accompanied by some mental process such as meaning or imagery or intention to communicate, for which they neglect or are unable to supply the behavioral evidence, to be looked for in both chimp and man. It does not make you a behaviorist (in, say, a Skinnerian sense) to recognize that the comparative psychological question must be expressed in behavioral terms, or else no question is being asked.

The primate research center in Georgia (directed by Duane Rumbaugh and Sue Savage-Rumbaugh) has from the start used an artificial language system rather than ASL, but it is still a system in which the possibily linguistic responses are manual. The chimp and his trainer work with a keyboard mounted on a wall panel and always available. Each key is embossed with a distinctive geometric figure (compounded from a small set of elements), and the manual response is simply depression of a key. The geometric figures on the keys are in one-to-one associative relation with real-world objects, such as foods and tools. In some experiments there are also implicit grammatical rules for the acceptable sequencing of key presses. A key when touched lights up, and the geometric figure is projected on a screen above the board and also optimally on monitors elsewhere. One or another trainer typically spends most of the day with the chimp (Lana was the first, with Sherman and Austin arriving later), and a large amount of spontaneous communication goes on by way of the keyboard, but that spontaneous interaction is distinguished from controlled experimental tests. A picture of the keyboard appears as Figure 12–1.

ASL has the clear advantage of portability; all communicators carry their language apparatus in their bodies, and so interaction can closely resemble that of parent and child. Recording of responses in the chimp ASL studies has, like the naturalistic studies of first language development in children (e.g. Brown, 1973), necessarily been far from complete and also more or less "richly interpreted." The Georgia keyboard lacks portability, and use of it does not look much like any sort of parent–child language use. However, the "look" of the process is of no importance since response topography is not part of the definition of any language capacity, and the keyboard has the advantage of being linked with a computer that automatically and without interpretation records everything. In experiments the keyboard can also be used without any human being present, and so the always worrisome problem of unintentional cueing or prompting from a trainer is removed.

The chimp language studies enjoyed almost ten years of relatively uncritical appreciation (e.g. Fouts, 1973; Gardner and Gardner, 1971, 1975, 1978, and many more; Patterson, 1978; Rumbaugh, 1977; Rumbaugh, Warner, and Von Glasersfeld, 1977; Savage-Rumbaugh, Rumbaugh, and Boysen, 1978). All the chimps learned to produce large numbers of signs (either ASL signs or distinctive key pressings) in response to the intended referents of the signs, whether real or photographed. Washoe, at the end of her four years with the Gardners, was said to have 132 signs, and Roger Fouts was quoted in *The New York Times*

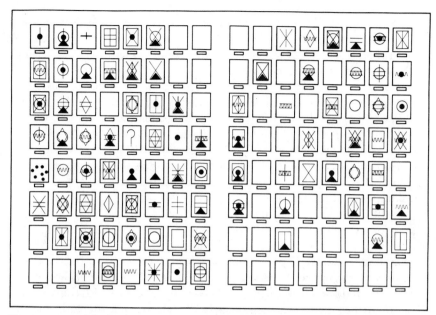

Figure 12–1. The keyboard used with Lana, Sherman, and Austin

All symbols are white on a black background. Blank spaces are nonfunctioning keys or photographs of teachers. (From E. S. Savage-Rumbaugh, J. L. Pate, J. Lawson, S. T. Smith, and S. Rosenbaum, Can a chimpanzee make a statement? *Journal of Experimental Psychology: General, 112* [1983], p. 470, Fig. 1. Copyright 1983 by the American Psychological Association. Reprinted by permission of the publisher and author)

of March 25, 1984, as saying she had by then learned 260, but Koko, the gorilla, beat that with 400 (Patterson and Linden, 1981). In writing about this selective responding, the authors used terms like *name, referent, symbol,* and *vocabulary,* so quite naturally their readers assumed that the performances in question were like those of the young child who marches around the house, naming one thing and another, announcing his intentions, reporting information to someone in another room, and so on. It was easy to forget that in the controlled tests of chimp vocabulary the trainer presented the referent or picture, the chimp signed in an offhand abstract way that suggested indifference to communication, and the trainer tossed the animal a peanut or equivalent as reward. It was also easy to overlook the fact that, in the supposedly language-like behavior, the chimp almost always was on the response production end; almost no evidence of sign comprehension appeared in the reports and films; the Georgia research team is a partial exception, and they reported in 1980 that comprehension does not necessarily follow from production, but must be trained as such.

In the uncritical decade that ended abruptly in 1979 just about everyone took it for granted that a capacity for symbolism had been demonstrated beyond any doubt. What arguments there were concerned syntax. Brown

(1970) seriously doubted that any syntactic capacity had been demonstrated, but in 1973 he was willing to concede, in rudimentary form, the capacities of a Stage I child (about 18–24 months old). However, the Gardners (1975) claimed for Washoe a Stage III, or beyond, development, and Fouts (1974) and Patterson (1978) were equally ambitious for their young ones. Students of child language were growing incredulous, because if a chimpanzee had the linguistic abilities of a Stage III child, it was really impossible to understand why no significant chimpanzee culture had developed and how it could happen that the species lives today much as it has lived for millions of years. However, scientists less equipped to judge the probability of the whole thing, for instance Carl Sagan, were listing the chimp language research as one of the great breakthroughs of recent science.

In 1979 the market crashed, and you couldn't sell stock in a linguistic chimp for a nickel a share. What did it was the outcome of Project Nim. Nim was yet another chimp reared as a child and set the task of learning ASL, in and around Columbia University in New York City. Herbert Terrace (1979), who directed the project, expected Nim to pick up ASL signs quickly and then planned to study problem-solving as related to sign, but he ended thinking Nim had not learned diddley-squat—or maybe diddley, but not squat. Terrace did several things differently. He and his associates (Thomas Bever and Laura Petitto) circulated to interested scientists (including me) two progress reports (1976a, 1976b) which, for the first time ever in this kind of research, exposed very large samples (called "corpora" in linguistics) to people equipped to analyze them for themselves. In child language research such large samples, though never published, are also informally circulated so that persons not committed to a project can see what the unedited data are like. In our longitudinal study of three children in their preschool years, for instance, we always made multiple copies of transcriptions, and those were sent to more than twenty independent researchers. Terrace, also for the first time in this kind of research, made videotapes of his subject's performances so that they could be studied in a leisurely, analytic way. Finally, he calculated an index of language development that is standard in child language research, the mean length of utterance (MLU), charted it over the course of several years, and reported the results.

Probably those who were disillusioned about linguistic chimps by the reports of Terrace and his associates were disillusioned for a variety of reasons. For me the important thing was that three aspects of Terrace's data removed all evidence of syntactic capacity. By syntactic capacity I mean (roughly) the ability to put symbols into construction so as to express compositionally meanings that are other than the sum of the meanings of the individual symbols. A simple paradigm for English is the contrast between *dog chase cat* and *cat chase dog*; the sum of meanings is the same in both sequences, but the constructions, differing in word order, have completely distinct meanings. Word order is only one of a very large number of syntactic devices for expressing meaning by composition.

The studies of ASL in the great apes had all been developmental, and my way of trying to understand their results had been by comparison with what appear to be invariant features in the early stages of development of spoken and sign language in present-day *Homo sapiens*. The data base for *Homo sapiens* is, of course, far from adequate. In 1979 it included studies of a large number of historically unrelated spoken languages: Finnish, Japanese, Samoan, Luo, and Mayan Cakchiquel, among others (see, for example, Bloom, 1970; Blount, 1969; Bowerman, 1973; Brown, 1978; Tolbert, 1978), but the studies of sign language were all of the America Sign Language (ASL) (see, for example, Klima and Bellugi, 1972; Collins-Ahlgren, 1975; McIntire, 1977; Olson, 1972). There were three differences between child language and Nim's sign language that led me to think that young children have a syntactic capacity and that young apes do not.

1. *Mean length of utterance (MLU)*. The MLU in morphemes for a sample of child speech or of child sign language is calculated in a standardized way, and this index of linguistic development rises steadily with age for several years for all normal children (Brown, 1973). Terrace calculated MLU values for Nim, and they did not rise at all but held steady at values between 1.1 and 1.6. MLU most directly reflects the complexity of construction that the child's brain is able to accomplish, and its steady rise probably results both from the maturation of the brain and the accumulation of linguistic information. A failure to increase suggests that the symbol combinations being produced are not in construction at all but are only strings of single signs.

In young children, for several years, the longest construction produced in a sample is closely related to the mean length of construction and is not much above the mean. Terrace reports for Nim that the upper bound or longest unbroken string is unrelated to the MLU and may assume very large values when the MLU is not greater than 2.0. That fact suggests that utterance length does not reflect complexity and so reinforces the impression that Nim's strings were only strings and not constructions. Nim's longest string was made of sixteen signs and reads in English: "Give orange me give eat orange me eat orange give me eat orange give me you." There is no evidence in this string or in the other long strings reported for any great ape that the information transmitted increases with the length of string.

2. *Symbol sequencing.* In many languages word order has syntactic significance, and children learning such languages, from the time when they first begin combining words, follow the ordering rules of the model language. Probably, sequencing is the first syntactic device that children can utilize, and it is largely because they utilize it that the constructions of child speech are roughly intelligible from the start (Brown, 1970, 1973). It is fair to look at sign sequencing in Nim and all the other nonhuman primates for evidence of syntactic construction as opposed to symbol stringing, because all of them had been taught a kind of pidgin signed English that preserves English word order (Terrace et al., 1979). The simplest fair summary is that chimpanzees tend to

produce their multisign combinations in all possible orders, and that suggests the absence of syntax (Brown, 1970; Terrace, 1979).

3. *Prompting and imitation.* A number of sessions between Nim and one or another teacher were put on videotape. A frame-by-frame examination of those permanent records revealed to Terrace that Nim had seldom signed spontaneously, on his own initiative, but almost always required human prompting to sign at all, and when he signed with a teacher, the signs he produced were very often complete or partial imitations of those produced by his teacher. Child speech, by contrast, is characteristically spontaneous rather than responsive, and imitations constitute a small proportion of all utterances, a proportion that rapidly approaches zero. Insofar as prompted imitation accounts for multisign combinations, there is, of course, no reason to invoke creative syntax.

In retrospect, I think I can see how the students of chimp signing and the students of child language came to misunderstand one another as badly as they did and suffered mutual disillusionment (Brown, 1981; Van Cantfort and Rimpau, 1982). Nobody had done both sorts of study at the same time, and as far as I know no one has as yet. We learned about one another's results from published papers, edited films, and occasional conversations. In naturalistic studies it is never possible to record all conceivably relevant variables and not possible to publish the full transcriptions that are the primary data. There had been no exchange of transcriptions, and so perhaps each kind of investigator imagined that the data he had not seen would, in unrecorded aspects, be like his own. We were wrong. Where a chimp's six-sign sequence might read like this: "You me sweet drink give me," a child's six word sentence might read like this: "Johnny's mother poured me some Kool-Aid." It makes a difference (example from Savage-Rumbaugh, Rumbaugh, and Boysen, 1980).

But there remains one final difference between the methods of Terrace and all the others, and it is a difference that could account for Nim's seeming underachievement. Nim might be said to have been the product of a "broken home" or, rather, of many broken homes. He had instruction from something like sixty different signers (Terrace calls them "babysitters"), and a lot of it was in a Columbia University classroom, which no one could call "home." Those were the vicissitudes of a project for which Terrace could not get steady adequate funding. However, several of Nim's teachers, notably Laura Petitto, were with him over long periods of time. He became firmly attached to Petitto and to Terrace and a couple of others.

In general the Gardners, Fouts, and Patterson have taken the position that Nim was an underprivileged chimp, subjected to routine drills, not reared like a child at all, and for that reason his achievement in ASL was below the level set by Washoe and others. That stand is not fully convincing, because none of the people taking it has published MLU results to show that their chimps were different, and none has published or circulated lists of long sign sequences to show that Nim's "Give orange me give eat orange me," et cetera, is atypical. Indeed, looking back at the 1975 paper in which the Gardners claimed Washoe could answer in a grammatically correct way questions of the *who, what, where* variety, one now notices that the responses published had been edited in ways that would tend to make them appear to be more childlike than they were.

I was disillusioned about syntax, but some linguistically sophisticated members of the Columbia group (e.g. Petitto and Seidenberg, 1979; Seidenberg and Petitto, 1979) doubted that Nim had demonstrated any linguistic capacities at all, including symbolism. They also doubted that any other chimp-signing study had demonstrated more. Probably they did not convince the Gardners, Fouts, or Patterson, but the group at Georgia's primate center reviewed the whole picture in 1980 and concluded that to date there was no evidence that Washoe, Lana, Koko, Nim, or any other nonhuman primate had achieved symbolization. If the signs of ASL and the key pressings produced by Lana were not symbolic, then there is no possibility that linguistic syntax has been demonstrated, because linguistic syntax, by definition, operates with symbols.

What is a symbol? A classic definition (Charles Sanders Pierce and many others) would read: A symbol is a token that is associated with and represents a referent on the basis of arbitrary convention. The evidence for association is strong; the problem is with representation. Savage-Rumbaugh and collaborators (1980) point out that when a pigeon is trained to peck a red key to get food and a green key to get water (Jenkins and Moore, 1973), one does not feel inclined to say that it has learned to *name* red and green with its discriminating pecks. Those pecks are just Skinnerian operants, or instrumentally conditioned responses (Chapter 10). But when a chimp makes one sign for red and another sign for green (and is rewarded for both), investigators have called the discriminating responses *names* and have considered the performance to be one of linguistic reference. But why are they not simply operant conditionings?

Clearly, the temptation to call manual responses names derives mainly from the fact that the responses in question belong to a system (ASL) in which, for humans, they function as symbols. What does this mean operationally or behaviorally? To state just one small difference: The human child learning those signs will not produce them only when a trainer sets the problem and delivers rewards but will sometimes spontaneously produce them to report something to someone who has not seen it or, in the absence of something desired, will produce the sign to request the missing object.

The work of Savage-Rumbaugh and her associates (1983) has recently taken an interesting tack in searching for symbolic capacity in chimps. They begin by trying to specify the kinds of behavior in children that are characterized as symbolic by such students of early communication as Bates (1979) and Bruner (1983). The goal essentially is to find an operational definition for the representational function of a symbol, a function beyond association, which Pierce and most philosophers of language have used in defining the symbol. It is not an easy thing to do, but the Georgia group has made an impressive start.

Suppose you tell a child that in the next room he will find five objects on a tray and that he is to have just one of them. He is to make his choice mentally, without speaking, and then go across the room to a microphone where he is to say the name of the object preferred, thereby reporting to you his intention of claiming it, and then retrace his steps to the tray, pick out the one he has named, and bring it to you. Only if the name matches the toy may he have it. That is a task that goes beyond simple conditioned association. The child does not speak the name upon seeing the object, and when he does speak the name, the object is out of sight. It certainly looks as if the name in the task functions as a surrogate or "vehicle" for the referent object. It looks as if the object is mentally encoded into a name, which is retained for a period, even mentally rehearsed, and then decoded back into the referent.

Savage-Rumbaugh and associates created a model of the task described designed for chimpanzee. Some thirty different foods and tools were used in varying sets of five, and Sherman selected and named seventeen, Austin twenty-three, across fifty-odd trials with almost perfect success. It is interesting to notice how close this test for symbolism in chimpanzees comes to Turing's test for intelligence in a computer. In both cases, one picks some task that everyone will agree entails, respectively, symbolism or intelligence. The question, then, is—abstracting away the fact that chimps look hairy and computers look metallic, whereas humans are human—could one distinguish the recorded performance of the beast or machine on trial from a human performance? In fact, the questions "Can a machine be said to be intelligent?" and "Can a chimp be said to use symbols?" are logically equivalent in the sense of the kinds of tests that are relevant.

What is the relevance of the linguistic capacities of chimpanzee to the origins of language? Other animal species have communication systems, which they use naturally, without human instruction, that resemble human language in function, in what they accomplish, much more closely than chimp symbolizing does. Most notable is the so-called language of the honey bee by which a finder bee signals to those in the hive the distance and direction of a nectar source. What the chimpanzee does in a linguistic way is more interesting than anything a honey bee or any other nonprimate does, because it can arise from *homology* and not just *analogy*. A homology is a correspondence of structure or function that arises out of common ancestry, whereas analogy is just an accidental similarity.

Present-day *Pan troglodytes* is not an ancestor of present-day *Homo sapiens*. We are, as it were, the ends of our respective evolutionary lines, and those lines diverged at least 5 million years ago and perhaps more like 10 million years ago. Still, the lines were once joined and, on the scale of geological time, actually not long ago. We are of the same order and superfamily and separate only at the level of the biological family into great apes (the *Pongidae*) and hominids (the *Hominidae*).

The common ancestor of man and chimpanzee did not, some 5–10 million years ago, invent human language. If he possessed the characteristics that man

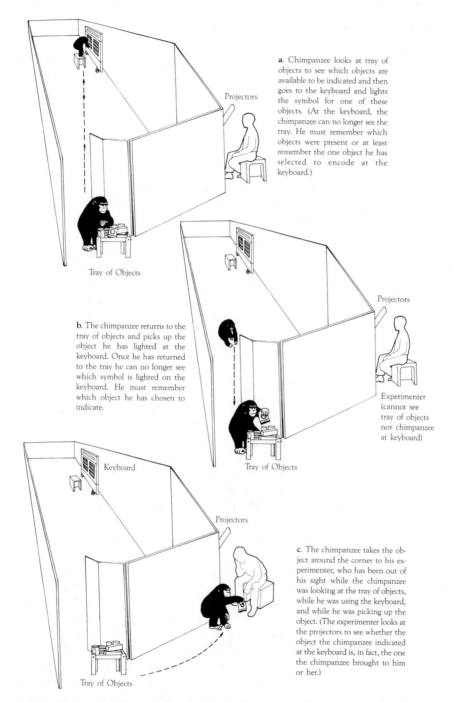

a. Chimpanzee looks at tray of objects to see which objects are available to be indicated and then goes to the keyboard and lights the symbol for one of these objects. (At the keyboard, the chimpanzee can no longer see the tray. He must remember which objects were present or at least remember the one object he has selected to encode at the keyboard.)

Projectors

Tray of Objects

b. The chimpanzee returns to the tray of objects and picks up the object he has lighted at the keyboard. Once he has returned to the tray he can no longer see which symbol is lighted on the keyboard. He must remember which object he has chosen to indicate.

Projectors

Experimenter (cannot see tray of objects nor chimpanzee at keyboard)

Tray of Objects

Keyboard

Projectors

c. The chimpanzee takes the object around the corner to his experimenter, who has been out of his sight while the chimpanzee was looking at the tray of objects, while he was using the keyboard, and while he was picking up the object. (The experimenter looks at the projectors to see whether the object the chimpanzee indicated at the keyboard is, in fact, the one the chimpanzee brought to him or her.)

Tray of Objects

Figure 12–2. A demonstration of symbolic function in chimpanzee

(From E. S. Savage-Rumbaugh, J. L. Pate, J. Lawson, S. T. Smith, and S. Rosenbaum, Can a chimpanzee make a statement? *Journal of Experimental Psychology: General, 112* [1983], pp. 481–82. Copyright 1983 by the American Psychological Association. Reprinted by permission of the publisher and author)

and chimpanzee share today, and probably he did, we may guess that some of those predisposed him to language and that some would have made even the least rudiments of language adaptive. Probably he had the hand and opposable thumb that man and chimpanzee have and also the manual dexterity that makes it possible to make many sign configurations. Probably he had the stereoscopic and color vision that both species have today, which makes possible a certain world of object referents. Whether or not he walked erect as the hominids all did or was a knuckle-walker like the present-day chimpanzee (with, however, the easy possibility of standing on his hind limbs) we do not know. A mode of walking is, most importantly, a means of locomotion adapted to the entire way of life of a species (on the ground, arboreal, in the air, and so on), but walking erect does, incidentally, free the hands for both tool use and gesture.

The vocalization of our common ancestor was probably more like that of the present-day chimp than like human speech, and chimp vocalization and human speech are only analogous, not homologous. The natural calls and cries of the chimp are emotional expressions controlled in the limbic area of the midbrain. They are homologous with involuntary screams and curses in man (Myers, 1976) but not with speech, which is voluntary and organized at the level of the cerebral cortex.

Socially the chimpanzee is the most humanlike of all the primates (Wilson, 1975). It does not reproduce frequently and in great quantity, as do many insects and fishes, but infrequently (every five or six years), and just one offspring at a time. That makes possible a long period of infant dependency, as in man, and it practically necessitates the relatively large brain of the species, because it is important that every individual learn enough to survive.

Chimps today live in bands of fifty to a hundred individuals, and their economy is of the hunting and gathering sort. They range freely over fairly large territories (in Equatorial Africa) and defend the borders of those territories against other bands—though not in a very combative way. Their families and larger groups manifest a social structure of dominance and submission (see Chapter 3), with the male in a family dominant over the female and young. The chimpanzee is unique among the nonhuman primates in the amount of cooperation manifest; males cooperate in the hunt, and food is shared. Much of this social life is remote from that of man in the modern nation-state, but it is exactly like that of man in the most primitive surviving preliterate societies and is presumed to be like that of our common ancestor.

If modern chimp and man do share a capacity to maintain an active repertoire of symbols that can be used to report something and not simply as an immediate reaction to a stimulus, it is clear that such a capacity would have had powerful survival value for the mode of social life described. It would certainly be more advantageous to say *what* (food, enemy, relative, a tool) is just around the corner than to use a call signalling that *something* is. It is possible, then, that the first step toward language was the reporting symbol, presumably in a gestural–visual modality since vocalizations are not homologous.

There is, however, one large difference between the chimpanzee's thus far demonstrated symbolic capacity and that of man in childhood. Savage-Rumbaugh and her associates (1983) say it well:

> The path to symbolic indication for the chimpanzees Sherman and Austin has been long and arduous, and they arrived there only with considerable help from members of another species. We do not view this as a negative comment on the intelligence of chimpanzees. Quite the contrary, it emphasizes the ease with which children achieve this skill and suggests that in human children there must be a strong predisposition to engage in communicative indication, and the predisposition apparently antedates the emergence of language.

It takes training by the human species to bring out any symbolic *capacity* in chimpanzees. For children, symbolizing is extremely natural. Above an early critical age it is sufficient to name an instance or so of a referent category to cause the child to use that name, not only in naming but in reporting and requesting, and soon in various semantic roles in sentences. Furthermore, if the child is interested in the referent and does not know the name, he or she will ask for it. The child not only treats symbols as representations but seems to know the general principle that things have names.

Since symbolizing is congenial and inevitable in *Homo sapiens* but not in *Pan troglodytes*, the similar performances might not really be homologous. The chimpanzee might simply be learning an analogous "trick"; chimps can also be trained to ride bicycles and wear hats. In the natural communications of the species, as they have been described by Jane Goodall (1965), the symbolic capacity demonstrated in the laboratory does not seem to operate. However, the capacity might still be homologous to the human capacity, but not manifest in communication. It could be manifest in some other type of behavior: recognition of individuals, tool use, whatever. The ultimate answer must come from neurology. If the same structural organization underlies easy symbolism in man and a capacity for symbolism in chimpanzee, then the two are homologous.

Language Invention in Recent Time

Recent time will range from about six thousand years ago, when writing was invented, until 1985 (Goldin-Meadow and Morford, 1985), when a report appeared of ten congenitally deaf children (in ten different families) who independently invented a manual sign language. It is usual to think of early writing itself as an independent invention of language, because the modern writing systems we know are almost all secondary to speech, indeed a way of transcribing speech, and so necessarily came later than the spoken language. No alphabetic or syllabic writing system can be thought of as an instance of the invention of language. However, the earliest writing systems were all independent of speech and were not alphabetic or syllabic in character but were all pictorial or representational in character (Gelb, 1980). The symbols in those systems were, to use the term we shall use henceforth, "iconic," which is to say that the forms in some way suggest their associated meanings.

The Principle of Iconicity

The symbols in iconic writing have what is called in the theory of signs the "mnemonic (or memory) advantage." Because the form of the sign is not arbitrarily related to its referent but is more or less suggestive of it, iconic signs are easy to learn and to remember. For instance, in the Zapotec writing from 600 B.C. (Marcus, 1980) one can easily tell the hill-of-the-bird glyph (carved figure) from the hill-of-the-jaguar glyph (Figure 12–3). These icons are highly "transparent"; most of us today, remote though we are from Zapotec culture, can guess at their meanings and hold them in memory indefinitely. However, it is not part of the definition of an icon that the similarity linking the symbol with its meaning should be universally apparent. Iconicity generally is time-bound, culture-bound, age-bound, and, in general, experience-bound. The pictogram from Ancient Egypt in Figure 12–3 may obviously to us have something to do with a bird and a human, but we could not guess that it meant the falcon-god Horus taking captive the land of the papyrus (Egypt), with papyrus represented by six lotus plants, the plant from which papyrus was made. For the Egyptians in ancient time, however, it would have been fairly easy to understand on sight and unlikely to be forgotten.

The alphabetic principle (of which the syllabic principle is a form) is one of the greatest of human inventions. It makes writing derivative from speech by setting conventional symbols in one-to-one relation with the sound elements of speech, either the vowels and consonants or the syllables. The resultant economy in achieving literacy is enormous. Everyone naturally learns to talk before learning to read and write, and children usually know thousands of words before beginning to become literate. In principle, with an alphabetic writing one could at once know how to read and write all the thousands of spoken words already in memory by simply learning the small number of rules that link forms with sounds. The reason that is not quite the case in English, and many other languages today, is that our writing has developed very many exceptions and irregularities. English is still fundamentally alphabetic, however, and the consequent economy in achieving literacy is manifest in the fact that those who cannot take advantage of the alphabetic principle but must learn words as if they were arbitrary shapes, the congenitally deaf, seldom learn to read above about the fourth-grade level, however long they study.

Figure 12–3. Zapotec and ancient Egyptian iconic glyphs

(Zapotec glyphs from J. Marcus, Zapotec writing, *Scientific American*, p. 59. Copyright 1980 by Scientific American, Inc. All rights reserved. Egyptian glyph from E. S. Meltzer in *Processing of Visible Languages 2*, p. 48, Fig. 11. Copyright 1980 by Plenum Publishing Corp.)

The alphabetic principle is a powerful economy, but the mnemonic principle is also a considerable economy, far better than a completely arbitrary linkage of symbol and sense. With respect to the origins of language, the important point is that the earliest writing systems were, without exception, pictorial or iconic. Since the first writing was independent of speech, it is a form of language invention, and since it *need* not have been iconic but could have been perfectly arbitrary, it follows that iconicity is, as far as written language is concerned, the primary principle of symbol invention.

There is just one other kind of language invention in recent time, and that is sign language, primarily manual but also often involving facial expression and posture. Concerning sign languages, a very strong generalization can be made; they are *always* iconic (Hewes, 1976; Kendon, 1980; Mandel, 1977; and many others). As it happens, that statement can give grave offense but will not if we are very explicit about just what is and is not meant. Those who can be offended are the deaf for whom a sign language is the native and primary means of communication, and that includes 2 million or so people in North America, all those whose first language is the American Sign Language (ASL), and their many sympathizers.

The basis for possible offense lies in the fact that the great linguists of a certain period considered arbitrariness, or complete conventionality, of symbols to be part of the essential definition of language. Ferdinand de Saussure, for instance, held that the linguistic symbol is "arbitrary" or "unmotivated" actually has no natural connection with the signified. If that principle is accepted and ASL and other sign languages have a large nonarbitrary or iconic aspect, then they cannot by definition be true languages. And deaf people well remember that in the recent past there were linguistic scholars who thought just that, and they know many nonscholars today who still think it. If your primary means of communication is not in every respect a human language, that makes you yourself less than fully human. For that very good reason, any talk about iconicity in sign language can register as a threat. In fact it is no threat, but that takes some explaining.

The congenitally deaf person, however intelligent and well educated, can seldom speak quite like the hearing, and the deaf who attempt speech are likely to be thought retarded. In fact, normally intelligent deaf small children have quite often been discovered in institutions for the severely retarded because of mistakes of diagnosis. If your intelligence and wit and poetry can be fully manifest only in a sign language, you naturally care a lot about the status of that language. The deaf in the United States have become a community bound together by their shared language, ASL, and "Deaf Pride" is just as unsteady as Black Pride. So let us be clear that the iconic aspect of a sign language is no threat to its full status as a language, which, in the case of ASL, has been established beyond doubt. Iconicity even adds a distinctive beauty to ASL, which has been effectively brought out in poetry readings and in the performances of the Theater of the Deaf.

The facts are these. The iconic element in manual signs is most evident to the hearing amateur, to the person first becoming acquainted with a sign system. For him it will be salient and impossible to doubt. If he is, as a hearing person, taking lessons in, for instance, ASL, his teacher is very likely to point out the iconic element as a way of fixing a sign in memory, and manuals of sign language do the same (see Figure 12–4 for examples of iconic signs in what is called "citation form"). As the pictured examples will convince you, the amateur is not imagining things.

In a series of controlled experiments at the Salk Institute, Klima and Bellugi (1979) have proved that there are important limits on the iconicity of ASL.

Figure 12–4. Signs for "butterfly" and for "cat" in the sign languages of Israel and of Victoria, Australia; all iconic but in different ways

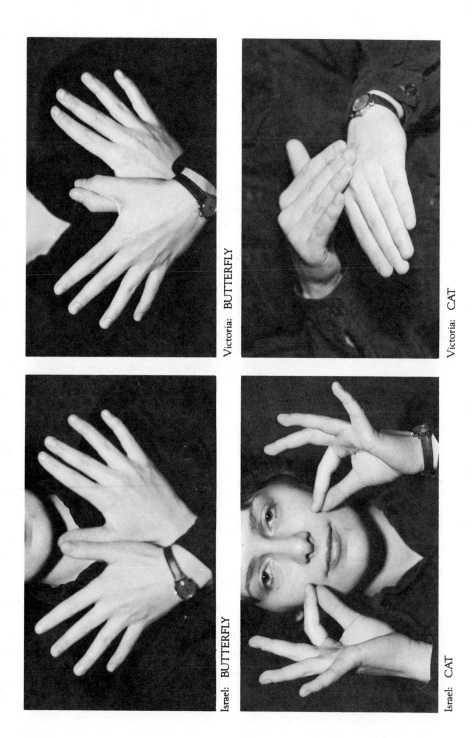

Victoria: BUTTERFLY

Victoria: CAT

Israel: BUTTERFLY

Israel: CAT

Almost no ASL signs are so iconic that their meanings can be correctly guessed from the sign alone; ASL signs and manual signs generally are not so iconic as to be "transparent" in meaning. Even for the highly iconic signs of Figure 12–4 you probably could not, on the basis of the sign alone, guess the correct meaning. Some ASL signs (no one knows how many) are sufficiently iconic so that a person given the sign and its spoken-word equivalent can say what the basis of the relationship between the two is. Notice that you could do this for the very iconic signs pictured: the butterfly's wings, the cat's whiskers, and the act of stroking a cat. Klima and Bellugi call this weaker level of iconicity, by contrast with "transparency," "translucence." The most important discovery is that for fluent deaf signers of ASL, iconicity plays no role at all in language processing. The fluent signer has been shown in memory experiments, using error analysis, to store signs in terms of the parameters of configuration, location, and movement (analogous to the vowels and consonants), and not in terms of iconic quality. The fluent signer is just like the fluent speaker in that he encodes symbols in terms of arbitrary formal qualities. Finally, Klima and Bellugi have shown that information is transmitted in signed ASL at almost exactly the same rate as in spoken English. There is no indication anywhere that ASL is inferior to English as a medium of communication.

For the fluent signer, then, iconicity simply does not matter; the language is processed as if there were no iconicity, and certainly the rapid signer is totally unaware of it. However, our interest here is not in the language processing of fluent signers but in the invention process, ultimately in prehistoric invention. There is much evidence that even today when new signs are invented, iconicity plays a role. In a fully developed sign language, the invention of new signs is in many ways governed by conventional rules (allowable hand configurations, allowable locations in space, and so on), but there is often also a clear iconic element (Schlesinger and Namir, 1978). When manual signs are invented and there is no preexistent full sign language, iconicity is everything. Since all signs in sign languages were newly invented at some time, it is not surprising that there is still far more iconicity in sign languages than in spoken languages.

Recently Invented Sign Languages

Now we are ready for sign languages that have been recently invented—by deaf children, by an isolated deaf adult, by hearing adults working in a sawmill with a high noise level, and by hearing adult aborigines in Australia developing a manual language for special ritual purposes. In all those cases and in all comparable cases, the principle of invention has been iconicity. And from this fact I mean to argue that the first forms of language were probably iconic manual gestures developed by early hominids 2 to 3 million years ago. I think those first symbols would have been manual in part, because iconicity is the principle of symbol invention and the hands are far more effective for representing the shape and motion of referents than are the vocal cords and organs of articulation. In other words, I see iconicity not as an incidental feature of manual signs but as the main reason why the first symbols are likely to have been manual.

In the field of deaf education there is a distinctly acrimonious controversy between the oralists and the signers, a controversy that has lasted more than a century in this country. The extreme oralist position is that when a deaf child is born to two hearing parents (and 90 percent of deaf children are), the parents should take every precaution not to develop a system of signing communication with the child lest he or she become attached to the manual–visual modality, but should, from the first, orient the child to speech—since the oral–auditory modality is most desirable for the child's future adaptation. That means early fitting with the best possible hearing aid and early enrollment in an oralist school. It is an approach that hearing parents naturally find appealing, because a child who does not learn to speak and to read well must always be psychologically distanced from them and eventually is likely to be economically and socially underprivileged. The problem is that if the hearing loss is nearly complete in both ears, the child will only rarely succeed in learning to speak. The deaf child of deaf parents, other things being equal, is better off in all ways, even, usually, in learning to read English. Probably the exposure to a language from the start, even though it must be a sign language, brings such enormous benefits in socio-emotional adaptation, parental identification, information about the world, and so on, as to give the child of deaf parents a better start on everything than the child of hearing parents.

Goldin-Meadow and Morford (1985) have identified ten severely deaf children who are being reared by parents with such strong oralist convictions as to try not to sign to their children at all. The investigators have studied those children in their preschool years and on after their entry into oralist schools and have made a comparison study of three hearing children. Conceive of the problem of the deaf child in a hearing family. The child must invent his or her own means of communication since it is necessary to communicate, and the parents provide no medium. The parents are not, of course, unkind and will try to understand the child's efforts at communication.

All ten children have independently invented the same kind of system. It comprises two categories of manual signs: pointings used to designate present objects and persons, and "characterizers" used for actions or attributes, occasionally for out-of-sight objects. An example of a characterizer is moving the fist back and forth in front of the mouth to convey "brush teeth." Concerning the characterizer signs, the investigators say that "the form of the gesture was transparently related to its referent" (p. 20). Probably they do not mean strictly "transparent" (translatable on sight), but simply highly iconic. How else could the child hope to communicate with a linguistic community he cannot join?

The *hearing* children studied by Goldin-Meadow and Morford also did some pointing and also used some iconic characterizers. Both hearing and deaf children combined gestures to make simple two-symbol sentences. It is significant that the hearing children made such manual sentences two to five months before they made such spoken sentences, and that is consistent with other work (Bates, 1979) in showing that manual symbols precede spoken symbols in the development of hearing children. For the hearing children, of course, manual symbols were used much less with time, but for the deaf children, even after they were in oralist schools, signing steadily increased.

The language invented by the deaf children does not simply employ single symbols or symbols in sequences (such as Nim produced). The children put their manual symbols into simple grammatical constructions using sequential order in consistent contrastive ways. In other words, they expressed meanings in a compositional way and not by means of single symbols only and so showed a capacity for syntax. There is much that suggests that symbol sequencing is the most primitive of all syntactic devices (Brown, 1973), and if we were attempting to construct a full evolutionary sequence for the origin of language, it would be a good guess that manual symbols were used with a syntax of sequence before they developed any speech at all.

At least one adult has been in a position comparable to that of the deaf children of oralist parents. On the Polynesian island of Rennell, the an-thropological linguist Kuschel (1973) found a congenitally deaf man, Kangobai by name, who was said to be the first deaf person born on that island in twenty-four generations. Kangobai had, all his life, the necessity of com-municating with people whose language he could not learn. He invented a large number of signs but not, as far as Kuschel noticed, a syntax. Kangobai's signs were all iconic (see Figure 12-5).

It has sometimes happened that a group of adult hearing humans has for a long period of time worked together in circumstances so noisy that speech was impracticable. Meissner and Philpott (1975) found such a situation in a sawmill in British Columbia and discovered that a manual sign language had been in-vented. Actually, a high noise level is not alone sufficient to produce a sign language. Workers in the press room of a newspaper, being free to move about, as sawmill workers are not, stick with speech and walk over to one another, cup the ear, and shout. The language of the sawmill started with a few gestures essential for coordinating work operations but then broke free of that technical requirement and was used to gossip and joke and spread the news. It consisted of 127 single signs and another 7,500 or so compounds, and all were iconic. Se-quence tended to copy English sequence. There was no expression of tense, aspect, specificity (articles), conjunction, and the like. All those things are also universally missing from the first sentences of children, hearing or deaf (Brown, 1973). Early child speech is a speech of nouns and verbs, which gives it a "telegraphic" quality, and of course the things left unexpressed are not essential in the life of a small child. It would be a good guess that they were also not essential for early hominids and not expressed.

Hearing sawmill workers started with a shared medium of communication and could, of course, have taken counsel together and agreed on a set of ar-

Figure 12–5. Kangobai's sign "drink"

(Courtesy William C. Stokoe [ed.], *Sign Language Studies*, 1973)

bitrary but simple and highly visible manual symbols, but that is not what they did. Instead, the medium developed gradually on consistent iconic lines, which, of course, carries a mnemonic advantage. The iconic principle is often said to be adequate only for a small number of meanings, but the sawmill workers apparently found it adequate for about two hundred meanings.

Finally, we have a community of hearing adults, with a shared spoken language and no technical necessity to sign, developing a sign language nevertheless: the Warlpiri, who are aborigines of the Northern Territory of Australia and one of the most primitive societies on earth. The Warlpiri sign language is used for certain ritual purposes, especially by women in mourning. Adam Kendon (1980), an anthropologist who has made a specialty of sign languages, reports a lexicon of six hundred signs in Warlpiri; the nature of the grammar is still to be described. Kendon finds some overlap of Warlpiri sign shapes with ASL and even with the system of the Plains Indians (West, 1960). As to the nature of Warlpiri signs, we know what to expect: "[I]n a majority of cases they can be said to be derived from some kind of depiction of visible features of the referent" (Kendon, 1980, p. 105).

In what circumstances does a human being with a normal brain who is not exposed to a language fail to invent one? In circumstances of extreme social isolation when there is, in effect, no community. The best-studied case is the modern one of the child Genie (Curtiss et al., 1974) who spent most of her first thirteen and a half years strapped to a child's potty seat in seclusion from a blind mother and a brutal, possibly psychotic father. Genie, when first rescued from that terrible bondage, had neither speech nor gestures. It is reported, however, that she began to initiate gestural communication in the hospital well before speech and, indeed, ASL has been used in an effort to help her with the transition to speech.

There is an apparent contradiction between the way in which the concept of symbol was used in discussing signing chimpanzees and the way it has been used in the discussion of language invention in recent times. While the definition, by Pierce and myself, of the symbol specified that it must be related to its referent by purely arbitrary convention, the evidence from the deaf children, from Kangobai, from the Warlpiri, from heiroglyphs and pictograms and modern sign languages is that the primary principle of symbol invention is iconicity, a certain kind of nonarbitrariness. However, the point of the stipulation of arbitrary convention in definition of the symbol, by Pierce and everyone else, is not to exclude invented icons but, rather, to exclude "indices" that are naturally related to referents in the manner of smoke to fire and a scream to a wound. There is usually a secondary intent to specify arbitrary convention, because only that kind of association allows for an infinite variety of symbols. Iconicity is somewhat limiting, but—very much to our present point—it is far less limiting when the organs of response are the hands than when they are the vocal cords and articulators.

However, when we speculate about the origins of language, we cannot know just how hominid (manlike) and how pongid (apelike) a creature we are talking about. Therefore, a case that the first symbols would have been manual and iconic must reckon with the ability of modern apes, notably chimpanzees, to detect iconicity or similarity where modern man detects it. Only if the iconicity can be appreciated will there be any mnemonic advantage over arbitrary symbols. Experiments that speak very directly to this point have not been done. Of course, the chimpanzees in the Washoe tradition who were trained to produce the signs of ASL were taught many signs a human finds iconic and some that a human does not find iconic, but there is no report on the relative ease with which the two were learned. The chimpanzees in the Lana tradition in Georgia learned to recognize visual symbols that had been deliberately made arbitrary and composed from a small number of repeating elements in order to maximize the analogy with human speech. What would happen with iconic symbols? There is a small amount of evidence from the work of David Premack (1976). Premack generally used arbitrary plastic tokens in his experiments with chimpanzees, but he did first try plastic icons resembling various fruit referents, and he reports that they were learned more easily and better retained than were arbitrary tokens. Indeed, they seem to have been learned so easily as to make the task seem unlike language in its most salient form—speech.

Chimpanzee has stereoscopic color vision, as does man. The two species also seem to have very similar systems of pattern recognition. One piece of evidence for that is the fact that chimpanzees taught to use some manual signs formed, from small sets of instances, just the same "natural categories" of apples and babies and soda pop and cars and flowers and sandwiches as humans do. That strongly argues that the human and chimpanzee perceived visual worlds are much the same. In addition, chimpanzees easily recognize photographs in either color or black-and-white. They recognize them so easily that the Gardners have used photographs in naming tests (rather than three-dimensional objects), because they are more convenient. A photograph is already an icon—though a very "transparent" one to us. Still, it is a two-dimensional representation of a three-dimensional reality with the absolute sizes of objects reduced, and so only a representation after all. It seems reasonable to assume that the hominids who originated language would have had a shared sense of iconicity.

The Fossil Record

The organ of language, spoken or signed, is the brain, and the brain does not fossilize, but its cradle, the cranium, does, so we look to the sequence of skulls in prehistory as the best empirical window on the origins of language. Paleoneurology, which is the science that attempts to trace the descent of the human brain, is a field plagued with difficulties: For long stretches of time there are as yet no fossils at all; sample sizes are always quite small; most specimens are fragmentary or damaged; and absolute dating is unreliable. There are even sharp differences of opinion on how to represent the family tree of *Homo sapiens*, and there are therefore disagreements on taxonomy. What I present in Figure 12–6 is my own attempt at a conservative consensus (Holloway, 1983b; Pilbeam, 1984) as of 1984.

The taxon levels of Figure 12–6 are terms from the Linnean taxonomy of biological science, and they move progressively from the more inclusive and abstract (Order) to the less inclusive and abstract (species). The starting point is the Primate Order, which is a branch of the Mammal Class. The Old World Monkeys are peeled away first (as the Primates most remote from man), and that leaves the hominoids, which include only humans, the great apes, and the extinct australopithecines, which were neither ape nor human, but more humanlike than apelike. The great apes are peeled off next as the Pongid Order of which *Pan troglodytes* is a present-day member, not an ancestor of man. From

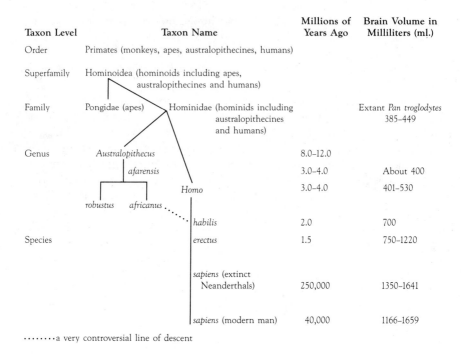

Taxon Level	Taxon Name	Millions of Years Ago	Brain Volume in Milliliters (ml.)
Order	Primates (monkeys, apes, australopithecines, humans)		
Superfamily	Hominoidea (hominoids including apes, australopithecines and humans)		
Family	Pongidae (apes) Hominidae (hominids including australopithecines and humans)		Extant *Pan troglodytes* 385–449
Genus	*Australopithecus*	8.0–12.0	
	afarensis	3.0–4.0	About 400
	Homo	3.0–4.0	401–530
	robustus *africanus*		
	habilis	2.0	700
Species	*erectus*	1.5	750–1220
	sapiens (extinct Neanderthals)	250,000	1350–1641
	sapiens (modern man)	40,000	1166–1659

········a very controversial line of descent

Figure 12–6. One view of the descent of the human brain

some ape precursor about 8 to 12 million years ago one group became bipedal (walked erect), retained a small ape-sized brain, and evolved into *Australopithecus*. *Australopithecus* is one hominid species (homin*id*, not homin*oid*), and *Homo* is the other. Apes are hominoids but not hominids.

There is in 1984 considerable disagreement as to the number of species of australopithecines and especially which species of them, if any, was ancestral to man. *Australopithecus afarensis* is a recent discovery of Donald Johanson and his colleagues (Johanson and Edey, 1981) in Hadar, Ethiopia, and appears to be older than the two familiar forms of australopithecine, the large, strong *robustus* and the smaller, weaker *africanus*. Johanson and some others believe that *afarensis* (represented by the nearly complete half skeleton called "Lucy" and associated remains) was ancestral to both *Australopithecus robustus* and *Australopithecus africanus* and that early man descended from the latter. There is considerable debate as to whether *afarensis* is truly distinct at the species level from *africanus* and whether any australopithecine is ancestral to Genus *Homo* (Holloway, 1983a; Kimbel, Johanson, and Coppens, 1982; Olson, 1981; Tobias, 1981; White, Johanson, and Kimbel, 1981). There is no disagreement at all that *robustus*, the large, heavy australopithecine, was an evolutionary dead end, not in the direct line of human descent, and there is little disagreement that *Homo habilis*, *erectus*, and *sapiens* emerged in that order. Neanderthal man is most commonly regarded as a now extinct race of *Homo sapiens*, larger and heavier of body and also with a slightly larger brain than modern man.

Brain Size

The numbers in Figure 12–6 should all be regarded as "ball park" figures, but representative ball park figures. For the brain volumes, ranges are appropriate, because individuals in the same species do vary considerably in brain size. Individual variations in modern man, incidentally, have not been shown to be correlated with IQ or any aspect of cognitive activity. Absolute brain size has roughly quadrupled from the australopithecines to modern man, and early australopithecine values are close to those for present-day chimpanzees (not a human ancestor). Brain size varies with body size, and so the numbers given in Figure 12–6 are less meaningful than would be some sort of brain-weight/body-weight ratio—a number representing *relative* brain size. There are problems in calculating relative brain sizes for fossils, because body weights have to be estimated, often with little to go on. However, relative brain sizes, technically "encephalization quotients" (Holloway and Post, 1982) leave no doubt that extreme encephalization has occurred in the primate line and at a very rapid rate. Primates have developed much bigger brains with no commensurate increase of body size. What can the progressive encephalization tell us about the origins of language? Almost nothing.

We know something in a direct (behavioral) way about just two relevant species: *Pan troglodytes* and *Homo sapiens*. Of those it can be said that chimpanzee certainly does not have language, though it may have a rudimentary symbolic capacity, and that man in society always does have language, either spoken or gestural. But where, between the great apes and modern man, is what Jerison (1976) calls the "linguistic Rubicon," or, better, "Rubicons"? One might think, at an absolute minimum, that an adult brain volume above 500 milliliters was called for, since that is an upper value for chimpanzee. Alas, not even that is clear. There exists a clinical condition called *nanocephalic dwarfism* (in English, bird-headed dwarfism) in which in the adult years the brain size is within the chimpanzee range. This sort of human dwarf, though severely retarded, always acquires rudimentary verbal skills, sometimes attaining the skills of a normal five-year-old, and that means the greater part of the language.

Eric Lenneberg (1967), a distinguished pioneer in the modern study of the biological foundations of language, spelled out the implications. Since the brain size of one species (chimpanzee) totally lacking language (as he thought) overlaps that of some specimens of a species in total possession of language, mere brain size, even relative size, cannot be the critical factor that makes language possible. It is not the quantity that ultimately matters, Lenneberg argued and all now agree, but the organization of the brain. And what can we learn about the organization of brains in prehistoric hominids when all we have are endocasts of the inner cranium? Fifteen years ago the answer would have been clear: Nothing. The fascinating thing is that the answer today is: Possibly something.

Brain Organization

In the majority of right-handed hearing adults, the left cerebral hemisphere is functionally specialized for speech. A brain injury in Broca's area of the left hemisphere just above what is called the Sylvian fissure in the frontal lobe results in some degree of expressive aphasia or impairment of speech production. A brain injury in Wernicke's area at the posterior end of the Sylvian fissure results in some degree of receptive aphasia or impairment of speech comprehension (see Figure 12-7). Areas in the right hemisphere corresponding to Broca's and Wernicke's in the left are not similarly involved in speech. Speech is, therefore, said to be lateralized or located on one side. There is also marked preference with respect to side in the use of limbs (right-handedness) and sense organs. None of those hemispheric specializations is absolute, only relative, and within certain constraints functions localized in one area can, if necessary, be taken on by another area.

Probably a function comes to be lateralized in evolution for reasons of efficiency when there is a complex sequence of fine movements to be performed requiring a single program in one hemisphere. Birdsong is such a complex sequence, and birdsong, though otherwise not much like speech, is lateralized.

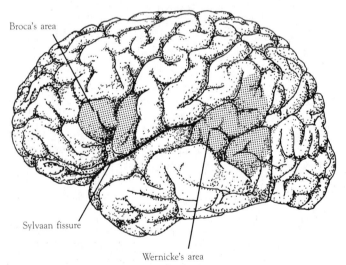

Broca's area

Sylvaan fissure

Wernicke's area

Figure 12-7. The left hemisphere of the human cerebral cortex, showing speech areas (Adapted from Geschwind, 1979, p. 186)

The manufacture of stone tools that have *arbitrary* design rules and are symmetrical and regular, such as the handaxe of 1.5 to 2 million years ago, also involves a sequence of fine movements and probably entails lateralization. From stone tools of that type made by Homo erectus about 1.5 million years ago it is possible to demonstrate that most of those who made them were right-handers, and that strongly suggests (though it does not necessarily entail) left cerebral dominance. Many archaeologists and paleoanthropologists (e.g. Isaac, 1976) have argued that there is an abstract analogy between the manufacture of standardized tools and language: Both involve a kind of general plan, or mental template, as well as serial control of precise movements. Those analogies are vague, however, and seem to encompass much besides toolmaking and language. So while toolmaking probably was lateralized by the time of Homo erectus (1.5 to 2 million years ago) and even earlier (Holloway and de LaCoste-LaReymondie, 1982), it is not necessarily the case that such lateralization is evidence that language existed.

Until about 1970 neurologists (e.g. Lenneberg, 1967) thought that whatever anatomical differences there might be constituting the substrate for the functional differences between the speech areas of the left hemisphere and the parallel nonspeech areas of the right hemisphere, those differences must be so small as to be discernible only by microscope. That idea has been overturned by modern work (Geschwind and Levitsky, 1968; LeMay and Culebras, 1972; LeMay, 1976; Gallaburda et al., 1978; Holloway and de LaCoste-LaReymondie, 1982). It is now clear that there are rather gross structural differences associated with the speech areas, involving both shape and size, but most clearly and reliably discernible in the Sylvian fissure, the deep horizontally rising cleft in Figure 12–8. On the left side the cleft is longer, and on the right the posterior end shows a kind of upward twist (see Figure 12–7). With x-ray computerized tomography (CT scan), it is possible to see the difference today in living persons. If those differences are the outward sign of lateralized speech, then it would be enormously interesting to know at what point in the fossil record the hominid brain first showed the sign, and one might interpret that point as marking the origin of speech as we know it. Is there any possible way of finding out when that happened in long-vanished prehistoric brains?

In the lifetime of the individual the cerebral cortex exerts pressure on the vault of the skull and leaves a more or less readable imprint. If the fossil skull is filled with rubber latex, then on the outside of the resultant "endocast" it will be possible to see something of the gross pattern of the brain that once was there (Holloway, 1981). The distinguished radiologist Marjorie LeMay (1976) first showed that the asymmetry of the Sylvian fissures could be seen on the endocast of the La-Chapelle-aux-Saints fossil of Neanderthal man, which would put the origin somewhere between 40,000 and 100,000 years ago. With less certainty, LeMay believed it could be discerned in the skull of Peking man, which is a specimen of Homo erectus, and that takes us back 1.6 to 2 million years, when stone tools first give clear evidence of handedness. However, LeMay also provided data that seemed to divest the asymmetry of the Sylvian fissure of any value as a marker of language, for she found that asymmetries were also present in the great apes, who lack language and do not clearly manifest handedness.

The functional specialization of the left hemisphere (in right-handed persons) for speech is, of course, only one aspect of the left hemisphere–right hemisphere specialization in man, roughly characterizable as a difference between symbolic-communicative functions (left hemisphere) and visuospatial functions (right hemisphere). There is steadily mounting evidence that there are many correlated anatomical asymmetries, some of which can be read, by modern methods, from fossil endocasts. In 1982 Holloway and de LaCoste-LaReymondie reported on a total sample of 190 hominoid endocasts, including extant gorilla and chimpanzee specimens as well as modern man, Neanderthal man, *Homo erectus*, and some small-brained early australopithecines. They arrived at a startling conclusion.

LeMay had shown in 1976 that an asymmetry of the Sylvian fissure appeared in present-day apes, and that fact seemed to eliminate any possibility that the asymmetry in question was a sign of speech. Some still think that it does so. However, Holloway and de LaCoste-LaReymondie (1982) find that the patterns of asymmetry in ape brains are *characteristically different* from the patterns of asymmetry in the human brain. Their analyses lead them to suggest that the organization of the brain, even in early small-brained australopithecines, may have been characteristically human and qualitatively different from the organization of ape brains. It is possible, though far from proved, that hemispheric specialization goes all the way back to the early australopithecines and possibly, therefore, the potential for language.

The demonstrated localization of language functions in the left hemisphere applied, until very recently, exclusively to *spoken* language. The evidence for iconicity in symbol invention has been interpreted as suggesting that language began in the visual–manual modality. That suggestion is in apparent conflict with the idea that there is a left hemisphere specialization for language and a right hemisphere specialization for visuospatial tasks and the possibility that the specialization is nascent in even the earliest hominids. How could a visual–manual language get started in a brain in which one hemisphere is specialized for language and the other for visuospatial tasks? Recent important evidence from the Salk Institute for Biological Research (Bellugi, Poizner, and Klima, 1983; Poizner, Bellugi, and Iragui, 1984; Poizner et al., 1984) suggests the answer. It appears that for fluent deaf signers of the American Sign Language, this language—a visual and manual language—is lateralized in the left hemisphere. It is apparently more like speech—in that it is a language—than it is like other kinds of visuospatial tasks (Kimura, 1974, 1979). This means that nothing in the evidence up to the mid 1980s excludes the possibility of a gestural beginning.

The complications of evidence described here, and there are many more that have not been described, mean, I fear, that answers to the origins of language question are still mainly speculative. It is exciting, nevertheless, to have a "vision" of the kinds of evidence that may some day provide the answers.

A Speculative Answer

My own speculation goes like this. Probably the symbolic function, in the sense of the demonstration with Sherman and Austin by Savage-Rumbaugh and her collaborators, goes all the way back to the australopithecines (2–3 million years). The symbolic function may initially not even have been used for interindividual communication. It may have arisen as a memory function. Suppose Sherman or Austin had picked out one of five foods for eventual consumption and encoded it internally in symbolic form and then gone off somewhere, eventually returning and picking out the food coded in memory; that would be a use of a symbol not involving report or communication.

The first reports, I believe, are likely to have been gestural and iconic. The australopithecines walked upright as the great apes do not, and so the hands were free. We have seen many kinds of evidence that iconicity is the sovereign principle of symbolic invention; it has the mnemonic or memory advantage. The hands offer far more possibilities for icon creation than do the articulators and vocal cords. There is no reason to suppose, of course, that the australopithecines were mute. The best guess (Hewes, 1976) is that their calls functioned as they do in the present-day great apes to communicate affect and were not controlled by the cerebral cortex, but at the level of the midbrain (Myers, 1976). Lieberman (1973) has some fossil evidence that the vocal tract above the larynx of the australopithecines could have produced a few vowel-consonant contrasts, but far from all of those needed for speech as we know it.

If we say that language officially began with symbolic function in *Australopithecus*, then it must have had a long period of gradual evolution. The shift from iconicity to arbitrariness probably developed when language was still manual, with newly invented signs being clearly iconic and older signs becoming conventionalized. Increased cephalic capacity and neocortical control would have been necessary for the long-term retention of a large lexicon and for speedier communication. The advantages of speech over sign are many: It works at night; it gets around obstacles in the line of sight; it does not interrupt useful manual work.

It does seem certain that spoken language as we know it existed by 50,000 B.C. and probably 100,000 B.C. It is just possible that it did not exist, in the form we know, until then. In that period the brain had attained its contemporary size. In that period there was an explosion of new and different tools (Isaac, 1976) suggesting easy transmission of information and cultural evolution. After 50,000 B.C. there appears the first prehistoric art, body adornment, evidence of ritual burial (suggesting religion), and representational or iconic stone statuettes (Marschack, 1976). Humankind was dispersed over most of the world: Africa, Eurasia, and later the Americas (Jaynes, 1976). That very general increase in the tempo of change suggests, though it does not prove, that some final Rubicon of the evolution of language was crossed within the most recent 100,000 years.

From the standpoint of social psychology the fundamental importance of language consists in its ability to make rapid cultural evolution possible and biological evolution almost irrelevant. Language does that because it causes individual life experiences to become cumulative both across individuals at one time and across generations. Each of us today knows far more than could have been learned by direct personal experience. In fact, most of what we know has come to us by way of language: our science, law, religion, economics, trade, history, geography, and also, of course, our follies, superstitions, and undying enmities. The invention of writing vastly increased the rate of cultural evolution, and printing increased it again, and radio, telegraphy, and telephone again and again and again. To compare the rate of biological evolution and cultural evolution, think first of the fact that it took roughly 200 million years for the first marine animals of the Cambrian Epoch to evolve biologically into the amphibians of the Devonian Epoch. Think, then, of the fact that it has taken only about fifty years of cultural evolution for humankind to move from flying in the air to travel in space.

Summary

One way to try to learn something about the origins of language is to study the linguistic capacities of the chimpanzee, the present-day species closest to man and to prehistoric hominids, which does not, in its natural state, use language. After more than twenty-five years of inventive and painstaking study, utilizing manual rather than vocal responses, it can be said that there is evidence of some symbolic capacity in chimpanzees, in the sense of an ability to use a token to represent a referent. That capacity apparently plays no role in the communications of chimpanzees living in a natural state and can be demonstrated only by way of deliberate training. As yet there is no evidence at all of a capacity for syntax.

A second way to learn something about the prehistoric origins of language is by studying instances of language invention in recent times. These include representational writing systems and manual sign languages invented by deaf children of oralist parents and by hearing adults in special circumstances in which speech cannot be employed or, for ritual reasons, is not employed. All known examples of language invention in recent times converge on the conclusion that iconicity is the prime principle in the creation of symbols. An iconic symbol is not arbitrarily related to its referent but suggests it for people at a given time, and with much shared experience, by depiction or representation.

Iconic symbols can rarely be decoded on sight; they are not transparent. However, the sense of an iconic symbol can be roughly guessed at, or selected correctly, from a set of alternatives. Icons have a mnemonic or memory advantage over completely arbitrary symbols. It is much easier to create icons with the hands than with the articulatory organs of speech. It is therefore plausible that the first prehistoric symbols, like the symbols invented in recent times, would have been manual precisely because they could then be iconic and take full advantage of the mnemonic principle. It is likely that the representational character of many icons is evident also to present-day chimpanzees and could have been evident to prehistoric humans.

A final way to learn something about the prehistoric origins of language is from the study of prehistoric skulls. Brain size generally is correlated with body size, and so elephants and whales have much larger brains than man but do not, nevertheless, have language. When there is an increase of brain size with no commensurate increase of body size in an evolutionary sequence of species, one speaks of a process of encephalization. In the evolution of present-day *Homo sapiens* from earlier species of the genus *Homo* and possibly from still earlier members of the species *Australopithecus*, over a period of about 3–4 million years, a great deal of encephalization has occurred. There has been approximately a fourfold increase in the brain-weight:body-weight ratio. The lower values are comparable to those of present-day chimpanzees. While the encephalization process certainly made language possible, one cannot identify any minimal value that is the lowest value able to support language, because there are human dwarfs with brains smaller than chimpanzees who have language capacities that the chimpanzee does not have. It is not brain size alone, nor relative brain size (encephalization), that ultimately matters but, rather, the organization of the brain.

It is possible to learn something about the organization of the brain in prehistoric ancestors of man because of the following circumstances. The brain in life presses against the internal vault of the cranium and leaves an imprint that can be studied on fossilized skulls (converted into endocasts). Language in right-handed humans is organized primarily in certain areas of the left cerebral hemisphere, and it has recently been discovered that there are anatomical differences between the hemispheres correlated with the functional specialization. Those anatomical differences can sometimes be seen on the endocast of the internal cranium. It appears that there is cranial evidence of brain lateralization as far back as *Homo erectus* (1.5 million years ago) and probably as far back as the australopithecines 3 million years ago. One problem with concluding that the brain substrate for language goes back to those remote dates is that the great apes also have anatomical asymmetries of the cerebral hemispheres but do not have language. However, the work of Ralph Holloway indicates that the ape asymmetries are not the same as the human and so appears to remove that difficulty. Evidence of lateralization does not decide between a manual–visual and a vocal–auditory origin of language, because it now appears that both language modes are lateralized. Nothing in the fossil record establishes a date for the origin of either manual or spoken language. However, nothing excludes the possibility that language began as iconic manual symbols used by the australopithecines and underwent a long period of evolution, possibly not attaining its present spoken, elaborately syntactic form until 100,000 years ago or even more recently.

13

Language and Thought

THIS CHAPTER IS CONCERNED with two large topics: (1) the degree to which all languages are constrained by the nature of human thought and (2) the degree to which the structural properties peculiar to individual languages influence the thinking of those who speak each language. It is obvious to everyone that languages differ, especially if they are not historically cognate, because the differences are maximal at the surface, in pronunciation, in the way languages sound, and there has been a lot of interest in the possibility that the language a person learns might have effects on the way he perceives and thinks of the world. Translators between languages have often asserted that something easily expressed in one is really untranslatable into another because of deep differences of world-view. If anything of the kind is true, it must be tremendously important, because it would set limits to international understanding. In fact, however, it has proved difficult to come up with hard evidence that the structural differences between languages cause speakers of the respective languages to think differently.

The idea that all languages are in some abstract ways exactly the same is less obvious than language differences, and indeed very few people are in a position to form an independent judgment on the matter. However, linguistic science in this century has established the existence of many universals of struc-

The organization of this chapter was in part suggested to me by the organization of the first draft of a chapter on a similar range of topics by Miss Terry Kit-fong Au.

ture in the languages of the world. The next questions are: Where do these universals come from? Why do they exist? A likely answer is that they exist because of cognitive constraints, because the mind of the human species creates a kind of abstract blueprint that all languages must fit. With respect to cognitive categories or concepts especially, a strong case has been made. It appears that all languages name categories of a certain type, natural categories with fuzzy boundaries, and that all languages classify plants and animals into taxonomies of such natural categories, with just three to six vertical levels, of which one level has the special status called *basic* or *generic*. And there are still more ways in which the structure of human cognition seemingly constrains all languages to be the same.

We begin with the effects of cognition on language, because it is the more substantial of the two topics. The ideas are important for social psychology, but they are also fairly new and difficult, and a discussion of the nature of human object categories is unavoidable if the case is to be made clear.

Cognitive Constraints on Language

If the General Assembly of the United Nations were suddenly bereft of all its translators, the Tower of Babel would be restored—everybody seeming to speak unintelligibly, exotically, and rapidly. On first hearing the world's languages are wildly various. Prodigious polyglots who learn ten or twelve languages, some of them not historically related, have a different impression. To them it seems that while each language has distinctive qualities, in some hard-to-specify way they are all alike; they are almost trivial variations on a basic design. All such prodigies that I am acquainted with say that adding on a new language gets easier and easier, and there is even a little experimental evidence (Reed, 1983) that this is true: What is universal in languages is no doubt partly pure syntax, of little interest for social psychology, but in addition there are universal qualities that arise out of the way in which humans everywhere perceive and think about the world.

Categories and the Lexicon

The lexicon of a language is (roughly) the list of words, and a word may be simple, or unanalyzable semantically, as *bird* and *fish* and *fruit* are in English, or complex (analyzable into meaningful parts), as *bluejay* and *catfish* and *breadfruit* are in English. The lexicons of all languages include very many words of the grammatical type called nouns, which (again, roughly) name animals, vegetables, persons, objects, and places. Except for proper nouns, which name individuals, nouns refer to categories. Of course the categories named by nouns are not identical in all languages. One society may need to have a word for a certain kind of stone axe but not for spacecraft, and vice versa. The plant and animal worlds must, however, be named in all languages. For preliterate societies, those most like prehistoric societies, it is estimated (Berlin, 1978) that the lexicon for the biological world is larger than the lexicon for all other domains of knowledge combined. In several important ways, all known languages are alike in their treatment of the biological world, and that appears to be because of an interaction between cognitive characteristics, universal in the species, and the nature of the biological world.

A category is a number of objects considered to be equivalent, and categories are designated by names like *dog, cat, animal; lemon, orange, fruit; carrot, peas, vegetable*. A taxonomy is a hierarchy of categories such that categories are related to one another in terms of class inclusion. The category called *animal* includes *dogs* and *cats* but no other item in the sample list above; just as the category called *fruit* includes *lemon* and *orange* but not the rest; and the category called *vegetable* includes *carrot* and *peas* but not the rest. The term "level of abstraction" in a taxonomy refers to a particular level of inclusiveness. For our examples, animal, fruit, and vegetable are at a higher level of abstraction than the categories they include; they would be called "superordinate" to their respective "subordinate" pairs. Categories sharing a common superordinate but not themselves related by class inclusion are called "coordinate."

The sciences of botany and zoology classify plants and animals in taxonomic hierarchies having many levels of abstraction. For example, we move from the most abstract and inclusive level to less and less abstract and inclusive levels when we use the words *animal–mammal–primate–hominid–man*. The higher level of abstraction, the larger the population included in a category but the fewer the distinctive attributes shared by the members of the category; there is not much you can say that is true of all animals and no plants. The lower the level of abstraction, the smaller the population included but the larger the number of distinctive attributes shared by the numbers of the category; all men (also women, of course) walk erect, can reproduce sexually, use language, and so forth.

The first strong universal statement that can be made about biological lexicons is that all languages, including those of preliterate societies that have no sciences, organize the plant and animal world in terms of taxonomic hierarchies. That statement summarizes the results to date of the fields of anthropology called *ethnobotany* and *ethnozoology* (Berlin, 1978). Ethnobotanists and ethnozoologists work out the folk vocabularies and categories in the domains of, respectively, plants and animals. Folk categories of plants and animals are those that can be perceived directly without such technical aids as the microscope. Of course, not all languages have been studied in the detailed way required, and not all ever can be. The claim that taxonomies are universal fits all known cases and generalizes beyond them as inductive principles always must.

Categorization is a cognitive economy. The human senses can make indefinitely fine discriminations in several modalities, but it does not pay to discriminate more finely than is necessary. By categorizing we treat as equivalent stimuli or objects that we are able to distinguish because, for certain purposes, they are equivalent and *also different* from other categories of discriminable objects.

Until about 1973 psychological experiments on category formation conceived of human categories on the model of a "proper set." Triangles are a proper set, which means that members of the triangle class are precisely definable in terms of a conjunction of attributes true of all members of the set and of no nonmembers. A triangle is a three-sided closed figure. From the fact that a clear definition exists, it follows that membership in the set is not a matter of degree; one triangle is no more essentially triangular than any other. An entity either is or is not a triangle.

In retrospect, it is amazing that psychology was for so long able to think of real-life categories as proper sets. We ought to have worried more over the extreme difficulty everyone has in defining anything "natural," and natural, as used here, includes not only dogs and carrots but also artifacts like chairs, cars, and pencils. I know you can tell one when you see one, but just try listing the attributes that are true of all dogs and of no cats or wolves or hyenas, or of all carrots and no radishes or turnips, or of all chairs and no small tables, hassocks, benches, or slings.

PROTOTYPICALITY

In the early 1970s, Eleanor Rosch started to study categories using a new sort of instruction:

> This study has to do with what we have in mind when we use words which refer to categories. Let's take the word "red" as an example. Close your eyes and imagine a true red. Now imagine an orangish red . . . imagine a purple red. Although you might still name the orange-red or the purple-red with the term "red," they are not as good examples of red (as clear cases of what "red" refers to) as the clear "true" red. In short, some reds are redder than others. The same is true for other kinds of categories. Think of dogs. You all have some notion of what a "real dog," a "doggy dog" is. To me a retriever or a German shepherd is a very doggy dog while a Pekinese is a less doggy dog. Notice that this kind of judgment has nothing to do with how well you like the thing; you can like a purple red better than a true red but still recognize that the color you like is not a true red. You may prefer to own a Pekinese without thinking that it is the breed that best represents what people mean by dogginess. [Rosch, 1973, pp. 131–32]

Rosch then went on to ask people to rate instances of a category for "goodness of category membership" or what she called "prototypicality" on a scale from 1 (high) to 7 (low). With respect to fruits, how would you rate apple? How about lemon? Pineapple? Strawberry? Fig? Olive? With respect to vegetables, how would you rate carrot? Celery? Onion? Pickle? Rice? In the first place, no subject in 1973 said, and no subject in the many studies since (reviewed by Mervis and Rosch, 1981) has said: "I don't know what you are talking about. Either something is a fruit or it is not a fruit." Everyone always knows what those instructions were talking about. Furthermore, for members of a single culture, ratings of prototypicality of instances for every sort of category agree very closely. Which is the more prototypical science: chemistry or geology? Which is the more prototypical sport: football or weightlifting? Which is the more prototypical crime: murder or blackmail? You know and so does everyone else.

To begin the study of concept formation with proper sets like geometrical figures was rather like beginning the study of thought with logic. The proper set is a kind of *ideal type* of category. Words name proper sets, well-defined categories, only where usage is carefully policed as it is in mathematics, logic, and some branches of science, in the law (sometimes), and in government (sometimes). Whenever a name is used without careful monitoring, its meaning tends to drift, with the result that it comes to name not a proper set but a "fuzzy" set. The term "natural category" is used for the fuzzy sets of everyday life—whether biological, like plants and animals, or manufactured, like furniture and vehicles.

The strength of the human tendency to construct natural categories may be judged from the fact that we do it even when the starting point is a proper set. Armstrong, Gleitman, and Gleitman (1983) have shown that "4" is considered to be a much better even number than "34" or "106" and the square a more prototypical geometrical figure than a trapezoid or an ellipse. Female is a well-defined category but, among female roles, mother seems more prototypical than waitress, and waitress is better than policewoman, and cowgirl is rated as quite marginal. U.S. Senators are exactly defined in law, but Senator Ernest Hollings (tall, white-haired, male, Southern, courtly) probably seems more essentially senatorial than Senator Gary Hart (youthful-looking, dark hair, Western, breezy), and Margaret Chase Smith when she was a Senator was like a "dolphin among the fishes." When we have well-defined categories like geometrical figures, legal positions, sexes, races, and nationalities, the human mind seems to construct a natural category, in addition, as a kind of superstructure, and the concept of prototype comes close to that of stereotype (see Chapter 16).

Books for very young children as well as illustrations in dictionaries are good sources to consult for examples of prototypes. Figure 13–1 shows the picture that accompanies the entry *bird* in the ninth edition of Merriam-Webster's *New Collegiate Dictionary*. Was there ever a more quintessential bird? It seems the very essence of all that is avian, but how can it be so when *bird* is the abstract name for a large number of species that vary greatly in appearance. Certainly the picture in Figure 13–1 does not do justice to chickens or penguins and is very unfair to the ostrich and emu. How have dictionary-makers managed convincingly to picture what cannot in principle be pictured? They have

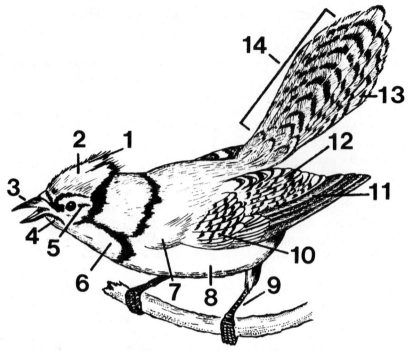

bird 2 (blue jay): *1* crest, *2* crown, *3* bill, *4* throat, *5* auricular region, *6* breast, *7* scapulars, *8* abdomen, *9* tarsus, *10* upper wing coverts, *11* primaries, *12* secondaries, *13* rectrix, *14* tail

Figure 13–1. Dictionary drawing used to illustrate the entry bird

(By permission. From *Webster's Ninth New Collegiate Dictionary*, © 1985 by Merriam-Webster Inc., publisher of the Merriam-Webster Dictionaries)

not drawn an abstraction, but rather a particular kind of bird—in considerable detail. The kind of bird pictured to represent all birds was not chosen at random. It is the bluejay we see, and the bluejay, Rosch has shown, is one of the most prototypical of all birds; it ranks with the sparrow and the robin. How odd it would be if the same dictionary read "bird (flamingo)" with a long-legged illustration to match. Yet why not if dictionary-makers had no sense of prototypicality?

The fact that members of a natural category vary in prototypicality is in accord with the fact that natural categories are not clearly defined. However, something must bind together the instances of a natural category. There is no single distinctive attribute shared by all and no conjunction of attributes. What there is is some set of attributes, none true of all instances, but each true of some, a collection of overlapping short-range similarities. Wittgenstein (1953) called this a "family resemblance" structure and convincingly argued that natural categories are held together by family resemblance and not by defining attributes. He conveyed the same idea in another wonderful metaphor—a natural category is like a rope of many strands, such that no single strand runs the full length.

Figure 13-2 takes the notion of family resemblance quite literally and pictures the Smith Brothers. If you saw the faces on the perimeter around the dining room table, you would know they belonged to one family, but there is no single distinctive feature common to all. Rather, there is a set of attributes more or less characteristic of the lot: six have white beards, two black; three have white moustaches, one black; five wear spectacles, three do not; six have large ears, two small. A face combining white beard, white moustache, spectacles, and large ears will be a maximally prototypical Smith brother, and he appears in the center. Natural categories, like dogs, apples, chairs, professors, Irishmen, Nazis, and most of the categories we operate with, are more like the Smith brothers than they are like triangles.

How do the taxonomies of scientific biology relate to the many ethnobotanies and ethnozoologies, including the everyday categories of American English? The great taxonomist was Linnaeus (early eighteenth century) and his *Systema Naturae* arranged plants and animals in terms of anatomical and physiological attributes, essentially how they looked and how they functioned, which is the way that folk systems also have been constructed.

Figure 13-2. The Smith Brothers

(S. L. Armstrong, L. R. Gleitman, and H. Gleitman, What some concepts might not be. *Cognition*, 13 [1983], p. 269, Fig. 3. By permission of North-Holland Publishing Co., Amsterdam)

Linnaeus wrote before Darwin, so he believed in simultaneous creation and thought, for example, that the 4,235 species of animals he identified were all the "kinds" the Creator had made. What is most interesting is that for the taxonomists of this time the

> . . . essential thing, the ultimate or transcendent reality of a species was believed not to be material or tangible, but a pattern, a divine idea, a *type*, or, as then often designated, an archetype ("primeval pattern"). The way for a systematist to look at organisms, then, was supposed to be to ignore individuals, to brush aside variation and all characteristics of populations, as such, but to abstract an idea of what the individuals have in common. [Simpson, Pittendrigh, and Tiffany, 1957]

Clearly, the Creator's kinds were the layman's natural categories, and the Creator's archetype seems to live again as psychology's prototype.

The theory of natural selection changed the basis for classification from morphology to common ancestry. This often left the general picture largely unaltered except in such cases as the marsupial mouse, which had to be put with kangaroos instead of rodents (Quine, 1969). Later on a population concept developed, along with Mendelian genetics and population genetics, and the identification of countless new species. The result is that scientific biological taxonomy is vastly more finely differentiated than any folk system and at some points organized in ways that would not arise out of unaided visual perception.

There is a strong universal proposition that can be made about natural categories. The plant and animal taxonomies of all languages are composed of terms that name natural categories, that is, categories with internal structure, with variation of prototypicality from one instance to another. Prototypicality or internal structure applies to categories at every level of a taxonomy: among carrots a bright orange, spindle-shaped, 5-inch-long specimen is more prototypical than is a yellowish, warped, 1-inch specimen. Among vegetables carrots are more prototypical than rice or mushrooms. Prototypicality has to do with the horizontal dimension of a taxonomic hierarchy—with internal structure at each level. With respect to the vertical dimension in plant and animal taxonomies, there are additional human cognitive constraints making all languages alike.

THE LEVEL OF THE BASIC OBJECT OR GENUS

Plants and animals are everywhere organized into hierarchies, which grow increasingly inclusive as the level of abstraction rises. Brent Berlin, the cognitive anthropologist who has played the leading role in discovering taxonomic universals, estimates (1978) that the number of levels is never less than three nor greater than six. The names Berlin proposes for the six levels of a maximally differentiated system appear in Table 13–1, together with examples from English ethnobiology.

TABLE 13-1. Proposed Taxonomic Hierarchy

Folk Biological Ranks	Examples from English Ethnobiology
Kingdom	Plant, animal
Life form	Tree, fish
(Intermediate)	Evergreen, fresh water fish
Generic	Pine, bass
Specific	White pine, black bass
Varietal	Western white pine, large-mouthed (black) bass

SOURCE: Berlin (1978), Table 1.1, p. 12.

Three very powerful propositions can be made about folk taxonomies, for which Table 13-1 represents the most differentiated extreme: (1) The classification of biological diversity at the generic level and above arises directly out of gross differences of form and, in the case of animals, behavior. (2) It is, therefore, not the case that preliterate man names and classifies only those organisms that have functional significance in his culture (e.g. edible plants versus poisonous plants), but *subgeneric classes (species or varieties) do usually have definite cultural utility*. (3) The level of the genus, therefore, has a special status. It is the lowest level at which classes "cry out to be named" (Berlin's phrase) because of perceptual discontinuities. It corresponds to what Rosch and associates (1976) call the "basic object level." These are generalizations about human cognition and the constraints it places on language. They need to be refined and elaborated.

The best place to begin is with the generic or basic object level, represented in Table 13-1 by *pine* and *bass* for English ethnobiology. Berlin's *genus* does not correspond with the *genus* of scientific biological taxonomy, which is based on genetic principles; it is closer to the biologist's *species*, but there is no exact science-to-folk translation anywhere in Table 13-1 except at the highest level of the plant and animal kingdoms.

Different cultures live in different biological environments, so there can be no standard list of plant and animal genera. How, then, does one identify the level of the genus in any given language? Most fundamentally it is the lowest level at which biological discontinuities of form and function are easily perceived without close inspection. In linguistic terms categories at the generic level are named by simple unanalyzable words (such as *oak, birch, bass, trout,* and so on), and in general this is the lowest level at which such names are found. At the vertical level just below, most names are complex (modifier plus noun in English). For instance: *white oak, red oak, silver birch, sea bass, striped bass,* and *rainbow trout.* The ethnobiologist in the field finds that the generic or basic object names for plants and animals are the first ones elicited, and informants give the impression that they think these are the "real names" ("x" is better named a *pine* than a *tree* or a *plant,* and "y" is better named a *bass* than a *fish* or an *animal*). Finally, all languages have a generic level in their biological taxonomies. Where they vary is in the number of higher and lower levels in various domains.

To the anthropological and linguistic criteria defining the level of the genus, or basic object, psychology has added many others. Rosch and associates (1976) worked with nine three-level taxonomies of the type illustrated in Figure 13-3. The most abstract level (fruit, clothing) is labeled "superordinate," the least abstract "subordinate," and the one in the middle "intermediate." Notice that Figure 13-3 includes a nonbiological class of objects (clothing), and in the full research there were others (vehicle, musical instrument, furniture, tool, and so forth), and this research makes it clear that inanimate objects also have a generic or basic object level. However, cognitive anthropology has not yet determined whether all the principles that apply universally to plants and animals apply also to things, but I would bet that they do.

In the two hierarchies of Figure 13-3 the intermediate level is destined to be revealed as the basic object level by a new set of psychological operations, but notice that it also satisfies Berlin's linguistic criterion. Apple, peach, grapes, pants, socks, and shirt are the lowest levels in the hierarchies at which names are unanalyzable simple words. They are also at a level of perceptual discontinuity that "cries out to be named," but the Rosch group describes the perceptual distinctiveness of the basic object level somewhat otherwise than Berlin does. They emphasize the fact that many attributes shift together on this level. Contrasting apple with peach, there is within-category similarity and between-category distinctiveness in many attributes at once: texture, shape, seeds, internal color, juiciness, fragrance, flavor, and so on. At subordinate levels (Delicious apple versus Mackintosh) there are many fewer *differentiating* attributes, and at superordinate levels (fruit) there are few *shared* attributes. The basic object level from this point of view is the set of categorical cuts that maximizes intracategory uniformity and intercategory difference. The basic object categories give us maximal information with minimal cognitive effort because they "cut Nature at the joints."

The cognitive-informational analysis is the basic idea, but the definition of the basic object level is ultimately also defined in operational and behavioral terms. There are many convergent operations, but one will suffice. Subjects were given a set of nine words drawn from one level of abstraction and were asked to list all the attributes of the object named that they could think of (in $1\frac{1}{2}$ minutes per object). The results were as predicted: Categories at the intermediate level had maximal intracategory common attributes and maximal intercategory differences. Superordinate categories had few, if any, attributes common to all instances (or category members). Subordinate categories had many attributes common to all instances intracategory but shared most of them with their contrasting subordinate and so had few distinctive attributes. The behavioral definitions make explicit and objective one's sense that, at the

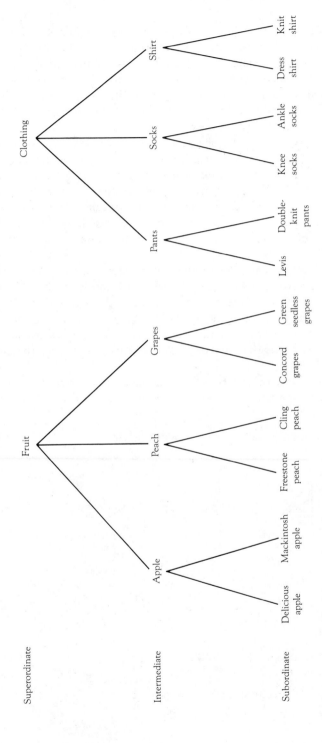

Figure 13–3. Three-level taxonomies
(Based on Rosch et al., 1976)

level of the basic object, within-category similarity of attributes is maximized, and at the same time so is between-category distinctiveness. Figure 13–4 lists attributes for the superordinate clothing, for two basic objects (pants and shirt), and for two subordinate kinds of pants (levis and double-knit pants), and two subordinate kinds of shirt (dress shirt and knit shirt). The point of Figure 13–4 is that in the domain of clothing the distinction between pants and shirt is more "basic" than that between their subvarieties.

From the fact that concrete objects are organized in taxonomies, it follows that any individual object has membership in a set of increasingly inclusive levels and, since there is a name for each level, that any thing, any entity, has more than one name that can be correctly applied to it. Any single particular shirt in a drawer or closet can quite appropriately be called a *dress shirt, a shirt,* or *an article of clothing,* because it is all of those. Notice, however, that *shirt* is the only simple unanalyzable name in the hierarchy of three, and from that fact we could correctly guess that the word *shirt* names the object at the basic or generic level. It is the same with any particular object, plant or animal. There are always appropriate names at several levels which categorize the object more or less broadly, but the simple, unanalyzable name that categorizes the object so as to maximize common attributes inside the category and distinctive attributes between categories is basic. *Piano* rather than *musical instrument* or *grand piano; apple* rather than *fruit* or *Mackintosh apple; truck* rather than *vehicle* or *dump truck;* and so on.

The name of any thing that falls at the basic level seems to be the *real* name, the name one would provide if asked. Rosch and collaborators asked

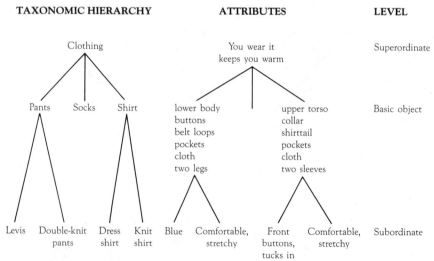

Figure 13–4. Attributes listed for three taxonomic levels

(Based on Rosch et al., 1976)

adults to shuffle through the deck of pictured objects in their nine taxonomies and name each one; they received 530 names at the basic level (*pants*, *shirt*, *piano*, *apple*, and so on) and just ten at any other level, though all 530 could have been named alternatively at either the superordinate or subordinate level. Jeremy Anglin (1977) has had mothers name things for their small children and found again that the basic object name is the one given. Finally, Mervis (in Rosch et al., 1976) has determined that the first names children learn are at the basic level. From that work (and more) it is now possible to answer a long-standing question about the growth of vocabulary in childhood: Does it move from the concrete (subordinate) to the abstract (superordinate), or does it move in the opposite direction? The answer is: Both at once. Object names start at the basic level and then develop gradually in both the more abstract and the more concrete directions.

Berlin, you may recall, said that generic (or basic object level terms) were the first terms elicited by anthropologists from native-speaking informants asked to name particular plants and animals. Berlin (1978) has also said that the growth of vocabulary in a language in historic time is from the basic level toward the more abstract levels of life forms and kingdoms and, simultaneously, toward the more concrete specific and vertical levels. In short, the development of language lexicons over many generations appears to follow the same law as the development of vocabulary in each person's lifetime: from the generic or basic in both vertical directions.

Berlin (1978) finds that categories more abstract than the generic are, like the generic, named because they represent major perceptual discontinuities that "cry out to be named" (like *shrub*, *vine*, *evergreen*). Categories less abstract than the generic (e.g. *black pine*, *white pine*) do not, by contrast, correspond to major discontinuities but, rather, require rather careful attention to perceptual detail and are usually named for reasons of cultural utility. It is on the subgeneric levels that we find the principal language differences that correspond to cultural differences: the many words for varieties of snow in Eskimo, for kinds of camel in Arabic, and in American English the lexicon of the automobile: *Torino*, *Camaro*, *Volare*, *Cougar*, and so forth. Berlin adds that lexical loss or decay also occurs chiefly on the subgeneric levels.

The principle that the subgeneric (or subbasic) differentiation of categories and names is closely related to cultural emphases when put together with the principle that lexical loss is subgeneric enables us to understand a third generalization: The overall size of the lexicon of a language is positively related to societal complexity. Preliterate, low-technology societies with minimal occupational differentiation have much smaller lexicons than the languages of modern nation states, and we are now in a position to see why that should be so.

In a complex society like the United States there is an almost endless differentiation of occupations, interests, and hobbies, and each subculture develops its own vocabulary. Gardeners can identify and name zinnias, poppies, asters, marigolds, and so on. Designers of clothing have a color vocabulary that includes aqua, puce, magenta, fuchsia, blueberry, mauve, and so on quite indefinitely. Connoisseurs of drugs know what *red devils* and *smack* are, as well as *reefers* and *tokes* and *ludes* and so on. Connoisseurs of contemporary music can distinguish *heavy metal* from *funk* and *R and B* from *pop, punk,* and *reggae.* Skiers even have names for many kinds of snow, and for all I know there may be camel fanciers who can differentiate twenty kinds of camel. Societies that are less differentiated by occupation, where the mode of life is more uniform, will not have elaborate vocabularies in every conceivable area but will have some one or more areas that represent local specialties, like the Eskimo's varieties of snow, usually closely tied to habitat and economy. Such specialized vocabularies do not result in a total lexicon that is large by world standards. So if we just assume that socially differentiated groups develop their own vocabularies, it seems obvious that size of lexicon must increase with societal complexity. However, there is also the matter of lexical loss.

Janet Dougherty (1978) investigated the biological taxonomies of urban twentieth-century Americans (in San Francisco) and found that some life forms were known (*bird, fish, tree, shrub*) and just a few generic terms like *sparrow* and *robin, goldfish* and *sardine, oak* and *maple,* and almost no subgeneric or more concrete terms. Dougherty's explanation is that urban Americans simply do not have much significant interaction with the biological world and so either have not learned to categorize and name in a finely differentiated way or else have forgotten what they once knew. Quite significant lexical loss goes on in complex societies, and it occurs where it is supposed to, at the lower levels of abstraction. However, those losses are not total losses in a complex and literate society as they might be in a simple and preliterate society. Urbanites may lose vocabulary in the biological domain, but gardeners, farmers, and fishermen will not, and certainly botanists and zoologists will not. In addition, literacy guarantees records (e.g. dictionaries) from earlier times, which preserve lexical items even if whole occupations or hobbies are eliminated. For these reasons also the size of language lexicon will be positively correlated with the complexity of the society that uses the language.

The American Sign Language (ASL) provides an interesting test of the generality of the principles describing the effect on language of the basic object level. Newport and Bellugi (1979) investigated the ASL expressions for the English terms at each of the three levels (subordinate, intermediate, superordinate) of six of the taxonomies of Rosch and colleagues: musical instruments, fruits, tools, clothing, furniture, and vehicles. In terms of Berlin's linguistic criterion the intermediate level proved to be the basic object level just as it is in English. For words at the basic level, ASL provides simple, unanalyzable signs, whereas the superordinate and subordinate levels could be named only by compounding signs.

The ASL signs for categories at three taxonomic levels bring us back to the speculation (Chapter 12) that the first linguistic symbols were iconic and manual. Certainly the signs for basic objects illustrated by Newport and Bellugi are highly iconic: for *piano*, finger movements as if playing; a sawing motion for *saw*; indication of pant legs for *pants*; for *grapes*, the hands shaped like a hanging cluster. The signs at the superordinate level cannot be very iconic, because there are no shared attributes to represent, and the signs at subordinate levels have to use some arbitrary specifiers for color and size. I suggest that it must be so, that basic object level categories must generally be more iconically signed than categories at other levels, and that this follows from the very definition of the basic object level.

Recall that the basic object level is the level at which the largest number of distinctive perceptual attributes (shape, legs, motions, and so on) involving the object exist. Distinctive attributes and distinctive movements are the raw material from which iconic signs can be created. How could one iconically represent in a simple sign such abstract categories as musical instrument or tool? It would seem to follow that if the first linguistic symbols were iconic and manual, they ought also to have symbolized objects at the basic level of categorization, and there are two reasons for saying this. In the first place the basic level is the level of maximal perceptual discontinuities. In the second place it is the level that supplies the best raw materials—distinctive attributes and motions—for the invention of icons.

SUMMARY

The world's languages seem to be constrained by human cognition in many ways. The plants and animals of the biological world and apparently also the objects made by man are organized as natural categories, which are not well defined but are bound together by attributes in a family-resemblance manner. From the externally given family resemblance structure of a category, the human mind generates a mental structure internal to the category such that instances vary in prototypicality. The natural categories of plants, animals, and objects are universally organized into taxonomies of class inclusion; for plants and animals at least, levels of abstraction range from three to six.

Among the vertical levels of abstraction there is one, called the generic or basic object level, that has a number of special properties. Words at that level will be simple and unanalyzable. At that level intracategory similarity and intercategory difference, in perceptible attributes, are maximal. At the basic object (or generic) level and above, categories are named because they are perceptually obvious, not because of cultural significance, but below the basic object level categories usually have clear cultural utility. Names at the basic level are the ones most readily elicited by anthropologists and also the ones parents give first to children. The vertical (levels of abstraction) development of the child's vocabulary begins at the basic object level and thereafter moves both up and down; the vertical development of the lexicon of a language in the course of history apparently follows the same law. Because categorization below the basic object level is primarily determined by the special attention of occupations, hobbies, and interests, it follows that the size of language lexicons will be positively correlated with societal complexity. It finally seems likely that if language began with manual iconic symbols, those symbols would have been at the level of the basic object for the reason that perceptual distinctiveness and distinctiveness of motion are greatest there.

In very many ways it seems the naming of plants, animals, and objects in the world's languages follows a universal blueprint. The variation that exists is limited and lawful, and as you learn one language after another, you learn what is bound to be the case and what may or may not be the case. The world of objects is an external physical reality, which it is not surprising to find fitted in a certain way to our perceptual and cognitive apparatus.

Linguistic Relativity

Linguistic relativity is the reverse of the view that human cognition constrains the form of language. Relativity is the view that the cognitive processes of a human being—perception, memory, inference, deduction—vary with the structural characteristics—lexicon, morphology, syntax—of the language he speaks. Of course, both can be true, but in different domains of language and cognition. It has proved to be more difficult, however, to find convincing examples of language affecting cognition than of cognition affecting language, but then it is very difficult to invent a really good experiment on linguistic relativity, and I myself think the first was Alfred Bloom's (1981) study of English and Chinese.

Despite the lack of confirming evidence, linguistic relativity is a very old and rather widely held view. It has been most effectively championed in this century by two anthropological linguists: Edward Sapir (1949) and Benjamin Lee Whorf (1956). Edmund Glenn and Maung Gyi, two chief translators for the United Nations, have both said that one thinks differently in different languages and have supported their position with stories of highly consequential misunderstandings. Khrushchev, it seems, when he said "We will bury you" did not mean, as the translation suggested, "in atomic dust," but rather something like "in the dust of our national chariot as we pass you in the economic race."

George Orwell passionately believed that language played an important role in shaping political thought, and in his futuristic 1984 there is a language, Newspeak, which is explicitly designed not simply to provide a medium of expression for the world-view of Ingsoc (English Socialism) but to make all other modes of thought impossible. In nonfuturistic 1982 there appeared a book Nukespeak, which argues that the elite that is technically qualified to talk about nuclear war uses a lexicon well designed to keep the "unthinkable" unthought, a lexicon of clean bombs, preemptive first strikes, and normal aberrations (Three Mile Island). The kind of linguistic determinism attributed to Newspeak and to

Nukespeak presupposes the truth of linguistic relativity and goes beyond it. The claim is not simply that cognitive structures covary with language structures, but that the latter shape and limit the former.

In history generally linguistic relativity has more often operated as an assumption than as an explicit hypothesis, but it has usually figured as an assumption in revolutionary libertarian thinking rather than in the thinking of established power (Newspeak and Nukespeak). Programs of social reform very often include reforms of language. The most easily accomplished item on the civil rights agenda was the displacement of the term *Negro* by the term *black*; it happened in little more than a year. Not so easy, in fact not yet accomplished, is the displacement of both *Miss* and *Mrs.*, in both writing and speech, by *Ms.* (pronounced MIZ), which is favored by some. The hitch is, of course, that unless married women insist on being addressed as *Ms.* the form will, like *Miss*, mean unmarried, and marital status continues to matter to many women. However, quite a few women now keep their maiden names after marriage, and they find *Ms.* more accurate than either *Mrs.* or *Miss*.

It was a part of the program of the French Revolution to extirpate the deferential use of plural *vous* to a single person; Malbec called it a remnant of feudalism. Equality and fraternity called for the use of *tu*, the pronoun of friends and family, in all circumstances, by each person, to each person. Frenchmen made the effort to change their linguistic habits as long as revolutionary fervor lasted, but when it waned they relapsed into unthinking pronominal acknowledgement of status. Communism in modern Europe had the same pronominal reform program as the French Revolution (against such forms as *vy*, cognate to *vous*, and in favor of *ty*). In China the traditional honorific *Nin* was the target of attack. In seventeenth-century England the Society of Friends (Quakers), an equalitarian reformist movement, tried to eliminate deferential *ye* in favor of universal *thou* and *thee*. The fact that those changes were thought to be essential for a revolutionary consciousness seems to imply belief in linguistic relativity and, indeed, determinism. The fact that none of those reforms has endured tells us something about the inertia of certain aspects of language and also something about the inertia of some aspects of social structure. It may also tell us something about linguistic relativity and determinism.

Only in the present decade, in the psychologically self-conscious United States, has the link between linguistic relativity and language reform been explicitly recognized. In the effort to win full equality for women "sexist" language has been attacked on the ground that it embodies and transmits from generation to generation sexist thought. Those attacks have come from linguists (Lakoff, 1973; Bodine, 1975) and psycholinguists (Henley, 1977) as well as from laypersons, and Whorf's name has been invoked. It is a pronoun once again that most offends, but this time not a pronoun of address. In English we have the third person masculine *he* as a generic substitute for nouns of indefinite gender, such as *somebody*, *person*, *reader*, and *child*. Bodine (1975) contends that

that usage reflects and helps to maintain an "androcentric" view of the world, and socially alert speakers, writers, and publishers are attempting to eliminate generic *he*. An increasingly common expedient in textbooks is to alternate *he* and *she* as replacements for *child* or *person* in a more or less random manner. The reader experiences an initial vertiginous incohesion, but it wears off.

What is completely new about the present-day attack on *he* is the recognition by some that the existence of the linguistic form alone, which would have satisfied Whorf as evidence of the related sexist thought, is not evidence enough. When *he* is used for *child* or *somebody*, it may suggest a person of masculine gender, but it need not since all words are understood not as isolated entities but in context and in fact it is an answerable empirical question whether *he* in the generic sense conjures up a masculine image. There is some psycholinguistic research aimed at answering that question (Crawford and English, 1984; MacKay, 1980; MacKay and Fulkerson, 1979), and it does look as if generic *he* tends to suggest a masculine referent, but it is still unclear what effect that has on the world-view of those who use it.

In this book I have usually used *he* as the generic pronoun, switching to *he or she* or to *she* only where it seemed likely to do some good. That decision does not reflect any lack of sympathy with the goals of the Women's Movement but, rather, some doubt that the pronoun does harm and, especially, the absence of a good alternative. To the linguist *he and she, his and hers* are more invidious than the generic *he*, because the "frozen" word order (masculine first, feminine second) derives historically from a position that the "masculine gender is more worthy than the feminine" (Poole, 1646, p. 21). The thinking behind *he and she* is nicely and comically illustrated by this paragraph from the year 1553:

> Some will set the Carte before the horse, as thus. My mother and my father are both at home, even as thoughe the good man of the house ware no breaches, or that the graye Mare were the better Horse. And what thoughe it often so happeneth (God wotte the more pitte) yet in speaking at the leaste, let us kepe a natural order, and set the man before the woman for maners Sake. [Wilson, 1553, p. 189]

I did not want to hitch myself to this Carte. Still, I suppose I might have done what many students do in their papers and used *s/he*, but then one ought also to use *her/him* and *hers/his*, and the look of all those slash marks on the printed page is not pleasing. Another alternative is *they*, which violates number instead of gender, and still sounds ungrammatical: "Any writer whose ear does not change with evolving usage should lay down their pen." I could get used to that and expect to, but have not yet.

Counterfactual Conditionals in English and Chinese

In 1972–73, a young social psychologist named Alfred Bloom was in Hong Kong administering a questionnaire designed to investigate political thinking. In his interviews he asked the following question: "If the government had passed a law requiring that all citizens born outside of Hong Kong make weekly reports of their activities to the police, how would you have reacted?" Since he was interviewing speakers of Chinese, that was not the question he asked but, rather, its Chinese equivalent. Alfred Bloom is himself bilingual in Chinese and English, and he made his own translations. This particular Chinese translation, however, regularly elicited a surprising answer. One Chinese-speaking interviewee after another, asked how he or she would have reacted if the Hong Kong government had passed a certain law, answered: "It hasn't."

Bloom's experience with his questionnaire was the starting point of a program of research that eventuated in his 1981 book, *The Linguistic Shaping of Thought: A Study in the Impact of Language on Thinking in China and the West*. In 1983 the *Journal of Asian Studies* published an extremely enthusiastic review of Bloom's book by Benjamin A. Elman of Kyoto University: "It is clear that we can no longer be armchair linguists pontificating about the 'Chinese mind' or the 'Western mind.' Bloom has demonstrated that what we have long suspected to be the case can be evaluated and measured with a great deal of precision" (Elman, 1983, p. 613).

The questionnaire sentence about the Hong Kong government carries a counterfactual conditional meaning. It states a premise (or condition or supposition) and asks about a conclusion; that is the conditional part. At the same time the sentence negates the premise or condition; that is the counterfactual part. In English the counterfactual meaning and the conditional meaning are not expressed in sequentially distinct clauses or sentences but are simultaneously expressed with "if . . . then" and the verbs in what is (loosely) called the subjunctive mode. The linguistic mechanism can be more effectively dissected if we use simple declarative sentences as examples rather than the question about Hong Kong.

A simple conditional $(p \supset q)$ is expressed in English by starting the suppositional clause with "if" and the main clause with "then," though "then" is optional and often omitted, and putting the verb in the appropriate tense. Thus: "If interest rates go down, (then) housing will recover." Suppose one asks, "Have interest rates gone down?" or "Will interest rates go down?" The appropriate answer, given only the conditional sentence, is "I have no idea." Let us say instead, "If interest rates were to go down, (then) housing would recover" or, alternatively, "If interest rates had gone down, then housing would have recovered." Suppose now one asks, "Have interest rates at this time gone down?" The appropriate answer is "No, they have not." For the subjunctive, verb forms (*were . . . would*; *had . . . would have*) signal the contrary-to-fact status of the supposition. This is a construction that asks us to entertain implications of premises not now true. In English it is a simple, compact construction. Bloom's study of Chinese grammar led him to believe that things are otherwise arranged in that language.

In Chinese the form *ru guo* identifies a supposition, and *jiu* is the word for *then*. This form is used in implicational sentences which imply nothing about truth values, and it is also used in counterfactual cases. One might hear the equivalent of "*ru guo* President Carter not admitted the Shah of Iran into the United States, Carter *jiu* been reelected" with the contrary-to-fact premise not marked linguistically. The speaker might nevertheless expect a listener to arrive at a counterfactual reading, because the listener might reasonably be expected to know the facts. When the listener or reader cannot be expected to know the facts, Chinese does mark the supposition as contrary to fact but does so not with a verb form, but in an independent statement. Thus: "James not speak Chinese. *Ru guo* James speak Chinese, James *jiu* get a good job in American Consulate, Hong Kong." Very like: "~p; p⊃q" or "Not p. If p, then q."

In Hong Kong and in Taiwan Bloom formed the impression that while the Chinese language, of course, provides a construction for the explicit expression of counterfactual conditionals, the construction is rarely used. He reports making a content analysis of a Taiwan newspaper over a period of three weeks and finding only a single instance of the construction, and that instance was in a translation of a speech made by Kissinger. His Chinese informants, many of them scholars, told him that there was something "un-Chinese" about counterfactual reasoning. Certainly there is nothing "un-American" about such reasoning. We do it all the time. For instance, any important unhappy event on the national level (an election lost, an assassination attempted) or on the personal level (an illness, an accident, a quarrel) elicits a flow of counterfactuals of the post mortem type: "If it were not for the deficit . . ." "If Mondale had not asked: "Where's the beef?" . . ." "If I had put on the snow tires yesterday . . ." We positively *go in for* working out the implications of contrary-to-fact suppositions, and Bloom's impression was that the Chinese considered this to be a rather bootless business. He speculated that the compact English construction used for counterfactuals somehow encouraged the creation of an integrated, easily triggered schema for counterfactual thought in a way that the separate sequential clauses in Chinese did not.

To test his hypothesis Bloom made up certain story problems in both English and Chinese. Something was first established as not the case. Then, from that contrary-to-fact "something" a series of implications was drawn. Finally, with the story in front of them, readers read the implications and were to mark those that were factually true or else to indicate that none of them could be said to be true and to explain why this was so. They ought to have said none was true since all were marked as counterfactual. Here is one story in English (Version Two of Bier) and also the questions that followed it:

> Bier was an Eighteenth Century European philosopher who wanted very much to investigate the principles of the universe and the laws of nature. Because there was some contact between China and the West at the time, works of Chinese philosophy could be found in Europe, but very few had been translated. Bier could not read Chinese, but if he had been able to read Chinese, he would have discovered that those Chinese philosophical works were relevant to his own in-

vestigations. What would have most influenced him would have been the fact that Chinese philosophers, in describing natural phenomena, generally focused on the interrelationships between such phenomena, while Western philosophers by contrast generally focused on the description of such phenomena as distinct individual entities. Once influenced by that Chinese perspective, Bier would then have synthesized Western and Chinese views and created a new philosophical theory which focuses on natural phenomena both in terms of their mutual interrelationships and as individual entities. He would have overcome a weakness in Western philosophical thought of that Century and, moreover, deeply influenced German, French and Dutch philosophers, encouraging Western philosophy to take a step forward and at the same time approach more closely to science.

Please indicate, by choosing *one or more* of the following answers what contribution or contributions Bier made to the West, according to the paragraph above:

1. Bier led Western philosophy to pay attention to natural phenomena as individual entities.

2. He led Western philosophy to pay attention to the mutual interrelationships among natural phenomena.

3. He led European philosophy closer to science.

4. He led Western philosophy one step closer to Chinese philosophy.

5. None of these answers are appropriate. (Please explain your own opinion briefly.)

In the story about the philosopher Bier, in the sentence beginning "Bier could not read Chinese, but if he had been able to read Chinese, he would have . . .," we have the signals of the counterfactual condition: "If . . . had + *past participle* . . . would have . . ." Besides those signals, the sentence explicitly asserts "~ p": "Bier could not read Chinese." In the rest of the paragraph we find one implication after another all marked as counterfactual by the form *would have*:

        . . . would have discovered . . .
        . . . would have most influenced him . . .
        . . . would have been the fact . . .
        . . . would then have synthesized . . .
        . . . would have overcome . . .

Would have, would have, would have—and so, to the reader of English, did not. Which means that none of the statements 1–4 can be endorsed. One must check 5. None of the answers offered is appropriate, because the story does not say that Bier, in fact, did any of the things listed, but only that he would have—if he had been able to read Chinese.

When fifty-five Americans, both students and nonstudents, read the paragraph about Bier, 98 percent checked the fifth alternative and, in nontechnical terms, explained why. When, however, a Chinese translation was read by 120 native speakers of Chinese in Taiwan and Hong Kong, only 7 percent gave counterfactual interpretations. How did they explain their answers? A great many said that by the end of the story they had lost track of the fact that Bier could not read Chinese. About the same number said that they remembered Bier could not read Chinese, but when so many implications were spelled out they concluded that the author must intend them to be understood as true. "Otherwise, why write it?" The counterfactual realm does seem to be un-Chinese, not in the sense that the Chinese are *unable* to think about contrary-to-fact matters and to draw out contrary-to-fact implications, but rather in the sense that it is not a congenial, familiar way of thinking.

The Bier story quoted here (called "Version Two") does not in its Chinese version absolutely exclude conclusions 1–4. The story says of works of Chinese philosophy that ". . . very few had been translated." Those very few translated works constitute a narrow but possible channel of communication from Chinese philosophy to a Bier who could not read Chinese. To be sure, the implications that follow all take the form *ru guo . . . jiu* (if . . . then) and so build on a premise that has been said to be untrue, but since the Chinese verb is not marked for counterfactuality (as the English verb is), conclusions 1–4 could be taken as true in the Chinese story but not in the English story. Bloom's Version Two of the Bier story was intended to *permit* either interpretation in Chinese and so to expose a predilection for the factual over the counterfactual. However, Bloom also wrote a Version Three of the Bier story, which might be said to "plug the leak" in Version Two and make more salient for Chinese readers the counterfactual logic. In Version Three, *no* works of Chinese philosophy had been translated. This version was read by 102 native speakers of Chinese in Hong Kong and Taiwan and by 52 native speakers of English. As Bloom had predicted, the more salient counterfactual logic made no difference to English-speaking subjects (96 percent counterfactual answers) but significantly increased the counterfactual responses of Chinese-speaking subjects (50 percent). There still remained a large significant difference between the two groups.

There is a third piece of evidence using the Bier stories, which Bloom finds most compelling of all. Some (twenty-one) of the Taiwanese students who had not given counterfactual answers to Version Two of the Bier story spoke English as well as Chinese and spoke it every day in their businesses. They were all nonstudents. Three months after the first reading, Bloom contacted them again and gave them Version Three in English. Of the twenty-one bilinguals who read in English this story of counterfactual implications, 86 percent rejected all of the implications as untrue and checked the fifth alternative. Apparently it is possible for someone who thinks as a Chinese when using the Chinese language to think as a speaker of English when using that language. To be sure, the story in English was the leakproof Version Three, whereas the story in Chinese had been Version Two, but the 86 percent counterfactual responses to Version Three in English is significantly above the 50 percent obtained from a comparable group when Version Three was in Chinese.

A Research Response

Bloom's work on counterfactual reasoning interested Miss Terry Kit-fong Au, then an undergraduate concentrator in psychology at Harvard, born in Hong Kong, whose first language is Chinese. Miss Au doubted that there really was a difference in the availability of counterfactual reasoning that depended on whether one was thinking in English or in Chinese, so she designed a set of experiments (Au, 1983) to be conducted with Hong Kong subjects bilingual in Chinese and English. Eventually Au had 989 subjects, which probably sets a numerical record for undergraduate research.

Most of Bloom's work compares speakers of English in the United States with speakers of Chinese in either Hong Kong or Taiwan, and while there is no clear reason to expect culture to make a difference in comprehension of the Bier stories (all subjects lived in cities and were about equal in schooling), the fact remains that in those studies language and culture are confounded. The more powerful design, using bilinguals in a single culture who receive the problem in English or in Chinese, was used once, but the design was less than ideal. In Au's studies comparing problem-solving in English and in Chinese, all subjects were bilinguals in the same culture: Anglo-Chinese secondary schools in Hong Kong. Subjects (aged 15-25) had studied English as a second language for about twelve years. They were always randomly assigned on an individual level to receive materials in Chinese or else in English.

The Bier story (both Version Two and Version Three) seemed to Au, as indeed it does to most people, convoluted in structure and esoteric in subject matter, and she thought it possible that a more concrete and "lively" story that retained the counterfactual structure would not show so large an English language–Chinese language difference simply because the story as such would be more readily understood. She composed the following "good" tale:*

> Once a Dutch explorer ventured into Central Africa and saw a tribe of natives gathered around a fire. Hoping to make some interesting discoveries, this Dutch explorer held his breath and observed the natives attentively from behind the bushes. He heard one of the natives shout in a language, which he unfortunately did not know. He then saw the natives throw a dead human body into a big pot of boiling water. And when the "human broth" was done, the natives all hurried to drink some of it. Upon seeing this event, the explorer was absolutely astonished, and fled as soon as he could. If this explorer had been able to understand the language spoken by the natives and had not fled so quickly, he would have learnt that the dead native was actually a hero of the tribe, and was killed in an accident. The explorer would also have learnt that the natives drank the "broth" of their hero because they believed that only by doing so could they acquire the virtues of their hero. If this explorer had been able to understand the language spoken by the natives and had not fled so quickly, he would have learnt that the natives were very friendly, and were not cruel and savage as he thought.

*T. K. Au, Chinese and English counterfactuals, Cognition, 15 (1983), p. 163. By permission of North-Holland Publishing Co., Amsterdam.

Please indicate, by choosing *one or more* of the following answers, which thing or things about the natives the Dutch explorer knew according to the above paragraph:

1. The dead native was a hero of the tribe.

2. The dead native was killed in an accident.

3. The natives believed that they could acquire a dead hero's virtues only by boiling the dead hero's body in water and then drinking the "broth."

4. The natives were friendly and not cruel and savage as the Dutch explorer thought.

5. None of the above. (Please explain your opinion briefly.)

The Human Broth story has exactly the same logical structure as Version Three of the Bier story. The English version reduces to: "A was not the case; if A had been the case, B would have been the case; C would have been the case. If A had been the case, D would have been the case." The premise A is explicitly negated, and implications B, C, and D are stated but marked counterfactual in each instance by *would have*. The Chinese version of Human Broth has the same logical structure, but since the verb is not marked for counterfactuality, there are no repeated reminders that A is not the case. It reduces to: "A not being the case. If A being the case, then B will be the case; C will be the case. If A being the case, then D will be the case."

Version Three of Bloom's Bier story in both the English and Chinese versions was also administered. If the concreteness and clarity of the story were important, then the results with Human Broth would be more often correct, which is to say counterfactual, than the results with the Bier story. It seemed likely that the English versions of both stories would produce more counterfactual answers than the Chinese versions but that the Chinese versus English difference would be greater for Bier than for Human Broth.

The results were a surprise. Counterfactual answers on the two versions of the two stories ranged from 88 percent to 100 percent, and no differences between stories or versions approached statistical significance. Quite simply, Au's bilingual subjects had no problem understanding the counterfactual nature of either story in either language; they just about always gave the correct (counterfactual) answer. The research question became: What could account for the difficulty Bloom's Chinese-speaking subjects had had with the Chinese version of the Bier story?

In all of Au's samples the largest difference had been between Human Broth in Chinese (100 percent correct) and Bier in Chinese (88 percent correct). Several Chinese bilinguals, including Au, thought that there was a difference in the quality of the language in the two stories. The Chinese of Human Broth impressed them as fully idiomatic, whereas the Chinese of the Bier story seemed to them quite unidiomatic. Bloom's Chinese version of the Bier story was written by a Chinese research assistant under Bloom's guidance as to content. It appeared to be possible that if the Bier story were revised so as to make it fully idiomatic, the 12 percent difference between the two stories in Chinese would be reduced. The story was revised, and everything was run once more with new samples from Hong Kong secondary schools. Human Broth in Chinese elicited 100 percent correct responses, and the revised fully idiomatic Bier story was only slightly below: 97 percent.

It seems likely that an unidiomatic translation had contributed to the seeming deficiency associated in Bloom's studies with the Chinese language. That cannot have been the only factor, however, because the overall rate of correct answers he obtained for this Chinese story was only 55 percent correct. There are many possibilities: Au's subjects wrote their answers at school with their teachers present and so may have tried harder than did Bloom's adults; Bloom did his studies between 1975 and 1977 whereas Au did hers in 1981, and the westernization of Hong Kong Chinese in that interval may have made counterfactual thought congenial. Au weighed the possibilities and found an ingenious way to provide evidence on the degree of westernization hypothesis.

The Hong Kong Chinese westernized to the 1975-77 level, when Bloom did his study, are gone forever; adult Chinese who do not know any English are superabundant on the mainland but hard to find in Hong Kong. What could be found in 1981, however, were Hong Kong young people whose knowledge of English did not yet extend to the subjunctive counterfactual, and one could see whether such young people—monolingual with respect to the construction of interest—had more problems with counterfactual reasoning than the secondary school children. This time subjects were 12–15 years old rather than 15–21. Their knowledge of the English subjunctive was tested at Time 1 by asking for a simple translation from Chinese to English: "Mrs. Wong does not know English. If Mrs. Wong knew English, she would be able to read English." With a very liberal definition of the subjunctive that accepted *could*, *would*, *would have*, and so on, only one student could be credited with knowledge of the subjunctive. At Time 2, one month later, the same students were given the Human Broth story in Chinese in a version developing just one counterfactual implication (not described here), which had also been given to secondary school students. The secondary school students (presumed to know the English subjunctive) gave 99 percent correct counterfactual answers; the younger students (ignorant of the subjunctive on the evidence of the translation test) gave 98 percent correct counterfactual responses. Evidently knowledge of the English counterfactual construction is not a necessary condition for correct counterfactual reasoning on story problems presented in Chinese.

The possibility that unidiomatic materials can introduce noise, which causes the performance of one set of subjects but not the other to be unrepresentative of real logical competence, inspired Au to a language and thought study originating on the Asian side of the Pacific. What if, she reasoned (showing no impairment of counterfactual thought), a Chinese psychologist had undertaken a Chinese–English contrast using the Bier story?

Version Three of the Bier story, in the fully idiomatic form, was translated into English by two Chinese bilinguals who had studied English for about twelve years. The translations were judged to be similar in content to the originals but less idiomatic. Those two story problems (others also, for which see Au, 1983) were administered to monolingual speakers of English, aged 15–18, in a public high school in the United States. To account for the unidiomatic English, subjects were told (truly) that some stories had been written by Hong Kong high school students.

The less idiomatic translation of the two used is quoted here just to show the kind of thing that can happen:*

> Bier was a German philosopher in the 18th century. To study about the theory of the Great Harmony and the laws of nature was his greatest interest. In those days, the communication between China and Europe had already developed to some extent. Chinese works could be found in Europe but the translations of them were still not available. If Bier had known about the technique to master the Chinese language, he would certainly discover the different attitudes between the Chinese philosophers and the European philosophers when describing the natural phenomena: the Chinese stressed the interrelationships among these aspects while the European ignored them and studied each aspect separately. Suppose Bier had learnt about Chinese philosophy, he would certainly develop his own theory, which included not only a thorough study about the nature of natural phenomena, but also a clear explanation of the relations among various natural aspects. Such theory not only patched up the disadvantages of the Western philosophy, but also influenced deeply and furthered the development of philosophy in Germany, France, and Holland toward science.
>
> From the above article, what new influence had Bier brought to the West? Please choose one or more of the following answers:
>
> 1. Awakened the consciousness of the Western philosophers about the nature of natural phenomena.
>
> 2. Awakened the consciousness of the Western philosophers about the interrelationships among the natural phenomena.
>
> 3. Pushed the European philosophy a step towards science.
>
> 4. Pushed the Western philosophy a step towards Chinese philosophy.
>
> 5. None of the above. (Please explain your opinion briefly.)

Notice that the counterfactual starts out in nearly perfect form with: "If Bier had known . . . he would certainly discover . . ." However, the verbs in the last two sentences have shed *would have*; it is Bier "included" and "patched up" and "influenced." It is not surprising then that some of the English-speaking subjects thought some of the implications were factual.

Back in Hong Kong, our imaginary Chinese psycholinguist receives the

---

*T. K. Au, Chinese and English counterfactuals, *Cognition, 15* (1983), pp. 186–87. By permission of North-Holland Publishing Co., Amsterdam.

result for the English language version of the Bier story, which is 60 percent correct for the two translations combined, and he compares this outcome with the result obtained in China with the original: 97 percent counterfactual answers. The conclusion is that the Chinese language facilitates thinking in the counterfactual mode whereas English makes it difficult.

The comparative research on counterfactual reasoning started in a spirit of linguistic relativity and with evidence to sustain it, but it has come in 1984 to a (not necessarily final) conclusion of cognitive universality. Counterfactual logical competence seems to be the same for speakers of English and speakers of Chinese once the noise of unidiomatic translation (and probably other situational factors) is removed. We may be sure, however, that Bloom will publish a response to Au, and so we remain open to new data and new arguments.

In summary, we are still without any convincing scientific evidence in 1984 that language structure affects human cognition, though there is quite a bit of evidence that cognition affects language. Some language changes in the interest of social reform are made easily (*black* for *Negro*) while others are difficult (a new generic pronoun to replace *he*). Whether easy or difficult, there is reason to question whether language change alone can alter thought and feeling.

Summary

While the many languages of the world today are superficially very different from one another, in certain deep semantic ways they are all alike. Characteristics common to all languages include the following:

1. All organize the plant and animal kingdoms into vertical hierarchies of three to six levels in terms of class inclusion.
2. The categories named in all languages are almost all fuzzy, ill-defined categories, rather than proper sets. The members of natural categories are held together by overlapping short-run attributes, which constitute a family resemblance structure. The family resemblance scores of category instances predict their ratings for prototypicality. In natural categories membership is not an all-or-none matter as it is in proper sets; instead, instances vary in prototypicality.
3. Among the vertical levels of plant and animal taxonomies (probably also artifacts) there is, in all languages, one level of special significance called the "generic level" in cognitive anthropology and the "basic object level" in psychology. The categories at the basic object level have maximal similarity among instances within the category and maximal distinctiveness between categories. There are numerous convergent operations, both linguistic and psychological, that serve to identify the basic object level in any taxonomy.
4. Categories at the basic object level or above do not usually have utilities

peculiar to a given culture, but categories below the basic object level usually do have such utilities (e.g. snows for Eskimos).

5. Basic object level names are the first names acquired by children and are probably the first terms coined in the history of any language. In the case of a sign language, the basic object level, because it provides the maximal number of distinctive attributes, offers the best raw material for iconic signs.

6. Complex societies with many differentiated roles, occupations, and interests have larger lexicons or vocabularies than simple societies, because they have more kinds of specialist vocabularies at levels below the basic object level.

Linguistic relativity is the view that perception and thought vary with the structural characteristics of the native language; it is the reverse of the view that human cognitive processes in conjunction with the properties of the physical world constrain all languages to be in some ways the same. Many social movements have taken for granted the principle of linguistic relativity and, indeed, the stronger principle of linguistic determinism, and so programs of social change have often included linguistic reforms. Nevertheless, hard evidence for the truth of linguistic relativity does not as yet exist. The most imaginative effort to provide such evidence has been Alfred Bloom's work on counterfactual conditional problems solved by English-speakers and by Chinese-speakers. He found Chinese-speakers less likely to answer correctly than English-speakers and attributed the cognitive difference to a difference in the facility with which the Chinese and English languages express counterfactual conditions. However, Terry Au, in attempting to replicate Bloom's work, found that the Chinese–American difference was probably due to the fact that the Chinese translation used by Bloom was not fully idiomatic. Au's data show no difference at all in competence for counterfactual reasoning when problems are presented in English and when they are presented in Chinese. As yet, then, there is no firm experimental support for the linguistic relativity hypothesis.

14

Nonverbal Communication and Speech Registers

A NONVERBAL COMMUNICATION is any communication that does not use words. Voice quality is nonverbal, and so are the personally expressive aspects of handwriting, but speech and written, printed, or telegraphed words are all verbal. The nonverbal channels (e.g. face, voice quality) are continually attended to and seem to communicate information that is primarily affective in quality and connected with personal relationships, but that is not the same as saying that the nonverbal channels are inherently better able than the verbal to communicate such information. The nonverbal channels do seem to be less controllable than the verbal, more likely to "leak" information about feelings.

Display rules are cultural prescriptions as to the feelings or emotions that it is proper to display on given occasions (e.g. marriages and funerals) and in given roles (experimenter, teacher). Distinguishing display rules from natural expressions has, we shall see, made it possible to answer the ancient question as to whether the expression of emotions in the face is entirely cultural or is universal. When subjects in experiments penetrate the experimenter's display that is intended to mask his expectancy as to how the experiment will turn out, and then proceed to give him what he is looking for, we have the phenomenon of "experimenter bias." Expectancies are "leaked" by nonverbal cues, which the experimenter cannot easily control. Teachers have expectancies with respect to their students, expectancies about how well or how poorly each is likely to do in schoolwork, and we shall see that those risk becoming self-fulfilling prophecies.

In discussing the origins of language (Chapter 12) and language and thought (Chapter 13), we have been concerned with language insofar as it is the same for the entire human species or for large natural communities, but there are also special "registers" within one language, which are specialized ways of talking to particular kinds of listeners. The first social register to be carefully studied was the baby talk register and then foreigner talk, sickroom talk, and sports announcer talk. It has become clear that someone who "controls" a language actually controls very many social registers and effortlessly shifts from one to another. We begin, however, with nonverbal communication.

Nonverbal Communication

Not all human communication is linguistic or verbal; the face, the body, and voice quality also carry messages. No one can doubt this, but it is surprising to me to find statements of the following kind: "In other words, the tonal component makes a disproportionately greater contribution to the interpretation of the total message than does the content component" (Mehrabian and Wiener, 1967). "It was found that when verbal cues and nonverbal cues of equivalent strength were combined, the nonverbal cues accounted for 12.3 times as much variance as verbal cues and produced 4.3 times as much shift on relevant rating scales" (Argyle, Alkema, and Gilmour, 1971). "In fact, the current study provides no indication that verbal transcripts of interactions provide any independent contribution to accurate interpretation" (Archer and Akert, 1977).

Statements of the kind quoted come out of experiments in which subjects have been asked to make inferences on the basis of messages presented as written transcripts (verbal only) or of messages spoken (verbal + vocal) or of messages in full-channel form on videotape. The inferences always have been limited to a narrow set having to do with the feelings, affect, or personal relationships of the authors of the messages. Those are, of course, the kinds of things that *can* be communicated nonverbally. Sensibly enough, no investigator has asked subjects to paraphrase the content of a lecture after exposure to vocal quality or facial expression alone, since cognitive content in general cannot be communicated nonverbally. Everyone knows that, but sometimes the enthusiastic researcher writes as if he were claiming a universal advantage for nonverbal communication. Pressed to it, no one could claim that.

The claim is, rather (Argyle et al., 1970; Argyle, Alkema, and Gilmour, 1971), that the nonverbal channels (facial expression, body posture and movement, vocal quality) are especially effective at communicating attitudes, feelings, and relationships, while the verbal channel (language) is normally used to communicate information about events external to the speaker. I think it is nonsense to suggest that the nonverbal channels are better adapted to the expression of affect and relationship than the verbal channels. Certainly, good actors can contribute something to the emotional impact of *Romeo and Juliet*, but it is generally supposed that Shakespeare's exclusively verbal contribution (the written transcript) is not negligible.

The idea that nonverbal channels can communicate attitudinal meanings better than can language arises out of a subtle misplacement of emphasis in experimental results. Argyle, Alkema, and Gilmour (1971), for example, worked with three verbal messages (Friendly, Neutral, Hostile) and three nonverbal styles of delivery (Friendly, Neutral, Hostile) and crossed content and style in all possible pairs to produce nine content-style combinations. When subjects were asked to rate the source of a message on a seven-point scale from Hostile to Friendly, they proved to give far greater weight to nonverbal style than to verbal content. Let me bring this experiment a little closer. We can ignore the Neutral messages and consider only the Friendly and Hostile extremes:

Verbal Friendly. "I enjoy meeting the subjects who take part in these experiments and find I usually get on well with them. I hope you will be able to stay on afterwards to have a chat about the experiment. In fact, the people who have come as subjects in the past always seemed to be very pleasant" (p. 388).

Verbal Hostile. "I don't much enjoy meeting the subjects who take part in these experiments. I often find them rather boring and difficult to deal with. Please don't hang around too long afterwards and talk about the experiment. Some people who come as subjects are really rather disagreeable" (p. 386).

Nonverbal Friendly Style. Warm, soft tone of voice, open smile, relaxed posture.

Nonverbal Hostile Style. Harsh voice, frown with teeth showing, tense posture.

The verbal passages were individually rated in advance of the experiment on a Hostile (1)–Friendly (7) scale, and the printed Friendly passage was rated at 5.95; the Hostile passage at 2.25. In order to rate the styles, free of content, the communicator (an attractive female student) read numbers in the styles indicated (Friendly or Hostile) while being videotaped, and the tapings were rated: Friendly at 6.10 and Hostile at 1.75. From these materials, four content + style messages were created: Verbal Friendly + Nonverbal Friendly; Verbal Friendly + Nonverbal Hostile; Verbal Hostile + Nonverbal Hostile; Verbal Hostile + Nonverbal Friendly. In two of the four combinations, message and style are congruent, and in two they are incongruent. Table 14–1 presents the individual advance ratings and the ratings of the four combinations.

There are two very different outcomes in Table 14–1. The congruent pairs (*a* and *d*) yield ratings that fall between the ratings of the constituent message and style, are not much different from either, and across all the data are not consistently closer to the ratings for one channel than to the ratings for the other channel. There is no sign of nonverbal (or verbal) prepotency in the con-

TABLE 14-1. Individual Ratings of Verbal Messages and Nonverbal Styles and Ratings of the Four Combinations

	Verbal	
	Friendly (5.95)	Hostile (2.25)
Nonverbal Friendly (6.10)	6.03 *a*	5.17 *b*
Nonverbal Hostile (1.75)	1.60 *c*	1.80 *d*

Congruent messages: *a* and *d*.
Incongruent messages: *b* and *c*.
SOURCE: Based on Argyle, Alkema, and Gilmour (1971), Table 2.

gruent ratings. The action is all in the incongruent ratings (*b* and *c*), and it is the nonverbal style that exerts the greater effect. If you imagine the Verbal Friendly message quoted above delivered with a "harsh voice, frown with teeth showing, tense posture," it probably comes across as blatant hypocrisy or sarcasm. The Verbal Hostile message delivered with "warm, soft tone of voice, open smile, relaxed posture" would seem to elicit a reaction like "She's just kidding; she doesn't mean it."

It is perfectly correct to summarize results like those of Table 14-1, as Argyle and associates do, by saying that the nonverbal component exerted a much greater influence on the attitude ratings than did the verbal component. That is what happened in the experiment as designed. The experiment as designed is not, however, able to show that the verbal channel *in general* is less suited to the communication of affect than are nonverbal channels. It depends, as we shall see, on what you put in the channels. What the experiment does demonstrate is that when verbal and nonverbal components of a message both primarily communicate affect (or feeling) and contradict one another, without the contradiction being verbally acknowledged, the nonverbal channel will be prepotent. It will be prepotent in this kind of case because we believe that the nonverbal is less controllable than the verbal, less available for dissimulation or masquerade, and so we trust it more. That generalization is not at all the same as saying that nonverbal channels are better always at communicating affect than are verbal channels, nor does it say that nonverbal affect will always prevail over verbal when the two contradict one another in the same message. We shall shortly have examples to the contrary.

It is clear that many who have read the results of Argyle and colleagues (1970, 1971), of Mehrabian and Wiener (1967), and of Mehrabian (1972) have understood results like those of Table 14-1 as estimates of the relative contribution of verbal and nonverbal levels to the communication of "social meanings" generally. One finds, for example, Mehrabian (1972) cited as having shown that only 7 percent of the total impact of an emotion is attributable to the verbal channel—though Mehrabian himself never made such unqualified statements. Archer and Akert (1977) criticize the earlier work of Mehrabian and of Argyle for using highly unnatural situations and intentionally posed or enacted expressive styles and for relying largely on incongruent message–style combinations. Archer and Akert invented a wonderfully natural task with congruent information on verbal and nonverbal channels. However, those investigators seem still to believe that it makes sense to search for a generalization about the relative importance of the two kinds of channel and seem to believe that their own research demonstrates the greater importance of the nonverbal. It is instructive to put one part of that procedure under the magnifying glass.

The Social Interpretations Task (SIT) is a videotape that presents twenty very brief natural interactions about which subjects are to answer multiple choice questions. The sequences were extracted from long videotapes (five to fifteen minutes) of naturally occurring scenes. For instance, two women are seen playing with a baby, and the viewer is asked to say which woman is the baby's mother. Another scene shows two men talking about a basketball game, and viewers are asked to say which man was on the winning team. The full-channel spontaneous interactions are compared with purely verbal transcripts.

The method has many excellent qualities. Answers to the questions are objective. The verbal transcript and the tape are congruent in that the same correct answer is entailed. There is a no-information chance level of success defined by the number of persons interacting (two or three), and one can determine how much better than chance, performance is, with just the verbal transcript and how much better performance is with the videotape than with the transcript alone.

The results seem clear-cut: With the transcript only, answers were actually below the chance level, whereas with videotapes they were, for almost all sequences, significantly above chance. It looks as if the information on personal relationships and feelings is in the nonverbal channels conveyed on videotape and absent from the purely verbal channel, and as if the authors are justified in concluding: "In fact, the current study provides no indication that verbal transcripts of interactions provide any independent contribution to accurate interpretation" (p. 449).

The real question is whether the conclusions of Archer and Akert as well as those of Mehrabian and of Argyle are legitimate conclusions about what *can* be accomplished by linguistic and nonverbal means or what happened to be accomplished in particular circumstances. Archer and Akert, describing the rules they followed in extracting their short sequences from longer videotapes, write that "since we did not want a simple test of audition, we avoided explicit mentions of the correct answer (e.g. 'I won the game because . . .')" (p. 446). You might like to read the previous sentence again. Why would it be a simple test of *audition* to include explicit mentions of the correct answer? It would not be a test of audition only, but, rather, a fair test of the powers of the linguistic channel. It would be a perfectly legitimate use of language if one of the two women playing with the baby were to say: "This here is my baby." By excluding such expressions, they deprived the linguistic channel of its usual power. Of course, if they had permitted such expressions, the videotape full-channel messages would have enjoyed no advantage whatsoever over the verbal transcripts.

I believe that the correct answer to the question about the relative powers of the verbal and nonverbal channels is that language is a universal medium that can express anything that can be thought or felt, whereas the nonverbal channels are specialized to a restricted class of meanings. In the experiment described above of Argyle, Alkema, and Gilmour, the meanings of the incongruent combinations, if we were clear what they were, could be fully expressed verbally. The Friendly passage with the Hostile style might be captured by first speaking the lines about enjoying meeting experimental subjects and then appending: "This is what they tell me I have to say, but, in fact, I detest the chumps who volunteer for these experiments." The Hostile passage with the Friendly style could be rendered by adding: "Of course, I'm kidding when I say this; in fact, I'd love to talk with you afterwards." It could all be in print, as it is here, and the message would get across without benefit of nonverbals.

Robert Krauss and his associates (Krauss et al., 1981) did several experiments to make the point that the verbal channel may be, in the right circumstances, more expressive of attitudes than the nonverbal channels. They drew their stimulus materials from the telecast of the 1976 debate between Senator Walter Mondale and Senator Robert Dole, who were, respectively, in that year, the Democratic and Republican candidates for the office of vice-president. They chose that debate rather than any of the debates between presidential candidates because it was unusually spirited and, in fact, referred to in *The New York Times* as a "slugfest."

Subjects rated the emotional quality of debate segments on such bipolar scales as: "nice . . . awful"; "good . . . bad"; and so on. Some rated from the transcript only (verbal); some from the video without the sound track (visual); some from the sound track only with content filtering to make the speech unintelligible (audio); and some from the full-channel audiovisual. Since the audiovisual presentation contains everything usable, one can take the ratings based on that version as a kind of criterion and score the ratings based on the three single channels (verbal or visual or audio) for their degree of agreement with the criterion. Ratings on the verbal transcript alone correlated a high .77 with ratings on the full presentation, whereas ratings on the visual correlated only .15 and ratings on unintelligible audio correlated only .32. In that situation the emotional meanings were carried primarily by the verbal channel.

If it is true that language *can* express attitudes, feelings, and relationships just as well as the nonverbal channels can, where does the idea come from that there is some special affinity between feeling and the nonverbal? I do think language has the potential to express all shades of feeling, and I do not think you have to be a Shakespeare to exploit that potential; read any good irate letter to the editor and you will see how easy it is. Still, the nonverbal channels do have a kind of "special relationship" with feeling for two reasons. In the first place, speakers sometimes seek to deceive. When they do, the nonverbal channels (avoidance of eye contact, not smiling, postural shifts, high vocal pitch) combine with speech (slow rate, longer pauses, slips of the tongue) to signal a deception attempt. Where a deception attempt is identified, the affect-attitudinal content of the most controllable channel, the verbal, is discounted and the less controllable or "leakier" nonverbal channels (Blanck and Rosenthal, 1982; DePaulo and Rosenthal, 1979; DePaulo et al., 1978; DePaulo, Zuckerman, and Rosenthal, 1980; Zuckerman, DePaulo, and Rosenthal, 1981) are looked to for the true answers.

Deception attempts alone do not fully account for the continuous attention given to the face, hands, body posture, and vocal quality of a communicator. The nonverbal channels often contain information that is incongruent with the verbal when there is no conscious attempt at deception and no conscious interest on the receiver's part in playing the detective or eavesdropper. That is because there are culturally defined "display rules" (Ekman and Friesen, 1969) which successfully govern the relatively controllable verbal and facial channels but do not so successfully govern hands, legs, body, and vocal quality. For full understanding of a message, a receiver needs to attend both to the display and to the involuntary nonverbal commentary. A nurse is required by his role to smile and speak optimistically even to patients whose prognoses he knows to be bad; the patients will usually be interested also in signs of what he really thinks. In a psychological experiment, the experimenter is not supposed to reveal to subjects what result she expects and/or hopes for, but subjects are interested in knowing. Everyone is expected to speak sadly and look somber at funerals; everybody is expected to speak affectionately to and look fondly at both nurslings and old people in nursing homes, but not everybody can feel like it all the time. Some display rules apply to everyone ("Don't blow your own horn"), and some to particular roles (nurse, patient, parent, teacher, priest). Communication attempts are almost always affected by display rules, but those rules leave the less controllable channels free to modulate the meaning of the intended message.

The affective modulations of meaning that arise from uncontrollable facial expression, body postures, and vocal qualities are not necessarily secondary to cognitive appraisal, let alone conscious formulation. Robert Zajonc (1980, 1984) has put together a substantial amount of data suggesting that affect, liking and not liking, is sometimes primary, can sometimes occur in the absence of any interpretation or recognition. In the clearest case preferences were established by repeated exposure to stimuli (e.g. tones, polygons) degraded to prevent recognition (Kunst-Wilson and Zajonc, 1980). Richard Lazarus (1984), in particular, has argued that affect or feeling is always secondary to cognition, secondary, that is, to the processing of stimuli for recognition and meaning. The issue was unresolved as of 1984, but we need not wait upon its resolution to understand that a voluntary display of feeling can be modified or contradicted by stimuli from uncontrolled sources. Those stimuli might enter into the interpretation of the complete communication as primary positive or negative affects or might enter into it only after substantial cognition processing as, for instance, a well-meant or a treacherous attempt at deception.

Deception

An attempt at deception occurs when someone deliberately expresses what he knows to be false. Prototypical life cases include a crime suspect under interrogation; a job applicant trying, in an interview, to conceal something in his past record; labor–management negotiations and negotiations between representatives of unfriendly nations: "faking out" in basketball and "bluffing" in poker; and so on. In genuine deception attempts, the possibility of deception tends to be salient for both parties; interests are opposed and the stakes are high (Ekman and Friesen, 1969). Most students of nonverbal communication, including Paul Ekman, Wallace Friesen, Phoebe Ellsworth, Robert Rosenthal, Judith Hall, Miron Zuckerman, Bella DePaulo, and their various associates find it useful to postulate a controllability-leakage hierarchy in connection with deception. That hierarchy is best explained in connection with the most widely used standardized test of sensitivity to nonverbal cues, the PONS, or "Profile of Nonverbal Sensitivity" (Rosenthal, Hall, Archer et al., 1979; Rosenthal, Hall, DiMatteo et al., 1979).

THE PONS

The creation of the PONS starts really with Judith Hall, at age twenty-four, acting out twenty different scenes: talking to a lost child, trying to seduce someone, saying a prayer, admiring nature, and so on. Those videotaped scenes were chopped up and otherwise operated upon to produce 220 segments, each two seconds long and comprising one or more "channels" from Dr. Hall's various enactments. Since this is a test of *nonverbal* sensitivity, no sequence includes the words spoken, in an intelligible form. The single channels are defined as: face, body, randomized spliced voice (preserves only pitch and intensity), content filtered voice (preserves sequence and rhythm). Those four single channels for each of the twenty scenarios occur in isolation and in all possible pairs and triads to make up the 220 segments. The segments appear in random order on a forty-five-minute tape, and if you watch and listen to it your experience is of a very rapid succession of faces, bodies, muffled talk, and unreal squawks.

For each segment you have to make a choice between two alternative affects that might be expressed in the segment: dominant or submissive, positive or negative. The original twenty scenes enacted were classified as: Positive-Dominant (e.g. expressing motherly love); Positive-Submissive (helping a customer); Negative-Dominant (e.g. nagging a child); and Negative-Submissive (asking forgiveness). The classification provides the right answer for each segment, and individual accuracy rates may be compared with a "pure guess" level of 50 percent since there are always just two alternatives. It all goes very fast. There is no time to deliberate, and for most segments you feel that your answer is a pure guess.

The PONS has been taken by some three thousand-odd persons from twenty nations. Performance is not highly correlated with intellectual ability. High scorers tend to be better adjusted, more interpersonally democratic and encouraging, more extroverted, more popular, and more interpersonally sensitive as judged by acquaintances, clients, spouses, and supervisors. Of the various special groups that have been tested with the PONS, the best scores have been attained by actors, students of nonverbal communication, and students of the visual arts. It is a reliable and valid instrument (Rosenthal and Benowitz, 1985).

The two firm results with the PONS that seem to me to have the greatest theoretical importance concern women and brain localization. Females have proved superior to males on the PONS in 133 samples comprising 2,615 subjects (Hall, 1980, 1984; Rosenthal and Benowitz, 1985). One might think this a manifestation of the general edge that women have over men in linguistic skills (Maccoby and Jacklin, 1974), were it not for another finding. Language, spoken or signed, is (for right-handed persons) lateralized in the left hemisphere, but the nonverbal skills tested in the PONS have turned out to be lateralized in the right cerebral hemisphere. That is most clearly true of the "reading" of the face channel, which is quite precisely localizable, but it is generally true of success in reading nonverbal cues (Benowitz et al., 1983). Signed languages (e.g. ASL) operate with the visual modality, as do most nonverbal cues, but the languages are lateralized in the left hemisphere, just as spoken language is, rather than with other visual functions. That discovery suggests, as one would in any case suspect, that nonverbal cues, though they communicate, are not a language.

The finding of female superiority is consistent with the conception of female temperament as high on interpersonal sensitivity (see Chapter 9), and the brain localization discovery suggests the possibility of a biological substrate for the difference. There is considerable evidence (McGlone, 1980) that male and female brains do differ both anatomically and functionally, but the evidence points to a difference in *degree* of lateralization or asymmetry (male brains more asymmetrical), not to a difference in degree of development of particular areas and functions. Since women's superiority on the PONS lies primarily in the identification of negative affect, the possibility comes to mind that women as a disadvantaged group have learned to identify unfavorable sentiments that are not verbally expressed.

Studies using the PONS have found that the individual channels contribute to accuracy of judgment in this order, from most controllable to least: face, body, voice quality (combination of the two vocal channels). There is no deception in the PONS; all of Dr. Hall's "channels" worked congruently to express a certain feeling. We know then that the order—face, body, vocal quality—represents an order of accurate informativeness when channels are congruent. Verbalization is not included in the PONS, but it is included in a later (Blanck and Rosenthal, 1982) similar test, the MOVANS, or Measure of Verbal and Nonverbal Sensitivity, which retains the verbal transcripts of the original twenty enactments. The verbal channel turns out to head the hierarchy as the most informative channel.

Many kinds of evidence (Blanck and Rosenthal, 1982; DePaulo et al., 1978; DePaulo and Rosenthal, 1979; Ekman, Friesen, and Scherer, 1976; Krauss, Geller, and Olson, 1976; Rosenthal and DePaulo, 1979a, 1979b; Scherer, et al., in press; Zuckerman et al., 1979; Zuckerman, DePaulo, and Rosenthal, 1981) converge on the conclusion that leakage reverses the controllability hierarchy, ranging from high to low: vocal quality, body, face, verbal.

The best operation for assessing leakage is as follows: Determine the ratings for some affect (e.g. positive versus negative) of each of two channels in isolation (e.g. face and vocal quality) and then put the channels together in highly discrepant pairs (e.g. face as very positive and vocal quality as very negative). The rating for the combined channels will be closer to the rating for one or the other channel in isolation. The individual channel that seems to carry greater weight in the combination (e.g. voice if face + voice is negative) may be said to have "primacy," to be the more trusted channel in the communication. The presumption is that the channel that dominates the combination does so because it is known to be less controllable, or leakier, and so less manageable by a would-be deceiver.

THE CONTROLLABILITY–LEAKAGE HIERARCHY

Ekman and Friesen (1969), who introduced the idea of a controllability-leakage hierarchy, tried to define the terms conceptually and not just by operations. The word *controllability* itself gives away the underlying conception; it is meant to be a hierarchy of decreasing voluntary control, decreasing ability to express what one intends to express, and nothing else. The problem with that underlying conception is that it is very difficult to identify intentions and pin down the voluntary in psychology. Volition, of all the classical functions of the mind, is the one that makes the most trouble for a science of psychology, and that is because science is deterministic and so has no place for will, which must be free. What Ekman and Friesen proposed, however, by way of definition of controllability, is very valuable.

A more controllable channel, they suggest, is (1) a channel that has the capacity to transmit a large number of distinct meaningful messages; (2) a channel that is perceptually salient; (3) a channel that elicits external feedback, especially comment; and (4) a channel that delivers clear internal feedback to the sender. Contrast the face and the legs. Ekman and Friesen (1982) have developed a Facial Action Coding System (FACS), which makes possible the coding of all the discriminable muscle action units and, with much practice, voluntary control over them all. The number of discriminable combinations of action units the face can send is large, between four thousand and five thousand (though small by comparison with language, which has the possibility of sending infinitely many different messages). The face is salient; it elicits external feedback—people comment on expressions—and its many movements and positions can be felt. The legs can do little more than jiggle nervously; they are not salient but, rather, usually under the table and clothed; they rarely elicit comment, and the distribution of the nerves is such that internal feedback is only very coarse-grained.

Controllability entails accountability. One can be held maximally responsible for one's words but also accountable for facial expression. Meanings picked up from hands, legs, body, vocal quality are much more *deniable*. Since they were not intended, were not voluntarily controlled, one can hardly be held accountable, and, indeed, the existence of meaning itself can be denied.

Figure 14-1 represents the controllability-leakage hierarchy with voice quality functioning, as Scherer and associates (in press) have shown, as a cover term for many physically distinct nonverbal aspects of speech. While the research literature suggests that many qualifications may be necessary, the controllability–leakage hierarchy is thought generally to operate in the follow-

Most Controllable (voluntary, intentional, high accountability, with many discriminable messages, high perceptual salience, much external feedback, and much internal feedback. Thought to be highly informative in congruent combinations)

Verbal—Linguistic

Facial Expression

Body—Hands—Legs—Feet

Vocal Quality

Maximally leaky (involuntary, unintentional, low accountability, with few discriminable messages, low perceptual salience, little external feedback, and little internal feedback. Thought to be true and trustworthy in deception attempts because not manageable)

Figure 14-1. The controllability-leakage hierarchy

ing way. Reading Figure 14-1 from top to bottom, channels appear in the order of their accurate informativeness in full congruent messages, as revealed by the PONS. Reading from bottom to top, channels appear in the order of trust placed in their content, an order of primacy in combinations under circumstances of suspected deception. In short, the order of reliance on different channels in deception reverses that in circumstances of congruent communication.

Deception may be signaled in either of two ways: (1) extreme discrepancy in the messages carried by different channels, or (2) a set of cues specific to the effort to deceive (DePaulo and Rosenthal, 1979; Zuckerman, DePaulo, and Rosenthal, 1981). Cues perceived to be or thought to be signs of an effort to deceive include avoidance of eye contact, little smiling, postural shifts, long latency of response, slow speech, high vocal pitch, and speech slips. In substantial degree it turns out (Zuckerman, DePaulo, and Rosenthal, 1981) that the real signs of deception are the same as the perceived signs. As you can see, the signs of deception may appear in any channel. In addition, large discrepancies of content between channels also serve as signs of deception. When a deception effort is detected, the leakier channels (passing over certain qualifications) are likely to be the more trusted channels.

How accurate are human detectives at detecting acts of deception? Better than chance generally, but in terms of absolute success not very good (Zuckerman, DePaulo, and Rosenthal, 1981). Generally speaking, the more channels available, the better the chance of picking up signs of deception. Somewhat surprisingly, the verbal channel, though relatively controllable, contributes substantially to the signs of deception. Just what those signs are has not been determined. One that I have noticed is "semantic seepage." Suppose a person who is feeling depressed is giving a learned lecture that leaves room for a certain number of spontaneous examples. The selection of examples will quite usually be affected by the mood; the stream of talk insofar as it has not been planned is likely to show the dark stain of the speaker's feeling.

THE POLYGRAPH AS LIE DETECTOR

There is a mechanism, the polygraph, that is supposed to be better than the unaided human at detecting deception. Its prototypical use is in the interrogation of persons suspected of crimes, though the conclusions of a polygraphist (a trained reader of polygraph records) are not often admitted as evidence in criminal trials. Many polygraphists find their principal employment in industry either screening job applicants for honesty or, in businesses plagued with pilferage, periodically screening all employees. Additional uses are easily imagined: Congressional committees that review presidential nominations could certainly benefit from valid polygraphy, and the addition of a polygraphist to debates between candidates for the presidency would enliven that rather stale form of show business.

The polygraph does not record data from the leaky channels of face, body, and vocal quality. Those data are accessible to the unaided senses of the polygraphist, who is widely supposed to be especially skilled at reading them, a kind of expert on veracity. What the polygraph provides is a continuous record of certain physiological data thought to be relevant to deception: the galvanic skin response (GSR), cardiovascular data, and respiration measured at the chest and at the abdomen.

The theory of the polygraph is extremely simple. The suspect must answer "yes" or "no" to a series of questions (twelve or so) of which some are intended to be control questions and some guilt-relevant questions. A control question might be: "Have you ever stolen anything from a hotel or store?" A guilt-relevant question might be: "Did you steal Mrs. Smith's diamond ring last Friday?"

The control question is intended to reveal that level of nonverbal activation which, for this person, goes with lying about something of which almost everyone is guilty, or, if he does not lie, simply being asked about a generally "touchy" matter. If he is truly innocent of the theft of Mrs. Smith's diamond ring, he should be able to say "no" to the guilt-relevant question with no more, and perhaps less, physiological perturbation than he manifests in answering the control question. If he is truly guilty and says "no" to the guilt-relevant question, his nonverbal indices should "jump" and give him away to the polygraphist. Since acceptable answers are limited to "yes" or "no," in the polygraphist's case the detection of deception is coincident with learning the right answer (the one not given). In everyday detection of deception from nonverbal channels those two pieces of information are usually separate.

The theory of the polygraph, as stated, seems full of holes. Any accused person, whether innocent or guilty, will know the crime of which he is accused and so should overreact to relevant questions. That is a serious problem, but an attempt is made to minimize it, in a prepolygraph interview, by talking about the crime so that the innocent will get over being startled by mention of it. Well, but does not that mean that the guilty suspect, by rehearsing questions to himself, could become so habituated as to make no telltale response when hooked up to the polygraph (Lykken, 1979)? Possibly, but apparently not easily (Raskin and Podlesny, 1979).

Not only the guilt-relevant question but also the control question involves problems. Perhaps the general question about whether one has ever stolen anything will be understood by the guilty suspect as a direct question about the diamond ring, and so his baseline disturbance would not differ from that of his guilt-relevant disturbance. It is once again the prepolygraph interview that is critical. Questions are asked about the suspect's life history and values in an effort to obtain a data base from which to construct control questions that will tap general sensitivities but not specific guilty knowledge. Unfortunately, the pretest interview is largely an art, not a science, since every crime and suspect is unique.

In general the theory seems to be about equally likely to work and not to work, and so we look to empirical validation studies for a pragmatic answer. The majority of these studies involve mock crimes and college student subjects, and it can reasonably be argued, as Lykken (1979) has argued, that they are simply irrelevant because the level of concern in the suspects cannot be high enough. It is possible, however, to test the value of the polygraph in real cases. For instance, suspects who were given polygraph tests may subsequently confess and so be known to be guilty or may be cleared by another's confession. Horvath (1977) had ten experienced polygraphists independently score the charts of twenty-eight suspects who turned out definitely to be guilty and twenty-eight who turned out definitely to be innocent. Of the 560 blind scorings, with 50 percent being the chance level of success, only 64 percent were correctly judged. Experts like Lykken (1979) and Raskin and Podlesny (1979) disagree as to whether that result and others less directly testing the value of the polygraph are good enough to justify admission of the results of a polygraph test as evidence. Lykken says definitely not, but Raskin and Podlesny, who believe that many other studies yielding better accuracy must be considered, say definitely that the polygraph test should be admitted as evidence in law, although for ethical reasons they oppose its use in industry.

One thing everyone agrees about is that a polygraph test is more likely to make the innocent seem guilty (because of overreaction to the guilt-relevant questions) than to make the guilty look innocent. In the Horvath study, for instance, only 23 percent of the guilty were mistakenly identified as truthful, whereas 49 percent of the innocent were mistakenly called deceptive, and that disproportion is representative. If the results of a polygraph test are to be admitted as evidence, this bias in the instrument must be explained to the jurors.

Experiments on the validity of the polygraph are difficult to evaluate, in part because the polygraphist has been free to base his judgment on everything he knows about the evidence and has observed in the demeanor of the suspect (all the leaky nonverbals) and not on the polygraph record alone. It is essential that basic research on the polygraph remove the polygraphist from the procedure, and that can be done only by relying on one or another form of objective, not globally impressionistic, scoring. Polygraphists are sure to vary in skill, just as clinical psychologists and psychiatrists vary in clinical skill, and so an accumulation of evidence on the instrument that lets the individual polygraphist be a functioning part of the instrument cannot have any bearing on the probable value as evidence of a new reading in a new case with a new polygraphist. There are in existence several methods of objective scoring and some evidence that such scoring is as good as or better than subjective impressions (Ginton et al., 1982; Szucko and Kleinmuntz, 1981). Of course, polygraphists have considerable vested interest in maintaining the mystique of their role as "veracity experts" and so are likely to resist objective scoring.

Several states ban the use of the polygraph in private industry. Most courts do not allow the introduction of polygraph evidence unless prosecution, defense, and judge all agree to it, and that rarely happens. I think it should stay that way until, if ever, there is a substantial literature showing that objectively scored polygraph records do a much-better-than-chance job of distinguishing truth from falsehood in real, not mock, circumstances. I favor the admission of expert testimony on eyewitness identification, because jurors generally have a lot to learn from psychological research on that subject, but I do not favor admission of expert testimony on polygraph records, as of now, because I think the lesson from research is that such records ought to inspire little confidence. But that might not be the message the expert would deliver.

Display Rules

The term "display rules" was coined by Ekman and Friesen (1969) specifically in connection with the facial expression of emotion. Display rules are cultural norms regarding the proper management of the facial expression of emotion. I shall broaden the term to include the management of other controllable channels, most notably the verbal, and also to include not only completely general cultural norms but also the status-specific norms called "roles" (nurse, patient, teacher, undertaker, and so on). First, however, let us have the Ekman and Friesen sense. The distinction they made between facial display rules and unmanaged emotional expressions enabled psychology to answer the ancient question, Are there universal facial expressions of emotions?

Ekman and Friesen thought that display rules served three general ends: intensification in expression of felt emotion, de-intensification, and masking. We see an intensification display in our culture when a deplorable gift gives rise to beaming smiles and squeals of pleasure. We see a de-intensification display whenever a grief-stricken person puts on a "brave front" that is still clearly sorrowful. We see masking when a strong man, feeling fearful, acts boldly. The rules are cultural and so variable and learned. The striking cultural variability in emotion displays led many (e.g. the anthropologist W. LaBarre, 1947) to argue that there were no universally human emotional expressions. Charles Darwin, however, had argued that there were universal facial expressions in man and gave a plausible account of how they might have evolved (Darwin, 1872).

THE UNIVERSALITY HYPOTHESIS

Many psychologists in this century have sought to determine how much agreement there is among judges on the identification of emotions expressed in the face. Almost all studies used posed still photographs, usually of actors, and so the faces they collected must have mixed, in unknown ways, display rules and natural expressions. That literature has been summarized by Ekman, Friesen, and Ellsworth (1982c), and while it cannot answer the universality question, it does reveal an interesting convergence. In spite of variations in the emotion terms used and in the stimulus faces, some six emotions seemed to be reliably (not necessarily accurately) identified: happiness (joy), surprise (startle), fear (suffering), anger, disgust (contempt), and sadness (grief).

There have been quite a few studies of the spontaneous expression of emotions by ordinary people, not actors, and with some criterion as to the actual emotion felt. The criterion has been sometimes a stimulus judged adequate to create an emotion (a disgusting or horrifying film) and sometimes the verbal report of the person having the emotion. Ekman, Friesen, and Ellsworth (1982a) have also reviewed that literature and found that spontaneous expressions can be accurately judged and that *accuracy* is best for the same six emotions as *reliably* identified in posed photographs.

The studies so far reviewed do not directly address the question of universality in emotional expression, but there are many studies that do. The experimental design easiest to carry out is one using some standard set of posed emotions and showing them to subjects in various easily accessible cultures like the United States, Greece, Mexico, Germany, France, and Britain. The emotion expressed by each face is named in the native language. Of course, responses have to be translated, and back-translation (English to Greek; Greek back to English) is a desirable check on ambiguity. Such studies have been done, and the results are consistent: high pancultural agreement on the six emotions already familiar: happiness, fear, anger, sadness, disgust, and surprise. As an answer to the universality question, however, all of those studies fall short of proof for the same reason. The cultures studied are in close visual contact (travel, film, books, television), and so persons in all the cultures could have learned the same set of conventional display rules for the facial expression of emotions, none of which need be natural or universal. Some other kind of evidence is needed.

A critical study of Darwin's universality hypothesis ought to have all of the following properties. The emotions studied should be limited to the short list that is reported everywhere: happiness, fear, anger, sadness, disgust, and surprise. The expressions of the emotions should be not governed by display rules but natural. The subjects should be drawn from cultures lacking all visual contact. Ekman and Friesen and their associates managed to realize such a design and even to improve upon it (Ekman, 1973, 1982).

The most difficult part of the procedure was locating subjects out of visual contact with the Western world. Ekman and his associates found them among the Fore of New Guinea. They picked men and women who had seen no movies or magazines, understood no English or Pidgin, and who had lived in no Western settlement and worked for no Caucasian. Pictures that were not conventionalized by display rules were selected in accordance with a theory of the natural association between certain muscle units and the six basic emotions (Tomkins, 1982, 1984). The method of posing the task was particularly good. Subjects were shown the pictures in sets of three and asked not simply to pick the face expressing a particular emotion (named in Fore) but given the emotion word in a context that would universally fix its sense. For example, with the leftmost face of Figure 14–2: "how he would look if his child died and he felt sad." For this problem, 79 percent of 189 subjects in New Guinea selected the correct face (A).

Subjects in New Guinea, the majority of the time, selected the same faces for each word-in-story-context as subjects had done in the United States. The investigators then asked persons among the Fore to express emotions like "the way you look when your friend has come and you are *happy*" or "your child has died and you are sad" (see Figure 14–3). Videotapes of those faces were shown to college students in the United States and correctly identified most of the time. Members of two cultures that had no visual contact successfully identified one another's emotional expressions, so the universality hypothesis seems to be true for the fundamental six: happiness, fear, anger, sadness, disgust, and surprise.

One last experiment beautifully separates display rules from natural expressions; it was done by Ekman and his associates in collaboration with Richard Lazarus and his associates (Ekman, 1982). The comparison was made between American subjects and Japanese subjects (both groups in their home countries), because Japanese and American display rules are different for some situations. However, display rules do not apply when people are in the dark and believe themselves to be unobserved. Both groups were shown two films, a neutral film and a shocking film that induced stress. It was demonstrated that the films had unlike effects on such physiological indices of emotion as are recorded by the polygraph, and, indeed, subjects thought those physiological records, taken in the dark, were the point of the procedure. What they did not know was that their facial expressions were being videotaped. The faces were scored using

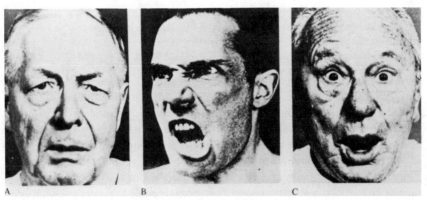

Figure 14–2. Three faces shown to subjects in New Guinea

"A" represents "his child died and he feels sad." (P. Ekman [ed.], *Emotion in the Human Face*, 2d ed., 1982, p. 135. By permission of Cambridge University Press. Photo by Ed. Gallob)

Figure 14-3. Faces from New Guinea shown to U.S. college students

The instructions for the top left photograph were "your friend has come and you are happy"; for the top right "your child has died"; for the bottom left "you are angry and about to fight"; and for the bottom right "you see a dead pig that has been lying there for a long time." (P. Ekman [ed.], *Darwin and Facial Expression*, 1973, p. 213. By permission of Academic Press)

Ekman's Facial Affect Scoring Technique (Ekman and Friesen, 1982). The two films produced very different sets of expressions in both groups, and the Japanese expressions were, muscle-group by muscle-group, close matches for the American expressions. Surprise, disgust, and sadness were registered by both groups in response to the stress film. But then the private experience ended, and an interviewer came in to talk with each group about their feelings. The Americans showed their stress when talking about the stress film, whereas the Japanese, talking about the same film, politely smiled. You know what kind of smile a display smile is; it is the kind that leaves your face aching after a mirthless dinner party dominated by an indefatigable raconteur.

BEYOND FACIAL DISPLAY

For the Japanese smiling when he feels some distress and the American dinner guest smiling when he is bored, there is some discrepancy of affect. Probably an acute observer of leaky nonverbal channels would have picked up the
discrepancy from the hands twisting under the table or the legs crossing and
uncrossing in too rapid succession. Yet one hesitates to classify these cases with
deception such as a criminal suspect may practice. Deception proper is salient
for both sender and receiver; the former is consciously monitoring his communications, and the latter is consciously playing the detective. With display
rules the whole thing is more automatized and less salient. There is no sharp
opposition of interests, and the stakes, in any case, are low. The defining
distinction between deception and display is, I suspect, that in the former case
there is not just channel discrepancy but also one or more of the telltale signs of
an effort at deception, whereas in the latter case such signs are absent. Display
does not feel like deception. It feels like politeness.

Display rules affect facial expression because it is a controllable channel,
and they affect verbal behavior because it is still more controllable. The display
rules that govern the talk of upper-class New Englanders are obvious to me,
because I never learned to use them. One such rule is to de-intensify the
speaker's own troubles. An elderly gentleman, very dear to me, suffered a
stroke late in his life and then a year later had to have an operation without
anesthetic (because of the neurological damage caused by the stroke). I thought
it must have been an excruciatingly painful experience and said so. But this
Boston Brahmin replied: "It—was—(searching for just the right word)—
vexing." I never learned how to de-intensify, growing up in Detroit, Michigan,
and am inclined, if I have so much as a common cold, to ask, "Why me?" The
Brahmin code also calls for intensification of the pleasure felt at the prospect of
your company. However boring one may be, acceptance of an invitation elicits:
"How super!" It's a nice set of manners, really.

I know there are verbal display rules for everyone and not just Boston
aristocrats, because I have sometimes asked for one. For years I did not know
what to say when a mother showed me her new baby. "Well done" would come
to mind, or "How very small," but I knew those were wrong. So I asked a friend
who has great experience admiring babies, "What are you supposed to say?"
"You are supposed to say," he told me, "*What a beautiful baby!*" He was right,
and I have been saying it for years. You have to keep track of the babies,
however, and not say just the same thing on a second meeting—or a third.

EXPECTANCY LEAKAGE

In addition to the display rules that apply to all members of a culture or of a
social class, there are display rules specific to roles; nurses are obliged to sound
and look cheery and undertakers the reverse. One very general display rule, a

rule that applies to research psychologists, teachers, and clinicians, is a masking rule. A psychologist dealing directly with experimental subjects, if he expects or hopes for a given outcome, is required to mask that expectancy lest subjects wishing to be obliging produce the predicted result for the wrong reason. The rationale for the masking rule in experimental psychology is simply good scientific procedure. Notice that the masking of such expectancies is not an effort at deception of the kind sometimes necessary in social psychology, e.g. the experimenter and "victim" in Milgram's obedience research seek actively to deceive the "teacher" subject into the belief that he is delivering strong electric shocks. The expectancy masking rule is not deception but simply proper performance of a role.

Teachers, clinicians, and employers dealing, as they do, with numerous students, clients, and employees are supposed to mask expectancies of another sort. Those in the superordinate roles are bound to have varying individual expectancies for those in the subordinate roles. A teacher expects some students to do excellent work and some not to do very well; a clinician expects some clients (or patients) to respond well and some less well, and so on. The reason why such expectancies ought to be masked is ultimately the same as the reason for masking experimenter expectancies: the danger of the self-fulfilling prophecy. In an experiment that means drawing a mistaken conclusion as to cause and effect. In school, business, and the clinic the problem with self-fulfilling expectancies is one of injustice to those who do not make promising first impressions.

In the volume *Experimenter Effects in Behavioral Research*, a classic work in psychology, Robert Rosenthal (1966) demonstrated beyond any possible doubt that experimenters who deal directly with subjects often do not fully succeed in masking their expectancies. They succeed with the most controllable channel, the verbal, but expectancies are very often given away by the leakier channels, especially the face and tone of voice. Furthermore, subjects respond cooperatively and tend to confirm the expectancies they pick up. The entire process is unconscious for all concerned. The leakage is unwitting and the cooperation also. Those discoveries have made necessary procedural precautions in experimental psychology designed to exclude expectancy effects. Expectancy effects have also been clearly established in teaching, and the probability is strong that they operate also in clinical treatment, medicine, business, and wherever people try to mask expectancies.

In a prototypical experiment (Rosenthal and Fode, 1963), each of ten advanced psychology students in a laboratory course, playing the role of experimenter, was assigned twenty undergraduate subjects. The experimenter was to show a series of ten faces to his subjects, and each face was to be rated for the level of success or failure the person pictured had been experiencing, from + 10 through zero to − 10. It had been determined in advance that each face used elicited an average rating close to zero, neither successful nor unsuccessful. However, five experimenters were told (falsely) that the purpose of the experiment was to replicate well-established findings that the faces tended to be judged, on the average, as quite successful (+5). In short, a "+5" expectancy was planted in their minds. The remaining five experimenters were given the opposite expectancy, a "−5" rating on the average. All experimenters received written instructions to be read to their subjects without deviation. When the results came in, the subjects of the experimenter who expected higher ratings had all produced higher ratings than had any of the subjects of the experimenter who had expected lower ratings. Those results and comparable results in many, many experiments (Rosenthal, 1966, 1985) were not produced by unprofessional behavior of any kind; the experimenters did not falsify the data, did not make enough "honest" errors of tabulation to account for the effect, and did not significantly depart from the written instructions.

The induced expectancies were somehow unwittingly communicated. But how? Adair and Epstein (1968) replicated the original success–failure induction and, in the process, tape-recorded each experimenter's reading of the instructions. Then a second experiment was done in which subjects received their instructions from the tape recordings alone without directly contacting any experimenter. When the experimenter whose voice was recorded had expected high (success) ratings, that is what the subjects who heard the recording produced. When the experimenter whose voice was recorded had expected low (failure) ratings, that is what the subjects who heard the recording produced. Since the verbal instructions were fixed, it was established that vocal qualities (intonation, inflection, emphasis) were alone sufficient to produce an experimental bias. That outcome, many times replicated now, is especially unnerving because vocal quality is a channel not easily controlled.

Qualities of vocalization in an experimenter who has a definite expectancy are alone sufficient to produce an experimenter bias. They are sufficient causes of a bias, but they are not necessary. Vocal qualities can be excluded by giving subjects written instructions to read for themselves. If the experimenter is visible, however, it turns out that visual cues (mostly facial) are also alone sufficient to produce bias in line with expectancy. In general it now appears (Badini and Rosenthal, 1982) that visual cues produce somewhat stronger expectancy effects than do vocal cues.

Exactly *how* expectancy effects are communicated has still not been determined (Rosenthal, 1985). The cues must sometimes be immediate, because even the first responses of subjects can be biased. The failure to find, so far, any general cueing system suggests that individual experimenters may have personally peculiar modes of nonverbal leakage, and there may be modes peculiar to individual experimenter–subject dyads. There are experiments in which the bias grows stronger with successive series of trials, and that suggests that experimenters may sometimes (unintentionally) *learn how* to influence a particular subject. The quest for the medium of communication of expectancies led Robert Rosenthal to the second stage of his research career—the development of the PONS and the study of nonverbal encoding and decoding as personal skills. It is a reasonable prediction that when good encoders are assigned the experimenter role and good decoders the subject role, expectancy effects should be maximal, and Zuckerman and associates (1978) found that to be the case. However, decoding skill alone, as assessed by the PONS, has not consistently been related to the size of the expectancy effects obtained (Rosenthal, Hall, DiMatteo et al., 1979).

In his 1966 book Rosenthal describes procedures for safeguarding psychological research against expectancy effects. Many of them were already standard practice in careful research. Experimenters who directly contact subjects can be kept "blind" as to research hypotheses and "blind," where group differences are expected, as to the experimental or control group membership of particular subjects. Instructions to subjects even when individually presented can be held constant by putting them on audiotape or videotape. A procedure not yet common with human subjects in 1966 that has since then become standard for many kinds of cognitive research is completely automated data collection in a computer-based laboratory. In addition to his close scrutiny of the more or less standard practices of high-quality research, Rosenthal describes a variety of new control groups specifically designed to exclude expectancy effects.

Knowing that expectancies can be communicated and exert an effect even when the only "open" channels are the face and vocal quality, we ought not to be surprised that expectancy effects occur in school where teachers are completely free to communicate, on all channels and over long periods of time, that they look for great accomplishments from student A, but not from Student B. In ordinary life, however, the causal role of expectancies is unclear because a principal ground of expectancy must be prior performance of the student, and good or bad prior performance should be consistent with later performance, since both depend on ability and effort. To test for a causal role of expectancy as such is ethically delicate since one certainly cannot induce negative expectancies for students and risk their welfare. It has been possible to demonstrate teacher expectancy effects without ever doing anything to damage the prospects of any student.

The most famous, but also the most controversial, work is *Pygmalion in the Classroom* (Rosenthal and Jacobson, 1968). The title refers back to George Bernard Shaw's play, *Pygmalion* (on which the musical My Fair Lady was based), and Shaw's play refers further back to the Greek legend of a king of Cyprus who sculpted an ivory statue of a woman and then fell in love with it. In Shaw's play, a Cockney flower girl is transformed into a fine lady by a misanthropic phonetician who *believes that she can become one.* More exactly, Professor Henry Higgins believes that *with the benefit of his teaching* Liza can become a lady. Still more exactly, what Professor Higgins believes is that with the benefit of his teaching, the flower girl will be able to "pass" as a lady.

The classroom Pygmalions were created in a public elementary school in South San Francisco (called by the pseudonym "Oak School") by causing teachers to believe that a certain 20 percent of their students could be expected in the next year or so to show an academic "spurt," to "bloom" intellectually. For those students a positive expectancy was induced. For the remaining 80 percent teachers were simply left with whatever expectancies they had formed in the usual way; no negative expectancies were created.

In May of 1964 the "Harvard Test of Inflected Acquisition" was administered to all of the children of Oak School (eighteen classes in grades 1–6) who would be returning the next fall. This test was actually an IQ test with which the teachers were unfamiliar, but it was alleged to be a test able to identify those youngsters who were about to reach an "inflection point" in their development and bloom intellectually. It was explained to the teachers that such imminent bloomers might be at any academic level at the present time. As school began in the fall of 1964, a randomly chosen 20 percent of the children were designated as "spurters." Each of the teachers received a list of one to nine names identifying those spurters who would be in his or her class. All of the children were retested with a comparable form of the same IQ test after a full academic year, and those who had been expected to spurt gained IQ points significantly in excess of the control children. That effect was confined to children in the first and second grades, but for those children it was quite dramatic. However, on retesting one year later, the first and second graders had not retained their advantage.

The possible social implications of the positive teacher expectancy effect reported in *Pygmalion* seemed very great and drew the attention of educators, policy-makers, and journalists as well as psychologists. Reviews in such general periodicals as *Time*, *The New York Review of Books*, and the *Saturday Review* were hypermanic. Some even guessed that the negative expectancies of teachers might be the whole explanation of the low academic achievement of various ethnic minorities. The reception of *Pygmalion* in professional psychological and educational journals was quite different. Richard Snow in *Contemporary Psychology* (1969) and Robert L. Thorndike in *Educational Research Journal* (1968) wrote blisteringly critical reviews. The problems with the study include the use of an IQ test not standardized for the lower grades, verbal summaries that sometimes overstated what the data showed, and a failure to highlight aspects of the data that embarrassed the expectancy hypothesis. Elashoff and Snow (1971) published a full book in criticism of *Pygmalion*. Throughout the storm Robert Rosenthal responded frankly and knowledgeably to his critics.

By 1982 there were more than a hundred studies of teacher expectancies (Brophy, 1982), including a number by Rosenthal and various associates (e.g. Babad, Inbar, and Rosenthal, 1982), and it was clear that teachers communicated their expectancies to individual students even when they intended not to and that expectancies could produce modest effects. The *Pygmalion* book was misleading insofar as it suggested that a single expectancy intervention could work wonders. Teachers' expectancies are not shaped once and for all by a single test score. Some do not believe in IQ scores, many forget how well individual students have done on such tests or never understand the scores in the first place. The most important limitation on what can be accomplished by manipulating expectancies is, of course, the day-to-day reality of student performance. Teachers adjust their expectancies in response to performance, and prior performance affects the credibility of attempts to create new expectancies. Nevertheless, a limited teacher expectancy effect has stood the test of time (Brophy, 1982).

Social Registers

My office in William James Hall is next door to the Child Development Research Laboratory. We are pretty well insulated against sound transmission, so the voices in the laboratory are content-filtered for me, but I can nevertheless always tell when someone is talking to a baby. That is because everyone, all adults and even children as young as 3–4 years (Dunn and Kendrick, 1982; Shatz and Gelman, 1977), speaks to babies in a special "register" (the baby talk register or BT), and that register has six prosodic or intonational features (Garnica, 1977), which penetrate and sometimes pierce the insulation.

1. A significantly higher than normal fundamental frequency (about 267 Hz.)
2. A greater than normal range of pitch
3. A rising final intonation on imperatives (*push in?*)
4. Occasional whispering
5. Longer than normal duration in speaking separable verbs (puuu—sh—in)
6. Two primary syllabic stresses on words calling for one (pú—úsh—ín)

Can you hear it? It is difficult to produce the baby talk register (BT) to order in the absence of a baby, but if you speak to a baby you will automatically shift into BT. The six prosodic features, which in combination are called "nursery tone," are just the most penetrating features of BT; the register as a whole has something like a hundred documented characteristics (Hoff-Ginsberg and Shatz, 1982; Snow and Ferguson, 1977). They include simplification of consonant clusters (stop—top, pretty—pwetty); short, simple sentences and a small concrete vocabulary; the use of proper names or kin terms in place of pronouns (*that's Mommy's good girl*); diminutive affixes (*doggie, kitty*); cute euphemisms (*make pee pee*), and about ninety other things. The effect on the printed page of sayings like: "Does our tummy hurt?" is kind of disgusting, but that's because BT is for babies.

Some very ideological parents (the ones who will not *permit* TV and insist that the wallpaper in baby's room must be "stimulating") intend never to use baby talk, but they cannot succeed. It is possible to eschew the stereotypical "choo-choo" features, such as diminutives and euphemisms, but most of the register is out-of-awareness and fully automatized, and that is a good thing because, while BT may (Cross, 1977; Furrow, Nelson, and Benedict, 1979) or may not (Gleitman, Newport, and Gleitman, 1984) facilitate language acquisition, it does seem important for capturing attention and sustaining communication between parent and child.

Baby talk is a social speech "register," with both verbal and nonverbal components. A "social register" is a way of talking that is specialized to a certain class of addressee. Baby talk is not the only social register, but it is the most striking and most fully documented. Extensive ethnographic research (Ferguson, 1977) indicates that a BT register is a linguistic universal. It was noted as early as the first century B.C. and has been described in diverse languages, including some of preliterate communities (Gilyak and Comanche) and many world languages (English, Arabic, Chinese, and so on). In some respects, including high pitch, exaggerated intonation, and simple sentences, the BT register is the same in all languages.

When it is pointed out to parents that they use the BT register and they are asked why, the usual response is: "To teach my child to talk." Probably that is not quite right, however. Brown (1977), reviewing the features of BT, pointed out that they were of two kinds: simplification features (e.g. short sentences, consonant cluster reduction, reference to what is here and now), and affectionate features (e.g. diminutives, pet names, nursery tone). It seems probable that the simplification features are a response to low linguistic and cognitive competence in the addressee and the affectionate features to lovability. Brown went on to suggest that one or both aspects of BT might appear in speech to other kinds of addressee for whom language teaching was either unnecessary or else totally impossible. Speech to adult foreigners and to retarded adults seems to be simplified, though not usually affectionate; talk to pets and even to plants seems to resemble talk to babies. On the whole, those impressions have proved correct.

While older siblings as young as three years are able expertly to shift from three-year-old English to BT, not all older siblings feel uncomplicated love for baby, and Dunn and Kendrick (1982) have shown that when rivalrous sentiment is strong, the affection features are dropped. A foreigner register, mainly simplifying and not affectionate, has been well established (Clyne, 1981). Hirsh-Pasek and Treiman (1982) unobtrusively taped the speech of four ladies talking to their pooches and discovered a register, which they wittily named "Doggerel," that is much the same as Baby Talk.

The distinguished social and developmental psychologist Harry Levin (Levin, Snow, and Lee, 1984), has described the features of a sickroom register, which is primarily nurturant in quality. I think the idea for that register may have developed in the year that Professor Levin spent as a Visiting Scholar at Harvard, when he had to have coronary bypass surgery and so spent time in Massachusetts General Hospital. Harry Levin and I have been friends since we were graduate students, and one day when I visited him at the hospital he quipped: "Roger, I'm going to get better so you can drop the 'memorial service register'." A good social psychologist can always find something to observe.

Lynn Caporael (1981) had the good thought that speech in nursing homes might be something like speech in nurseries since the institutionalized aged stand in relation to their caregivers rather as a child stands to a parent. Of course the content would be different, so she content-filtered the speech she taped in a nursing home and also the speech she taped at a nursery school. Not all speech in the nursing home resembled baby talk, but on the average 22 percent did. When judges heard the content-filtered tapes, they thought the speech to the elderly must be addressed to a small child. One would guess (with Friedman, 1979) that elderly adults would find BT either offensively condescending or else an encouragement to dependency, and it may be so, when the verbal as well as the prosodic or vocal channels are heard. Maybe not, however. Caporael had judges rate the content-filtered speech to the elderly, and they judged it to be more "comforting" and less "irritating" than ordinary adult-to-adult speech.

Some speech variation, called "dialectal," is associated with geographic region, and some, called "stratificational," is associated with social class. A group-slang or *argot* is a way of speaking that identifies speakers *and hearers* as members of a particular in-group or subculture. Slang expressions typically label outsiders with whom there is routine contact. Hospital staff slang has terms for three main patient categories: *crocks* are patients who demand more attention than is warranted by their physical condition; *gomers* are patients belonging to such stigmatized groups as derelicts and alcoholics, whose personal hygiene is extremely bad and illness possibly feigned; *gorks* are comatose patients beyond recovery. An outsider might think that those "in" terms, never used to patients or visitors, reflect a general callousness or else an attempt to deal with an overload of empathy on the part of hospital personnel, but a sensitive analysis by David Gordon (1983) shows that neither interpretation is quite correct. There are no hospital slang terms for seriously sick patients who cannot be considered responsible for their trouble and who arouse sympathy, no slang for small children, little old ladies, and so on. Crocks, gomers, and gorks are all types of patient whose care arouses some resentment—because they are excessively demanding (crocks), socially stigmatized (gomers), or beyond any response or hope (gorks). In using the slang terms, hospital staff express a shared—not quite professional—sentiment that unites them and promotes a kind of camaraderie.

A register has usually been defined as a way of speaking *to* addressees of a particular category: babies, pets, foreigners, patients, the institutionalized elderly. Charles Ferguson, a sociolinguist who has led the way in the study of speech variation, uses "register" somewhat more broadly. For Ferguson (1983) a register is simply a systematic variation with the occasion of use. He considers register variation to be all-pervasive in language use, and his detailed analysis of

SAT, or Sports Announcer Talk (1983), is really my favorite paper in this new field.

Do you think because you have been listening to sportscasts most of your life that you would be able to be a sportscaster yourself on a moment's notice? Forget it. Sportscasting is a genre almost as rigid as the sonnet. Here are some of the rules:

1. Omit the copular verb, forms of *be*: *Klutts* [*is*] *in close at third; McCarthy* [*is*] *in difficulty; The A's* [*are*] *now hoping to get* . . . [p. 159]

2. Make frequent use of inversions, sentences in which the predicate precedes the subject: *Holding up at third, is Murphy; And all set again is Pat Harden; And out right is Drew Hall.* [p. 160]

3. In order to indicate that an event leads to a particular state use *for*, even though this particular use of *for* is not recognized by either the Oxford English Dictionary or Webster's Third: *Joe Ross's caught it for a touchdown; He throws for the out.*

4. Make heavy use of modifiers in the form of appositional noun phrases: *David Winfield, the 25-million-dollar man, who is hitting zero, five, six in this World Series; Big David, beleaguered not only because of his failure to hit in the Series as well as he did in the regular season, but for other reasons as well; Bobby Watson, with a 3-run homerun last night and a single* . . . [p. 163]

5. Use such prefabricated routines as the count of balls (first) and strikes (second) in baseball: *One and one; Two balls and two strikes; Three and two.* [p. 166]

Perhaps, however, I am wrong in thinking that someone could not pick up Sports Announcer Talk just by listening. Most kinds of language learning proceed unconsciously without knowledge of the rules.

That's all from James Hall for today, fans. Upsetting all forecasts, the verbals romped over the nonverbals as a general medium. However, the nonverbals held on as league-leaders in leakiness. The very famous, always controversial polygraph still does not meet professional standards for admission as evidence. Brilliant Bob Rosenthal, with a historic first in experimenter expectancy, tried for another with *Pygmalion in the Classroom* but met tough opposition. Strong backup made the difference, and teacher expectancies are here to stay. Darwin, world famous for Natural Selection, right again on the universality of emotional expression. Paul Ekman credited with a strong assist on that play. Seemingly simple sportscaster talk eludes academic author.

Summary

Nonverbal communication is communication by facial expression, hands, feet, body, and vocal quality. Without doubt, the nonverbal channels are continuously attended to and do communicate information—primarily affective in quality and connected with personal relationships. An inappropriate inter-pretation of some results that combine verbal messages and nonverbal cues in various ways has led some investigators to assert that the nonverbal channel is more informative than the verbal either in general or with respect to affect. That cannot be the case, because language is a universal medium able to ex-press anything that can be thought or felt. However, nonverbal channels do have a special relationship with affect or feeling, because they are likely to "leak" information deliberately concealed in the controllable verbal channel. Channels of communication can be ranked in a hierarchy from high con-trollability (verbal) to low controllability or highly leaky (vocal quality). In general, when channels are congruent, as they are on the PONS, the more con-trollable the channel, the more informative it is, but when messages are in-congruent, because of a deception effort, the leakier, or less controllable, chan-nels are the more informative.

It is an ancient question whether the expression of emotions in the face is entirely culturally determined or is, as Charles Darwin thought, in some respects universal. Ekman and Friesen and their associates found the key to an answer in distinguishing display rules (cultural) from the natural expressions the face shows when unobserved. For six emotions—happiness, fear, anger, sadness, disgust, and surprise—universality of facial expression has been established by showing that members of cultures having no visual contact can correctly recognize one another's expressions.

Certain roles—especially those of psychological experimenter and teacher—have display rules requiring that some expectancies be masked. In the psychological laboratory the experimenter ought not to reveal his scientific ex-pectations, his anticipated and hoped-for results, lest subjects deliberately pro-duce them in order to be accommodating. In a long series of experiments, Rosenthal has shown that experimenters often do leak their expectancies nonverbally and subjects do often pick them up and respond to them—with neither party knowing what has occurred. With various careful controls, expec-tancy leakage on the part of experimenters can be prevented.

Teachers in elementary schools are not professionally bound to mask the differential expectancies they have for "good" and for "bad" students, but out of simple fairness to the student, they usually try to do so. In fact, however, students learn what teachers expect of them and are somewhat affected by the knowledge. It is not possible to produce good outcomes for all students by the simple device of implanting good expectancies for the reason that expectancies are not totally malleable but largely dependent on student performance.

Social speech registers are ways of speaking specialized for particular classes of addressee. The baby talk register is the most fully documented, elaborate, and universal of registers. Others that have been so far identified include the foreigner register, the sick room register, the sports announcer register, and "doggerel."

References for Part V

ADAIR, J. G., and J. S. EPSTEIN. 1968. Verbal cues in the mediation of experimenter bias, *Psychological Reports, 22*: 1045-53.

ANGLIN, J. M. 1977. *Word, Object, and Conceptual Development.* New York: Norton.

ARCHER, D., and R. M. AKERT. 1977. Words and everything else: Verbal and nonverbal cues to social interpretation, *Journal of Personality and Social Psychology, 35*: 443-49.

ARGYLE, M.; F. ALKEMA; and R. GILMOUR. 1971. The communication of friendly and hostile attitudes by verbal and nonverbal signals, *European Journal of Social Psychology, 1*: 385-402.

ARGYLE, M.; V. SALTER; H. NICOLSON; N. WILLIAMS; and P. BURGESS. 1970. The communication of inferior and superior attitudes by verbal and nonverbal signals, *British Journal of Social and Clinical Psychology, 9*: 222-31.

ARMSTRONG, S. L.; L. R. GLEITMAN; and H. GLEITMAN. 1983. What some concepts might not be, *Cognition, 13*: 263-308.

AU, T. KIT-FONG. 1983. Chinese and English counterfactuals: The Sapir-Whorf hypothesis revisited, *Cognition, 15*: 155-87.

BABAD, E. Y.; J. INBAR; and R. ROSENTHAL. 1982. Pygmalion, Galatea, and the Golem: Investigators of biased and unbiased teachers, *Journal of Educational Psychology, 74*: 459-74.

BADINI, A. A., and R. ROSENTHAL. 1982. Visual cues and student gender as mediating factors in teacher expectancy effects. Paper read at Eastern Communication Association, Hartford, Connecticut, May.

BATES, E. 1979. *The Emergence of Symbols: Cognition and Communication in Infancy.* New York: Academic Press.

BELLUGI, U.; H. POIZNER; and E. S. KLIMA. 1983. Brain organization for language: Clues from sign aphasia, *Human Neurobiology,* special issue, D. Kimura (ed.), *2*: 155-70.

BENOWITZ, L. I.; D. M. BEAR; R. ROSENTHAL; M. M. MESULAM; E. ZAIDEL; and R. W. SPERRY. 1983. Hemisphere specialization in nonverbal communication, *Cortex, 19*: 5-11.

BERLIN, B. 1978. Ethnobiological classification. In E. Rosch and B. B. Lloyd (eds.), *Cognition and Categorization.* New York: Wiley, pp. 9-26.

BLANCK, P. D., and R. ROSENTHAL. 1982. Developing strategies for decoding "leaky" messages: On learning how and when to decode discrepant and consistent social communications. In R. S. Feldman (ed.), *Development of Nonverbal Behavior in Children.* New York: Springer-Verlag, pp. 203-29.

BLOOM, A. H. 1981. *The Linguistic Shaping of Thought: A Study in the Impact of Language on Thinking in China and the West.* Hillsdale, N.J.: Erlbaum.

BLOOM, L. 1970. *Language Development: Form and Function in Emerging Grammar.* Cambridge, Mass.: MIT Press.

BLOUNT, B. G. 1969. Acquisition of language by Luo children. Unpublished doctoral thesis, University of California, Berkeley.

BODINE, A. 1975. Androcentrism in prescriptive grammar: Singular "they," sex-indefinite "he" and "he or she," *Language in Society*, 4: 129–46.

BOWERMAN, M. 1973. *Early Syntactic Development: A Cross-Linguistic Study with Special Reference to Finnish*. Cambridge, England: Cambridge University Press.

BROPHY, J. E. 1982. Research on the self-fulfilling prophecy and teacher expectations. Paper delivered at annual meeting of the American Educational Research Association, New York City.

BROWN, R. 1970. The first sentences of child and chimpanzee. In R. Brown (ed.), *Psycholinguistics*. New York: Free Press, pp. 208–31.

———. 1973. *A First Language*. Cambridge, Mass.: Harvard University Press.

———. 1977. Introduction. In C. E. Snow and C. A. Ferguson (eds.), *Talking to Children: Language Input and Acquisition*. Cambridge, England: Cambridge University Press, pp. 1–27.

———. 1978. Why are signed languages easier to learn than spoken languages? Part two, *Bulletin of the American Academy of Arts and Sciences*, XXXII: 25–44.

———. 1981. Symbolic and syntactic capacities, *Philosophical Transactions of the Royal Society*, B292: 197–204.

BRUNER, J. S. 1983. *Child's Talk: Learning to Use Language*. New York: Norton.

CAPORAEL, L. R. 1981. The paralanguage of caregiving: Baby talk to the institutionalized aged, *Journal of Personality and Social Psychology*, 40: 876–84.

CLYNE, M. G. (ed.). 1981. Foreigner talk, *International Journal of the Sociology of Language*, No. 28.

COLLINS-AHLGREN, M. 1975. Language development of two deaf children, *American Annals of the Deaf*, 120: 524–39.

CRAWFORD, M., and L. ENGLISH. 1984. Generic versus specific inclusion of women in language: Effects on recall, *Journal of Psycholinguistic Research*, 13: 373–81.

CROSS, T. G. 1977. Mothers' speech adjustments: The contribution of selected child listener variables. In C. E. Snow and C.A. Ferguson (eds.), *Talking to Children: Language Input and Acquisition*. Cambridge, England: Cambridge University Press, pp. 151–88.

CURTISS, S.; V. FROMKIN; D. KRASHEN; D. RIGLER; and M. RIGLER. 1974. The linguistic development of Genie, *Language*, 50: 528–54.

DARWIN, C. 1872. *The Expression of the Emotions in Man and Animals*. London: John Murray.

DEPAULO, B. M., and R. ROSENTHAL. 1979. Ambivalence, discrepancy, and deception in nonverbal communication. In R. Rosenthal (ed.), *Skill in Nonverbal Communication: Individual Differences*. Cambridge, Mass.: Oelgeschlager, Gunn, & Hain, pp. 204–48.

DEPAULO, B. M.; R. ROSENTHAL; R. A. EISENSTAT; P. L. ROGERS; and S. FINKELSTEIN. 1978. Decoding discrepant nonverbal cues, *Journal of Personality and Social Psychology*, 36: 313–23.

DEPAULO, B. M.; M. ZUCKERMAN, and R. ROSENTHAL. 1980. Detecting deception: Modality effects. In L. Wheeler (ed.), *The Review of Personality and Social Psychology*. New York: Sage, pp. 125–62.

DOUGHERTY, J. W. D. 1978. Salience and relativity in classification, *American Ethnologist*, 5: 66–80.

DUNN, J., and C. KENDRICK. 1982. The speech of two- and three-year-olds to infant siblings: "Baby talk" and the context of communication, *Journal of Child Language*, 9: 579–95.

EKMAN, P. (ed.). 1973. *Darwin and Facial Expression*. New York: Academic Press.

——. (ed.). 1982. *Emotion in the Human Face*. 2d ed. Cambridge, England: Cambridge University Press.

EKMAN, P., and W. V. FRIESEN. 1969. Nonverbal leakage and clues to deception, *Psychiatry*, 32: 88–106.

——. 1982. Measuring facial movement with the Facial Action Coding System. In P. Ekman (ed.), *Emotion in the Human Face*. 2d ed. Cambridge, England: Cambridge University Press, pp. 178–211.

EKMAN, P.; W. V. FRIESEN; and P. C. ELLSWORTH. 1982a. Does the face provide accurate information? In P. Ekman (ed.), *Emotion in the Human Face*. 2d ed. Cambridge, England: Cambridge University Press, pp. 56–97.

——. 1982b. What are the similarities and differences in facial behavior across cultures? In P. Ekman (ed.), *Emotion in the Human Face*. 2d ed. Cambridge, England: Cambridge University Press, pp. 128–43.

——. 1982c. What emotion categories or dimensions can observers judge from facial behavior? In P. Ekman (ed.), *Emotion in the Human Face*. 2d ed. Cambridge, England: Cambridge University Press, pp. 39–55.

EKMAN, P.; W. V. FRIESEN; and K. R. SCHERER. 1976. Body movement and voice pitch in deceptive interaction, *Semiotica*, 16: 23–27.

ELASHOFF, J. R., and R. W. SNOW. 1971. *Pygmalion Reconsidered*. Worthington, Ohio: Charles A. Jones.

ELMAN, B. A. 1983. Review of *The Linguistic Shaping of Thought: A Study in the Impact of Language on Thinking in China and the West* (A. Bloom), *Journal of Asian Studies*, XLII: 611–14.

FERGUSON, C. A. 1977. Baby talk as a simplified register. In C. E. Snow and C. A. Ferguson (eds.), *Talking to Children: Language Input and Acquisition*. Cambridge, England: Cambridge University Press, pp. 219–36.

FERGUSON, C. A. 1983. Sports announcer talk: Syntactic aspects of register variation, *Language in Society*, 12: 153–73.

FOUTS, R. S. 1973. Acquisition and testing of gestural signs in four young chimpanzees, *Science*, 180: 978–80.

FRIEDMAN, H. A. 1979. Nonverbal communication between patients and medical practitioners, *Journal of Social Issues*, 35: 82–99.

FURROW, D.; K. NELSON; and H. BENEDICT. 1979. Mothers' speech to children and syntactic development: Some simple relationships, *Journal of Child Language*, 6: 423–42.

GALLABURDA, A. M.; M. LEMAY; T. L. KEMPER; and N. GESCHWIND. 1978. Right-left asymmetries in the brain, *Science*, 199: 852–56.

GARDNER, B. T., and R. A. GARDNER. 1971. Two-way communication with an infant chimpanzee. In A. Schrier and F. Stollnitz (eds.), *Behavior of Nonhuman Primates.* New York: Academic Press, *4*: 117–84.

——. 1975. Evidence for sentence constituents in the early utterances of child and chimpanzee, *Journal of Experimental Psychology: General, 104*: 244–67.

GARDNER, R. A., and B. T. GARDNER. 1978. Comparative psychology and language acquisition. In K. Salzinger and F. Denmark (eds.), *Psychology: The State of the Art. Annals of the New York Academy of Sciences, 809*: 37–76.

GARNICA, O. K. 1977. Some prosodic and paralinguistic features of speech to young children. In C. E. Snow and C. A. Ferguson (eds.), *Talking to Children: Language Input and Acquisition.* Cambridge, England: Cambridge University Press, pp. 63–88.

GELB, I. J. 1980. Principles of writing systems within the frame of visual communication. In P. A. Kolers, M. E. Wrolstad, and H. Bouma (eds.), *Processing of Visible Language 2.* New York: Plenum, pp. 7–24.

GESCHWIND, N. 1979. Specializations of the human brain, *Scientific American, 241*: 180–99.

GESCHWIND, N., and W. LEVITSKY. 1968. Human brain: Left-right asymmetries in temporal speech region. *Science, 161*: 186–87.

GINTON, A.; N. DAIE; E. ELRAD; and G. BEN-SHAKAR. 1982. A method for evaluating the use of the polygraph in a real-life situation, *Journal of Applied Psychology, 67*: 131–37.

GLEITMAN, L. R.; E. L. NEWPORT; and H. GLEITMAN. 1984. The current status of the motherese hypothesis, *Journal of Child Language, 11*: 43–79.

GOLDIN-MEADOW, S., and M. MORFORD. 1985. Gesture in early child language: Studies of deaf and hearing children. *Merrill-Palmer Quarterly.*

GOODALL, J. 1965. Chimpanzees of the Gombe Stream Reserve. In I. DeVore (ed.), *Primate Behavior: Field Studies of Monkeys and Apes.* New York: Holt, Rinehart & Winston, pp. 425–81.

GORDON, D. P. 1983. Hospital slang for patients: Crocks, gomers, gorks, and others, *Language in Society, 12*: 173–86.

HALL, J. A. 1980. Gender differences in nonverbal communication skills. In R. Rosenthal (ed.), *Quantitative Assessment of Research Domains.* San Francisco: Jossey-Bass, pp. 63–77.

——. 1984. *Nonverbal Sex Differences: Communication Accuracy and Expressive Style.* Baltimore: Johns Hopkins Press.

HAYES, K. H., and C. HAYES. 1951. Intellectual development of a home-raised chimpanzee, *Proceedings of the American Philosophical Society, 95*: 105.

HENLEY, N. M. 1977. *Body Politics.* Englewood Cliffs, N.J.: Prentice-Hall.

HEWES, G. W. 1976. The current status of the gestural theory of language origin. In S. R. Harnad, H. D. Steklis, and J. Lancaster (eds.), *Origins and Evolution of Language and Speech. Annals of the New York Academy of Sciences, 280*: 482–504.

HIRSH-PASEK, K., and R. TREIMAN. 1982. Doggerel: Motherese in a new context, *Journal of Child Language, 9*: 229–37.

HOFF-GINSBERG, E., and M. SHATZ. 1982. Linguistic input and the child's acquisition of language, *Psychological Bulletin, 92*, pp. 3–26.

HOLLOWAY, R. L. 1976. Paleoneurological evidence for language origins. In S. R. Harnad, H. D. Steklis, and J. Lancaster (eds.), *Origins and Evolution of Language and Speech. Annals of the New York Academy of Sciences, 280:* 330–48.

———. 1981. Exploring the dorsal surface of hominoid brain endocasts by stereoplotter and discriminant analysis, *Philosophical Transactions of the Royal Society London, B292:* 155–61.

———. 1983a. Cerebral brain endocast pattern of *Australopithecus afarensis* hominid, *Nature, 303:* 420–22.

———. 1983b. Human paleontological evidence relevant to language behavior, *Human Neurobiology, 2:* 105–14.

HOLLOWAY, R. L., and M. C. DE LACOSTE-LAREYMONDIE. 1982. Brain endocast asymmetry in Pongids and Hominids: Some preliminary findings on the paleontology of cerebral dominance, *American Journal of Physical Anthropology, 58:* 108–10.

HOLLOWAY, R. L., and D. G. POST. 1982. The relativity of relative brain measures and hominid mosaic evolution. In E. Armstrong and D. Falk (eds.), *Primate Brain Evolution: Methods and Concepts.* New York: Plenum, pp. 57–76.

HORVATH, F. S. 1977. The effect of selected variables on interpretation of polygraph records, *Journal of Applied Psychology, 62:* 127–36.

ISAAC, G. L. 1976. Stages of cultural elaboration in the Pleistocene: Possible archeological indicators of the development of language capabilities. In S. R. Harnad, H. D. Steklis, and J. Lancaster (eds.), *Origins and Evolution of Language and Speech. Annals of the New York Academy of Sciences, 280:* 275–88.

JAYNES, J. 1976. The evolution of language in the late Pleistocene. In S. R. Harnad, H. D. Steklis, and J. Lancaster (eds.), *Origins and Evolution of Language and Speech. Annals of the New York Academy of Sciences, 280:* 312–25.

JENKINS, H. M., and B. R. MOORE. 1973. The form of the autoshaped response with food or water reinforcers, *Journal of the Experimental Analysis of Behavior, 20:* 163–81.

JERISON, H. D. 1976. Discussion paper: The paleoneurology of language. In S. R. Harnad, H. D. Steklis, and J. Lancaster (eds.), *Origins and Evolution of Language and Speech. Annals of the New York Academy of Sciences, 280:* 370–82.

JOHANSON, D., and M. EDEY. 1981. *Lucy: The Beginnings of Humankind.* New York: Simon & Schuster.

KELLOGG, W. N., and L. A. KELLOGG. 1933. *The Ape and the Child.* New York: McGraw-Hill.

KENDON, A. 1980. The sign language of the women of Yuendumu: A preliminary report of the structure of Warlpiri sign language, *Sign Language Studies, 27:* 101–12.

KIMBEL, W. H.; D. C. JOHANSON; and Y. COPPENS. 1982. Pliocene hominid cranial remains from the Hadar Formation, Ethiopia, *American Journal of Physical Anthropology, 57:* 453–500.

KIMURA, D. 1974. Motor functions of the left hemisphere, *Brain, 97:* 337–50.

———. 1979. Cases of "aphasia" in the deaf. In *Recent Developments in Language and Cognition: Sign Language Research.* Copenhagen: NATO Advanced Study Institute.

KLIMA, E. S., and U. BELLUGI. 1972. The signs of language in child and chimpanzee. In T. Alloway, L. Krames, and P. Pliner (eds.), *Communication and Affect: A Comparative Approach.* New York: Academic Press, pp. 67–96.

———. 1979. *The Signs of Language*. Cambridge, Mass.: Harvard University Press.

Krauss, R. M.; W. Apple; N. Morency; C. Wenzel; and W. Winton. 1981. Verbal, vocal, and visible factors in judgments of another's affect, *Journal of Personality and Social Psychology, 40:* 312–19.

Krauss, R. M.; V. Geller; and C. Olson. 1976. Modalities and cues in the detection of deception. Paper presented at the meetings of the American Psychological Association, Washington, D.C.

Kunst-Wilson, W. R., and R. B. Zajonc. 1980. Affective discrimination of stimuli that cannot be recognized, *Science, 207:* 557–58.

Kuschel, R. 1973. The silent inventor: The creation of a sign language by the only deaf-mute on a Polynesian island, *Sign Language Studies, 3:* 1–28.

LaBarre, W. 1947. The cultural basis of emotions and gestures, *Journal of Personality,* 16: 49–68.

Lakoff, R. 1973. Language and woman's place, *Language in Society, 2:* 45–80.

Lazarus, R. 1984. Thoughts on the relations between emotion and cognition. In K. R. Scherer and P. Ekman (eds.), *Approaches to Emotion.* Hillsdale, N.J.: Erlbaum, pp. 247–57.

LeMay, M. 1976. Morphological cerebral asymmetries of modern man, fossil man, and nonhuman primate. In S. R. Harnad, H. D. Steklis, and J. Lancaster (eds.), *Origins and Evolution of Language and Speech. Annals of the New York Academy of Sciences, 280:* 349–66.

LeMay, M., and A. Culebras. 1972. Human brain morphologic differences in the hemispheres demonstrable by carotid angiography, *New England Journal of Medicine, 287:* 168–70.

Lenneberg, E. H. 1967. *Biological Foundations of Language.* New York: Wiley.

Levin, H.; C. E. Snow; and K. Lee. 1984. Nurturant talk to children, *Language and Speech,* part 2.

Lieberman, P. 1973. On the evolution of language: A unified view, *Cognition, 2:* 59–94.

Lykken, D. T. 1979. The detection of deception, *Psychological Bulletin, 86:* 47–53.

Maccoby, E. E., and C. N. Jacklin. 1974. *The Psychology of Sex Differences.* Stanford, Calif.: Stanford University Press.

MacKay, D. G. 1980. Psychology, prescriptive grammar, and the pronoun problem, *American Psychologist, 35:* 444–49.

MacKay, D. G., and D. Fulkerson. 1979. On the comprehension and production of pronouns, *Journal of Verbal Learning and Verbal Behavior, 18:* 661–73.

Mandel, M. 1977. Iconic devices in American Sign Language. In L. Friedman (ed.), *On the Other Hand: New Perspectives in American Sign Language.* New York: Academic Press, pp. 57–107.

Marcus, J. 1980. Zapotec writing. *Scientific American, 242:* 50–64.

Marshack, A. 1976. Some implications of the Paleolithic symbolic evidence for the origin of language. In S. R. Harnad, H. D. Steklis, and J. Lancaster (eds.), *Origins and Evolution of Language and Speech. Annals of the New York Academy of Sciences, 280:* 330–48.

McGLONE, J. 1980. Sex differences in human brain asymmetry: A critical review, *Behavioral and Brain Sciences*, 3: 215–27.

McINTIRE, M. L. 1977. The acquisition of American Sign Language hand configuration, *Sign Language Studies*, 16: 247–66.

MEHRABIAN, A. 1972. *Nonverbal Communication*. Chicago: Aldine-Atherton.

MEHRABIAN, A., and M. WIENER. 1967. Decoding of inconsistent communications, *Journal of Personality and Social Psychology*, 6: 109–14.

MEISSNER, M., and S. B. PHILPOTT. 1975. The sign language of sawmill workers in British Columbia, *Sign Language Studies*, 9: 291–308.

MELTZER, E. S. 1980. Remarks on ancient Egyptian writing with emphasis on its mnemonic aspects. In P. A. Kolers, M. E. Wrolstad, and H. Bouma (eds.), *Processing of Visible Languages 2*. New York: Plenum, pp. 43–66.

MERVIS, C. B., and E. ROSCH. 1981. Categorization of natural objects. In M. R. Rosenzweig and L. W. Porter (eds.), *Annual Review of Psychology*, 32: 89–115.

MYERS, R. E. 1976. Comparative neurology of vocalization and speech: Proof of a dichotomy. In S. R. Harnad, H. D. Steklis, and J. Lancaster (eds.), *Annals of the New York Academy of Sciences*, 280: 745–57.

NEWPORT, E., and U. BELLUGI. 1979. Linguistic expression of category levels. In E. Klima and U. Bellugi (eds.), *The Signs of Language*. Cambridge, Mass.: Harvard University Press, pp. 225–42.

OLSON, J. R. 1972. A case for the use of sign language to stimulate language development during the critical period for learning in a congenitally deaf child, *American Annals of the Deaf*, 117: 397–400.

OLSON, T. R. 1981. Basiocranial morphology of the extant hominoids and Pliocene hominids: The new materials from the Hadar Formation, Ethiopa, and its significance in early human evolution and taxonomy. In C. B. Stringer (ed.), *Aspects of Human Evolution*. London: Taylor & Francis, pp. 99–128.

ORWELL, G. 1949. *1984*. New York: Harcourt Brace; Signet, 1955.

PATTERSON, F., and E. LINDEN. 1981. *The Education of Koko*. New York: Holt, Rinehart, & Winston.

PETITTO, L., and M. S. SEIDENBERG. 1979. On the evidence for linguistic abilities in signing apes, *Brain and Language*, 8: 162–63.

PILBEAM, D. 1984. The descent of hominoids and hominids, *Scientific American*, 250: 84–96.

POIZNER, H.; U. BELLUGI; and V. IRAGUI. 1984. Apraxia and aphasia in a visual-gestural language, *American Journal of Physiology: Regulatory, Integrative and Comparative Physiology*, 246: R868–R883.

POIZNER, H.; E. KAPLAN; U. BELLUGI; and C. PADDEN. 1984. Visual-spatial processing in deaf brain-damaged signers, *Brain and Cognition*, 3: 281–306.

POOLE, J. 1646. *The English Accidence*. Menston, England: Scholar Press Facsimile.

PREMACK, D. 1976. *Intelligence in Ape and Man*. Hillsdale, N.J.: Erlbaum.

QUINE, W. V. 1969. Natural kinds. In W. V. QUINE, *Ontological Relativity and Other Essays*. New York: Columbia University Press, pp. 114–38.

RASKIN, D. C., and J. A. PODLESNY. 1979. Truth and deception: A reply to Lykken, *Psychological Bulletin*, 86: 54–59.

REED, A. 1983. *Parlez-Vous le Metalanguage*. Unpublished senior honors thesis, Harvard University.

ROSCH, E. 1973. On the internal structure of perceptual and semantic categories. In T. E. Moore (ed.), *Cognitive Development and the Acquisition of Language*. New York: Academic Press, pp. 111–44.

ROSCH, E.; C. B. MERVIS; W. GRAY; D. JOHNSON; and P. BOYES-BRAEM. 1976. Basic objects in natural categories, *Cognitive Psychology*, 8: 382–439.

ROSENTHAL, R. 1966. *Experimenter Effects in Behavioral Research*. New York: Appleton-Century-Crofts.

——. 1985. Nonverbal cues in the mediation of interpersonal expectancy effects. In A. W. Siegman and S. Feldstein (eds.), *Nonverbal Communication*. Hillsdale, N.J.: Erlbaum.

ROSENTHAL, R., and L. I. BENOWITZ. 1985. Sensitivity to nonverbal communication in normal, psychiatric, and brain-damaged samples. In P. D. Blanck, R. W. Buck, and R. Rosenthal (eds.), *Nonverbal Communication in the Clinical Context*. Univ. Park, Pa.: Penn State Press.

ROSENTHAL, R., and B. M. DEPAULO. 1979a. Sex differences in eavesdropping on nonverbal cues, *Journal of Social and Personality Psychology*, 37: 273–85.

——. 1979b. Sex differences in accommodation in nonverbal communication. In R. Rosenthal (ed.), *Skill in Nonverbal Communication*. Cambridge, Mass.: Oelgeschlager, Gunn & Hain, pp. 68–103.

ROSENTHAL, R., and K. L. FODE. 1963. Three experiments in experimenter bias, *Psychological Reports*, 12: 491–511.

ROSENTHAL, R., and L. JACOBSON. 1968. *Pygmalion in the Classroom*. New York: Holt, Rinehart & Winston.

ROSENTHAL, R.; J. A. HALL; D. ARCHER; M. DIMATTEO; and P. L. ROGERS. 1979. The PONS test: Measuring sensitivity to nonverbal cues. In S. Weitz (ed.), *Nonverbal Communication*. New York: Oxford University Press, pp. 357–70.

ROSENTHAL, R.; J. A. HALL; M. R. DIMATTEO; P. L. ROGERS; and D. ARCHER. 1979. *Sensitivity to Nonverbal Communication: The PONS Test*. Baltimore: Johns Hopkins Press.

RUMBAUGH, D. M. (ed). 1977. *Language Learning by a Chimpanzee: The LANA Project*. New York: Academic Press.

RUMBAUGH, D. M.; H. WARNER; and E. VON GLASERSFELD. 1977. The Lana project: Origin and tactics. In D. M. Rumbaugh (ed.), *Language Learning by a Chimpanzee: The LANA Project*. New York: Academic Press, pp. 87–90.

SAPIR, E. 1949. *Selected Writings of Edward Sapir*. D. G. Mandelbaum (ed.). Berkeley and Los Angeles: University of California Press.

SAVAGE-RUMBAUGH, E. S.; J. L. PATE; J. LAWSON; S. T. SMITH; and S. ROSENBAUM. 1983. Can a chimpanzee make a statement? *Journal of Experimental Psychology: General*, 112: 457–92.

SAVAGE-RUMBAUGH, E. S.; D. M. RUMBAUGH; and S. L. BOYSEN. 1978. Symbolic communication between two chimpanzees (*Pan troglodytes*), *Science, 201*: 641–44.

——. 1980. Do apes use language? *American Scientist, 68*: 49–61.

SCHERER, K. R.; S. FELDSTEIN; R. N. BOND; and R. ROSENTHAL. In press. Vocal cues to deception: A comparative channel approach. *Journal of Psycholinguistic Research.*

SCHLESINGER, I. M., and L. NAMIR (eds.). 1978. *Sign Language of the Deaf.* New York: Academic Press.

SEIDENBERG, M. S., and L. A. PETITTO. 1979. Signing behavior in apes: A critical review, *Cognition, 7*: 177–215.

SHATZ, M., and R. GELMAN. 1977. Beyond syntax: The influence of conversational constraints on speech modifications. In C. E. Snow and C. A. Ferguson (eds.), *Talking to Children: Language Input and Acquisition.* Cambridge, England: Cambridge University Press, pp. 189–98.

SIMPSON, G. G.; C. S. PITTENDRIGH, and L. TIFFANY. 1957. *Life; An Introduction to Biology.* New York: Harcourt, Brace.

SNOW, C. E., and C. A. FERGUSON (eds.). 1977. *Talking to Children: Language Input and Acquisition.* Cambridge, England: Cambridge University Press.

SNOW, R. 1969. Unfinished Pygmalion, *Contemporary Psychology, 14*: 197–99.

SZUCKO, J. J., and B. KLEINMUNTZ. 1981. Statistical versus clinical lie detection, *American Psychologist, 36*: 488.

TERRACE, H. S. 1979. *Nim.* New York: Knopf.

TERRACE, H.; L. PETITTO; and T. BEVER. 1976a. *Project Nim: Progress Report I.* Distributed by Columbia University Psychology Department.

——. 1976b. *Project Nim: Progress Report II.* Distributed by Columbia University Psychology Department.

TERRACE, H. S.; L. A. PETITTO; R. J. SANDERS; and T. G. BEVER. 1979. Can an ape create a sentence? *Science, 206*: 891–902.

THORNDIKE, R. L. 1968. Review of R. Rosenthal and L. Jacobson, *Pygmalion in the Classroom, Educational Research Journal, 5*: 708–11.

TOBIAS, P. V. 1981. The emergence of man in Africa and beyond, *Philosophical Transactions of Royal Society London B292*: 43–56.

TOLBERT, M. K. 1978. The acquisition of grammatical morphemes: A cross-linguistic study with reference to Mayan (Cakchiquel) and Spanish. Unpublished doctoral thesis, Harvard University.

TOMKINS, S. S. 1982. Affect theory. In P. Ekman (ed.), *Emotion in the Human Face.* 2d ed. Cambridge, England: Cambridge University Press, pp. 353–95.

——. 1984. Affect theory. In K. R. Scherer and P. Ekman (eds.), *Approaches to Emotion.* Hillsdale, N.J.: Erlbaum, pp. 163–95.

VAN CANTFORT, T. E., and J. B. RIMPAU. 1982. Sign language studies with children and chimpanzees, *Sign Language Studies, 34*: 15–72.

WEST, LAMONT. 1960. The sign language: An analysis. Unpublished doctoral dissertation, Indiana University.

WHITE, T. D.; D. C. JOHANSON; and W. H. KIMBEL. 1981. *Australopithecus afarensis*: Its phyletic position reconsidered, *South African Journal of Science, 77*: 445–70.

WHORF, B. L. 1956. *Language, Thought and Reality: Selected Writings of Benjamin Lee Whorf.* T. B. Carroll (ed.). Cambridge, Mass.: MIT Press and New York: Wiley.

WILSON, E. O. 1975. *Sociobiology: The New Synthesis.* Cambridge, Mass.: Harvard University Press.

WILSON, T. 1553. *Arte and Rhetorique.* Gainesville: Scholars Facsimiles and Reprints.

WITTGENSTEIN, L. 1953. *Philosophical Investigations.* New York: Macmillan.

ZAJONC, R. B. 1980. Feeling and thinking: Preferences need no inferences, *American Psychologist,* 35: 151–75.

——. 1984. On primacy of affect. In K. R. Scherer and P. Ekman (eds.), *Approaches to Emotion.* Hillsdale, N.J.: Erlbaum, pp. 259–70.

ZUCKERMAN, M.; R. S. DeFRANK; J. A. HALL; D. T. LARRANCE; and R. ROSENTHAL. 1979. Facial and vocal cues of deception and honesty, *Journal of Experimental Social Psychology,* 15: 378–96.

ZUCKERMAN, M.; R. S. DeFRANK; J. A. HALL; and R. ROSENTHAL. 1978. Accuracy of nonverbal communication as determinant of interpersonal expectancy effects, *Environmental Psychology and Nonverbal Behavior,* 2: 206–14.

ZUCKERMAN, M.; B. DePAULO; and R. ROSENTHAL. 1981. Verbal and nonverbal communication of deception. In L. Berkowitz (ed.), *Advances in Experimental Social Psychology.* New York: Academic Press, 14: 1–59.

spent in cooperative activities: hiking, pitching tents, making meals, a treasure hunt. In each group an overall leader emerged as well as a fairly stable status hierarchy. The two groups developed distinct culture-defining norms. In one group a norm of being "tough" and not complaining about slight injuries became so strong that the counselors had to take care that several who had bad bruises should not stoically go forward with every activity. In that same group cursing a lot became the thing to do. In the other group it became the norm to swim nude and, after two boys withdrew because of bad homesickness, any expression of homesickness became taboo. At the end of the week the boys got unmarked caps and T-shirts. The tough and cussing bunch stenciled the name "Rattlers" and a snake on theirs; the others called themselves the "Eagles."

Near the end of the week the Rattlers and the Eagles were allowed to become aware of one another's existence, seeing paper cups where they had left none and hearing distant voices. The in-group, out-group language of *us* and *them* promptly developed. "They better not be in our swimming hole." "Those guys were using our diamond again."

Stage II, five days long, was initiated with the announcement that there was to be a grand tournament between the Rattlers and the Eagles. There would be ten sports events including baseball, touch football, and tug-of-war. In addition counselors would inspect the two cabins and award points for cleanliness and neatness, and counselors would judge performance competitions involving skits and songs. The category of "counselor-judged" events was included so that team scores could be juggled as necessary to keep the Rattlers and the Eagles in neck-to-neck competition to the very end. There was a splendid trophy to be awarded the winning team and eleven medals and eleven four-bladed knives for individual members of the winning team. The teams inspected the prizes and found them very desirable. Because the Eagles had lost two members through homesickness the rule was made that the Rattlers must exclude two members for certain events (e.g. tug-of-war). Beginning with the second day the teams were to take their meals together in one mess hall, and points earned for the day would be added to two giant thermometers registering competitive progress.

The best name for the independent variable introduced in Stage II is "competition," and it is necessary to say something about how competition relates to the unfair distribution of resources. The resources or rewards are the trophy, medals, and knives, which are in short supply, deliberately so, and will all go to the winning team. When that distribution shall have been made, we may count on it that the losing team will find the outcome unfair, because they think better of themselves than they do of the out-group and because, as it turns out, the teams do not stick to the rules but in many ways go outside the bounds of sports competition. The suggestion I want to make is that the creation of competition that is not constrained by rules that all accept promises to produce a distribution of rewards that is perceived as unjust. A competition of that sort

VI

Ethnic Conflict

"W HENEVER individuals belonging to one group interact, collectively or individually, with another group or its members in terms of their group identification, we have an instance of intergroup behavior" (Sherif, 1966, p. 12). There may be only two parties to an interaction, but so long as the individual does not act, and is not reacted to, *as an individual* but as a group member, it is group interaction. The Pakistani immigrant inquiring about a room in Kensington Gardens, London, who is told falsely that the vacancy has been filled is not treated so because he is a certain medical student, slightly built, bright, but not very well prepared for his studies. He is reacted to as a black by a white.

Conflict between groups is like a sturdy three-legged stool. It is sturdy because two legs are universal ineradicable psychological processes, ethnocentrism and stereotyping, and the third leg is a state of society, unfair distribution of resources, which has always existed everywhere. For theoretical reasons, therefore, it ought to be extremely difficult to reduce group conflict, and that it certainly is.

Ethnocentrism was defined by William Graham Sumner in his book *Folkways* (1906) as "the technical name for the view of things in which one's own group is the center of everything. . . . Each group nourishes its own pride and vanity, boasts itself superior . . . and looks with contempt on outsiders" (p. 12). Sumner provided abundant ethnographic examples of in-group preference and out-group derogation, and Brewer (1979a, 1979b) carried out a worldwide survey of ethnocentrism, starting with twenty field sites ranging from Northern

Canada to the South Pacific to West Africa. The people in those sites were, by definition, the in-group, and informants were interviewed to obtain attitudes toward the in-groups and attitudes toward fifteen out-groups. On the average the ratings of trait attributions to in-group members were positive, and significantly more so than average ratings of out-group attributions, for each trait dimension. It is not just the seeming universality of ethnocentrism that makes us think it ineradicable but rather that it has been traced to its source in individual psychology (Tajfel, 1981; Tajfel and Turner, 1979), and the source is the individual effort to achieve and maintain positive self-esteem. That is an urge so deeply human that we can hardly imagine its absence.

Ethnocentrism alone, that is thinking more highly of the in-group than of an out-group, is not sufficient to bring about hostile action between groups. In addition it is necessary that groups be similar enough so that they compare their outcomes, the distribution of rewards and costs, and find that it is unfair or inequitable. *Unfair* or unjust disadvantage or frustration is the sovereign cause of anger and aggression. Disadvantage or frustration will not alone do it; perceived injustice is critical. Since good things and bad things are never distributed equally, the perception of injustice is pretty well guaranteed for any groups that compare their outcomes. Ethnocentrism is just the turn of the screw that guarantees that both parties to a social comparison will feel unfairly treated. In being ethnocentric each group sets a higher value on its own assets or investments than it does on the assets or investments of the other (see Chapter 2). The result must be that even complete equality of outcomes, complete even-handedness, will be perceived as unfair disadvantage—by both groups.

Stereotypes go beyond ethnocentrism in that they are not simply expressions of in-group preference but qualitatively distinct character profiles attributed to in-groups and out-groups. Because of ethnocentrism, in-group profiles are generally going to be more favorable than out-group profiles. Like ethnocentrism, stereotypes are not the cause of group hostilities. They serve primarily to justify and explain, with cartoonlike simplicity, hostilities that derive from conflicts of interest leading to unjust outcomes. To some extent national and ethnic stereotypes are *responsive* to changing policies, to new alliances and new enemies. To some extent, however, stereotypes manifest inertia and once in existence have effects of their own on social behavior.

Ethnocentrism, perceived injustice of outcomes, and stereotypes converge not only in serious hostilities like wars, riots, and strikes but in competitive team sports. The difference is that team sports are conducted within a set of rules set by a superordinate authority. Those rules limit the expressions of hostility, and penalize those who go too far, and provide the possibility that this year's loser will be next year's winner. When we dream of international peace we dream of a supranational authority, the League of Nations or the United Nations, that will be able to make rules, set limits, and penalize violators. That is basically a dream of turning wars into games. Clearly, com-

petitive team sports do not serve the hydraulic function of draining energies that might go into serious conflict; there seems to be ample en both. Sport is not the "moral equivalent of war" in the sense that substitute for war, but it is the moral equivalent in the sense that it psychological equivalent conducted morally.

The Robbers Cave Experiment

Muzafer Sherif's Robbers Cave is the most successful field experiment eve ducted on intergroup conflict (Sherif et al, 1961). With eleven-year-old b summer camp at Robbers Cave, Oklahoma, real ethnocentrism, real s types, and real perceived injustice were all experimentally created, an result was truly hostile action that would have gone beyond the safe level researchers had not moved fast, like referees in a game, to control it. At no did the boys suspect that an experiment was in progress, so we are relieve this case of our usual worry that the results may have been artificial. hostility created at Robbers Cave was, in the last days of the study, success eliminated, but I will not describe that last stage until the start of Chapter

Twenty-two middle-class, white, Protestant, well-adjusted boys who doing average schoolwork constituted the final set of subjects. Initial proaches were to school authorities and then parents to whom the study described, accurately but not exhaustively, as a three-week summer camp perience to see how the boys would work together within teams and betwe teams, under adult supervision. There was a small fee and a stipulation that visits would be permitted during the three-week period, though of course bc who wanted to go home would be allowed to do so. It was essential that tl boys be mutually unacquainted, and that requirement together with all tho designed to guarantee a kind of "normality" meant that it was necessary begin with a pool of two hundred potential candidates to get a final twent two.

The campsite was a 200-acre, densely wooded area in Robbers Cave Stat Park. The boys were divided in advance into two groups of eleven each roughly matched in terms of sports ability, camp experience, and general popularity. One set of eleven was picked up by bus at two stops in Oklahoma City on June 19, and the second set on June 20. Each set was driven to a cabin with swimming, boating, and cooking facilities, but the two cabins were out of sight of each other. The data were collected by the method called "participant observation," which in this case meant that all researchers had roles in the camp life (mainly counselors). They took advantage of "rest times" during the day to scribble notes on everything that happened and each evening wrote out a full account.

Stage I, about one week, was devoted to the creation of in-groups. For most of the week neither group knew of the existence of the other. The time was

can be thought of as the incipient stage in unfair distribution and so as a stimulus to anger and hostility.

At the start of the grand tourney between the Rattlers and the Eagles, the first baseball game, the norm of good sportsmanship that is supposed to control competitive team sports pretty well prevailed. The Eagles lost and were very dejected; one boy started to cry, and one said he thought the Rattlers were older and bigger. Then they spotted the Rattlers' flag flying from the backstop. They seized it, burned it, and hung up the scorched remnant. Their leader said: "You can tell those guys I did it if they say anything. I'll fight 'em" (Sherif et al., 1961, p. 104).

Next morning when the Rattlers discovered the remnant of their flag they were furious. The plan was that the Rattler captain should go to the Eagles, ask if they had burned the flag, and if they admitted it, as expected, he would begin fighting and the others would join in. All this came to pass, and the counselors had to break up the fight. The Eagles won the next ballgame and, much elated, attributed their victory to the prayer they had said before the game and to the fact that the Rattlers were such "bad cussers." They concluded that they should not even talk to the Rattlers any more if they could help it.

After that the war between the Rattlers and the Eagles becomes a little hard to keep track of. I think of scattered skirmishes between the Blue and the Gray, with a puff of smoke on one hill and the rattle of musketry on another, though of course they had no firearms and the research team somehow managed to bring them back repeatedly to the events of the tournament. In the tug-of-war the Eagles used the strategy of sitting down and digging in their feet. The Rattlers thought that was completely unfair, so that night, when the Eagles were asleep, made a commando raid on their cabin, overturning beds and ripping mosquito netting. The following day, while the Rattlers were in the mess hall, the Eagles, armed with sticks and bats, made a retaliatory raid and then returned to their own cabin, where they entrenched themselves with new weapons—rocks in socks. The counselors hastily intervened.

In the end, with a little undetected connivance by the counselors, the Eagles won the tournament. They gave the trophy to the staff for safekeeping and went off for a celebratory swim. And the Rattlers? Did they accept their defeat like good sports? No, they raided the Eagles' cabin and stole the knives and medals, later telling them they could have them back if they got down on their bellies and crawled for them. As I have said, there was a Stage III in which all the antagonism was resolved, but I am postponing its description until the end of this section. Nobody got seriously hurt, the kids felt they had had the time of their lives, parents apparently found nothing extraordinary in the events recounted, and committees to review research with human subjects had not yet been invented.

In Stage II group hostility to the point of combat was experimentally created. The day following the end of the tournament the research team collected quantitative data, using clever cover stories, on just what had happened, and their data are just the facts needed to check on the three-legged stool theory. There was strong ethnocentrism or preference for the in-group and overevaluation of its products relative to the out-group. All members of the camp were asked to rate all others in terms of desirability as friends. Friendship preferences of this kind are called "sociometric ratings." The explicit ratings reflected the sharp cleavage expected: 93 percent of friendship preferences for both Rattlers and Eagles were in-group preferences. To assess evaluation of group products, a bean pickup game was devised in which each person was to pick up as many beans as he could in one minute's time from an assigned stretch of terrain. Afterward the teams guessed how many each individual had managed to pick up from an opaque projection on the wall of each individual's collection. In fact, just thirty-five beans were always projected, but Rattlers reported more for Rattlers and fewer for Eagles, whereas Eagles reversed the counts. Those guesses did not reflect the actual count but were a pure manifestation of in-group overevaluation. Besides those quantitative demonstrations of ethnocentrism there were countless qualitative observations. Perhaps the clearest evidence of out-group derogation is that the Rattlers and the Eagles held their noses when passing one another.

Stereotyping was assessed using the traits: brave, tough, friendly, sneaky, stinker, smart alecks. Those were traits suggested by spontaneous in-group pep talks and out-group insults. Rattlers thought all Rattlers were brave, tough, and friendly and that all, or almost all, Eagles were sneaky, stinkers, and smart alecks. The Eagles reciprocated in kind. There were also some stereotyped attributions unique to each group: Eagles thought Rattlers were "rotten cussers" and Rattlers thought Eagles were "crybabies."

The competition of the tournament threatened an unfair distribution of rewards (the prizes) in short supply. No outcome could have been perceived as fair; neither team could think the other deserved to win since its members were sneaky, stinkers, and smart alecks. The boys on each team had to think they deserved to win since they were brave, tough, and friendly. The researchers had been prepared to introduce some unfairness attributable to a team to be sure to get anger going, but that had proved not necessary. Each team saw the other as unfair from the start, and the raids, flag burnings, and fights were totally outside the frame of competitive sports. When the prizes were finally awarded to one team (the Eagles) the other (the Rattlers) thought the outcome unjust and proceeded to steal the prizes for themselves.

The Robbers Cave experiment is a rich example of all the factors involved in group hostilities: ethnocentrism, stereotyping, and unfair distribution of scarce resources. The findings have been confirmed by Blake and Mouton (1962, 1979) with groups of a very different kind: adults from industrial organizations meeting for two-week periods that began with a cooperative stage and moved on to competition. Blake and Mouton also succeeded in resolving the conflicts they created, using the techniques used for that purpose with the Rattlers and the Eagles. Now that we have seen everything happening at once, all three predisposing factors converging to produce hostile action between groups, we shall look at the factors one at a time in some depth: ethnocentrism and hostility in Chapter 15 and stereotypes in Chapter 16. Chapter 17 deals with conflict resolution.

15

Ethnocentrism and Hostility

THE POSITIVE HALF OF ETHNOCENTRISM is in-group pride, and there seems to be more of it, or perhaps only more advertisement of it, more vigorous affirmation of it, in the 1980s than ever before. Every sort of group is asserting its distinctiveness, even exaggerating its distinctiveness, and insisting that this distinctiveness be valued—valued first and most importantly by group members themselves. There is Black Pride in the United States, Brown Pride among the Maori (a Polynesian minority) in New Zealand, and Bantu Pride in South Africa. There is Deaf Pride and Gay Pride and Women's Liberation in many places. In Britain the people of Wales are trying to learn Welsh as they press toward nationalism and the Scots grow more Scottish while the Catholics in Northern Ireland are famous for being more Catholic than the Pope; the Protestants in the same area are just as extremely Protestant. In Quebec the Québecois, no longer content with official bilingualism, have passed a law making French the one "official" language in the province. In Israel a linguistic miracle has been performed and a previously dead language, Hebrew, revived to become the primary unifying tongue of 2 million people.

In-group pride and cultural assertion cannot be constrained to follow just the boundaries that those who helped to create them may have wished. Frantz Fanon (1967) worked to create a Black African identity but what has ensued is a host of national and even tribal identities. Muslims divide into Shi'ite and Suni varieties; Israelis into the Ashkenazic, the Sephardic, the Yemenite, and other varieties, and as for Christians the denominations and sects are almost beyond counting.

There is something paradoxical about in-group pride or cultural assertion. Many of the people who favor it in connection with one or another group will tell you that their ideal creed is: no discrimination by reason of race, color, sex, religion, or national origin. Surely there is a contradiction here, since every sort of cultural assertion, whether Black Pride, Gay Pride, Algerian Pride, or Mormon Pride, emphasizes and may exaggerate some sort of group difference. A certain kind of liberal will think that he has caught out groups that are too militant for his taste in an ideological inconsistency here. Even many of those who are in the forefront of cultural assertion do not seem to be quite clear about what it is *good for*, given that the ultimate goal is to eliminate unjust discrimination. Fanon (1967) is one leader who did know what group pride was good for, and so shall we by the end of this section.

It would be absurd to suggest that psychology can explain much about ethnocentrism in particular cases; economics, history, and investigative journalism will all have more to offer on the details. Still, I think there must be a psychological theory of ethnocentrism generally, and I have strong intuitions about what that theory should be like. It must, I think, start with motives deeply rooted in individual psychology, motives that are primitive and universal. The principal goal of the theory should be to explain why those motives sometimes give rise to individual behavior and sometimes to group behavior.

The only theory that satisfies my intuition is the theory of social identity developed between 1971 and 1981 by the late Henri Tajfel of the University of Bristol. While there is no doubt that Tajfel (1978, 1979, 1982a, 1982b) was the main architect of the theory, it is also very clearly a collective creation, and the creative collectivity is European social psychology. Elaborations, disagreements, and experimental tests have come from colleagues at Bristol, from all over Britain, from France and Switzerland, the Netherlands and Scandinavia, and elsewhere. A list of important contributors should certainly begin with John Turner and Michael Billig, who were close associates of Tajfel, but after identifying those two I do not know how to continue, except by citation of papers. Almost all of the papers first appeared in the *European Journal of Social Psychology*, which fact further identifies the theory of social identity, and its variants, as a European product. That adds credibility, in a way, because Europeans have plenty of experience of group conflict. Henri Tajfel himself belonged to the minority of European Jews who survived World War II. That minority came in "from very cold and very far" (Tajfel, 1981), and Tajfel never forgot the extremities that must ultimately be explained.

With an ultimate goal that includes the explanation of extreme violence it is odd that our starting point should be a very tepid, rather artificial laboratory demonstration—odd also that our method will be almost meditative: to hold up the demonstration in one light and another, to ponder it, to take it in, to apprehend its mystery.

The Minimal Group Experiment

Long before Tajfel began his work, Sherif in the Robbers Cave experiment, and others following his lead, had shown that it is possible to produce ethnocentrism and all the phenomena of group conflict by assigning unacquainted strangers to groups and putting those groups into competition. The American work stressed the importance of competition, and Donald Campbell (1965; Levine and Campbell, 1972) gave it the name "realistic group conflict theory." Certainly it had been established that objective group competition was a *sufficient* condition for the creation of ethnocentrism. The first question Tajfel asked was whether competition was a *necessary* condition, whether it was the minimal case.

In 1971 Tajfel and his co-workers made their first experimental approach and found an answer that was so nearly correct as to require only a minor emendation. Chapter 13 of the present book discusses at length the categories that human beings impose on the animal, vegetable, and artificial world but does not discuss at all the categories imposed by humans on humans. Between the categories for humans and nonhumans there are many similarities; all are natural categories organized as taxonomic hierarchies with basic object levels. There is, however, one important difference between the categories for humans and the categories for nonhumans. With respect to categories for humans, the categorizer himself will be either in or out of any given category, whereas the categorizer will always be outside the nonhuman categories. A great deal hinges on the in–out distinction.

Bristol schoolboys, fourteen or fifteen years old, were the subjects for Tajfel and his associates (1971). They were shown slide projections with varying numbers of dots on them, a fraction of a second each, and asked to estimate the number of dots seen. While one experimenter ostentatiously scored the responses, the boys were told that some people were chronic "overestimators" on the task and some chronic "underestimators." Neither underestimators nor overestimators were consistently more accurate: They were just two different response tendencies. There was a second task to be performed, and for purposes of convenience the boys would be divided into two groups for the task: the group of underestimators and the group of overestimators. In fact, group assignments were made at random, but the subjects could not know that. The task was to allocate points, as in a game, points exchangeable at the end for one-tenth of a penny each. No boy allocated points to himself but only to other individuals whose identity was always unknown but who were known to be members of either the group of underestimators or the group of overestimators. Each boy worked through a booklet or sets of points (exchangeable for pennies), worked on his own in a private cubicle, and was told before he started which group he himself was *in*. The basic result is in-group favoritism. The average number of points assigned by both underestimators and overestimators was much larger for the assigner's in-group, and almost every single boy showed this favoritism. In-group favoritism is a sign of preference for the in-group over the out-group, and so is a form of ethnocentrism, a form easily created in the laboratory with new groups having no history of antagonism. Afterward, as the boys emerged from their cubicles, each was asked, "Which were you?" and the answer was greeted with a mixture of cheers and catcalls.

While in-group favoritism in the distribution of pennies or points in a game has been the index of ethnocentrism most commonly used in minimal group experiments, other indices have also been used, and it is all the indices considered together that make it clear that a real in-group preference is established by categorization alone. In at least five studies (Brewer and Silver, 1978; Doise et al., 1972; Kahn and Ryen, 1972; Locksley, Ortiz, and Hepburn, 1980; Turner 1978) subjects have been asked to rate in-group and out-group on such evaluative scales as *likable–unlikable* and *fair–unfair*. The in-group has always been valued more highly. Tasks have been assigned to in-groups and out-groups (Ferguson and Kelley, 1964), and subjects have been asked to evaluate the products; they evaluate the work of the in-group more highly, just as the Rattlers and Eagles did in the bean pickup game. Ethnocentrism with real-life groups (e.g. Hindus and Moslems) involves not only in-group preference but an attributional bias comparable to the self-esteem bias on the individual level (Chapter 5): Good deeds are attributed to the in-group and bad to the out-group. Real ethnocentrism also biases memory so that the good actions of the in-group are better remembered than the bad and for the out-group the bad better remembered than the good. Howard and Rothbart (1980) have shown that the minimal group situation produces both the attributional and the memory bias. So it is real ethnocentrism that the minimal group produces.

The Bristol schoolboys who took part in the 1971 experiment were all acquainted in advance of the experiment and no doubt were linked in various ways on sports teams, as friends, as near-neighbors, and so on, but none of those advance meaningful functioning groups had any connection with the new imposed and arbitrary classification. As underestimators and overestimators the boys had no prior history. Furthermore, they had no knowledge of the membership of the new groups. Each one was told his own membership privately and given a code number, so that when points were allocated they were allocated to anonymous underestimators and over-estimators. There was no face-to-face interaction in the experiment; each boy worked alone. It was a truly Kafkaesque social system in which there was no meaning at all except the meaning the boys themselves imposed. What they imposed was ethnocentrism.

Just to be sure that nothing about the dot estimation task made it peculiarly liable to induce ethnocentrism, another task was used as the supposed basis for actually random groupings in a second 1971 experiment. Reproductions of paintings by either Klee or Kandinsky were projected in pairs, and subjects expressed a preference. All the paintings were abstract, and while the subjects knew that some were by Klee and some by Kandinsky (with the painters' names being written on the board) they didn't know which artist had produced any particular work. Subjects were then randomly assigned to a group of either Klee fanciers or Kandinsky fanciers, told their group membership, but not that it had been randomly determined, and given the point allocation task for individuals by group membership only. Both groups showed consistent in-group preference.

It might seem that a group membership, actually randomly determined but thought to be based either on a preference between two painters or a consistent tendency either to underestimate or to overestimate, would be as minimal a membership as imaginable, but it is not so. There are two grouping factors operating: (1) explicit group assignment by the experimenter; (2) the supposed similarity on which that grouping was said to be based. Those two factors were pulled apart by Billig and Tajfel (1973) and by Locksley, Ortiz, and Hepburn (1980). It is only mildly surprising that supposed similarity alone, with no talk about groups, can suggest groups and create in-group preference. What is very surprising is that when subjects were told that they were being assigned to groups on a purely random basis and shown that the toss of a coin or a ticket in a lottery determined group membership, and the names of the groups were obviously meaningless (the "A's" and the "B's" or the "Kappas" and the "Phis"), they still showed a full group preference effect. The ultimate minimal condition is assignment to a group—on a random basis.

What are we to make of the minimal group favoritism effect? What causes it? It was not, to begin with, in any way guaranteed by the nature of the task. The points did not have to be divided so as to advantage one group and disadvantage the other. When we look at the actual setup of the problems, we shall see that both groups might have been rewarded equally or both groups might have been rewarded in such a way as to extract from the experimenter the largest possible number of pennies to be divided among one's schoolfellows. Even though the standard setup, shortly to be described, does not compel discrimination but permits other principles to operate, one might think it suggests discrimination, because it does have a kind of forced-choice format, and so think the format responsible for the result. That notion can be discarded, however, because Locksley, Ortiz, and Hepburn (1980) in the United States created explicitly random minimal groups and gave each subject five piles of chips to be divided as he liked among anonymous members of the in-group and out-group, with no forced choice at all. The result was the usual: strong in-group favoritism.

What about other artifactual explanations? Might not the discrimination result be produced, for instance, because the experimenter expected it (Rosenthal, 1966)? Experimenter expectancy effect (discussed in Chapter 14) is unlikely, in the first place, because in-group favoritism was precisely not expected by Tajfel and co-workers in 1971. They created the minimal situation as a kind of baseline condition in which no group effects would occur, and the intention was to lay on additional group-forming properties until discrimination did occur but, as matters turned out, nothing additional was needed. Some of the later experiments on minimal categorization introduced one or another control to try to exclude expectancy, but it was left for St. Claire and Turner (1982) to deliver the *coup de grace* to expectancy. They had some subjects go through the usual minimal categorization procedure and others who went through it all, except that they themselves were not assigned to any group but were given the job of predicting how subjects who *were* assigned to groups, would divide the points. Actual group members showed in-group favoritism, but ungrouped predictors did not predict that outcome at all but thought group equality or fairness the likeliest outcome. So expectancy cannot be the cause.

Among artifactual explanations that leaves what Orne (1962) has called the "demand characteristics" of the situation. For instance, surely it is likely that when English schoolboys are divided into groups by an adult they will automatically interpret those groups as teams and think at once in terms of competition. Several things argue against that hypothesis. One is the St. Claire and Turner (1982) finding that schoolchildren in the role of predictors did not predict in-group favoritism, which is the only form competition could take. In addition, in that same experiment the real subjects, the grouped subjects, were asked if they had awarded the points in any special way, following any rule, and if so what rule? In fact they had followed the rule of in-group favoritism, but only four of twenty-three said that that was what they had done. Most thought they had followed no rule; some thought they had tried to be fair. So you see it is really a rather mysterious effect: a "pull" or force to favor the in-group, without usually even knowing you are doing it.

An explanation in terms of English schoolboy norms is finally improbable because of the fact that many kinds of subjects in several nations have shown the minimal group effect. They include adults in Cardiff, Wales (Branthwaite and Jones, 1975); women undergraduates in Santa Barbara, California (Brewer and Silver, 1978); men and women undergraduates in Oregon (Howard and Rothbart, 1980) and New York City (Locksley et al., 1980); college preparatory students (*collégiens*) and trade school students (*apprentis*) in Geneva, Switzerland (Doise and Sinclair, 1973); soldiers in the West German army (Dann and Doise, 1974); and Maori children in New Zealand (Vaughan, 1977).

The problem of point allocation, as it was presented, did not by virtue of its format favor discrimination over generosity or even-handedness or any of several other possibilities. To appreciate that, we must sample the problems. Table 15-1 presents the simplest sort of penny payoff matrix in which three strategies are possible: in-group favoritism, fairness, or generosity. The subject reads that he must choose one from among fourteen payoff boxes such that a given number of points will be given to an anonymous member of the Klee group (let that be his in-group) when a given number of points is given to an unknown member of the Kandinsky group. The same matrix, the same fourteen sets of paired numbers, will appear twice in the text booklet, not close together, and with the rewards of the in-group and out-group reversed. As

TABLE 15–1. Payoff Matrices Permitting In-Group Favoritism, Fairness or Generosity

These numbers are rewards for:
Member No. 74 of Klee group
Member No. 44 of Kandinsky group
   Please select one box:

1	2	3	4	5	6	7	8	9	10	11	12	13	14
14	13	12	11	10	9	8	7	6	5	4	3	2	1

These numbers are rewards for:
Member No. 12 of Kandinsky group
Member No. 50 of Klee group
   Please select one box:

1	2	3	4	5	6	7	8	9	10	11	12	13	14
14	13	12	11	10	9	8	7	6	5	4	3	2	1

Maximal in-group favoritism for a member of the Klee group: $\dfrac{14}{1}$; $\dfrac{1}{14}$

Maximal fairness for a member of the Klee group: $\dfrac{7}{8}$; $\dfrac{8}{7}$

Maximal generosity for a member of the Klee group: $\dfrac{1}{14}$; $\dfrac{14}{1}$

SOURCE: Based on Tajfel et al. (1971), Table 2, p. 157.

Table 15-1 indicates, it is clear how to show maximal in-group favoritism and obtain a total of twenty-eight points for the Klees while yielding only two to the Kandinskys. It is equally clear how to be fair or even-handed, giving a total of fifteen points to each group, and also how to be maximally generous. A subject would seldom elect the extreme position of any of the three strategies, but the relative-pulls or strengths of the strategies could be determined from matrices like Table 15-1 and other less transparent matrices. The statistical methods for determining which strategies exerted significant pulls are too complicated to discuss here (see Bornstein et al., 1983a, 1983b, and Turner, 1983, for a thorough discussion).

Subjects were told that their choices would in no way affect the number of points they themselves received but that in the end they would be given the number of points allocated them by others. No one could know how others would act, and there seemed to be, and in fact was, nothing one could do to cause others to maximize one's own gain. As for norms or values, it is a good thing to be fair, we are told, and a good or better thing to be generous. What subjects dominantly were is *selfish* for the in-group. It is interesting that though that was the dominant strategy subjects afterward said it would be regarded as the socially undesirable thing to do. The fact that they knew this and yet chose the strategy is strong evidence that they were not doing what the experimenter expected or what the situation demanded.

The dominant strategy in the thirty or more experiments with the minimal group situation on matrices like Table 15-1 has been in-group favoritism but not all-out, unqualified in-group favoritism. The fairness principle has always also had a significant effect, mitigating favoritism. What has not appeared is generosity to the out-group.

Given the fact that the Bristol schoolboys in the first experiment were all acquaintances and the experimenter a stranger, and this has been true also in subsequent experiments, there is something like a rational strategy that each subject might pursue even in his ignorance of the membership in his group and the identities of particular individuals to whom points are assigned. That strategy cannot be realized in the matrices of Table 15-1, however, but requires a different sort of matrix, which was also included in the test booklet.

Since all subjects were acquainted beforehand with one another but not with the experimenter, it would be rational for subjects as a collectivity to try to extract as many points, ultimately pennies, as possible from the experimenter and work out an equitable distribution afterward. That strategy involves ignoring the imposed new groups and simply choosing the pair of points that comes to the greatest sum. In Table 15-2 that means choosing the rightmost box, totaling 44 points, more points than any other box, and doing so whether one is a Klee or a Kandinsky. The strategy is rational, of course, only if other subjects can be counted on to see the point and make the choice. Quite a few subjects did appreciate the rationality of a maximal joint outcome, and yet it never exerted a significant overall pull.

TABLE 15–2. Payoff Matrices Permitting Maximal Joint Profit and Maximal Group Difference

These numbers are rewards for:
Member No. 24 of Klee group
Member No. 44 of Kandinsky group
    Please select one box:

7	8	9	10	11	12	13	14	15	16	17	18	19
1	3	5	7	9	11	13	15	17	19	21	23	25

These numbers are rewards for:
Member No. 12 of Kandinsky group
Member No. 50 of Klee group
    Please select one box:

1	3	5	7	9	11	13	15	17	19	21	23	25
7	8	9	10	11	12	13	14	15	16	17	18	19

Maximal joint profit for a member of either group: $\dfrac{19}{25}$; $\dfrac{25}{19}$ or vice versa

Maximum in-group difference for a member of the Klee group: $\dfrac{7}{1}$; $\dfrac{1}{7}$

SOURCE: Based on Tajfel et al. (1971), Table 6, p. 164.

The leftmost box of Table 15-2 offers a very different prospect. The difference between 7 and 1 is the largest proportionate difference available in matrices of this type. Notice that the largest differential favoring the in-group is quite distinct from the largest total reward to the in-group. If the Klees just wanted as many pennies as they could get they ought to choose the rightmost box, because 19 points is the greatest number the matrix allows them. Of course in doing so they would earn fewer points than the Kandinskys, who would get 25 points each time the Klees got 19. One of the most consistent and psychologically telling results in all this research is the preference for a maximal in-group advantage over the out-group, even at the sacrifice of total in-group rewards. It is above all the social *comparisons* between the groups that matters to subjects.

This reminds me of a story about the great singer Maria Callas. Her single salary stipulation was, they say, that any opera house she sang in must pay her one dollar more than the next highest paid singer in the company. She was less interested, according to the story, in money as a medium of exchange than in money as a symbol—establishing her as what the Italians call "Prima Donna Assoluta." So are groups interested in the symbolic value of money and not just imposed minimal groups. Rupert Brown (1978) has shown that three groups of workers in a British aircraft factory—toolroom, development, and production workers—were at least as concerned about relative group wages as absolute wages, and we all know that for our own work groups.

The matrices we have seen in Tables 15-1 and 15-2 all require subjects to assign points simultaneously to an anonymous in-group member and an anonymous out-group member, with the numbers assigned to one always linked to numbers assigned the other. The minimal group experiment has typically included two other sorts of matrix. In one the subject must assign some number of points to one anonymous member of the in-group (e.g. a Klee) and, at the same time some number of points to a different anonymous member of the in-group (another Klee). That sort of matrix alone affords no possibility for expressing in-group favoritism, but that possibility arises when results for in-group/in-group matrices are compared with results for out-group/out-group matrices. In fact comparing those two kinds of matrix provides an alternative, rather less obvious, way of testing for in-group favoritism.

What subjects tend to do when both sets of points are going to the in-group is to select the largest total sums. In Table 15-2 they might pick the rightmost box, which delivers 44 points to the in-group as a whole. That is to say that they tend to favor the maximum joint profit for their own group. That is not what they do when both recipients are members of the out-group. In that case they favor smaller total sums and thereby indirectly, by means of a comparison of the two kinds of matrix, establish a relative advantage for the in-group. When all the variations of matrix are combined in one test booklet it is not always obvious to a subject what he is doing, but what he usually does is favor the in-group over the out-group both directly and indirectly, both absolutely and, most significantly, relatively.

The Theory of Social Identity

If in-group preference cannot be explained by experimenter expectancies or demand characteristics, and it cannot, what is the explanation? The fundamental claim made by Tajfel (1981) and by Tajfel and Turner (1979) is that when people are assigned to a group, any group, they immediately, automatically, and almost reflexively think of that group, an in-group for them, as better than the alternative, an out-group for them, and do so basically because they are motivated to achieve and maintain a positive self-image (see the self-esteem bias in Chapter 5). The self-image has two components: a personal identity and many social identities, as many as the groups with which the individual is identified. Identity is a concept no one has defined with precision, but it seems we can move ahead anyway, because everyone roughly understands what is meant. The theory of social identity (Tajfel, 1981; Tajfel and Turner, 1979; Turner, 1975) assumes that an individual can make an effort to improve his or her self-image either by trying to enhance personal identity or by trying to enhance social identity, and the theory undertakes to explain when the one sort of effort will be made and when the other.

If in-group preference or ethnocentrism raises the value of a social identity and ultimately of the self-image, then we have a partial answer to the question: What is cultural affirmation good for? It is good for the individual pride of all the persons whose culture is being affirmed. Fanon and many others who have exhorted their groups to be themselves, to be different, and to be proud of what they are have understood the benefit on the level of individual psychology that would result. That is the beginning of an answer to the paradoxical fact that people who oppose group discrimination of any kind sometimes favor group assertion. Such people sometimes explain the paradoxical combination by saying that group assertion or group pride is for some reason a necessary beginning. You have to have a Black Studies Program or a Women's Studies Program at first, but only for a while, it is sometimes said. But why only at first or only for a while? What is going to change that will make the assertion of the value of group distinctiveness less important?

It is premature to offer an answer at this point, but it would be frustrating to defer even an outline of it. A positive social identity in an underprivileged group, a minority pride, has the power to change the perception of justice. In equity theory (Chapter 2) as long as a group believes that its assets or investments (its identity) are less valuable than the assets (or identity) of a group with which it compares outcomes, then lower outcomes or disadvantages will be perceived as equitable, fair, or just. So long as women or blacks think they have less to offer, they will think they deserve what they get, which is less. Raising the value of social identity is a way of awakening a sense of injustice and so of unwillingness to submit to discrimination. It can be in the ultimate interest of nondiscrimination to insist on group distinctiveness and on the value of the distinctiveness. The sense of injustice awakened en route is the main stimulus in humans to anger and aggression. We shall come back to this subject.

Self-Image as Personal Identity Plus Social Identity

The central idea is that a positive self-image can be affected by social identity, so I think we had better establish the plausibility of that axiom before laying out the full theory in a systematic way. One experiment speaks very directly to this point. Oakes and Turner (1980) carried out the familiar Klees-and-Kandinskys paradigm and obtained the usual in-group favoritism, but in addition all experimental subjects described their current level of self-esteem on three different paper-and-pencil measures. Both the Klees and the Kandinskys had had a chance to achieve positive social identities, so their levels of self-esteem were compared not with one another but with control subjects, who had simply spent the time reading an irrelevant newspaper article. The members of the two minimal groups reported significantly higher levels of self-esteem than did the controls. Apparently the expression of a preference for the new in-group over the alternative out-group quite automatically boosted self-esteem.

An experiment by Turner (1978) shows that in the minimal group situation, when subjects have a chance to work very directly on the self-image by favoring themselves over anonymous members of either the in-group or the out-group, they will take the direct route. The design was ingenious but complex. Subjects did not allocate pennies (giving money to oneself rather than any other is all too easy to understand) but rather points in a game where the rule was "the more points the better." Subjects might have played the game as if it were a team game and divided all the points evenly among self and other members of the in-group, but they played it in a completely selfish way, given the chance to do so. Except—there is a qualification. Some subjects started out with matrices of the usual type that did not allow points to be assigned to the self but forced choices between anonymous in-group members and anonymous out-group members. Those subjects, in this condition, showed the usual in-group preference. They were then given the opportunity to award points to themselves or to in-group members or to out-group members. It was as if the prior in/out experience had created an identification with the in-group strong enough to curb complete selfishness, as if the self-image had come to be constituted of a social identity as well as a personal identity, because they assigned points to members of the in-group as well as the self. It is a long leap, unsupported by research, but think of black American singers like Stevie Wonder, Lena Horne, or Leontyne Price, who take every occasion of personal triumph to express their identification with blacks and pride in that social identity. The self-image can be enhanced in both ways at once, both individually and so-cially.

The two experiments make it plausible that social identities are a compo-nent of the self-image in the minimal group experiment, but anecdotes from life outside the laboratory will probably be more effective in starting a flow of rele-vant personal experiences. As a preliminary it must be said that the evaluation of both personal identity and social identities involves social comparison. In Leon Festinger's (1954) influential theory of social comparison the important point is made that comparisons are not made between incomparables but only between fairly similar cases. A teacher does not compare his or her knowledge with that of a pupil to evaluate professional competence but with a peer, and the Boston Celtics do not compare themselves with the Cambridge High basketball team but with other teams in the National Basketball Association, especially the Philadelphia 76ers and the Los Angeles Lakers.

In June of 1984 the Boston Celtics won the NBA title from the Los Angeles Lakers in a close game at the Boston Garden. The picture of Larry Bird (Figure 15-1) shows how the players felt: "Celts Supreme!" It was not just the players who felt supreme but all their fans. There was ecstasy in the North End. The fans burst out of the Garden and nearby bars, practically break dancing in the air, stogies lit, arms uplifted, voices screaming. The hood of a car was flattened, about thirty people jubilantly piled aboard, and the driver—a fan—smiled hap-pily. An improvised slow parade of honking cars circled through the neighborhood. It did not seem to me that those fans were just sympathizing or empathizing with their team. They personally were flying high. On that night each fan's self-esteem felt supreme; a social identity did a lot for many personal identities.

Notice that identification with a sports team has in it something of the ar-bitrariness of the minimal groups. To be a Celtics fan you need not be born in Boston or even live there, and the same is true of membership on the team. As individuals, or with other group memberships salient, both fans and team members might be very hostile. So long as the Celtic membership was salient, however, all rode the waves together. Minimal group favoritism is to be understood as a minimal and so rather pallid version of the same thing.

The Celtic celebration is a case of positive social identity contributing to positive self-identity, but there is also, of course, the possibility of negative social identity contributing to negative self-identity. We had such a case in 1984 in the much-publicized New Bedford gang rape that occurred in Big Dan's Bar. Of six defendants, four were found guilty. All six were immigrants from Por-tugal, members of the large Portuguese population of New Bedford, and seemed always to be identified as such in stories on the trial. Of course, other members of the group felt the impact of the negative social identity and seemed to feel it

Figure 15–1. Larry Bird celebrates the Celtics victory over Los Angeles in final game of the NBA Championship Series

(Courtesy *The Boston Globe*, June 13, 1984; photo by Stan Grossfeld)

very personally. When the guilty verdicts were brought in, Portuguese men tore out of the courthouse, wounded and enraged, and some pounded on the roofs of cars to express their frustration. Probably they would have done more had there not been many police present. They could hardly stay cool when their social identities had been so denigrated.

Tajfel and his associates have written only about social identities that involve *groups* outside the self, but I believe the process is exactly the same in cases of identification not with a group but with some single other person, especially that interesting, if somewhat abject, state in which someone becomes a "fan" of an actor, an athlete, or a singer. Objects of fanhood seem usually to be performing artists (or athletes) rather than creative artists like writers or composers. I

am not sure why that should be so, but perhaps it is because performers experience big highs and big lows in public rather than private, and riding that
roller coaster with them is the thrill of fanhood. Apparently not everyone is
susceptible—I have asked around—but teenagers certainly are, and I was when
young and have been again in recent years. For fans of Michael Jackson or
Frank Sinatra I have the impression that the collectivity is important, as it is
also for fans of sports teams, so those cases combine group identities with
fanhood. I have never been a groupie, I am the solitary fan type, like John Hin-
ckley only less extreme.

For most of my life I have enjoyed classical music, especially opera, but by
the age of fifty or so I had heard most of the works that really spoke to me so
often that they had become overfamiliar and a bit boring. Then I saw and
heard for the first time the beautiful Italian soprano Renata Scotto, beautiful of
voice but also of appearance, especially her face. I had heard and seen many
great singers but had never encountered any whose facial expressions and
movements seemed to me really to reflect the music and enhance its effect, and
I was thrilled. Happily for me, James Levine, the music director of the
Metropolitan Opera, was also much impressed and for some years the telecasts
"Live from the Met," beginning with the first (La Boheme with Scotto and
Pavarotti), included at least one a year with Renata Scotto in the soprano lead.
The televised closeups were even better than the stage performances; they
refreshed my interest in the whole repertoire of Italian opera, and I was grateful
and half in love.

I remained a psychologist and all the time bemusedly observed my
ridiculous state. The test of being a fan is very simple. Your own self-esteem
must rise and fall with the successes and failures of your object of admiration.
In addition, though you may be a solitary fan with no nearby like-minded
group, a fan cannot rest content with his private opinion but must try to convince others that his evaluation is objectively correct. That means he must
make propaganda to build a social consensus that will establish the reality he
believes in. And I did that—firing off letters (shameless abuse of the Harvard
letterhead) to educate critics who thought Renata Scotto's voice too light for
some role or her acting too mannered or her high notes increasingly shrill. I
even wrote James Levine a couple of times to assure him that he was right to
feature Miss Scotto in new productions, telecasts, and opening nights because
she just knew more about how Italian opera should go than any living singer. I
wrote because there were many signs of impending trouble. All the other
sopranos at the Met were said to be furiously jealous. Miss Scotto, after a career
of more than twenty years, was enlarging her repertoire to sing new, heavy
roles, and most people thought she was damaging her voice.

Renata Scotto is an artist of tremendous ambition. She is a diminutive
figure, not well suited in appearance to some of the greater tragic roles, and
when I heard her say to an interviewer that her hobby is collecting Napoleonic
memorabilia, I thought, "It figures." On the opening night of 1981 she was to

sing the role of *Norma* (with Placido Domingo, who I think was as impressed as myself and Mr. Levine). This is, to put it briefly, the most difficult role in Italian opera and the role most closely associated with Maria Callas. I knew there would be trouble, and there was. The soprano does not come on until about twenty-five minutes into the first act, and her entrance is very well prepared in both the drama and the music. She is the Druid high priestess and will first sing the beautiful invocation *Casta Diva*. There is a long hush; she stands in the moonlight, her arms raised high; the strings begin the rum-ti-tum simple background. And some execrable oaf shouted: "Viva Callas!"

I read about it in *The New York Times* the next day. There had been laughs and boos as well as some applause. The critic for the *Times*, a man of abysmal taste who had clearly been waiting his opportunity, ridiculed the performance. I wrote my first note to Renata Scotto, telling her how bad I felt about her experience and adding that I hoped she would have the courage to carry out her commitments—many *Normas* in New York and later on tour, plus other roles. She wrote back a note that made it clear that she was moved to learn that someone she had never met was so involved in her fortunes.

Well, Renata Scotto is not just ambitious; she is also very brave and a trouper. She met all her commitments that season and several seasons after, including a new production each year, always with James Levine conducting. The critics outnumber the admirers by far, and Mr. Levine has taken a lot of criticism for championing her. Ever since the *Norma* opening I have flown to New York for her opening night just to make sure there will be at least one supporter in the house. My self-esteem has suffered many painful bruises because of the identification with another person. There has been more pain than pleasure in the reviews of recent years. But once attached I have found myself not free to detach. Fans everywhere, whether of sports teams, singers, actors, or others, will know what I mean and will agree that it really is the self that rises and falls with a social identification.

Overview of the Theory

I have attempted a graphic representation (Figure 15–2) of the theory of social identity. Figure 15–2 is necessarily unintelligible at this point but will gradually become meaningful as its parts are explained, if you will continually consult the figure in connection with what now follows.

The principal axioms of the theory are, we know: (1) Individuals strive to achieve and maintain a positive self-image. (2) The self-image has two components, a personal identity and a social identity. In Figure 15–2 the self-image appears as the tall rectangle on the right, and arrows pointing in its direction are meant to represent efforts at achieving and maintaining positive evaluation. The two axioms and their representation in Figure 15–2 assert that any im-

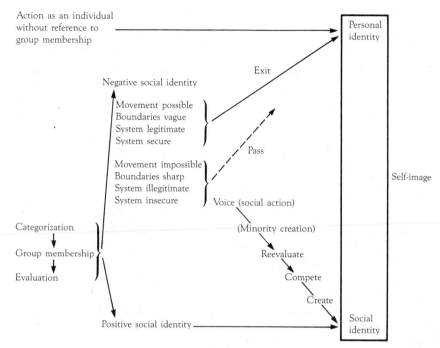

Figure 15–2. Graphic representation of the theory of social identity

provement in either personal identity or social identity will be experienced as an improvement of the self-image.

POSITIVE AND NEGATIVE SOCIAL IDENTITIES

In the lower-left section of Figure 15–2 we have "categorization → group membership → evaluation." That is meant to be a sequence of events in time, and the arrows represent temporal succession, not striving for positive self-esteem. The events are those of the minimal group experiment in which subjects are categorized by the experimenter and thereby made into members of one of two groups (the Klees or the Kandinskys) and then proceed to evaluate their groups by social comparison. In the experiment the evaluation is totally within the subject's control (allocation of points or attribution of traits) and both groups create positive social identities by some simple act of in-group preference. The sequence of events in the experiment is meant to model a sequence that occurs many times in the life of every individual, as many times as there are membership groups relevant to self-esteem and occasions for thinking about them.

Between the minimal groups of the experiment and the ethnocentrism of real-life groups are two fundamental differences. In the first place the many studies (e.g. Turner, 1978) that asked for ratings of in-group and out-group on traits such as likability always found that the out-group was rated as less likable but *never actually disliked*. In the entire body of work on the minimal group there is no evidence of *hostility* to the out-group but only mild derogation. Consequently the minimal group experiment, standing alone, cannot explain even the little wars of the Eagles and the Rattlers, let alone the great wars of nations, tribes, and races. Something must be added, namely perceived injustice, to generate hostility, and we shall return to this point.

The second difference between the minimal groups of the laboratory and real groups outside the laboratory is that members of randomly created groups—underestimators or overestimators, Klees or Kandinskys—are completely free to fix the value of their social identities as superior since all they have to do is think so. And that is what they always do. That is the invariable experimental finding: in-group preference or favoritism and out-group derogation. Minimal groups have no history, however, and exist outside of social systems. For real groups the case is otherwise, and the constraints under which real groups operate often make it difficult or impossible to believe in the superiority of one's own group.

Within a social system there may be a general consensus on the relative value of a group, a consensus involving many groups other than the one being evaluated. From attribution theory (Chapter 4) we know that a high social consensus defines social reality. As a result ethnocentrism is often reversed. Subordinate groups like black Americans, South African Bantus, the Mayans of Guatemala, and the lower castes of India either do, or until recently did, derogate or look down on the in-group and show positive attitudes toward the depriving out-group (Milner, 1975; Giles and Powesland, 1975). Probably serious groups are like minimal groups in that they strive to be ethnocentric, but they labor under handicaps unknown to the minimal groups. In a social vacuum thinking positive makes it so, but in life it is not so easy.

A single famous demonstration of in-group derogation and out-group elevation (Clark and Clark, 1947) will serve to fix in mind that sad condition. The subjects were black and white children, three to seven years old, living in interracial neighborhoods in either the Northern or Southern United States. The children were shown two dolls, one black ("colored" in 1947) and one white, and were asked:

1. Give me the doll that you want to play with.
2. Give me the doll that is a nice doll.
3. Give me the doll that looks bad.
4. Give me the doll that is a nice color.

The results appear in Table 15-3. Approximately 60 percent of the black children thought the nice doll, the doll that was the nice color, and the one they wanted to play with was white. The doll that looked bad to 59 percent of the black children was the black doll. Do not suppose that the children did not

TABLE 15-3. Racial Preferences in Doll Play of Black Children in Different Years

Item	Clark and Clark (1947)	Hraba and Grant (1970)
1. (Play with)		
White doll	67%	30%
Black doll	32%	70%
2. (Nice doll)		
White doll	59%	46%
Black doll	38%	58%
3. (Looks bad)		
White doll	17%	61%
Black doll	59%	36%
4. (Nice color)		
White doll	60%	31%
Black doll	38%	69%

SOURCE: Based on Hraba and Grant (1970), Table 1.

know they themselves were black; the experiment demonstrated that they knew. This is the reverse of ethnocentrism; this is in-group derogation and out-group elevation, and there are many similar demonstrations for other subordinate groups (Milner, 1975; Giles and Powesland, 1976).

However, much research since about 1970 indicates that things have changed, and all over the world subordinate groups that once derogated themselves do so no longer. There is evidence on Americans (Brigham, 1971b; Ward and Braun, 1972; Hraba and Grant, 1970; Paige, 1970; Patchen, Hofmann, and Davidson, 1976), French Canadians (Berry, Kalin, and Taylor, 1977), New Zealand Maoris (Vaughan, 1978, 1978a), and the Welsh (Bourhis, Giles, and Tajfel, 1973; Giles and Powesland, 1976).

The historic change is dramatically manifest in a replication of the 1947 doll preference study reported in 1970 by Hraba and Grant. The new percentages appear in Table 15-3. Approximately 60 percent of the black children preferred the black doll. That is ethnocentrism restored. The title of the 1970 article: "Black is Beautiful."

The black pride result in doll preference found by Hraba and Grant in 1970 in Lincoln, Nebraska, has not been found everywhere in the United States ever since 1970. In Boston, for instance, Porter in 1971 found that black children manifested primarily white preference, and in 1985 Jenkins found the same. Brand, Ruiz, and Padilla (1974), surveying all doll studies to date, found that since about 1970 both sorts of preference had been found with the probable determining factors including the proportionate size of the black population and the vigor of the local black pride movement. The historical change is that until 1970 no studies at all found black preference in American children whereas that result has been often reported since. In 1980 in *Ebony* magazine Clark and Clark reported that 90 percent of black Americans thought blacks had become prouder of their race since the 1950s. The result in the doll preference studies that is most directly relevant to social identity theory is the occasional finding (Jenkins, 1985; Ward and Braun, 1972) that those black children who show black doll preference had higher self-esteem than those who showed white preference. This relationship is predicted by social identity theory, but the finding, being only correlational, does not prove the theory.

In New Zealand about 10 percent of the population nowadays call themselves "brown"; they are the Maori, an indigenous Polynesian group. Graham Vaughan (1978a, 1978b) of the University of Auckland carried out doll-preference studies with more than 1,400 Maori children from the early 1960s to the early 1970s. He found that just as the Maori people had coined the slogan "Brown Power" by analogy with "Black Power" in the United States, so had the Maori children changed their preferences in a decade from the out-group to the in-group.

The historical change in Maori children and in black American children is important in several ways for the theory of social identity, but at this point it serves merely as a strong example of the fact that the evaluation process in Figure 15-2 can have a negative (or neutral or ambiguous) outcome and need not lead, as it always does in the social vacuum of the experiment, to a positive social identity. Positive social identities are those that result from membership in dominant groups—familial, national, racial, or sexual—groups that are compared favorably with contrast groups, not just by themselves but by a majority. Positive social identities influence self-esteem (see Figure 15-2), and that is about all there is to say about them. The negative social identity is the interesting one.

OUTCOMES OF A NEGATIVE SOCIAL IDENTITY

A negative social identity can have any of three outcomes that will serve the maintenance of positive self-esteem. Two of the outcomes are directed at a positive personal identity: "exit" and "pass." Exit means moving out of the group that creates a negative social identity for you and is most clearly manifest in the improved social mobility, movement from the lower classes, that occurs in open societies like Britain, France, West Germany, the United States, Australia, and others. Exit is *real* movement out of a group and so is available as an alternative only where movement is possible. To pass is not the same as exit. It is to be thought a member of a higher group while privately thinking oneself a member of a lower group: to pass as Aryan in Nazi Germany while believing oneself Jewish; to pass as heterosexual while thinking oneself homosexual; to pass as white in the United States while believing oneself to be black.

The great alternative to exit and pass, which are both individual strategies for dealing with a negative social identity, is *social* action, called "voice" by Tajfel, which is aimed at the elevation of the group and so of the social identity. The terms "exit" and "voice" were used originally in economics (Hirschman, 1972) to name alternative reactions to decline in either a business organization or a nation.

While exit, pass, and voice are the only arrows issuing from a negative social identity, in Figure 15-2 they do not exhaust the possible reactions to negative social identity. They exhaust the *positive* reactions, the efforts to act so as to achieve and maintain self-esteem. The alternative to all three is stagnant acceptance of the negative social identity. That was the 1947 reaction of the black American children and of Maori children: assigning higher value to the out-group. It was for centuries the reaction of subordinate groups in feudal Europe, caste-governed India, South Africa, and the United States.

Four variables are thought to determine positive reactions to negative social identity: the possibility or not of personal movement, the sharpness of boundary definition, the perceived legitimacy of the system, and the perceived security of the system. Those variables are the heart of the theory, since they are used to explain the choice between the two kinds of reaction to a negative social identity: individual movement out (exit) or social action to raise the value of the group identity (voice). We shall consider one variable at a time and illustrate its operation.

The possibility of moving from one group to another in the minimal group experiment does not even come to mind, because there is no reason to move when you can make your group better than the other by thinking it is. In life one can resign from a stupid committee or move from a bad neighborhood and, possibly but not so easily, leave a failing or dishonest business, move from a declining city, or shift allegiance when your basketball team or political party or opera singer begins to disappoint. But the group memberships called race, nationality, sex, religion, and sexual orientation pretty much exclude the possibility of real movement (though perhaps not passing) and so voice, or social action to raise the value of the group, is a likely response if other necessary conditions are realized. Movement may, incidentally, *seem* more possible in the case of a social identity such as religion or nationality than it really is. Among the real obstacles to movement must be included the psychological inability to violate values central to self-respect. Not everyone is psychologically capable of being a "*renegade.*"

Group membership is clearly defined in the experimental paradigm, but some real-life memberships are vaguely defined. The Jew who is an atheist and has no strong family ties is Jewish only if he and others think he is. The person with bisexual interests is either gay or straight as he and others decide. The "colored" person who could pass as white if he or she chose has an option. Insofar as definitions of negative identities are fuzzy, individual action (exit or pass) is possible, but insofar as the definitions are sharp the only way to raise up the self is to raise up evaluation of the group.

A set of social arrangements is legitimate where it is in accordance with values accepted by all concerned. If the citizens of a country agree that those who are to exercise power are to be selected by a given process (whether democratic voting or "legitimate" family succession), then those selected will govern with the consent of the governed. So long as *slavery* and *apartheid* and *segregation* and *caste* were perceived as legitimate, there was little action on behalf of the group, though some individual efforts were made to enhance personal identity. When arrangements are shown to be inconsistent with general values, and so illegitimate, efforts to enhance social identity begin.

The security of a social system has two aspects. One concerns power. Concentration of military power in a dominant group can totally discourage group action. The Jews under Nazi domination mobilized very little collective resistance. There were revolts in Treblinka and other death camps, but for the most part individuals only hoped to escape the worst—as individuals, by getting out or passing—because they judged that the military power arrayed against them was invulnerable. Most Czechs today do not think there will ever be another "Prague spring," and Hungarians do not expect to rise up again. The system seems militarily totally secure. In South Africa the Afrikaans minority has been able to dominate the black majority because they have all the wealth and military power.

There is another sense of security in Tajfel's theory, a psychological, more interesting sense. A dominant group is secure when a subordinate group cannot imagine things otherwise arranged, when the subordinate group lacks "cognitive alternatives" (Turner and Brown, 1981). How are cognitive alternatives created? Initially by imaginative, utopian thinkers who can conceive of them and try to persuade others that they are possible. But real alternatives, things that *can* happen, are best created by the power of example. We have seen what the example of Black Pride and Black Power did for the Maori, but it worked also for feminists, Hispanic Americans, Native Americans, gay men, and lesbians in this country to create cognitive alternatives. And before Black Power in America there was black nationalism in Africa, and Frantz Fanon (1967) who helped create it, knew what the power of even a single successful example would be: "The Algerian people knows that the people south of the Sahara are watching the struggle against French colonialism. The Algerian people is quite aware of the fact that every blow struck against French oppression in Algeria dismantles the colonialist power" (p. 105).

Tajfel identified the factors that favored voice (or social action) as a reaction to negative social identity: Personal movement is impossible, group definitions are sharp, the dominant power is perceived as illegitimate, the dominant power is somewhat insecure. So far as I have discovered, Tajfel did not offer an explanation for the tremendous upsurge of voice, of cultural assertion, in our time. I do think there is an upsurge, greater than any in prior history, of affirmation of group distinctiveness and insistence on being valued as distinct. Assimilation is not a popular idea nowadays. I think the main factor accounting for the upsurge is the creation of cognitive alternatives—by *example*. That suggestion cannot explain how the first successful examples came to succeed, but perhaps the rate of successful "firsts" has not been higher in recent years than at other times. What is definitely higher is the rate and completeness of diffusion of information. Through the media a successful cultural affirmation in one part of the world rapidly becomes known in all parts of the world, except where a canny tyranny controls the diffusion of information.

MINORITY INFLUENCE

Tajfel (1981) makes a very good distinction in his discussion of voice between a minority that is only numerical and a minority that is psychological. A psychological minority is a segment of society that feels bound together by common traits that are held in low esteem. The creation of a psychological or self-conscious minority is the first task of voice. In the extreme case of South Africa the self-conscious, dominated "minority" is actually a *numerical* majority. In the United States red-haired persons and left-handed persons are numerical but not psychological minorities.

Why do not the conformity pressures exerted by numerical majorities bring all dissident minorities, especially those lacking power and prestige, into line? In Chapter 1 I reviewed Asch's studies (1951) demonstrating that even clear perceptual judgments of the length of lines are influenced by a majority of confederates reporting falsely. People look to the majority, especially a high-status majority, to define what is correct and true (Jones and Gerard, 1977) and strongly tend to conform to that standard. Conformity is so strong a force that one must ask how it is ever possible for the *status quo* to change, and yet we know that it does change. Furthermore, profound change on a world scale has sometimes resulted from the efforts of a small minority or even one person: Newton, Pasteur, Jesus.

In recent years we have had experimental demonstrations, beginning with the work of Serge Moscovici and his colleagues at the University of Paris, that minorities can also exert social influence. There are excellent recent summaries of work on minority influence by Moscovici (1980), Nemeth (1979), and Nemeth and Wachtler (1983). Several general propositions are well established. Majority influence of the kind Asch used affects response at the public level, which we call *compliance*, but often leaves response at the private level, which we call, following Moscovici (1980), *conversion*, unaffected. Asch (1951) and also Allen (1965) found that while many subjects could be brought to make the same reports as a falsely reporting majority—to comply, in short—their minds had not been changed by the majority, and they would so report afterward in private; no *conversion* had occurred. By contrast, when a minority has any effect on public response, it also usually changes private opinion (Moscovici, 1976;

Nemeth and Wachtler, 1974; Moscovici and Lage, 1976). Furthermore a minority may influence private belief—may produce conversion—when there is little or no public compliance (Moscovici, Lage, and Naffrechoux, 1969; Moscovici and Lage, 1976; Moscovici and Personnaz, 1980; Mugny, 1974–75, 1975; Nemeth and Wachtler, 1974, 1983; Personnaz, 1981).

A numerical minority with a negative social identity that undertakes to improve that identity (blacks or gay persons) must first of all convince its own members and become what Tajfel calls a psychological minority. It must work at internal consistency first, not just because that is good for the self-esteem of the individual members but also because minority consistency is a prerequisite to the exertion of influence on out-groups. A numerical minority must in the end, however, seek to convert nonmembers, because a favorable social evaluation that is limited to the in-group and denied by out-groups is like a flicker of flame in danger of being snuffed out. There are two kinds of outsiders to be concerned with: the dominant majority that denies the affirmative claims of the minority and all the comparatively unconcerned independents. Research shows that both sorts of outsider can be influenced by a minority, but only by a minority that presents a solid front, a high internal consensus as well as consistency over time (Moscovici and Lage, 1976; Nemeth and Wachtler, 1974; Nemeth, Swedlund, and Kanki, 1974). Why should high consensus and consistency in the minority be prerequisite to successful influence?

In attribution theory (Part II) actions on which there is a high consensus and high consistency are likely to be attributed to a reality external to the actors. A minority that consensually and consistently asserts its own value is likely to be presumed to know such a reality. It will give the appearance of having the correct answer. In a way that kind of minority will operate like the one just juror, the Henry Fonda figure in *Twelve Angry Men* (Chapter 6). The just juror was consistent and uncompromising and radiated confidence because he had the right answer, both intellectually and morally. There is no intellectual right answer in conflicts between groups, no right answer of the sort involved in a legal case, but a minority in order to influence outcomes must give the impression that there is. Numerous experiments have shown that an inconsistent minority is perceived as incompetent or inaccurate, whereas a consistent minority is perceived as confident (Moscovici and Faucheux, 1972; Nemeth and Wachtler, 1974; Nemeth, Swedlund, and Kanki, 1974). Confidence is a powerful persuader, because it suggests knowledge of the right answer (see Chapter 7).

Most of the work on minority influence has involved either perceptual judgments or else jury decisions rather than minority affirmation, but a study by Maass and Clark (1983) is the exception; it deals with the issue of gay rights and was inspired by the Trask–Bush Amendment in the state of Florida. The amendment mandated the withdrawal of all public funds from institutions that provide facilities for groups advocating extramarital sex. The gay liberation movement must, as marriage is defined in present laws, approve of sex outside marriage. The Trask–Bush Amendment was interpreted as an indirect assault on that movement. The amendment has, incidentally, been declared unconstitutional by the Florida Supreme Court.

The experiment was done twice, once with only female undergraduates and once with both males and females. Some hundreds of students answered a set of questions in the area of gay rights, including job protection, homosexual marriages, and rights of child adoption. The answers reduced to a seven-point scale where 7 represented a strong "con" position and 1 a strong "pro" position. From the total set of responses approximately four hundred persons who scored as moderate, or close to 4 on the scale, were selected to be subjects.

The majorities and minorities to which subjects were exposed were entirely on paper. A subject read a purported summary of a sixty-minute group discussion of gay rights held by five undergraduates like themselves. In all cases a majority of four members of the imaginary group favored one position and a minority of one consistently favored the opposite position. The same number of arguments, eight, was always put forward by both the majority and the minority. The independent variable was the position espoused by each; for some subjects the majority was pro gay rights and the minority con; for others the situation was reversed, with the majority con and the minority pro. The dependent variable of interest was public expression, or compliance, versus private expression or conversion.

The results showed substantial public compliance with the majority view, whether pro or con, and that is a pure conformity effect. The results also showed that private confidential beliefs actually shifted away from the majority (whether pro or con) in the direction of the minority. Exactly how those processes work is not known. Latané and Wolf (1981) argue that Social Impact Theory (Chapter 1) can explain influence by both majorities and minorities, but they admit that it cannot explain the difference between private expression and public expression. Moscovici (1980) argues that majority opinion does not inspire much thought but simply a compliant response, whereas minority ideas, consistently put forward, cause people to think more deeply about the ideas involved.

The creation of a true psychological minority is the first step in an effective reaction to a negative social identity. The next step is to work at making the identity positive, the reaction called "voice." What are the ways in which it can work? Tajfel and his associates have identified three, and they appear in Figure 15-2 as a succession of arrows aimed at raising social identity. The first is the most important: the reevaluation in a positive direction of attributes the group undoubtedly has. A distinctive appearance and a distinctive language are the two attributes most central to social identities. How do people go about raising the value of the way a group looks and talks? It clearly begins in the mind of the individual member who must think positively about his own group's attributes and cease to acknowledge superiority in the dominant group. Striking examples of good looks from within the group may help. A broader historical and geographic perspective on beauty can help. For language pride linguistic science has been invaluable, because it strikes down the claims to intrinsic superiority of languages that happen to be used by dominant groups. Above all, reevaluation of group traits requires propaganda. If enough people say that a certain kind of appearance is good, or a certain language, then they are good, because the only reality is social.

The second way to push a social identity higher is by way of direct competition. Political competition is the most effective but is not always possible. Individual competition in athletics, art, science, and beauty helps with social identity only if the individuals who compete successfully assert their solidarity with the group; if they do not, then they are just "exiting" as individuals. The third way to advance social identity is the most unusual: the invention of new attributes for the group, attributes that will be positively valued.

This is the end of the explication of the theory of social identity as represented in Figure 15-2. What follows is a set of examples, brief case studies, of efforts to improve a social identity. Most of these efforts are of the positive reevaluation type. The examples do not add anything conceptual but simply illustrate what is meant by elevation of social identity.

Examples of Efforts to Raise the Value of Social Identities

The slogan "Black is Beautiful" has had some success in causing the reevaluation of black appearance. It has put a halt to extreme self-defeating efforts to bleach the skin and straighten the hair ("conking") on the part of blacks and has even resulted in occasional prideful exaggerations of difference (the Afro hairdo). Countless black public figures are thought of, by whites, as highly attractive: Grace Jones, Diana Ross, Eddie Murphy, Bill Cosby, Bryant Gumbel, and, in her own special majestic way, Jessye Norman. However, insofar as the attractiveness is acknowledged to be specifically sexual, attractive blacks have been largely limited to those who might pass as nicely tanned Caucasians such as Lena Horne, the 1984 Miss America, Michael Jackson, and so on. It as as though marginal cases, differing from the white ideal in only one or two features, were reevaluated first. There is more to sexual attraction than acknowledged beauty, however, and blacks in America have been sufficiently attractive over the centuries to produce a population in which just about every technical black has at least one white ancestor. Dominant groups always profess to find subordinate groups physically distasteful, but that is just a part of the policy of domination and not a fact about either sexual appeal or the distribution of beauty in races.

Language is the trickiest attribute to reevaluate in a productive way. So far as linguistic science is concerned all languages are of equal value in the sense that none has ever been shown to be better than any other as a vehicle for logical thought (Chapter 13), and yet in any multilanguage society the language, dialect, or accent of subordinate groups is likely to be held in lower esteem. The first, or native language, is the one in which one's personality and intellectual potential will be most fully and ideally expressed and so members of subordinate groups, the deaf who use the American Sign Language (ASL), the Québecois in Canada, and black Americans who use the Black English Vernacular, are likely to challenge the necessity of becoming bilingual. It is possible, however, to be self-defeatingly "militant" about a minority language. The best antidote I know to such militancy is the knowledge that in South Africa the ruling white minority encourages the learning of tribal languages and tribal languages only. Complete local self-determination in linguistic matters sounds like a good thing. The drawback is that the language of economic and social power is not any tribal language, it is Afrikaans.

The problem of the language of black Americans is a subtle one. Until the mid 1960s (Labov, 1966) it was not even clear that there was a problem peculiar to blacks. The usual assumption was that black Americans spoke the dialect of the region in which they grew up, the same dialect spoken by whites from that region. The present understanding (Labov, 1982), based on much linguistic research, a substantial part of it done by linguists who are black, is that the Black English Vernacular is a part of the English language that is distinct in significant respects from the standard English of the schools, business, government, and the professions. It is and has been used by about 80 percent of the black people in this country, from one coast to the other, largely in casual talk among themselves. Some educators, black and white, who were very militant about minority rights, fell into the South Africa trap and argued that the Black English Vernacular should be taught to black children in the public schools. When that view surfaced in Boston some years ago the parents of the children stopped it fast with the unanswerable argument: "We don't want them taught something they already know, something that won't help them to get ahead."

Teaching the Black English Vernacular in the schools is not the same as having the schools know about it and know what effects it can have on the work of black pupils. The issues came to a focus in the historic Black English trial in Ann Arbor, Michigan (Labov, 1982). In the 1960s the city of Ann Arbor (where the University of Michigan is located) built a low-income housing project, the Green Road project, in a middle-to-upper-class area, and some black children from that project went to the nearby Martin Luther King elementary school. About 80 percent of the children in the King school were white. After a number of years it became clear that many of the Green Road youngsters were not doing well in school. Some were labeled "mentally handicapped," some "learning disabled," some held back in grade, some passed on to junior high without basic reading and arithmetic skills. The mothers got together, enlisted the aid of a public interest law firm, and brought suit in Federal Court against the King School, the Ann Arbor School District, and the Michigan Board of Education.

The cause of legal action, which was accepted by the court, was that the school authorities had failed to take action to overcome language barriers and so were in violation of Title 20 of the U.S. Code, Section 1103(f), which reads in part:

> No state shall deny educational opportunity to an individual on account of his or her race, color, sex, or national origin by . . . (f) the failure by an educational agency to take appropriate action to overcome linguistic barriers that impede equal participation by its students in its instructional programs.

The plaintiffs called expert witnesses to testify on the nature of Black English Vernacular, including the noted sociolinguist William Labov. In making the case that the vernacular could impede a pupil's progress in school, the linguists took great care not to fall into the error of advocating the vernacular as the target of instruction, since that could only impede the social mobility of students. The case was that teachers ought to be able to identify students who used the vernacular and know enough about its structure to avoid errors in interpreting test scores. They ought also to know enough about the vernacular to take account of problems it would create in learning to read standard English. The court found for the plaintiffs and gave the School Board thirty days in which to submit a plan for helping the teachers to deal effectively with the problems posed by the Black English Vernacular. Unfortunately the court's exactly correct opinion was so distorted by the national press that many thought the judge had ordered the King School to teach Black English.

In some countries the language of the subordinate group is a world language with a great literature, but that does not prevent the dominant group from holding it in low esteem. The Province of Quebec was a French colony until 1763, when the British acquired it as a result of having won the Seven Years' War. The upper classes went back to France, leaving a peasantry, their seigneurs, and the Catholic Church. The British moved in, forming a dominant urban Protestant class. The French maintained their cultural and linguistic identity, grew to a large numerical majority, and created an urban proletariat. That is the way things were until about 1960 (Heller, 1982), when the French began to rise in socio-economic status and threaten Anglo dominance.

It was just in 1960 that Wallace Lambert and some colleagues at McGill University (Lambert et al., 1960) reported a study of evaluational reactions to English and French speech in Montreal and obtained a result that is reminiscent of the first doll preference study with black children, a result that does not show in-group favoritism or ethnocentrism. The method, called the method of "matched guises," was a beautiful one, invented by Lambert for the experiment. Subjects heard ten speakers read a short passage of philosophy—always the same passage. Some read it in English and some in French. One sample of subjects had English as their primary language and the other French, but most were in some degree bilingual. The task was to characterize each person who spoke, from the sound of his voice, in terms of fourteen characteristics including: height, good looks, leadership, sense of humor, and intelligence. Of course there was something subjects were not told: The same persons spoke twice, at well-spaced intervals on the tape, once in carefully coached "perfect" English and once in "perfect" French. Each person came in two linguistic guises, and that fact was detected by almost no subjects. A comparison of any one person's characterization in his French guise with his characterization in English guise was, therefore, a comparison of reactions to the two languages.

Subjects whose primary language was English ("Anglophones" they are called in Montreal) rated the English guise more favorably on seven traits: height, good looks, intelligence, dependability, kindness, ambition, and character. The person in French guise was granted the trait subordinate groups are usually granted, and surely need: "sense of humor." The Anglophones were ethnocentric, in the usual way. The Francophones were a surprise. They evaluated the English guise more favorably than the Anglophones did: English-speakers were rated higher on ten traits, practically everything but sense of humor. In 1960 in Montreal both sets of ratings could be said to reflect faithfully the existent social structure; English-speakers were on top in Quebec.

Things have changed a lot since 1960. The Francophone majority has asserted its superiority and the superiority of its language, has won political control, and has developed a strong Separatist movement. In the late 1970s the provincial government made French the official language. That does not mean French must be spoken in every sort of situation (McGill is an English-speaking university, and there are hospitals where the doctors speak only English) but rather that French must be used in all official matters.

Because French Canadian assertion has been successful in politics and business, I at first supposed that own-language derogation must have ended in Quebec. However, I had also thought that black pride must have eliminated white preference in doll choice and then learned (Jenkins, 1985) that white preference survived in Boston in 1985. So I checked on Quebec since 1960 with Professor Wallace Lambert. It turns out that since 1960 there have been a number of studies of language evaluation in Quebec using the method of matched guises (Lambert, 1984) and that even in 1985 (Maurice) French Canadians continue to derogate their own language.

White preference in doll choice seems incompatible with the "Black is Beautiful" slogan and French-language derogation with the language pride of the Canadian Francophone. What must be remembered in both cases is that the contrasting evaluations are on different psychological levels. Subjects studied by the method of matched guises do not know that they are evaluating languages; they believe they are rating individuals (who happen to speak English or happen to speak French) on various personal traits. It is only because each individual is represented in two linguistic guises that the results represent implicit comparative evaluations of English and French. The method of matched guises is exceptionally impenetrable. Doll preference, as a method for studying racial attitudes, would be transparent to adults but much less so to young children though probably not so opaque to them as the double guise is to adults. What both sets of results show is that high positive evaluation of group traits on an explicitly ideological level can coexist with negative, derogatory evaluations on an implicit private level.

Sometimes it is neither language nor appearance that is reevaluated in asserting social identity but some other acknowledged trait. The musicality and "sense of rhythm" that used to turn up in stereotypes of the American Negro have been rather successfully redefined as musical art, and many musicians, white as well as black, believe that the most important distinctively American contribution to music is black jazz. The traits of sensitivity, caring, and nurturance, which have always turned up in stereotypes of female temperament (see Chapter 9), have been rather deftly reevaluated within psychology itself. It was Carol Gilligan's book *In a Different Voice* (1982) that best did the trick, though reevaluation of the traits assigned a subordinate group was not Gilligan's explicit intention.

Gilligan studies moral reasoning in the tradition created by Lawrence Kohlberg (1958, 1981). Kohlberg's method is to present subjects with moral dilemmas in the form of story problems and to analyze the moral reasoning they do in a way that eventuates in assignment of the subject to one of six developmental stages. The claim is made, and there is some evidence to support it, that Kohlberg's six stages constitute a universal developmental progression. However not everyone, by any means, in a given culture attains the highest stages of universal principle, and in some cultures no one does. Paramount among those who rarely reach the higher stages in this culture are women. Women seem usually to exemplify Stage 3, in which morality is conceived in terms of sympathy with others and helping others rather than in terms of universal principles of justice. Early in her book Carol Gilligan points out something that I, and apparently all, students of Kohlberg's work had overlooked. The core group of subjects Kohlberg followed for a period of over twenty years were all male; "in the research from which Kohlberg derives his theory, females simply did not exist" (Gilligan, 1982, p. 18). What a devastating put-down for male psychologists!

Gilligan goes on to argue that women's moral reasoning is not deficient at all, that from their perspective responsibility and compassion are the highest moral requirements. The separate-self and moral principles unconstrained by reality seem to her to be adolescent ideals. It is possible to argue with her position, but it seems graceless to me to put up a defense when she has so definitely caught us in sexist error. Of course Carol Gilligan's goal was not to reevaluate positively the traits of women but rather to make a correction in developmental theory. But what she has incidentally accomplished is an elevation of a social identity.

Direct competition is a way to improve social identity that is different from reevaluation of acknowledged traits. Competition for political power has worked well for black Americans. In the 1960s black voting rights were established in those states where they had been jeopardized or effectively denied. In the 1970s black Americans were not optimistic about political competition, and many did not vote. By 1984 that had changed. The mayors of four of the largest American cities were black: Los Angeles, Philadelphia, Chicago, and Detroit. In Boston an impressive candidate, Mel King, came close. Most notably we had the first black presidential candidate with a serious following, the Reverend Jesse Jackson. He stayed the full course of the Democratic primaries and appeared in nationally televised debates alongside the two leading white contenders. None of those successful political leaders shows any renegade tendencies. They know the source of their power and they carry their social identity with them. In his speeches Jesse Jackson sometimes does exactly what the theory of social identity says he should do. He asks the members of his audience to repeat with him, "I am somebody," and thereby makes explicit what positive social identity is about.

It was also competition, but not political competition, that produced a black Miss America and a first black astronaut. Those are first competitive successes to add to the long-standing successes in athletics and music. At the Metropolitan Opera House today, with Leontyne Price, Shirley Verett, Leona Mitchell, Kathleen Battle, Simon Estes, and others on the roster of leading singers, it is difficult to believe that there had never been a black singer until Rudolf Bing hired Marian Anderson in 1955. I see those competitive achievements as enormously important, and I am not forgetting that the median income of blacks in 1984 is only 55 percent that of whites and that the unemployment rate is twice that of whites. There is a psychological power in the competitive successes of a few blacks ultimately to improve the lot of the majority, and I will shortly say what I think it is.

Women, gay men, and lesbians have been less successful at political competition. Of course blacks constitute about 20 percent of the electorate, whereas gay men and lesbians probably constitute 15 percent at most, but women are actually a numerical majority. The lesser political success is not, I think, mainly because of numbers but because those groups are not psychological minorities in the powerful sense that blacks are. Gay men and lesbians can "pass" and so are not subject to pervasive discrimination as groups. Women, acting as individuals, are increasingly able to accomplish most of the things they want to accomplish. From a social identity point of view, ignoring all other values, you might say that what those groups lack is a major-group-directed persecution.

Pluralistic Equality

Somehow our discussion of the minimal group experiment and the theory of social identity has made it seem likely that a certain liberal social ideal, the ideal of pluralistic equality, is on the verge of being realized. In a condition of pluralistic equality *different* is simply different, not *better than* or *worse than*.

Each person takes pride in his or her group membership and is supported in that pride by everyone else. Subcultures are like exhibits at a World's Fair, ways of life to be savored and respected. What has made this ideal of tolerance seem inevitable if not immediate? In stripped-down laboratory conditions randomly created group memberships seem to lead everyone—whether underestimator or overestimator, Klee or Kandinsky—to prefer his own group and in that preference enhance his own self-esteem, an undoubted benefit for any human, a benefit as basic as any. At the same time the theory of social identity concentrating on real-life cases of negative identity, or subordinated races, nationalities, language groups, and sex groups, has shown the ways in which such groups can attain positive identities and participate in the blessings of self-esteem.

In fact the minimal group experiment and the theory of social identity do not predict a state of worldwide pluralistic equality. They only seem to do so because our treatment has been selective. The invariable outcome of the experiment is, to be sure, in-group preference, but that preference is relative and always accompanied by out-group derogation. Equal treatment of the two groups has never been the outcome, so the experiment, far from predicting pluralistic equality, predicts pluralistic inequality of the ethnocentric sort. The theory of social identity is most fully developed for the case of negative identity, so we have dwelt on black Americans, black South Africans, the Maori, the hearing-impaired, women, and gays. For all those disadvantaged groups a positive identity is clearly desirable—at least up to the point of equality with contrasting group identities. But nothing in the theory says that efforts to enhance identity will cease at equality, and nothing in the theory says that groups already enjoying positive evaluation will fail to lust after more positive and indeed superior identities. And that is what has often happened. The Nazis had the conception of the superior Aryan race, Fascist Italy had its noble Roman identification, the Russians in the Union of Soviet Socialist Republics certainly think themselves better than the Moslem republics in Asia, and Jews believe themselves to be God's chosen people, and chauvinism is not absent from the American national character.

It is a good thing for the credibility of the minimal group effect and the theory of social identity that they do not predict an imminent triumph of pluralistic equality, because that is not the way things are going. The Rattlers and Eagles did not live side by side in peaceful equality but rather reviled each other, glorified themselves, fought battles, and destroyed possessions. Boston is a culturally diverse city, and that makes a Sunday stroll in June attractive, but Orlando Patterson, a Harvard sociologist, makes gentle fun of this idea:*

> How much better it is, we are told, to live in a city such as Boston in which, within a few blocks, it is possible to move from the lively Mediterranean clutter of the Italian

---

*Copyright © 1977 by O. Patterson, from *Ethnic Chauvinism*. Reprinted with permission of Stein and Day Publishers.

North End to the throbbing intensity of Roxbury, and not much farther on, the impish charm of Old Southie. The suicidal nature of such a promenade, whatever its sociological delights, should be obvious to anyone who has had anything to do with Boston lately or, for that matter, any of America's pluralist cities. [p. 177]

"Suicidal" is a bit strong, but the fact is that young men from each of those lively subcultures have killed people from the others just because of the groups they belong to.

Patterson's brief world summary of what positive group identity has come to goes like this:

There can be no doubt that we are living through a period of the most intense ethnic revival. In all the continents of the earth, men and women who for ages related to each other on other terms, or else did not relate at all, now struggle with each other in murderous combat as a result of conflicting ethnic loyalties. The disastrous consequences of this revival should be obvious to anyone who reads the newspapers with any regularity. In Black Africa, ethnic and tribal rivalries remain a source of permanent instability and the most unspeakable inhumanities, while in southern Africa a gang of fanatical ethnic thugs murders the minds and bodies of the native people with a cold-blooded efficiency that rivals that of Nazi Germany. In the Middle East, Arab fanaticism and Israeli nationalistic extremism remain at daggers drawn, resulting in the brutal displacement of a whole people, the displacement and denaturalization of Jews by Arabs and of Arabs by Jews, and the constant threat to the peace of the world. In Southeast Asia, Chinese, Indian, and other native peoples each day come to loathe each other more and more. In Soviet Central Asia, the one possibly liberal feature of Soviet policy—its attempt to unite the various nationalities into a unified, though not necessarily uniform state sharing a common industrial civilization—has been completely undermined by the revival of conservative chauvinistic forces in the provinces, forces which, in their support of the lowly status of women, to give but one example, cannot be condoned by any civilized man or woman. In Latin America, where official ideology proclaims the existence of racial and ethnic harmony, whole tribes of Indians are still being decimated, while others face the cruel paradox of being romanticized in the abstract by "indianist" poets, novelists, choreographers, and other intellectuals, while treated like brutes in face-to-face contact or simply excluded altogether. In continental Europe, after the stunned, post-Nazi lull, economic forces have led to the creation of yet another dangerous revival of ethnic rivalry. France, Germany, and Switzerland, having invited southern Italians, Turks, Spaniards, and Algerians to migrate into their societies in order to meet critical labor needs and help sustain the "economic miracle" of the postwar years, now find themselves incapable of and unwilling to absorb these alien workers. And even if they were able to do so, it is doubtful whether the impending ethnic tragedy would be averted, for the migrants themselves cling to their national loyalties, wanting it both ways: the rewards of an industrial culture and the preindustrial cradle of their ethnic groups. [pp. 147–48]

Pluralistic inequality and hostility is the predominant picture in the world in 1986, but that does not count against the minimal group effect or the theory of social identity since they do not really predict peaceful equality. But do they predict universal cultural assertion, hostility, and aggression? Taken alone they do not. The problem is that minimal groups, though they have expressed in-group preference in about thirty experiments, have never actually expressed dislike of or hostility toward the out-group. Ratings of the out-group have always been either neutral or slightly favorable. That is not the way the Rattlers and Eagles felt about each other, nor does it describe Arab and Israeli, Sikh and Hindu, South African, Caucasian and black. As mentioned earlier, the minimal group in its mild derogation of outsiders is not a good model for ethnocentrism in the real world, which entails hostility, anger, aggression, and violence against out-groups.

What the minimal group lacks as a model of intergroup hostility is an imposed unjust distribution of resources or failing that, a competition that threatens to create such a distribution. However, elevating the identity of a subordinate group is the first step in creating real hostility. That is the below-the-surface psychological connection between Leontyne Price, Stevie Wonder, Jesse Jackson, and the black astronaut on one side and the millions of black Americans who are underpaid or unemployed on the other. A positive social identity makes individual group members feel better about themselves, but it also prepares the way for real social change by affecting two additional psychological changes:

1. Because social comparisons are never made between incomparables, between very unlike cases, a dominated group with a negative identity is likely to compare its outcomes either with other dominated groups (black Americans with Hispanic Americans) or with itself at an earlier time (blacks today with blacks ten years ago). So long as downward comparisons are made, a dominated group will feel justly treated and not press for change. Raising the value of social identity changes the selection of comparison groups to a higher level. Not blacks today with blacks ten years ago, but blacks today with whites today. Not women professionals today with women professionals ten years ago, but with men professionals.

2. So long as downward comparisons are made, there can be gross inequality of outcomes between dominant and superior groups and yet no sense whatever of injustice. When comparisons are made at the same level and group assets (or social identities) are judged to be equal, then inequality is transformed into perceived injustice. And it is perceived injustice, either as a stable state or as a state that competition is likely to produce, that fires up discontent, anger, and aggression.

Because the elevation of social identity can change comparison groups and the perception of justice, it is a revolutionary act. The ultimate goal of cultural affirmation is not a dreamy self-content but discontent with unfairness. For that reason it is not ultimately contradictory to believe that subordinate groups should insist on their distinctiveness and that the distinctiveness has high value while also believing that group discrimination ought to end.

Hostility

I think the most general social psychological causes of group hostility are known. In addition to the most general causes there are always in individual cases particular historical events, and in addition to social causes there are, in extreme cases, personality causes, especially the personality called "authoritarian" (see Brown, 1965, for a full review), but I mean to disregard those and discuss only the most stubborn, general, and social causes of hostility.

The fundamental idea is not new in this chapter, having been exhaustively explored in Chapter 2 under the rubric of equity theory. Equity between either individuals or groups is a state of perceived fairness or justice and does not produce hostility or aggression. Using the formulation of George Homans (1974) as in Chapter 2, a state of perceived equity exists when

$$\text{Profits} = \text{Rewards} - \text{Costs}$$

$$\text{Equity} = \frac{\text{profits}_p}{\text{investments}_p} = \frac{\text{profit}_o}{\text{investments}_o}$$

In the formula, the symbols p and o stand for "person" and the "other" with whom person compares himself. Now we are concerned with groups and comparison reference groups (Runciman, 1966), so the symbols might better be g and r. Rewards are anything desirable, including not only economic rewards and tangible possessions but such intangibles as respect, good access to higher education, good jobs, and desirable residential neighborhoods. Costs are anything undesirable, such as physical pain, psychological insult, hard work, and stress. Investments are any properties that *entitle* individuals or groups to rewards; they are assets, perceived assets.

In considering hostility between groups we are concerned not with the state of fairness or equity but with perceived inequity. And we are concerned with groups that see an existent or threatened inequity as disadvantageous to themselves: the disadvantaged group. The emotional response to perceived unfair disadvantage has been variously named *anger, resentment, hostility* and *aggression* (Adams, 1965; Homans, 1974; Runciman, 1966).

It is important to stress that the equity formula describes a state of *fair* or *just* distribution of resources, a distribution of resources that is fair because, for both parties that compare themselves, the ratio of profits to investments is the same. Anger is not posited as a strong and reliable reaction to disadvantage or hardship, as such, but only to *unfair*, or *illegitimate* disadvantage, in short to inequity.

Unfair disadvantage or inequity is not, of course, the only stimulus to anger and aggression. In man and almost all animal species physical pain is a stimulus to anger and aggression (Brown and Herrnstein, 1975). It is quite possible that "aversive," or disagreeable, stimuli of any kind stimulate aggression (Berkowitz, 1976). Illegitimate disadvantage or inequity is simply that stimulus to anger, hostility, and aggression that is most relevant to our problem—the understanding of group hostilities. We shall cite evidence that unfairness or illegitimacy is an essential property of strong anger and not hardship alone.

If anger and aggression are to result from unfair disadvantage there is an attributional (Part II) condition to be satisfied. The disadvantaged group must not attribute the disadvantage to themselves, must not take responsibility for the unfairness. It would be too much to say, however, that they must attribute the disadvantage to the truly responsible group. Anger and violence can be displaced from real sources or problems to more available and vulnerable targets. In the United States that has repeatedly happened in race riots; black Americans have suffered most from black American violence.

There are, for any group, almost an infinity of other groups with which comparisons might be made. Quite a lot has been learned about the choice of a comparison other (Form and Geschwender, 1962; Goethals and Darley, 1977; Wheeler and Zuckerman, 1977), but I shall not try to summarize it here. It is enough to say that comparisons are not made with very dissimilar, remote groups but with those that seem comparable, and the comparison group can be the same as the comparing group but imagined at another time, in the past or in the anticipated future.

Those are all the main ideas of the theory of group hostility, but now I shall state them as a set of propositions and relate them to the minimal group experiment and the theory of social identity. For each proposition there is quite a lot of evidence, and I shall only sample it.

Group Comparison

Each group evaluates its condition, judges itself well off or badly off, by comparing its rewards and costs with those of some reference group, including itself at another time. The modern source of this idea is Leon Festinger's (1954) theory of social comparison processes. While Festinger's theory is written in terms of the individual's effort to evaluate his opinions and abilities by comparison with others, the ideas are all translatable into group terms. Festinger discusses several of the important points, including the selection of a reference other that is similar and the instability of evaluation in the absence of a social consensus.

The term *reference group* was introduced in 1942 by Herbert Hyman in connection with the study of subjective social status. Hyman (1942) asked subjects to locate themselves on a scale of (for example) economic status that ranged from 0 to 100, and he shifted reference groups from (for instance) all persons in the United States to all persons "in your occupation." He found (as we social psychologists often do) the obvious: An individual shifts his own placement on the scale with that of the assigned reference group. Every kind of status involves a social comparison, and, if reference groups are assigned, self-evaluation shifts in a predictable way. Other pioneering studies did not assign reference groups in the laboratory but studied social comparison in natural circumstances, letting informants select their own reference groups.

W. G. Runciman (1966) made a survey study of manual and nonmanual workers in Britain and came up with the first powerful demonstration that objective inequalities of income went unnoticed or were perceived as fair as long as people compared themselves with reference groups at the same level or with groups at their levels that had appropriately different qualifications. One question he asked workers was whether they could think of "any group of people doing better than you are." Though their weekly wages were extremely modest, some 20 to 30 percent said that *they could not.* What those workers surely meant was not that they were unable to think of people richer than themselves (e.g. film stars, nobility, industrial magnates) but that they could not think of people who earned more money with assets equal to their own. Using the concepts of social comparison and reference group, Runciman enables social psychology to understand the phenomenon of the respectable poor and reactionary peasantry. The possible inequities that could make for a sense of injustice and social revolution are not necessarily perceived. People acquiesce in inequality that is disadvantageous to them unless they compare themselves with reference groups that are better off without having proportionately better investments. The rich who deserve to be rich may be envied, but they are not hated.

All evaluation involves social comparison. One group can be better off or worse off, advantaged or disadvantaged only with reference to some other group or groups. Even equality entails comparison. Equality and inequality, however, are not the same as equity and inequity, and the former do not necessarily give rise to any emotions or social actions at all. What must be added is a conception of *deservedness,* and in equity theory that translates as investments or assets, the denominator of the ratio.

Social Equity

Group comparison that takes account of investments leads to judgments of equity (fairness) or of inequity (unfairness). In all of the history of the United States race, black or white, has been counted as an investment, with black being assigned a lower value than white. It has been counted in that way when making judgments as to the fairness or not of such rewards as income, freedom, access to schools, access to residential neighborhoods and public facilities of every kind. Since the Civil War race has not been considered a relevant investment in calculating the justice of slavery, and in this century, especially since the Civil Rights protests of the 1960s, the role of race has declined in the calculation of equity in other areas. The official position of the American government and of black Americans is that race ought not to count as an investment in any calculations at all, but to some extent it still does.

In social comparison generally the selection of the reference group is everything; there is always some group better off and some group worse off. In the special case of social comparison that we call equity the selection of the reference group continues to be an important determinant of the conclusion drawn. With respect to the reward of annual income a black American today can, if he picks his reference group carefully, actually feel well off or advantaged, but most comparative references are going to leave him feeling unjustly treated. In 1980 the United States Department of Commerce published a comparative historical study of the incomes of blacks and whites. Table 15-4 is derived from that report. It provides rich possibilities for feeling either glad or mad, but the latter is more likely.

In the quarter-century 1947-74 blacks enjoyed moderate increases in real dollars of annual income. If a black American in 1974 chose to select as his reference group blacks in 1947 he might smile and say: "See how far we have come." Well, but white incomes have also increased since 1947. I was surprised to learn that the percentage increase for whites has actually been less than for blacks: 92 percent over the years, as compared with 112 percent—yet another reason for the group and the system to congratulate themselves. Even the mildly militant black will consider this an example of how to lie with statistics, but it is not lying, it is just a careful selection of reference groups.

The black American today is not much interested in comparisons with his own past or with percentage increases, since black incomes started at about half the level of white. The black man is probably most likely to compare himself with the white man for any given year. That, of course, changes the story. The black man has earned an average annual income between 47 and 61 percent of the income of the white man. That looks like gross inequity. The black woman and white woman are closer in income, but then we know that women generally only earn about 61 percent as much as men.

TABLE 15-4. Some Evidence of Racial Inequality in Income

Year	Black Men	White Men	Median Income Ratio Black Men to White Men
1947	2,793*	5,143	0.54
1953	3,450	6,266	0.55
1959	3,345	7,120	0.47
1964	4,447	7,847	0.57
1969	5,296	9,105	0.58
1974	5,370	8,794	0.61

*Adjusted for price changes in 1974 dollars.
SOURCE: Derived from United States Department of Commerce (1980), Table 30, p. 46.

The income ratios of Table 15-4 between black and white are certainly going to seem to be the most relevant comparison to blacks today, and they seem
to establish inequity and to provide ample cause for righteous anger. They do,
in fact, produce plenty of righteous anger, but the income ratios of Table 15-4
are not the end of the story. They take no account of investments or entitlements other than race, such as education, and until we do that we shall not
fully understand the source of the hostilities that exist.

Inequity, Anger, and Aggression

A state of inequity exists when a person fails to receive a reward for which he is
qualified or incurs some cost he has not deserved or, generally, when rewards
or costs are not in the expected ratio with investments. There is much evidence
that inequity produces more intense anger or hostility and active aggression
than does disappointment or injury alone (Kulik and Brown, 1979). The most
precise tests were made by Pastore (1952) and Cohen (1955) using a paper-and-
pencil format. They described to subjects pairs of situations that were identical
in the disappointment or injury suffered but different in deservedness, and subjects freely described what actions they would take and sometimes rated the
hostility or anger they would feel. In a prototypical example a subject is to imagine himself a private in the army who has applied for a promotion for which
he is fully qualified but is passed over while a less qualified private receives the
promotion. In the comparison situation everything is the same except that the
promotion goes to a private still better qualified than himself. The former story
describes an inequity, whereas the latter only describes an unpleasant outcome.
Subjects rated themselves as about twice as angry and twice as hostile over the
inequity than they would be over the simple disappointment. The actions they
said they would take were also considered more aggressive.

Other inequities invented by Pastore and by Cohen included such familiar
aggravations as being deliberately passed up by a bus when you are standing on
the right corner at the right time and having someone cut ahead of you in line
when you have been waiting a long time. Both registered as really infuriating,
whereas simply missing a bus or failing to get something you had lined up for
were just disappointing. It may not be obvious what the "investments" are in
these inequitable ratios. In the case of the bus the investments or qualifications
are just knowing where to stand and when and taking care to do it. In the case
of standing in line the investment is the time spent in line, and the rule of equity is that one's "turn" or chances of getting a desirable ticket should be proportionate to the investment.

Paper-and-pencil evidence is fairly satisfying when the experiences involved
are familiar to everyone, but we are not limited to paper-and-pencil evidence.
Leon Mann (1969) has observed people and interviewed them in twenty-two
queues (or waiting lines) formed in August 1967 in Melbourne, Australia, for

tickets to the "world series" of Australian-rule football. Some queues lasted a very long time, and numerous attempts were made at "cutting in" or "queue-jumping." If they occurred by day they were met by jeers and catcalls, and the power of concerted disapproval was ordinarily enough to force out the miscreant. At night, however, the social force could not be brought to bear in full strength, and on one night four brawls sent five people to the Melbourne hospitals.

Ross, Thibaut, and Evenbeck (1971) set up a game with fifth-grade boys as subjects, some designated to be workers and some managers. The managers set the workers the job of pulling on a rope at intervals to produce a precise force to match a target force and promised them a prize if they did well. Some workers were repeatedly told they were doing fine and so had every reason to think their investments had earned them their prize, but other workers were told they were doing a poor job and so thought they would not deserve the prize. In the end none got the prize expected, but only the workers who thought they deserved it got angry. They got very angry, called the managers unfair, and found several ways to retaliate aggressively. In labor–management relations in life, workers who perceive inequity go on strike, picket, quit, and throw rocks at scabs (Adams, 1965; Patchen, 1961).

In the summer of 1964 there were race riots in the cities of New York, Detroit, Los Angeles, which involved not only great property damage but personal injuries and lost lives, and there were riots again in the late 1960s in Cleveland and Miami. Several social psychologists were able to do large-scale interview studies with black Americans in those and other cities, one purpose of which was to distinguish militant blacks from more conservative blacks. The definitions of militancy varied from study to study, including strong antagonism to whites, a belief in taking action against the oppressor, and identification with such black radical groups as the Black Muslims. Militancy involved real anger, lasting anger, a strong sense of injustice, and serious aggression. The correlates of militancy discovered in those survey studies seem to me generally to support an inequity analysis.

There are three essential factors in the perception of inequity: the numerator of the ratio, which is rewards minus costs; the denominator of the ratio, which is investments; and the choice of a higher reference group, which will lead to a sense of disadvantage. Consider the numerator first. Tomlinson (1970) found that militants perceived much more antiblack discrimination (higher costs) than did nonmilitants. Practically all blacks were aware of discrimination in jobs, housing, and schooling, but militants were more likely to see discrimination also in welfare administration, the Fire Department, the Parks Department, and garbage collection. Militants also thought the city police guilty of much more antiblack malpractice than did nonmilitants. In sum, militant blacks thought that blacks as a group suffered far greater costs (or injuries) than did more conservative blacks. How well deserved did they think these costs were?

Deservedness concerns the denominator of the ratio: investments. Militant blacks had the higher investments. Gary Marx (1969) found that militants had more education, had more sophistication, and were of a higher social class than nonmilitants. Most directly and importantly, both Marx and Tomlinson found that militant blacks had a more positive image of their race, a higher social identity, in Tajfel's terms. Tomlinson's militants listed more ways in which blacks were equal or superior to whites. Marx summarizes his impressions: "An unstated assumption made by militants is that Negroes are every bit as capable as whites, if not superior. . . . To believe otherwise would seem to justify differential treatment of Negroes and to shift the blame away from changing the social situation to changing individuals" (p. 70). In short, the militants, who saw blacks as suffering the worst costs, were those who thought they deserved it least with respect to investments. It is still necessary to have a reference group since low costs and high investments can be unfair only by comparisons with some other persons.

Marx (1969) finds much to suggest that militants more than nonmilitants compared themselves to whites and, in fact, to the more privileged whites. In the first place militants were in all ways more in contact with the nonblack world. For instance, they read more newspapers and general magazines and had greater knowledge of world affairs. Marx's own summary is:

> The fact that militancy is more pronounced among the privileged than among the underprivileged suggests that the privileged have a broader perspective, derived from their greater education and social participation. With this perspective, an individual can evaluate his own and his group's position in relation to the more privileged segments of white society rather than the limited framework of the ghetto world. [p. 68]

All relevant factors converge to identify the same group of blacks as highest in perceived inequity: maximal costs (or injuries), highest investments, and the most advantaged, and so punishing, reference group. And those who are highest in perceived inequity are highest in militancy, which involves anger, hostility, and aggression. Abeles (1976), in his study of blacks in Cleveland and Miami, puts it all together in this summary: The greater the unjust difference they saw, the more militant they were.

What Happened to Pluralistic Equality?

The minimal group result does not predict pluralistic equality, a society of groups that are different but not better or worse. On the other hand the minimal group result also does not predict hostilities, since the minimal outgroup is never hated but only less preferred. What we find in the serious groups that are not minimal is widespread but not universal in-group preference and also widespread out-group hostility. What ideas have been added to get from the minimal group to where we are?

The important addition is equity theory. Even if the minimal group result were invariably obtained with real groups, namely moderate in-group preference, the best possible outcome would be the universal perception of mild inequity. Suppose, very, very contrary to fact, that all resources, all good things, were distributed with perfect equality among all the groups of the world. A state of injustice would still be the universal perception, because each group, thinking better of itself than of all others, would think, in accordance with equity theory, that it deserved and ought to have *more* of the available resources than other groups. There is no way to distribute goods so that each group has more than all the others and therefore no way to put together equity theory and the minimal group result so as to produce perceived justice. The ethnocentrism or in-group preference of the minimal group, however, is moderate, and so we might suppose that goods distributed equally would produce only very mild perceptions of inequity and no real anger or aggression— just a lot of grumbling discontent.

What we live with is a lot worse than grumbling discontent. That must be because resources—not just goods but power and prestige—are not equally but very unequally distributed. That ought to be and is enough to turn discontent into riot and war. The way to reduce hostility and move toward the best attainable idea, which is probably grumbling discontent, would seem to be to distribute resources more equally among groups. We need some wise power in charge to do this, but there does not seem to be one. The theory of social identity, however, suggests a possible way in which to work at the goal.

Groups that have long been maintained on short supplies of goods, power, and/or respect seem not to have been able to hang on to their natural in-group preference but to have in some degree accepted the negative evaluation of the larger society, as witness black American doll preferences in the past and Montreal language preferences and anti-Semitic Jews and self-contemptuous homosexuals. If groups with negative social identities would adopt the path Tajfel calls "voice" and work at developing positive social identities, there should be two advantageous consequences for them.

The first consequence of an improved social identity is an improved individual self-image. And that seems to work. Women, blacks, gay persons, the hearing-impaired, and members of many other subordinated groups do seem to feel more individual pride as a consequence of working at group pride. The second consequence of an improved social identity involves equity theory. The group that thinks better of itself will think it deserves a larger share of goods, power, and respect. It will become angry if it does not get that larger share and also aggressive, or perhaps only strongly assertive. It is likely as a result to win a larger share, so working at positive social identity ought to produce increased benefits, tangible and intangible. So far, however, it has not worked just that

TABLE 15-5. Black and White Family Incomes with Level of Education of Family Head Constant

Years of School Completed by Family Head	1974		1975		1976	
	B	W	B	W	B	W
8 years	$ 7,237*	$ 9,790	$ 7,568	$10,166	$ 7,995	$10,909
High school	10,516	14,316	10,453	15,083	11,297	16,311
4-year college	17,316	20,711	19,966	22,116	20,733	23,356

*In current dollars.
SOURCE: Derived from United States Department of Commerce (1980), Table 142, p. 197.

way for black Americans. Black Pride is a psychological success but has not been effective in eliminating economic underprivilege. That is clear from Table 15-4, where we see that even in recent years the black man's income has only been about 60 percent as great as the white man's.

The reason why the assertion of a positive social identity, of Black Pride, has not been effective in achieving economic equality is, I think, that in this domain thinking does not make it so. Table 15-5 compares black and white family incomes for several recent years with the education of the head of the household held constant. Education is an investment. A higher education in our society is an entitlement to higher rewards. Race is also an investment, black supposedly less good than white, and in Table 15-4 it appears that the effect of race as an investment is enormous. In Table 15-5 however, with education constant, the effect of race is much reduced, though everywhere present. Consider the most favorable and I hope prophetic comparison: college-educated blacks and whites in 1976. The black family income is 89 percent of the white family income. The values seem to be approaching equality.

The huge differences of income between blacks and whites that we see in Table 15-4 must in considerable degree arise from differences of education, and that means differences of occupation. The problem is partly still one of thinking black less good than white *if all other things are equal*, for there are differentials even with education constant (Table 15-5). The problem in considerable degree, however, is that other things, other investments, especially education and occupation, are not equal. And that suggests that equality of opportunity, of access to schools, is the problem today more than Black Pride is. But we know it is a more difficult matter than desegregating the schools and affirmative action can solve, because equality of opportunity goes back to aspirations and habits that are established in childhood.

I must be even more pessimistic, or realistic, and tell you that occupational, educational, and income equality are not everything. Black professionals earning excellent incomes still experience residential discrimination and social discrimination of many kinds, even here in civilized Boston. And it almost seems to hurt more the nearer the ideal is approached.

Summary

It is the thesis of this section that hostility between ethnic groups results from two very primitive psychological processes and one universal and probably in-eradicable condition of society. The psychological processes are ethnocentrism and stereotype-formation. The condition of society is the inequitable distribu-tion of goods or resources. In the Robbers Cave experiment two groups of boys, the Eagles and the Rattlers, were put into a competition that promised to create an inequitable distribution of resources (prizes) and eventually did so. The in-equity combined with ethnocentrism (in-group preference) and stereotyping to produce active hostilities.

In connection with the Robbers Cave experiment Tajfel wondered whether competition was a necessary condition for ethnocentrism. In the minimal group experiment he showed that competition was not necessary but that categorization alone, even on an explicitly random basis, was sufficient to pro-duce ethnocentrism in the sense of in-group preference, favoritism, and over-valuation. That robust effect cannot be explained by experimenter expectancies or demand characteristics of the situation. A largely unconscious "pull," or force, to favor the in-group seems to be a consequence of categorization into an in-group and an out-group.

Tajfel's theory of social identity holds that the self-image has two com-ponents: personal identity and social identity. In-group preference and favoritism (ethnocentrism) are thought to enhance self-esteem by increasing the value of a social identity. Social identities resulting from serious real-world group memberships may be either positive or negative in value. Two of the principal reactions to a negative social identity involve individual movement out of a group: They are called *exit* and *pass*. The third reaction, called *voice*, is social and aims at elevation of an in-group as a means ultimately of enhancing self-esteem.

The first step in a social reaction to a negative social identity is the creation of a psychological minority. Psychological minorities that are consistent within themselves and over time have been shown to be effective in producing private change of belief (conversion) in the absence of public conformity and even, where there is substantial public conformity, in a direction contrary to that conformity. A psychological minority works to elevate group identity chiefly by making propaganda in favor of group appearance, language, and abilities.

The theory of social identity is often associated with an ideal of pluralistic equality on the implicit assumption that once all negative social identities become positive, groups will be able to affirm their distinctiveness and have it valued by others. A closer look at the theory of social identity and the minimal group experiment, on which the theory builds, however, shows that neither ex-periment nor theory predicts the attainment of pluralistic equality. The objec-tive result always obtained in the experiment is not that in-group and out-group are perceived as different but equal but that the in-group is perceived as better than the out-group. The theory of social identity only seems to point toward pluralistic equality because the examples discussed in connection with the theory all concern the negative identities of disadvantaged groups, which if elevated would move toward equality. However the theory has no stop rule as far as group, especially ethnic, assertion is concerned and so does not rule out competing clamorous chauvinisms rather than pluralistic equality as the outcome.

The chauvinism in the modern world has one characteristic not found in the minimal group experiment and not explained by the theory of social identity. The out-group in the minimal experiment is not hated but only liked less than the in-group. What needs to be added to account for hostility, anger, and aggression is equity theory. Raising a negative social identity is a revolutionary act, because it leads not to a placid "live and let live" attitude but to a new conception of injustice. If a group receiving less than its share of resources thinks of itself as inferior (negative identity), it will then feel that it deserves its lesser share and will not get angry, because deprivation alone does not cause anger. It is deprivation perceived as undeserved that causes anger.

The perception of inequitable deprivation depends on the choice of a high-level comparison group and on a positive social identity that makes disadvantage unfair. Militant black Americans, in contrast with conservative black Americans, have been shown to count their costs more heavily, to assess their investments more highly, and to compare themselves with whites. All of those findings are as they should be if the equity-theory analysis of anger and hostility is correct. In the case of black Americans today there is less inequity of income where education and occupation are counted as investments, but access to higher education and occupation is very limited, so those are the resources that need to be made more available.

16

Stereotypes

THE EAGLES AND THE RATTLERS, those summer campers who hated and fought each other, also developed conceptions of each other. The members of the in-group were thought to be *brave, tough* and *friendly* and the out-group members *sneaky, smart-alecs,* and *stinkers.* Those beliefs qualify as stereotypes, since a stereotype is defined as a shared conception of the character of a group. Concerning stereotypes there are three interesting questions: (1) Are they irrational beliefs? (2) Are they important causes of hostility between groups or primarily rationalizations of hostilities that arise out of real conflicts of interest? (3) Do beliefs about a group affect the way someone treats an individual member of the group when relevant individual information is available?

Irrational or Not?

The term stereotype was introduced by the political commentator Walter Lippmann in his book *Public Opinion* (1922) and defined as an oversimplified picture of the world, one that satisfies a need to see the world as more understandable and manageable than it really is. It is clear that Lippmann thought stereotypes of races and nationalities, and ethnic groups generally, were both irrational and pernicious, and it is equally clear that Katz and Braly, the authors of the first important empirical study of stereotypes (1933), thought the same. There are a number of subtle ways in which stereotypes may be thought less than ideally rational, but the principal objection has always been this: "But it is obvious that there are wide individual differences within any nationality group—that is, not all Englishmen are alike, nor are all Frenchmen, nor are all Russians" (Katz and Braly, 1933, p. 281). The view that generalizations about ethnic groups were obviously false and in that sense irrational was a cornerstone of the General Semantics Movement (Hayakawa, 1941; Korzybski, 1933), which sought to reform society by reforming everyday thinking. To free oneself from the harmful effects of overgeneralization, the movement recommended the use of index numbers and the ritual incantation: Jew_1 is not Jew_2 is not Jew_3; $Communist_1$ is not $Communist_2$ is not $Communist_3$; and even, cow_1 is not cow_2 is not cow_3 (Hayakawa, 1941).

Because the flaw in stereotyped thinking seemed obvious—there are no characterological generalizations true of all members of any ethnic group, no true exceptionless generalizations—its correction promised to be easy. And so semanticists, and sociologists, and social psychologists patiently explained to their student audiences that it was stupid to believe that Jews were thus-and-so and Negroes this-and-that, and those students grew up to be editors of *Time* magazine, which enabled them to explain their point to all respectable urban Americans. I am not sure how the message reached farmers, cowboys, and racketeers. Perhaps it never *did* reach them.

In spite of all the well-intentioned effort, something clearly went wrong. The Katz and Braly study in 1933 was done with Princeton students. When Gilbert replicated the study at Princeton in 1951, stereotyping showed a significant decline, which made social scientists feel good, but a third replication in 1967 (Karlins, Coffman, and Walters, 1969) showed a rebound to 1933 levels. And in the 1980s our minds are probably more richly stocked with stereotypes than ever in history. One thing was accomplished by the persuasion blitz: Middle-class Americans have learned that it is bad form to express stereotypes in some kinds of company. Of course, with your own good buddies the slight impropriety of ethnic jokes just adds spice. Politicians try hard to remember that ethnic remarks can be disastrous for them, but they keep slipping (as Jesse Jackson and James Watt both did in 1983–84), and the hypocritical majority cries "*shame!*"

Today it seems clear that the original analysis was quite wrong. The stereotype beliefs people really held never were irrational in the way we thought. As a matter of fact social psychology created the appearance of irrationality by assigning subjects an irrational task, which subjects carried out just because subjects will carry out almost any paper-and-pencil task they are assigned, and besides the psychologist was always urging them not to think about it too much but just put down the first thing that came to mind. Then he turned around and, in print, used the results as evidence of irrationality—in *them*. Our wiser view today is that stereotypes are natural categories, an intrinsic essential and primitive aspect of cognition, and anyone who attempts to "jawbone" natural categories out of existence has chosen not just an ineffective means but also an end whose realization would be disastrous.

Why do I think that stereotypes, in the sense of beliefs about the characters of groups, are in the 1980s, as always, universal and inevitable? Let us postpone the obvious nationality, race, and religion examples and think of our own immediate worlds. Of course I do not know yours, but it probably includes some or all of the following: the reputations of your own and others' universities and colleges, residential groupings of some sort, concentrators in various academic departments, athletes who go out for different sports, female students at your school as contrasted with female students at other nearby schools, and also male students. Probably you have fairly definite ideas about the distinctive characteristics of all the groups that matter to you. At Harvard the undergraduate residences (called "Houses") all have distinctive reputations, even though assignment to a House is by a lottery only somewhat influenced by preferences. There is the "preppy" House and the "laid back" House and the "jock" House and the "minorities" House and even the "gay–lesbian" House. Trafficking in those stereotypes becomes intense in the spring of each year, when freshmen (who live in the Yard the first year) must list their House preferences for the remaining undergraduate years. Everyone thinks there is something absurd about the stereotypes, but everyone knows them.

In Federico Fellini's movie *Orchestra Rehearsal* the members of an orchestra describe in a detailed way what oboists are like, and tympanists and violinists and bassonists. Every professional group I know has characterological conceptions of its subgroups. Ask doctors to tell you about surgeons, optometrists, psychiatrists, or proctologists. And I can assure you that psychophysicists are a different tribe from social psychologists.

Then there are the many conceptions we have in our heads that we happen never to have to talk about. I suggest to you that there are two kinds of people in the world: "night people" or "nocturnals," who like to go to bed late and wake up late, and "day people" or "diurnals" who like to go to sleep early and wake up early. Which group is more responsible? More unconventional? More depressed? More self-controlled? No one knows, of course, and no one even talks about it, but most people think nocturnals are unconventional, unpredictable, rebellious and depressed whereas diurnals are responsible, self-controlled, dependable, and healthy (Locksley, Hepburn, and Ortiz, 1982).

But wait, I can think of a crazier question to ask you. I will list the first names of some people I know and ask you to guess the age of each person as either "under forty" or "over forty": *Elizabeth, Christopher, Jason, Michelle, Ruth, Lisa, George, Joseph, Brian, Jennifer, Charles,* and *Mary.* In fact I had no particular people in mind but the correct answers to this hallucinatory exercise are: *Elizabeth, Ruth, Mary, George, Joseph* and *Charles* are all over forty, while *Michelle, Lisa, Jennifer, Christopher, Jason,* and *Brian* are under forty. You can feel the generational difference and the basis for it is the fact that the over-forty names were among the most popular names assigned infants in 1900, whereas the under-forty names are among the most popular in 1975 (Dunkling, 1977). Two inventive students in our introductory social psychology, Missy Karas (1983) and Alyssa Eisenacher (1983), established the fact that almost everyone guesses those names right. So we have conceptions even of the sets of people with particular first names. No "Chaunceys" should try to join street gangs, and "Fifis" need not apply for partnerships in conservative law firms.

The 1933 study of ethnic stereotypes (Katz and Braly) began with the collection of a very large list of trait terms and then asked Princeton undergraduates to select for each of ten ethnic groups (e.g. Germans, Italians, Jews, Negroes) the terms "typical" of the group. The procedure was repeated in 1951 by Gilbert and in 1967 by Karlins and associates. Table 16–1 lists the five traits most commonly assigned to four especially interesting groups. The traits are listed in order of frequency of assignment; for example, 79 percent of the sample in 1933 said Jews were shrewd, and 49 percent said Jews were mercenary.

The method of Katz and Braly is definitely a method for documenting

TABLE 16–1. The Five Traits Most Frequently Assigned to Four Ethnic Groups in the Years 1933, 1951, and 1967

Group	1933	1951	1967
Americans	industrious intelligent materialistic ambitious progressive	materialistic intelligent industrious pleasure-loving individualistic	materialistic ambitious pleasure-loving industrious conventional
Japanese	intelligent industrious progressive shrewd sly	imitative sly extremely nationalistic treacherous	industrious ambitious efficient intelligent progressive
Jews	shrewd mercenary industrious grasping intelligent	shrewd intelligent industrious mercenary ambitious	ambitious materialistic intelligent industrious shrewd
Negroes	superstitious lazy happy-go-lucky ignorant musical	superstitious musical lazy ignorant pleasure-loving	musical happy-go-lucky lazy pleasure-loving ostentatious

SOURCE: Adapted from Karlins, Coffman, and Walters (1969), Table 1, pp. 4–5.

shared or social stereotypes only, since a trait can only appear in the stereotype if it is assigned by many people. The sharpness of the social stereotype, or closeness of agreement, was measured by simply counting the least number of traits (starting with the most frequent) necessary to account for 50 percent of all attributions. In 1933 the stereotype of the Negro was the one on which agreement was highest; only 4.6 traits were needed to account for 50 percent of all attributions to Negroes. The adjectives were also used to measure the esteem in which the groups were held by obtaining favorableness ratings for the adjectives in isolation.

The most interesting changes in stereotypes across three generations of Princeton students concerned the amount of agreement or sharpness of the stereotypes and the preference values of the ten ethnic groups. Between 1933 and 1951, all ten stereotypes declined in sharpness or uniformity, which meant that it took larger numbers of traits to account for 50 percent of the attributions to each group. That is the decline in stereotyping which came as good news. However, between 1951 and 1967 almost all stereotypes sharpened again to become about as uniform in 1967 as they had been in 1933. The uniformity or degree of agreement returned to prewar levels, but there were important changes of content and especially of esteem. In 1933 and 1951 Princeton students were most complimentary to Americans, much less to Jews, and distinctly uncomplimentary to Negroes. The change in 1967 is striking. The self-portrait has become fairly critical, with *materialistic* and *conventional* ranking high and *intelligent* fairly low. The characterization of Jews is more favorable than the characterization of Americans in 1967, and in fact the Jews of 1967 look very much like the Americans of 1933. Negroes are no longer superstitious and ignorant, and the picture is rather neutral.

The persuasion efforts that did not succeed in eliminating stereotypes may nevertheless have accomplished something valuable if they are responsible for the reduction in in-group preference and out-group antagonism and if the reductions are real and not only verbal. Sigall and Page (1971) have given us reason to be somewhat skeptical on that point. They had some subjects rate Americans and Negroes on various traits under the usual circumstances, in which a person feels free to represent himself as unprejudiced if he thinks he should, and other subjects under circumstances involving a lie-detection apparatus, which made a person feel he had better tell the truth. With a lie detector operating, Negroes were rated less favorably than usual and Americans more favorably.

In the detailed results of the Princeton studies there is much that suggests stereotypes really are irrational. For instance, Turks were characterized by three generations of Princetonians as *cruel, treacherous, sensual, ignorant,* and *dirty,* but hardly a single Princetonian had ever met a real-life Turk. That was a conception derived from reading or movies, not personal experience, but that fact does not make it irrational, because we have many conceptions, of past times and remote places, that are not based on personal experience and yet are accurate and useful.

Many of the traits attributed to out-groups are not really descriptive terms at all and so are not open to testing for truth value. What does it mean to call the Chinese *superstitious* (a trait low on desirability) and the Italians religious (a trait high on desirability)? It means that large numbers of both nationalities subscribe to supernatural beliefs *plus* the ethnocentric difference that the supernatural ideas of Italians are respected by most Americans. What does it mean to say that the Italians are *impulsive* and the British *reserved*? It means they are at opposite poles of a scale of impulsivity plus the ethnocentric judgment that Princetonians occupy the ideal intermediate position. In short, much of the content of stereotypes is ethnocentrically evaluated, that is, judged by the standards of the in-group, and insofar as that is the case the truth or falsity of the content cannot be established. That is certainly correct and does mean at the least that stereotypes cannot be considered *rational* because they are demonstrably true. It would be wrong, however, to say that they are irrational because they are ethnocentric, for there is nothing maladaptive or stupid about judging others by your own standards—unfair, perhaps, but hardly irrational.

The subtler reasons for thinking stereotypes irrational (see McCauley, Stitt, and Segal, 1980, for an elegant discussion of them) were never the important reasons. The important reason was that the Katz and Braly instruction to list the traits typical of each group was thought to have been understood by subjects as an instruction to list the traits *true of all members* of each group. And when the traits are listed as they are in Table 16-1 underneath the names of the groups, and that is the way they appear in the original reports, one tends to read the tables as propositions of this form: "Americans (all of them) are industrious"; "Negroes (all of them) are superstitious"; "Japanese (all of them) are imitative." It is no wonder that when we read tables like 16-1 we smile a little and feel slightly superior. Anyone who thinks *all* Americans are industrious or *all* Negroes superstitious is just plain *stoopid*, and that is why stereotypes are irrational! An exceptionless generalization is disconfirmed by a single exception, and everyone knows exceptions.

The hitch is that the early studies never actually found out what subjects understood by *typical*. By 1951 and 1967 some subjects had grown sensitive to the topic and insisted on telling the social psychologists what they thought: "I must make it clear that I think it ludicrous to attempt to classify various ethnic groups"; "I don't believe that any people can accurately be depicted as having, in total, certain characteristics" (Karlins, Coffman, and Walters, 1969, p. 9)". Fairly substantial numbers of subjects actually refused to carry out the task in 1951 and 1967 because they sensed that *characterizing* ethnic groups at all would be interpreted as an ignorant and immoral thing to do.

In 1978 McCauley and Stitt looked into the question: What do subjects really mean when they say that a trait is *typical* of a group? The group they chose was the Germans, a nationality included in the Princeton studies, and as traits they used some that were always considered typical of Germans (e.g. *efficient, extremely nationalistic, scientifically minded*) and some that never were (e.g. *pleasure-loving, superstitious*). Subjects were told that they would be asked questions they could not answer exactly, such as, "What percent of American cars are Chevrolets?" Subjects were junior college students not sophisticated mathematically. The questions they were asked (the ones that matter here) were: (1) What percent of Germans are *efficient, extremely nationalistic* (etc.)? (2) What percent of people in the world generally are *efficient, extremely nationalistic* (etc.)? The results were very interesting, and a subset that makes the important points appears in Table 16–2.

Please look first at the percentages of Germans estimated to have the three traits that belong to the core of the stereotype of Germans: *efficient, extremely nationalistic, scientifically minded*. None of those values is even close to 100 percent, so it is clear that *typical* does not mean "true of all," does not mean an exceptionless generalization. Perhaps I have not been quite fair in suggesting that social psychologists were attributing to subjects that sense of *typical*. I do think it is definitely fair, however, to say that many of us attributed to subjects the sense "true of a majority—more than 50 percent." Brigham (1971a) explicitly says this. And so it is interesting to see that *scientifically minded* is not even attributed to a majority of Germans, and in still other results of McCauley and Stitt it is clear that *typical* does not mean "true of more than 50 percent." Furthermore, *pleasure-loving* is attributed to a large majority of Germans but does not belong to the stereotype.

What does *typical* mean when used nontechnically in a study of stereotypes? From Table 16–2 and additional results of McCauley and Stitt, *typical* means true of a higher percentage of the group in question than of people in general. The traits of the stereotype of Germans (*efficient, extremely nationalistic,* and *scientifically minded*) all satisfy that condition, whereas *pleasure-loving* and *superstitious* do not. The phrase *characteristic of* pretty well conveys

TABLE 16–2. Percentage Estimates Concerning Certain Traits for Germans

Trait	Percent People in World	Percent German	Diagnostic Ratio
Efficient[a]	49.8	63.4	1.27
Extremely nationalistic[a]	35.4	56.3	1.59
Scientifically minded[a]	32.6	43.1	1.32
Pleasure-loving	82.2	72.8	.89
Superstitious	42.1	30.4	.72

[a]A trait in the stereotype.
SOURCE: Derived from McCauley and Stitt (1978), Table 1, p. 932.

the understanding of *typical*. The precise sense can be conveyed using a symbolism we shall need again in this chapter: $p(A/B)$. That is to be understood as "the probability of A, given B." A trait (T) is then typical of a group (G) whenever $p(T/G) > pT$, which means: The probability of the trait, given the group, is greater than the probability of the trait generally (in people in the world).

The diagnostic ratio in Table 16–2 is obtained by dividing the percentage of Germans having a trait (or $p[T/G]$) by the percentage of people in the world having the trait (or pT). For the trait *efficient*, $p(T/G)$ is .634 and pT is .498, which yields a diagnostic ratio of 1.27. We can say that a trait belongs to a stereotype of a group whenever the diagnostic ratio is substantially greater than 1.0, and that is true of the diagnostic ratios for the three traits in Table 16–2 that belong to the stereotype of Germans. A diagnostic ratio of 1.0 would mean that subjects thought the trait in question was no more probable in the group in question than in people generally, hence totally nondiagnostic. It is interesting that, in the McCauley and Stitt (1978) experiments, whereas quite large numbers of subjects of various kinds estimated percentages, just two subjects held that no traits were more probable in any particular ethnic group than in the world generally. I think those two may have been a bit oversold on equalitarianism; all groups equally worthy is admirable, but all groups indistinguishable?

Two traits in Table 16–2 do not belong to the stereotype of Germans: *pleasure-loving* and *superstitious*. Subjects estimated that 82.2 percent of the world's people were *pleasure-loving* and that a slightly smaller percentage of Germans were, but still far more than a majority. The fact that more than 50 percent of Germans are thought to be *pleasure-loving* does not suffice to make that trait a part of the stereotype since a majority of people in general are believed to be *pleasure-loving*. *Superstitious* is a trait thought to be substantially less true of Germans than of people generally. *Scientifically minded* is a trait that is almost opposite in meaning to *superstitious*, and the diagnostic ratio of the former is about as far above 1.0 as the diagnostic ratio of the latter is below 1.0. If you were trying to predict whether a given person would turn out to be *superstitious* or not it would be worthwhile knowing that the person was German since that fact makes it less likely (presumably) that he is *superstitious* than does the simple fact that he is human. With respect to *superstitious* there is information in nationality. In short, diagnostic ratios substantially below 1.0 are like those above 1.0 in that they are evidence of stereotyping in the sense of group characterization, but a lower ratio means that it is characteristic of the group not to have the trait; Germans are *typically* not *superstitious*.

McCauley and Stitt propose the diagnostic ratio as an index of the degree to which a given trait belongs to the stereotype of a given group, and that seems to be a good idea. Notice that it is an index that can be used to assess *individual* stereotypes and not only social stereotypes. Notice also that the beliefs in Table 16–2 are not at all extreme. If the diagnostic ratios in that table were translated into words you would say that the traits belonging to the stereotype were thought to be "somewhat" or "slightly" more typical of Germans than of people generally. If the stereotypes people hold are all, like those of Table 16–2, simply beliefs in moderate tendencies, then it is going to be extremely difficult to maintain that stereotypes are irrational in the sense of being obviously or demonstrably false. It may be that stereotypes outside the laboratory are more extreme than the results you get when you ask people to estimate percentages and so put them on guard not to say stupid things. But even if the unguarded diagnostic ratios are somewhat higher than those of Table 16–2 it is clear from statements volunteered in the Princeton studies and in other work that *typical of a group* means usually "somewhat characteristic" and not either "true without exception" or "true of a majority." Beliefs about groups that are probabilistic in nature, as are those of Table 16–2, are certainly not obviously or necessarily untrue, but furthermore their truth or falsity is never going to be known, because the research needed to find out will never be done. Is anyone interested in a project designed to find out whether approximately 49.8 percent of the people in the world and 63.4 percent of Germans are *efficient* (whatever *efficient* means)? Now that we have a more exact idea of the meaning of *typical* we realize that we shall never know what traits are *really typical* of groups and so never know whether group characterizations are true or false, rational or irrational.

Having a more exact sense of the nature of the beliefs that have been pejoratively labeled stereotypes has a deeper consequence. In Chapter 13 I claimed that the study of concept formation did not begin in psychology with representative natural categories like birds and trees and vegetables, which are fuzzy categories that cannot be exactly defined. It began with well-defined proper sets, such as geometrical figures, which are not at all representative of the categories people mostly use but are a kind of idealization. Natural categories, the categories people use, such as fruits, furniture, tools, clothing, and the like, are fuzzy or indefinable because there are no attributes true of all instances and of no noninstances. What holds a natural category together is a collection of short-run attributes that are like the fibers of a rope in that none runs the full length and like the resemblances in a family (e.g. the Smith Brothers) in that no feature is found in all family members. Natural category formation is a very primitive process and also a nondeliberate, almost effortless process that requires nothing more than attention to an array of instances. Finally we found in Chapter 13 that natural categories with instances varying in prototypicality are formed even for a well-defined proper set. An equilateral triangle is a more prototypical triangle than an isosceles, and "4" is a more prototypical even number than "358," and Ernest Hollings is a more prototypical United States Senator than Gary Hart. A prototype, I said in Chapter 13, is very much like a stereotype.

In the context of category theory generally I think we can really understand what has happened in the study of stereotypes since Katz and Braly started it off in 1933. The idea that subjects understood *typical* to mean *true of all* seems simply to be a consequence of psychology's mistaking the proper set for the usual thing. The defining attributes of a proper set, such as triangle, are *true of all* instances: three-sided closed figure. A nationality like German is a well-defined proper set with citizenship criteria being the attributes true of all instances. If now we learn that Germans are believed typically to be *nationalistic* and *efficient,* and if our only model for such categorical ideas is the proper set, then it is inevitable that we should fall into thinking that what people who hold such beliefs mean is that *all* Germans are *efficient* and *nationalistic.* It is obviously not true that all Germans are *efficient* and *nationalistic,* and those subjects who think it is true are irrational. Now, however, McCauley and Stitt have found out that nobody believes all Germans are *nationalistic* and *efficient.* What many do believe is that *nationalistic* and *efficient* are attributes more likely to be found in Germans than in other people, that *nationalistic* and *efficient* are short-run attributes, family resemblances, just like the large ears and white beards of the Smith Brothers. Stereotypes are natural categories in the domain of ethnic groups.

Of course there are differences between natural categories for ethnic groups and natural categories for the nonhuman world. The main difference is that in the latter domain there is no one to take offense if you use a highly prototypical example to stand for the category. When Merriam-Webster's *New Collegiate Dictionary* (9th edition) used the bluejay to stand for all birdsville, emus and ostriches and penguins and eagles did not go on the attack. Imagine what would happen, however, if *Webster's* used a picture of Doris Day to illustrate the general entry *woman* and perhaps John Wayne for *man.* Of course, people would be right to take offense since a prototype can never represent the variation that exists in natural categories. It is just that birds don't care but people do.

If, however, stereotype formation is essentially the process of natural category formation, then it is bootless to protest it. It will take place whether or not ideology approves and is neither more nor less rational than concept formation generally. What can effectively be protested, and it has been, is the exaggeration of stereotypes, especially of unfavorable ones in presentation by the media. And what can truly be called irrational is taking any serious action, such as hiring or firing an individual on the basis of knowledge of nothing but group membership when more diagnostic information is obtainable. Characterizations of groups are probabilistic in nature and of unknown validity and so do not provide a rational basis for serious action. How much stereotypes affect actions is the topic after next.

Cause or Reflection?

The social anthropologist Robert Levine is reported (Tajfel, 1981, p. 224) to have challenged a conference on ethnic and national loyalties with this assertion: "Describe to me the economic intergroup situation and I shall predict the content of the stereotypes." It is nowhere reported whether anyone took up that challenge, but I do not think that Levine could have met it. Economics is a strong determinant but not that strong. If you were to add political and social relations you would be able to come closer to predicting stereotypes. Buchanan and Cantril (1953) made a survey study for UNESCO of stereotypes in nine nations, of the nine nations themselves, Russia, and the United States. The Russians were regarded as *cruel* and *domineering* and the Americans as *peace-loving*. In effect this was the NATO pole of a bipolar world. It would be absurd to suggest that the stereotypes caused the bipolarity, and the authors of the study are quite sure that stereotypes follow and rationalize political relations. To suppose that national character causes political relations seems to be the Fundamental Attribution Error (Chapter 5) applied on a grand scale to group personalities. It has all the cartoon simplicity of Uncle Sam wrestling the Russian Bear.

There is a lot of evidence that stereotypes are reflections of political relations at any given time. In addition to the UNESCO survey there is, for instance, a report on the stereotypes held by the student body at the American University in Beirut, Lebanon, in the 1950s (Prothro and Melikian, 1954). The students were from the countries in the Middle East, excepting Israel. Their characterization of Jews was: *base, stingy, deceitful, rich,* and *materialistic.* As a form of apology to the Turks, who were held in such low esteem by Princeton students, I am glad to report that Beirut students, who were more closely acquainted with Turks, called them: *strong, militaristic, nationalistic, courageous,* and *progressive.*

Studies of stereotypes over time suggest that they are not just reflections of stable political relations but responsive to changing political relations. The Princeton studies took snapshots of the Germans and Japanese before World War II (1933) and very soon after (1951). The Germans in 1951 looked *aggressive, arrogant,* and extremely *nationalistic* just after the war but not before. The postwar Japanese were *treacherous* and *sly* (remember Pearl Harbor!) and also extremely *nationalistic,* but in 1933 they were mainly *intelligent, industrious,* and *progressive.* It is not likely that the two national characters really changed in that period.

The most rapid adjustment of stereotypes on record occurred in India before and after India and China had a border dispute (Sinha and Upadhyaya, 1960). Stereotypes of eight nationalities were elicited from students at Patna University in February 1959 and again in December of the same year. Seven groups did not change in national character in ten months. The Chinese did. Before the dispute they were believed to be *artistic, religious, industrious, friendly* and *progressive,* but when the dispute occurred they became *aggressive, threatening, cheating, selfish, war-mongers* who, however, remained *artistic* in Indian eyes.

Stereotypes are not, nevertheless, only reflections of political alliance and hostility. For one thing the traits are not all purely evaluative, not simply synonyms for good and bad. Most of them also have a descriptive component: The Irish are thought to be *witty* and *quick-tempered,* the Italians *musical* and *talkative.* There is, in addition, a considerable amount of stability over time. The Princeton studies recorded stereotypes long after World War II (1967) as well as shortly after (1951) and well before. Twenty years sufficed for our wartime enemies, the Germans and Japanese, to recover their prewar characters. The Japanese were once again thought to be *industrious, intelligent* and *ambitious*; in 1967 almost no one said they were *treacherous*. And the new postwar Germans (very prosperous in 1967) were mainly *industrious* and *efficient*.

There is even one result that shows stereotype stability in spite of a sharp political change and a strong effort by a new leadership to rationalize the change on a characterological level (Beattie, Agahi, and Spencer, 1982). In Iran the Islamic Revolution required that the British and Americans who had been allies be recast as the "Great Devil" and that Iranians look favorably on those Arab states that were Islamic brothers. In 1980, stereotypes were documented in Isfahan, Iran, from university lecturers, taxidrivers, and factory workers for Americans, the British, Iranians, and Arabs. The new religious leaders in Iran had made intense efforts to improve the image of Iranians and Arabs while vilifying Americans and the British. The investigators thought that university lecturers, because they had been educated in the West, and taxi drivers, because they had had quite a lot of contact with Westerners, would show some resistance to the new propaganda but that factory workers would unquestioningly take it in. Quite surprisingly, Iranians at all three levels, including factory workers, gave very favorable impressions of the Americans and British (*progressive, practical, industrious*) and not very favorable impressions of either Arabs or Iranians (*lazy, talkative, happy-go-lucky*). The factory workers cannot have derived their impression of the two Western countries from contact with individuals. One suspects that many years of American movies had stabilized the image, especially since it included the trait *musical* (personally, I can't even carry a tune). There is another possibility: 25 percent of the Iranians approached for the questionnaire refused, and we do not know what they would have said about the Western nationalities.

Stereotypes are, in short, reflective of existent political relations and responsive to changes but also in some degree stable, and some ethnic groups even have rather uniform reputations in most of the world. Americans seem *ambitious* and *materialistic* to most nationalities, and the Japanese reputation as *progressive* and *industrious* is worldwide. It is probably best to think of the stable and widely shared learned "traits" of ethnic groups not as personality characteristics in individuals but as the impact of one culture on many others through movies, literature, and travel. The American culture strikes much of the world as both *rich* and *materialistic*, the British culture as *conservative*, and the Italian as *artistic*, but of course none of those "traits" fits all or even most of the people stereotyped.

Stereotypes and Behavior to Individuals

There is a remark prejudiced people make which though intended to deny prejudice has become its very hallmark: "Some of my best friends are . . .". There is a real phenomenon, a paradoxical one, behind the remark. People who are well stocked with unfavorable beliefs about group X do nevertheless make friends of individuals who are members of X. There is always in such friendship an almost unconscious trace of uneasiness on the part of the befriended one, which stems from his or her suspicion that, if they two were to fall out, the other would voice those things that are part of the culture. And, of course, who knows what things he or she subvocalizes at times of friendship strain?

Anne Locksley and her associates (Locksley et al., 1980; Locksley, Hepburn, and Ortiz, 1982) have discovered what may be the theoretical foundation of the "some of my best friends" effect, and that foundation turns out to be very surprising from the point of view of general psychology. In describing the work I have taken the unusual liberty of substituting my numbers for those of the experiments. The substitute numbers correctly represent the effects obtained, but they sharpen the effects, and the numbers are picked so that simple arithmetical complexity will not slow our thinking. The argument to be made is important but not easy, at first, to grasp.

The stereotype we shall be concerned with is familiar from Chapter 9; it is the idea that males are more likely to be *assertive* than are females. That idea, by the way, has been steadily documented, as a belief, not a fact, for at least twenty years (recently by Ruble and Ruble, 1980). In one of the Locksley studies the exact nature of the belief was obtained in quantitative form. In sharpened numbers, both men and women informants guessed that 70 percent of males are assertive and 30 percent of females. In terms of diagnostic ratios, assuming 50 percent of humans in general are assertive, the values would be $+1.4$ and $-.6$, equidistant in the two directions from 1.0. The percentages (70 percent and 30 percent) can be alternatively and more conveniently represented as conditional probabilities: $p(\text{assertive/male}) = .70$ which means the probability of being assertive if male is .70 and in parallel fashion by $p(\text{assertive/female}) = .30$. That is the same notation introduced in connection with diagnostic ratios.

Assertiveness as a trait in individuals, that is, as an enduring disposition to act assertively across time and occasion, may be attributed to an individual on some basis other than sex, especially on the basis of one or more assertive actions (see Part II). An assertive action used in the Locksley research, as a description not an observation, is:

> The other day Nancy (or Tom) was in a class in which she (or he) wanted to make several points about the readings being discussed. But another student was dominating the class discussion so thoroughly that she (or he) had to abruptly interrupt this student in order to break into the discussion and express her (or his) own views. [Locksley et al., 1980, p. 827]

Let us suppose that this single act (act 1) of Nancy's (or Tom's) is thought by someone to be diagnostic of the *trait* of assertiveness with the conditional probability $p(\text{assertive/act 1}) = .60$, which means that a person (male or female) who performs act 1 is thought to be likely to have the trait assertiveness with a probability of .60. Information of that sort, information about the individual, is called *individuating information.*

We can conceive of two contrasting extreme ways of using the information described in attributing assertiveness. Someone might completely ignore the individuating information and operate solely on the basis of group membership and the belief about what that membership implies. Whoever did so would judge that the probability of Nancy's (a female) being assertive was .3 and the probability of Tom's being assertive .7. That would be behavior toward an individual based solely on a belief about the characteristics of a group. It is the pure case of stereotypic *behavior.* Behavior not belief; the beliefs are p(assertive/male) $= .7$ and p(assertive/female) $= .3$, and the belief need not necessarily lead to the behavior.

It is vital that we be clear about the fact that pure stereotypic behavior, in certain circumstances, would actually be rational, but in other circumstances irrational. If someone did not know the individuating information but had only the group characterization beliefs and had to judge whether Nancy or Tom was more likely to be assertive, then it would be rational to judge in accordance with the beliefs. Of course, the beliefs might be false, and it is not rational to act on beliefs known to be false, but then, as argued previously, we can almost never know about *probabilistic* beliefs of this kind whether they are true or false, so judging by the belief would be rational.

It is less obvious that even a decision about employment or promotion based on pure stereotyping can in a sense be rational. *If* all an employer knew, or thought he or she knew, was the sex of applicants plus: p(assertiveness/female) $= .30$; p(assertiveness/male) $= .70$, plus the fact that the position to be filled required assertiveness, then it would be rational to favor Tom over Nancy. Of course, there is also something weirdly irrational about making a business decision on the basis of sex alone, but given the strange constraints the decision would be rational.

The extreme contrast to purely stereotypic behavior is behavior based on individuating behavior alone in the absence of any beliefs about groups. If individuating information were the only information available, then it would be rational to make estimates or to act on that information alone—for just the same reason that acting on beliefs about groups would be rational. If only one sort of information exists, it is rational to use it. It probably does not seem weirdly irrational, as pure stereotyping does, for the reason that it is in accord with liberal values. To use only individuating information is to judge a person on his or her merits. You have to fly in the face of that value to say that it would be more rational also to get information on sex, race, and attractiveness (a photo). Indeed, we have laws against soliciting such information. Behind those laws lies the belief that there are no true generalizations to be made about group characteristics plus the idea that inborn characteristics, things a person cannot affect, ought not to influence prospects in life. Those are important values, but they do not determine rationality in decision-making.

If both kinds of information exist, beliefs about assertiveness in males and females as well as relevant individuating information (act 1), then Bayes's Rule in decision theory says that an optimal decision will take account of both kinds of information, will integrate the two sorts of information in a specific way. We first need to feel intuitively that the general thrust of Bayes's Rule is correct. Consider the case of Nancy and imagine that the two kinds of information are learned sequentially. The first thing one knows is that Nancy is female, the belief about females suggest that the probability of assertiveness is .30. In the decision-making literature that sort of belief is called either the *prior probability* or the *base rate*, and the value of the *prior probability* of assertiveness is .30, or the *base rate* of assertiveness for females is .30. Suppose one next learns that Nancy has performed act 1, which implies assertiveness with a probability of .60. It is obvious, I think, that the prior probability ought to be raised upward. Exactly how far upward involves more mathematics than I want to go into, but clearly the new probability that Nancy will prove assertive should be higher than the base rate or prior probability. It ought also to be lower than .60, because Nancy after all is female, and for females the base rate of assertiveness is only .30. Some account must be taken of the possibility that Nancy's act 1 is not characteristic of her, that it belongs with those occurrences of act 1 (40 percent of them) that do not entail assertiveness. Therefore the best estimate will use both kinds of information and will be a probability value lying between the prior probability and the individuating information.

Tom's case is less obvious to intuition. The prior probability (based on the fact that he is male) is .70, and individuating information entails a probability of .60, which is lower than the prior. Does that mean that where the two are ideally integrated the probability will be between the two, lower than .70? It does not. The individuating information implies assertiveness with a probability greater than that for humans generally (.50). It reduces the probability that Tom is among the 30 percent of males who are not assertive. Therefore the new probability integrating both kinds of information ought to be greater than .70, though not very much so.

Now we come to a conclusion that is downright subtle—or "counterintuitive," as we social psychologists like to say. A number of studies have investigated the existence of (or degree of) sex discrimination in business (Rosen and Jerdee, 1974) and academic psychology (Fidell, 1970; Friend, Kalin, and Giles, 1979; Mischel, 1974) in men and women in several countries. The method is always essentially the same. Evaluators of some sort (business executives, department chairmen, and so on) are presented with some form of professional achievement or some record of it, such as journal articles or professional résumés, which include pairs exactly matched except for sex. The neat trick Fidell (1970) played on 228 chairmen of departments of psychology is representative. They received in the mail either the male or the female form of ten professional résumés such as this one:

Dr. Patrick (Patricia) Clavel received his (her) doctorate in clinical psychology from Western Reserve University. He (She) is considered both highly intelligent and very serious about his (her) academic goals. His (Her) students feel that he (she) is more interested in them than in his (her) research. He (She) works well with his (her) colleagues on committees, but has added only three articles to his (her) vita since graduation. These articles have, however, been well received professionally. Dr. Clavel is married. [Fidell, 1970, p. 1098]

The chairmen were asked to make various evaluative judgments such as desirability for employment and level at which employment should be offered. Rosen and Jerdee (1974) had managers decide on promotions. The general result, varying with the date of the study, the nature of the job, is that (no surprise) discrimination in favor of men exists and (some surprise) exists whether the evaluators are themselves male or female. There is just a suggestion of evidence (Mischel, 1974; Friend, Kalin, and Giles, 1979) that there is more sexism in Britain than in the United States and more in the United States than in Israel.

Discrimination by sex is morally wrong but not necessarily irrational. Résumés are individuating information, and when two are matched the probability of a given level of expertise must be assumed to be, on the average, the same. The fact of discrimination by sex shows that there are beliefs about women and men as groups and that those beliefs assign lower probabilities of professional expertise to women. Those beliefs may be, and in my opinion probably are, false. However, as beliefs that exist they qualify as prior probabilities or base rates, and that means, by Bayes's Rule, that optimal decision-making should take them into consideration—along with individuating information. That means it is *not irrational* for today's evaluators, with the beliefs they have, to value differently sets of credentials that are perfectly matched except for sex. I do not make this quaint point as a contribution to conservatism but because it helps exactly to locate the problem—which is in the beliefs about groups. It also shows how the beliefs are self-perpetuating. Expertise is often guessed at from success, and if beliefs about expertise guarantee that men will be more successful than women, those beliefs will endure.

What were the experiments like (Locksley et al., 1980) that bear on all this logic-chopping? This is where the real surprise comes. Subjects were undergraduates at New York University. Their beliefs about the assertiveness of males and females, their base rates, were determined and conformed to the stereotype. One independent sample of subjects were given paragraphs to read like the Nancy–Tom paragraph above, but *without identification by sex,* and asked to evaluate the *diagnosticity* of each paragraph of individuating information for the trait of assertiveness. The paragraph you have read, of course, implied assertiveness fairly strongly, as did some others, but there was also a paragraph intended to be completely uninformative about assertiveness, neutral or nondiagnostic. In the experimental form, with names inserted, it reads like this:

> Yesterday Tom went to get his hair cut. He had an early morning appointment because he had classes that day. Since the place where he gets his hair cut is near the campus, he had no trouble getting to class on time. [Locksley et al., 1980, p. 827]

The paragraph was, in fact, judged to imply nothing at all about assertiveness.

Without names, to reveal sex, the paragraph was judged to be non-diagnostic for the trait of assertiveness. In short, preliminary operations established quantitative base rate beliefs for assertiveness in males and females (stereotypes) and also present the estimates of the diagnosticity for assertiveness of various paragraphs in which the sex of the protagonist was not known. The question posed by the experiment was: How would subjects integrate their base-rate information with individuating information of known diagnosticity?

As a kind of baseline, subjects estimated assertiveness from no information but proper names (e.g. *Tom* or *Nancy*), which, of course revealed sex. Under those conditions their estimates mirrored their sex stereotypes or base rates, as they sensibly should. When subjects had entirely nondiagnostic individuating information—the paragraph immediately above—their estimates continued to reflect sex stereotypes or base rates, as one would think they should, since no useful information about individuals had been provided. By contrast, when subjects were given diagnostic individuating information (e.g. the Nancy–Tom paragraph), any effect of base rates or sex stereotypes was completely eliminated. Estimates for male or female, Tom or Nancy, were almost identical when useful individual information was provided.

We need to take a moment to let that result sink in, because it is profoundly contrary to what social psychologists have long believed. We have tirelessly documented the existence of beliefs about group characteristics—groups of many kinds, but especially ethnic groups and the sexes. It has been our generally *implicit assumption* that those beliefs must affect the way individuals in the groups are treated, and indeed that assumption has been the principal reason for condemning stereotypes, since beliefs that do not eventuate in discrimination are not socially very significant. And *implicit assumption* is not the whole story. Discrimination on the basis of ethnicity has often been documented, and we have just reviewed a set of studies showing clear sexist discrimination when highly diagnostic individuating information has been provided. In Chapter 11 we reviewed a sample of the many studies showing that physical attractiveness stereotypes produce discrimination when there is excellent individuating information (e.g. essays alleged to have been written by attractive or unattractive authors). For those reasons the Locksley result is very unexpected; it clashes sharply with much that has been both demonstrated and assumed in social psychology.

One might quite reasonably think that the explanation of the anomalous result lies in the values of New York University students in 1980. At most universities today students disapprove of sexist discrimination, and it must have been obvious to them that this was what the experiment with its matched paragraphs and related names was after. Tom and Nancy would not qualify as "best friend" exceptions to stereotypes, but the attack on sexist discrimination has been so forceful at liberal universities that discrimination as such is thought to be immoral, and if you know people as individuals they need not be best friends to be exempted from group stereotypes. However, Locksley, Hepburn, and Ortiz (1982) have countered that superficial explanation with an experiment showing the same disregard of stereotypes when diagnostic individuating information is available in the case of the noncontroversial, never discussed stereotypes concerning "nocturnal" people and "diurnal" people, which was described earlier in the chapter.

The really odd thing is that while the Locksley results are anomalous for social psychology, they are entirely consistent with well-established results in the general psychology of decision-making. Beginning with a seminal paper by Daniel Kahneman and Amos Tversky (1973) many experiments (Ajzen, 1977; Lyon and Slovic, 1976; Nisbett et al., 1976; Slovic, Fischoff, and Lichtenstein, 1977) have shown that base rates or prior probabilities are *characteristically* disregarded where diagnostic information is available. To be sure, the base rates in those experiments have not concerned stereotypes. One experiment by Kahneman and Tversky can be used to represent many others.

The base rates (you may not recognize them at first, for they are not stereotypes) were explicitly given to subjects rather than elicited from them. The instructions read as follows:

> A panel of psychologists have interviewed and administered personality tests to 30 engineers and 70 lawyers, all successful in their respective fields. On the basis of this information, thumbnail descriptions of the 30 engineers and 70 lawyers have been written. You will find on your forms five descriptions, chosen at random from the 100 available descriptions. For each description, please indicate your probability that the person described is an engineer, on a scale from 0 to 100.
>
> The same task has been performed by a panel of experts, who were highly accurate in assigning probabilities to the various descriptions. You will be paid a bonus to the extent that your estimates come close to those of the expert panel. [Kahneman and Tversky, 1973, p. 241]

The instructions came in two forms, with the difference being that the second form reversed the numbers and said there were seventy engineers and thirty lawyers. If you had received the description quoted above you would have actually been provided with base rates or prior probabilities of the following sort: For any person now to be described (some sort of individuating information) the prior probability that that person will be a lawyer is .70. Those prior probabilities do not seem to be beliefs about groups, and certainly they are not stereotypes. In fact, however, they are newly created beliefs about groups (nothing to do with character traits) where the group is simply the group psychologists are said to have interviewed and so in our familiar notation: p(engineer/interviewed person) = .30; p(lawyer/interviewed person) = .70. Given that someone has been interviewed, the probability that that someone is an engineer, in the absence of any individual information, is .30, and so on. For those subjects who read the alternative paragraph the two probabilities were: p(engineer/interviewed person) = .70; p(lawyer/interviewed person) = .30.

The design is elegant. There were two groups of subjects with exactly reversed base rates (I chose the values .7 and .3 for assertiveness in order to facilitate comparison between Locksley's work and that of Kahneman and Tversky). Both groups of subjects received the same sets of five paragraphs, which, as in Locksley's studies, conveyed individuating information of varying diagnosticity. Since the individuating paragraphs were the same for both groups of subjects while the base rates were reversed, the guessed probabilities as to whether a given person is an engineer or a lawyer would be sharply different for the two groups if base rates were in fact used but would be about the same if base rates were ignored and individuating information relied upon exclusively.

Here now is an example of a paragraph (individuating information) designed strongly to suggest that the protagonist is an engineer, not a lawyer.

> Jack is a 45-year-old man. He is married and has four children. He is generally conservative, careful, and ambitious. He shows no interest in political and social issues and spends most of his free time on his many hobbies which include home carpentry, sailing, and mathematical puzzles. The probability that Jack is one of the 30 engineers in the sample of 100 is _____%. [Kahneman and Tversky, 1973, p. 241]

Remember that both sets of subjects, those thinking there were 30 engineers and those thinking there were 70, read the paragraph. Optimal decision-making in accordance with Bayes's Rule requires that the base rates or prior probabilities be taken into account, however suggestive the paragraph. If there are 30 engineers instead of 70 it is less likely that Jack is an engineer. You will feel in yourself the tendency to disregard the base rate, but that means assuming the information is accurate and assuming it is really true that conservative, careful, apolitical people are very likely to be engineers, and you do not know those things at all, really.

A completely nondiagnostic paragraph was also included:

> Dick is a 30-year-old man. He is married with no children. A man of high ability and high motivation, he promises to be quite successful in his field. He is well liked by his colleagues. [Kahneman and Tversky, 1973, p. 242]

The results are clearest in graphic form and appear as Figure 16-1. The two groups of subjects are represented by their respective assigned base rates for engineers: .30 on the horizontal and .70 on the vertical. The points plotted refer to probabilities that persons would be engineers. Lawyers can be omitted, because the results for them are simply the reciprocal of the results for engineers.

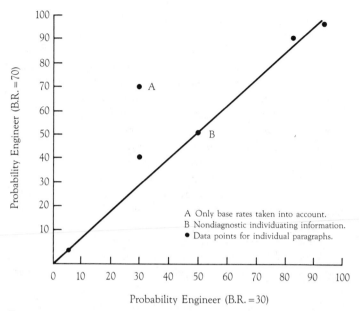

Figure showing plot with y-axis "Probability Engineer (B.R. = 70)" from 0 to 100, and x-axis "Probability Engineer (B.R. = 30)" from 0 to 100.

A Only base rates taken into account.
B Nondiagnostic individuating information.
● Data points for individual paragraphs.

Figure 16–1. Median judged probability (engineer) for five descriptions and for the null description (square symbol) under high and low probabilities

(From D. Kahneman and A. Tversky, On the psychology of prediction, *Psychological Review, 80* [1973], p. 242. Copyright 1973 by the American Psychological Association. Reprinted by permission of the publisher and author)

Notice first the 45° straight line from the origin. On that line all guesses, for all paragraphs of individuating information, would be identical for both groups. That line therefore represents *total disregard* of base rates, and to the degree that actual points plotted approach this line, we may say that base rates were ignored. As you can see, the points fall very near the line, and there was a barely significant reliance on base rates; they exerted far less effect than they should according to Bayes's Rule. The plotted point corresponding to the paragraph strongly suggesting that Jack was an engineer must be one of the two in the top-right section of the figure.

There is more that is worth notice in Figure 16–1. Suppose base rates had been all-important and individuating information totally disregarded. In that case the probability of being an engineer would always be the same, whatever the paragraph, so all data points would fall at the intersection of $p = .30$ (horizontal) and $p = .70$ (vertical), marked as point A in the figure. Clearly that is far from the case: the individuating paragraph had large effects. It is important, however, to know that the investigators included a kind of baseline condition such that subjects were asked to guess the probability that a person, with no individuating characteristics, would be an engineer. In that condition point

A *was* the result. Subjects knew how to use base rates if they did not have to integrate them with other information.

The locus of the completely nondiagnostic paragraph is also interesting. Subjects who read the paragraph about Dick decided that he was equally likely to be either a lawyer or an engineer and *disregarding supposed base rates* assigned him a probability of .50 of being an engineer. Useless individuating information is evidently not the same thing as no individuating information. When base rates only are supplied they are used, but when base rates are combined with useless individuating information the base rates are ignored, and estimates that utilize the individuating information in a way that recognizes its uselessness are made (probability of .50 in a two-choice situation). That particular result, for reasons unknown, is different from Locksley's results with sex and assertiveness. The nondiagnostic paragraph in that case led subjects to use base rates or sex stereotypes.

If you have a taste for paradoxes, the confrontation of research on stereotyping with research on decision-making will either prove deeply interesting or else cure you of the taste. Taking the findings in order of discovery, it goes like this:

1. Social psychology has generally supposed and sometimes explicitly demonstrated that beliefs about group characteristics (stereotypes) influence the treatment of individuals who belong to those groups and that this is both irrational and unfair.

2. Kahneman and Tversky (1973) and others have shown that base rates or prior probabilities when combined with individuating information tend to be almost ignored, and *this* is irrational because Bayes's Rule for integrating such information says that base rates should be taken into account along with individuating information.

3. Locksley et al. (1980) and Locksley, Hepburn, and Ortiz (1982) point out that beliefs about group characteristics are, after all, base rates or prior probabilities and so by Bayes's Rule should be utilized in rational decision-making, but that is contrary to what social psychology has always said about stereotypes.

4. Locksley et al. (1980) and Locksley, Hepburn, and Ortiz (1982) find in several experiments utilizing base rates that are stereotypes that what subjects do, apparently, is largely ignore base rates when there is individuating information, and those experiments suggest that the decision-making literature is correct, not the social psychological literature, and that humans are not Bayesian decision-makers.

How can one make sense of those contradictions? The confusion about whether it is rational or irrational to use base rates that are beliefs about group characteristics is easily cleared up. Social psychologists have generally assumed that stereotypes or beliefs about group characteristics are false, ethnocentric, or unverifiable and so it is irrational to utilize them in making decisions about individuals. It cannot be rational to rely on false beliefs no matter what Bayes's

Rule says. In addition social psychologists have been at least as much concerned about fairness or justice as about rationality. Such group membership as
race and sex are not chosen or achieved but are assigned at birth, and beliefs
about the characteristics of such groups *ought* not to effect the fate of individuals belonging to the groups, whether the beliefs are true or false, rational
or irrational. By sharp contrast with social psychologists, decision theorists
have dealt with problems in which fairness or justice is not an important consideration and with base rates assumed to be accurate for the purpose of studying decision-making.

Still open is the question whether the two studies of Locksley and her
associates, showing disregard of stereotypes when dealing with individuals, correctly represent human use of stereotypes. I think they cannot be representative
of the usual case, because that would be tantamount to claiming that there is
not now and has not been discrimination on the basis of race, sex, and nationality, which is of course absurd. Decisions that result in residential segregation by race are made all over this country and Britain every day; they are
made every time an individual (like the Pakistani medical student of the opening paragraph in this section) has had individuating data (degree, recommendations, good manners) overridden by beliefs about his group membership. And
of course all the studies showing discrimination by race, sex, or attractiveness,
with matched résumés or journal articles or whatever, constitute experimental
demonstrations of the use of stereotypes in ways that are both irrational and
unfair. Finally, Mary Amanda Dew demonstrated in a 1984 dissertation that
while base rate beliefs about sex and managerial style did not directly affect
decision-making about individuals when good individuating information was
supplied they did have an indirect effect mediated by recall.

I think that Anne Locksley's work has identified a phenomenon that occurs in the world outside the laboratory. In her studies subjects were undergraduates at New York University, and it seems likely to me that such subjects
would believe it unfair to discriminate by sex when individual information is
available, and that that would account for the 1980 results. The 1982 results
show no group discrimination (use of base rate) in terms of the categories "nocturnal" and "diurnals." While those categories are noncontroversial and indeed
never discussed, I think the student subjects might well have been opposed to
any discrimination of individuals on the basis of supposed group characteristics
and might have recognized the experimental situation as one designed to tempt
them into just that sort of unfairness. Unwillingness to discriminate between
individuals on the basis of group membership is after all only the abstract form
of the value. In the many experiments that did find discrimination (matched
résumés and so on), subjects would not have been able to recognize the discriminatory element.

My guess is that the student subjects of Locksley and her associates figured
out the point of the experiments and made socially desirable nondiscriminating
responses, but in life outside the laboratory there is much behavioral

discrimination based on group memberships. The Locksley experiments do call attention to one effect that seems to be common outside the laboratory. When information is available about an individual that is thought to be highly relevant or diagnostic, it can overcome the effects of prejudice or group base rates and become the exception that breaks the rule.

The utilization or not of base-rates in decision-making unrelated to stereotypes has turned into a complicated and fascinating story. Ajzen (1977) and Tversky and Kahneman (1980) have found that base rates that are *causally related* to the variable to be predicted are fully utilized. The engineers–lawyers problem used base rates that had no causal relevance, but beliefs about group characteristics do have a kind of causal relevance. In general the question of whether human decision-makers are Bayesian or not has become: In what circumstances and in what degree are we Bayesian? (Nisbett and Ross, 1980). To be Bayesian in decision-making is to utilize both individuating and base rate information according to a certain optimal rule.

Summary

Ethnocentrism and out-group hostility are accompanied by stereotypes of the out-group. One interesting question about stereotypes is whether they are irrational. It used to be thought that ethnic stereotypes were obviously irrational, because no characterological traits assigned to ethnic groups were true of all members, and it was assumed that when subjects said a trait was "typical" of a group they meant true of all members. However, new research has shown that what subjects mean by "typical" is not "true of all" but rather "somewhat" or "slightly" characteristic of the group in question. In that form the truth or falsity of ethnocentric stereotypes is at present unknown and never will be known, so the beliefs cannot be condemned as irrational on the ground that they are false. As probabilistic attributes of categories beliefs about ethnic groups become natural categories and as inevitable as the formation of natural categories generally is.

A second interesting question about stereotypes is whether they simply reflect political, economic, and social relations or have some causal role. The answer is that they are primarily reflections, mirroring contemporary alliance and enmities and shifting as those shift. There is, however, some stability over time and some international consensus on the reputations of Americans, English, Japanese, and so forth. Probably that stability and consensus are to be understood as the impact of a stable culture on most other cultures through its movies, literature, history, and television.

A third interesting question about stereotypes is whether or not they affect decisions about individuals when useful (or diagnostic) information on the individuals is available. Social psychology has generally assumed and sometimes explicitly demonstrated (as with matched résumés with attached female or male names) that beliefs about groups do affect treatment of individuals, and that is the impossible-to-doubt phenomenon of discrimination by sex, race, or nationality. However, in the general psychology of decision-making, beliefs about groups or stereotypes are examples of base rates, and there is considerable evidence that base rates that are not beliefs about groups are used hardly at all when individual diagnostic information is available. In two experiments Anne Locksley has found that contemporary university students who had beliefs about groups (or stereotypes) did not rely on them when given individual information, and those results suggest that general decision-making theory is correct rather than social psychology concerning the use of stereotypes. That cannot be generally so, however, because it would deny the existence of discrimination by sex, race, or nationality. The most likely resolution of the problem is that contemporary university students are very alert to identify any occasion for discrimination and recognize the Locksley experiments as such occasions; since those same students oppose discrimination of any kind they produce results in which group beliefs, or base rates, are disregarded. That amounts to a claim that Locksley's experiments are only representative of a special segment of the population operating in a special situation.

17

Conflict Resolution

WE LEFT THE EAGLES AND THE RATTLERS transformed by the black magic of group competition into opposed armies. Their minds stocked with hate-filled stereotypes, raiding one another's quarters by night and always ready for battle, it was time for Sherif to work some white magic, and he had some in mind. The large research literature on reducing group tensions suggested that two factors were more effective than any other: (1) noncompetitive contact with the two antagonistic groups having equal status, and (2) a superordinate goal that was important for all, not attainable by the efforts of either group alone but attainable by universal cooperation (Deutsch, 1949, 1973; Allport, 1954). Sherif doubted that equal status contact alone would be effective with really antagonistic groups, and in the absence of a superordinate shared goal might even exacerbate group tensions. Therefore the first part of Stage III was a test of what contact alone could accomplish.

In all, seven equal status contact situations were created: filling out questionnaires at the same time, looking at movies together, shooting off Fourth of July firecrackers together, taking meals in the same mess hall at the same time, and others. None of those contacts, nor *all* of them together, did anything to reduce group friction. When filling out questionnaires, the Rattlers read on their yellow pencils the hated name *Eagle* and refused to use that brand. For the movies and firecrackers the two groups stayed apart from one another and lobbed across the occasional insult. Meals in the mess hall turned into "garbage fights," with rolls and napkins and potatoes as projectiles. What had been twenty individual eleven-year-olds were now all either little Rattlers or little Eagles, as fixed in their opposition as Hatfields and McCoys or Montagues and Capulets.

Superordinate goals worked, but not fast. The first common problem was created by knocking out the supply of drinking water. All their water came from a storage tank about a mile up the mountain, and when the faucets stopped flowing the boys were told that the problem could be a leakage in the pipe from the tank, at any point along its route. The area was divided into four segments to be inspected and, while everyone offered to help, the volunteers for each work detail were either all Eagles or else all Rattlers. The problem turned out not to be in the pipe but in the valve on the tank, and they all came together there. When a staff member fixed the valve there was general rejoicing and the Eagles, who had no canteens and so were thirstier than the Rattlers, were permitted to drink first. On the hike back there was, for the first time, some good-natured intermingling. Nevertheless, there was another garbage fight at dinner that night.

The second superordinate goal was rental of the movie *Treasure Island*. Everybody wanted to see it, but the sum of seven dollars was needed, and the question was how to divide that among eleven Rattlers and nine Eagles (remember that two Eagles got homesick). Various proposals were made and the one that all could agree to was that each of the eleven Rattlers should contribute thirty-one cents and the nine Eagles each thirty-nine cents, with the counselors adding the odd pennies to bring each group total to $3.50. The agreement was peaceably arrived at, but it is important to notice that equity between groups, not equity for each individual was the goal, so the organization into groups still dominated their thinking. At the movie they adopted segregated seating.

The great event of the last days was a trip by truck to Cedar Lake, a camp-out there, and then an additional 30-mile drive to the Arkansas border—so they could say they had been in another state. It was taken for granted that they would travel separately in two trucks. Meal preparation and tent-pitching were so arranged as to require the campers to cooperate with one another. One truck was in bad shape, and when it got stuck all twenty boys pulled together on the former tug-of-war rope to get it started (Figure 17–1). In those last days the group lines sometimes disappeared and then, with some change in the external situation, reappeared. After a last evening back at the "house camp," the twenty boys themselves proposed that they return to Oklahoma City in a single bus, and the self-chosen seating did not reflect the Eagles and the Rattlers. One boy cried because camp was over and it had been so much fun.

The many naturalistic observations showing the end of antagonism, the development first of group cooperation and then the fading of group consciousness, were supplemented with quantitative data. Using subtle procedures that never suggested a "study," each boy was led to make friendship choices (sociometric choices). At the end of Stage II, when group opposition was at its

Successful effort to start the truck: Both groups have tug-of-war against the truck.

Getting ready to return home: *All together.*

Figure 17–1. The end of the war between the Eagles and the Rattlers

(M. Sherif, O. J. Harvey, B. J. White, W. R. Hood, and C. W. Sherif, *Intergroup Conflict and Cooperation: The Robbers Cave Experiment*, 1961, Stage 3. Courtesy University of Oklahoma Book Exchange, Norman)

peak, almost 100 percent of the friendship choices were made within the same group. At the end of Stage III it was still true that in-group choices were more frequent than out-group choices, but the ratio had become about 65 to 35 percent. Stereotypes were also obtained a second time, and some said they were glad as they had changed their minds. Rattlers now thought that almost all Eagles had become like the Rattlers themselves: *brave, tough,* and *friendly.* The Eagles said as much for the Rattlers. There were no more *sneaky, smart-aleck stinkers.* Just as attribution theory (Part II) says they should, the boys as observers of one another saw personality change as the cause of the new order, but Sherif, of course, knew better. He knew that the boys had changed their thoughts and feelings because of a succession of situations designed to require cooperative effort.

The Robbers Cave and Desegregation

The Robbers Cave experiment was carried out in 1954, and it was in 1954 that the Supreme Court ruled (*Brown* v. *Board of Education*) that in public education the doctrine "separate but equal" has no place and school desegregation was undertaken. In that same year Gordon Allport published his classic *The Nature of Prejudice* and summarized the conditions that reduce prejudice and tension between groups in these words: "Prejudice (unless deeply rooted in the character structure of the individual) may be reduced by equal status contact between majority and minority groups in the pursuit of common goals. The effect is greatly enhanced if this contact is sanctioned by institutional supports (i.e., by law, custom, or local atmosphere) . . . " (p. 281).

Allport's statement of the conditions necessary to reduce group prejudice— equal status contact in the pursuit of common goals with institutional support —was his elegant distillation of research prior to 1954. It remains, in the early 1980s, an excellent statement of research wisdom on the reduction of group hostilities (e.g. Amir, 1976; Austin and Worchel, 1979; Cook, 1978; Deschamps and Brown, 1983; Deutsch, 1949, 1973; Deutsch and Krauss, 1962; Pettigrew, 1969; Schofield, 1982; Sharan, 1980; Slavin, 1980; Sole, Marton, and Hornstein, 1975; Worchel, 1979; Worchel, Andreoli, and Folger, 1977). Allport's statement incidentally describes the conditions that eliminated hostility between the Eagles and the Rattlers. The two groups after one week of pursuing common goals, with equal group status and the support of authorities, ceased to attack one another, gave up their negative group stereotypes, voluntarily chose to desegregate at meals and on the bus ride home, and began to treat one another as individuals, choosing friends on the basis of personal qualities. Although the Supreme Court heard testimony from social scientists on school desegregation (e.g. Floyd Allport et al., 1953), it cannot be said that desegregation efforts have eliminated group hostilities in the wonderful way that Sherif's Stage III did for the Eagles and the Rattlers.

Gerard and Miller (1975) report on a very thoroughgoing longitudinal study in Riverside, California, that, long after the schools there desegregated, white, black, and Hispanic-American students continued to "hang out" in clear ethnic clusters. Stephan (1978) carefully reviewed all the research evidence on the impact of school desegregation some twenty-five years after the Court's decision and drew several tentative conclusions. The achievement level of blacks did sometimes increase after desegregation and only rarely decreased. Desegregation as such seemed not to reduce the prejudices of whites toward blacks, though most national surveys have shown some reduction of such prejudice as a result of all social forces combined. As for the prejudice of blacks toward whites, that seemed usually to increase after desegregation. Janet Ward Schofield (1982) in a detailed study of a model integrated school found that interaction and friendship, at first totally governed by group attitudes, did very slowly start to take account of personal qualities over a period of three years, and yet racial attitudes changed very little. Wax (1979) found a similarly complex pattern in an intimate portrait of five desegregated schools.

In general I think social psychologists have been disappointed in the impact of school desegregation on intergroup hostilities, but it cannot be said that this great national experiment disconfirms the hypothesis that equal status contact in the pursuit of common goals, with institutional support, reduces group hostility. The hypothesis is not disconfirmed by desegregation because it is not tested by desegregation. Institutional support from families, school boards, and neighborhoods has, to put it mildly, often been absent. Even more seriously, however, equal status contact in the pursuit of common goals is not what goes on in desegregated schools. What goes on is poignantly described by Schofield in this vignette:

> The teacher says, "If you have 400 and 90 and $7\frac{1}{2}$, how much would that be total?" He calls on Dan (black), whose hand is not raised. Dan doesn't know the answer. Three children, all white, are waving their hands in the air. Mr. Little persists with Dan and writes the three figures on the board. By this time there are six white and two black children waving their hands in the air. You can hear little moans of excitement and pleas like, "Call on me." Finally, Dan gets the answer. This class is roughly two-thirds black. [Schofield, 1982, p. 22]

Gordon Allport does not, in his 1954 book, say much about the nature of the status that must be equal, if prejudice is to be reduced, but he seems mainly to have had formal status in mind. Formal status applies to organizational roles such as manager and employee or teacher and pupil, and in the desegregated classroom that kind of organizational status is equal for white and black students. However there are other kinds of status in which majority and minority students are not equal. The socioeconomic status of blacks (income, life-style, and so on) is on the average lower than the socioeconomic status of whites, an inequality that children are aware of. Most important, the scholastic achievement status of black students is, on the average, lower than that of white students; that fact was a major reason for the desegregation decision. However the difference in achievement levels means that the contact in the desegregated classroom is, like the interracial contact in Schofield's little vignette, not equal status contact. The black students were doing less well, on the average, than the white students in the incident described.

The students in Schofield's story are also not cooperating in pursuit of a common goal. They are *competing* in pursuit of individual goals. You may have forgotten the fierce competitiveness of small children, but Schofield's description of the pants-wetting eagerness to be called on by the teacher should bring it all back. There is the effort not to let the teacher catch your eye when you do not know the answer. There is the shame at giving the wrong answer and the resentment felt for the student who gleefully corrects you. Worst of all, if you habitually do not know the right answer the teacher comes to feel awkward about calling on you and may eventually not do so at all, and you become a kind of public embarrassment.

In a cooperative social situation the attainment of one person's goal enhances the probability of attainment of the goals of others in the group. In a competitive situation, however, the attainment of one person's goal lowers the probability of the attainment of the goals of others (Deutsch, 1949; Slavin, 1980; Worchel, 1979). Competition, therefore, threatens to produce unequal distribution of rewards or resources. The important rewards or resources in a classroom are the approval of the teacher and of peers. The entitlements or relevant investments are supposed to be achievements, academic primarily, but also athletic and social. Probably those investments are seldom the only ones considered, since teachers do find one student more likable than another and may find one race more likable than another. Usually, however, the distribution of classroom rewards is proportional to classroom achievements.

The lower average achievement of minority students and resultant lower rewards and higher costs can be perceived as fair or legitimate, but in that case minority students must suffer low self-esteem. Alternatively, minority students can perceive their lower rewards and higher costs as unfair, as undeserved, but in that case they must feel anger and behave in a hostile way. It is possible for a minority student to cope with inequity of which he or she is the victim by limiting social comparison to a group doing no better than oneself and to restrict social contacts to that group, which is likely to be a same-race, same-class group. It is also possible to respond to perceived inequity on the individual level by developing what Tajfel calls a group "voice" designed to elevate social identity. All of those things happen in circumstances of competition (Deutsch, 1973; Worchel, 1979), and none of them reduces intergroup hostility, stereotyping, and segregation.

The desegregated classroom is almost always a highly competitive situation in which minority students receive less than their share of rewards and so occupy a lower status. In short, desegregation of the schools as such does not produce equal status contact and cooperative pursuit of a common goal. In a few cases, however, efforts have been made to alter the classroom experience so as to realize the conditions—equal status contact and cooperation—that social psychology identifies as necessary for the reduction of group hostility. The most interesting of those efforts is the introduction by Elliot Aronson of the "jigsaw classroom" into schools in Austin, Texas.

The Jigsaw Classroom

When the schools in Austin were desegregated by extensive busing, the result was increased racial tension among blacks, Mexican Americans, and Anglos, which erupted into violence in the high schools. The superintendent of schools consulted with Aronson, an eminent social psychologist, then at the University of Texas. Aronson thought it was both more possible and more important to try to prevent racial hostility than to try to control incidents in the high schools, so he concentrated on the elementary school classroom. It did not take him long to recognize that what was going on in these classrooms was not what Allport had recommended in 1954 but was fierce competition between persons of unequal status.

Aronson undertook to change the reward structure of the elementary school classroom from one of unequal competition to one of cooperation among equals without making any changes at all in curriculum content. The "jigsaw classroom" is a way of learning that can be employed with any content whatever. Suppose, for example, that we had a class of thirty, some Anglos, some black, and some Hispanic Americans, and that the lesson the teacher has assigned is to learn the main facts in the life of Joseph Pulitzer. The class might be broken up into five groups of six each, with the groups equated as nearly as possible in ethnic composition and in scholastic achievement levels. The lesson, Pulitzer's life, would be divided into six parts, with one part given to each member of the six-person groups. The parts might be paragraphs from Pulitzer's biography: (1) how the Pulitzer family came to the United States, (2) Joseph's childhood and education, (3) Joseph's early jobs,—and so forth. The parts are like pieces of a jigsaw puzzle in that they fit together to create a total picture.

Each group member would be given time to study his or her portion of the full biography. The group would then convene, and each member in turn would undertake to teach his part of the whole. Eventually, perhaps an hour later, everybody would be tested on the full life of Joseph Pulitzer and would receive an individual score—not a group score. Each person therefore must learn the full lesson, but each would be dependent on five others—the members of his group—for parts of the lesson that could be learned only from them. They in turn would be dependent on him. There is complete mutual interdependence. The attainment of one member's individual goal (learning his part well) facilitates the attainment of every member's goal (learning the full life). The jigsaw classroom calls for cooperation in pursuit of a common super-

ordinate goal. If you recall that point in Sherif's Stage III, when the water supply failed and Rattlers and Eagles alike were given individual segments to
search, for the path of the water pipe, it should be clear that the jigsaw classroom is an abstract equivalent of Stage III. Is it comparably effective in reducing
group hostilities?

Aronson, with various groups of associates, did a pretest (Aronson et al.,
1975), a large-scale experiment (Blaney et al., 1977), a replication with additional controls (Geffner, 1978), and a replication focused on the effect of the
jigsaw classroom on academic performance (Lucker et al., 1977). In addition to
the reports on individual studies there are several general summaries (Aronson
et al., 1975, 1978; Aronson and Bridgeman, 1979; Aronson, Bridgeman, and
Geffner, 1978). Control groups in one experiment or another have included
small groups taught by teachers in traditional competitive fashion and small
groups taught in new ways which did not entail cooperation. Dependent
variables, typically assessed before and after the learning experiences, have
included liking for group members as opposed to liking for class members generally, liking for school, self-esteem, perceptions of the academic abilities of ethnic
groups, prejudice toward ethnic groups, and academic performance on the
lessons assigned. The jigsaw classroom was not introduced as a trivial one-time
intervention. In the main experiment, for instance, fifty-three groups from
seven schools met for forty-five minutes a day, three days a week, over a total
period of six weeks.

What did the jigsaw classroom accomplish? Apparently quite a lot. "Summarizing all the research on the jigsaw technique [e.g. Blaney et al., 1977; Geffner, 1978; Lucker et al., 1977], it appears that this interdependent learning
method enhances the students' self-esteem, improves their academic performance, increases liking for their classmates, and improves some of their inter-
ethnic and intraethnic perceptions" (Aronson et al., 1978). Of course this is a
summary statement taken out of context, and the full context adds many qualifications. I find, however, that the idea of the jigsaw classroom seems so right
and the metaphor so powerful that I resist reading the qualifications, let alone
the numbers in the tables in the original articles, because I feel that the jigsaw
classroom must work. Besides, I want it to. The only thing is—If, indeed, it
accomplishes all the good effects described, how does it happen that the jigsaw
classroom has not been put into effect everywhere and race prejudice eliminated?

In part the answer lies in the magnitude of the effects obtained. If you look
at the numbers, you find that most effects were small. In the main experiment
(Blaney et al., 1977) jigsaw students liked their groupmates better, on the average, than they did the other members of the class, but on a scale from 1 to 7 the
values were 4.26 for groupmates and 4.22 for other classmates. In the same
experiment jigsaw students increased in self-esteem from pretest to posttest,
from 20.62 to 21.98 on a scale from 4 to 28. Those and other results are statistically significant when proper comparisons are made with control subjects, but

the levels of significance are not very high and the effects are not whopping. Of course it is our own fault that we were so taken with the idea of the jigsaw classroom that we imagined larger effects.

The impact of research on the jigsaw method is also diminished by the fact that the results that turn out to be significant are not quite the ones we most hoped for. Geffner (1978) found that Anglo students' perceptions of how Hispanic American students view themselves and their classmates improved. You have to read that sentence twice to notice that it does not say, as we would have most hoped, that Anglo students improved their perceptions of Hispanic Americans, or came to think more highly of them. Blaney and associates (1977) found that Hispanic American students in the jigsaw groups like school better after the learning experience than before. However, Hispanic American students in control groups taught by traditional methods also liked school better after the six-week trial, only the increased liking registered by the controls was about eight times as great as that registered by the experimental subjects.

It is not the fault of the investigators that their results are modest in size and complicated to interpret. They make the qualifications clear, and the modest magnitude of the results is perhaps a good match for the modest magnitude of the intervention—a mere forty-five minutes a day, three days a week, for a few weeks. A larger intervention might well produce larger and more interpretable effects. Ultimately I do not think it is disappointment with results that accounts for current neglect of the jigsaw classroom. My guess is that there is a problem with the jigsaw plan, a problem, interestingly enough, that is concealed by the metaphor of the jigsaw puzzle.

If the pieces of a real jigsaw puzzle were doled out—one to a person—and then assembled by the group, one would expect any one person to do about as well as any other in adding his bit to the total. There is almost no skill element involved in fitting a particular piece and so assembling a real jigsaw puzzle would be a case of cooperation among equals in achieving a superordinate goal. Suppose, however, that we shift the metaphor and call the same group learning arrangement by a different name: the "baseball classroom."

Why baseball? What has the procedure in common with the game? Nothing superficial; no parts that are fitted together. However, the members of a baseball team do cooperate in the interest of a superordinate goal: winning the game. The attainment of each individual's goal (pitching a no-hit inning; catching a fly ball; hitting a home run) increases the probability of attaining the group goal. While individuals do not contribute distinct pieces of a picture, they do play distinct roles in a process, and the roles are called by such names as pitcher, catcher, first baseman, and so on. So the interdependent classroom has about as much abstract resemblance to baseball as it does to a jigsaw puzzle. In one respect, however, the two metaphors, or models, are very unlike. There is a very large skill element in playing the various roles in baseball, much larger than there is in fitting the various pieces of a jigsaw puzzle.

Is baseball cooperative or is it competitive? It is both, but it certainly is not purely cooperative. Suppose someone is not very good at baseball. A high school team would probably make him the right fielder. A team depends on its right fielder, but the occasions of critical dependence are not numerous. Still they do arise, as with the fly to right that might easily—most would think— be caught. Baseball, unlike soccer, football, or hockey, has the interesting property of repeatedly exposing individual performance in maximal degree. The right fielder positioning himself to catch the ball is the object of universal attention—and assessment. If the individual fails to perform up to some standard, then the interdependence of the players on the team ceases to be an agreeable feature and becomes an excruciatingly painful one. If you drop that fly ball you not only let yourself down, you *let down the team!* Few social experiences are more painful at high school age.

In the research on the interdependent classroom there are indications that it was sometimes more like a baseball game than like assembling a jigsaw puzzle. For instance, in the main experiment those Hispanic American students who were controls and received six weeks of traditional teaching liked school better at the end than did the Mexican-American students who had six weeks of interdependent small group learning. The authors write: "It seems possible that the latter result may be due to the language and communication problems of many Hispanic American students, problems which initially may be exacerbated by being forced to teach material and speak with classmates in English" (p. 126). And in an article for *Psychology Today* Aronson and his collaborators (1975) describe the plight of a student whom they call "Carlos." Carlos, they suggest, stammers and hesitates in presenting his part of the lesson because of a language problem, and the other kids resort to ridicule and teasing. "Aw, you don't know it," accused Mary. "You're dumb; you're stupid. You don't know what you're doing" (p. 47). Carlos was, it seems, in the position of an inept right fielder.

The inventors of the jigsaw classroom suggest that Carlos would benefit in the end from having his language problem repeatedly exposed. In a traditional classroom it might simply go unexposed by a teacher who is embarrassed for him or perhaps considers him beyond help. That could well be true of any particular Carlos trying to improve his English, but Carlos is only a sign of a general problem intrinsic to the design of the jigsaw classroom. There is inevitably an element of skill in the task of teaching the group your portion of the lesson, an element of skill greater than is required to fit a piece into a jigsaw puzzle. With the Joseph Pulitzer lesson the main skill would be English fluency, and all students could be expected soon to attain a minimal competence in that skill, but the lessons in successive grades would have to become progressively more difficult, extending to literature, sentence-diagramming, algebra, and so forth, and the skill element in teaching a portion of a lesson ever greater. What would happen then?

Academic achievement is necessarily not a team sport; it is a game of individual competition, because it is the game that introduces all the serious games that come later and determines the level of individual entry into those games: blue collar jobs, nursing, business, teaching, medicine, and so on. And it is evidently not easy to make academic achievement into a team sport by altering the form of the national government or social structure; school is just as competitive in Communist Russia or somewhat-Socialist Britain as in the United States. In Aronson's jigsaw classroom exam grades are assigned to individuals, not to interdependent groups, and that is the way it must be if the learning method is going to be adopted by real schools. Imagine now that an academically advantaged Anglo student starts bringing home lower grades than usual. What is he likely to say if his classroom has recently been jigsawed? What attribution will he make?

"The teacher has us teaching each other and in our group we've got this kid Carlos who can't hardly even speak English." Irate parent: "You mean you're being taught by a little Chicano!" Or—another possibility—"You mean the black children are doing the teaching! What are we paying the teachers for?" Or some other equally nasty scene. It seems inevitable, given the initial academic inequalities, the dependence of each member on each other member, and the self-esteem bias which causes failures to be attributed externally. The very interdependence that is the point of the jigsaw plan would become a force for group hostility, so the jigsaw classroom contains, I think, a "self-destruct" feature.

An Ideal School

Social psychology's ideas about the conditions necessary to reduce group hostility—equal status contact in the cooperative pursuit of a superordinate goal—are not unknown to educators, and, when external circumstances have permitted, attempts have been made to operate an entire school program in accordance with them. The best-conceived of those was the Wexler Middle School in the city of Waterford (names are fictitious), and we are all fortunate that a sensitive psychologist, Janet Ward Schofield, studied the first three years of Wexler's operation using the ethnographic methods of participation, observation, and interviewing. When the school opened, a local newspaper wrote: "If anything, Wexler may be too good . . . . But the administration is putting its best foot forward and worrying later about future successes" (Schofield, 1982, p. 1). Less than four years later another paper characterized Wexler as "a racial timebomb ticking toward disaster." It was not the social psychology applied in the school that brought about the change but the impingement on a beautiful experiment of forces in the external situation.

In Waterford the Board of Education had not yet, in the 1970s, devised a workable plan of desegregation, and it was under pressure from the state to do so. Therefore when a new, lavishly outfitted middle school (grades 6-8) was built, the board committed itself to the goal in this school, not of desegregation only, but of positive racial integration. The target enrollment was 58 percent white and 42 percent black, a ratio reflecting that of the school system as a whole. Admission was to be on an open first come, first served basis from twenty-four elementary schools in the district. Applications from black students came in much faster than applications from white students, and when the school first opened in the fall of 1975 the white quota had not been filled; the ratio was almost exactly 50–50. There were many things that made Wexler attractive to both black and white families including, besides the superlative physical facilities, a superior faculty and an enriched program for high-IQ students, but it was more attractive to blacks, because the schools otherwise available to them were much worse than those available to whites.

While Wexler School did not officially adopt Gordon Allport as its guide to effective integration, its efforts certainly matched his recommendations. In the interest of equalizing formal status 25 percent of the faculty were black, including the vice-principals in charge of the sixth and seventh grades. The school requested more black faculty, but none were available within the system. Neither race was a minority within the school, and neither race had the status of "outsiders," which black students usually have, because the school had no history as a segregated institution, the residential area was racially neutral, and no students had to be bused in.

Equality of achievement status was not attained, but more was done to deemphasize inequality than is usual. Honor rolls were discouraged, and students were not assigned to "fast" and "slow" tracks. Still, there were some hard facts of unequal achievement that no one could fail to see. The enriched high-IQ class, instituted to attract white students, was in fact 75 percent white, whereas the unavoidable special class for retarded students was 70 percent black. Of sixty-eight sixth-grade students who had an "A" average, sixty were white. Behind those differences of student achievement were differences of parental education; most of the black parents had not graduated from high school, whereas most of the white parents had some post–high school education. And there were the attendant large differences of income and life-style.

Institutional support for integration and the goal of racial harmony was unusually strong. The Board of Education was unequivocal in its statements, the opening day ceremonies were a dream of equal dignity, but best of all was the school's principal, a white male to be sure, but an equalitarian idealist with great practical wisdom. The teachers were all supportive of integration, and the parents were at least sufficiently supportive to send their children to a racially mixed school.

Institutional support was good, equality of formal status was good, achievement was unequal between races, but the inequality was less emphasized than usual. Of the general prescription, that leaves only cooperation in pursuit of shared goals to be satisfied. In connection with the jigsaw classroom I suggested that real schooling, with grades that count, cannot be only cooperative with no competition at all. However there can certainly be some cooperation. The school's principal believed in the importance of interracial cooperative activities and urged his faculty to develop them. One teacher organized a class into racially mixed groups of six students and rewarded them *as a group*, not as individuals, for some activities. For example a group as a whole would be dismissed as soon as it had cleaned up its work space. The great opportunity for cooperation came, however, in extracurricular activities. Students worked to raise funds to buy special equipment for the use of all—just like the Eagles and Rattlers putting their money together to rent *Treasure Island.* Preparation of a Broadway musical was a particularly great cooperative success, because there were many different things to be done requiring a variety of talents.

It should not be thought that the various efforts to facilitate interracial harmony always went smoothly. A white student, fed up with racially mixed groups, complained: "I came here for my own education, not for somebody else's" (p. 43). The belief of the teachers was that academics came first and group relations second, so they would temporarily divide classes into fast and slow learners because, of course, such groups are more teachable. The fact that such groupings also temporarily reintroduced segregation seemed secondary. One teacher (black) posted in the front of the room an honor roll of "Super Mathematicians" despite the general policy of minimizing comparisons.

Even in Wexler's best years, the first two, Allport's conditions for reducing group hostility were a goal unevenly approached and never reached. It is not surprising, therefore, that the results were quite mixed. On the one hand racial "incidents" were extremely rare. On the other hand black and white students tended to resegregate themselves whenever groupings were voluntary, as in the cafeteria and on the playground. At the end of three years there were numerous black–white friendships, but they were limited to school hours; the friends did not go to one another's homes or meet on weekends.

Interracial behavior changed more than beliefs did. The stereotypes of the blacks, in the minds of both black and white students, was that they were physically tougher, more combative, and more assertive, outstanding at athletics but poor at academics. Whites were thought by all students to be smarter, harder working and more rule-abiding. Blacks also thought whites conceited; whites found blacks intimidating. And yet, as the three years at Wexler passed, there was more voluntary racial mixing, and almost all students interviewed at the end of three years thought relations between the races had either improved or stayed the same; very few said they had deteriorated. Black students saw substantially more improvement than did the white students.

One lesson was learned perfectly: to speak of race at all was taboo. Friends of mine who teach in the Boston public schools tell me that that taboo operates in all racially mixed schools. It is not an impressive achievement, because it is simple verbal compliance and is limited to mixed-race school settings. Another facet of Wexler's school culture that is common in racially mixed schools was the belief of the teachers that they themselves had become "color blind." A teacher in such schools will often say, running over the names in his class-book, that he could not tell you whether a given student is black or white, because he treats each as an individual. That may sometimes be true, but what is most clear about the claim is that it expresses what many teachers think of as a teaching ideal. However the taboo on any talk about race and the teachers' contention that they themselves are color blind may be unhealthy in view of the abundant evidence from voluntary resegregation and social stereotypes that race is attended to by everyone in the schools. Superficial compliance with school ideals may simply mean that real problems cannot be discussed or, perhaps, even thought about.

Beliefs about race and beliefs about gender (masculinity and femininity) interacted in a very interesting way at Wexler Middle School. If black males are more assertive, athletic, and combative than white males, then, in accordance with the usual stereotype of masculinity (Chapter 9) blacks are also more masculine. At Wexler it was clear that the combined stereotypes called into question the masculinity of the white boys and that they sometimes felt intimidated yet unable to make such "feminine" responses as submission or withdrawal. The result was a social–psychological innovation. About forty boys formed a social club called the "Mice." When people think *mice*, they think *white*, but thinking is not saying and so does not violate the taboo against reference to race. What was the club for? Well, it was supposed to be for parties and so on, but mainly it was for protection. If one mouse got beat up, the whole collective would go after his attacker. A number of black students then formed a club called the "Dogs" and for a while it looked as if the Eagles and the Rattlers had been reincarnated, but the school's principal, working adroitly with the parents, got the clubs to break up before they turned into gangs.

If blacks are more athletic, assertive, and combative, and so more masculine, then it is conceivable that they will be more attractive to girls, including white girls. While Wexler school authorities promoted interracial contacts in general, they made a definite exception of romance and sex. The principal explained that the school's existence was conditional, as far as parents were concerned, on opposition to interracial love affairs. Still, there were some star-crossed cases. One white girl, from a wealthy and prominent family, was so seriously in love that the teachers had to keep her under constant surveillance. It is interesting that the cross-race romances all involved a black male and white female, never a black female and white male, and the same asymmetry applies to other schools and to interracial marriages. Janet Schofield suggests that the asymmetry may result in part from the fact that the supposed black traits, which make the black male seem more masculine, also have the effect of making the black female seem less feminine.

The approximately Allportean social climate at Wexler Middle School produced in its first three years what Schofield calls "a definite, but relatively modest, improvement in relations between black and white students" (1982, p. 157). Some of those at the school who were most committed to the ideal of integration were hoping soon to bring off a genuine success story. However, events external to the climate of the school were developing in a way that would eventually change the climate. Wexler at the end of its first year was perceived as a great success, and then the Board of Education announced a plan to open another middle school, the Maple Avenue School, in a converted building nearly three-quarters of a century old. Maple Avenue School would receive assigned students from several all-black elementary schools, so Maple Avenue, a very inferior facility, would be all-black, while excellent Wexler had a 50–50 ratio. Several groups of people began to make social comparisons, and they came to different conclusions about equity or justice.

Black parents saw it this way: Wexler in its first year had had difficulty meeting its target percentage for whites (58 percent) and in the end enrolled only 50 percent whites, which included *all who had applied* right up to the last minute. Hundreds of black applications had been turned down, and, for the second year of Wexler's operations, the hundreds of blacks turned down were mostly assigned to Maple Avenue. Why should white children all have the alternative of Wexler or some school they wanted still more (since none were turned down) when most black children could not get into a school as good as Wexler. In the words of one father:

> "Where is the financing coming from to make the school [Maple Avenue] as good as Wexler? . . . The Board is committed to keeping blacks in their place . . . . We are charging the Board with fraud and genocide by unscrupulous administration. You have . . . for over twenty years planned the death of black children. You have killed our children mentally." [Schofield, 1982, p. 186].

A group of black parents brought a class action suit charging that the board had no right to open a segregated inferior facility in view of the availability of Wexler. The judge agreed with them and ordered the board to close Maple Avenue and reassign the students, some of them to Wexler. The board appealed the verdict but, in the second year, yielded to the pressure by increasing the total size of the entering sixth grade and increased the black percentage to 64 percent. The evidence is that the second year went very well, but the image of the school in the city began to change. There was talk of a racial "tipping point" and there were threats of "white flight" from Wexler, two terrible catch phrases which so easily transform reality.

In the third year of its operation Wexler School's total enrollment was only 61 percent black, which is not much above the 58 percent original target figure for whites. Next year it would be 71 percent black, but it was already believed to be at least 80 percent black, and white children, finding themselves with more blacks in school than anywhere else, talked of—another terrible catch phrase—"wall to wall blacks." At the same time the increased total enrollment at Wexler had begun to overload its facilities and change its goals. Cooperative programs and racially balanced classes were being given up. The visionary school principal was fired. By the sixth year, the last of which Schofield gives an account, Wexler seemed destined to become a racially imbalanced, largely black school, with little in the way of innovative teaching or high ideals.

How can anyone possibly fix the blame? The black parents were right in saying that it was unjust for white students to have Wexler or better when the black students had Wexler or worse. Yet in pressing their rights they set in motion a set of processes sure to make Wexler fail in its goal of interracial harmony and likely to make it fail in its goal of intellectual excellence. But those processes were not inevitable mechanical processes. They went as they did only because people thought and felt certain things. The external processes are not necessarily outside the domain of social psychology, though some are economic and some political, but they are outside the domain of Wexler's Allportean social climate—and beyond the control of those who worked at creating that climate.

Summary

The general prescription for resolving group conflict is equal status contact in the cooperative pursuit of a superordinate goal. The conflict between the Rattlers and the Eagles was resolved not by equal status contact but by cooperation over several days aimed at attaining shared goals. Desegregated schooling in the United States produces some contact, with equality of formal status as pupils, but there is usually serious inequality of academic achievement and always individual competition rather than cooperation. Therefore the small success of desegregation in reducing racial conflict does not disconfirm the value of the general prescription. The jigsaw classroom is a learning situation designed to replace individual competition with group cooperation. It has had some success but is severely limited by a residual competitive feature.

When Wexler Middle School in the city of Waterford first opened in 1975 a serious effort was made to satisfy the conditions of the general prescription for reducing interracial conflict. While it proved impossible fully to realize the ideal, Wexler probably came as close as any public school has managed to, and the result, after three years, was a definite but modest improvement in race relations. However, forces in the external community made it necessary for Wexler to admit too many students, to desert its 50–50 racial balance, and eventually give up its innovative programs and high ideals.

Conclusions

Part VI has been a pessimistic section. Ethnic hostilities seem to be rooted in ethnocentrism, inequitable distribution of resources, and stereotyping, which is simply natural category formation. None of those three can be easily changed, hence it is not surprising that the reduction of group hostility has turned out to be a discouraging task. But of course a discussion of the social psychology of ethnic hostility that was not pessimistic could hardly be realistic. The history of man and, I will guess, the newspapers on the day that you read this, though I cannot know what day that will be, confirm the universality and resistance to change of ethnic hostility.

> We can easily reduce our detractors to absurdity and show them their hostility is groundless. But what does this prove? That their hatred is *real*. When every slander has been rebutted, every misconception cleared up, every false opinion about us overcome, intolerance itself will remain finally irrefutable. [Moritz Goldstein, "Deutsch-jüdischer Parnass"]

I had intended to let Moritz Goldstein's words end Part VI, but then in June of 1984 I participated in a trifling episode which I would rather end with. My good friend of many years, the painter Dorothy Iannone, who lives in Berlin, was visiting Boston. There are not many people like Dorothy. She lives for art and love and friendship. She has never compromised her goals and somehow this has made her radiantly cheerful and spontaneous. We were walking in the Back Bay area of Boston near midnight. On the stairs of a rundown government building, in the otherwise unpeopled scene, we saw two black boys sitting, one about ten and the other about 5, staring glumly at the ground. Instead of looking aside and politely passing by, in the manner of Americans, Dorothy said: "Hi, darlings, what are you doing?" and gave them a dazzling smile. They looked startled and made no answer, but when we were about 20 feet past them Dorothy looked back and saw the little one looking at her and smiling shyly. She immediately blew him a kiss and he blew one back—from the palm, not the fingers, since he was just a shaver. That was June, and June is the month of promise.

References for Part VI

ABELES, R. D. 1976. Relative deprivation, rising expectations, and black militancy, *Journal of Social Issues, 32*: 119–37.

ADAMS, J. S. 1965. Inequity in social exchange. In L. Berkowitz (ed.), *Advances in Experimental Social Psychology.* New York: Academic Press, 2: 267–99.

AJZEN, I. 1977. Intuitive theories of events and the effects of base-rate information on prediction, *Journal of Personality and Social Psychology, 35*: 303–14.

ALLEN, V. L. 1965. Situational factors in conformity. In L. Berkowitz (ed.), *Advances in Experimental Social Psychology.* New York: Academic Press, 2: 133–75.

ALLPORT, F. H., et al. 1953. The effects of segregation and the consequences of desegregation: A social science statement, *Minnesota Law Review, 37*: 429–40.

ALLPORT, G. W. 1954. *The Nature of Prejudice.* Cambridge, Mass.: Addison-Wesley.

AMIR, Y. 1976. The role of intergroup contact in change of prejudice and ethnic relations. In P. A. Katz (ed.), *Toward the Elimination of Racism.* New York: Pergamon, pp. 245–308.

ARONSON, E.; N. T. BLANEY; J. SIKES; C. STEPHAN; and M. SNAPP. 1975. Busing and racial tension: The jigsaw route to learning and liking, *Psychology Today,* February, pp. 43–59.

ARONSON, E.; N. T. BLANEY; C. STEPHAN; J. SIKES; and M. SNAPP. 1978. *The Jigsaw Classroom.* Beverly Hills: Sage.

ARONSON, E., and D. L. BRIDGEMAN. 1979. Jigsaw groups and the desegregated classroom: In pursuit of common goals, *Personality and Social Psychology Bulletin, 5*: 438–46.

ARONSON, E.; D. L. BRIDGEMAN; and R. GEFFNER. 1978. The effects of a cooperative classroom structure on student behavior and attitudes. In D. Bar-Tal and L. Saxe (eds.), *Social Psychology of Education.* New York: Wiley, pp. 257–72.

ASCH, S. E. 1951. Effects of group pressure upon the modification and distortion of judgments. In H. Guetzkow (ed.), *Groups, Leadership, and Men.* Pittsburgh: Carnegie Press, pp. 177–90.

AUSTIN, W. G., and S. WORCHEL (eds.). 1979. *The Social Psychology of Intergroup Relations.* Monterey, Calif.: Brooks/Cole.

BEATTIE, G. W.; C. AGAHI; and C. SPENCER. 1982. Social stereotypes held by different occupational groups in post-revolutionary Iran, *European Journal of Social Psychology, 12*: 75–87.

BERKOWITZ, L. 1982. Aversive conditions as stimuli to aggression. In L. Berkowitz (ed.), *Advances in Experimental Social Psychology.* New York: Academic Press, 15: 249–88.

BERRY, J. W.; R. KALIN; and D. M. TAYLOR. 1977. *Multiculturalism and Ethnic Attitudes in Canada.* Ottawa: Minister of Supply and Services.

BILLIG, M., and H. TAJFEL. 1973. Social categorization and similarity in intergroup behaviour, *European Journal of Social Psychology, 3*: 27–52.

BLAKE, R. R., and J. S. MOUTON. 1962. The intergroup dynamics of win–lose conflict and problem-solving collaboration in union–management relations. In M. Sherif (ed.), *Intergroup Relations and Leadership.* New York: Wiley.

———. 1979. Intergroup problem solving in organizations: From theory to practice. In

W. G. Austin and S. Worchel (eds.), *The Social Psychology of Intergroup Relations.* Monterey, Calif.: Brooks/Cole, pp. 19–32.

BLANEY, N. T.; C. STEPHAN; D. ROSENFIELD; E. ARONSON; and J. SIKES. 1977. Interdependence in the classroom: A field study, *Journal of Educational Psychology,* 69: 121–28.

BORNSTEIN, G.; L. CRUM; J. WITTENBRAKER; K. HARRING; C. A. INSKO; and J. THIBAUT. 1983a. On the measurement of social orientations in the minimal group paradigm, *European Journal of Social Psychology,* 13: 321–50.

——. 1983b. Reply to Turner's comments, *European Journal of Social Psychology,* 13: 369–81.

BOURHIS, R. Y.; H. GILES; and H. TAJFEL. 1973. Language as a determinant of Welsh identity, *European Journal of Social Psychology,* 3: 447–60.

BRAND, E. S.; A. RUIZ; and A. M. PADILLA. 1974. Ethnic identification and preference: A review, *Psychological Bulletin,* 81: 860–90.

BRANTHWAITE, A., and J. E. JONES. 1975. Fairness and discrimination: English vs. Welch, *European Journal of Social Psychology,* 5: 323–28.

BREWER, M. B. 1979a. Ingroup bias in the minimal intergroup situation: A cognitive motivational analysis, *Psychological Bulletin,* 86: 307–24.

——. 1979b. The role of ethnocentrism in intergroup conflict. In W. G. Austin and S. Worchel (eds.), *The Social Psychology of Intergroup Relations.* Monterey, Calif.: Brooks/Cole, pp. 71–84.

BREWER, M. B., and M. SILVER. 1978. Ingroup bias as a function of task characteristics, *European Journal of Social Psychology,* 8: 393–400.

BRIGHAM, J. C. 1971a. Ethnic stereotypes, *Psychological Bulletin,* 76: 15–38.

——. 1971b. Views of white and black schoolchildren concerning racial differences. Paper presented at the meeting of the Midwestern Psychological Association, Detroit.

BROWN, ROGER. 1965. *Social Psychology.* Glencoe, Ill.: Free Press.

BROWN, RUPERT. 1978. Divided we fall: An analysis of relations between sections of a factory workforce. In Tajfel, H. (ed.), *Differentiation Between Social Groups.* New York: Academic Press.

BROWN, R., and R. J. HERRNSTEIN. 1975. *Psychology.* Boston: Little, Brown.

BUCHANAN, W., and H. CANTRIL. 1953. *How Nations See Each Other.* Urbana: University of Illinois Press.

CADDICK, B. 1980. Equity theory, social identity, and intergroup relations. *Review of Personality and Social Psychology,* 1: 219–45.

CAMPBELL, D. T. 1965. Ethnocentric and other altruistic motives. In D. Levine (ed.), *Nebraska Symposium on Motivation.* Lincoln: University of Nebraska Press, 13: 283–311.

CLARK, K. B., and M. P. CLARK. 1947. Racial identification and preference in Negro children. In T. Newcomb and E. L. Hartley (eds.), *Readings in Social Psychology.* New York: Holt, pp. 169–78.

——. 1980. What do blacks think of themselves? *Ebony,* pp. 176–82.

COHEN, A. R. 1955. Social norms, arbitrariness of frustration, and status of the agent of frustration in the frustration–aggression hypothesis, *Journal of Abnormal and Social Psychology*, 51: 222–26.

COOK, S. W. 1978. Interpersonal and attitudinal outcomes in cooperating interracial groups, *Journal of Research and Development in Education*, 12: 97–113.

DANN, H., and W. DOISE. 1974. Ein neuer methodologischer Ansatz sur experimentellen Erforschung von Intergroupen-Beziehungen, *Zeitschrift für Sozialpsychologie*, 5: 2–15.

DESCHAMPS, J. C., and R. BROWN. 1983. Superordinate goals and intergroup conflict, *British Journal of Social Psychology*, 22: 189–95.

DEUTSCH, M. 1949. An experimental study of the effects of cooperation and competition upon group process, *Human Relations*, 2: 199–231.

——. 1973. *The Resolution of Conflict*. New Haven: Yale University Press.

DEUTSCH, M., and R. M. KRAUSS. 1962. Studies of interpersonal bargaining, *Journal of Conflict Resolution*, 6: 52–76.

DOISE, W., and A. SINCLAIR. 1973. The categorization process in intergroup relations, *European Journal of Social Psychology*, 3: 145–57.

DOISE, W.; G. CSEPELI; H. D. DANN; C. GOUGE; K. LARSEN; and A. OSTELL. 1972. An experimental investigation into the formation of intergroup representations, *European Journal of Social Psychology*, 2: 202–4.

DUNCKLING, L. A. 1977. *First Names First*. London: Dent.

EISENACHER, A. 1983. You are old, Father William: An exploration of age and name stereotypes. Research paper on file with Roger Brown, Harvard University.

FANON, F. 1967. *Toward the African Revolution*. New York: Grove.

FERGUSON, C. K., and H. H. KELLEY. 1964. Significant factors in over-evaluation of own group's product, *Journal of Abnormal and Social Psychology*, 69: 223–28.

FESTINGER, L. 1954. A theory of social comparison processes, *Human Relations*, 7: 117–40.

FIDELL, L. S. 1970. Empirical verification of sex discrimination in hiring practices in psychology, *American Psychologist*, 75: 1094–98.

FORM, W. A., and J. A. GESCHWENDER. 1962. Social reference basis for job satisfaction: The case of manual workers, *American Sociological Review*, 27: 228–37.

FRIEND, P.; R. KALIN; and H. GILES. 1979. Sex bias in the evaluation of journal articles: Sexism in England, *British Journal of Social and Clinical Psychology*, 18: 77–78.

GEFFNER, R. A. 1978. The effects of interdependent learning on self-esteem, inter-ethnic relations, and intra-ethnic attitudes of elementary school children: A field experiment. Unpublished doctoral dissertation, University of California at Santa Cruz.

GERARD, H., and N. MILLER. 1975. *School Desegregation*. New York: Plenum.

GILBERT, G. M. 1951. Stereotype persistence and change among college students, *Journal of Abnormal and Social Psychology*, 46: 245–54.

GILES, H., and P. F. POWESLAND. 1976. Speech style and social evaluation. *European Monographs in Social Psychology* (No. 9). London: Academic Press.

GILLIGAN, C. 1982. *In a Different Voice*. Cambridge, Mass.: Harvard University Press.

GOETHALS, G. R., and J. M. DARLEY. 1977. Social comparison theory. In J. M. Suls and R. L. Miller (eds.), *Social Comparison Processes*. New York: Wiley, pp. 259–77.

HARRIS, S., and J. R. BRAUN. 1971. Self-esteem and racial preference in black children,

Proceedings of the 79th Annual Convention of the American Psychological Association, vol. 6.

HAYAKAWA, S. I. 1981. *Language in Action*. New York: Harcourt, Brace.

HELLER, M. S. 1982. Negotiations of language choice in Montreal. In J. Gumperz (ed.), *Language and Social Identity*. Cambridge, England: Cambridge University Press.

HIRSCHMAN, A. O. 1972. *Exit, Voice, and Loyalty: Responses to Decline in Firms, Organizations, and States*. 2d ed. Cambridge, Mass.: Harvard University Press.

HOMANS, G. C. 1974. *Social Behavior: Its Elementary Forms*. Rev. Ed. New York: Harcourt Brace Jovanovich.

HOWARD, J., and M. ROTHBART. 1980. Social categorization and memory for in-group and out-group behavior, *Journal of Personality and Social Psychology*, 38: 301–10.

HRABA, J., and G. GRANT. 1970. Black is beautiful: A re-examination of racial preference and identification, *Journal of Personality and Social Psychology*, 16: 398–402.

HYMAN, H. H. 1942. The psychology of status, *Archives of Psychology*, No. 269.

JENKINS, A. 1985. Hearts and minds: The relationship between racial attitudes and self-esteem in young children. Unpublished honors thesis in the Department of Psychology and Social Relations, Harvard University.

JONES, E. E., and H. B. GERARD. 1977. *Foundations of Social Psychology*. New York: Wiley.

KAHN, A. S., and A. H. RYEN. 1972. Factors influencing the bias towards one's own group, *International Journal of Group Tensions*, 2: 33–50.

KAHNEMAN, D., and A. TVERSKY. 1973. On the psychology of prediction, *Psychological Review*, 80: 237–51.

KARAS, M. 1983. A names survey. Research paper on file with Roger Brown, Harvard University.

KARLINS, M.; T. L. COFFMAN; and G. WALTERS. 1969. On the fading of social stereotypes: Studies in three generations of college students, *Journal of Personality and Social Psychology*, 13: 1–16.

KATZ, D., and K. W. BRALY. 1933. Racial stereotypes of one hundred college students, *Journal of Abnormal and Social Psychology*, 28: 280–90.

KOHLBERG, L. 1958. The development of modes of thinking and choices in the years 10 to 16. Unpublished doctoral dissertation, University of Chicago.

———. 1981. *The Philosophy of Moral Development*. San Francisco: Harper & Row.

KORZYBSKI, A. 1933. *Science and Sanity: An Introduction to Non-Aristotelian Systems and General Semantics*. Lancaster, England: Science Press.

KULIK, J. A., and R. BROWN. 1979. Frustration, attribution of blame, and aggression, *Journal of Experimental Social Psychology*, 15: 183–94.

LABOV, W. 1966. *The Social Stratification of English in New York City*. Washington, D.C.: Center for Applied Linguistics.

———. 1982. Objectivity and commitment in linguistic science: The case of the Black English trial in Ann Arbor, *Language in Society*, 11: 165–201.

LAMBERT, W. E. 1980. The social psychology of language; A perspective for the 1980s. In H. Giles, W. P. Robinson, and P. A. Smith (eds.), *Language; Social Psychological Perspectives*. Oxford: Pergamon Press.

———. 1984. An overview of issues in immersion education. In California State Department of Education, *Studies on Immersion Education*. Sacramento, pp. 8–30.

LAMBERT, W. E.; R. C. HODGSON; R. C. GARDNER; and S. FILLENBAUM. 1960. *Journal of Abnormal and Social Psychology*, 60: 44–51.

LATANÉ, B., and S. WOLF. 1981. The social impact of majorities and minorities, *Psychological Review*, 88: 438–53.

LEVINE, R. A., and D. T. CAMPBELL. 1972. *Ethnocentrism: Theories of Conflict, Ethnic Attitudes, and Group Behavior*. New York: Wiley.

LIPPMANN, W. 1922. *Public Opinion*. New York: Harcourt, Brace.

LOCKSLEY, A.; E. BORGIDA; N. BREKKE; and C. HEPBURN. 1980. Sex stereotypes and social judgment, *Journal of Personality and Social Psychology*, 39: 821–31.

LOCKSLEY, A.; C. HEPBURN; and V. ORTIZ. 1982. Social stereotypes and judgments of individuals: An instance of the base-rate fallacy, *Journal of Experimental Social Psychology*, 18: 23–42.

LOCKSLEY, A.; V. ORTIZ; and C. HEPBURN. 1980. Social categorization and discriminatory behavior: Extinguishing the minimal intergroup discrimination effect, *Journal of Personality and Social Psychology*, 39: 773–83.

LUCKER, G. W.; D. ROSENFIELD; J. SIKES; and E. ARONSON. 1977. Performance in the interdependent classroom: A field study, *American Educational Research Journal*, 13: 115–23.

LYON, D., and P. SLOVIC. 1976. Dominance of accuracy information and neglect of base rates in probability estimation, *Acta Psychologica*, 40: 287–98.

MAASS, A., and R. D. CLARK III. 1983. Internalization versus compliance: Differential processes underlying minority influence and conformity, *European Journal of Social Psychology*, 13: 197–215.

MANN, L. 1969. Queue culture: The waiting line as a social system, *American Journal of Sociology*, 75: 340–54.

MARX, G. T. 1969. *Protest and Prejudice*. New York: Harper & Row.

MAURICE, S. 1985. Evaluative reactions to spoken languages: Attitudes of French Canadians, *McGill Student Journal of Psychology*, 1: 84–97.

MCCAULEY, C., and C. L. STITT. 1978. An individual and quantitative measure of stereotypes, *Journal of Personality and Social Psychology*, 36: 929–40.

MCCAULEY, C.; C. L. STITT; and M. SEGAL. 1980. Stereotyping: From prejudice to prediction, *Psychological Bulletin*, 87: 195–208.

MILNER, D. *Children and Race*. 1975. Harmondsworth, Middlesex: Penguin.

MISCHEL, H. 1974. Sex bias in the evaluation of professional achievements, *Journal of Educational Psychology*, 94: 237–41.

MOSCOVICI, S. 1976. *Social Influence and Social Change. European Monographs in Social Psychology*, No. 10. London: Academic Press.

———. 1980. Toward a theory of conversion behavior. In L. Berkowitz (ed.), *Advances in Experimental Social Psychology*. New York: Academic Press, 13: 209–39.

MOSCOVICI, S., and C. FAUCHEUX. 1972. Social influence, conformity bias and the study of active minorities. In L. Berkowitz (ed.), *Advances in Experimental Social Psychology*, New York: Academic Press, 6: 149–202.

MOSCOVICI, S., and E. LAGE. 1976. Studies in social influence III: Majority versus minority influence in a group, *European Journal of Social Psychology*, 6: 149–74.

MOSCOVICI, S.; E. LAGE; and M. NAFFRECHOUX. 1969. Influence of a consistent minority on the responses of a majority to a color-perception task. *Sociometry*, 32: 365–80.

MOSCOVICI, S., and B. PERSONNAZ. 1980. Studies in social influence v. minority influence and conversion behavior in a perceptual task, *Journal of Experimental Social Psychology*, 16: 270–82.

MUGNY, G. 1974–75. Majorité et minorité: Le niveau de leur influence, *Bulletin de Psychologie*, 28: 789–93.

——. 1975. Negotiations, image of the other, and the process of minority influence, *European Journal of Social Psychology*, 5: 209–28.

NEMETH, C. 1979. The role of an active minority in inter-group conflict. In W. G. Austin and S. Worchel (eds.), *The Psychology of Intergroup Relations*. Monterey, Calif.: Brooks/Cole, pp. 225–36.

NEMETH, C.; M. SWEDLUND; and B. KANKI. 1974. Patterning of the minority responses and their influence on the majority, *European Journal of Social Psychology*, 4: 53–64.

NEMETH, C., and J. WACHTLER. 1974. Creating the perceptions of consistency and confidence: A necessary condition for minority influence, *Sociometry*, 37: 529–40.

——. 1983. Creative problem solving as a result of majority vs. minority influence, *European Journal of Social Psychology*, 13: 45–55.

NISBETT, R. E.; E. BORGIDA; R. CRANDALL; and H. REED. 1976. Popular induction: Information is not necessarily informative. In J. S. Carroll and J. W. Payne (eds.), *Cognition and Social Behavior*. Hillsdale, N.J.: Erlbaum.

NISBETT, R. E., and L. ROSS. 1980. *Human Inference: Strategies and Shortcomings in Social Judgment*. Englewood Cliffs, N.J.: Prentice-Hall.

OAKES, P. J., and J. C. TURNER. 1980. Social categorization and intergroup behaviour: Does minimal intergroup discrimination make social identity more positive? *European Journal of Social Psychology*, 10: 295–301.

ORNE, M. T. 1962. On the social psychology of the psychological experiment with particular reference to the demand characteristics and their implications, *American Psychologist*, 17: 776–83.

PAIGE, J. M. 1970. Changing patterns of anti-white attitudes among blacks, *Journal of Social Issues*, 26: 67–86.

PASTORE, N. 1952. The role of arbitrariness in the frustration–aggression hypothesis, *Journal of Abnormal and Social Psychology*, 47: 728–31.

PATCHEN, M. 1961. *The Choice of Wage Comparisons*. Englewood Cliffs, N.J.: Prentice-Hall.

PATCHEN, M.; G. HOFMANN; and J. D. DAVIDSON. 1976. Interracial perceptions among high school students. *Sociometry*, 39: 341–54.

PATTERSON, O. 1977. *Ethnic Chauvinism*. Briarcliffe Manor, N.Y.: Stein & Day.

PERSONNAZ, B. 1981. Study in social influence using the spectrometer method: Dynamics of the phenomena of conversion and covertness in perceptual responses, *European Journal of Social Psychology*, 11: 431–38.

PETTIGREW, T. F. 1969. Racially separate or together, *Journal of Social Issues*, 25: 43–69.

PORTER, J. D. 1971. *Black Child, White Child. The Development of Racial Attitudes.* Cambridge, Mass.: Harvard University Press.

PROTHRO, E. T., and L. H. MELIKIAN. 1954. Studies in stereotypes: III. Arab students in the Near East, *Journal of Social Psychology, 40*: 237–43.

ROSEN, B., and T. H. JERDEE. 1974. Influence of sex roles stereotypes on personnel decisions, *Journal of Applied Psychology, 59*: 9–14.

ROSENTHAL, R. 1966. *Experimenter Effects in Behavioral Research.* New York: Appleton-Century-Crofts.

ROSS, M.; J. THIBAUT; and S. EVENBECK. 1971. Some determinants of the intensity of social protest, *Journal of Experimental Social Psychology, 7*: 401–18.

RUBLE, D. N., and T. L. RUBLE. 1980. Sex stereotypes. In A. G. Miller (ed.), *In the Eye of the Beholder: Contemporary Issues in Stereotyping.* New York: Holt, Rinehart & Winston, pp. 188–252.

RUNCIMAN, W. G. 1966. *Relative Deprivation and Social Justice.* London: Routledge & Kegan Paul.

ST. CLAIRE, L., and J. C. TURNER. 1982. The role of demand characteristics in the social categorization paradigm, *European Journal of Social Psychology, 12*: 307–14.

SCHOFIELD, J. W. 1982. *Black and White in School: Trust, Tension, or Tolerance?* New York: Praeger.

SHARAN, S. 1980. Cooperative learning in teams: Recent methods and effects on achievement, attitudes and ethnic relations, *Review of Educational Research, 50*: 241–72.

SHERIF, M. 1966. *Group Conflict and Cooperation: Their Social Psychology.* London: Routledge & Kegan Paul.

SHERIF, M.; O. J. HARVEY; B. J. WHITE; W. R. HOOD; and C. W. SHERIF. 1961. *Intergroup Conflict and Cooperation: The Robbers Cave Experiment.* Norman: University of Oklahoma Book Exchange.

SIGALL, H., and R. PAGE. 1971. Current stereotypes: A little fading, a little faking, *Journal of Personality and Social Psychology, 18*: 247–55.

SINHA, A. K. P., and O. P. UPADHYAYA. 1960. Change and persistence in the stereotypes of university students toward different ethnic groups during the Sino-Indian border dispute, *Journal of Social Psychology, 52*: 31–39.

SLAVIN, R. E. 1980. Cooperative learning, *Review of Educational Research, 50*: 315–42.

SLOVIC, P.; B. FISCHOFF; and S. LICHTENSTEIN. 1977. Behavioral decision theory, *Annual Review of Psychology, 28*: 1–39.

SOLE, K.; J. MARTON, and H. A. HORNSTEIN. 1975. Opinion similarity and helping: Three field experiments in investigating the bases of promotive tension, *Journal of Experimental Social Psychology, 11*: 1–13.

STEPHAN, W. G. 1978. School desegregation: An evaluation of predictions made in Brown vs. The Board of Education, *Psychological Bulletin, 85*: 217–38.

SUMNER, W. G. 1906. *Folkways.* Boston: Ginn.

TAJFEL, H. (ed.). 1978. *Differentiation Between Social Groups.* New York: Academic Press.

——. 1979. Individuals and groups in social psychology, *British Journal of Social and Clinical Psychology, 18*: 183–90.

——. 1981. *Human Groups and Social Categories.* Cambridge, England: Cambridge University Press.

——. 1982a. *Social Identity and Intergroup Relations.* Cambridge, England: Cambridge University Press.

——. 1982b. Social psychology of intergroup relations. In M. R. Rosenzweig and L. W. Porter (eds.), *Annual Review of Psychology,* 33: 1–39.

TAJFEL, H.; M. G. BILLIG; R. P. BUNDY; and C. FLAMENT. 1971. Social categorization and intergroup behavior, *European Journal of Social Psychology,* 1: 149–78.

TAJFEL, H., and J. C. TURNER. 1979. An integrative theory of social conflict. In W. Austin and S. Worchel (eds.), *The Social Psychology of Intergroup Relations.* Monterey, California: Brooks/Cole, pp. 33–47.

TOMLINSON, T. M. 1970. Ideological foundations for Negro action: A comparative analysis of militant and non-militant views of the Los Angeles riot, *Journal of Social Issues,* 26: 93–119.

TURNER, J. C. 1978. Social categorization and social discrimination in the minimal group situation. In H. Tajfel (ed.), *Differentiation Between Social Groups.* London: Academic.

TURNER, J. C. 1975. Social comparison and social identity: Some prospects for intergroup behaviour, *European Journal of Social Psychology,* 5: 5–34.

——. 1983. Some comments on . . . "the measurement of social orientations in the minimal group paradigm," *European Journal of Social Psychology,* 13: 351–67.

TURNER, J. C., and R. J. BROWN. 1981. Social status, cognitive alternatives, and intergroup relations. In H. Tajfel (ed.), *Social Identity and Intergroup Relations.* Cambridge, England: Cambridge University Press.

TVERSKY, A., and KAHNEMAN, D. 1980. Causal schemata in judgments under uncertainty. In M. Fishbein (ed.), *Progress in Social Psychology.* Hillsdale, N.J.: Erlbaum, 1: 49–72.

UNITED STATES DEPARTMENT OF COMMERCE. 1980. *The Social and Economic Status of the Black Population in the United States: An Historical View, 1790–1978.* Washington, D.C.: Bureau of the Census.

VAUGHAN, G. M. 1978a. Social categorization and intergroup behaviour in children. In H. Tajfel (ed.), *Differentiation between Social Groups.* London: Academic Press.

——. 1978b. Social change and intergroup preferences in New Zealand, *European Journal of Social Psychology,* 8: 297–314.

WARD, S., and J. BRAUN. 1972. Self-esteem and racial preferences in black children, *American Journal of Orthopsychiatry,* 42: 664–67.

WAX, M. L. 1979. *Desegregated Schools: An Intimate Portrait Based on Five Ethnographic Studies.* Washington, D.C.: U.S. Government Printing Office.

WHEELER, L., and M. Zuckerman. 1977. Commentary. In J. M. Suls and R. L. Miller (eds.), *Social Comparison Processes.* New York: Wiley, pp. 335–67.

WORCHEL, S. 1979. Cooperation and the reduction of intergroup conflict: Some determining factors. In W. G. Austin and S. Worchel (eds.), *The Social Psychology of Intergroup Relations.* Monterey, California: Brooks/Cole.

WORCHEL, S.; V. ANDREOLI; and R. FOLGER. 1977. Intergroup cooperation and intergroup attraction: The effect of previous interaction and outcome of combined effort, *Journal of Experimental Social Psychology,* 13: 131–40.

18

Health and Social Behavior

"I SPEND MOST OF MY TIME trying to keep my patients from killing themselves." This is an internist speaking, a man with a family practice, and he is expressing his irritation at being called upon to play doctor in a way for which neither history nor medical school has prepared him. Where are the patients with pneumonia, diphtheria, tuberculosis, and gastrointestinal infections? Those are diseases he can cure, and at the beginning of the century they were the leading causes of death (Surgeon General, 1979). Of course, medicine has conquered them and so deposed them. In 1980 the Center for Disease Control of the U.S. Public Health Service estimated that 50 percent of the mortality from the leading causes of death could be traced to life-styles: smoking, dietary preference, abuse of alcohol, environmental poisons, and stress. It is that fundamental change in the nature of illness and health that has propelled psychology into behavioral medicine—ready or not (Miller, 1983).

Mental illness has, of course, always been in the psychological domain, but the somatic illnesses have not, not the various cancers, cardiovascular diseases, not the diseases of gall bladder, kidney, liver and lights. But now it is known that about one-third of all cancers in this country derive from cigarette smoking, a habit, and while 30 million people a year try to quit smoking, only about 3 million manage permanently to eliminate this—behavior. The Type A personality, the competitive, hard-driving, pressed-for-time American entrepreneurial ideal, at first only for males but now increasingly also for females, is at least twice as likely to develop coronary heart disease as is his or her relaxed counterpart. Obesity (being really fat) is a risk factor for diabetes, gall bladder diseases, and cardiovascular diseases, and obesity comes from behavior—overeating and underexercising. Cirrhosis of the liver, Korsakoff's brain syndrome, and several other terrible things come from yet another kind of behavior: chronic overuse of alcohol. All of the habits that can lead to mortal illness were learned and can be unlearned, but unlearning has proved very difficult, and the successes of behavior modification and the cognitive therapies taken all together are still not very impressive.

The habits one cannot easily eliminate all have the same abstract properties. Actions like smoking a cigarette, having a drink, eating a candy bar, and working overtime to "catch up" all lead to immediate and certain gratification, whereas their bad consequences are remote in time, only probabilistic, and still avoidable now. It is no contest: Certain and immediate rewards win out over probabilistic and remote costs, even though the rewards are slight and the possible costs lethal. Those are *behavioral traps*, and a present-day Pilgrim's Progress is strewn with them. All learning theories predict that such traps, once they take hold, will be hard to shake, and avoidance or prevention may be more effective than any behavioral therapy, but psychology's power to create healthful environments is small. Most behavioral traps are rewarding because they relieve stress, and stress has many uncontrollable sources. For instance, the 14 percent increase in unemployment just prior to the recession of 1974–75 has been linked with a 2.8 percent increase in cardiovascular mortality and a 1.4 percent increase in cirrhosis mortality (Brenner, 1984). Social psychology could do nothing to prevent unemployment but is limited to promoting modes of stress relief (e.g. the relaxation response, meditation) that do not have deleterious remote consequences.

The problem of obesity is an instructive example of the interaction among biology, culture, and psychology that makes it difficult to change a maladaptive life style (Hall, 1984; Nisbett and Temoshok, 1976; Rodin, 1981; Schachter and Rodin, 1974). Anyone who is obese not only risks somatic illness but suffers a social stigma second only to race, among physical characteristics. Almost any obese person can lose weight, but few can keep it off. Why should that be so?

The biology of the state is, in the first place, cruelly self-maintaining. Overeating causes fat cells to increase in size so as to store more fat, and when they can store no more the actual number of fat cells increases. Once that happens, undereating can never reduce the number of cells, but only shrink them. When the obese person complains, "But I eat so little," he is telling the truth in the sense that it takes less food to maintain obesity than to achieve it in the first place. In addition, obesity directly lowers the rate of metabolism even when the body is at rest, because fat tissue is metabolically more inert than lean tissue. Finally, extra weight makes exercise more effortful and probably less pleasurable. In short, obesity strongly tends to be self-sustaining by virtue of its biology alone.

What characterizes fat people psychologically? A formulation that fits many familiar cases is external responsiveness as opposed to internal responsiveness (or control). This is the person who says: "I can't have anything sweet in the house" or "Please move those nuts before I eat them all." This is also, by my observation, the person who subtly pressures his friends either to order the dessert themselves or to urge him to do so on pain of spoiling his good time if they fail to oblige. As formulated by Stanley Schachter and Judith Rodin (1974), the external responsiveness of fat people was thought to be a general responsive style not limited to food cues. Rodin (1981) says that the best measure is a within-person difference between the magnitude of response (whether eating, attention, emotionality, or whatever) to highly salient external cues and cues of low salience in the external environment. As this formulation suggests, the externality hypothesis, though very popular and well known, has run into both empirical and conceptual difficulties (e.g. Nisbett and Temoshok, 1976). Rodin (1981) and Hall (1984) say it is now clear that not all fat people are "externals" and that there are multiple psychological paths to the common endpoint of obesity.

The ultimate irony involves genetics, social psychology, and culture. Speculating on the possible sources in evolution for a genetic tendency to overeat, Rodin (1981) suggests that it makes good sense, in terms of the theory of natural selection, for all the millennia when our species and its forebears lived in conditions of food scarcity. Any individual programmed genetically to overeat and store fat in times of plenty would have a survival advantage. For unknown reasons, women generally are programmed to store more fat cells than are men. Today in the more fortunate societies and social classes, where food is plentiful, it is maladaptive to overeat. In addition, just those societies and classes have perversely adopted an ideal of feminine beauty that is extremely slim. In the United States today, Rodin (Hall, 1984) finds, the majority of women consider themselves to be on a diet at any given time, and the continual cultural emphasis on being thin can cause even a woman who is five pounds underweight to feel too fat. The combination of a Twiggy ideal of beauty, a genetic tendency to overeat that is biologically self-maintaining, and a supply of delectable foods, everywhere available and everywhere advertised, make obesity an unhappy life condition that is not easily improved.

Making bad habits salient and attempting change are themselves an aspect of contemporary life-style, an aspect that ironically enough carries its own danger—the overriding problems of stress. In this chapter we shall use the topic of stress as our point of entry into the boundless subject of health and social behavior. We shall set aside very extreme short-term stress such as the blitz bombing of London (Stewart and Winser, 1944), POW incarceration in Korea (Spaulding and Ford, 1976) and in Vietnam (Helzer, 1981), and the atomic disasters in Hiroshima and Nagasaki (Janis, 1976). The chapter opens with research that conceives of stress as resulting from life events that require readjustment or change and assumes that such stresses (possibly weighted for magnitude, possibly only those resulting from undesirable life events) can be meaningfully summed to yield an index of the total stress sustained by an individual over a given period of time. The approach to illness in this research story is equally global, including every sort of psychiatric and somatic illness and even some accidents (all weighted for magnitude and summed). The first research question asked is: Does an index of total stress for some earlier period predict scores on an index of total illness for a later period?

The answer to the first question is that stress, conceived of as a kind of psychic Agent Orange raining down upon passive persons, is only a weak predictor of global illness or health. The effects of stress are mediated by coping mechanisms and personality resources, and the most important of those is perceived *control*.[1] Stresses that a person believes he can control are far less injurious than those he believes are uncontrollable. Putting it differently, feeling helpless makes a stress worse. Control is something one can learn to exercise and experience, to use as a coping mechanism. It is also a relatively stable personal characteristic: Some individuals have a general sense of being in control of their lives, and others lack that sense. The "same" amount of stress, externally defined, will damage less the person with a strong sense of control.

There is a personality resource called *hardiness*, which includes control as one of its components, that seems to be especially important in distinguishing, among individuals subjected to the same high stress, those who will fall ill from those who will not. It is clear that hardiness is thought of as a highly desirable thing. The hardy business executive is committed to his work, welcomes challenge, and feels in control of his life, especially his work, and the hardy individual is less likely to fall ill under stress, with illness defined globally over 126 commonly recognized symptoms and diseases.

At this point we turn from the prediction of global illness to a particular illness, coronary heart disease, and become acquainted with the "Type A Behavior Pattern." The establishment of Type A behavior as a risk factor for coronary heart disease is the principal accomplishment of behavioral medicine to date. In 1984 a report was published of a three-year effort to modify Type A Behavior, and that is the only study of an attempted therapy that will be included here.

---

[1] To see yourself as having a high degree of personal control is arguably the same thing as believing you have a high degree of freedom; seeing yourself as in control of some particular behavior is the same thing as believing you are free to engage in that behavior. The absence or loss of freedom, either general or particular, is very disagreeable, and it is eminently reasonable to propose that threats to or losses of freedom constitute a kind of negative drive state. That proposal was made by Jack Brehm (1966), and the negative drive that is reduced by attaining or restoring freedom was christened *reactance*. Reactance theory (Brehm and Brehm, 1981) has a well-developed logical structure and has stimulated much research. In a general way control and reactance are working the same territory, since reactance is the drive that results from perceived loss or absence of control. Control theory is named for the desired state (control or freedom) and reactance theory for the undesirable state, which is postulated to be a drive. Between the two formulations there are, however, numerous differences, and it is quite possible that reactance theory will ultimately prove to be the better formulation. I have chosen to present control theory because it is the simpler of the two and also more accessible to intuition.

Stress from Recent Life Events

In 1956 Hans Selye published an enormously influential book, *The Stress of Life*. In it he described a syndrome, or correlated set, of physiological reactions occurring in organisms in response to a wide variety of noxious agents. It was a general or nonspecific syndrome, which occurred in response to diverse injuries and poisons and was not peculiar to any particular disease. Selye at first called it the *general adaptation system* since it represented the body's generalized effort to mobilize resistance to threat. Later on Selye called it the *stress syndrome*. Selye's book awakened medicine to the importance of stress and prepared the way for the view that social events could produce stress and that stress might be a factor not only in the conventionally recognized psychosomatic illnesses, but in all illnesses, even those that are infectious.

Thomas H. Holmes of the UCLA Medical School and Richard H. Rahe, a physician and Commanding Officer of the Naval Health Research Center at San Diego, moved life stress research a long step forward by creating a quantitative measure. They first examined some five thousand patient records and made a list of forty-three life events, of varying seriousness, which seemed to cluster in the months preceding the onset of illness. That list became the Schedule of Recent Events (SRE), a self-administered paper-and-pencil measure on which a subject simply checked all those things that had happened to him or her in some specified period of time—most often the immediately preceding six months or one year. The simple sum of life changes checked (from 0–43) became the subjects' stress score, and the question was whether or not such scores would predict the number of episodes of illness in some time period subsequent to the life changes (Holmes and Rahe, 1967).

Table 18–1 is the Schedule of Recent Events (SRE), if you disregard the mean values in the rightmost column and think of the events as a forty-three-item checklist with the number of items checked being the individual's score. If the score on the SRE is to be interpreted as an index of the amount of social stress sustained in a specified time period, some strong assumptions must be made. In the first place a social stress must be any personal circumstance, desirable or undesirable, that requires change in the individual's ongoing life pattern. In the second place one must think of stressors as additive in their impact, and in the third place one must think it reasonable to assign the same weight or value (a weight of 1) to each stressor in obtaining the sum. Very many investigators have been willing to make those assumptions and have used the SRE to predict scores on an illness rating scale that includes somatic illnesses as well as psychiatric illnesses, and even accidents (Wyler, Masuda, and Holmes, 1968) or on some other global index of illness. Life Events Research that does not use the SRE mainly uses instruments related to the SRE but which change one or another of the original assumptions (Rabkin and Struening, 1976).

The assumption that seems most bizarre is the equal weighting of all stres-

TABLE 18–1. The Social Readjustment Rating Scale
(Without the Mean Values, the Schedule of Recent Events)

Rank	Life event	Mean value
1	Death of spouse	100
2	Divorce	73
3	Marital separation	65
4	Jail term	63
5	Death of close family member	63
6	Personal injury or illness	53
7	Marriage	50
8	Fired at work	47
9	Marital reconciliation	45
10	Retirement	45
11	Change in health of family member	44
12	Pregnancy	40
13	Sex difficulties	39
14	Gain of new family member	39
15	Business readjustment	39
16	Change in financial state	38
17	Death of close friend	37
18	Change to different line of work	36
19	Change in number of arguments with spouse	35
20	Mortage over $10,000	31
21	Foreclosure of mortgage or loan	30
22	Change in responsibilities at work	29
23	Son or daughter leaving home	29
24	Trouble with in-laws	29
25	Outstanding personal achievement	28
26	Wife begin or stop work	26
27	Begin or end school	26
28	Change in living conditions	25
29	Revision of personal habits	24
30	Trouble with boss	23
31	Change in work hours or conditions	20
32	Change in residence	20
33	Change in schools	20
34	Change in recreation	19
35	Change in church activities	19
36	Change in social activities	18
37	Mortgage or loan less than $10,000	17
38	Change in sleeping habits	16
39	Change in number of family get-togethers	15
40	Change in eating habits	15
41	Vacation	13
42	Christmas	12
43	Minor violations of the law	11

SOURCE: Reprinted with permission from T. H. Holmes and R. H. Rahe, The social readjustment rating scale, *Journal of Psychosomatic Research*, 11. Copyright 1967, Pergamon Press, Ltd.

sors, which suggests that parking tickets are as stressful as death of spouse. Holmes and Rahe themselves thought that assumption probably wrong, and in 1967 they brought out a modified form of the SRE in which stressing events are assigned differential weights. That instrument (which appears in Table 18-1) is called the *Social Readjustment Rating Scale*. The item weights were obtained empirically using the psychophysical method called *magnitude estimation* (Stevens and Galanter, 1957). Several hundred judges were told that the life change *Marriage* had been assigned the arbitrary value 500, and it was their task to assign a number to each other event so as to rate it proportionately as requiring more or less change than marriage in someone's life pattern. The average of numbers assigned each event was divided by 10, and the resultant values became the weights (mean values in Table 18-1) of each stressor. Thus *Marriage*, which had been arbitrarily assigned the value 500 for all judges, finally assumed a weight of 50, and *Death of spouse*, which was on the average thought to require twice as much readjustment as *Marriage*, assumed a value of 100 (the highest value on the scale) and *Minor violations of the law* (considered to call for only about one-fifth as much readjustment as *Marriage*) assumed the lowest value of the scale, 11. An individual's score on the Social Readjustment Rating Scale (SRRS) was the sum of the weights of the stresses checked.

A great deal of research has been done with the SRRS as Holmes and Rahe originally published it, but the question of event weighting, once raised, has proved difficult to settle, and indeed is still controversial more than fifteen years later. On the one hand there is the question whether it is a good idea to use the same set of standard weightings for all groups and all individuals. Dohrenwend and Dohrenwend (1974; 1978) found that male judges assigned a greater weight than did female judges to *Marital infidelity*, and persons in a higher social class assigned lower weights than did persons in a lower class to *Expanded business or professional practice*. Carrying the relativity of weights to its logical extreme, some (e.g. Ander, Lindstrom, and Tibblin, 1974) have argued that each individual should assign his own personal weights. That sounds right, but there is another side. It turns out that the correlation between unweighted sums (the Schedule of Recent Events) and weighted sums (the SRRS or some variant) is generally so high (.90 or above) that one might almost as well use the simple unweighted checklist (Lorimer et al., 1979; Zimmerman, 1983).

The assumption underlying both of the Holmes and Rahe measures, that stress is created by events that require change, whether the events be desirable or undesirable, is an interesting departure from common sense, but is it correct? That issue is not quite settled (Dohrenwend and Dohrenwend, 1978), but the weight of the evidence (e.g. Suls and Mullen, 1981; Vinokur and Selzer, 1975) is that undesirable events are more potent stressors than are desirable events.

How well does the measure Holmes and Rahe themselves prefer, the checklist with weighted items both desirable and undesirable, which is the Social Readjustment Rating Scale, predict illness onset? There have been many studies, mostly with very large numbers of subjects (e.g. Holmes and Masuda, 1974; Rahe, 1981; 1974; Rahe and Arthur, 1977). Subjects have often been U.S.

naval shipboard personnel (Rahe is a Navy Captain). In a representative study 2,500 naval personnel filled out the SRRS for life events that had occurred in the six months preceding a six-month tour of sea duty, and their shipboard medical records were then compared with their life events scores. For those in the highest quartile (25 percent) of the SRRS the mean rate of illness was 2.1, and for those in the lowest quartile (lowest life events score) it was 1.8 (Rahe, 1974). In absolute terms that is not a great difference, but with 2,500 subjects it is a statistically significant difference.

Most published studies have found modest but significant relationships between number and intensity of life events and illness episodes. In addition to naval personnel, employees of large corporations and clinic or hospital patients have been popular subjects because of the availability of long-term records. Life events have been related to sudden cardiac death, heart attacks, tuberculosis, diabetes, leukemia, accidents, and even athletic injuries. It is not of course suggested by anyone that the stress from change is a sufficient or necessary cause of any of those outcomes but only a predisposing vulnerability factor.

The correlations between weighted life event scores and number of illness onsets are always low, generally well below .30, and in Rahe's (1974) naval data they were consistently around .12 (Rabkin and Struening, 1976). There is even a serious possibility that the life events checklist method has given us no evidence at all of a *causal* relation between life events stress and illness, because there is one last difficulty with the measure.

In Table 18–1 we find such stress as: 8. *Fired at work*; 13. *Sex difficulties*; 24. *Trouble with in-laws*; and 38. *Change in sleeping habits*. We also found items like these: 5. *Death of close family member*; 17. *Death of close friend*; 27. *Begin or end school*; and 42. *Christmas*. What is the difference between the two sets? The second set, and items like them, seem to be things that happen willy-nilly, life events that would be independent of any possible, slow-developing still subclinical illness. The events of the first set, and many others like them, might very well be early manifestations of illness, either psychiatric or somatic. The changes in the first set are possibly confounded with the illness outcomes they predict and so not causes of illness at all. Hudgens (1974) argues persuasively that twenty-nine of the forty-three items on the life events checklist are not independent of developing illness. Almost none of the studies finding significant correlations between life event scores and illness onset counts has used a checklist composed exclusively of independent events. I agree with Schroeder and Costa (1984) that the causal case will not be fully convincing until more significant relations are found between uncontaminated measures.

Do not suppose that life events research has begun to wane because of the various shortcomings of the Holmes and Rahe self-administered checklists. The journals that include stress and illness within their purview are filled with new contributions on stress as life events. Many of them attempt to improve on the early checklists with revised checklists, which retain the appeal that stems from ease and economy of administration.

Minor Hassles and Uplifts

The life events of the Holmes–Rahe checklists are not such extreme situations as combat duty or confinement in a prisoner-of-war camp, but they are fairly major, as compared, at least, with misplacing your glasses, waiting for a plumber, or agonizing over an untimely pimple—but do not those minor daily hassles also take their toll? People certainly think so. I recently told some friends that psychologists had developed a measure of daily hassles and that the idea was abroad that hassles might be more injurious to health than major life changes. Well, one friend had lost a contact lens that morning and later learned from the optometrist that she had put two in the same eye. Another had waited from noon till 7 P.M. on a beautiful Saturday for the delivery of a new chest of drawers, which was brought at last by the modern-day equivalents of Mr. Laurel and Mr. Hardy. A third had just had her apartment repainted and found all the windows stuck shut. Those three were very enthusiastic about Hassle Theory. "That's it!" "You've got the answer there!" "Daily hassles are what's killing me!"

It does *feel* right. Especially when you add that not only daily hassles are measured but also minor uplifts—a compliment on loss of weight, a cigarette successfully forgone, a needed book actually retrieved from the library stacks. Uplifts seem to do one good; make it possible to smile; they positively improve the circulation. Richard Lazarus and his associates (Kanner et al., 1981) have created self-administered checklists for hassles (117 of them) and uplifts (135) and tested the possibility that they are related to psychological symptoms, more closely related, perhaps, than major life events.

One hundred respondents, both men and women, aged 45–64, took part in a twelve-month study. For each of nine successive months they filled out both the Hassles Scale and the Uplifts Scale, checking the things that had occurred and rating them for intensity on a three-point scale. In the tenth month they filled out a major life events questionnaire comparable to the SRRS, with events assigned standard weights. In months 2 and 10 they filled out the Hopkins Symptoms Checklist, a list of psychological symptoms defined in such a way that the symptoms are not confounded with hassles, uplifts, or major life events. Lazarus and his associates broke with the increasingly untenable view of Holmes and Rahe that desirable and undesirable events alike are stressful and instead tested the commonsense hypothesis that hassles would be positively related to undesirable symptoms and uplifts negatively related. The hassles and uplifts most frequently reported are listed in Table 18–2.

The 1981 paper is the first on hassle research, but the results are already interesting. Hassle frequency proved to be quite substantially correlated with psychological symptoms. The various correlations ranged between .49 and .66. Hassles were a more powerful predictor of symptoms than life events in every comparison made. In addition it was shown that the predictive power of life

TABLE 18-2. The Ten Most Frequently Reported Hassles and Uplifts

	Item[a]	% of Times Checked
	Hassles	
1.	Concerns about weight (91)[b]	52.4
2.	Health of a family member (7)	48.1
3.	Rising price of common goods (70)	43.7
4.	Home maintenance (29)	42.8
5.	Too many things to do (79)	38.6
6.	Misplacing or losing things (1)	38.1
7.	Yard work or outside home maintenance (112)	38.1
8.	Property investment, or taxes (110)	37.6
9.	Crime (115)	37.1
10.	Physical appearance (51)	35.9
	Uplifts	
1.	Relating well with your spouse or lover (18)	76.3
2.	Relating well with friends (22)	74.4
3.	Completing a task (19)	73.3
4.	Feeling healthy (11)	72.7
5.	Getting enough sleep (1)	69.7
6.	Eating out (35)	68.4
7.	Meeting your responsibilities (24)	68.1
8.	Visiting, phoning, or writing someone (17)	67.7
9.	Spending time with family (51)	66.7
10.	Home (inside) pleasing to you (52)	65.5

[a] Items are those most frequently checked over a period of nine months. The "% of times checked" figures represent the mean percentage of people checking the item each month averaged over the nine monthly administrations.   [b] Item scale number is in parentheses following the item.
SOURCE: From A. D. Kanner, J. C. Coyne, C. Schaefer, and R. S. Lazarus, Comparison of two modes of stress measurement: Daily hassles and uplifts versus major life events, *Journal of Behavioral Medicine, 4* (1981), p. 14, Table 3. Used with permission.

events was totally encompassed by hassles. The authors suggest that a major undesirable event like *Divorce* may exert stress by any of a number of component molecular hassles such as making one's meals, keeping house, handling finances, and getting the car repaired.

Initial results with daily hassles are certainly interesting, but I will feel more persuaded of their importance to health when we have predictive results for somatic rather than psychological symptoms. Psychological symptoms are after all temporally close to hassles, and there is not much surprise in learning that irritability and depression go with frequent daily annoyances.

Control as a Mediating Variable in Life Events Stress

Suls and Mullen (1981) had respondents mark undesirable life changes on a Holmes–Rahe checklist as either "controllable" or "uncontrollable." Controllable life changes were not significantly correlated with subsequent illness onsets, but uncontrollable life changes were correlated $+.23$, which was highly significant. Stern, McCants, and Pettine (1982) found a still stronger effect: Uncontrollable life changes predicted illness with a correlation of .59, whereas controllable life changes were not a significant predictor. Perhaps uncontrollability is what makes stress dangerous to health. Not *real* uncontrollability— we do not know about that—but perceived uncontrollability.

Johnson and Sarason (1978) used a different approach to control as a possible mediator in life events stress. Instead of having subjects classify events as controllable or not, they categorized subjects into those having a strong general sense of control over their lives and those who felt that their lives were mainly controlled externally. To make the classification they used Rotter's Locus of Control Scale (Rotter, 1966) of which more will be said at a later point. To evaluate life event stressors Johnson and Sarason created a new scale that has come to be very widely used: The Life Events Scale. Assessing various psychiatric symptoms, they found that life events stress was more closely related to illness among persons of low control than among persons of high control. Their strongest relations, those for depression and anxiety in low-control individuals, were at the high end of the range of all results on record for life events and illness onsets.

Control, by all the evidence, is the principal mediating variable in stress from recent life events as assessed by paper-and-pencil questionnaires. Control can operate either as a coping mechanism (a kind of behavior) or as a personality resource and will be looked at in both ways. A good feature of the control literature is that it takes us away from questionnaires and into the field, to Three Mile Island and the stress that followed the nuclear accident there, to the New Haven Hospital and patients awaiting surgery there, to nursing homes and ways of introducing more control into the lives of elderly people.

Perceived Control as a Coping Mechanism

To introduce control as a coping mechanism we consider dental practice as it is and as it might be improved. The dentist in the course of filling teeth is certain, despite the use of a local anaesthetic, to cause his patient some pain, some sharp stabs of sensitivity, not easy to distinguish from pain, and a good deal of nervous anticipation and tension. How might those unpleasant effects be reduced by introducing control? The patient could be given a button, controlling a light that would act as an absolute imperative on the dentist, causing him instantly to cease drilling, picking, pressing, or whatever aversive business he might be up to. The patient would be encouraged not to press the button so long as his discomfort was tolerable since some discomfort would in the end be unavoidable, but, it would be stressed, whether he pressed or not was up to him. The button would give him absolute behavioral control in the sense that he would believe that there was a response he could make that would eliminate the aversive stimulus. It might happen in any given session that the patient would never press the button, but he would know that he could and so know that pain beyond his power to endure would not be delivered. Would the patient with behavioral control experience less stress than a patient who underwent exactly the same procedures but without the control button?

For several kinds of aversive stimulus, including loud noise and extreme cold as well as shock, the evidence is that the patient in the dentist's chair who was promised behavioral control would experience much less anxiety while awaiting the unpleasantness than a person identically situated who was not promised behavioral control (e.g. Bowers, 1968; Gatchel and Proctor, 1976; Geer, Davison, and Gatchel, 1970; Glass, Reim, and Singer, 1971; Houston, 1972; Szpiler and Epstein, 1976). It is also clear from relevant research (Kanfer and Seider, 1973; Glass, Singer, and Friedman, 1969; Sherrod et al., 1977) that the patient with the button would actually tolerate *more* pain than the patient without that kind of control and would often not use the button at all. As to whether the patient who believed himself in control would actually *feel* less discomfort upon the impact of the disagreeable stimulus, as assessed either physiologically or by self-report, evidence is divided (Björkstrand, 1973; Geer, Davison, and Gatchel, 1970; Glass and Singer, 1972; Glass, Reim, and Singer, 1971; Glass, Singer, and Friedman, 1969; Glass et al., 1973; Mills and Krantz, 1979; Staub, Tursky, and Schwartz, 1971). There is then good reason to believe that a STOP DRILLING button in the dentist's office would reduce anticipatory anxiety, cause the patient to tolerate more rather than less pain, and, possibly, reduce the intensity of the pain itself (Thompson, 1981). None of the existing evidence was actually collected in a dentistry situation, but the implications are clear, so we wonder why dentists do not install stop buttons.

Perhaps buttons are not installed because dentistry is often advertised as "painless," and in the circumstances handing patients a button to stop the pain would seem odd. More probably, however, dentists feel that patients already have a perfectly adequate behavioral control: A person can always scream. In fact we rarely scream but instead signal that the limits of what can be endured are not far off by gurgling, moaning, and twitching. Those behavioral controls are less than perfect, however, because we know the bastard will ignore them if he has just one tiny bit more to grind away. I urge the installation of STOP buttons that set off loud alarms in the dentist's office—and in his waiting room.

With behavior control you know you can do something that will turn off the stimulus, and dentists and physicians rarely supply that kind of control, but there is another kind that is usually supplied to some extent: information control. The dentist provides control through information when he warns: "This may hurt just a little bit." Signals that warn of something unpleasant are intended to provide a kind of control by enabling one to anticipate discomfort and somehow or other get ready for it. Another sort of intended information control is provided when the physician explains the causes and nature of your disease, its prognosis, and the procedures that will be used to arrest its course.

Much of the work on information control builds on the assumption that knowing is better than not knowing, that forewarning is better than surprise. The literature yields mixed findings (Thompson, 1981), but I think we need not wait for all the studies to be done to guess what one outcome will be. Probably it is better to know than to imagine, to predict than to be surprised, just in case what you can imagine is much worse than what you will be told. It is possible, however, that there is some value in information as such, so long as it combines realistic warnings with adequate reassurance (Janis, 1958, 1971).

There is a third kind of control, cognitive control. Incidentally, we owe this useful classification of control mechanisms (by behavior, information, or cognition) to Suzanne Thompson (1981). Cognitive control is like behavior control in that you believe there is something you can do that will directly influence the aversiveness of a stimulus, but what you can do is *think* a certain way, not press a button or make any other overt response. Cognitive control is like information control in that it concerns mentality, not action, but cognitive control is a belief in direct instrumentality whereas the idea of information control leaves the mode of action a bit vague.

Control at Three Mile Island and in the New Haven Hospital

When the accident occurred in the nuclear energy plant at Three Mile Island, it created for people living in the area acute short-term stress since there were immediate possibilities of explosion and radiation. We are not, in this chapter, talking about the kind of acute stress produced by disasters, but the disaster at Three Mile Island also produced chronic long-term stress, because long after the reactor stabilized, local residents worried about possible delayed effects on themselves and their children, effects like sterility and leukemia. Fischoff (1983) has shown that the risks from nuclear radiation that frighten people most are those that are unobservable, delayed, and unknown to science. More than one person interviewed seventeen months after the disaster at Three Mile Island said the chronic stress was the worst thing in the entire episode. Residents were not explicitly provided with any mechanism of control, but of course they did not remain passive under stress, but found their own ways of coping. Baum, Fleming, and Singer (1983) interviewed a sample of residents with the Ways of Coping Inventory (Folkman and Lazarus, 1980) and also a sample of people living near an undamaged nuclear plant more than 100 miles from Three Mile Island. Besides inquiring about coping strategies, they administered a ninety-item inventory of stress symptoms (nausea, headache, nervousness, and so on) and a biochemical assessment of stress (urine levels of epinephrine and norepinephrine).

The coping mechanisms were of two kinds: (1) problem centered, information-seeking mechanisms, and (2) response-centered mechanisms concerned with control of the individual's own thoughts and emotions. While not exactly coincident with information control and cognitive control, the conceptual distinction made by Baum, Fleming, and Singer (1983) is similar. The measure of stress combined symptomatic and biochemical indicators. The important result is that emotion-centered coping was associated with much lower stress levels than was problem-centered coping. The authors suggest: "Having control or believing that one has control can reduce the aversiveness of stressing events.... At Three Mile Island, the likelihood of actually succeeding in regulating one's emotional response is far greater than the possibility of gaining control over the damaged power plant or the events surrounding it" (Baum, Fleming, and Singer, 1983, p. 128).

Information control and cognitive control, very explicitly defined, have been compared in effectiveness in a field study by Langer, Janis, and Wolfer (1975), with patients who were in the Yale-New Haven Hospital for various kinds of elective surgery, including hernia repairs, hysterectomies, and cholecystectomies.

Irving Janis (1958, 1971) is the pioneer of research on stress in patients awaiting surgery and also on the uses of information control, though he did not call it by that name. Janis showed that if a patient is given accurate prior information about impending pain and discomfort along with sufficient reassurances so that the fear does not reach too high a level, the patient is less likely to suffer acute emotional disturbance after the operation than one who has not been warned. Janis reasoned that the patient had a certain amount of "work of worrying" to get through, by analogy with the "work of mourning" in psychoanalytic theory, and that warning with reassurances set the process going and kept it realistic. The new question asked in 1975 by Janis and by Ellen Langer was how well information control compared with a more direct cognitive control.

The cognitive control invented as a coping strategy for the New Haven surgery patients was in part founded on an established truth about pain: The experienced severity of pain is enormously dependent on attention (Melzack, 1973). The stories about soldiers in combat failing to notice terrible wounds until afterward are true. The hospital patients were invited to think for themselves of a time when some engrossing activity (e.g. rushing to prepare a dinner for fifteen people or carrying the football in the last minutes of a close game) had kept them from attending to a minor cut and to compare such circumstances with their reactions to a comparable cut when they had been free to lavish concern on it. Pain and discomfort were, they were told truthfully, extremely subjective, and in the usual range the stress is likely to be worse than the actual pain. One can learn to control stress by controlling attention, they were told, and nothing is ever either wholly bad or wholly good. Any event, including elective surgery, has both good and bad aspects. Think of the chance to withdraw for a time from daily hassles, to rest, to take stock of your lives, and—probably—to lose some unwanted weight.

Patients given information control were told what the preoperative steps would be and warned of postoperative discomforts but reassured about the quality of the hospital and safety of all procedures. What they were not given was practice in perceiving events positively by way of the control of attention. A comparison set of patients was interviewed by an interested psychologist, but the interview was limited to rather neutral content (e.g. "Have you ever been in the hospital before?").

Nurses and all hospital staff members were kept blind to (or ignorant of) the treatment to which patients had been assigned, and they provided outcome data in the form of ratings (e.g. on level of patient anxiety) and such objective matters as the frequency with which patients requested sedatives and tranquilizers. The results indicate that both cognitive control and information control were effective devices for coping with stress, the former more effective than the latter. Of the neutrally interviewed patients, for instance, a full 93 percent requested both pain relievers and sedatives at least once; 73 percent of those receiving preparatory information did so, and just 50 percent of those trained to cope by means of cognitive control. Perceived control is evidently a useful mechanism for coping with the acute unpleasantness of minor surgery and a stay in the hospital. Can control somehow facilitate coping with chronic mundane problems?

Control in Nursing Homes

In Chapter 4 we became acquainted with the work of Martin Seligman and his associates (e.g. Seligman, 1975) on learned helplessness in animals and in man and helplessness is the absence of control. Extensive experimental work with both animals and humans convinced Seligman that learned helplessness was the basis of neurotic depression. In his more recent work (e.g. Seligman et al., 1979) Seligman has been mainly interested in arriving at an accurate understanding of depression. He has found in attribution theory some essential additions to the simple relationship between control and helplessness (Chapter 4). The psychology of control as set forth, for instance, by Ellen Langer (1983) and by Judith Rodin (Rodin, Bohm, and Wack, 1982) derives in part from the learned helplessness formulation (Seligman, 1975) but does not follow Seligman into attribution theory. The psychology of control has stayed with its own powerful concept, perceived control, and the elaboration of the more serious consequences of control and the loss of control.

About 5 percent of Americans over sixty-five years old live in residential care facilities, nursing homes of one variety or another. That is a smaller percentage than most would guess, but it is a large absolute number and is destined to become larger in the near future. Putting an elderly relative in a nursing home is a last resort for loving families, because, as everyone who has visited nursing homes knows, there is something terrible about them. Elderly people tend to become depressed and apathetic in nursing homes and often rapidly deteriorate both physically and mentally.

If we ask what it is about nursing homes that is terrible the list is long, and yet if we ask which items on the list are most destructive of human life we cannot say for sure. In many nursing homes there are distressing sights and sounds, bad smells, bad food, dingy quarters, poor medical attendance, and hard-boiled, resentful staff members. A good nursing home, the kind that is expensive and gets a high rating from the state, will whisk away the worst sights, sounds, and smells; will have decent food and medical attention and a busy schedule of activities and a relatively cheerful staff; and, to me, will still seem terrible. Probably it is my moderately somber nature, but I believe there are several ineradicable awful aspects of residential living for the elderly. It is, you see, the end—the last status—not for just one person, in a group of young and middle-aged and old, but for all inmates. They have been warehoused together and deprived of the privacy that makes it possible to deteriorate with dignity.

In Tolstoy's *Anna Karenina* the character Levin is called to the bedside of his brother Nicolai, who is dying of tuberculosis. He was as useless there as I am with the very sick and even with the not so very sick who have, however, had to go into a nursing home:

> More than that, he did not know what to say, how to look, how to move. Talk of irrelevant things seemed to him shocking, impossible. To talk of death and depressing subjects was likewise impossible. To keep silent, equally so. "I am afraid to look at him in case he thinks I am watching him. If I don't look, he will imagine my thoughts are elsewhere. If I walk on tiptoe he won't like it; to tread firmly seems wrong." [Tolstoy, (1878) 1982, p. 524]

Fortunately for Nicolai, persons less helpless than Levin were also there, especially his wife, Kitty:

> But Kitty evidently did not think, and had no time to think, about herself. Occupied with the patient she seemed to have a clear idea of something, and so all went well. She would even talk to him about herself and about her wedding, smile, sympathize, and pet him, cite cases of recovery, and all went well so then she must know what she was about.
> . . . "Do you really think he can recover?" asked Levin. . . . "I asked the doctor. He says he cannot last more than three days. But how can they be sure? . . . Everything is possible," she added. [pp. 524–25]

Not all social psychologists are as useless in extreme situations as Levin and I, and in recent years some have tried to see what might be done to make nursing homes less terrible. Ellen Langer, Judith Rodin, and Richard Schulz have discovered that the nursing home is an environment in which small changes can have large effects.

One thing that characterizes nursing homes that might be changed is chronic loss of perceived control. A person going from his own home to a "residence" must eat his meals on a schedule he does not set, often with no dietary choices and an assigned seating place. He may also be wakened at a set time and, in general, be required to conform his life to an institutional routine. In all these ways, in every area of his life, he must relinquish control, give up the power of choice. Before anyone attempted to change that aspect of nursing homes there were indications that the sudden loss of control on entering a home was harmful. In the North Carolina Cancer Institute, a terminal care facility for indigent persons, patients who came directly from a home environment very unlike the institution did not survive as long as patients who came from the institutional environments of other hospitals. With everything else the same, the patients who experienced a sharp loss of control over their lives died sooner. The authors of the study (Schulz and Aderman, 1973) attributed the more rapid decease to "feelings of helplessness."

Langer and Rodin (1976) picked a high-quality nursing home, Arden House in Connecticut, for their benign intervention. It had good medical, recreational, and residential facilities and was rated among the finest care units in the state. There were four floors, and the plan was to do a field experiment by enhancing perceived control for the residents of the fourth floor and use the residents of the second floor as a comparison group, treated the same except for the control manipulation. Langer and Rodin were not able to make great changes in the routine of one floor as contrasted with another, but they could attempt to affect the way in which existent, largely identical circumstances were perceived, and they had the enthusiastic help of an outgoing, friendly, thirty-three-year-old male chief administrator. Eventually that man gave two different pep talks on the two floors; for the group on the fourth floor he stressed choice, control, and responsibility, whereas for the group on the second floor he stressed arrangements made by the staff for the benefit of patients.

The character of the contrast is best conveyed with a few nearly matched quotations from what was said to the patients on four (enhanced control) and what was said to the patients on two (comparison):

4: I was surprised to learn . . . that many of you don't realize the influence you have over your lives here.

2: I was surprised to learn . . . that many of you don't realize all you're allowed to do here.

4: You should be deciding how you want your room to be arranged—whether you want it to be as it is or whether you want the staff to help you rearrange the furniture.

2: We want your rooms to be as nice as they can be, and we've tried to make them that way for you.

4: You should be deciding how you want to spend your time, for example, whether you want to be visiting your friends who live on this floor or on other floors, whether you want to visit in your room or your friend's room, in the lounge, the dining room, etc., or whether you want to be watching television, listening to the radio, writing, reading, or planning social events.

2: For example, you're permitted to meet people on the other floors and to use the lounge on the floor for visiting as well as the dining room or your own room.

4: In other words, it's your life and you can make of it whatever you want.

2: We feel that it's our responsibility to make this a home you can be proud of and happy in, and we want to do all that we can to help you.

As you can see, the two talks were very nicely equated in terms of information and even wording, with the difference that the residents of four were told that everything depended on them; they were responsible and must make their own choices, whereas the residents of two were told of the ways in which the staff took responsibility for them. In addition the residents of four chose to see a movie or not and if they wanted to see it, they chose the night; the residents of two were assigned nights—in accordance with standard procedure in most nursing homes. Residents of four were offered a small gift, a plant, which they might want or not (all did) and then each had to make his or her selection. The plant, once chosen, had to be looked after by its owner. Residents of two had plants handed to them and were told the nurses would look after watering them.

The director of the home reinforced his divergent messages just once, three days later. Otherwise, so far as the staff was concerned all the residents were treated in the same way. It was a pretest, posttest experimental design with an interval of three weeks. Residents were interviewed and rated themselves on happiness and degree of activity. Nurses rated residents on time spent visiting others, talking to staff, and general improvement. Behavioral measures were taken of such things as attendance at the movies and participation in other activities. Before the intervention there were no significant differences between the residents of four and two, and the floors had been selected because the two patient populations were well matched in sex distribution, age, severity of illnesses, and so on. A single pair of numbers will serve to represent the general difference on the posttest. Of the patients on two (the comparison group), in just three weeks in this high-quality facility, 71 percent were rated as having become more debilitated. By startling contrast, of those urged to take control and responsibility (for themselves and plant) 93 percent were actually rated as improved.

There was an eighteen-month followup (Rodin and Langer, 1977). Nurses rated residents once again on happiness, sociability, vigor, and so forth, and a physician made independent health ratings. The residents exposed to the control-responsibility manipulation were in just about all respects in better condition than the comparison residents. Most surprising of all were the comparative mortality ratings. Of the responsibility group 15 percent had died in eighteen months, and of the comparison group 30 percent.

The results of the experiment by Langer and Rodin might be said to be embarrassingly good. Is it really possible for so trifling an intervention to affect happiness, health, and mortality? It seems likely to me that some of the incredulity inspired by the Rodin–Langer results stems from the incredulous person's unfamiliarity with nursing homes. In that setting I can believe that almost any change would have large consequences. I think too that Rodin (1980) is right in saying that the intervention they used had the potential to keep having effects after the investigators were gone. Once the patients became more responsive to the environment, then friends, family, nursing staff and others became more responsive to the patients. It was undoubtedly some aspect of that process rather than the somewhat trivial manipulation *per se* that led to the long-term benefits that were evidenced. The Langer–Rodin results were independently replicated in 1980 by Pohl and Fuller.

Langer and Rodin manipulated *perception* of control rather than actual conditions of control, but Richard Schulz (1976) was ingenious enough to think of a way to manipulate real control without having to modify institutional routine. Old folks in nursing homes are generally very lonely, and a visit from a friendly college student can be a very big thing for them. Schulz had Duke University students pay visits over a two-month period according to one of three plans. In the *behavior control* condition residents were free to schedule the time and direction of visits; in the *information control condition* residents were advised beforehand of the visiting schedules (which matched the various schedules created under behavior control); in the *random visit* condition residents neither determined schedules—nor knew of them beforehand. Behavior control and information control were both effective in making patients happier and healthier; random visits, though enjoyed, did not have the same general good effects. However, in a long-term followup Schulz and Hanusa (1978) found that the groups originally benefited showed a relative decline. The most likely reason for that unhappy outcome was the eventual, inevitable, cessation of the student visits.

In terms of control the big difference between the Langer–Rodin (1975) intervention and the Schulz intervention is that the perceived control created in the former case was general in scope and could last indefinitely, whereas control over visits was specific and time-limited. The difference is elegantly captured (Schulz points out) by attribution theory. Using the three dimensions of Seligman et al. (1979), the Langer–Rodin personal responsibility manipulation ought to have caused residents to attribute control internally (themselves), stably (lastingly), and globally (generally). The visitor manipulation should have produced, by contrast, a sense of internal control that was unstable (it would end) and specific (over only one outcome).

Thoughts about the debilitating effect of chronic loss of control were in my mind in July 1984, when a ninety-year-old woman, who has been my friend for thirty years, decided to enter a residential home. It was called (not exactly) Saint Jerome's Residence for Elderly Ladies and was directed by four Sisters. The genteel name and affiliation with the Church were features that made it attractive to my friend Mary Kelley (a pseudonym). Mrs. Kelley is one of the most original, humorous, sharp-witted people I have known in my life, though she had, as she would often say, no education, and her brogue was as fresh as the day she got off the boat.

To her friends Mary Kelley is a kind of folk hero. There are many tales about her. When she visited Ireland at the age of seventy-five, she presented me with a souvenir, which turned out to be a small metal facsimile of the Eiffel Tower; she had bought one gift too few and so picked up mine in the Central Square dime store. When she visited Rome and saw the Pope she reported: "He was lovely, but you know he's Italian!" And if I ever refused a drink at her house the sarcasm would be heavy: "Oh sure, I suppose you're used to canapés and cocktails." When I asked her how she felt about the attempted assassination of President Reagan she said: "Oh Ray-gun (withering scorn), who cares about him? They've canceled my stories all day." Such remarks would be quickly followed with: "May God forgive me."

Mrs. Kelley had lived for the past ten years in her own very nice little apartment in a building for the elderly, where rents are partly subsidized by the city. She called it her "castle" and loved it, but as time went on, though her health stayed good, she could not do much walking any more, had to give up going to mass, and was dependent on her busy married son to get groceries for her and on a niece who visited every few weeks for cleaning the apartment, odd jobs, and cooking things that would keep in the refrigerator. Mrs. Kelley's family and friends worried about her living alone and thought she would be safer and less lonesome in St. Jerome's. She decided to move there. I was worried and went to visit her on the first Sunday.

The building is old but well maintained and has a lawn in back. There are about sixty elderly ladies living there, but the halls were almost empty and completely silent. Everything had been scrubbed to the bone. There were four or five flavors of disinfectant in the air, so that just when you got habituated to one, another hit you. The lounges were intended to be cheerful but seemed ugly to me. Everywhere you went statues of Our Lord kept an eye on you. Everybody was awakened early and went to mass at 9:15. Seats in the dining hall were permanently assigned and carried little cards with special dietary consideration. Mrs. Kelley thought hers said 18 calories a day, which worried her, and no one with better eyesight had told her that it said 1,800.

"Isn't it beautiful?" she asked. I lied and said it was. "Who wouldn't be happy here? I'm happy here." I thought her eyes glistened with tears when she said it, and when I left I was very worried. I did not think I would have lasted even one week in St. Jerome's. So I called two days later. She had to be looked for and brought to the phone. With unmistakable sincerity she said, "Oh, Professor Brown, I'm *so* happy to be here." Several of the ladies had been out on the lawn—singing songs! She is still very happy there.

What about the debilitating effects of absence of control? Waking and going to bed on a schedule, eating no-choice meals at scheduled hours in assigned seats, daily mass, and all the rest of the routine had seemed to me to represent a shockingly abrupt loss of behavior control. And so they would have been for me. But then I thought about her recent life in the apartment. She had always *wanted* to go to mass every day but never could unless someone took her. For her shopping and her meals and her housecleaning she had been dependent on others who always came often enough but had not had enough free time to come whenever she wanted them and could not even plan their lives far enough ahead so that she would know just when to expect them. She was a sociable person who liked company, but she had few visitors in the apartment.

I think, really, that the nursing home expanded Mary Kelley's control. Mass was held in the building, so she could go as often as she liked, and meals were available three times a day. There was always plenty of company. In calculating the perceived control someone has in a given new setting, you have to take account of the amount of perceived control in the prior setting. Probably expanded control is not the whole explanation of Mrs. Kelley's happy acceptance of her nursing home; she is healthy at ninety years, a person of exceptional *hardiness*, and that is an important factor.

Judith Rodin's early work on perceived control in nursing homes inspired her to continue along several related lines. She has studied the physiological connections among stress, coping, and aging. It seems likely that stress operates on the pituitary-adrenal system to elevate corticosteroids, which tend to suppress the immune system, and the result is increased susceptibility to illness. Good coping mechanisms reduce the pituitary-adrenal effect (Rodin, 1980). Rodin has continued work in nursing homes with so much success that it is said to have become difficult to find, in Connecticut, homes that still practice the institutional routines that contribute to decline (Hall, 1984).

Ellen Langer, having seen enhanced control and responsibility improve happiness and health and, apparently, defer death itself, became convinced that many of the changes of old age, both psychological and physical, that have conventionally been considered inevitable and given the medical label *senility* might be quite avoidable consequences of social psychological processes. She and her associates (Langer et al., 1979) produced large improvements in tested short-term memory in elderly persons in nursing homes by the simple method of motivating them to work at acquiring information (e.g. number of male residents on the floor, activities scheduled each day, food eaten at each meal) and retaining the information for several weeks. The kind of memory practiced was not the kind tested, so the change was not one of direct training but, in Langer's view, a consequence of increased cognitive activity or mindfulness. Langer has forged ahead, testing the limits of what increased mindfulness can do to reverse the changes physicians take to be inevitable consequences of aging (Langer et al, in press). Her high confidence is expressed in the title of one of her papers: "Old Age: An Artifact?" (Langer, 1981).

Perceived Control as a Personality Resource

Control as a coping mechanism can be made available on a time-limited basis by altering situations with a STOP button, by a technique for diverting attention from pain, or by the introduction of visits whenever someone wishes. Perceived control also exists, in individually varying degree, as an enduring personality characteristic, as a very general outlook on life events, and it appears that this characteristic or outlook, for those who have it in high degree, operates to moderate the impact of whatever stresses are encountered.

The original instrument for assessing perceived control as a personality resource is a self-administered questionnaire called the *Locus of Control Scale* (Rotter, 1966; Rotter, Seeman, and Liverant, 1962). To forestall confusion it is necessary to say, first off, that the scale contrasts control perceived as external and control perceived as internal (the two loci of control are external and internal), and it is internal control that means the same thing as our perceived control. External control, or control exercised by factors external to the individual, is simply the absence of perceived control in our sense. The *Locus of Control Scale* is composed of twenty-three items, each of which offers two opposed statements which one is asked to choose between. A few sample items convey a sense of the scale:

> 2. a. Many of the unhappy things in people's lives are partly due to bad luck. (E)
>   b. People's misfortunes result from the mistakes they make. (I)
> 4. a. In the long run people get the respect they deserve in this world. (I)
>   b. Unfortunately, an individual's worth often passes unrecognized no matter how hard he tries. (E)
> 28. a. What happens to me is my own doing. (I)
>   b. Sometimes I feel that I don't have enough control over the direction my life is taking. (E)

The locus of control concept, which is the same as a concept of generalized perceived control, has inspired a very large amount of research (e.g. Lefcourt, 1973, 1981, 1982, 1983, 1984). While Rotter's original scale has been more often used than any other, the construct, or conception, is not to be equated with the scale. Individual researchers have developed other scales more directly relevant to our present interests. Wallston and Wallston (1981) created a scale specifically concerned with control of health; Reid and Zeigler (1981) a scale for the elderly; and Worell and Tumilty (1981) a scale for alcoholics. One general proposition about the relation between high control, as a personality resource, and experienced stress is fairly well supported by research: When individuals of high and low control are subjected to the same extreme stress the individuals of high control feel it less and are less disrupted by it; when individuals of high and low personal control are studied over long periods the correlation between life changes (in the Holmes and Rahe sense) and experienced stress or illness is lower for those with higher control, because they tend to be more stable.

When Hurricane Agnes struck in 1972 it caused extensive flooding in a small Pennsylvania town and extensively damaged more than four hundred different small businesses. Carl Anderson (1977) of the School of Business and Management at the University of Maryland picked a random sample of ninety entrepreneurs who had suffered comparable damage and undertook to find out how experienced stress and coping styles were related to individual perceived control. In a set of interviews conducted eight months after the disaster very strong reactions appeared. The extremity of emotional reaction was correlated .61 with scores on the Rotter scale (low content went with high stress). In addition, the low-control persons were strongly disposed to react to the disaster in noninstrumental, ineffective ways, including withdrawal and hostility, whereas the persons with high perceived control made instrumental coping responses aimed at dealing with the objective situation. Those reactions were all extremely strong and certainly suggest that high control moderates the experience of stress and, as a personality resource, gives rise to directly instrumental coping. However, all the data were obtained from the same interviews and were essentially subjective, so we cannot be completely confident of the findings. More impressive is the fact that the businesses of the high-control entrepreneurs were objectively rated (e.g. an independent national credit rating agency) as having performed better over a two-and-a-half-year recovery period than did the businesses of low-control entrepreneurs!

Numerous other studies have started with some extreme form of stressor, falling alike on persons of high and low control, and found that the high control individuals (internals) gave less evidence of perceived stress. Cromwell and associates (1977), examined the reactions of cardiac patients to the procedures in hospital intensive-care units and found that on three physiological indices the high-control individuals (internals) had better prognostic ratings. Cook, Novaco, and Sarason (1980), studied the impact of Marine Corps recruit training on 254 individuals and found that only 1 percent of high-control individuals dropped out, whereas 17 percent of low-control individuals did so. Novaco and co-workers (1979) examined the effects of commuting to work on employees of two companies and found that those who traveled the greatest distance and had low-control were maximally distraught. In all those studies it is pretty clear that high-control moderates the impact of a potential stressor, and, as a first approximation, that is a good generalization. However, not all studies have supported this generalization and not every detail of those cited is consistent with it. For a more critical analytic discussion see Lefcourt (1983).

Hardiness as a Personality Resource

By 1979–80 it had become clear that direct relations between life change stressors as assessed by the Holmes—Rahe questionnaire and subsequent illness were generally weak, that most people exposed to high stress did not become ill, and so the field of health and social behavior had turned to the study of "resistance resources" (Antonovsky, 1979). The first thing found that made a difference was personal control (internal locus of control), but its value as a buffer of stress was still only moderate. Hardiness has proved more important.

Much of the work on hardiness has been done by Suzanne Kobasa (then at the University of Chicago) and Salvatore Maddi in connection with the Chicago Stress Study. The Chicago Study (as I will call it) has been concerned with stress and health in middle- and high-level executives in a large utility company. The company had become worried about the high levels of stress experienced by its personnel due to promotions and demotions, the institution of performance evaluations, affirmative action policies, and so on, and work-related stress was the subject of many articles in company publications and many executive seminars. The longitudinal stress study initiated by the comany had an initial subject pool of all executive personnel, some 837 persons.

The first step (Kobasa, 1979) was to determine whether two samples of executives, both exposed to comparable high levels of stress, but with one group falling ill and the other not, could be clearly distinguished in terms of personality characteristics. To assess stress Kobasa used the modification of the Holmes–Rahe Social Readjustment Scale, which assigns weights to various life changes. The instrument was made better suited to the utility executives by adding fifteen stressors identified by the executives themselves as common in their lives and also weighted for seriousness by a subgroup of executives. To assess illness the Illness Rating Scale (Wyler, Masuda, and Holmes, 1962), originally developed in conjunction with the research of Holmes and Rahe, was used. It includes 118 illnesses rated for seriousness by physicians. Those two measures—a life events questionnaire and an illness questionnaire—were mailed out to the entire pool of 837 subjects and were to be answered for the preceding three years. About three months later they all received a number of personality measures.

Two samples of high-stress executives were selected (scores above the median on the Social Readjustment Rating Scale). One sample (n = 100) also had high illness scores (above the median on the Illness Rating Scale), and the other sample had low illness scores (below the median). Here, then, were the two crucial groups to compare in personality: high stress/high illness versus high stress/low illness.

Kobasa's hypothesis was that the hardy personality, able to undergo high stress without becoming ill, would have three characteristics: control, commitment, and challenge. Persons with high perceived control are those, we know, who believe they can strongly influence the events of their lives. Commitment means high involvement in and appreciation of self, family, work, and society; it is the opposite of alienation. A person high in challenge thinks of change as an exciting opportunity rather than as something to be feared. For each of the concepts Kobasa used multiple candidate measures, all standard paper-and-pencil questionnaires, of which only the Locus of Control Scale is familiar to us. The results were promising. Measures of all three concepts (control, commitment, and challenge) very significantly distinguished between the two groups: high stress/high illness and high stress/low illness. The five measures (sometimes six) of the concepts that distinguished best between those who fell ill and those who did not ultimately became the standard assessment of personality hardiness. The instrument has been shown (by principal components analysis) to have a single large factor (hardiness) and to be quite stable over as long as five years (Kobasa and Puccetti, 1983).

The first analyses, those that discovered how well each measure discriminated, were made on just half of the total sample. That left a "holdout sample" that could be used as a form of replication. The question was: How well would the tests of control, commitment, and challenge that had been discovered with one sample serve to discriminate between the members of a second sample? The result was downright exciting: 80 percent of the high stress/low illness executives and 75 percent of the high stress/high illness executives were correctly identified as such on the basis of hardiness scores.

To convey a livelier sense of the hardy executive I quote from Kobasa's characterization of his (they were all males) reaction to a job transfer.

> Hence, the hardy executive does more than passively acquiesce to the job transfer. Rather, he throws himself actively into the new situation, utilizing his inner resources to make it his own. Another important characteristic of the hardy executive is an unshakable sense of meaningfulness and ability to evaluate the impact of a transfer in terms of a general life plan with its established priorities. . . . For him, the job transfer means a change that can be transferred into a potential step in the right direction in his onreaching career plan, and also provide his family with a developmentally stimulating change. [A sense of control] allows the hardy executive to greet the transfer with the recognition that although it may have been initiated in an office above him, the actual course it takes is dependent upon how he handles it. [Kobasa, 1979, p. 9]

The 1979 study assessed stress and illness retrospectively (the prior three-year period), and a critic might reasonably suspect that any individual who *felt stressed* might like to be *thought sick* (more sympathy) and so inclined to report such symptoms of illness as digestive upsets and headaches. That is a reasonable suspicion but Kobasa (1979, p. 10) assures us that high illness scores reflected such things as heart attack, cancer, detached retina, and hypertension, which require medical diagnosis. Even so, it is a good thing that the retrospective study was followed by a prospective study (Kobasa, Maddi, and Kahn, 1982) from which it appears that stress foreshadows illness unless a high level of hardiness functions as a buffer.

The current strategy in the Chicago Stress Study is to consider the personality resource of hardiness together with one or more possible resistance factors outside the domain of personality. Kobasa and Puccetti (1983) studied, besides hardiness, social assets (e.g. status, love, money, and safety) and social support (e.g. backing from the boss). As in previous studies hardiness of personality was a significant buffer against stress, and so was support from the boss; social assets (e.g. status, money, love) turned out not to be significant buffers.

Kobasa, Maddi, and Puccetti (1982) considered hardiness together with physical exercise as possible buffers in the stress–illness relationship. Both proved significant. When the stress–illness correlation is separately calculated for individuals high and low on each buffer, a group is identified for which there is *no* significant relationship (−.08) and a group for which the relationship is very high (+.64) as well as two intermediate groups. Those results appear in Table 18–3. For individuals who exercise frequently and who have hardy personalities, individuals who have the benefit of both buffers, stress is unrelated to illness (−.08). For individuals lacking both buffers stress is highly related to illness (+.64).

The Chicago Stress research has put together a compelling picture in which the usually very low correlation between reported life events and illness onsets appears to be much increased when the personality resource of hardiness as well as social support and exercise are taken into account as illness resistance factors. However, it is still the case that most of this research is retrospective rather than prospective and that some of the self-report measures may be contaminated. Until those shortcomings are corrected it is not possible to be sure that the Chicago results are really as powerful as they appear to be.

TABLE 18–3. Hardiness and Exercise as Buffers
in the Stress–Illness Relation

	Correlations Between Stress and Illness	
	High Hardiness	Low Hardiness
High Exercise	−.08	+.39
Low Exercise	+.33	+.64

SOURCE: Based on Kobasa, Maddi, and Puccetti (1982), Table IV, p. 401.

Coronary Heart Disease and Type A Behavior Pattern

Up to this point we have conceived of the health–illness balance in a global way, adding together the symptoms and diseases for a given time period to produce a single weighted index. Now we consider a single illness, or small set of related illnesses, coronary heart disease, and the aspects of social behavior that are a risk factor for this particular disease: the Type A Behavior Pattern. The A pattern is not an environmental stress score but a characteristic pattern of thought and action—resembling a personality type—that has become common in the twentieth century in societies that have industrialized and urbanized. Type A is a pattern that seems over many years, most of a lifetime, to put those manifesting it at risk specifically for coronary heart disease.

Death by heart attack is an easier exit than most but an extremely shocking one for those left behind because it can occur with no forewarning and seems downright partial to the twenty-four hours immediately following a reassuring medical checkup that includes an electrocardiogram. The condition that predisposes to heart attack is atherosclerosis, or coronary artery disease, in which the innermost layer of the coronary artery has been grossly thickened by fatty deposits. The thickening process is especially unnerving to think about, because it is silent or symptomless and very gradual, beginning in early childhood and lasting many decades. The effect of atherosclerosis is to narrow the central passage open to blood flow. An attack (technically a *myocardial infarction*) occurs when the inner wall develops scarlike masses called *arterial plaques* and one of these gives rise to a blood clot that obstructs an artery, cuts down blood supply to the left ventricle, and so causes some portion of the heart muscle to die from lack of oxygen. A heart attack can be silent, but when it is not it is experienced as extreme pain and oppression in the chest, shoulder, and left arm. Sometimes an attack quickly leads to death, but often not, and when it does not the individual may live for many years, more or less as before, depending upon the amount of damage the heart has sustained.

In the United States in the 1980s heart disease is the main cause of death, but it was not always so here and is not so everywhere now. The mortality rate from cardiovascular disease in white American males is about five times as great today as it was in the early 1920s. For Japanese males living in Japan it is much lower than for American males, whereas Japanese males living in America have rates intermediate between the two. Rates for white American males are higher than for white American females, and in the latter group women who are employed full time have higher rates than women who are full-time housewives. Black American males have lower rates than white American males and also slightly lower rates than black American females (Friedman and Rosenman, 1974). Among the Amish people in Pennsylvania heart attacks almost never occur in anyone younger than seventy, and the Amish eschew the use of radio, television, movies, telephone, cars and most of the other toys of the twentieth century. Variations in the incidence of a disease from one culture to another and from one subcultural group to another are called the *epidemiological patterns* of a disease, and they often suggest causal hypotheses. It was epidemiological evidence that first pointed to a causal connection between cigarette smoking and lung cancer.

Epidemiological studies such as the Heart Disease–Epidemiology Study of the National Heart and Lung Institute carried out for more than thirty years with 5,500 people in Framingham, Massachusetts (Dawber and Kannel, 1961), long ago showed that the individual prone to cardiovascular disease can be identified by certain characteristic features. The best-established features are: (1) aging; (2) sex (being male); (3) heavy cigarette smoking; (4) elevated systolic blood pressure; (5) serum cholesterol; (6) left ventricular hypertrophy (from electrocardiological evidence); (7) diabetes mellitus. In general the more factors present the greater the risk, but even the best combination of those traditional risk factors predicts only about half the incidence from an epidemiological point of view (Keys et al., 1972). The traditional risk factors leave something out, and one thing they leave out is the coronary-prone behavior pattern, also called the Type A behavior pattern (Friedman and Rosenman, 1974). Concerning the pattern, C. David Jenkins has written: "Never before in the history of medicine has a behavioral rating that is not an expression of subclinical disease, ever successfully predicted future emergence of a physical illness, let alone done so repeatedly in large study populations" (Jenkins, 1978, p. 72).

Sir William Osler in his 1897 Lectures on *Angina Pectoris and Allied States* seems already to have had intimations of Type A in addition to a strong sense of the dramatic irony of cardiovascular disease:

> Angeio-sclerosis [i.e. atherosclerosis or coronary artery disease], creeping slowly but surely with "no pace perceived" is the Nemesis through which Nature exacts retributive justice for the transgression of her laws. Nowhere do we see such an element of tragic sadness as in many of these cases. A man who has early risen and late taken rest, who has eaten the bread of carefulness, striving for success in commercial, professional or political life, after twenty-five or thirty years of incessant toil reaches the point where he can say, perhaps with great satisfaction, "Soul thou has much good laid up for many years; take thine ease", all unconscious that the fell sergeant has already issued the warrant. [Osler, 1897]

The rhetoric is a bit orotund, but "early risen and late taken rest," "the bread of carefulness," "striving for success," and "incessant toil" anticipate Type A.

Sometime between 1955 and 1958 Meyer Friedman and Ray Rosenman, San Francisco cardiologists who had been seeing patients for more than a decade, began to consider seriously the possibility that behavior and mental life might be factors in cardiovascular disease. As they tell it, the then president of the San Francisco Junior League told them flat out why husbands had heart attacks and wives did not. It did not seem to her to be because of any hormonal difference or differences of diet or smoking: "It's stress, the stress they received in the work, that's what's doing it" (Friedman and Rosenman, 1974, p. 73).

From careful observation of the verbal and nonverbal behavior of their patients Friedman and Rosenman discovered what they took to be the central characteristics of the coronary-prone American middle-class male: a chronic sense of time urgency, excessive competitive drive, and hostility gave way eventually to this more formal statement:

> Type A Behavior Pattern is an action-emotion complex that can be observed in any person who is *aggressively* involved in a *chronic, incessant* struggle to achieve more and more in less and less time, and if required to do so, against the opposing effort of other things or other persons. . . . Persons possessing this pattern also are quite prone to exhibit a free-floating but extraordinarily well-rationalized hostility. [1974, p. 85; emphasis in original]

B may be as ambitious as A, have as much desire to achieve as A, but it seems to steady him, give him confidence, rather than goad and irritate him.

In their nontechnical book, *Type A Behavior and Your Heart* (1974), Friedman and Rosenman expand informally at some length on "how to tell a Type A from a Type B. Type A is always setting deadlines for himself; he has the hurry sickness." He cannot bear waiting in line, and he blows up when a car ahead of him in his lane goes too slow. A tends to measure his achievements in numbers; during the school years it will be the number of A grades in courses or IQ or number of plays directed or touchdowns scored; later on it might be thousands of dollars in annual income or size of budget managed or number of experiments done, poems written, furrows plowed, or tricks turned. Because A is always under time pressure he tends to do several things at once: to read while eating, to dictate while driving, to study a foreign language via Walkman while jogging. A is insecure about his status and needs the admiration of his peers to bolster his self-esteem. In telling A's from B's it helps to borrow ahead from Friedman and Ulmer (1984), who confidently class as presidential A's Nixon, Johnson, and Kennedy, and as B's Truman, Reagan, and Lincoln.

Friedman and Rosenman tell the reader of their 1974 book that he can diagnose himself as Type A or Type B, if he is honest in his self-appraisal, and certainly the characterizations seem clear. From just what is written here it is perfectly clear to me that I am a classic Type A person and I must expect Osler's "fell sergeant" to issue his deadly warrant at any moment. I am always under time pressure; I hate standing in line and do blow up in slow traffic; I am certainly insecure and in need of admiration. In writing this book I have always set myself deadlines nested in deadlines, some nearer in time, some remote, and some intermediate. And whenever I have become jumpy about finishing on time I have reassured myself by thinking of the many hundreds of pages already written. "Fell sergeant, what delays your deadly warrant?"

Probably you are as confident as I am that you can type yourself as A or B on the basis of what is written here; if Friedman and Rosenman are right about the prevalence of the two types, roughly 45 percent of you will think yourself A's, 45 percent B's, and 10 percent intermediate X's. But then we find this statement by Friedman and Rosenman, which is absolutely astonishing in the context of the rest of their book:

> The questions themselves, of course, are far less important than the *manner* of response to them. We found it necessary to emphasize this point repeatedly to those asking to have our list of twenty or so questions in order to run their own tests. Type A and Type B persons may give identical answers, but the *way* they give them is sufficient for our interviewers to differentiate the types almost all of the time. [1974, p. 97]

This casual paragraph makes me splutter with indignation. If A's and B's can give *identical answers* to content questions and are distinguishable only in terms of manner of response, or style, then we are completely deceived in thinking we can diagnose ourselves on the basis of the descriptions contained in the 1974 book. In their 1984 book Friedman and Ulmer make just the same sort of statement: It is style that is primarily diagnostic, not content.

Assessment of Type A and Type B

There are two principal measures: the Structured Interview (SI) of Friedman and Rosenman and the Jenkins Activity Survey of C. David Jenkins.[2] The Structured Interview is essentially a behavior sample (ten minutes) produced in a challenge situation created by a face-to-face interview. It is not a self-administered test but a rating or classification made by a trained interviewer who must be certified by the authors of the measure. A good interviewer (and not everyone can become one) must be able to *bring out* Type A behavior, if the potential for it exists, and be able to recognize it when it appears and also recognize when A behavior does not appear and B does. The interviewers assign the interviewees to one of four (sometimes five) categories: A-1 (the extreme A type); A-2 (less extreme); X (equally A and B); and B (or B3 and B4). Certified interviewers agree between 75 and 85 percent of the time (Rosenman, 1978), so the measure is respectably reliable.

To create an interview you must ask questions and questions must have content and the content of the (approximately twenty-five) questions asked for the SI is directly relevant to the general characterizations you have read of Types A and B. For instance:

> 4. Does your job carry *heavy* responsibility?
>   a. Is there any time when you feel particularly *rushed* or under pressure?
> 5. Would you describe yourself as a *hard-driving, ambitious,* type of man (*woman*)?

---

[2]There is a third measure, a ten-item questionnaire, called the Framingham Type A Behavior Scale (FTA), which has been used in the long term Framingham study. That measure also predicts coronary heart disease. It has been omitted from the discussion in the chapter because it has not usually been included in theoretical disputes (Haynes et al., 1978).

19. How do you feel about waiting in lines: *Bank* lines or *Supermarket* lines? [Rosenman, 1978, p. 68]

The italicized words in the questions are to be *emphasized* in the interview and it is *known* (Scherwitz, Berton, and Leventhal, 1977, 1978; Schucker and Jacobs, 1977) that these *emphases* give A's a feeling of being *rushed* and are *annoying* and so elicit Type A behavior!!

The content of the SI questions is just like the content of the informal characterization of A and B given above and from the questions above one would think it perfectly possible to do a self-assessment without any interview at all, but remember we have been told that "Type A and Type B persons may give identical answers" (Friedman and Rosenman, 1974, p. 97), so the content cannot be the only significant aspect of the outcomes. In addition to recording answers to questions, interviewers make a large number of notations and ratings on the interviewee's nonverbal behavior and speech stylistics: explosiveness, volume, and speed of speech; his stride, handshake, gestures, and general vigor. Also, and most important, the interviewer is directed sometimes to interrupt, sometimes to go too slow and to hesitate, sometimes to take a challenging tone—all in order to bring out Type A behavior. Finally, in assigning the interviewer to one of four (or five) categories, the behavior *observed* is to be weighted more heavily, given greater importance than the content of answers to questions. The interview functions as a stimulus to behavior that is either Type A or Type B in content and, more important, style, and it is a certified interviewer's overall assessment of a behavior sample that determines the interviewee's category. Self-assessment or assessment by paper-and-pencil questionnaire would not be the same thing at all, and we uninterviewed readers cannot tell what types we are.

I became so curious about the diagnostic procedure of the Structured Interview that I wrote Dr. Friedman to request audio tapes of representative interviews. He kindly complied, and now that I have played the tapes several times I can attest that it is indeed quite possible to get answers that would in print seem equally competitive, time-urgent, and aggressive but when you hear them spoken are startlingly different. One mildly subtle difference in the tapes is that an A seldom allows the interviewer to finish his questions but jumps in with his answers; the B's seem better able to wait.

We have arrived at a somewhat puzzling position. A pattern of behavior conceptualized as competitive, time-urgent, hostile, and impatient is not diagnosed as such because the person has been observed regularly to behave in those ways or because he has so described himself but rather because his speech, when he is asked questions relevant to competition, time urgency, hostility, and impatience in a challenging way becomes emphatic and loud and because he also tends to interrupt and talk over the interviewer. What evidence is there that speech style in a certain kind of interview is related to general competitiveness, time urgency, hostility, and impatience?

There is practically no evidence that the usual everyday behavior of persons diagnosed as Type A on the basis of the SI, and therefore mainly on the basis of speech stylistics, is marked by competitiveness, time urgency, hostility, and impatience (Matthews, 1982). What about the self-descriptions given in response to the interviewer's twenty-five questions? Although classification as A, X, or B pays little attention to this content and is largely determined by speech stylistics, appropriate content could be somewhat associated with the speech stylistics. In fact it is, but in barely significant degree (Matthews, 1982). That means Type A, as defined by the SI, most clearly means an explosive, loud speech style in reaction to challenging questions on touchy subjects and *much less clearly* means a general style of life that is competitive, time urgent, hostile, and impatient.

The Structured Interview (SI) has shortcomings as a measure. A special sort of person—an interviewer trained and certified—is literally part of the measure; it takes time and money to create such persons, and that severely limits the quantity of research that can be done. In addition, scoring is not objective and so cannot be made mechanical. In the early 1960s C. David Jenkins developed the Jenkins Activity Survey (JAS), a paper-and-pencil self-assessment that was objectively scorable (by electronic means), with the intended capability to replace the SI, as it would closely approximate SI scores (Jenkins, Rosenman, and Friedman, 1967). In form the JAS is a set of multiple-choice items, some of them direct rewrites of questions on the SI and the remainder closely based on the content characterization of Type A behavior by Friedman and Rosenman. There are approximately fifty items, and they yield quantitative scores for A and B.

Because the multiple-choice items on the JAS were based either on questions in the SI or on general characterizations of Types A and B, they had a certain presumptive validity as items predictive of SI assessments. However, Friedman and Rosenman knew from clinical experience that content answers were often inaccurate either because a Type A person lacked insight and so could not make accurate self-appraisals or because a Type B person, judging it socially desirable to be a competitive, hard-driving A, as indeed it often is, misrepresented himself in the socially desirable direction. Consequently it was necessary to go beyond presumption or face validity in selecting items that would predict SI categorical assessments.

Beginning in 1964 C. David Jenkins, working with Rosenman and Friedman (1967) carried out a succession of psychometric studies designed to select from a large pool of multiple-choice questions just those that best predicted A or B diagnosis based on the Structured Interview (SI). The outcome was an objective, mechanically scorable, test that furthermore proved to have a reasonably high test–retest reliability over one to four years, which meant that what it measured was a reasonably stable personal characteristic. In subsequent years forms were developed appropriate for women as well as men and also a student form (Jenkins, 1978; Matthews, 1982). The JAS has been often described as an alternative (to the SI) measure of Type A, more economical and fully objective. Certainly that had been the intention motivating its creation, but how well had the various psychometric procedures designed to produce an equivalent measure actually worked?

In its final standardization the 1965 JAS predicted the A or B assessment of the SI 73 percent of the time (Jenkins, 1978). That would be its best performance, because the sample used belonged to the sample of subjects used to select and weight multiple-choice items in the first place. Matthews (1982), reviewing many studies relating the JAS and the SI, says that the two measures agree on A–B classification about 70 percent or less of the time. With A's and B's being about equally common, the two measures should agree by chance 50 percent of the time, so they agree at a better than random level only 20 percent of the time (or less). Factor analytic studies by Matthews and collaborators (1982) and Musante and associates (1983) establish the conclusion to which all evidence now points. It is, in exact terms, this: While JAS total scores and the content scores on the SI agree quite closely, JAS total scores and final SI assessments are *largely independent measures*. That is so because SI scores are mainly based not on content at all but on speech stylistics. Therefore, even though the JAS and SI have often been called alternative measure of one thing, Type A coronary-prone behavior, in fact they are barely related and should be considered independent measures.

The evidence is consistent and the conclusion is clear—but puzzling when we try psychologically to conceptualize the Type A person. What is he? Someone who describes himself (herself) as ambitious, time urgent, hostile, and impatient, or someone who responds to annoyance and challenge with explosive, loud speech? Is it necessary to choose between the measures?

The construct or conception called Type A was not originally a part of any psychological theory but was simply a descriptive effort, on the part of two cardiologists, to capture the kind of person (from their clientele of middle-class white males) who developed cardiovascular problems. Type A is important only because it has turned out to be a serious risk factor for coronary heart disease and (probably) for coronary artery disease. It has, or until recently had, no theoretical interest. For that reason, if we are going to choose between two measures, the JAS and the SI, we ought to do so in terms of their comparative value as predictors of cardiovascular disease rather than their comparative ability to capture a particular *ad hoc* construct.

Prediction of Cardiovascular Disorders

The cornerstone of the evidence for an association between coronary heart disease (CHD) and A–B behavior is the Western Collaborative Group Study (Rosenman et al., 1975; Brand et al., 1978). Initiated in 1960–61, the Western Collaborative Group Study (WCGS) was a prospective epidemiological study of the incidence of coronary heart disease in about three thousand men who were well at the start and aged between thirty-five and fifty-nine. At the start, and annually for eight and a half years, comprehensive data were collected for those men: social, dietary, biochemical, clinical, and behavioral data, including the Structured Interview from the start and, in the last four years, the Jenkins Activity Survey. Both measures significantly and substantially predicted CHD. The SI proved to be the better predictor, but there were trends in the data (Brand et al., 1978) suggesting that the two measures might be responsive to somewhat different risk factors.

Type A subjects as diagnosed by the SI were 2.37 times as likely to develop CHD as their Type B counterparts. That is a highly significant difference, but in absolute numbers fewer than two hundred A's developed CHD, whereas the sample was about evenly divided between A's and B's, which means that about 1,300 diagnosed A's did not develop CHD in the years of the study. The association between A–B behavior and CHD does not prove direct causality. There were, in the WCGS, a number of risk factors in addition to A–B behavior, especially age, heavy cigarette smoking, serum cholesterol, systolic blood pressure, and parental CHD history. Some of the "traditional" risk factors were associated with Type A behavior, so it was necessary to consider the possibility that the A–B association with CHD simply reflected a correlation between behavior and known risks. When statistical adjustments were made for traditional risk factors, however, A's still had an incidence of CHD about twice as great as B's, which means that however the behavior pattern works, it is not through an indirect association with traditional factors.

The WCGS provided the first large-scale demonstration that Type A behavior was an independent risk factor in cardiovascular disease. Since it was done there have been very many studies, both clinical and epidemiological (see Cooper, Detre, and Weiss, 1981, and Dembroski et al., 1978, for reviews) largely consistent in showing Type A to be a risk factor in coronary heart disease and angina pectoris and probably in coronary artery disease (diagnosed either *post mortem* or by angiography). The Activity Survey (JAS) has been used in more large-scale studies, including studies in Sweden, Belgium, Honolulu, England, New Zealand, and Canada because of its economy and objectivity. However, except for the economy of the JAS, neither measure has demonstrated any consistent advantage, and both predict cardiovascular diseases. Because the two measures both predict the same diseases there is good reason, after all, to think of both as measures of one thing, Type A personality, even though the two measures are only very slightly related to each other.

How could the SI and the JAS both be indices of Type A, both predict cardiovascular disease, and yet be largely independent of each other? It is important to have a conception that would result in such a set of relationships even though no one knows in 1986 what the correct conception is.

The SI assessment is mainly based on a sample of vocal and nonverbal response to a challenging, irritating interviewer, so perhaps we should think of it as an index of relative reactivity to such challenges. What kind of reactivity? There are many studies relating SI-defined A behavior to neuroendocrine, metabolic, and cardiovascular response (Matthews, 1982). All of the following responses have been found: elevated systolic blood pressure, elevated plasma levels of the neurotransmitters epinephrine and norepinephrine, and accelerated heart rate. Those are responses of the *sympathetic* division of the autonomic nervous system, which (roughly) functions to mobilize the body for emergencies by contrast with the parasympathetic division, which operates to conserve or store resources. There are lines of evidence suggesting, though not proving, that high levels of sympathetic activation induce myocardial lesions and are implicated in cardiovascular disease. Let us suppose that that is so and suppose further that the SI is mainly an index of the individual's sympathetic nervous system reactivity—a kind of psychophysiological *potential* for stress (see Krantz et al., 1982).

Sympathetic arousal is a response to environmental events, including the Structured Interview but more generally including frustrating, challenging, moderately competitive situations (Matthews, 1982). The frequency with which such situations arise varies widely from one person to another and one time period to another. Friedman and Rosenman (1974) have always said that even the most extreme Type A may be relaxed when on vacation or when in the hospital with a serious illness. In those and other nonchallenging circumstances competitive, time-urgent, hostile, and impatient behavior may disappear. It seems likely also that environmental challenge would vary with occupation and with sex, age, and culture.

The JAS is, after all, an Activity Survey. Let us suppose, though it has not been proved, that self-appraisals of competitiveness, drive, and impatience are mainly reflective not of basic sympathetic reactivity but of the frequency in a given person's life at a given time of challenging situations. Perhaps the Type A that predicts and helps to cause cardiovascular disorders has two largely independent components: basic sympathetic reactivity mainly assessed by the SI behavior sample and amount of environmental challenge mainly assessed by the JAS.

It now becomes easy to imagine several varieties of Type A person. I know individuals who appear to be about equally overreactive to challenge or stress but who are exposed, or who have so arranged their lives as to be exposed, to very different amounts of challenge. A highly reactive person may be in a position that involves continual individual competition, striving for high standards, time pressure, and so on. Perhaps that is true for many business executives, senior medical students, taxicab drivers, and star athletes but not for civil servants, some kinds of scholars, postmen, housewives, and librarians. Perhaps it is more true in the United States than in Japan since, though hard work is a value in both cultures, individual as opposed to group competition is a more general value in the United States than in Japan. A highly reactive person may use his recreational time in competitive games, or else he may jog, read, meditate, or narcotize his sympathetic nervous system. Highly reactive persons, whether or not their environments provide steady high challenge, would all be expected to register as Type A on the SI, which is sensitive to physiological reactivity, but only reactive persons who have steadily challenging environments would score as Type A on the JAS, which reflects the amount of competition, time urgency, and striving of daily life. If both sympathetic reactivity and a continually challenging environment are components of the Type A behavior pattern and predictors of coronary heart disease, then SI scores and JAS scores would both be significantly related to CHD, but the two measures could be largely independent of each other.

I also know individuals who seem to be about equally low in general sympathetic reactivity, but while one has a slow, steady, unchallenging job (some librarians) the other is in a very intensely competitive, time-pressured job (manager of a rock music group). The prediction would be that both would score as X or B on the Structured Interview and so not at risk for CHD as far as that measure is concerned, but the person in the competitive job should score as an A on the JAS and, as far as that measure is concerned, be at risk for CHD. The SI and JAS scores could then be largely independent, and yet Type A on both would be at risk for CHD whereas B would not.

The conception is that Type A has two components, general sympathetic reactivity and amount of challenge in the everyday environment, that the SI is mainly an index of the former and the JAS of the latter, and that both components are predictive of CHD but largely independent of each other. The conception is motivated by the established independence of SI and JAS and by the fact that both predict CHD. It is a long way from having been established by research, but it is at least consistent with several general trends. Matthews, in her 1982 review of Type A research, finds a lot of evidence that the SI-defined A–B distinction has neurophysiological correlates and little evidence that it has general behavior correlates, whereas the evidence for the JAS-defined A–B distinction is the exact reverse, many behavioral correlates but few that are neurophysiological. In recent studies using both measures (e.g. Krantz et al., 1982; Corse et al., 1982) the SI has regularly proved to be closer to physiological arousal (e.g. systolic blood pressure) than the JAS.

One implication of the two-component conception of Type A is that persons who are diagnosed as Type A on both the SI and the JAS should be at maximal risk for CHD, persons scored as Type B on both at minimal risk, and persons scored as A on one measure and B on the other at intermediate risk. There is a small amount of evidence from the Western Collaborative Group Study that this implication is empirically correct, and it appears in Table 18–4. In the first place note that both measures predict CHD: for SI-defined types, the A incidences are both higher than the B incidences; for JAS scores, the higher A score is associated with the greater incidence. Notice in addition that the largest incidence in the table, 15.68, is for individuals who are A's in terms of both measures, and the lowest incidence, 7.86, is for individuals who are B's

TABLE 18–4. JAS Type A Scores, Type Assignment from the SI and CHD Incidence in the Western Collaborative Group Study, 1965–69: Annual Incidence Rate for Employed Men, Ages 44–64

JAS Type A Score	SI Interview Type	
	A	B
+5.0	15.68	11.78
−5.0	8.25	7.86

SOURCE: Adapted from Jenkins (1978), Table 5.3, p. 80.

in terms of both measures. The other two entries represent combinations of A on one measure and B on the other and are intermediate between the extreme incidences.

In the late 1970s and early 1980s we have had several serious attempts to understand coronary-prone behavior in terms of systematic psychological theory. These include the self-involvement approach of Scherwitz and colleagues (Scherwitz, Berton, and Leventhal, 1978; Scherwitz et al., 1983), the ambiguous standards of evaluation theory of Karen Matthews and her colleagues (1982), and David Glass's (1977) control theory. The last of those is the most systematic and has the best experimental support. Glass proposes, roughly, that A's when faced with a stressful event (defined as potentially harmful and uncontrollable) first try very hard to cope, manifesting the characteristic A behavior, but if their efforts at control meet with repeated failure, lapse into helplessness. He suggests that cardiovascular damage results from the attendant abrupt extreme shifts between sympathetic and parasympathetic activity. In addition to the several serious attempts at theoretical understanding there is much work in progress on the development in childhood of Type A behavior (Matthews, 1982) and on the possibility of changing A's into B's through medication or behavioral therapy (Gentry and Suinn, 1978; Schmieder et al., 1983).

Modification of Type A

Evidence that coronary heart disease is significantly related to cigarette smoking, age, sex, Type A Behavior Pattern, and so on is only correlational and so cannot prove causality. If correlation were sufficient to demonstrate causality, we should have to conclude that owning a Cadillac and wearing reading glasses are both causes of CHD, since both are correlated with CHD, but we would be mistaken; Cadillacs are correlated because they are an aspect of a certain lifestyle, and reading glasses because they are associated with age. There is more evidence than epidemiology provides for the causal roles of the major risk factors, but there is not much of the very best sort of evidence: experimental change. In 1984 Meyer Friedman (a cardiologist) and Diane Ulmer (a nurse) of the Harold Brunn Institute reported the results of a large-scale prospective effort to modify Type A behavior and reduce the incidence of heart attacks.

In order to change Type A behavior, the Brunn Institute team reasoned, you would have to have a cohort of persons willing to work hard for some years at transforming themselves, and Type A persons who had never had a heart attack would not be interested because they would be "too busy" and, in addition, would probably credit their Type A qualities with whatever occupational successes they had achieved. In addition, it would seem that a study would have to run for many years to accumulate enough heart attacks to mean anything, since the average annual rate for males between thirty-five and sixty-five was only 10 in 1000. Both problems were solved by recruiting as subjects persons who had already had one or more heart attacks. They would be likely to have the motivation, and the incidence of attack subsequent to a first is 75 to 100 per 1,000. So the San Francisco Recurrent Coronary Prevention Project began in 1977 with 1,012 volunteers, almost all of them Caucasian and 90 percent of them men.

The essence of the design is a comparison of both Type A behavior and heart attacks in a control group (I), which was given cardiovascular counseling of a conventional kind, including advice on diet, exercise, caffeine, alcohol, and the like, with an experimental group (II), which was given the conventional counseling and, in addition, counseling on how to change Type A behavior together with behavior modification drills to be done at home. The study ran for three years, and the two interventions were continuing, at first on a very frequent basis (ninety minutes a week) and much less frequently (e.g. monthly) later on. Type A behavior, assessed both by questionnaires and by Structured Interview diagnosis, was initially high in almost all subjects (90 percent), and after three years it had been reduced substantially (by 30 percent) in Group II and much less, though a little, in Group I. Group I could hardly be expected nowadays to be totally ignorant of the significance of Type A behavior. The important outcome is that for heart attacks: for Group I the average annual recurrence rate for three years was 6.6 percent; for Group II it was only half as great, or 3.0 percent. That is statistically a highly significant difference, and the rejoicing expressed by Friedman and Ulmer is understandably great.

There seems never to be an experiment reporting therapeutic success with which no fault can be found. The possible fault in the present case derives from the fact that about 40 percent of all those who began the experiment dropped out before the end or were excluded because of noncompliance. The percentages falling out of I and II were about the same (roughly 40 percent), but it is necessary to ask whether they would probably have been the same sorts of patients. There is the danger that II may have lost "worse cases" than I and on that account turned up better outcomes *for those who remained*. Is there anything that makes such a possibility plausible? The experimental group (II) met more often than the control group; weekly at first instead of alternate weeks and, later on, monthly instead of alternate months. In addition, the members of II were supposed to carry out daily drills at home, and the members of I had no such drills. That just sounds as if the protocol for the experimental people had been more time consuming and so is perhaps a reason to expect a larger percentage dropout from II than from I, but that did not happen. However, the percentages could be the same and the types different. For whom would the more time-consuming protocol be especially onerous? For Type A persons and perhaps especially for the most extreme Type A persons, who might in addition, of course, be at the highest risk for recurrent heart attack. The research group reports with a certain satisfaction that the dropouts had a higher heart attack rate than those who stayed with the therapy, and they clearly believe that the therapy might have saved them. Alternatively, however, the dropouts who may have been "worst cases" destined to have attacks no matter what, and by selectively dropping out of II may have enabled II to look good. I hope this cavil is mistaken and that Type A can be changed and CHD reduced in frequency.

In some ways Type A behavior suggests hardiness. Both fit the harried but purposeful and successful man or woman: competitive, aggressive, time-urgent (A), plus control, commitment, and challenge. The assessment instruments are different, and so far as I know scores among them have not been correlated. It is clearly an altogether socially desirable thing in our culture to be hardy, whereas sentiments about Type A are somewhat ambivalent (because of the hostility), but in most modern economic settings A qualities are admired—even to the point where real B's sometimes paint themselves as A's because they think Type A is nearer the American ideal. Surely the big difference is that hardiness is a buffer against illnesses generally (an index based on 126 symptoms and diseases), whereas Type A behavior is a risk factor for disease. However even here A and hardiness are reconciled, because A behavior is not a risk factor for illness in general but very specifically for coronary heart disease, and for all we know the general index of 126 illnesses that hardiness tends to buffer may include an exception, coronary heart disease, which hardiness perhaps cannot help to prevent but may even help to cause. If that should be true, the person who develops control, commitment, and challenge and so builds some protection against illness generally would risk, specifically, coronary heart disease, which might be avoided by alienation, vegetativeness, and other non-hardy qualities. A close study of the instruments and concepts employed in the two research traditions suggests that hardiness does not entail Type A behavior. It is possible to be committed to yourself and your work and give to society and yet not be impatient, time-pressured, and insecure. One can aspire to be a John F. Kennedy or an Abraham Lincoln and Friedman and Ulmer (1984) say Kennedy was an A, Lincoln a B. How they managed to carry out the two structured interviews, the only trustworthy basis of diagnosis, I could not say.

Summary

In this century the leading causes of death have shifted from infectious diseases like pneumonia and tuberculosis to diseases like cancer and heart attack, in which life-style plays a principal causal part, and since life-styles are behavior psychology has become an important health science. Stress in the general sense of the frequent need to readjust or change and in the specific sense of Type A behavior has been the aspect of life-style most intensively studied. Holmes and Rahe devised an instrument that lists major life events compelling readjustment and hypothesized that as the number of such events increased in a given time period the number of illness onsets would also increase. A great deal of research has been done to test that hypothesis, and the most usual result is an extremely modest but statistically significant correlation.

The manifold hassles of daily life have been related to symptoms of psychological distress and minor uplifts to the absence of such symptoms. In an initial study the correlations were high, higher than those obtained in major life events studies, but that could be because the disturbances predicted were psychological in character. It remains to be seen whether hassles and uplifts predict somatic symptoms and illness.

The effects of environmental stressors are mediated by coping mechanisms (behavior) and personality resources. As a coping mechanism, it is useful to distinguish three varieties of control: behavioral, informational, and cognitive. There is a very large amount of evidence that giving someone behavior control over pain or other aversive stimulation reduces the stress of anticipation, leads to tolerance of higher levels of aversive stimulation, and may reduce the pain itself.

Perceived control, as a coping mechanism, reduces stress in patients awaiting surgery. Perceived control introduced into nursing homes for the elderly improves health, activity, and zest and can even favorably affect mortality rates. However, a control that is introduced for a short time and then completely withdrawn can have a net effect that is debilitating.

Hardiness is a personality resource that includes control but adds the variables of challenge and commitment. The work of the Chicago Stress Project on all executive personnel of a large utility company indicates that hardiness is a more powerful mediator of the relation between life events and illness than is control alone. When hardiness is supplemented with the illness resistance factors of social support and exercise, a picture emerges in which stress and illness are highly related in only those people who lack the resistance factors.

Type A Behavior Pattern is not itself an external stress but is a stressful way of struggling with modern urban life that constitutes a risk factor, not for illness generally but for coronary heart disease and probably coronary artery disease. A popular description of Type A suggests that self-diagnosis should be easy. A is excessively competitive and has a strong sense of time urgency and chronic hostility.

The primary method for assessing Type A and Type B is the Structured Interview (SI) of Friedman and Rosenman. The interview, a ten-minute sample of behavior, is rated or typed by a trained, certified interviewer who gives more weight to behavior style and speech stylistics than to the content of answers to questions and so self-diagnosis is not really possible at all.

There is a second instrument for assessing Type A and Type B: the Jenkins Activity Survey, a self-administered multiple-choice questionnaire that can be electronically scored. The content of the questions is similar to and based on the questions of the Structured Interview. After some years of psychometric study, however, it has become clear that the correlation between the two instruments is low and that they are best considered to be independent measures. The Jenkins Activity Survey has the advantage of ease, economy, and objectivity of administration, and scores on this measure appear also to be more closely related to Type A behavior outside the laboratory than do scores on the Structured Interview.

On large-scale prospective longitudinal studies both the Structured Interview and the Jenkins Activity Survey identify substantial risk factors for cardiovascular diseases. A conception that would reconcile all the data is as follows: Perhaps the Structured Interview, as a sample of behavior in response to challenge, is primarily a measure of sympathetic nervous system reactivity. Perhaps the Jenkins Activity Survey, as a survey of activities, is primarily a measure of the amount of challenge in a person's life. Both reactivity and challenge could be components of the Type A personality, independent components. There is some evidence that this is the case from the Western Collaborative Group Study.

In 1984 a report was published of a successful effort to modify Type A behavior over a three-year period. All subjects had had one or more heart attacks before entering the study, but the annual rate of recurrent attacks was only half as great in the patients whose Type A behavior was reduced as in control patients who were simply given standard cardiovascular counseling. While there is a possible flaw in that ambitious study, it gives some hope that Type A behavior and the risk it creates for coronary heart disease can be reduced.

References

ANDER, S.; B. LINDSTROM; and G. TIBBLIN. 1974. Life changes in random samples of middle-aged men. In E. K. G. Gunderson and R. H. Rake (eds.), *Life Stress and Illness*. Springfield, Ill.: Charles C Thomas, pp. 121–24.

ANDERSON, C. R. 1977. Locus of control, coping behaviors, and performance in a stress setting: A longitudinal study, *Journal of Applied Psychology*, 62: 446–51.

ANTONOVSKY, A. 1979. *Health, Stress, and Coping*. San Francisco: Jossey-Bass.

BAUM, A.; R. FLEMING; and J. E. SINGER. 1983. Coping with victimization by technological disaster, *Journal of Social Issues*, 39: 117–38.

BJORKSTRAND, P. 1973. Electrodermal responses as affected by subject-versus-experimenter-controlled noxious stimulation, *Journal of Experimental Psychology, 97*: 365–69.

BOWERS, K. 1968. Pain, anxiety, and perceived control, *Journal of Clinical and Consulting Psychology, 32*: 596–602.

BRAND, R. J.; R. H. ROSENMAN; C. D. JENKINS; R. I. SHOLTZ; and S. T. ZYZANSKI. 1978. Comparison of coronary heart disease prediction in the Western Collaborative Group Study using the Structured Interview and the Jenkins Activity Survey assessment of the coronary-prone Type A behavior pattern. Paper presented at the conference on cardiovascular disease epidemiology of the American Heart Association, Orlando, Florida, March.

BREHM, J. W. 1966. *A Theory of Psychological Reactance*. New York: Academic Press.

BREHM, S. S., and J. W. BREHM. 1981. *Psychological Reactance: A Theory of Freedom and Control*. New York: Academic Press.

BRENNER, M. H. 1984. *Estimating the Effects of Economic Change on National Health and Social Well-being*. Washington, D.C.: U.S. Government Printing Office.

CENTER FOR DISEASE CONTROL. 1980. *Ten Leading Causes of Death in the United States, 1977*. Washington, D.C.: U.S. Government Printing Office.

COOK, T. M.; R. W. NOVACO; and I. G. SARASON. 1980. *Generalized Expectancy, Life Experience, and Adaptations: Marine Corps Recruit Training* (AR-002). Seattle: University of Washington.

COOPER, T.; T. DETRE; and S. M. WEISS. 1981. Coronary-prone behavior and coronary heart disease: A critical review, *Circulation, 63*: 1199–1215.

CORSE, C. D.; S. B. MANUCK; J. D. CANTWELL; B. GIORDANI; and K. A. MATTHEWS. 1982. Coronary-prone behavior pattern and cardiovascular response in persons with and without coronary heart disease, *Psychosomatic Medicine, 44*: 449–59.

CROMWELL, R. L.; E. C. BUTTERFIELD; F. M. BRAYFIELD; and J. J. CURRY. 1977. *Acute Myocardial Infarction*. St. Louis: Mosby.

DAWBER, T. R., and W. B. KANNEL. 1961. Susceptibility to coronary heart disease, *Modern Concepts in Cardiovascular Disease, 30*: 671–76.

DEMBROSKI, T. M.; S. M. WEISS; J. L. SHIELDS; S. G. HAYNES; and M. FEINLEIB (eds.). 1978. *Coronary-Prone Behavior*. New York: Springer-Verlag.

DOHRENWEND, B. S., and B. P. DOHRENWEND. 1978. Some issues in research on stressful life events, *Journal of Nervous and Mental Diseases, 166*: 7–15.

———. 1974. *Stressful Life Events: Their Nature and Effect*. New York: Wiley.

FISCHHOFF, B. 1983. Strategic policy preferences: A behavioral decision theory perspective, *Journal of Social Issues, 83*: 133–60.

FOLKMAN, S., and R. S. LAZARUS. 1980. An analysis of coping in a middle-aged community sample, *Journal of Health and Social Behavior, 21*: 219–39.

FRIEDMAN, M., and R. ROSENMAN. 1974. *Type A Behavior and Your Heart*. New York: Knopf.

FRIEDMAN, M., and D. ULMER. 1984. *Treating Type A Behavior and Your Heart*. New York: Knopf.

GATCHEL, R. J., and J. D. PROCTOR. 1976. Physiological correlates of learned helplessness in man, *Journal of Abnormal Psychology*, 85: 27–34.

GEER, J. H.; G. C. DAVISON; and R. I. GATCHEL. 1970. Reduction of stress in humans through nonverdical perceived control of aversive stimulation, *Journal of Personality and Social Psychology*, 16: 731–38.

GENTRY, W. D., and R. SUINN. 1978. Section summary: Behavioral intervention. In T. M. Dembroski, S. M. Weiss, J. S. Shields, S. G. Haynes, and M. Feinleib (eds.), *Coronary-Prone Behavior*. New York: Springer-Verlag, pp. 220–23.

GLASS, D. C. 1977. *Behavior Patterns, Stress, and Coronary Disease*. Hillsdale, N.J.: Erlbaum.

GLASS, D. C., and J. E. SINGER. 1972. *Stress and Adaptation: Experimental Studies of Behavioral Effects of Exposure to Aversive Events*. New York: Academic Press.

GLASS, D. C.; B. REIM; and J. E. SINGER. 1971. Behavioral consequences of adaptation to controllable and uncontrollable noise, *Journal of Experimental Social Psychology*, 7: 244–57.

GLASS, D. C.; J. E. SINGER; and L. N. FRIEDMAN. 1969. Psychic costs of adaptation to an environmental stressor, *Journal of Personality and Social Psychology*, 12: 200–10.

GLASS, D. C., et al. 1973. Perceived control of aversive stimulation and the reduction of stress responses, *Journal of Personality and Social Psychology*, 41: 577–95.

HALL, E. 1984. A sense of control, *Psychology Today*, December, pp. 38–45.

HAYNES, S. G.; S. LEVINE; N. SCOTCH; M. FEINLEIB; and W. B. KANNEL. 1978. The relationship of psychosocial factors to coronary heart disease in the Framingham Study: I Methods and risk factors, *American Journal of Epidemiology*, 107: 362–83.

HELZER, J. E. 1981. Methodological issues in the interpretation of the consequences of extreme situations. In B. S. Dohrenwend and B. P. Dohrenwend (eds.), *Stressful Life Events and Their Contexts*. New York: Prodist, pp. 108–29.

HOLMES, T. H., and R. H. RAHE. 1967. The social readjustment rating scale, *Journal of Psychosomatic Research*, 11: 213–18.

HOLMES, T. H., and M. MASUDA. 1974. Life change and illness susceptibility. In B. S. Dohrenwend and B. P. Dohrenwend (eds.), *Stressful Life Events: Their Nature and Effects*. New York: Wiley, pp. 45–72.

HOUSTON, B. K. 1972. Control over stress, locus of control, and response to stress, *Journal of Personality and Social Psychology*, 21: 249–55.

HUDGENS, R. W. 1974. Personal catastrophe and depression: A consideration of the subject with respect to medically ill adolescents, and a requiem for retrospective life-event studies. In B. S. Dohrenwend and B. P. Dohrenwend (eds.), *Stressful Life Events: Their Nature and Effects*. New York: Wiley, pp. 119–34.

JANIS, I. 1958. *Psychological Stress*. New York: Wiley.

——. 1971. *Stress and Frustration*. New York: Harcourt, Brace.

——. 1976. Aftermath of the atomic disasters. In R. H. Moos (ed.), *Human Adaptation: Coping with Life Crises*. Lexington, Mass.: Heath, pp. 376–84.

JENKINS, C. D. 1978. A comparative review of the interview and questionnaire methods in the assessment of the coronary-prone behavior patterns. In T. M. Dembroski,

S. M. Weiss, J. L. Shields, S. G. Haynes, M. Feinleib (eds.), *Coronary-Prone Behavior*. New York: Springer-Verlag.

JENKINS, C. D.; R. H. ROSENMAN; and M. FRIEDMAN. 1967. Development of an objective psychological test for the determination of the coronary-prone behavior in employed men, *Journal of Chronic Diseases, 20*: 371–79.

JOHNSON, J. S., and I. G. SARASON. 1978. Life stress, depression and anxiety: Internal–external control as a moderator variable, *Journal of Psychosomatic Research, 22*: 205–8.

KANFER, F., and M. L. SEIDER. 1973. Self-control: Factors enhancing tolerance of noxious stimulation, *Journal of Personality and Social Psychology, 25*: 381.

KANNER, A. D.; J. C. COYNE; C. SCHAEFER; and R. S. LAZARUS. 1981. Comparison of two modes of stress measurement: Daily hassles and uplifts versus major life events, *Journal of Behavioral Medicine, 4*: 1–29.

KEYS, A.; C. ARAVNIS; H. BLACKBURN; F. S. P. VAN BUCHEM; R. BUZINA; B. S. DJORDJEVIC; F. FIDANZA; M. J. KAVONEN; A. MENOTTI; V. PUDOV; and H. L. TAYLOR. 1972. Probability of middle-aged men developing coronary heart disease in 5 years, *Circulation, 45*: 815–28.

KOBASA, S. C. 1979. Stressful life events, personality, and health: An inquiry into hardiness, *Journal of Personality and Social Psychology, 37*: 1–11.

KOBASA, S. C.; S. R. MADDI; and S. KAHN. 1982. Hardiness and health: A prospective study, *Journal of Personality and Social Psychology, 42*: 168–77.

KOBASA, S. C.; S. R. MADDI; and M. C. PUCCETTI. 1982. Personality and exercise as buffers in the stress-illness relationship, *Journal of Behavioral Medicine, 5*: 391–404.

KOBASA, S. C., and M. C. PUCETTI. 1983. Personality and social resources in stress resistance, *Journal of Personality and Social Psychology, 45*: 839–50.

KRANTZ, D. S.; J. M. ARABIAN; J. E. DAVIA; and J. S. PARKER. 1982. Type A behavior and coronary artery bypass surgery: Intraoperative blood pressure and perioperative complications, *Psychosomatic Medicine, 44*: 273–84.

LANGER, E. 1981. Old age: an artifact? In S. Kiesler and J. McGaugh (eds.), *Biology, Behavior, and Aging*. New York: Academic Press, pp. 255–81.

——. 1983. *The Psychology of Control*. Beverly Hills, Calif.: Sage.

LANGER, E.; B. CHANOWITZ; S. JACOBS; M. RHODES; M. PALMERINO; and P. THAYER. In press. Nonsequential development and aging. In C. Alexander, E. Langer, and R. Oetzal (eds.), *Higher Stages of Development: Beyond Formal Operations*.

LANGER, E. J.; I. L. JANIS; and J. A. WOLFER. 1975. Reduction of psychological stress in surgical patients, *Journal of Experimental Social Psychology, 11*: 155–65.

LANGER, E. J., and J. RODIN. 1976. The effects of choice and enhanced personal responsibility for the aged: A field experiment in an institutional setting, *Journal of Personality and Social Psychology, 34*: 191–98.

LANGER, E.; J. RODIN; P. BECK; C. WEINMAN; and L. SPITZER. 1979. Environmental determinants of memory improvement in late adulthood, *Journal of Personality and Social Psychology, 37*: 2003–13.

LEFCOURT, H. M. 1973. The function of the illusions of control and freedom, *American Psychologist, 28*: 417–25.

———. 1981. *Research with the Locus of Control Construct. Volume 1: Assessment Methods.* New York: Academic Press.

———. 1982. *Locus of Control.* 2 ed. Hillsdale, N.J.: Erlbaum.

———. 1983. *Research with the Locus of Control Construct. Volume 2: Developments and Social Problems.* New York: Academic Press.

———. 1984. *Research with the Locus of Control Construct. Volume 3: Extensions and Limitations.* New York: Academic Press.

LORIMER, R. J.; B. JUSTICE; G. W. MCBEE; and M. WEINMAN. 1979. Weighting events in life-events research, *Journal of Health and Social Behavior, 20*: 306–7.

MATTHEWS, K. A. 1982. Psychological perspectives on the type A behavior pattern, *Psychological Bulletin, 91*: 293–323.

MATTHEWS, K. A., and D. S. KRANTZ. 1976. Resemblances of twins and their parents in Pattern A behavior, *Psychosomatic Medicine, 28*: 140–44.

MATTHEWS, K. A.; D. S. KRANTZ; T. M. DEMBROSKI; and J. A. MACDOUGALL. 1982. The unique and common variance in the Structured Interview and the Jenkins Activity Survey measures of the Type A behavior pattern, *Journal of Personality and Social Psychology, 42*: 303–13.

MELZACK, R. 1973. *The Puzzle of Pain.* New York: Basic Books.

MILLER, N. E. 1983. Behavioral medicine, *Annual Reviews of Psychology, 34*: 1–31.

MILLS, R. T., and D. S. KRANTZ. 1979. Information, choice, and reactions to stress: A field experiment in a blood bank with laboratory analogue, *Journal of Personality and Social Psychology, 37*: 608–20.

MUSANTE, L.; J. M. MACDOUGALL; T. M. DEMBROSKI; and A. E. VAN HORN. 1983. Component analysis of the type A coronary-prone behavior pattern in male and female college students, *Journal of Personality and Social Psychology, 45*: 1104–17.

NISBETT, R. E., and L. TEMOSHOK. 1976. Is there an external cognitive style? *Journal of Personality and Social Psychology, 33*: 36–47.

NOVACO, R. W.; D. STOKOLS; J. CAMPBELL; and J. STOKOLS. 1979. Transportation, stress, and community psychology, *American Journal of Community Psychology, 7*: 361–80.

OSLER, WILLIAM. 1897. *Lectures on Angina Pectoris and Allied States.* New York: D. Appleton.

POHL, J. M., and S. S. FULLER. 1980. Perceived choice, social interaction and dimensions of morale of residents in a home for the aged, *Research in Nursing and Health, 3*: 49–54.

RABKIN, J. G., and E. L. STRUENING. 1976. Life events, stress, and illness. *Science, 194*: 1013–20.

RAHE, R. H. 1974. The pathway between subjects' recent life changes and their near-future illness reports: Representative results and methodological issues. In B. S. Dohrenwend and B. P. Dohrenwend (eds.), *Stressful Life Events: Their Nature and Effects.* New York: Wiley, pp. 73–86.

———. 1981. Developments in life change measurement: Subjective life change unit scaling. In B. S. Dohrenwend and B. P. Dohrenwend (eds.), *Stressful Life Events and Their Contexts.* New York: Wiley, pp. 48–62.

RAHE, R. H., and R. J. ARTHUR. 1977. Life-change patterns surrounding illness experience. In A. Monat and R. S. Lazarus (eds.), *Stress and Coping*. New York: Columbia University Press, pp. 36–44.

REID, D. M., and M. ZIEGLER. 1981. The desired control measure and adjustment among the elderly. In H. M. Lefcourt (ed.), *Research with the Locus of Control Construct. Volume 1: Assessment Methods*. New York: Academic Press, pp. 127–59.

RODIN, J. 1980. Aging, stress, and the immune system. In S. Levine and H. Ursin (eds.), *Coping and Health*. New York: Academic, pp. 171–202.

——. 1981. Current status of the internal–external hypothesis for obesity: What went wrong? *American Psychologist, 36:* 361–72.

RODIN, J.; L. C. BOHM; and J. T. WACK. 1982. Control, coping, and aging: Models for research and intervention, *Applied Social Psychology Annual, 3:* 153–80.

RODIN, J., and E. LANGER. 1977. Long-term effect of a control-relevant intervention, *Journal of Personality and Social Psychology, 35:* 897–902.

ROSENMAN, R. 1978. The interview method of assessment of the coronary-prone behavior pattern. In T. M. Dembroski, S. M. Weiss, J. L. Shields, S. G. Haynes, and M. Feinleib (eds.), *Coronary-Prone Behavior*. New York: Springer-Verlag, pp. 55–70.

ROSENMAN, R. H.; R. J. BRAND; C. D. JENKINS; M. FRIEDMAN; R. STRAUSS; and M. WURM. 1975. Coronary heart disease in the Western Collaborative Group Study: Final follow-up experience of $8\frac{1}{2}$ years, *Journal of the American Medical Association, 233:* 872–77.

ROTTER, J. B. 1966. Generalized expectancies for internal versus external control of reinforcement, *Psychological Monographs*, vol. 80. No. 1.

ROTTER, J. B.; M. SEEMAN; and S. LIVERANT. 1962. Internal vs. external locus of control of reinforcement: A major variable in behavior theory. In N. F. Washburne (ed.), *Decisions, Values, and Groups*. New York: Pergamon Press, pp. 473–516.

SCHACHTER, S., and J. RODIN. 1974. *Obese Humans and Rats*. Washington, D.C.: Erlbaum/Halsted.

SCHERWITZ, L.; K. BERTON; and H. LEVENTHAL. 1977. Type A assessment and interaction in the behavior pattern interview, *Psychosomatic Medicine, 39:* 229–40.

——. 1978. Type A behavior, self-involvement, and cardiovascular response, *Psychosomatic Medicine, 40:* 593–609.

SCHERWITZ, L., et al. 1983. Type A behavior, self-involvement, and coronary atherosclerosis, *Psychosomatic Medicine, 45:* 47–57.

SCHMIEDER, R; G. FRIEDRICH; H. NEUS; H. RUDEL; and A. W. VON EIFF. 1983. The influence of Beta Blockers on cardiovascular reactivity and Type A behavior pattern in hypertensives, *Psychosomatic Medicine, 45:* 417–23.

SCHNEIDER, M. 1975. The quality of life in large American cities: Objective and subjective social indicators. *Social Indicators Research, 1:* 495–509.

SCHROEDER, D. H., and P. T. COSTA, JR. 1984. Influence of life event stress on physical illness: Substantive effects or methodological flaws? *Journal of Personality and Social Psychology, 46:* 853–63.

SCHUCKER, B., and D. R. JACOBS. 1977. Assessment of behavior pattern A by voice characteristics, *Psychosomatic Medicine, 39:* 219–28.

SCHULZ, R. 1976. Effects of control and predictability on the physical and psychological well-being of the institutionalized aged, *Journal of Personality and Social Psychology*, 33: 563–73.

SCHULZ, R., and D. ADERMAN. 1973. Effect of residential change on the temporal distance of death of terminal cancer patients, *Omega: Journal of Death and Dying*, 4: 157–62.

SCHULZ, R., and B. H. HANUSA. 1978. Long-term effects of control and predictability enhancing interventions: Findings and ethical issues, *Journal of Personality and Social Psychology*, 36: 1194–1201.

SELIGMAN, M. E. P. 1975. *Helplessness: On Depression, Development and Death*. San Francisco: Freeman.

SELIGMAN, M. E. P.; L. Y. ABRAMSON; A. SEMMEL; and C. VON BAEYER. 1979. Depressive attributional style, *Journal of Abnormal Psychology*, 88: 242–47.

SHERROD, D. R.; J. M. HAGE; P. L. HALPERN; and B. S. MOORE. 1977. Effects of personal causation and perceived control on responses to an aversive environment: The more control the better, *Journal of Experimental Social Psychology*, 13: 14–27.

SPAULDING, R. C., and C. V. FORD. 1976. The *Pueblo* incident: Psychological reactions to the stresses of imprisonment and repatriation. In R. H. Moos (ed.), *Human Adaptation: Coping with Life Crises*. Lexington, Mass.: Heath, pp. 308–21.

STAUB, E.; B. TURSKY; and G. E. SCHWARTZ. 1971. Self-control and predictability: Their effects on reactions to aversive stimulation, *Journal of Personality and Social Psychology*, 18: 157–62.

STERN, G. S.; T. R. McCANTS; and P. W. PETTINE. 1982. Stress and illness: Controllable and uncontrollable life events' relative contributions, *Personality and Social Psychology Bulletin*, 8: 140–45.

STEVENS, S. S., and E. H. GALANTER. 1957. Ratio scales and category scales for a dozen perceptual continua, *Journal of Experimental Psychology*, 54: 377.

STEWART, D. N., and D. M. DE R. WINSER. 1944. Perforated peptic ulcer during the period of heavy air raids, *Lancet*, 1: 14.

SULS, J., and B. MULLEN. 1981. Life events, perceived control and illness: The role of uncertainty, *Journal of Human Stress*, 7: 30–34.

SURGEON GENERAL OF THE UNITED STATES. 1979. *Healthy People*. Washington, D.C.: Government Printing Office.

SZPILER, F. A., and S. EPSTEIN. 1976. Availability of an avoidance response as related to autonomic arousal, *Journal of Abnormal Psychology*, 85: 73–82.

THOMPSON, S. C. 1981. Will it hurt if I can control it? A complex answer to a simple question, *Psychological Bulletin*, 90: 89–101.

TOLSTOY, L. 1982. *Anna Karenina*. London: Penguin (1878).

VINOKUR, A., and M. L. SELZER. 1975. Desirable versus undesirable life events: Their relationship to stress and mental stress, *Journal of Personality and Social Psychology*, 32: 329–37.

WALLSTON, K. A., and B. S. WALLSTON. 1981. Health locus of control scales. In H. M. Lefcourt (ed.), *Research with the Locus of Control Construct. Volume 1: Assessment Methods*. New York: Academic Press, pp. 189–243.

WORELL, L., and T. N. TUMILTY. 1981. The measurement of control among alcoholics. In H. M. Lefcourt (ed.), *Research with the Locus of Control Construct. Volume 1: Assessment Methods.* New York: Academic Press, pp. 321–33.

WYLER, A. R.; M. MASUDA; and T. H. HOLMES. 1968. Seriousness of illness rating scale, *Journal of Psychosomatic Research, 11:* 363–75.

ZIMMERMAN, M. 1983. Weighted vs. unweighted life event scores: Is there a difference? *Journal of Human Stress, 9,* no. 4: 30–35.

Name Index

Subject Index